Including

the Poor

Proceedings of a Symposium

Organized by the World Bank

and the International Food

Policy Research Institute

WORLD BANK

REGIONAL AND

SECTORAL STUDIES

Including

the Poor

Proceedings of a Symposium

Organized by the World Bank

and the International Food

Policy Research Institute

EDITED BY

MICHAEL LIPTON

AND

JACQUES VAN DER GAAG

The World Bank
Washington, D.C.

The World Bank Regional and Sectoral Studies series provides an outlet for work that is relatively limited in its subject matter or geographical coverage but that contributes to the intellectual foundations of development operations and policy formulation. These studies have not necessarily been edited with the same rigor as Bank publications that carry the imprint of a university press.

The findings, interpretations, and conclusions expressed in this publication are those of the authors and should not be attributed in any manner to the World Bank, to its affiliated organizations, or to the members of its Board of Executive Directors or the countries they represent.

The material in this publication is copyrighted. Requests for permission to reproduce portions of it should be sent to the Office of the Publisher at the address shown in the copyright notice above. The World Bank encourages dissemination of its work and will normally give permission promptly and, when the reproduction is for noncommercial purposes, without asking a fee. Permission to copy portions for classroom use is granted through the Copyright Clearance Center, Suite 910, 222 Rosewood Dr., Danvers, Massachusetts 01923, U.S.A.

The complete backlist of publications from the World Bank is shown in the annual *Index of Publications*, which contains an alphabetical title list and indexes of subjects, authors, and countries and regions. The latest edition is available free of charge from Distribution Unit, Office of the Publisher, The World Bank, 1818 H Street, N.W., Washington, D.C. 20433, U.S.A., or from Publications, The World Bank, 66, avenue d'Iéna, 75116 Paris, France.

The map that accompanies the text has been prepared solely for the convenience of the reader; the designations and presentation of material in it do not imply the expression of any opinion whatsoever on the part of the World Bank, its affiliates, or its Board or member countries concerning the legal status of any country, territory, city, or area, or of the authorities thereof, or concerning the delimitation of its boundaries or its national affiliation.

Michael Lipton is Professorial Fellow in Economics at the Institute of Development Studies, Sussex University; at the time of the 1989 World Bank–IFPRI conference on poverty research, he was Program Director of the Food Consumption and Nutrition Program at the International Food Policy Research Institute in Washington. Jacques van der Gaag is Chief of the Human Resources Operations Division in the World Bank's Latin American and the Caribbean Regional Office.

Cover design by Sam Ferro

Library of Congress Cataloging-in-Publication Data

Including the poor / edited by Michael Lipton and Jacques van der
   Gaag.
     p. cm.—(World Bank regional and sectoral studies)
   Includes bibliographical references and index.
   ISBN 0-8213-2674-0
   1. Poor—Government policy—Developing countries. 2. Poverty—
Government policy—Developing countries I. Lipton, Michael.
II. Gaag, J. van der. III. Series.
HC59.72.P6I528   1993
362.5'8'091724—dc20
                                   93-34793
                                      CIP

Contents

Preface

The World Bank, the largest development lending agency, and the International Food Policy Research Institute (IFPRI), a group of social scientists who analyze food production, trade, consumption, and nutrition, are very different organizations. Yet the main objective of both institutions is to reduce poverty. This book reflects that shared concern.

During 1989 the World Bank and IFPRI cosponsored monthly workshops on poverty research. Each workshop focused on an issue that we saw as essential to understanding poverty or to assessing the efficiency or effectiveness of policies to reduce it. Although our agenda was tightly structured—along the lines sketched out in the book's introductory chapter—it led us to commission work on most of the key issues of economic development. These issues ranged from measuring poverty to analyzing events—such as agricultural development—that affect the severity of poverty to assessing the effectiveness of supposed cures—such as land reform and structural adjustment.

The monthly workshops culminated in a two-day conference at Airlie House, Virginia, in October 1989. Each draft paper presented at the conference was analyzed by two commentators and discussed by the participants. By this time we knew that the World Bank's *World Development Report 1990* would address poverty, with the intent of refocusing and realigning development policies to reduce it. The knowledge that our papers would serve as source materials for this crucial study sharpened our focus.

Armed with the contributions of the commentators and the results of the discussions, we began work. Some papers were extensively rewritten, and most were edited to avoid overlaps and to fit them into our structure of analysis. This structure is set out in the introductory chapter, which also introduces some issues that are not dealt with in the rest of the volume but that are nevertheless important in defining the effects on poverty of national policies and programs.

We would like to acknowledge the help of many people: the participants in the workshops and the conference; members of the "sharp end" of the staff at Airlie House, IFPRI, and the World Bank, especially those who managed our comforts so well as we discussed the problems of the less comfortable; the secretaries who typed the numerous drafts; the text editors, who brought the volume to its final form; and the authors, who patiently tolerated the long delays caused by our many requests to rewrite, reformat, reestimate, and otherwise relate their work more closely to the structure of the volume.

Poverty: A Research and Policy Framework

Michael Lipton
Jacques van der Gaag

1

The incidence of poverty has fallen in most regions of the world since 1945. Yet despite decolonization and an expanding world economy, huge numbers of people remain poor, even in some countries that have enjoyed unprecedented economic growth, such as Brazil, India, and Pakistan.[1] In 1985 about 600 million people in the developing world, including at least one in four Africans and Asians, were too poor to afford enough food on a reliable basis.[2]

In part because of the mixed record of the war on poverty proclaimed by many countries, the 1980s saw a reassessment of the role of governments in economic development, though by no means a retreat from antipoverty goals. The time was ripe to reassess the failures and successes of both developing countries and donors in attacking poverty. The World Bank attempted that reassessment in *World Development Report 1990*.[3]

The report concluded that governments in developing countries could best make sustainable progress against poverty by following a twin-track strategy.[4] The first element of the strategy is a growth-oriented policy that uses the poor's most abundant asset: labor.[5] It calls for the strengthening of institutions, infrastructure, and market incentives, and, to that end, the distribution of information and adoption of technology. The second element is the provision of basic social services to the poor: primary health care, education, nutrition, and family planning services.

The rationale behind the strategy is that an increasing number of the poor derive most of their income from labor.[6] Policies for employment-intensive growth create opportunities for poor households by increasing the demand for labor, thereby increasing employment, wage rates, and the political power of the poor. Social sector policies should provide the poor with enough human capital to exploit these new opportunities, and create a safety net for the most vulnerable— those who are poor because of such shocks as harvest failure, illness, or a large number of children, or because of a chronic inability to work due to disease or old age.

This conclusion recalls Singh's view of the so-called green revolution in South Asia. He argues that it has substantially reduced poverty, in the context of "policy reforms and action programs to accelerate rural growth," but that "a workable antipoverty strategy [also] involves...a rural works program aimed at the poor...and supplemental but well-targeted programs in the social sectors" (1990: 2, 7). The case for this approach in Latin America is developed in chapter 11 of this volume.

The World Bank (1990b: 134-37) argued that donors, including by implication itself, should give increasing assistance to the governments of developing countries to support their adoption of these antipoverty strategies. This stance has serious policy ramifications, not yet fully recognized. Aid would be reduced for countries without serious antipoverty policies (World Bank 1990b: 136). And through World Bank country policy statements on poverty (World Bank 1992), not only the Bank's structural adjustment lending[7] but also its major project loans, overall country assistance, and aid mobilization efforts would increasingly reflect the twin-track strategy, through precise guidelines or even conditions wherever feasible.

This book surveys the relevance to the twin-track strategy of recent poverty research, much of it undertaken under the aegis of the World Bank and the International Food Policy Research Institute. The authors provide general support for the strategy, but go beyond it.

First, they develop further some concerns raised in *World Development Report 1990* about *measurement*. This is not an academic exercise. Correct measures, used in allocating resources among groups of the poor, can save lives. Second, the authors stress the effect on poverty not only of policies, but of major *events*. These include normal concomitants of development, such as population change and imported technical advances in agriculture. Such events are not influenced mainly by domestic projects, or even by the policy conditions that a developing country government might negotiate with a donor. Yet antipoverty policy must allow for big events that alter its parameters, even if the events are largely exogenous. Third, the authors consider some overt *remedies* for poverty, including directly redistributive ones, such as land reform and social welfare payments. Such measures may seem old-fashioned—hostile to incentives, rent-creating (de Soto 1989: ch. 6), or politically inviable. Yet they seem likely to force their way back onto the political and economic agenda, for example, as populations age in South Asia or as land hunger presses in East Africa. Many developing countries cannot push through, or pay for, much of the twin-track strategy without some redistribution of income, assets, or power. Finally, the book closes with studies of antipoverty actions and outcomes in three big developing countries: India, Brazil, and Pakistan.

Does measurement matter?

Measuring poverty has proved crucial for antipoverty policy. But it has required research that goes beyond incidence—beyond counting the poor. It is necessary also to assess the intensity and distribution of poverty. At a global level, such assessments show where the problem is greatest, where and when it is increasing or decreasing, and perhaps what its correlates are. At national and regional levels, our contributors show that attributing poverty (as between incidence, intensity, and intrapoor distribution) tells us a lot about appropriate steps toward curing it. Lack of such measurement in much of Africa (until recently; see, for example, van der Gaag and Glewwe 1988; Glewwe and Twum-Baah 1991; and Glewwe 1990b) helps explain the weakness of antipoverty policy there.

An example from India illustrates how, conversely, even rather crude measurement can help guide policy where reliable data on poverty incidence, intensity, and distribution are available (table 1.1), but that such guidance must be used warily.

Table 1.1 Monthly expenditure per person (MEP), India, 1983
(rupees)

Category	Range of MEP	Percentage of population	Average MEP	Average short-fall in MEP
Poorest	<76.65	32.65	57.66	18.99
Fairly poor	76.65-89.00	11.25	82.71	6.29
All poor	<89.00	43.90	64.08	24.92
Nonpoor	>89.00	56.10	156.13	-67.13
All	n.a.	100.00	115.72	-26.72

n.a. Not applicable.
Note: The poverty line is Rs 76.65 MEP for the poorest and Rs 89.00 MEP in all other rows.
Source: Datt and Ravallion, chapter 4, tables 4.1, 4.2, and 4.3.

The lower poverty line, a monthly expenditure per person (MEP) of Rs 76.65,[8] permits an average Indian to obtain an adequate diet.[9] To reach this expenditure level, the average person below it would have required a transfer of 19 rupees (Rs) a month in 1983. Financing these transfers through a tax on the nonpoor would require that each pay on average Rs 19 times 32.65/56.10—the ratio of the poorest to the nonpoor—or about Rs 11. This Rs 11 poverty tax on the nonpoor would comprise just over 7 percent of their average monthly expenditure—probably about 5.5 percent of their income. At first, the nonpoor would have to transfer something like this 5.5 percent of their income to the poorest each year to keep extreme poverty at bay. But continued growth of per capita gross national product (GNP), plus some income from investment and education that poor people purchased out of their transfers, would steadily reduce the proportionate burden on the nonpoor.

Why isn't eliminating poverty as simple as that? Although a few places, such as Kerala state in India, have attacked poverty mainly through such transfers, the twin-track strategy (and most policies reviewed in this book) gives them only a minor role. Why?

The simplistic sum and poverty measurement

Before answering this question, we need to grasp how the simplistic sum relates to several measurement issues addressed in chapters 2-4. First, until the 1970s, most poverty measures simply counted the poor to derive the *head count ratio*:

about one in three were in extreme poverty in India around 1983. But to assess the arithmetical feasibility of eliminating poverty by (perfectly targeted and incentive-neutral) taxes and transfers alone, three other pieces of knowledge were needed: the shortfall of the consumption of the average poor person from the extreme poverty line—the extreme *poverty gap* (about Rs 19 a month); the proportion of nonpoor Indians, in principle able to pay some tax to alleviate poverty (56 percent); and their average monthly income (about Rs 156).

Though still widely used, the head count ratio is an unsatisfactory measure of poverty for two important reasons. First, it says nothing about how far below the poverty line the income of the average poor person is—the poverty gap. The head count ratio and the poverty gap can easily move in opposite directions. For instance, a study by Khan (1977) for Bangladesh showed that the proportion of the population living below the poverty line had declined, yet the remaining poor were, on average, poorer—the poverty gap had increased. Second, a poverty measure should decrease if the poorest receive a transfer from the moderately poor (Sen 1979 and 1981a). Neither the head count ratio nor the poverty gap does so.

Foster, Greer, and Thorbecke (1984) introduced a class of poverty measures that have the desirable properties. The FGT class of poverty measures, which includes the head count ratio and the poverty gap as special cases, is increasingly used (chapters 2, 18, and 20). We reproduce it here for ease of reference:

$$P_\alpha = \int_0^z \left(\frac{z-x}{z}\right)^\alpha f(x)\,dx,$$

where P_α is the poverty measure, depending on parameter α; z is the poverty line; x is income; and $f(.)$ the density function of the income distribution.

The parameter α determines the weight given to the severity of poverty. For $\alpha = 0$, $P_0 = F(z)$, the cumulative income distribution at the poverty line z. In other words, for $\alpha = 0$, all poor are given equal weight and P_0 equals the head count ratio.

For $\alpha = 1$, each poor person is weighted by his distance to the poverty line, $(z - x)$, relative to z. Thus P_1 measures the distance to the poverty line for the average poor person: the poverty gap.

For $\alpha > 1$, the weight given to each of the poor is more than proportional to the shortfall from the poverty line. Thus, an increase in income for the poorest of the poor is judged so important by the analyst or policymaker that poverty is said to decline even if such an increase comes at the cost of a decrease in income for the moderately poor. A value $\alpha = 2$ is often used.

The choice of measure is important for poverty policy. The head count ratio is most easily reduced by aiming policies at those just below the poverty line. Policies helping the poorest, however, may not reduce the head count ratio, but may nevertheless be desirable. Their effectiveness should be measured by P_α for values of $\alpha > 1$. The use of the appropriate measure is just one of the methodological issues that need to be dealt with in designing an antipoverty strategy.

Does the simplistic sum understate the problem?

If in 1983 only 5.5 percent of the income of India's nonpoor needed to be taxed away (or diverted from current uses of the existing taxes) in order to eliminate extreme poverty through transfers, and if this percentage decreases in the normal course of economic growth, why did extreme poverty persist?

Such a poverty tax might prove difficult in part because it might reduce domestic savings rates, and in part because the nonpoor wield much more political influence than the extremely poor. But if the tax does not discourage effort, and the revenue can be properly targeted toward the poorest, these reasons are not convincing. The 5.5 percent tax rate is equivalent to less than two years' ordinary growth in the incomes of the nonpoor, and comprises a fairly small part of their total taxes. Also, the poor would spend some of the transfer on improving their health, nutrition, or education, which contributes to growth. The main reason that there is no such poverty tax may instead be that a 5.5 percent tax on the incomes of the nonpoor was judged too small to abolish extreme poverty, for two principal reasons (see Besley and Kanbur, chapter 3): incentive effects and poor information.

The "simplistic sum" suggests that, from the poverty tax take, very poor workers are given exactly enough to fill the gap between earned income and the extreme poverty line. But this would lead to disincentive effects, causing many of them to work less. That reduces their pretransfer income to even further below the extreme poverty line, increasing the revenues needed to end extreme poverty—and therefore increasing the required poverty tax. The nonpoor, too, will work less if the extra taxes fall on their employment income.[10]

In addition, there is imperfect information about who is extremely poor. Thus, some of the revenue from a poverty tax would leak to the nonpoor,[11] increasing the tax take needed to abolish severe poverty. Leakage of one-third of the poverty tax would raise the tax needed to abolish extreme poverty from 100 to 150.

These factors militate against attacking poverty mainly through transfers. Most state spending to reduce poverty is best used to provide infrastructure, institutions, and research that stimulate labor-intensive production; self-targeting social services and safety nets, along the lines discussed in chapters 3 and 15; and some redistribution of assets to the poor that would complement labor. There is some scope for attacking poverty by direct current transfers to the poor, but usually not a lot. Yet longer-term investments in poor people do less to reduce immediate poverty than direct current transfers. That once more increases the poverty tax required: *efficient delay costs resources.*

Might the simplistic sum overstate the problem?

Problems of information, of incentives, and of inevitable inefficiencies, then, suggest that 5.5 percent of nonpoor people's annual income would not, around 1980-85, have sufficed to abolish extreme poverty in India. Yet there are offsetting factors that tend to reduce the poverty tax required (or efficient) to remove extreme poverty. This is in part for reasons implicit in Alderman's discussion (chapter 5). He shows that, even among rather poor populations (including in India), a 20 percent rise in income or outlay appears to induce, at the mean, only a 3 to 5 percent rise in calorie intake. Can most of the poor thus require much more income or outlay as a precondition for eating enough?

Alderman points out that, because of nonlinearities, the poorest group, who are the intended gainers from the tax transfer scheme, might raise calorie intake by more than average, say, by 5 to 7 percent, implying a calorie-income elasticity approaching 0.3. He also shows that, whereas most of the new evidence for low calorie-income elasticities is short-term and assumes that income improves nutritional status only through changes in food consumption, the paths from extra income to better nutritional status are in fact varied and often long-term. But if we recall that the lower poverty line is defined as expenditure below which the household cannot reliably attain a caloric norm,[12] Alderman's finding suggests the possibility of selecting policies in pricing, health, or nutrition education that would increase calorie intake, or other sources of nutritional adequacy, at given levels of outlay or income.

In the context of table 1.1, this would reduce the rise in MEP—and thus the poverty tax—needed to finance transfers sufficient to eliminate undernutrition due to poverty. Policy choices can then increase the effect of a given rise in MEP on the nutritionally based health and well-being of poor people. This depends in part on learning from the "positive deviance" that permits some poor households to convert low outlays into reasonable levels of energy intake (C. Shah 1979), or low energy intakes (even relative to requirements) into reasonable levels of infant and child health and nutrition (Zeitlin, Mansour, and Bajrai 1987). An even more important lesson, however, is that it is probably cost-effective, in reducing poverty, to use some of the poverty tax revenue not for direct transfers or indirect food price subsidies for the poor, but to pay for other goods that are vital in producing good health and nutrition. In such production, these goods—such as basic health care and safe drinking water—are likely to complement the extra food that poor people can "buy" with the transfers or subsidies that increase their MEP (Taylor and others 1978).[13] But once more, *efficient delay* reduces the power of the poverty tax money to relieve immediate need.

During the early 1980s, 5.5 percent of nonpoor people's annual income would probably not have sufficed to end even extreme poverty in India. In the early 1990s, however, it would come closer. Preliminary data for 1987-88 show that, compared with 1983, there were a smaller proportion of Indians in severe poverty, a larger proportion not poor, and a bigger gap between income per person in the nonpoor group and the moderate poverty line. As a result of all three facts, the poverty tax rate needed to make a given dent in severe poverty would be lower. But there is a tradeoff between relieving short-run poverty and reducing it sustainably in the long run. There is room in poverty programs for some immediate supplementing of consumption, but mostly they can, and increasingly do, complement poor people's own efforts, by building up human or capital assets that complement extra labor input. Yet again, *efficient delay costs resources* available for short-term transfers to the poor.

In summary, the simplistic sum is just that. The considerations of incentives and information (chapter 3), and the need to use antipoverty resources for long-run goals, mean that more money is needed to eliminate poverty. But such considerations also indicate ways to keep the long-term cost down—for example, through self-targeting, and through cost-effective steps to break the link between low income and ill health and malnutrition. Yet again, *efficiency costs resources*: not only income transfers, but often also expensive investments in sanitation and primary health, are required.

Measuring interaction effects on poverty

So far, our simplistic sum, and even the major modifications implicit in chapters 3 and 5, stop at the first round. But Thorbecke, in his commentary on these chapters, goes further:

> The extension of the budgetary decision rules to minimize societal poverty...within a computable general equilibrium (CGE) framework leads to significant modifications. Subsidies to certain groups not only reduce [their] poverty directly, but may also alleviate poverty indirectly among other groups...through responding. (personal communication to the editors)

Another CGE effect arises when an antipoverty program helps the poorest in part by stimulating their food growing. The extra food, and perhaps its reduced price, help people who spend a large part of their income on food. These are mainly other poor people, especially in cities.

Such CGE effects can also go the wrong way, raising the costs of poverty alleviation. The very poor, if they spend extra income on food (but without contributing more to its production), bid up its price for other poor. Also, potentially favorable CGE effects can be subverted. Cheaper food, if labor supply is real-wage elastic, enables employers to cut wage rates, so that the poor gain little—unless employers, because wage cuts are now possible, employ more of them. Chapter 16 discusses interactions between food price subsidies and real wages.

The importance of such effects, especially for staple food pricing, production, and employment, underlines the need for CGE approaches. They are used by de Janvry and Sadoulet (chapter 11) to evaluate antipoverty strategies in Latin America, and by Parikh and Srinivasan (chapter 17) to compare the cost-effectiveness of food subsidies and employment generation in alleviating poverty in India. These chapters also begin the urgent task of explaining to policy-makers why CGE approaches sometimes predict surprising poverty effects from alternative policies.

The need for targeting by region and other correlates of poverty

Directly measuring whether individuals are poor in income or outlay may be feasible for a small sample and for an independent survey team. It is extremely difficult for a large set of households, however, especially where official survey managers or respondents know that the answers determine eligibility for benefit.[14] This has motivated the efforts to find indicators of poverty, such as location or size of household. What criteria make good indicators?

Besley and Kanbur (chapter 3) divide the (given) cost of any antipoverty program into administrative costs, A, poor people's benefits, P, and benefits that leak to the nonpoor, N. They reason that the ratio $P/(P + N)$ can usually be raised at the cost of incurring higher A,[15] and show how $A/(A + P + N)$ might be optimized (not minimized) so as to maximize P, given total cost $(A + P + N)$. The more imperfect the information on poverty given by an indicator, the severer is the tradeoff between cutting A and raising $P/(P + N)$. So we should choose indicators of readily assessed characteristics, correlated with poverty, that are hard to simulate or misreport, and that therefore reduce the costs of targeting.

All four chapters in part 1 bear on this key measurement issue. Datt and Ravallion (chapter 4) experiment with the assumption that, in reallocating resources among forty regions—the urban and rural areas of each of twenty Indian states—policymakers have no information about exactly who (in the "universe") has what MEP, but perfect information (from the sample) for each region about the incidence and severity of extreme poverty (below the Rs 76.65 MEP line) and of moderate poverty (between the Rs 76.65 line and the Rs 89 moderate poverty line). Policymakers can redistribute income between regions, but must then let the chips fall where they may within each region. Under each of two assumptions—that the intraregional distribution of burden and benefits is additional or that it is proportional to each person's initial MEP—Datt and Ravallion demonstrate that, without any intraregional redistribution, interregional equalization of average MEP, or even the interregional redistribution that would minimize poverty, has surprisingly little effect on poverty.[16] Moreover, they show that, because poorer regions tend to have more equal distribution of income, the poverty impact of purely regional redistribution on the FGT measure, P_α for $\alpha = 2$, is smaller than that on the measures that are not sensitive to redistribution among the poor.

Region of residence is a better indicator of poverty in Indonesia: taxes and transfers to equalize average income among provinces, with no redistribution within any province, would reduce aggregate poverty by about one-third. This reduction is greater than that in India, but it is still surprisingly modest, especially as it assumes no limit on the power of the central government to tax any provinces and to disburse the revenues to other provinces. These strong results, even for implausibly radical redistributions, suggest that targeting poor regions alone is an unpromising antipoverty policy. But regional targeting has some advantages and should not be dismissed completely. For example, it is relatively cheap in terms of the information it requires. Furthermore, the simulation results in these studies make use of the administrative (and political) infrastructure, consisting of federal and regional or provincial units, without the further disaggregation to, say, the district or village level that would allow more precise regional targeting, and hence a greater effect on poverty. But regional targeting clearly needs to be supplemented by targeting based on other correlates of poverty.

At the international level the most commonly used correlates of poverty are the infant mortality rate, life expectancy, literacy rate, and, if available, malnutrition rate. Ravallion, Datt, van de Walle, and Chan (1991) regress the first two indicators on poverty measures in countries for which income distribution data are available; the fit is sufficiently good to be used to predict poverty in countries lacking income distribution data. This was part of the exercise that produced the count of the world's poor for *World Development Report 1990*.

At the household level, however, vital events are too rare to be used. Furthermore, undernutrition is seasonal and hard to observe clearly in adults, and it stems from causes other than poverty. But information from household sample surveys may be suitable for targeting in the universe. Kakwani (chapter 2) shows that poverty in Côte d'Ivoire is significantly associated with (1) rural residence, (2) remote areas, (3) large family size, (4) the household head's education, and (5) the household head's employment. It is not, however, associated with the household head's gender or nationality. These results are similar to those from South Asia (Visaria 1980; and Lipton 1983b and 1983c). Using the same data as Kakwani, Glewwe and Kannan (1989) show how these and other correlates, such as the characteristics of dwellings, can be used to improve on regional targeting alone. Ignoring implementation costs, they obtain results that are, in some cases, close to what would be possible if income were directly observable. Sometimes it is more cost-effective to base targeting on several characteristics associated with poverty rather than on one alone (chapter 3).

Kakwani (chapter 2) strengthens the case for a multidimensional approach to targeting. He develops, for the first time, tests for the statistical significance of bivariate comparisons (for example, for a statement that poverty is worse in female-headed than in male-headed households) using various poverty measures, such as P_0, P_1, and P_2. In Côte d'Ivoire, some apparently big differences between population subgroups in these measures have very low statistical significance.[17] This increases the importance of a multivariate "fix" on poverty.

Targeting is not simply a Scrooge-like way to limit the fiscal cost of reducing poverty. It can also prevent undue dependency among the poor (chapter 3) and wrong incentives. Conversely, incentives can be used to improve targeting. Where the rich avoid the use of public health clinics because of crowding or low-quality care, these clinics can be used as distribution centers for, say, food stamps. This kind of self-targeting scheme has proved effective in Jamaica. Ahmad (chapter 15) warns of the risk, however, that such a scheme, although it may avoid leakage to the rich, may exclude or deter many of the poor.

Alderman (chapter 5), in a similar vein, discusses the supply and demand effects of subsidizing foods that are grown or eaten mainly by the poor. Also self-targeting are subsidies for very small-scale productive assets that, because they are intensive in both labor and supervision, are unattractive to the nonpoor; handpumps for micro-irrigation around Islampur, Bangladesh, are an example (Howes 1982). Perhaps the most successful approach to self-targeting is the provision of low-wage public employment, as in the Maharashtra Employment Guarantee Scheme. Its effectiveness is compared with that of food price subsidies in chapter 17.

Events affecting poor people

Poverty measures and profiles allow analysts to identify groups of poor people, to assess the size of the groups and the severity of their poverty, and hence to model and track how changes in their "world" influence their poverty (chapters 2-5). This enables policymakers to see how their choices, by inducing such changes, are likely to affect poverty, and—if they wish—to change the choices accordingly. The components of the world of the poor can be changed in three main ways.

First, poor people may alter their preferences, or decisionmaking procedures. They can form cooperations, become less averse to risk, or process more or better information—and hence may obtain more resources, or turn a given amount into greater well-being. Other than chapter 14, which discusses education, the chapters in this volume say little about poor people's autonomous capacity to escape poverty. That is probably because most economic models in use assume that each person already maximizes expected utility, subject to external constraints (chapter 9). Any other assumption seems to suggest that some outside "expert" knows better than poor people themselves how they should use their scanty income. Yet sensible behavior by the poor does not render policy irrelevant to the parameters of their autonomous capacity to help themselves. For example, laws, knowledge, and enforcement of property rights affect poor people's capacity to handle risk, to cooperate discriminatingly, or to enter into contracts.

Second, the poor's world is altered by events other than direct antipoverty policies. Chapters 6-10 address events of two sorts: those that form part of developmental, labor market, and demographic *transformation*, both of a developing country as a whole and among its sectors (for example, farm and nonfarm) or regions (for example, rural and urban); and those connected with explicit state *policies* (on institutions, technology, and the international environment) not geared mainly toward poverty reduction. Most events affect poor people mainly by causing changes in the level or stability of their real per capita consumption of marketed or home-produced commodities. Also reviewed by these chapters are changes in the level or stability of poor people's consumption of nonmarketed goods, such as free health care; of their life expectancy; and of their conversion efficiency of lifetime consumption into well-being. And chapters 6-10 review the fiscal, administrative, and environmental sustainability of progress on these four fronts toward increasing, or stabilizing, poor people's welfare.

Third, the poor's world is altered by explicit remedies for poverty (chapters 11-17, and the section on remedies below).

Development as an event affecting the poor

All five chapters (6-10) on events affecting the poor recognize that one of the most important such events is development itself. Economists once signaled that recognition, even in the titles of such major works as *The Wealth of Nations* and *Progress and Poverty*. Recently, except for the long debate about the trickle-down theory, the analysis has shifted toward the impact on the poor of apparently local, exogenous, "poor-specific," and microeconomic events, usually linked to price changes or to particular projects.

This shift corresponds to the increasing incorporation and fragmentation of development studies, as reflected in several recent surveys of the topic,[18] into the standard microeconomics of trade and, to a lesser extent, of agriculture, industry, population, insurance, and so on. In this process the "magnificent dynamics" (Baumol 1969), for two centuries the core of development studies, has recently been squeezed aside by more rigorous but less magnificent microstatics. Although microstatics can handle some interactions (for instance, in Walrasian CGE models), it is ill suited to analyzing the central question of progress and poverty: how does a Great Transformation (Polanyi 1944; and Singh 1990) affect the poor?

Yet Carlyle's "Condition-of-England question" in 1852—how is it possible and preventable that "in the midst of plethoric plenty the people perish?"— remains the central demand that the outside intellectual community has always made, rightly, of economists. Economics was nearly discredited in the 1840s because it appeared, wrongly, to be irretrievably microstatic and unable, or unwilling, to address Carlyle's question. Today, as then, statements are often heard very like Candide's "all is for the best in the best of all possible worlds": implausible, and not amoral (as science perhaps should be), but immoral in the presence of poverty and famine so substantial still in Asia, and massive and unrelenting in Africa. Today, as then, development economics needs to return to Carlyle's challenge. It cannot do so through microstatics alone. A view of the Great Transformation as events affecting the poor—or as a mutual transformation of technology and poverty—may be a good beginning.

Demographic events, labor, development, and poverty

Past industrializations typically featured population growth of 0.5 to 1.5 percent a year, compared with 2.2 to 4.0 percent in today's developing countries. The earlier increases in growth rates were traced, until recently, to declines in death rates induced by better living standards. Recent research, however, shows that birth rates initially rose as well, and that the declines in death rates usually preceded the acceleration of industrial (and even, earlier, of agricultural) growth. The falling death rates can be traced largely to a sharp decline from 1665 to 1800 in epidemics, notably bubonic plague, which had recurred regularly and devastatingly from the early fourteenth to the mid-seventeenth centuries. This was analogous to the swifter and larger demographic changes in Asia and Africa that occurred after malaria was brought under control, beginning in the mid-1940s, also before modern industrial growth.

Effects on real (labor) income. For the poor, the effects of the earlier demographic transition differed from those of the transition in today's developing countries, for three main reasons. First, although extended families have been of little significance for most poor people in industrializing countries (chapter 10), family structure was very different during earlier periods of industrialization than it is now (Hajnal 1982). During early Western industrialization the poor tended to be in smaller, later-marrying families compared with the nonpoor, and hence to feel fewer of the direct losses (and gains) from population increase. In today's developing world the poor are heavily concentrated in larger households.

Second, the few medical and public health improvements before and during early Western industrialization (deliberate smallpox and cowpox immunization, the fortuitous retreat of bubonic plague) did not selectively raise population growth among the poor, but attacked mostly "equal-opportunity diseases."[19] In today's developing countries, however, falling death rates accompany the spread, to poorer (and especially rural) people, of access to preconditions for adequate health formerly confined largely to better-off city dwellers: antibiotics, sanitary childbirth, and better nutrition and preventive care. Thus, even the nonselective expansion of health-related outlay does much more for the poor than for the rich (because the rich already enjoyed health care), much more than was possible in early Western development (when medicine had much less to offer). So Kakwani, Makonnen, and van der Gaag (chapter 6) can use trends in average incidence of premature death and malnutrition, for example, as indicators of trends in poor people's health. This means that medical progress tends to reduce mortality more among the poor than among the nonpoor in developing countries, unlike in the West during early industrialization.

Third, the growing populations of poor in the developing world probably face an even less favorable employment environment than did the poor during early Western industrialization, despite widespread unemployment then (chapter 10). Today's population growth, at rates two or three times faster than those during Western industrialization, is more concentrated among the poor, and fastest among those of working age,[20] so the supply of unskilled labor is growing faster still. In further contrast to the nineteenth-century West, today's developing countries are set in a developed world economy. The demands and savings of that economy largely dictate the path of technical progress because they determine what research results are available for transmission to all countries. Because firms in developed countries face incentives to replace unskilled labor with human and physical capital, global technical progress tends to retard the demand for unskilled labor. Even in India, for example, the unit cost of farming with tractors and combines has been reduced relative to that of more labor-intensive, but less researched, farming methods.[21]

These trends can be overcome. The incidence and severity of poverty have fallen in the last forty years—even in the difficult 1980s, as improvements in Asia outweighed deterioration elsewhere. But the stylized facts about demographic events "now" as against "then"—faster population growth, concentrated more among workers and the poor, and more labor-displacing technical change; medical changes favoring especially fast growth in poorer groups; and changes in family structure resulting in a concentration of big families among the poor—do tighten the constraints against continued poverty reduction. Expanding exports, growing aggregate domestic activity, and labor-demanding events in agriculture (the green revolution in some areas, land expansion in others) have overcome the downward pressures exerted by demography and technology on the employment and real wage rates of the working poor since 1945. Yet such offsetting events are more precarious than are demography and world labor-saving research.

Effects on nonmarket consumption. The nonmarket consumption of poor people has also behaved surprisingly favorably, given these demographic events. Even in Sub-Saharan Africa, the region with the most rapid population growth, and even during its worst period of economic setbacks (1980-86),[22] there was a slight rise in real public sector health and education outlays per person. Because of the still-increasing child-adult ratio however, outlays per child may not have risen (chapter 6, table 6.9).[23] Birdsall and Griffin (chapter 9), while accepting that faster growth in population or in the child-adult ratio might shift public education outlays from the deepening to the widening of human capital (or even reduce outlays per child), find little evidence for this.[24]

Effects on life expectancy. Males in low-income countries enjoyed a rise in life expectancy at birth between 1972 and 1987 of 13.3 percent in Africa, 17.4 percent in Asia, and 12.8 percent in Latin America. The improvements for females were even higher—13.6 percent, 19.9 percent, and 12.8 percent (chapter 6, tables 6.10-6.11). The improvements[25] were proportionately greater for the poor (chapter 6).

The same health improvements that have increased the life expectancy of the poor and their capacity to transform income into well-being tend to lower real wage rates and increase profits as a share of GNP. Economists' practice of measuring poverty (or real consumption per person) over an average year, rather than over the life span, catches the downward effects of population growth on poverty (through lower real wage rates) in a given year. But it misses the upward effects of the lower death rates on longevity and hence on the total lifetime well-being of persons initially poor. Poor people's expected real consumption over their life span likely rose more than 25 percent in developing countries as a whole since the early 1970s, although measures of poverty in a typical year of life fell much more slowly.

The decline in death rates in most developing countries in 1950-90—in sharp contrast to the increase in the nineteenth-century West (chapter 10, table 10.3)—shows that the poverty impact of the Great Transformation has itself been transformed, for the better, in ways not captured in most poverty data. Moreover, health-related improvements, except in the Horn of Africa, are more stable in today's developing world than in nineteenth-century Europe. Life expectancy, and related social expenditures, are robust in the face of recession (though not, of course, in the face of war and famine)—much more robust than real private consumption among the poor (chapter 6). Looking only at single-year, labor market, or private consumption effects, we become too gloomy about the impact on the poor of the "new demography" of economic transformation. Longer life is a boon, even if it also involves a higher labor supply that restrains real earnings per year.

Demographic events and the composition of the poor. Demographic events change the composition of the poor by age and sex, which in turn changes the effects on the poor of other events in the process of economic transformation, and of policy responses to those events. In Britain by the end of the nineteenth century "the old, the sick, widows, children of single parents, and those in large families were much more likely to be very poor" (chapter 10). In early Western industrialization persons in large families did not belong on that list (Hajnal 1982), but they do in today's developing countries. The old are heavily underrepresented in the poorest deciles in India because, where work is physically demanding and health care rationed by price, the poor are much likelier to die before reaching old age than the nonpoor; this was probably also true in early-nineteenth-century Europe.

The most important implication of demographic events for the poor of the developing world, however, is probably the steady, worldwide shift in the incidence of poverty away from persons who derive most of their income from farmland, toward persons who rely for income mainly on their employed labor. Thus, the case for smallholder cash cropping as a means to alleviate poverty (chapter 7) depends mainly on its potential to create employment—directly through labor-intensive cash crops, or indirectly through the labor-intensive growth in food production that is often permitted by the acquisition of techniques and capital through cash cropping.

Gains to the poor from some forms of technical progress in agriculture have often gone mainly to rural laborers, through increased employment (chapter 8). Which cash crops, what technical progress, which nonfarm linkages are best designed to benefit the poor? That may depend mainly on demographic events that determine who the poor are: the old, the young, mothers who need work that can be done while watching small children, and so on. In nineteenth-century Britain the decline of rural cottage industry lessened the stability of real income, especially for children, women, and old people (chapter 10). In Asia, as rural artisan work gives way to urban factory work, the same selective effects are likely. Is this damaging? It depends on what categories of poor people are growing and who among the poor therefore needs more life chances. That, in turn, depends largely on demographic changes that occurred twenty to forty years ago.

Agricultural progress or industrialization?

Three lessons emerge from chapter 7. First, accelerated agricultural change—whether in technology or in market orientation—has usually benefited most poor groups absolutely. Second, agricultural commercialization and technical progress, though not necessarily linked, have in practice usually gone hand in hand. And third, there is usually little scope for orienting technical progress to benefit the poor. These lessons suggest that the fate of the poor (who depend heavily on farm work, and spend most of their income on food) is tied up with the speed and priority, not the technical fine-tuning, of the agricultural transformation. Are there state actions that greatly affect such events?

Chapter 7 nowhere suggests that state inaction suffices for propoor, accelerated agricultural commercialization and technical progress. The list of activities for which the state, not firms or communities, appears to have an advantage in providing during early stages of development is long, and not coextensive with public goods in any textbook sense. Many commodities are systematically undersupplied by the private sector, so that there is a case for their public provision, even though they are exhaustible, rivalrous, and price-excludable. This is especially true of producer goods consumed by large numbers of dispersed and poor rural people. Conversely, there exist many public goods and services, notably the management of several sorts of rural common property (Ostrom 1990), that are adequately provided by groups of individuals comprising a community, so that no state action is indicated. Rural roads, health, and education are not pure public goods, and the management of local grazing rights often is; yet the reduction of rural poverty through agricultural growth will benefit if, in general, the state provides the former sorts of commodities, and does not interfere with successful community provision of the latter.

Rural or urban? Does the sectoral distinction between agriculture and industry really reflect the distinction between labor-intensive, propoor activities and high-technology, late-transformation activities? Is a rural-urban distinction more appropriate? Hazell and Haggblade (chapter 8) emphasize the much greater gains in employment from extra units of nonfarm output—and allocation of capital—in the labor-intensive rural hinterland (including small rural towns) than in or around big cities.

State action can raise the urban share in activity, penalizing labor-intensive and propoor rural farm and nonfarm work, in two main ways. First, as Polak and Williamson (chapter 10) demonstrate, state action can result in antiagricultural price bias, as happened during Western industrialization (with the strong exception of British Corn Law policy in 1815-46). Second, it can lead to antirural "real" bias, which is much more significant in today's poor countries—and harder for the poor to escape. For example, in India, age- and sex-specific mortality is substantially higher in rural than in urban areas (Mitra 1978), and the gap has been widening. The opposite was true in nineteenth-century Europe. Chapter 10 stresses the absence of state commitment to the provision of major urban infrastructure during the first industrial revolution in Britain. Throughout most of the developing world today, there is a much deeper commitment to providing costly urban infrastructure. Since the incidence of poverty is now usually much higher in rural areas, this imbalance probably harms the poor, at least relatively, except for the few who can "vote with their feet" by migrating to cities.[26] Rural-urban (and farm-nonfarm) gaps in real income per person were much higher in almost all developing countries in the mid-1970s than in almost any of the ten to twelve industrial countries for which there are comparable data for their early industrialization (Lipton 1977: 437-38).

A comparison of the state's urban emphasis in today's developing countries with the emphases of states during nineteenth-century industrialization (chapter

10) leads to an important conclusion. The significant expansion of state action, which might have redressed the market power that allows wealthier people to steer the product mix toward their demands, has in fact been biased toward areas with less labor-intensive production, less food grown per person, and a lower incidence of poverty.[27] These policy biases, although not directly related to poverty, produce events that may subvert state remedies for poverty.

Regional events and policies

In 1983 the four states in India's "poverty square" (Bihar, Madhya Pradesh, Orissa, and West Bengal) contained 51 percent of India's poor, but only 34 percent of its nonpoor (Rao, Ray, and Subbarao 1988: 114).[28] The concentration of rural poverty at lower levels of disaggregation—for example, in the poorest of the fifty-six rural regions in India's National Sample Survey—is much greater still (Bardhan 1983). There is a rough negative relationship between the incidence of rural poverty and the level of agricultural productivity (and, though much weaker, the agricultural growth rate—Bardhan 1983; Dev 1985; and Howes 1990). This relationship is based on extreme observations, however: the Punjab and Haryana consistently have by far the lowest poverty incidence among India's states, and the six regions with dramatic agricultural growth prior to 1972-73 show very low poverty incidence (Dev 1985: A-135; and Bardhan 1984: 228-30).

In any transformation, some areas advance faster than others. Do poorer people in sluggish areas gain from growth in progressive areas—either as they migrate to work there or through demand for their products in the progressive areas? In several well-documented Asian examples, immigration to rapidly growing rural areas, largely by those seeking unskilled employment, has been an important way of transmitting between regions the benefits of growth to the poor (chapter 7). Because the elasticity of employment with respect to crop yield has tended to fall (Jayasuriya and Shand 1986), employment opportunities for poor, unskilled, rural-to-rural migrants depend heavily on the growth and labor intensity of the rural nonfarm sector. The fixed costs and risks of rural-to-urban migration reduce its scope for relieving the poverty of the worst-off in "backward" rural regions (Connell and others 1976; and Lipton 1982a). So rural-to-rural migration, especially toward areas with growing nonfarm employment, becomes crucial.

In nineteenth-century transformations the poorest, migrating from remoter rural areas, "bought into" better urban real private consumption at the cost of lower public consumption (relative to requirements), life expectancy, and income-to-welfare conversion (chapter 10). In today's developing countries those who move to the city expect to gain all around. Migration to cities normally increases not only expected consumption but also medical and educational prospects, even for poor migrants. But because migration is attractive, it is price-rationed, usually in the form of time and money used to obtain relevant education, to cultivate urban connections, or to acquire the capacity to bear costs and risks. The poorest, especially those from remoter regions, can seldom afford this.

Indeed, in today's developing world, the share of urban growth due to natural increase is much larger than it was in industrializing Britain (Williamson 1988: 428-30). Thus, poor people in sluggish rural areas depend on migrating to advanced rural areas with high labor-intensive demand for a share in the gains from growth.

Typically, a one dollar rise in technologically induced agricultural income generates about 30 to 80 cents of secondary, nonfarm income (chapter 8). If policy causes more of the extra primary income to go to small farms, such linkages generate secondary demands with high labor coefficients, and thus benefit the poor. But these models assume that the extra income will remain in the same (progressive) rural region. If a boost in primary farm incomes in, say, the progressive rural Punjab generated secondary demand for nonfarm activities in technologically backward rural Madhya Pradesh (with its much higher incidence of poverty) rather than in the Punjab itself, the effect on poverty would be much greater.

Agricultural growth can overcome many differences in regions, however. A credible simulation of the effects of the green revolution, allowing for interregional migration of labor and for the effects of technical progress on cereal prices, suggests that the poor in all major regions of India gained absolutely from the improved cereal varieties (chapter 7). They gained even though extra wheat sales from green revolution areas reduced farm prices, incomes, and employment on wheat-surplus farms in much poorer, technically backward areas.[29]

Events affecting institutions, including markets

In the next twenty-five years there will be sharp rises in the proportions of poor people who (1) depend for most of their income on employment rather than land ownership; (2) reside in cities and in Asia; (3) are adults; and (4) are old. How these events work out for the poor, and for those households with a chance of escaping poverty, depends substantially on institutions. The term *institution* includes two types of thing: first, the modes of law, custom, and conduct (such as rules for land tenure and inheritance) that affect claims on labor, commodities, and property; and second, the organized bodies of persons that act to influence, alter, enforce, or relax such modes and rules. The (changing) powers of such institutions are critical shift parameters in determining how given events, in given physical circumstances, affect a given incidence, severity, and group structure of poverty. For example, the rules of land inheritance alter the impact of any factor-neutral improvement in crop production on poor people, in this and the next generation.

Yet, at first sight, chapters 6-10 on events (other than antipoverty policies) that influence the poor have little to say about institutions, except to some extent markets as they constrain or alter these influences. That is in part because the new institutional economics has, since 1970, either interpreted institutions as methods of assigning economic rents or endogenized them, given initial factor endowments and asset distributions. For example, the institution *sharecropping* is usually analyzed either for its effect on outputs and their factor distribution or as an outcome of the initial allocation of land, labor, and preference structures among households, given the risks of farming and the costs of screening laborers (or sharecroppers) and of supervising inputs and outputs. This tends to leave out the empirical investigation of *how* an institution affects the poor.

Economics researchers, to grasp how development events affect the poor, may need to engage much more with the specifics of institutions at the village, suburb, farm, and factory level than they now do. Investigations in the spirit of Bliss and Stern (1982), Bell (1977), Hart (1986), or Wade (1982) are too rare: what is needed are not limited, one-time ethnographies, but hypothesis-testing, localized inputs to comparative "anthropoeconomics" along the lines of Pryor (1977) or, in a different vein, Bardhan and Rudra (1981), Dasgupta and others (1977), or Connell (1976). Such comparative work seeks generalizations about the community and institutional contexts in which particular events—such as migration, free labor contracts, or monetization—are likelier to happen, or likelier to help or harm particular poor groups.

In this vein, Binswanger and von Braun (chapter 7) summarize evidence showing that "where technology or commercialization have been blamed for declines in the income of the poor, additional antipoor interventions or policies ... have usually been responsible." Their evidence on the needless linkage of desirable crop improvements to evictions and labor-displacing mechanizations in Ethiopia, Pakistan, and the Sudan illustrates that appropriate institutions of land tenure and of related political influence are a crucial but neglected "filter" between such improvements and the realization of potential gains by the poor (Prahladachar 1983).

The institutions of the state have an important influence—through events that affect nonmarket incomes—on the stability of poor people's well-being. Drèze (1990a) has analyzed the nineteenth-century origins of rural public works in India. The central role of workhouse relief in England and Wales in 1834-1939— and of much more generous outrelief in 1608-1795 and, especially, in 1795-1834— is described in chapter 10; the "state dependence" of many of the U.S. and European ultrapoor (especially women, children, and the old) during early industrialization is also well documented. Today there is widespread acceptance across the ideological spectrum of a public goods rationale for state safety nets that provide at least the essentials for physical survival to the extremely poor,[30] even in developing countries with a weak fisc or substantial corruption. The applied economics of alternative safety net schemes are explored in chapters 14-15, and the "pure" economics of targeting them in chapter 2.

Several of the chapters focus on poor people's institutional relationship to the market. They can draw on very little exploration of poor people's involvement in, or benefits from, physically identifiable markets, such as Epstein's (1982) analysis of the Tolai of Papua New Guinea. Chapter 9, however, considers how "market failures" might cause poor people to select fertility levels above the private, internal optimum. Causes, in rising order of importance, include ignorance of contraception; lack of information about recent or pending declines in infant and child mortality; overinsurance by risk-averse couples against the failure of children to survive to working age, obtain rewarding work, or support their parents; and Sen's (1967) "isolation paradox," in which each poor couple has to optimize by aiming at a large family size because poor couples cannot jointly agree on, or enforce, a contract to restrict fertility (and hence unskilled labor supply) in a way that would help them all. Apart from such true market failures, there are many circumstances (chapter 9) in which interpersonal or intergenerational externalities, or nonappropriabilities, reduce the appeal to the poor of socially profitable incentives to reduce fertility; this is less market failure than a problem outside the scope of market responses.

As mistaken as attempts to attribute all poverty to market failure is neglecting the fact that market responses often operate through institutions that permit the exercise of market power. In the Gambia, commercialization and technical improvements in the production of rice, a crop that women traditionally produce, provided incentives for men to use their power to take over production. Poor women did benefit, however, because of the increase in household income (chapter 7).

The increasing reliance of poor people on employment renders the working of labor markets especially important to them. Chapter 7, confirming Berry and Sabot (1981), shows that the rural poor are usually integrated into well-performing rural labor markets and the exchange economy. Indeed, the diagnosis of most of the chapters in this volume, consistent with the balance of professional judgments (for example, Binswanger and Rosenzweig 1984), is that poverty is seldom due mainly to market failure.

This diagnosis, in conjunction with the persistence of mass poverty, implies at least one of three things. First, the costs of supporting a market through infrastructure, which may include health and education as well as transport and telephones, may be too high to be profitably provided by private enterprise, and fiscally or politically forbidding to the public sector. Second, the distribution of income, assets, or political or customary power may prevent many poor people from participating in, or otherwise benefiting from, some well-functioning markets. Third, price or technical inefficiency may be too pervasive—among the poor or more generally—for the poor to gain much from such markets. If the state can do no better, or seeks (or seizes) economic rents without sufficient offsetting benefit, the alternatives are grim: revolution toward an undefined new order, or passive acceptance of the living conditions—and death rates—that accompany persistent mass poverty, which neither states nor markets can do much about.

Poverty and technical progress

A deus ex machina has classically been supposed to permit escape from that persistent poverty. Rapidly accelerated technical progress, embodied in investment, makes increased investment profitable, raises farm and nonfarm output faster than it cuts employment per unit of output, and yet allows labor to move from agriculture to secondary and tertiary sectors.[31] It is this process, represented by the steam engine, the spinning jenny, or even four-field rotation with marling and horse hoeing, that most scholars see as the central events that linked the Great Transformation to the reduction of poverty in the West.

In nineteenth-century Britain, however, there was relatively slow technical progress in production to meet poor people's main food and housing needs (chapter 10). Along with fast but labor-saving progress in products that provided unskilled industrial employment, this made the wage-price terms of trade less favorable for the nineteenth-century Western poor than would have been the case with more balanced technical progress. But this only delayed, and did not prevent, a long-run decline in poverty.

Is the contribution of technical progress in today's developing countries similar? The much higher cost of modern urban infrastructure sharpens the problem of financing the new investments; so does the capital intensity of global technical progress. Yet chapters 11-17 maintain that technical progress, backed by education, is the key to development accompanied by poverty reduction, despite widespread state and market inadequacy. Despite tragic but transitional losses suffered by, for example, handloom weavers, and indigenous people displaced in newly irrigated areas, most evidence from Asia and Latin America since 1950 (chapters 18-20), as from Britain after 1847 (and, more generally, from the West in the late nineteenth century), does show a large reduction in the incidence and severity of poverty.

Yet doubts remain about the current power of conventionally transformative technical progress to benefit the poor, despite the arguments made in chapters 7 and 8. Those chapters stress the positive effects on the poor of what is today *unconventionally* transformative technical progress in smallholder agricultural commercialization and cereal production, and in the spending of income gained from such small-farm innovations on nonfarm commodities produced nearby. Global pressures of, and for, technical progress, and investments to embody it, remain geared toward *conventionally* transformative, and very low-employment, sectors and techniques: heavy industry and urban and administrative infrastructure. The negative effect of the sectoral imbalance in technical progress on the transmission to the poor of the gains from growth in Britain in 1815-47 was broadly similar to that in South Asia in 1947-65. Subsequently, in both cases, the poor gained much more, but this had to take place where most of them were: in urban industry in Britain in 1848-1900, and in rural activities, mostly agriculture, in South Asia since 1965. Does the scope for continuing such gains from (unusually) labor-intensive technical progress, in a research world that is seeking to reduce unskilled labor costs, still suffice to greatly reduce poverty in the rural and urban informal sectors of the developing world?

What matters critically, if the gains from transforming technical progress are to benefit today's mainly rural poor, is the presence of a stream of labor-using agricultural innovations, and a shift of investment toward informal and small-scale industry and services. Although the share of industry in employment (as opposed to output) rose hardly at all in 1967-90, South and East Asia were "lucky" because green revolution innovations raised total factor productivity in cereals fast enough to restrain food prices, yet not so fast and not in a way that displaced so much labor as to prevent net growth in agricultural employment. Plainly this is something of a tightrope act. The international transmission of technology helps by cutting unit costs, but harms through its labor-saving bias.

International events and poverty during transformation

Three main types of international event affect the outcomes of economic transformation for poor people. Only one type, events associated with international trade, is even roughly the same for developing countries today as it was for the nineteenth-century West. The second type, events associated with international capital flows, has been transformed completely, both by concessional aid and by the treatment of interest; the poverty impact of these events is not treated here (but see Lipton and Toye 1990: ch. 2). The third type, events associated with technology generation and diffusion, is discussed above.

Discussions in this book of the role of trade in linking transformation to poverty reduction are largely implicit. Chapter 6, however, makes three poverty-related points that are seldom considered in discussions of growth through trade. First, the correction of distortions due to past excesses of protectionism affects poor people because it involves raising the domestic price of tradables relative to that of nontradables. The poor suffer to the extent that they are net buyers of tradables or net sellers of nontradables—or both. But such suffering can be outweighed (or occasionally intensified) by other consequences of adjustment. Second, the correction of price distortions that favor nontradables affects the stability of poor people's real private consumption. After protection is lifted, local shortages can be met by extra net imports, resulting in smaller price rises. At the same time, however, income from production becomes more closely linked to international price fluctuations. Third, real public consumption by the poor may be affected if governments cut spending to reduce a structural balance of payments deficit.

The evidence presented in chapter 6, however, undermines the proposition that adjustment has harmed the poor (or selectively reduced public outlays for them), or that the poor suffered greatly from the adjustments of the 1980s or from the shocks that triggered them. This conclusion, that the poor are substantially insulated from even quite large fluctuations in and adjustments to a developing country's external balances, is in marked contrast to that of several other studies (for example, Cornia, Jolly, and Stewart 1987; and Commander 1989). But it is perhaps less surprising than it seems. Many analysts have reached two conclusions that would support this theory. First, poverty is deeply rooted in social and economic structures, for example, of access to land and to appropriate technology for the poor. Second, much structural adjustment, in addressing mainly the price distortions underlying structural disequilibrium in the balance of payments, tends to underemphasize the more genuinely structural causes of economic segmentation and exclusion. Therefore (because the poor are often structurally impeded from responding to the new incentives), such adjustment often leads to disappointing growth outcomes—for example, because of persistently low price-elasticities of aggregate agricultural output.[32] Thus, nonstructural private adjustments, however desirable (or overrated) they are as measures to address a developing country's external imbalances, will not greatly affect the incidence and severity of that country's poverty, which is mainly structural in origin.

Reducing public investment expenditure is often recommended as the least painful way of cutting back domestic absorption until balance of payments equilibrium is restored. Despite exceptions in some countries (Commander 1989; and Mosley and Smith 1989), however, it does not seem to be a general truth that the poor have owed their partial protection against cutbacks in public *consumption*, in the face of adjustment to international imbalances, to dramatic and lasting cuts in public *investment*. The aggregate evidence (chapter 6) suggests that real public consumption, and health and education among the poor, have not clearly deteriorated under adjustment during the 1980s, even in most African and Latin American countries.[33]

The relevance of trade liberalization (as opposed to adjustment) to poverty reduction has received little attention, despite the mass of literature on outward-looking, trade-led growth.

Remedies for poverty

Chapters 6-10 address partly exogenous events, and related or independent domestic policies, that affect the poor in a developing country through their effect on the country's rate of growth and on the labor-intensity of its production techniques and product mix. These, along with the balance of political power and asset ownership, are doubtless the most important influences on the time path of poverty. Chapters 11-17 evaluate experience with a range of more poverty-specific remedies: targeted health and education interventions, social security and safety net measures, public works programs, food price policies, and land reform. The country studies (chapters 18-20) disentangle the effects on poverty reduction of growth and of changes in inequality, in general and among the poor, and attribute these effects to events affecting the rate or pattern of growth or to remedies for poverty.

Economic policies that foster growth need not reduce poverty. Unless the growth pattern includes the poor, both by creating employment opportunities for low-skilled workers (and thus pulling up the demand for labor and hence employment and wage rates) and by enabling them to improve their health and skills (and thus meet the emerging demands), the poor will be left behind when the country moves on. This appears to have been the case in the United States in the 1970s, in Pakistan in the 1960s, and in Brazil since 1980 (chapters 19-20).

Including the poor in the growth process

Chapter 11 addresses this point most explicitly. Restating the major components of an antipoverty strategy (employment-enhancing growth, investment in human capital, and social safety nets), the authors flesh out a strategy for including the poor in Latin America, along with resuming growth. The key to reducing rural and, to some extent, migratory urban poverty is to include the poor in rural development, both in agriculture and through rural farm-nonfarm linkages (see also chapter 8). In part because of protection-driven attempts at import-substituting industrialization, the growth of agriculture in Latin America lagged behind that of the rest of the economy from at least the 1940s through the 1970s. But this was reversed during the 1980s: agriculture grew 1.8 percent annually, and nonagricultural GDP only 1.1 percent (chapter 11). In some Latin American countries (Chile, Ecuador, Peru), agricultural growth rates were higher during the crisis years of the 1980s than they were in the 1970s.

This reemergence of agriculture as "the engine of growth" was in part the result of real exchange rate depreciation, which favored agricultural exports despite falling commodity prices.[34] In Latin America, as in Africa, adjustment measures have concentrated on reducing internal and external imbalances and improving productive incentives by "getting the prices right" through devaluation and changes in the often pro-urban tax and price subsidy structures. The supply responses following early attempts at adjustment, however, fell short of expectations.

The problem is not that adjustment packages were antipoor. Contrary to the impression given by the sometimes heated debate about adjustment and poverty, many of the price measures in a standard adjustment package favor agriculture and, therefore, on balance, favor labor-intensive employment and the production of food, and are thus propoor. Rather, the problem is that the adjustment policy package was not really structural enough. Thus, the benefits of better price policies failed to emerge in countries in which the complementary state activities were not in place. In such cases the poor, harmed by the inevitable inflation, were unable to reap the offsetting benefits. This was because, by and large, such policies were accompanied by a contraction of public investment in rural and social service infrastructure and in agricultural technology. This, together with credit constraints and other nonprice factors, limited the potential benefits of improved incentives. Chapter 11 emphasizes the need for the new political forces representing the rural poor—forces formed in response to adjustment and democratization in Latin America—to use their power to press for state action in support of rural infrastructure, skill formation, and asset distribution, rather than the old pseudopopulist giveaways to nonpoor client groups.

In Africa, where there has been no such realignment of civil society, the economic forces producing reasonably high aggregate price elasticities of agricultural supply, and hence propoor adjustment policy outcomes, have proved particularly disappointing (Lipton 1987). There, the quality of much of the infrastructure is well below that in other regions at similar levels of development (Lemer 1990). Yet in Africa, too, there are hopeful signs of change. Ghana is a case in point.

During the 1970s, Ghana's GDP declined by 0.5 percent a year; food production was 30 percent lower in 1981-83 than in 1975; and export earnings fell from 21 percent of GDP in 1970 to 4 percent in 1982 (Okyere 1990). Production of the main export crop, cocoa, declined from more than 500,000 metric tons in the mid-1960s to less than 200,000 metric tons in the early 1980s. Cocoa production employs about one-fifth of Ghana's labor force, so its performance is crucial to Ghana's poor.

External shocks and adverse climatic conditions are partly responsible for the agricultural decline, but faulty policies also played a role. High inflation rates eroded real farm incomes. Export crops were overtaxed to finance the deficit in the recurrent budget, which resulted in part from a generally overstaffed civil service (though staffing was inadequate for many critical agricultural tasks (Commander 1989). The currency was highly overvalued, and rural development was neglected. This, in turn, accelerated rural-to-urban migration and led to a shortage of agricultural labor.

With this plethora of antiagriculture (and thus antipoor) policies, price adjustments alone could not turn the tide. In 1983 Ghana's government initiated a comprehensive economic recovery program that contained the necessary price measures, including progressive exchange rate adjustments. It also contained nonprice measures to revitalize the agricultural sector—measures requiring and receiving more public spending, with more aid inflows to support it. The program included—in the short term—better agricultural producer incentives, better, more reliable farm inputs, and rehabilitation of transport infrastructure. In the medium term,

> agricultural strategy was aimed at (i) improving the consistency between macro- and sectoral policies through measures that improve resource use efficiency, such as the reform of agricultural state-owned enterprises, further liberalization of agricultural pricing, marketing, and trade, and the rationalization of public investment programs; (ii) strengthening the capacity of the public sector to support agricultural development; (iii) revitalizing agricultural research and extension services; (iv) increasing the level and efficiency of rural financial intermediation in order to increase the role of the private sector in agricultural growth, especially small farmers and small rural entrepreneurs; and (v) increasing the productivity and incomes of the majority of the farmers through selective intervention in key areas, such as small-scale irrigation, output diversification, and increased artisanal production and marketing. (Okyere 1990: 75)

Supply responses have been modest but tangible. Cocoa production recovered to 219,000 metric tons in 1985-86. Officially estimated cereal production also shows modest recovery from levels in 1984 (Okyere 1990: 74-76).

The benefits of International Monetary Fund– and World Bank–supported stabilization and adjustment measures have generally been clearer in middle-income, modestly indebted developing countries—for example, Chile, Morocco, and Turkey. Elsewhere, especially in Africa, gains from such measures have fallen well below expectations, with recovery much slower than anticipated and with little difference between the performance of the adjusters and that of carefully matched controls (World Bank 1988a; and Corbo, Fischer, and Webb 1992).

Even "successful" adjustment, however, has sometimes harmed poor people. But where the poor fail to gain from adjustment, it is usually because adjustment fails, not because successful adjustment fails the poor. It would be wrong to construe the observed lack of supply response as an argument against adjustment. Rather, the failure of adjustment to meet expectations should draw attention to the need for it to be truly structural. Adjustment should include ensuring that the state plays an appropriate role in providing infrastructure, marketing structures, technology, and—where appropriate—credit to enhance the potential for agricultural development. And it should include developing institutions of "civil society" that assure the economic inclusion and political participation of the poor, enabling them to take part in monitoring the exercise of power, both in states and in markets.

In such a context, the enhanced role of agriculture in economic recovery can lay the foundation for a strategy to reduce rural poverty. The potential of such an approach is illustrated by an example in Guatemala, where some small farmers contract with export companies, to the benefit of both. The small farmers obtain credit, new crops, chemicals, fertilizers, and better marketing opportunities; the export companies can exploit the improved price and exchange rate regimes that result from adjustment (chapter 7). Multiplier effects spread the benefits of rural development and contribute to poverty reduction through linkages with rural processing and packaging industries (chapter 8).

But does including the poor in resumed development, during and after adjustment, mean only providing them with a level playing field, through unbiased prices, access to training, research oriented toward labor-intensive production methods, public infrastructure to improve transport and market access, and so on? Chapter 11 shows that efforts to include the poor in development are unlikely to be sustained unless they are supported in "the political kingdom." The experience of Malaysia shows the importance of legal and open political pressure by the poor in securing for themselves the fruits of growth. It also shows the importance of rapid growth, of a simmering threat of insurgency, and of an ethnic majority that is relatively poor, and that uses competitive politics to seek redress.

In Latin America the macropolitics of poor people's pressure were critical in increasing their potential to benefit from growth (chapter 11). The micropolitics matter too. Can or should the poor participate in identifying, selecting, designing, appraising, implementing, monitoring, or managing some development projects or programs? If so, which ones, and how? What outside support and training are required? What role should nongovernmental organizations (NGOs) play? Are the nonpoor always the enemy, or can they be bought off, split, or attracted by common interests and positive-sum games?

Access to land

For such symbiotic approaches to poverty reduction through rural development (chapter 11) to succeed, the poor need some autochthonous source of income and safety. That is, they need to have an alternative, in the marketplace and in the polity, to dependence on a patron or monopolist or bureaucrat. Providing the poor with access to productive land is usually regarded as crucial.

Providing the rural poor with access to land, to social services and educational infrastructure that enhance their market power, and to a favorable price environment sounds forbiddingly costly. Is it really necessary? Where land reform has been successfully implemented (China, Japan, Republic of Korea), the poor have clearly benefited. But most major land reforms were the direct result of social revolution or war. And even then, not all obtained the stated goal of reducing poverty (not, for example, in Bolivia and Mexico). Carter and Mesbah (chapter 12) diagnose this gap between promise and reality.

Land reform is of two types: collectivist and distributist. Collectivist land reform has almost always failed both to raise output and to reduce poverty. Distributist land reform—from rural families owning many units of land per person to those owning very few—is more likely to raise poor people's share in output. That is because small landowners are more likely to be poor than big ones, and total employment—and usually even hired employment—per hectare, especially of the poorest (casual, unskilled) workers, increases as farm size decreases.

Efficient distributist reform must also normally increase farm output. The argument that it does so is usually based on two facts: first, notwithstanding tenancy, large, privately owned farms tend to be large operated farms; and second, there is an inverse relationship between the size of an operated farm and its net annual output per acre.[35] If this inverse relationship is strong enough, everybody can gain from land distribution: those who lose land can be bought off with part of the extra production after the reform, and the poor gain new opportunities to use the family's resources. Even if the inverse relationship is weak or absent, multiplier effects of land reform—because of the greater propensity of smaller farmers to buy consumer goods (and producer inputs) from both local and labor-intensive suppliers—can enhance the poverty-reducing effect. Without land reform, extreme polarization between the very rich and the very poor, especially in remote rural areas, can lead to inefficient and inequitable distortion, segmentation, and interlocking of land, labor, and capital markets—such as in Latin America and in eastern India (Bhaduri 1973)—perhaps even to semi-feudalism.

Carter and Mesbah (chapter 12) pose what they call "the Chicago question": if the inverse relationship prevails, why do markets in land (especially tenancies) and labor not push the size of operational holdings to the optimum? Their review of possible answers in Latin America demonstrates that the issue of land reform deserves a more careful and subtle examination than can be expected from static comparison of the poverty and output effects of the three extreme forms of ownership: very large private ownership, equalized smallholdings, and full collectivization. In Latin America the trajectories of past rural development may well have carried the infrastructure, financial institutions, and technology for some crops far beyond the point at which a return to family smallholdings is feasible, let alone efficient. Intermediate strategies could experiment with measures directly encouraging stable tenancy at market rates, so that small, efficiently *operated* holdings might coexist with large, financially and commercially strong *privately owned* holdings. Contractual arrangements could enable the smallholdings to use the processing and marketing strengths of large holdings. This could be a politically more palatable and economically more efficient model for land reform—one that would still allow the poor to earn income by selling managerial skills, not just labor. Routes toward nonconfrontational land reform are explored in chapter 11.

Complacent and conservative land policies, on the other hand, even those with otherwise sensible growth strategies, carry risks that growth will bypass the poor. Sahn and Arulpragasam's country study of Malawi (chapter 13) illustrates the dangers of such policies. An array of land, marketing, and pricing policies together transformed Malawi's already unequal blend of traditional and colonial farming systems into a dualistic agricultural sector that gives huge special advantages to estate-based, capital-intensive tobacco production. Development of smallholder production was neglected, and resources were directed to the estates—which used their concomitant political power to maintain prohibitions against competitive burley tobacco production by labor-intensive smallholders.

Initially, the policy to make the estates the engine of growth appeared successful. During the 1970s estate output quadrupled, while smallholder production grew only 3.3 percent. But much of the estates' increased production can be explained by their increased land acquisition. Failure to increase output per acre, coupled with the increasing number of estates that proved unable to repay commercial bank loans in the 1980s, undermined Malawi's growth strategy. During the 1980s GDP growth was negative (–1.5 percent annually), and by 1989 Malawi's per capita income, at US$180, was the fifth lowest in the impoverished Sub-Saharan African region. Severe income inequality compounds the country's poverty problems.

This example shows that land is becoming scarce even in Africa. It also shows that in a land-scarce developing country the efficiency case—that a sustainable agricultural policy must almost always have a small-farm thrust—does not depend on the inverse relationship. Smallholders, with more "need" as well as more workers per acre (but with less access to capital markets), farm with higher labor-capital ratios than large farmers. A growth strategy centered on small farms is likely, in the medium term, to prove more sustainable fiscally, politically, and ecologically, especially since small farmers are well able to use improved biochemical inputs (Lipton with Longhurst 1989).

Land reform and land tenure will not soon disappear from the policy agenda, especially where there is a concern with poverty reduction. As populations grow, land scarcity is becoming an increasingly important problem. Everywhere, increased awareness of the environmental implications of deforestation and other forms of frontier land development will transform the debate on how to reform land policies to support a sustainable antipoverty strategy. This requires the creation of incentives, institutions, and, perhaps above all, profitable and safe technologies that make it attractive for rural labor, especially in the slack season, to develop and manage water, land, and capital inputs in ways that both use extra labor and reduce rates of resource depletion and, to a lesser extent, pollution and loss of biodiversity. Big corporate loggers maximizing profit in an era of unprecedentedly high real rates of interest, and microfarmers desperately seeking to feed growing families from dwindling private and commonly held resources, will both have to give ground to more equal, more labor-intensive, and more "managed" (Ostrom 1990) patterns of land ownership and use.

Successful reforms will more likely be consistent with the "New Wave" policies discussed in chapter 12, rather than with the more dramatic, but too often merely formal, changes in ownership rights that have been attempted in the past. But evidence on their success in reducing poverty will not be available until the future. Now is the need to enable the poor to earn income, not just with raw labor, but also with enhanced assets—land, cows, and skills.

Increasing the human capital of the poor

> The richest [decile or thereabouts] can well be, at most, four times better placed than the poorest to meet calorie requirements for a full and active life—yet three hundred times better placed in terms of [physical] asset ownership. This latter vast discrepancy naturally focuses, upon asset redistribution, the attention of fighters of wars against poverty. (Lipton 1985, quoted in chapter 12; on the 300-fold figure, see Pathak, Ganpathy, and Sarma 1977: 507)

Land reform remains politically controversial. In Bangladesh a farmer owning three hectares is "big," and may be denounced by an urban politician or academic ten times as rich and fifty times as safe. The rural near-poor resent and resist schemes to transfer their land, entirely at their expense, to the rural poor— schemes promoted, but not financed, by the urban rich. Moreover, although there has been much more land reform than is suggested by those who set limited successes against unlimited expectations (Lipton 1985: 38), it has made only modest contributions to poverty reduction, especially since the reduction of overt Western policy support for it in the 1980s.

Another form of supporting physical asset generation for the poor—providing credit, often subsidized, for the acquisition of new nonfarm assets—has recorded some recent successes in Bangladesh (see Wood 1984 on Proshika; and Hossain 1988a on the Grameen Bank), but on a limited, essentially local scale. The record of large, inevitably bureaucratic, nationwide schemes is mixed or worse (see Drèze 1990a on the Integrated Rural Development Program in India).

A less controversial form of state action that promotes asset accumulation by the poor, one that has seen steady progress over the past four decades, is the increased provision of medical and educational services. These services enhance longevity and health and nutritional status, and produce literacy, numeracy, and other productive skills. Because the rich can usually buy such services privately, public sector provision tends to favor the poor, unless it is unduly concentrated in facilities to which the rich (or the potentially rich) are much likelier to have access, such as universities and high-tech urban teaching hospitals. Malik's study of Pakistan (chapter 20) shows how public spending on social services has improved health and educational outcomes for the poor. Malik also shows, however, that the biases in public provision of social services—regional, gender, urban, and high-tech—have severely retarded growth in the public income of the poor, reducing the welfare effect of the big rises in their private real incomes.

The "human development gap" between rich and poor countries has been steadily narrowing, despite a widening of the "economic development gap" during the 1980s (UNDP 1990; and World Bank 1990b). In this context, the opposite trends within some poor countries are remarkable. The rural-urban human development gap has widened, as indicated by disparities between rural and urban age- and sex-specific mortality, and the rural-urban economic gap, as measured in poverty incidence (with a poverty line defined in terms of private consumption), has narrowed both in India and, recently, in Pakistan (Mitra 1978; and chapters 18 and 20).

Despite some progress, levels of health and education in developing countries are still well below those in the industrial world. Perhaps more important, for some countries they are well below what many developing countries and regions within countries (for example, Kerala in India) have achieved with relatively modest means. This achievement has been possible in part because of improved technology, especially in the health sector. Immunization, birth spacing, prolonged breastfeeding, oral rehydration during diarrhea, and other low-tech, low-cost health practices affordable at the lowest levels of development have resulted in increased longevity and reduced infant mortality and morbidity. These health practices must be sustained over the long run by administrations kept competent by good career incentives and by overview, praise, and criticism from the public. In education this is even more important, to ensure that teaching quality, textbooks, and buildings are maintained in dispersed rural primary schools.

Despite the proven effectiveness of public health intervention, health education, and basic curative care, many developing countries spend 60 to 80 percent of their health budget on hospital care, while large parts of the rural population lack basic services. Similarly, investment in education is often skewed to higher and tertiary schooling, although virtually all studies show that the highest returns are to primary education. Why?

The current providers and beneficiaries of "superior," tertiary education and medical care (and of subsidies to these services) are wealthier, more powerful, and more readily identified and organized than are the potential beneficiaries of primary rural health and education facilities. But there are subtler (and less malleable) reasons why political economy considerations cause governments, the largest actors in the social sectors, to provide an inefficient and antipoor mix of services (chapter 14).

The principal problem is not to define corrective action, but either to change the power structure that led to and maintains this situation (for example, by increasing the "voice" and research support available to the illiterate and dysentery-ridden poor), or to convince the rich and powerful, including key providers of health and education, and their "organizers" that a substantial shift toward primary care is in their own interests. These strategies can be very effective, especially in combination. Employers want literate, healthy workers who are not kept home by sick children. Politicians are shamed by bad performance in "league tables" of health and literacy. And university professors prefer to teach able, motivated children of the poor rather than only the children of the rich and urban, whether motivated and able or not. Poor villagers, if aware of their deprivation and unafraid to speak out, can use the press (and informed foreigners) to claim a more effective and more humane allocation of health and education resources.

Some governments, in their role as providers of public goods, have over-stepped their proper mandate in health and education (Akin, Birdsall, and Ferranti 1987; and Gertler and van der Gaag 1990). Private providers are sometimes prohibited by law from entering these markets, though many commodities provided there are private goods. Externalities, asymmetrical information, scale economies, and other "market failures" justify much of the market intervention, but the rationale for government as the sole provider of health care and education is weak, except perhaps where government has sufficient resources (and is sufficiently scrutinized, open, or internally competitive) to meet all reasonable demands efficiently.

Where governments monopolize the provision of a social service and eschew price rationing, yet must face budget constraints, other forms of rationing have taken over, usually to the benefit of the more powerful urban middle and upper classes. They enjoy highly subsidized or even free basic health care and primary education, as well as nearby subsidized public hospitals and universities. In such circumstances, a reduction in the public sector monopoly may well lead to a shift from urban to rural, and from tertiary to primary, services. Like land reform (only more subtly), such a shift in the provision of human capital increases efficiency by redistributing assets: the poor, having had little access to such assets, use them with higher marginal products (of health or of educational attainment) than the better-provided rich. Secondary education was used not only more, but proportionately more, by the poor in Kenya, which permitted private competition against government schools, than in Tanzania, which forbade such competition (Knight and Sabot 1990). Yet basic health and education are "merit goods," not to be rationed solely by price, or to be made so costly that poor users (if their demand is price inelastic) must forgo other basic needs, such as food or shelter. Exclusive or free public provision, however, may not achieve such goals, but may instead ration the scarce and subsidized services to the influential rich.

Chapter 14 addresses the political factors that impede reallocation of total social sector resources, private and public, toward primary education and health, even when such a shift would both reduce poverty and increase efficiency. Part of the solution it proposes is to broaden the political coalition favoring programs that benefit the poor. This implies less targeting, with obvious budgetary implications.

Safety nets: Remedies for vulnerability

The theme of how to determine the optimal level of targeting pervades this volume. It is particularly relevant for programs aimed at reaching those groups that cannot benefit (or cannot benefit in good time) from the first two components of an overall antipoverty strategy: employment creation and enhancement of human capital. For the aged, disabled, sick, or otherwise vulnerable, social safety nets need to be put in place, either to prevent them from falling below an acceptable level of well-being because of temporary or seasonal adverse economic conditions, or to guarantee them a more permanent minimum but acceptable living standard.

The problem is how to provide such safety nets at a tolerable and sustainable fiscal cost and without excluding poor people, who are likely to be part of the rural, unorganized, informal sector, perhaps in remote areas. Social security in Latin America, notably Brazil (chapter 19), and arguably in the United States too, has become a fiscal nightmare. It is politically almost unassailable, excluding most of the poor from benefit, but financed largely out of taxes highly elastic to inflation, which hits mainly the poor, who have a higher propensity to consume than the rich and are less able to shelter their savings in inflation-proof assets. Yet without safety nets the poor face intolerable risks; and those, rich or poor, unable to transact in insurance markets (often highly incomplete in poor countries) are driven to reorganize their entire consumption, family, and production strategies to avoid catastrophic risk, at a cost to growth and efficiency. Chapters 15-17 ask how safety net policy should avoid these pitfalls.

Traditional safety nets

Public policy to provide safety nets for the poor and vulnerable should usually avoid crowding out private safety nets. These seldom include formal private insurance, especially in rural areas. Rather, they comprise traditional sharing arrangements within communities, villages, small regions, or kinship groups. Such arrangements serve two different purposes: they ensure livelihoods to all, even the chronically vulnerable, especially by providing fairly equal access to productive assets (land, work, fishing rights); and they ensure reduced variability in the livelihoods of poor households.

The first purpose of safety nets is most explicit in traditional, mostly subsistence societies in which every household is entitled to sufficient land to support it (Platteau 1991). Such land sharing is under great pressure from population growth, which is driving newcomers to marginal land and, increasingly, generating landless poor. In general, nonrivalrous "pure public goods" are becoming contested, exhaustible "common property resources" (Ostrom 1990)—and the poor and the weak are being squeezed out (Jodha 1991).

Guaranteed access to work is often a viable alternative to guaranteed access to land. The most common example is a sharecropping arrangement between a landowner and laborers, who pay for access to the land with a percentage of the yield. Such an arrangement includes a form of risk sharing that partially protects the worker against the risk of bad harvests. The *bawon* system in Java, which guarantees a share of the crop to laborers participating in the harvest, is another example of a permanent safety net that provides income to the landless poor.

Such schemes should not be idealized, however. They are generally restricted to villagers, approved ethnic groups, or other insiders. The poorest casual laborers in Java work on nonrice crops with nonguaranteed income and employment. In Bengali villages with highly fluctuating output, known workers from the same village enjoy job preferences (and some guarantees) from known employers; the marginal and the outsiders, presumably the poorest, are left to struggle (Bardhan and Rudra 1981). And as rural economies grow and develop, such work-sharing schemes tend to be replaced by formal labor markets (see

Hart 1986 on Java). Although growth tends to reduce poverty (chapter 7), specific poor groups may lose out.

Chapter 15 (see also Platteau 1991) considers how traditional maritime communities use shared access to the sea to prevent members of the community from being marginalized because of poor fishing spots, or unfavorable weather or seasonal conditions. Such arrangements often include a form of pension plan under which old or sick fishermen receive a share of the catch. Like land-sharing arrangements, these schemes are under increasing pressure from population growth, as well as from more open, competitive fishing and marketing practices.

All these informal guarantee schemes are under pressure from markets, which encroach everywhere, reducing poverty and inducing growth, but leaving victims. Population pressures further increase the scarcity of (and hence disputes about) once-guaranteed benefits. Contractual rights and legal claims develop alongside modern economies. In that process older, informal rights need to be supplemented by formal claims on jobs, as in Maharashtra's Employment Guarantee Scheme; on land, following reform; and on other assets, through a distribution scheme such as India's Integrated Rural Development Program. The trick is to devise formal schemes that work with, not against, the incentives to provide and claim those older rights. Such formal supplementation by the state was much more important in Britain's early industrialization process—and community was much less helpful—than older and more sentimental writings (Engels 1845) suggest (chapter 10). Even the presumed role of extended families (in stabilizing income and providing other support) has been greatly downgraded by research, both in Europe (Laslett and Wall 1972; and Wachter, Hammell, and Laslett 1978) and in India (A. Shah 1979), and especially for the poor. A hard-pressed son is less likely to stay with, or to send remittances to, aged parents if they have little or no land to bequeath (Nugent and Walther 1981).

Personal reciprocity remains a potentially valuable weapon in creating rights for those at high risk of falling into poverty, however. Remittances in exchange for something (a village base, or bequests) are much less likely to be crowded out by public safety net provision than are purely altruistic private transfers to kin (Barro 1974).

Guaranteed access to land or other productive assets, work-sharing arrangements, education and contacts for international, rural-urban, or rural-rural migration,[36] remittances by immigrants, and transfers based on altruism or self-interest are all part of the "bewildering variety" (Platteau 1991) of the organizational forms in traditional societies that diffuse risk and insure against poverty. A better understanding of how these traditional arrangements contribute to the economic security of the participating households, and to what extent they can be complemented, or crowded out, by social security, insurance, transfers, or other interventions, is crucial for the effective design of public safety net policies. It has been argued that state provision for a group of poor persons, generally or as safety nets in emergency, may be partly or wholly negated if it induces cuts in private transfers to the poor from nonpoor persons or groups, in insurance or private savings for emergencies of the poor, or in work effort by the poor. It is clearly in the interests of wealthy taxpayers to overstate these arguments, however; the harmful effect that such overstatement had in Britain in the 1830s is well documented.

Modern safety nets

Like traditional schemes, modern, publicly organized safety nets for the poor aim at a guaranteed minimum standard of living and protection against unpredictable external shocks. Ahmad (chapter 15) discusses modern social security schemes with these goals. Most include food-linked interventions, public works programs, or cash transfers from social security funds.

Much public effort has gone into providing food security for the population at large or for specific groups. Such efforts date back to Pharaonic times and take a variety of forms. The most prevalent are food price interventions.

For food price subsidies effectively to benefit the poor, the commodities chosen should constitute a large part of the poor's food budget. To target the poor, however, one should choose commodities that loom large in the outlays of the poor, but not in the outlays of the nonpoor—inferior goods that are important in the average poor person's consumption bundle. Yet most food price subsidies leak to the nonpoor, with obvious budgetary costs. Chapter 15 evaluates alternatives to general subsidies, ranging from ration shops to food stamps; narrower targeting may avoid leakage to the rich, but at the cost of missing some of the poor.

Pinstrup-Andersen (chapter 16) discusses food price and other food-linked interventions in more detail, with explicit reference to the objective of alleviating malnutrition. The discussion in chapter 5 on the weak link between income and malnutrition is relevant here. Malnutrition is the result of a combination of four things: inadequate expenditure on food; inadequate calories (dietary requirements for dietary energy, especially due to pregnancy, lactation, and long and hard seasonal work, that are insufficiently met. Food subsidization and distribution affect these things in three ways. First, the direct increase in the recipients' real income enables them to obtain more health care (and to reduce excessive labor, and perhaps excessive pregnancies) and to purchase more food, but it also induces them to purchase more expensive foods per calorie, perhaps with some offsetting, negative effects on nutrition. Second, the reduction in the price of foods causes them to be substituted for nonfoods. And third, the improved availability of food (especially with direct distribution programs) reduces the transactions cost of obtaining food relative to that of obtaining nonfood.

All three of these results of food subsidization and distribution can, of course, affect any of the four determinants of nutrition. Moreover, food subsidies or rations distributed to one person can leak to other family members directly or indirectly, or even across households through transfers; such leakages may either lessen or enhance the effects of any of the four determinants. No wonder, then, that attempts to diagnose the effect of food subsidies or supplements tend to show disappointing results; only some of the paths to improvement, and short-run paths at that, get considered as a rule, and then only for direct beneficiaries (for example, for children fed at school, but not for their younger sisters). Moreover, the findings for some of these paths that suggest low responsiveness—for example, the apparently very low income elasticity of short-term demand for calories—are derived from observations made at the mean value of variables; they may therefore understate the responsiveness of the very poor, even along any one of the routes to response (which may be all that is measured). Thus, increased food intake may do more good than the surveys show (chapter 5). Also, it is demonstrably more cost-effective, in improving poor people's health, when it is integrated with better primary health care (Taylor and others 1978; and Berg 1987).

A food-linked program that seeks to provide food security while respecting the need for targeting (to avoid exceeding budgetary constraints) is food in exchange for work. Ahmad (chapter 15) discusses employment provision and public works programs in general as instruments to prevent famine or as relief measures for those affected by economic shocks. The use of such programs as relief measures is particularly relevant in Eastern European countries undergoing the transition to market economies, with the unavoidable side effects of massive labor turnover and hence unprecedented unemployment.

The central question for public works programs is to what extent they reach the target population. Crucial for ensuring this is paying low wages. This guarantees that only the needy will apply for jobs and allows greater coverage of the poor with a given budget. But poor applicants for these programs also lose something: the costs of seeking and finding extra work, and of supporting it with calories, and the income (net of similar costs) from work forgone in order to work on the scheme. If the scheme wage is too low, the net gains to the poor may be too small for the public works program (because of its administrative costs) to be a cost-effective attack on poverty.

On balance, though, the poor gain if the public works wage is kept fairly low. Ravallion, Datt, and Chaudhuri (1991) examine recent experience with Maharashtra's Employment Guarantee Scheme. The scheme had to double its wage rate in mid-1988 because of a doubling of the statutory minimum wage. Shortly thereafter it experienced a sharp fall in employment. Though other factors, such as excellent and timely monsoons, may have played a role, the evidence suggests that after the wage increased, scheme jobs were made harder to come by. They were often informally rationed by being located only within the district of applicants, and not as before, within five miles of the home village. The data suggest that at times the greater distances may have filtered out about half the demand. Thus, although those lucky enough to obtain a job benefited from the higher wages, many of the poor were left out.

Parikh and Srinivasan (chapter 17), using a general equilibrium framework, show that in India rural public works programs are more effective in increasing the energy intake of the poorest quintile in monthly expenditure per person than are food distribution programs of similar cost. But such small-scale programs as the Tamil Nadu Integrated Nutrition Program (and the local successes even of the Integrated Child Development Program) suggest that carefully planned nutrition programs can do much better than large-scale food distribution (Berg 1987; and Heaver 1989). Furthermore, it seems unlikely that India's National Rural

Employment Program and its successors—or even, since 1988, the Maharashtra Employment Guarantee Scheme—will achieve the high cost-effectiveness of the scheme in its earlier years. This raises a general point about antipoverty programs. Begun with high ideals and careful plans, their cost-effectiveness and the effectiveness of their targeting almost inevitably deteriorate as the nonpoor (both bureaucrats and unintended beneficiaries) learn to "use" them. Rapid turnover of such programs need not mean failure; it may represent courageous recognition of reality, and steady service to the poor.

Social security, as it is commonly available in the industrial world—through pensions, unemployment payments, and other benefits—covers only a small fraction of the population in the developing world. Most of the existing schemes are found in Latin America, where wage employment is widespread. The debate about safety nets for the poor and vulnerable pays scant attention to the implementation of formal social security schemes. This is in part because the budgetary resources for such schemes are lacking. Another reason is the negative experience of many of the Latin American schemes. They have generally been funded through trust funds, and many have run into financial trouble because of government orders to carry holdings of government bonds and other inappropriate investments at below-market rates, and other mandated forms of mismanagement. Moreover, these schemes are usually confined to (and vehemently defended by) organized employees of government and big private firms—that is, mostly middle and upper-middle wage earners, not the poor.

As Ahmad points out, however, the mismanagement of Latin American social security funds does not prove that such schemes cannot effectively cover the poor; even some very poor Asian countries (Sri Lanka) and regions (Kerala state, India) achieve this to some extent. Furthermore, even where the formal labor market accounts for only a small portion of the total labor force, this portion may still be large in absolute numbers, it is likely to grow, and it does contain some poor people. The aging of the population, especially in Asia, but also in many Latin American countries, will exert pressure on policymakers to consider public social security schemes with broad coverage as alternatives to the more commonly used price or public employment interventions. Much can be learned from successful programs, such as the pension scheme in Kerala. But much can be learned also from the traditional private transfer systems that, up to now, have largely escaped the attention of economists and other social scientists concerned with the design and implementation of safety nets.

Including the poor

Defining a set of projects, usually conveniently small, while planning ports, major highways, and industrial policy as if these did not affect the poor is inadequate for ensuring that the poor benefit from development. It is also inadequate to tack on poverty alleviation schemes to important macroeconomic policies that harm or ignore the poor. To ensure that development reduces poverty, policymakers need to ask, at every decision point, a central question: What will this policy or project do to the main groups of poor people, to landless rural laborers, to families with only one earner and several small children, and to casual laborers, both urban and rural?

This question should be asked at each stage of programs, of large projects, and of experimental pilots that may later be replicated: at identification; during the selection of alternative designs at preappraisal; at the point of financing or rejection; during implementation; and when evaluating, managing, and monitoring. The question also needs to be posed with respect to policy packages seeking stabilization and adjustment. It needs to be part of the discussion on fiscal policies, the pattern and location of industrialization, and the direction of urban development. It should influence the research agenda that fosters agricultural development and technological change. It should be addressed when countries shape their future through trade liberalization, exchange rate policies, and democratization. It needs to take a central place in the work portfolio of the international development community, and it needs to be at the core of a country's own efforts to improve the living conditions of its citizens.

Including the poor needs to go beyond their passive sharing in the benefits from projects and programs. Indeed, such sharing is unlikely unless poor people also share actively in identifying their needs, and in organizing to press for their fulfillment. Hegel was right to identify the inclusion of the poor in "civil society" as the central problem of a liberal polity.

If the poor are included, or include themselves, in all decisions that shape the national and regional economic, political, and social environment, then (as the following chapters reveal) there is huge scope for policies *including the poor* in the benefits from such decisions. Only thus can we expect to achieve sustainable progress against the enemy that threatens the very existence of more than 600 million people in the developing world: poverty. We brought this collection of essays together in the hope that everyone in the development community would benefit from it, *including the poor*.

Notes

1. For fuller discussion and evidence, see Fields (1989a); Drèze and Sen (1989); and World Bank (1990b). For detailed analysis of India, Brazil, and Pakistan, see chapters 18-20.

2. These numbers represent those below an extreme poverty line of $275 consumption per person per year at U.S. purchasing-power parity (World Bank 1990b: 29). Though harsh, this "Indian" poverty line exceeds the level at which a typical household avoids calorie deprivation (the "ultra-poverty line" in Lipton 1983c). The $275 includes consumed produce of family farms, but excludes free public services.

3. This book grew out of a series of meetings arranged jointly by the International Food Policy Research Institute and the World Bank, followed by a conference, in 1988-89. These meetings and the conference were attended by some of the staff preparing *World Development Report 1990* under Lyn Squire's direction.

4. Work is needed on whether one element in large quantities is as good at reducing various kinds of poverty as a judicious mix of two elements in lesser quantities, and on the opportunity costs of these alternatives.

5. This is taken to include both self-employment and wage employment, per unit of land or of capital.

6. The argument is as follows: first, in rural areas (largely because of rising person-land ratios) a growing proportion of people operate little or no farmland on their own account; second, in urban areas a growing proportion of people are employees (in the informal or formal sector); and third, urbanization involves movement from rural areas to places where a larger, and growing, proportion of the work force consists of employees.

7. See Corbo, Fischer, and Webb (1992) for an evaluation of World Bank–supported adjustment lending and its impact on the poor.

8. Expenditure fluctuates much less than income, and is used in most poverty studies to measure permanent income (or access to goods and services). Per-household data are useless as measures of poverty or well-being, because households differ greatly in size; per-person measures of expenditure are therefore generally used. Expenditure per adult equivalent, or per consumer unit, is a somewhat better measure, but in practice almost always produces results very similar to the per-person measure (Lipton 1983c).

The Indian National Sample Survey data, used in table 1.1 and in several chapters in this volume, report results from more than 150,000 households, interviewed in four rounds staggered over a year.

9. In fact, the Datt-Ravallion line of Rs 76.65 MEP lies somewhat above the ultra-poverty line that would command a minimum adequate diet (for a household dividing MEP among items typically purchased by households of its size, composition, and MEP). See Minhas (1991).

10. Chapter 3 reviews this issue too. If nonpoor people work less hard as a result of a proportional tax on income, the tax rate needed to raise a given sum from them increases. But taxes on the nonpoor, even more than transfers to the poor, can readily be imposed on purchases rather than incomes; even if they are direct, they can be scheduled so as to avoid severely discouraging effort.

11. Imperfect information is only one cause of such leakage. But if everyone knows when an unentitled (nonpoor) person receives benefits under a poverty program, abuse is discouraged. For a scathing review of leakage to the nonpoor from India's Integrated Rural Development Program, see Drèze (1990a).

12. As Thorbecke points out in his commentary on chapters 2-5 (personal communication to the editors), this caloric norm in the Indian data used by Datt and Ravallion, although correctly priced by them at local prices (in each Indian state), relates to calories derived from the typical national-level diet of each MEP group. When each region's poverty line is estimated as the MEP sufficient to buy a diet that is just sufficient given regional food purchasing patterns, results are rather different, at least in Kenya. This is in part because tastes differ regionally, as Thorbecke stresses, but also because people—especially the poor—will select locally cheaper food staples, not national average bundles. Therefore, estimation of poverty lines at the outlay just sufficient, for each (given) household size and composition, to purchase enough of a national diet—even of a national diet for the average poor person, and even at regional prices—overstates the poverty line and hence P_0, P_1, and other poverty-related measures.

13. This is not to question the intelligence with which households use scarce resources—or the danger that resources labeled "for the poor" may leak to the bureaucrats who administer them. Genuine public goods do exist in the area of poverty reduction, however. A further case for using the poverty tax partly to finance public activities is that intrafamily power structures in some regions, sometimes backed by religious and customary norms, depress below the optimum for health the proportion of private MEP that goes to the calorie intake, health, and leisure of women and small children.

14. The exercise normally requires more time, training, and resources than project officials have. Also they, like potential beneficiaries, have incentives to misreport or

short-circuit. Apart from this, surprising (and genuine) ignorance about professionally settled issues persists among administrators of antipoverty programs. In no country have scholars contributed more to our understanding of poverty measurement than in India. Yet its massive Integrated Rural Development Program (which distributes nonfarm assets to the rural poor on a one-third-subsidy, two-thirds-loan basis) defined the poor in terms of total family income, not MEP, and conducted a huge, costly concurrent evaluation of the poverty impact of the Integrated Rural Development Program without baseline studies.

15. They allow for decreasing returns—that is, for decreasing elasticity of $P/(P + N)$ to A as A rises—but a cynic might suggest that returns at some point become negative, if a bigger and better-paid bureaucracy is more well-endowed, skillful, and motivated when colluding with the well-off to share benefits meant for the poor.

16. The poverty-minimizing redistribution among regions—with no intraregional redistribution—is not, in general, the same as equalization of all regional mean incomes. This is because intraregional distributions—which, by assumption, cannot be altered—vary among regions. See chapter 4.

17. Moreover, the significance level varies greatly according to the poverty measure chosen. This again illustrates the importance for policy of deciding what concepts of poverty to measure, and how.

18. See, for instance, Chenery and Srinivasan (1988); Ranis and Schultz (1988); and even the much more developmentalist approach in Stern (1989).

19. The distinction is correct in sign, but not absolute. Even in 1348 the rich had a somewhat better chance of fleeing the Black Death and surviving in blockaded houses in rural areas.

20. Malaria control, improved nutrition, famine prevention, and urbanization permitting access to basic health care are the four main causes of the decline in death rates in the developing world since 1945. All reduce death rates most among those under age five. This leads to a bulge in the groups of working age, such that they outgrow other age-groups ten to thirty years after the improvement in health conditions.

21. Even a labor-using exception, such as the improved cereal varieties of the 1960s, is subject to these pressures. The elasticity of employment with respect to yield-based farm growth for rice and wheat in South Asia fell from about 0.4 in the early 1970s to about 0.1 in the mid-1980s (Jayasuriya and Shand 1986).

22. The period 1980-86 saw several droughts, peaking debt repayments, worsening terms of trade, and—worst of all—a decline in economic activity as foreign and budgetary deficits (owing in part to chronic economic mismanagement) demanded attention.

23. Education, like health, is a service that nonpoor children are likely to obtain anyway, so chapter 6 can use changing total or average public real outlays as an indicator of changing access for the poor. Public outlays were calculated in purchasing power parity dollars per person. The population of Kenya and most other African countries—in sharp contrast to that of South and East Asia—is projected to get younger until 2010.

24. See preceding note; if public human capital outlays did fall, the poor would lose most, because others can more often afford private health care and education, and have lower child-adult ratios.

25. Contrary to general belief, these increases in life expectancy are by no means all among those under age five. Male life expectancy in India rose from 31.0 years at birth to 52.5 in 1976-80, but life expectancy at age 15 rose from 40.7 years (1945-51) to 50.3 years (1976-80). For females the increases were from 31.4 years to 52.1 and from 40.8 years to 52.1 (Bhatt 1989; and United Nations 1988).

26. On major statistical overestimation of true net urbanization, and of its net benefits to the initially rural poor, see Lipton (1982b).

27. According to most measures, income distribution is more unequal within urban areas than within rural areas in the large majority of countries with available data, however (Lipton 1984). Therefore, the intensity of poverty is sometimes greater in urban than in rural areas.

28. Estimates vary because of slightly different poverty lines and deflators. See Howes (1990: 11) and the sources cited there.

29. Regional effects on the poor might be more fully captured by disaggregating a developing country into rural regions classified as follows: (1) those that are very progressive, with new wheat and rice technologies from the start; (2) those following later with new sorghum or ragi varieties; (3) those moving into crops (such as sugar, groundnuts, or alfalfa) abandoned by regions that find wheat and other crops relatively more profitable with the new technologies; and (4) those at an absolute disadvantage in all significantly demanded crops (Lipton with Longhurst 1989: 162-65).

30. The argument is that almost every citizen is ready to contribute a fair share to the provision of such guarantees (and that acceptable agreement can be reached on fair shares) if and only if she or he is reasonably confident that a large majority of other citizens also contribute their fair shares. Such a social contract conditional on widespread enforcement might be possible because of widespread altruism conditional on the limitation of free-riding, or because of widespread self-interested perception of a risk, not insurable by private markets, and capable of being much reduced by public action if and only if enough taxpayers lend support.

31. Nothing about this implicit classical model requires that the acceleration of technical progress be mainly industrial or mainly agricultural, provided that trade is free enough. In a closed and fully employed economy, as Adam Smith pointed out, initial nonfarm growth depends on a previously increased surplus of farm products: food-wage goods. In past practice accelerated agricultural growth has almost always preceded the transfer of surplus to finance and feed accelerated growth, but the rate of technical progress in industry has exceeded earlier rates in agriculture. In the world of the green revolution (and biotechnology) and rustbelts, this empirical rule, and its implicit welding of development (at least in the long term) to industrialization, may break down (Stiglitz 1988).

32. If the great majority of farmers have access neither to more land nor to improved technology, they cannot respond to better farm prices by substantially increasing their *aggregate* output. They are highly responsive in the sense of shifting their output *among* agricultural products so as to take advantage of changes in relative prices, but *aggregate* supply elasticities are notoriously low in these circumstances (Bond 1993; Lipton 1987; and especially Binswanger 1985).

33. However, the dramatic fall in real public sector wage rates in many African countries during these adjustments (see, for example, Klitgaard 1989; and van der Gaag, Stelcner, and Vijverberg 1989) not only hampers the recovery to sustainable growth by further eroding the quality of public institutions, it also creates a class of the "new poor," who may become a vocal opposition to the adjustment policies.

34. This path requires caution. It shifts GNP into sectors in which relative world prices are falling. The shift accelerates the price decline and can harm producers of commodities for which world demand is price inelastic (for example, beverage crops), especially if many growers shift at once.

35. This inverse relationship need not, and indeed mainly does not, depend on differences between large and small farms with respect to the yield of a particular crop in

a particular season. Most of the observed instances of the inverse relationship rest mainly on less fallowing, higher cropping intensity, and a more labor-intensive—and hence valuable—crop mix on small farms.

36. For risk sharing in migration, see Epstein (1973) on the "share family" in South India; for major analytical developments, see Stark (1991). Poor migrants' prospects of alleviating poverty are reduced for two reasons: first, they are mostly rural-to-rural migrants (Connell 1976) and therefore have little to remit; and second, they have few hopes of inheriting rural assets and hence few incentives (besides familial love) to remit even if they can (Nugent and Walther 1981). But a review of the empirical literature (Cox and Jimenez 1990) indicates how important transfers can be. In two Mexican villages gross remittances from migrants accounted for 16 to 21 percent of household income. In Malaysia remittances were almost half the total income in receiving households. The role of remittances in insuring against poverty is often overstated, however, because research concentrates on places in which they are unusually important, and because reverse—for example, rural-to-urban—remittances are often omitted, and only the gross inflows to (poor) rural households are counted. In a sample of almost 200 Indian villages not purposefully selected for migration studies, transfers into households were about 3 percent of total household income, and most (though not all) were offset by transfers out (Connell 1976). In Peru in 1985 average transfers in were 2 percent of average household income—and transfers out, 1 percent (Cox and Jimenez 1989).

Part I
Concepts and Measurements

Measuring Poverty: Definitions and Significance Tests with Application to Côte d'Ivoire

2

N. Kakwani

To formulate a program to combat poverty, it is often important to identify the poor and desirable to measure the intensity of their poverty. Thus, the measurement of poverty involves two distinct problems: (1) specification of the poverty line—the income level below which one is considered to be poor, and (2) construction of an index to measure the intensity of poverty suffered by those whose income is below that line.

Since the publication of Sen's (1976) article on the axiomatic approach to the measurement of poverty, several indices of poverty have been developed. The indices use three poverty indicators:
* The percentage of poor
* The aggregate poverty gap
* The distribution of income among the poor.[1]

The way in which poverty indices combine these three indicators reflects different assumptions about the welfare function implied by the indicators. For example, a policymaker concerned solely with reducing the percentage of the poor would concentrate on those just below the poverty line. If the intensity of poverty is the main concern, however, greater weight needs to be given to the poorest of the poor.

Because the poverty measures are estimated on the basis of sample observations, we need to test whether the observed differences in their values are statistically significant. The main focus of this chapter is the problem of statistical inference with estimated poverty measures. The problem is important because we are often interested in knowing whether poverty has increased or decreased over time or in comparing differences in poverty between countries or between socioeconomic groups within the same country. This chapter provides a more detailed discussion of the distribution-free asymptotic confidence interval and statistical inference for several poverty measures developed by Kakwani (forthcoming).

The methodology developed in this chapter is applied to the data obtained from the Côte d'Ivoire Living Standards Measurement Study Survey, conducted in 1985 by the World Bank's Living Standards Unit and the Direction de la Statistique, Ministère de l'Economie et des Finances of the Republic of Côte d'Ivoire. A description of the survey and sampling methodology is given in Ainsworth and Muñoz (1986).

A brief review of poverty measures

Suppose income x of an individual is a random variable with the distribution function $F(x)$. Let z denote the poverty line—the threshold income below which one is considered to be poor. Then $F(z)$ is the proportion of individuals (or families) below the poverty line. This measure, widely used as a poverty measure, is called the head count ratio.

The head count is a crude poverty index because it does not take account of the income gap among the poor. If the degree of misery suffered by an individual is proportional to how far short of the poverty line that individual's income falls, then the sum total of these income shortfalls may be considered an adequate measure of poverty. Such a measure is called the poverty gap ratio and can be written as

$$(2.1) \qquad G = \int_0^z g(x)f(x)\,dx = F(z)[\frac{z-\mu^*}{z}],$$

where $g(x) = (z-x)/z$, $f(x)$ is the density function, and μ^* is the mean income of the poor.

The measure G will provide adequate information about the intensity of poverty if all the poor are assumed to have exactly the same income, which is less than the poverty line. But because income is unequally distributed among the poor, G cannot be an adequate measure of the intensity of poverty. More inequality of income among the poor with the mean remaining unchanged should imply greater hardship for the extremely poor in a society; therefore, the degree of poverty should be higher than that indicated by the measure G.

To make G sensitive to the income inequality among the poor, Sen (1976) proposed the following poverty measure:

$$S = F(z)\,\frac{[z-\mu^*(1-G^*)]}{z},$$

where μ^* is the mean income of the poor and G^* is the Gini index of the income distribution among the poor. He arrived at this measure on the basis of rank order weighting, and showed that it captures some of the relative deprivation aspect of poverty.

Suppose that the population is divided into mutually exclusive groups according to certain socioeconomic and demographic characteristics of the households to which individuals belong. Let $f_i(x)$ be the density function of the ith group. Further, suppose that because of certain government policies, the density function of the ith group changes from $f_i(x)$ to $f_i^*(x)$ and the distributions of the remaining $(m-1)$ groups do not change. As a consequence, the poverty measure P_i of the ith group changes to P_i^*, such that $P_i^* > P_i$.

Intuitively, one would expect the poverty in the entire population to then increase. For this to happen to an indicator, it must rise (fall) for the entire population if it rises (falls) for any one group and remains unchanged for all other groups. But Sen's poverty measure violates this simple requirement in certain cases. This violation occurs because Sen's measure is not additively separable.

A class of additively separable poverty measures is given by

(2.2)
$$P = \int_0^z \theta(z, x) f(x) \, dx,$$

where $\theta(z, x)$ is a function of the poverty line z and income x. P is equal to the head count measure of poverty when $\theta(z, x) = 1$. The poverty gap measure in equation 2.1 is obtained when $\theta(z, x) = (z - x)/z$.

The probability density function $f(x)$ of the entire population may be written

(2.3)
$$f(x) = \sum_{i=1}^{m} \lambda_i f_i(x),$$

where $f_i(x)$ is the probability function of the ith subgroup, which has the λ_i proportion of individuals such that

$$\sum_{i=1}^{m} \lambda_i = 1;$$

in other words, all the subgroups are mutually exclusive. Multiplying both sides of equation 2.3 by $\theta(z, x)$ and integrating, we obtain

(2.4)
$$P = \sum_{i=1}^{m} \lambda_i P_i,$$

where P_i is the poverty measure for the ith subgroup. It implies that total poverty is a weighted average of the poverty levels of the subgroups, with the weights proportional to their share in the population. Poverty measures that satisfy equation 2.4 are called "additively decomposable" (Foster, Greer, and Thorbecke 1984). Thus, we have shown that all additively separable poverty measures are additively decomposable.

The additively decomposable poverty measures are useful because they allow the assessment of the effects of changes in subgroup poverty on total poverty. If the population is disaggregated according to some socioeconomic and demographic characteristics, it is of interest to know how much each subgroup contributes to total poverty. Sen's poverty measure is inadequate for analyzing such issues because it is not additively decomposable.

An important attribute of Sen's measure is that it captures the sense of "relative deprivation," which Sen considers to be an important part of the harm done by poverty. But for developing countries, where most people live below the subsistence level, this heavy emphasis on relative positions of the poor is not very appealing. Our main concern—at least in *measuring* poverty—should be with absolute rather than relative deprivation.

To make the poverty measures in equation 2.2 operational, we need to specify $\theta(z, x)$. We start by considering four general restrictions that may be imposed on this function.

First, Sen's monotonicity axiom (which implies that, given other things, a reduction in the income of a poor individual must increase the poverty measure) will be satisfied by equation 2.2 if $\theta(z, x)$ is a decreasing function of x; that is, if $\partial\theta/\partial x < 0$.

Second, Sen's transfer axiom states that "given other things, a pure transfer of income from a poor individual to any other richer individual must increase the poverty measure" (1976: 220). This axiom will be satisfied if $\theta(z, y + \delta) - \theta(z, x - \delta) > 0$ for $y > x$, or, in other words, if $\partial^2\theta/\partial x^2 > 0$.

Third, the transfer sensitivity axiom introduced by Kakwani states that "if a transfer of income takes place from a poor person with income x to a poor person with income $(x + h)$, then for a given $h > 0$, the magnitude of increase in the poverty measure decreases as x increases" (1980b: 439). This axiom gives more weight to transfers of income among the poorest than to those among the less poor. If a society is particularly averse to inequality among the poor, the poverty measure must give maximum weight to a transfer from the poorest of the poor, and the weight should decrease as the level of income increases. This axiom in the case of poverty measures in equation 2.2 implies that $\partial\theta/\partial x < 0$ where $Q = \theta(z, x + h + \delta) - \theta(z, x - \delta)$ for fixed $h > 0$ and $\delta > 0$, or, in other words, $\partial^3\theta/\partial x^3 < 0$.

Fourth, we require that a proportional increase in all incomes, together with a proportional increase in the poverty line, should leave the poverty measure unaltered. This requirement can be met by specifying $\theta(z, x)$ to be homogeneous of degree zero in z and x: $\theta(kz, kx) = \theta(z, x)$.

Specific poverty measures

Foster, Greer, and Thorbecke (1984) proposed a class of poverty measures that are additively decomposable. This class of measures is obtained if we substitute

$$\theta(z,x) = \left[\frac{z-x}{x}\right]^\alpha$$

in equation 2.2:

(2.5) $$P_\alpha = \int_0^z \left[\frac{z-x}{x}\right]^\alpha f(x)\,dx,$$

where α is a parameter to be specified. These measures satisfy Sen's monotonicity axiom if and only if $\alpha > 0$ and Sen's transfer axiom if and only if $\alpha > 1$. When $\alpha > 2$, P_α also satisfies Kakwani's transfer sensitivity axiom.

Watts (1968) proposed a poverty measure that can be obtained by substituting $\theta(z, x) = \log z - \log x$:

(2.6) $$W = \int_0^z (\log z - \log x) f(x)\,dx.$$

Although this is an extremely simple poverty measure, it has all the important attributes: it satisfies Sen's monotonicity and transfer axioms and Kakwani's transfer sensitivity axiom.

Finally, we consider the Clark, Hemming, and Ulph (1981) poverty measure, which can be obtained by substituting

$$\theta(z,x) = \frac{1}{\beta}\left[1 - \left(\frac{x}{z}\right)^{\beta}\right];$$

(2.7)
$$C_{\beta} = \frac{1}{\beta}\int_{0}^{z}\left[1 - \left(\frac{x}{z}\right)^{\beta}\right]f(x)dx,$$

where ß is a parameter to be specified. These measures clearly satisfy Sen's monotonicity axiom if and only if ß > 0. Both the transfer and the transfer sensitivity axioms will be satisfied for all ß < 1. Thus, ß must lie in the range 0 < ß < 1.

Confidence interval and hypothesis testing

Let $x_1, x_2,..., x_n$ be a random sample of n observations drawn from a population with mean μ and variance σ^2. Suppose that P given in equation 2.2 is a poverty measure defined in terms of the population distribution and that $\hat{P}$ is its sample estimate based on n observations. It will be demonstrated below that $\sqrt{n}(\hat{P} - P)$ is asymptotically normally distributed with zero mean and variance $\sigma^2(\hat{P})$. If $\hat{\sigma}^2(\hat{P})$ is a consistent sample estimator of $\sigma^2(\hat{P})$, then $\hat{\sigma}(\hat{P})/\sqrt{n}$ is the standard error of $\hat{P}$, which we denote by $SE(\hat{P})$. Then

(2.8)
$$t = \frac{\hat{P} - P}{SE(\hat{P})}$$

is distributed asymptotically normally with zero mean and unit variance. Thus, t can be used to form a distribution-free confidence interval for poverty measures.

Further, suppose $\hat{P}_1$ and $\hat{P}_2$ are estimates of a poverty measure P computed on the basis of two independently drawn random samples of sizes n_1 and n_2, respectively. Let $\hat{\sigma}_1^2$ and $\hat{\sigma}_2^2$ be the sample estimators of the variances of the asymptotic distributors of $\sqrt{n_1}\hat{P}$ and $\sqrt{n}\,\hat{P}_2$, respectively. Then the standard error of $(\hat{P}_1 - \hat{P}_2)$ will be

$$SE(\hat{P}_1 - \hat{P}_1) = \sqrt{\frac{\hat{\sigma}_1^2}{n_1} + \frac{\hat{\sigma}_2^2}{n_2}},$$

and the statistic

(2.9)
$$\eta = \frac{\hat{P}_1 - \hat{P}_2}{SE(\hat{P}_1 - \hat{P}_1)}$$

follows asymptotic normal distribution with zero mean and unit variance. Thus, η can be used to test the null hypothesis that the differences in poverty observed between any two samples are statistically insignificant. To calculate t

and η, we need to derive the asymptotic distributions of various poverty measures.

Asymptotic distribution of poverty measures

Suppose that q $(\leq n)$ is the number of people in a sample of size n who have income below the poverty line. Then $H = q/n$ is an estimator of the head count ratio $F(z)$. Let

(2.10)
$$I_i = 1, \, x_i < z$$
$$= 0, \, \text{otherwise}.$$

Then $Pr[I = 1] = F(z)$ and $Pr[I_i = 0] = 1 - F(z)$ and

$$H = \frac{1}{n} \sum_{i=1}^{n} I_i$$

where Pr stands for probability. H is a binomial variate with parameters n and $F(z)$. The central limit theorem implies that $\sqrt{n} \, [H - F(z)]$ follows an asymptotic normal distribution with zero mean and variance $F(z) \, [1 - F(z)]$ (Cramer 1946). Thus, the standard error of H will be $\sqrt{H(1-H)/n}$, which, in conjunction with equation 2.8, provides a distribution-free statistical inference for the head count ratio.

A sample estimate of the class of additively separable poverty measures P in equation 2.2 is given by

(2.11)
$$\hat{P} = \frac{1}{n} \sum_{i=1}^{q} \theta(z, x_i),$$

which, using equation 2.10, can also be written as

(2.12)
$$\hat{P} = \frac{1}{n} \sum_{i=1}^{n} M_i,$$

where $M_i = I_i \theta(z, x_i)$. Note that

$$E(M_i) = \int_0^z \theta(z, x) f(x) \, d(x) = P,$$

which implies that $\hat{P}$ is an unbiased estimator of P.

Because the sample observations x_i and x_j are independently distributed, this implies that M_i and M_j will also be independently distributed. Applying the central limit theorem to equation 2.12 (Cramer 1946) leads to the result that $\sqrt{n} \, (P - P)$ is asymptotically normally distributed with zero mean and variance

(2.13)
$$\sigma_M^2 = E \, [M_i - P]^2 = \int_0^z \theta^2 (z, x) f(x) \, dx - P^2.$$

A sample estimate is

(2.14)
$$\hat{\sigma}_M^2 = \frac{1}{n} \sum_{i=1}^{q} \theta^2(z, x_i) - \hat{P}^2.$$

It can be seen, when $\theta(z, x) = 1.0$, that P is identical to the head count ratio and that therefore σ_M^2 becomes $F(z)[1 - F(z)]$, which is in fact the variance of $\sqrt{n}H$ as derived above. Similarly, if we substitute $\theta(z, x) = (z - x)/z$, σ_M^2 in equation 2.13, it gives the variance of $\sqrt{n}\hat{G}$, where $\hat{G}$ is the unbiased estimate of the poverty gap ratio given in equation 2.1.

The above formulation allows us to find the asymptotic distribution of all the specific poverty measures discussed above. Thus, the sample estimates of the variance of these measures are:

$$\text{var}(\sqrt{n}\,\hat{P}_\alpha) = \hat{P}_{2\alpha} - \hat{P}_\alpha^2,$$

where
$$\hat{P}_\alpha = \frac{1}{n} \sum_{i=1}^{q} \left[\frac{z - x_i}{z}\right]^\alpha;$$

$$\text{var}(\sqrt{n}\,\hat{W}) = \frac{1}{n} \sum_{i=1}^{q} (\log z - \log x_i)^2 - \hat{W}^2,$$

where
$$\hat{W} = \frac{1}{n} \sum_{i=1}^{q} (\log z - \log x_i);$$

$$\text{var}(\sqrt{n}\,\hat{C}_\beta) = \frac{1}{\beta^2 n} \sum_{i=1}^{q} \left[1 - \left(\frac{x_i}{z}\right)^\beta\right]^2 - \hat{C}_\beta^2,$$

where
$$\hat{C}_\beta = \frac{1}{\beta} \left[H - \frac{1}{n} \sum_{i=1}^{q} \left(\frac{x_i}{z}\right)^\beta\right].$$

Application to Côte d'Ivoire

To analyze poverty, we need to measure the economic welfare of each individual in the society. Although income is widely used to measure economic welfare, it has many serious drawbacks.[2] In this chapter we have used per capita adjusted consumption as a measure of households' economic welfare. This measure, constructed by Glewwe (1988), includes the imputed value of owner-occupied dwellings and the depreciated value of consumer durables. It also corrects for regional price variation.

To take account of the differing needs of household members, Glewwe divided the total household consumption by the number of equivalent adults. His formulation of equivalent adults gives children a smaller weight than adults: children less than seven years old were given a weight of 0.2; those between the ages of seven and thirteen, a weight of 0.3; and those between the ages of thirteen and seventeen, a weight of 0.5.

The next step in constructing the index of household welfare is to determine the welfare of the individuals in the household. In this chapter individual welfare was derived by assigning every individual in a household a welfare value equal to the consumption per equivalent adult for that household. The validity of this approach—that is, of the implicit assumptions that household consumption is distributed among individuals in proportion to their weighted requirements, and that it yields the same marginal benefit for each individual—is discussed in Kakwani (1986).

Once we have decided on a suitable index of economic welfare for individuals, the next step is to find a threshold level of welfare below which an individual is poor. In this chapter we have considered two poverty lines: one with an annual adjusted per capita consumption of 91,394 Communauté Financière Africaine francs (CFAF) and another of CFAF 162,613.[3] The two poverty lines identify approximately the poorest 10 percent and the poorest 30 percent of the total population.[4] As measured in adjusted per capita terms, consumption for the poorest 10 percent of Ivorians is less than 20 percent of the consumption of the average Ivorian; the poorest 30 percent consume about one-third of the national average. The poverty line of CFAF 91,394 per year is probably close to a situation of extreme poverty, below which physical personal maintenance is unstable (Lipton 1988b).

The numerical values of different poverty measures and their standard errors are presented in table 2.1. The t-value in the table is equal to the value of the poverty measure divided by its standard error (see equation 2.8). This statistic follows an asymptotic normal distribution with zero mean and unit variance. If t exceeds 1.96, it means that the hypothesis of zero poverty is rejected at a level of significance of 5 percent. This method is valid if our sample is large. In practice, it is often difficult to know whether our samples are large enough so that these large-sample approximations are valid. But the approximation is usually good for samples larger than thirty (Cramer 1946). Because our analysis of poverty is based on samples larger than 250, the statistical inference based on asymptotic distributions is appropriate.

Among the poverty measures presented in table 2.1, the head count ratio gives the smallest confidence interval relative to its value. But the head count ratio is a crude measure of poverty because it does not take account of the depth of poverty.

The precise estimation of a poverty measure depends on how sensitive the measure is to income transfers among the very poor. For instance, in Foster, Greer, and Thorbecke's poverty measures, α is a measure of the degree of the aversion to inequality—the larger the value of α, the greater is the weight attached to the poorest of the poor. The numerical results suggest that the precision

**Table 2.1 Poverty measures and their standard errors,
Côte d'Ivoire, 1985**

Poverty measure	Poverty line = CFAF 162,613			Poverty line = CFAF 91,394		
	Value (percent)	Standard error	t-value	Value (percent)	Standard error	t-value
Head count ratio	27.76	1.13	24.57	9.36	0.73	12.82
Poverty gap ratio	9.34	0.48	19.46	2.42	0.24	10.08
Watts measure	13.22	0.75	17.63	3.22	0.35	9.20
Foster et al. measures						
$\alpha = 2.00$	4.42	0.28	15.79	0.98	0.13	7.54
$= 3.00$	2.43	0.19	12.79	0.49	0.08	6.13
Clark et al. measures						
$\beta = 0.25$	12.01	0.66	18.20	2.98	0.32	9.31
$= 0.50$	10.98	0.58	18.93	2.77	0.29	9.55
$= 0.75$	10.10	0.52	19.42	2.58	0.26	9.92
$= 0.95$	9.48	0.48	19.75	2.45	0.25	9.80

Source: Author's calculations.

of this class of poverty measures is a monotonically decreasing function of α. If our value judgment suggests that great weight should be attached to income transfers among the most poor, we must select a poverty measure with a high value of α. But if we cannot obtain a precise estimate of such a poverty measure from a given sample, its usefulness is limited even if it has all the desirable properties from the welfare point of view. Should we reject a desirable poverty measure because of its undesirable statistical properties—that is, because we have little confidence in our judgments about the value of this measure for large groups, for example, urban vis-à-vis rural populations? This is a difficult question to answer, particularly when the sample is small.

Socioeconomic and demographic characteristics

This section focuses on testing for the significance of differences in poverty between various socioeconomic and demographic groups. Comparisons of poverty by sex of household head for Côte d'Ivoire show that the mean consumption (adjusted) of female-headed households is about 20 percent higher than that of male-headed households (table 2.2). The difference between the mean consumption of the two household groups is statistically significant at the 5 percent level. With the exception of P_α for $\alpha = 3.0$, all the poverty measures show that poverty is significantly higher among male-headed households. This is a surprising result because it has often been hypothesized that in many countries—both developing and industrial—female-headed households are poorer than those headed by males. But a review of the South Asian materials by Visaria with Pal (1980) showed that this was generally not the case there either (see also Lipton 1983a: 52). Nor do Grosh, Louat, and van der Gaag (forthcoming) find evidence for this for Jamaica. Some explanation of the situation in Côte d'Ivoire has been provided by Glewwe (1988); he observed that female-headed households are disproportionately lo-

Table 2.2 Comparison of poverty by sex of household head, Côte d'Ivoire, 1985
(poverty line = CFAF 162,613)

| | Female-headed households | | | Male-headed households | | | |
Poverty measure	Value (percent)	Standard error	t-value	Value (percent)	Standard error	t-value	η
Head count ratio	16.96	3.37	5.03	28.46	1.19	23.92	-3.22*
Poverty gap ratio	5.73	1.38	4.15	9.57	0.50	19.14	-2.62*
Watts measure	8.10	2.16	3.75	13.55	0.79	17.15	-2.37*
Foster et al. measures							
$\alpha = 2.00$	2.70	0.81	3.33	4.53	0.30	15.10	-2.12*
$= 3.00$	1.49	0.54	2.76	2.49	0.20	12.45	-1.74*
Clark et al. measures							
$\beta = 0.25$	7.36	1.90	3.87	12.31	0.69	17.84	-2.45*
$= 0.50$	6.74	1.69	3.40	11.25	0.61	18.44	-2.51*
$= 0.75$	6.20	1.52	4.08	10.35	0.55	18.82	-2.57*
Mean consumption per person (CFAF)	406.96	34.21	11.90	337.64	9.47	35.63	1.95

* Poverty differences are significant at 5 percent level.
Source: Author's calculations.

cated in Abidjan and other urban areas, which are considerably richer than the rural areas.

Several nationalities live in Côte d'Ivoire, but nationals are dominant, comprising 85.7 percent of the surveyed population. For our comparisons of poverty by nationality of household head, we have placed all other nationalities into one group (table 2.3). Adjusted per capita consumption is almost identical in the two groups. The difference is insignificant at the 5 percent level, as shown by the value of –0.11 for η given in the last row of the table. Therefore, any significant difference in poverty indicators must be due to a difference in the inequalities in consumption within the groups.

Table 2.3 shows that among Ivorians, 28.38 percent are poor, as against 24.04 percent among other nationalities. But these differences are statistically insignificant at the 5 percent level. Thus we cannot reject the hypothesis that the two groups have the same proportion of poor people. The other poverty measures, however, show that poverty among Ivorians is significantly higher than that among other nationalities. These conflicting conclusions emerge because the head count ratio is insensitive to the poverty gap as well as to the distribution of income among the poor. From these observations, we conclude that the depth of poverty among the Ivorians is significantly greater than that among other nationalities. This is a typical example of how poverty analysis based on the head count ratio can lead to a misleading conclusion—here, that the two groups have the same poverty level.

Household size is an important demographic variable, and one that affects poverty. A large household has greater needs than a small household. Several studies have observed that larger households also tend to have higher incomes because such households probably have, on average, a greater number of persons

**Table 2.3 Comparison of poverty by nationality of household head,
Côte d'Ivoire, 1985**

(poverty line = CFAF 162,613)

Poverty measure	Ivorian			Other nationalities			
	Value (percent)	Standard error	t-value	Value (percent)	Standard error	t-value	η
Head count ratio	28.38	1.25	22.70	24.04	2.60	9.25	1.50
Poverty gap ratio	9.77	0.54	18.09	6.78	0.92	7.37	2.80*
Watts measure	13.94	0.85	16.40	8.89	1.29	6.89	3.27*
Foster et al. measures							
α = 2.00	4.70	0.32	14.69	2.75	0.46	5.98	3.48*
= 3.00	2.62	0.22	11.91	1.29	0.26	4.96	3.91*
Clark et al. measures							
β = 0.25	12.63	0.75	16.84	8.26	1.17	7.06	3.14*
= 0.50	11.52	0.66	17.45	7.71	1.08	7.14	3.01*
= 0.75	10.58	0.59	17.93	7.22	0.99	7.27	2.92*
Mean consumption per person (CFAF)	341.52	10.22	33.42	343.87	19.43	17.70	-0.11

* Poverty differences are significant at 5 percent level.
Source: Author's calculations.

in the work force—but that households in poverty tend to have more members than other households (Kakwani 1986; and Lipton 1983a). The question of whether larger households are better or worse off has important implications, because many government poverty reduction programs are geared toward households with high proportions of dependent persons (Datta and Meerman 1980).

Table 2.4 presents estimates of various poverty measures and their standard errors when the households are classified according to size. The three classifications used are small households (one to four members), medium-size households (five to six members), and large households (seven or more members). All the poverty measures show that small households have the least poverty and large households the highest poverty. In all cases the t-values are considerably larger than 1.96, showing that high and significant poverty levels exist in each of the three household size classifications. To test whether the differences in poverty between households of different sizes are statistically significant, we computed the values of η for all possible pairs of households classified according to their size (table 2.5).

All poverty measures in table 2.5 show that the large households have significantly higher poverty than the small and medium-size households. The differences in poverty between small and medium-size households are statistically significant only for the head count ratio and the poverty gap ratio. For the other poverty measures, the hypothesis of equal poverty levels in the two groups cannot be rejected at the 5 percent significance level. This analysis indicates that the large households are almost certainly more susceptible to poverty than the small and medium-size households.

Côte d'Ivoire may be divided into five regions: Abidjan, other urban, west forest, east forest, and savannah. The first two regions are urban, and the other

Table 2.4 Comparison of poverty by size of household, Côte d'Ivoire, 1985
(poverty line = CFAF 162,613)

Poverty measure	Small households			Medium-size households			Large households		
	Value (percent)	Standard error	t-value	Value (percent)	Standard error	t-value	Value (percent)	Standard error	t-value
Head count ratio	15.20	1.88	8.09	23.40	2.36	9.92	29.75	1.54	19.32
Poverty gap ratio	5.28	0.81	6.52	7.73	0.96	8.05	10.02	0.65	15.42
Watts measure	7.93	1.41	5.62	10.69	1.44	7.42	14.17	1.02	13.89
Foster et al. measures									
α = 2.00	2.66	0.52	5.12	3.55	0.54	6.57	4.75	0.39	12.18
= 3.00	1.58	0.39	4.05	1.87	0.34	5.50	2.61	0.26	10.04
Clark et al. measures									
β = 0.25	7.05	1.19	5.92	9.79	1.28	7.65	12.88	0.90	14.31
= 0.50	6.34	1.03	6.16	9.01	1.15	7.83	11.78	0.89	14.72
= 0.75	5.76	0.90	6.40	8.33	1.05	7.93	10.83	0.72	15.04
Mean consumption per person (CFAF)	529.69	31.05	17.06	422.62	28.0	15.09	309.43	9.68	31.97

Source: Author's calculations.

Table 2.5 Significance of differences in poverty among households of different sizes, Côte d'Ivoire, 1985

	Small households		Medium-size households
Poverty measure	Medium-size households	Large households	Large households
Head count ratio	-2.72*	-5.99*	-2.25*
Poverty gap ratio	-1.95*	-4.56*	-1.98*
Watts measure	-1.37	-3.59*	-1.97*
Foster et al. measures			
$\alpha = 2.00$	-1.19	-3.22*	-1.80
$= 3.00$	-0.56	-2.20*	-1.73
Clark et al. measures			
$\beta = 0.25$	-1.57	-3.91*	-1.97*
$= 0.50$	-1.73	-4.17*	-1.98*
$= 0.75$	-1.86	-4.40*	-1.96*
Mean consumption per person	2.56*	6.77*	3.82*

* Poverty differences are significant at 5 percent level.
Source: Author's calculations.

three are rural. About 60 percent of Ivorians live in rural areas. Table 2.6 presents the poverty estimates and their standard errors according to the geographical location of the household. The empirical results in the table show that poverty varies widely among the regions. For instance, only 5.25 percent of the population in Abidjan is poor, whereas in the savannah region as much as 61.62 percent of the population is poor. All the poverty measures tell the same story: poverty in the savannah region is distressingly high and in Abidjan it is relatively low. The values of t are considerably larger than 1.96 in all the regions, which implies that every region in Côte d'Ivoire has significant poverty.

To test whether differences in poverty between regions are statistically significant, we computed η given in equation 2.9 for all possible pairs of regions (table 2.7). The last row in table 2.7 provides the values of statistics for testing the significance of differences in mean consumption per person (adjusted for size and composition of the household). All the differences in mean consumption are significant at the 5 percent level. Thus, the observed differences in mean consumption among the regions are not due to sampling errors, but to "real" facts.

Almost all poverty measures show significant differences in poverty among the regions. An exception occurs when we compare Abidjan with the region designated as other urban, for which Foster, Greer, and Thorbecke's measures show insignificant differences. The results clearly indicate that poverty is significantly higher in rural areas than in urban areas. Differences in poverty between regions, however, are statistically significant even within rural and urban subregions. Thus, the geographical location of a household has a sizable effect on its poverty level.

The economic welfare of a household is closely associated with the age of its head. In many countries it has been observed that income per household shows a

Table 2.6 Comparison of poverty by region, Côte d'Ivoire, 1985

(poverty line = CFAF 162,613)

Poverty measure	Abidjan Value (percent)	Abidjan Standard error	Abidjan t-value	Other urban Value (percent)	Other urban Standard error	Other urban t-value	West forest Value (percent)	West forest Standard error	West forest t-value	East forest Value (percent)	East forest Standard error	East forest t-value	Savannah Value (percent)	Savannah Standard error	Savannah t-value
Head count ratio	5.25	1.22	4.30	11.94	1.78	6.71	18.40	2.51	7.33	39.13	2.57	15.23	61.62	2.79	22.09
Poverty gap ratio	1.26	0.36	3.50	2.68	0.52	5.15	5.30	0.93	5.70	12.52	1.05	11.92	24.38	1.49	16.36
Watts measure	1.58	0.47	3.36	3.41	0.72	4.74	7.21	1.36	5.30	17.25	1.64	10.52	36.01	2.52	14.29
Foster et al. measures															
$\alpha = 2.00$	0.44	0.16	2.75	0.96	0.25	3.84	2.34	0.51	4.59	5.56	0.62	8.97	12.68	1.00	12.68
$= 3.00$	0.19	0.08	2.38	0.42	0.15	2.80	1.21	0.31	3.90	2.91	0.42	6.93	7.41	0.72	10.29
Clark et al. measures															
$\beta = 0.25$	1.49	0.44	3.39	3.19	0.65	4.91	6.63	1.23	5.39	15.79	1.44	10.97	32.32	2.17	14.89
$= 0.50$	1.41	0.41	3.44	3.00	0.60	5.00	6.13	1.11	5.52	14.54	1.28	11.36	29.23	1.89	15.47
$= 0.75$	1.33	0.38	3.50	2.83	0.56	5.05	5.68	1.01	5.62	13.46	1.16	11.60	26.62	1.67	15.95
Mean consumption per person (CFAF)	614.39	32.11	19.13	392.23	17.25	22.74	295.96	13.00	22.77	244.63	11.49	21.29	175.40	8.19	21.42

Source: Author's calculations.

Table 2.7 Significance of differences in poverty among regions, Côte d'Ivoire, 1985

(poverty line = CFAF 162,613)

	Abidjan				Other urban			West forest		East forest
Poverty measure	Other urban	West forest	East forest	Savannah	West forest	East forest	Savannah	East forest	Savannah	Savannah
Head count ratio	-3.10*	-4.71*	-11.91*	-18.51*	-2.10*	-8.70*	-15.01*	-5.77*	-11.52*	-5.93*
Poverty gap ratio	-2.25*	-4.05*	-10.14*	-15.08*	-2.46*	-8.40*	-13.75*	-5.15*	-10.86*	-6.51*
Watts measure	-2.13*	-3.91*	-9.19*	-13.43*	-2.47*	-7.73*	-12.44*	-4.71*	-10.06*	-6.24*
Foster et al. measures										
α = 2.00	-1.75	-3.55*	-8.00*	-12.09*	-2.43*	-6.88*	-11.37*	-4.01*	-9.21*	-6.05*
= 3.00	-1.35	-3.19*	-6.36*	-9.97*	-2.29*	-5.58*	-9.50*	-3.26*	-7.91*	-5.40*
Clark et al. measures										
β = 0.25	-2.17*	-3.93*	-9.50*	-13.92*	-2.47*	-7.98*	-12.86*	-4.84*	-10.30*	-6.35*
= 0.50	-2.19*	-3.99*	-9.77*	-14.38*	-2.48*	-8.16*	-13.23*	-4.96*	-10.54*	-6.44*
= 0.75	-2.22*	-4.03*	-9.94*	-14.77*	-2.47*	-8.25*	-13.51*	-5.06*	-10.73*	-6.73*
Mean consumption per person	6.09*	9.19*	10.84*	13.25*	4.46*	7.12*	11.36	2.96*	7.85*	4.91*

* Poverty differences are significant at 5 percent level.
Source: Author's calculations.

marked rise, from a low for households in which the head is under the age of 26 to a peak for those in which the head is age 45 to 54, and then a sharp decline to a trough for those in which the head is age 65 and over (Kuznets 1974). There are problems, especially in the absence of long-term panel data, in sorting out the effects of (1) different ages of marriage for the poor and the nonpoor, (2) different wage rates, occupational patterns, and worker-dependent ratios over the life cycle, and (3) changing economic conditions (Lipton 1983a: 53-57 and 1983b: 72-73, summarizable data and the issues). Much of the phenomenon may be explained by the skills and experience acquired by a person before settling down to a particular field of work. At the age of 65, a person faces a sharp decline in income with retirement from the work force. The age of the head may also have a close relation to the household size, which increases with the age of the head as children are born and added to the family.

Poverty comparisons by age of household head are presented in table 2.8. The last row in the table presents the mean consumption per person. The incidence of poverty is highest among households in which the head is over age 65. This group has the lowest per capita consumption. The age group 46 to 65 also has a fairly high incidence of poverty. The absolute magnitude of t exceeds 1.96 in most cases, implying that significant poverty exists in all age groups.

Table 2.9 presents values of η for testing the significance of differences in poverty among households with heads of different ages. The results indicate that differences in poverty are insignificant in comparisons of pairs of the following age groups: under 26, 26 to 35, and 36 to 45. Poverty in the age group 46 to 65 is significantly higher than that in the three lower-age groups. The age group 65 and over has significantly higher poverty than any other age group. Thus, the age of the household head, when it exceeds 45 years, becomes an important determinant of poverty.

Tables 2.10 and 2.11 present numerical results for comparisons of poverty among households classified according to the employer of the household head. Poverty is zero among households whose head is employed by parastatal firms (government-owned corporations). The households whose head is self-employed are most susceptible to poverty. It is interesting to observe that households whose head is not working have lower poverty levels than those whose head is self-employed. The group of households whose head is not working has a much lower poverty level than the national average. Unemployment, defined as not working and actively looking for work, is more common among the nonpoor households. Glewwe (1988) points out that some of these households may be composed entirely of retired persons living on pensions or other sources of transfer income.

The numerical results in table 2.11 show that most of the differences in poverty are significant at the 5 percent level, suggesting that the employer of the household head is an important factor in determining poverty. Households whose head is unemployed, however, have significantly higher per capita consumption levels than those whose head is self-employed, although all poverty measures do not indicate a significant difference in their poverty levels. Foster-Greer-Thorbecke

Table 2.8 Comparison of poverty by age of household head, Côte d'Ivoire, 1985
(poverty line = CFAF 162,613)

Poverty measure	<26			26 to 35			36 to 45			46 to 65			>65		
	Value (percent)	Standard error	t-value	Value (percent)	Standard error	t-value	Value (percent)	Standard error	t-value	Value (percent)	Standard error	t-value	Value (percent)	Standard error	t-value
Head count ratio	22.13	5.27	4.20	18.59	2.19	8.49	19.22	2.13	9.02	31.50	1.77	17.80	42.40	3.86	11.11
Poverty gap ratio	5.40	1.67	3.23	5.24	0.76	6.89	4.72	0.68	6.94	10.85	0.77	14.09	18.82	1.98	9.51
Watts measure	6.99	2.40	2.91	6.88	1.07	6.43	6.09	0.94	6.48	15.51	1.23	12.61	28.04	3.30	8.50
Foster et al. measures															
$\alpha = 2.00$	2.03	0.88	2.31	2.12	0.39	5.44	1.80	0.33	5.45	5.24	0.47	11.15	9.98	1.29	7.74
$= 3.00$	0.96	0.53	1.81	1.00	0.22	4.55	0.82	0.19	4.32	2.93	0.32	9.16	5.87	0.92	6.38
Clark et al. measures															
$\beta = 0.25$	6.52	2.17	3.00	6.40	0.98	6.53	5.69	0.86	6.62	14.05	1.08	13.01	25.11	2.85	8.81
$= 0.50$	6.10	1.98	3.08	5.97	0.90	6.63	5.33	0.79	6.75	12.81	0.95	13.48	22.66	2.49	9.10
$= 0.75$	5.73	1.82	3.15	5.58	0.83	6.72	5.01	0.73	6.86	11.76	0.85	13.84	20.59	2.21	9.32
Mean consumption per person (CFAF)	357.94	36.06	9.93	487.91	24.55	17.71	392.26	23.07	17.00	298.38	10.99	27.15	220.91	15.14	14.59

Source: Author's calculations.

Table 2.9 Significance of differences in poverty among households with different ages of household head, Côte d'Ivoire, 1985

Poverty measure	<26				26 to 35			36 to 45		46 to 65
	26 to 35	36 to 45	46 to 65	>65	36 to 45	46 to 65	>65	46 to 65	>65	>65
Head count ratio	0.62	0.51	-1.69	-3.18*	-0.21	-4.58*	-5.48*	-4.43*	-5.37*	-2.68*
Poverty gap ratio	0.09	0.38	-2.96*	-5.18*	-0.51	-5.19*	-6.40*	-5.97*	-6.74*	-3.75*
Watts measure	0.04	0.35	-3.16*	-5.16*	0.55	-5.29	-6.10	-6.09	-6.40	-3.56
Foster et al. measures										
α = 2.00	-0.09	0.24	-3.22*	-5.09*	0.63	-5.11*	-5.83*	-5.99*	-6.14*	-3.45*
= 3.00	-0.07	0.25	-3.18*	-4.62*	0.62	-4.97*	-5.15*	-5.67*	5.38*	-3.02*
Clark et al. measures										
β = 0.25	0.05	0.36	-3.11*	-5.19*	0.54	-5.25*	-6.21*	-6.06*	-6.52*	-3.63*
= 0.50	0.06	0.36	-3.06*	-5.21*	0.53	-5.23*	-6.30*	-6.05*	-6.63*	-3.70*
= 0.75	0.07	0.37	-3.00	-5.19	0.52	-5.20*	-6.36*	-6.02*	-6.69*	-3.73*
Mean consumption per person	-2.68*	-0.80	1.58	3.50*	2.66*	6.39*	8.49*	3.67*	6.21*	4.14*

* Poverty differences are significant at 5 percent level.
Source: Author's calculations.

Table 2.10 Comparison of poverty of households by employer of household head, Côte d'Ivoire, 1985
(poverty line = CFAF 162,613)

Poverty measure	Not working			Government			Parastatal			Private			Self-employed		
	Value (percent)	Standard error	t-value	Value (percent)	Standard error	t-value	Value (percent)	Standard error	t-value	Value (percent)	Standard error	t-value	Value (percent)	Standard error	t-value
Head count ratio	21.95	3.49	6.29	3.31	1.34	2.47	0.00			7.07	1.79	3.95	36.54	1.51	24.20
Poverty gap ratio	8.73	1.57	5.56	0.45	0.20	2.25	0.00			1.59	0.48	3.31	12.35	0.65	19.00
Watts measure	12.25	2.33	5.26	0.49	0.22	2.23	0.00			1.94	0.61	3.18	17.56	1.04	16.88
Foster et al. measures															
$\alpha = 2.00$	4.24	0.89	4.76	0.07	0.03	2.33	0.00			0.51	0.19	2.68	5.90	0.40	14.75
$= 3.00$	2.27	0.54	4.20	0.01	0.06	0.17	0.00			0.19	0.08	2.38	3.27	0.27	12.11
Clark et al. measures															
$\beta = 0.25$	11.18	2.09	5.35	0.48	0.21	2.29	0.00			1.84	0.58	3.17	15.93	0.91	17.51
$= 0.50$	10.25	1.89	5.42	0.47	0.21	2.24	0.00			1.75	0.54	3.24	14.55	0.81	17.96
$= 0.75$	9.44	1.72	5.49	0.46	0.20	2.30	0.00			1.67	0.51	3.27	13.37	0.72	18.57
Adjusted mean consumption per capita (CFAF)	331.93	21.01	15.80	648.33	45.07	14.38	516.05	60.50	8.53	487.37	30.65	15.90	265.85	8.27	32.15

Source: Author's calculations.

Table 2.11 Significance of differences in poverty according to employer of household head, Côte d'Ivoire, 1985

Poverty measure	Not working				Government			Parastatal		Private
	Government	Parastatal	Private	Self-employed	Parastatal	Private	Self-employed	Private	Self-employed	Self-employed
Head count ratio	4.99*	6.29*	3.79*	-3.84*	2.47*	-1.68*	-16.46*	-3.95*	-24.20*	-12.58*
Poverty gap ratio	5.23*	5.56*	4.35*	-2.13*	2.25*	-2.19*	-17.50*	-3.31*	-19.00*	-13.32*
Watts measure	5.02*	5.26*	4.28*	-2.08*	2.23*	-2.24*	-16.06*	-3.18*	-16.88*	-12.96*
Foster et al. measures										
α = 2.00	4.68*	4.76*	4.10*	-1.70	2.33*	-2.29*	-14.53*	-2.68*	-14.75*	-12.17*
= 3.00	4.16*	4.20*	3.81*	-1.66	-0.17	-1.80	-11.79	-2.37*	-12.11*	-10.94*
Clark et al. measures										
β = 0.25	5.09*	5.35*	4.31*	-2.08*	2.29*	-2.20*	-16.54*	-3.17*	-17.51*	-13.06*
= 0.50	5.14*	5.42*	4.32*	-2.09*	2.24*	-2.21*	-16.83*	-3.24*	-17.96*	-13.15*
= 0.75	5.19*	5.49*	4.33*	-2.11*	2.30*	-2.21*	-17.28*	-3.27*	-18.57*	-13.26*
Adjusted consumption per capita	-6.36*	-2.87*	-4.18*	2.93*	1.75*	2.95*	8.35*	0.42*	4.10*	6.98*

* Poverty differences are significant at 5 percent level.
Source: Author's calculations.

measures show that differences in poverty between the two groups are insignificant. Similarly, differences in per capita consumption between households whose head is employed by government and those whose head is employed by a parastatal firm are not significant. But the government-employed households have significantly higher levels of poverty than those employed by parastatal firms. This is indicated by all poverty measures presented except the Foster-Greer-Thorbecke measures when $\alpha = 3.0$.

In Côte d'Ivoire the heads of 65 percent of households had no education. This proportion varied considerably among regions. For instance, in Abidjan such households accounted for about 36 percent of households, and in the savannah region, for as much as 93 percent of households. It is possible that the significant poverty differences observed earlier between regions are attributable to the education levels attained by the household head.

Tables 2.12 and 2.13 present comparisons of poverty among households by the education of the household head. As expected, poverty is highest among households whose head had no education. Poverty decreases monotonically with the highest education level reached by the household head. Households whose head attended senior high school have zero poverty, and those whose head had a university education have statistically insignificant poverty levels. Education (up to senior high school) of the household head has an important bearing on poverty. Education even up to elementary school can substantially reduce poverty.

Conclusions

The empirical results of the analysis of poverty in Côte d'Ivoire suggest that observed differences in the values of poverty measures may lead to misleading conclusions without the statistical tests. Some poverty measures may show significant differences in poverty; others may show insignificant differences. This is an important finding—one that may affect the selection of an appropriate measure for the analysis of differences in poverty between populations. The results also suggest that poverty measures that give greater weight to income transfers among the most poor may have larger confidence intervals. This raises a difficult question: Should a desirable poverty measure be rejected because of undesirable statistical properties? This issue is of crucial importance when the sample is small.

This chapter demonstrates how to use statistical inference to analyze poverty. These statistical tests are important because poverty measures are estimated on the basis of sample observations. But these tests are based on the assumption that samples used are representative of the population they are drawn from. In practice, this assumption may be invalid because of nonresponse errors,[5] or because of other systematic nonsampling errors. These may be so large that it makes little sense to worry about sampling errors. Greater attention should be paid to nonsampling errors in future work.

Table 2.12 Comparison of poverty by education of household head, Côte d'Ivoire, 1985
(poverty line = CFAF 162,613)

Poverty measure	None			Elementary school			Junior high school			Senior high school			University		
	Value (percent)	Standard error	t-value	Value (percent)	Standard error	t-value	Value (percent)	Standard error	t-value	Value (percent)	Standard error	t-value	Value (percent)	Standard error	t-value
Head count ratio	35.62	1.48	24.10	20.09	2.52	8.00	3.62	1.55	2.30	0.00	0.00		1.25	1.51	0.83
Poverty gap ratio	12.43	0.65	19.10	5.30	0.87	6.10	0.75	0.34	2.20	0.00	0.00		0.52	0.63	0.82
Watts measure	17.75	1.04	17.10	7.01	1.23	5.70	0.85	0.39	2.20	0.00	0.00		0.68	0.82	0.83
Foster et al. measures															
$\alpha = 2.00$	6.00	0.40	15.00	2.19	0.45	4.90	0.17	0.09	1.90	0.00	0.00		0.22	0.27	0.81
$= 3.00$	3.34	0.28	11.90	1.06	0.25	4.20	0.04	0.02	2.00	0.00	0.00		0.09	0.11	0.82
Clark et al. measures															
$\beta = 0.25$	16.08	0.91	17.70	6.50	1.12	5.80	0.82	0.38	2.20	0.00	0.00		0.64	0.77	0.83
$= 0.50$	14.67	0.81	18.10	6.06	1.02	5.90	0.80	0.36	2.20	0.00	0.00		0.60	0.72	0.83
$= 0.75$	13.46	0.72	18.70	5.66	0.94	6.00	0.77	0.35	2.20	0.00	0.00		0.56	0.68	0.82
Mean consumption per person (CFAF)	254.18	6.15	41.31	323.70	13.68	23.70	578.86	40.02	14.50	790.00	68.69	11.50	1,285.95	128.86	10.00

Source: Author's calculations.

Table 2.13 Significance of differences in poverty among households by education level of household head, Côte d'Ivoire, 1985

Poverty measure	None				Elementary school			Junior high school		Senior high school
	Elementary school	Junior high school	Senior high school	University	Junior high school	Senior high school	University	Senior high school	University	University
Head count ratio	5.32*	14.95*	24.10*	16.29*	7.19*	8.00*	6.41*	2.30*	1.10	-0.83
Poverty gap ratio	6.54*	16.00*	19.10*	13.09*	4.84*	6.10*	4.43*	2.20*	0.32	-0.82
Watts measure	6.67*	15.22*	17.10*	12.93*	4.77*	5.70*	4.28*	2.20*	0.19	-0.82
Foster et al. measures										
$\alpha = 2.00$	6.35*	14.22*	15.00*	12.04*	8.42*	4.90*	3.79*	1.90*	-0.18	-0.81
$= 3.00$	6.16*	11.78*	11.90*	10.83*	4.25*	4.20*	3.73*	2.00*	-0.50	-0.82
Clark et al. measures										
$\beta = 0.25$	6.65*	15.57*	17.70*	12.97*	4.81*	5.80*	4.31*	2.20*	0.21	-0.83
$= 0.50$	6.62*	15.58*	18.10*	12.91*	4.87*	5.90*	4.37*	2.20*	0.25	-0.83
$= 0.75$	6.61*	15.86*	18.70*	13.03*	4.89*	6.00*	4.40*	2.20*	0.28	-0.82
Mean consumption per person	-4.63*	-8.02*	-7.80*	-8.00*	-6.03*	-6.66*	-7.43*	-2.66*	-5.24*	-3.40*

* Poverty differences are significant at 5 percent level.
Source: Author's calculations.

Notes

The paper could not have been completed without the invaluable computational assistance of Kalpana Mehra. Thanks are also due to Maria Felix for typing and to Brenda Rosa for editing an early draft of the manuscript.

1. See, for instance, Sen (1979), Takayama (1979), Kakwani (1980a and 1980b), Clark, Hemming, and Ulph (1981) and Thon (1983). For a review of the literature on poverty indices, see Clark, Hemming, and Ulph (1981) and Kakwani (1984).

2. For a detailed discussion of this issue see Kakwani (1986).

3. The CFAF is tied to the French franc at the fixed rate of 50 CFAF = 1 FF.

4. Throughout the chapter all poverty measures are based on the number of poor people, not the number of poor households.

5. The Living Standards Measurement Study Survey data for Côte d'Ivoire, 1985, used in this chapter had a 92 percent response rate; therefore, the possibility of large nonresponse errors is very small.

The Principles of Targeting

3 *Timothy Besley*
      Ravi Kanbur

The question of how to design policies to alleviate poverty effectively has great
practical significance. In nineteenth-century England, J. S. Mill succinctly characterized the problem as one of giving the greatest amount of needful help with
the smallest amount of undue reliance on it. This characterization fits well with
the dilemma that policymakers face today. It is important to use available
resources efficiently. This means directing them as much as possible toward
those who need them most. This is the basic idea motivating discussion about
targeting.

Hence, it is often argued that the "best" solution to the problem of poverty
alleviation is one that identifies who is poor and then directs benefits toward that
group. The debate on targeting is an old one; moreover, it has been as controversial in industrial countries as in developing countries.[1] Many commentators have
emphasized the costliness of identifying the poor and the effects on incentives
that may attend income-tested programs.[2] This emphasis leads to the recommendation of universalist programs that provide benefits that are paid independent of
recipients' income. It is in the wake of macroeconomic and structural adjustment, however, that targeting seems to have attained a special significance in
developing countries, as more and more governments have come under pressure
to reduce expenditure. Indeed, targeting has come to be seen as a panacea in
poverty alleviation. This perception suggests that policymakers can have their
cake and eat it too—that improved targeting means that more poverty alleviation
could be achieved with less expenditure. But the real world is not so straightforward. There are good reasons why this best of all possible worlds is not available
to policymakers in developing countries and why hard decisions will have to be
made that weigh the costs and benefits of targeting.

This chapter provides a framework for considering the principles of targeting to alleviate poverty. Because the focus is on the *principles*, much of the
discussion will be at a general and abstract level. These principles are intended to
be applicable in particular developing countries, however, where the flesh of
institutional knowledge must be added. The chapter begins by stating the basic
problem in a very simple framework and then presents the ideal solution: a case
of "perfect targeting." It next takes up three central problems with this solution:

administrative costs, high marginal tax rates (incentive effects), and political economy considerations. Each of these militates against fine targeting and suggests the advantages of more universalist schemes. The chapter then considers the "intermediate" option of targeting by indicators and, finally, it considers self-targeting schemes.

The basic problem and the ideal solution

Any discussion on targeting for poverty alleviation presupposes agreement on what is meant by poverty—agreement on (1) a measure of the standard of living, (2) a poverty line that distinguishes the poor from the nonpoor, and (3) a poverty index that aggregates information on the standard of living of the poor. Each of these is an important and controversial topic that would demand a separate paper.[3] We assume that these problems have been solved in order to focus attention on targeting.

Let us suppose, initially, that we have a household income distribution that measures income correctly and adjusts for households facing different prices, household size and composition, and so on. Suppose further that the poverty line is given by z, so all those with incomes less than z are in poverty. The goal of policy is to reduce poverty to zero. The ideal solution would be one in which income can be observed accurately and without cost and in which no incentive effects prevent the state from bringing individuals' incomes up to the poverty line. The ideal solution is depicted in figure 3.1, which plots final income (post-transfer) against original income. Along the dotted 45° line there is no difference between original and final income.[4] A point above this line indicates a subsidy or transfer, and a point below indicates a withdrawal or tax. The ideal solution is given by the solid line. For anyone with original income y less than z, the government transfers exactly the amount $z - y$ so as to bring final income up to z. This eliminates poverty. The financial cost of this strategy is given by the sum of these transfers $z - y$. If the distribution of income were uniform, this cost would simply be depicted by the triangular area between the horizontal solid line and the 45° line.

Figure 3.1 The ideal solution

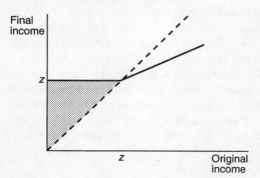

The structure of the scheme for those with income above z depends on the nature of the budget constraint. If the transfer scheme is to be self-financing, those with incomes above z must be taxed. This is shown in figure 3.1 by the solid line beyond z lying below the 45° line. The larger the tax revenue to be raised, the shallower this line will have to be in order to balance the budget. Figure 3.2 makes explicit the transfers to and from the government as a function of original income. Below z the transfers are from the government and are therefore shown as negative; above z they are to the government. The slope of the solid line in figure 3.2 is the *marginal* tax rate. Figure 3.2 shows that the ideal solution imposes a higher marginal tax rate on the poor than on the nonpoor. We return to this point in a later section, where the disincentive effects of high marginal tax rates are discussed.

If the government is perfectly informed, the ideal solution is clearly the least-cost method of alleviating poverty. If external resources were at stake, or if internal resources had to be raised to finance the poverty alleviation program, the ideal solution would be preferred. But is it feasible? It relies on being able to transfer exactly the right amount to each individual below the poverty line without affecting their incentives to earn. The administrative costs of this in a developing country context are taken up in the following section. Here we present the opposite extreme to the ideal solution, by way of contrast. This is a completely universalist scheme that gives *everybody* a transfer of z, regardless of income (figures 3.3 and 3.4). This scheme also eliminates poverty, but at a far greater budgetary cost. It is easy to see why this is so. Now everybody, even someone with an original income exceeding z, receives the transfer of z from the government (figure 3.4). The budgetary cost is simply z times the population. If the cost is to be recouped through taxation, the marginal tax rates on the nonpoor would need to be higher than those in the ideal solution, although the marginal tax rates on the poor are now lower. Fig-

Figure 3.2 The cost of the ideal solution

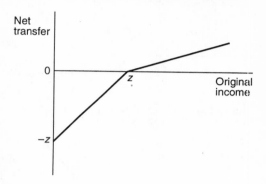

Figure 3.3 A uniform transfer scheme

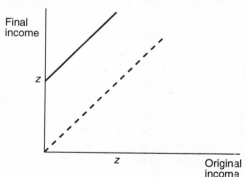

Figure 3.4 The cost of a uniform transfer scheme

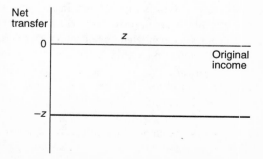

Figure 3.5 Allowing for financing through taxation of the nonpoor

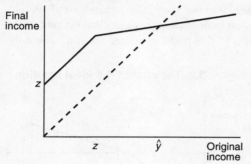

Figure 3.6 Costs of financing through taxation of the nonpoor

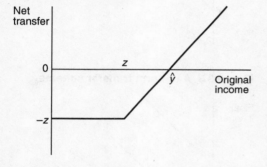

ures 3.5 and 3.6 depict such a scheme, which is discussed further below.

These two extremes (ideal means testing and universalist) anchor our discussion of the principles of targeting. As will become clear by the end of this chapter, neither extreme is particularly appealing. The benefits of the ideal solution are clear. The next four sections discuss some of its costs.

Administrative costs

Although the previous section developed its argument using the language of income transfers, it is also relevant to other institutional settings—for example, the analysis of food subsidy programs. Before the reforms of 1977, ration shops in Sri Lanka provided rice rations to all Sri Lankans at below-market prices. As Besley and Kanbur (1988) have argued, this is equivalent to an income transfer equal to the ration times the effective subsidy if any unwanted rice can be resold. Thus, it is like a universalist program. After 1977 this system was gradually replaced by a food stamp program that restricted benefits to those households whose incomes were below a critical value (see Anand and Kanbur 1990 for details). This involves a move toward the ideal solution described above. But a recent World Bank study points out some difficulties with this attempt to effect the ideal solution:

> One problem is inflexibility in the way a program determines who is eligible, as exemplified by Sri Lanka's food stamp program. The target group was identified by household size and earnings but, because households were never checked to see if they remained eligible, many stayed on the rolls even after their earnings increased above the eligibility cutoff. Households that became eligible after the program started, however, never had a chance to get on the rolls. (World Bank 1986a: 34)

This is not an isolated case. The same document provides other examples, such as in Brazil:

A coupon program that distributed food every two weeks through government-run supermarkets used income to determine who could participate in Recife, Brazil. The program revealed several problems....It is difficult to target income if income reporting is arbitrary....A coupon program requires extensive book keeping and administrative cost....Building on lessons from the evaluators, the Brazilian program was modified, with apparent success, to reach very low-income neighborhoods without coupons or down payments. Common basic foods are now subsidized for all customers of many small neighborhood stores in selected poverty areas. Any leakage of benefits to people not in need is much less expensive than administering the cumbersome coupon program. (World Bank, 1986a: 35)

One of the main lessons of the above is the difficulty of assessing and verifying low incomes. This is not easy even in industrial countries, despite their systems of regular employment and their literate populations accustomed to filling in tax returns (see, for example, Kay and King 1980). In developing countries, where much employment (especially that of the poor) is irregular, where there is agricultural production for home consumption, and where the definition of a "household" is problematic, one would suspect a priori that the administrative costs involved in the ideal solution are high. Frequent testing—which is costly—is necessary, as the Sri Lankan case illustrates, to ensure that those genuinely in need are in the scheme and to weed out those who are not. The administrative capacity to do this simply does not exist in many (perhaps most) developing—and possibly even industrial—countries. Macedo (1987) identifies instances in Brazil in which the authorities relied on local committees to identify the needy, and he points to the difficulties to which this gave rise.

Quantifying administrative costs by program will not be an easy task, particularly if costs are shared by several programs. Some allocation formulas might be feasible, however. The revenue required to implement a program, R, can be divided into three categories: $R = A + NP + P$, where A is administrative costs, NP is transfers (leakages) to the nonpoor or, more generally, to those not in the target group, and P is the effective transfer to the poor. A measure of the fineness of targeting is then given by $F = P / (P + NP)$, the fraction of total nonadministrative outlay that reaches the target group. The administrative costs as a proportion of the revenues are $C = A / (A + P + NP)$. It is hypothesized that C rises with F, and at an increasing rate. This is illustrated in figure 3.7, which also assumes that there is a minimum level of administra-

Figure 3.7 An administrative cost function

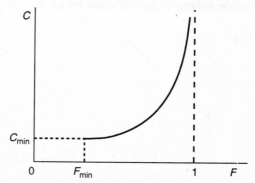

tive costs, C_{min}, needed to get any program going, and that a minimum level of targeting, F_{min}, can always be achieved. For example, if the total nonadministrative budget is divided equally within the population, with no attempt at targeting, the fraction of the outlay that goes to the pretransfer poor is given by the fraction of poor people in the population—that is, the incidence of poverty. This much targeting is always possible, even with the opposite extreme of the ideal solution. It is the shape of the curve between F and 1 on which we require more information; yet it is about this that we are most ignorant at present.[5] Quantifying the administrative costs of poverty alleviation programs is clearly an important issue for future research, since the efficacy of means-tested programs depends on it.

Individual responses and incentive effects

The incentive effects of the ideal solution must also be weighed in assessing its applicability. Besley (1990) examines one aspect of this—that certain individuals might not participate in a finely targeted program because of the costs to them in subjecting themselves to detailed assessment, filling out forms, and attending interviews, or because of the psychic costs of the social stigma of participating in programs meant specifically for the poor.[6]

   Besley (1990) hypothesizes that if an individual's costs of participating in a finely targeted poverty alleviation program are c, those with incomes greater than $z - c$ will not take part. This means that those with incomes between z and $z - c$ will remain below the poverty line. The alternative is to have a universal scheme that gives everybody an amount m, such that the total budgetary outlay is equal to that of the targeted program. These two alternatives are illustrated in figure 3.8. As can be seen, the finely targeted program tends to exclude those just below the poverty line, but provides greater benefits, compared with a universalist program with the same budget, to the poorest of the poor. Besley (1990) provides some quantification of these tradeoffs for assumed income distributions. His numerical simulations suggest that the introduction of take-up costs does not turn the tables against income testing.

   Incentive problems are insignificant measure related to problems of imperfect information. If the government found individuals transparent—that is, if it knew their tastes and abilities—taxes and benefits could be made to depend directly on immutable characteristics. In fact, only income is observable (perhaps not even this), and by altering their behavior to alter their income, agents can alter the amount of the tax or benefit that they pay or receive. This is the root of the incentive problem.[7]

Figure 3.8 Means testing versus universal provision with take-up costs

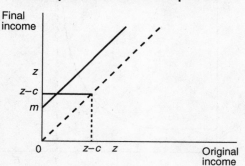

The ideal solution is also faced with the problem that it imposes a 100 percent marginal tax rate on all those below the poverty line. This can be seen from the fact that the slope of the solid line in figure 3.2 is below z. The advantage claimed for this is that, because it is the way of alleviating poverty at least cost (the shaded triangle in figure 3.1), in a self-financing scheme the high marginal tax rates on the poor would be offset by the lower marginal tax rates on the nonpoor. But there is an important caveat to be added if marginal tax rates affect the incentive to work, and hence to earn income—that income is endogenous and thus depends on the tax schedule implicit in the program. To see this, notice that with a 100 percent marginal tax rate there is no incentive for anybody with an original income below z to work. All these people would be better-off not working and receiving z from the government. But if the original income for these individuals falls to zero, the financial cost of the program is no longer depicted by the triangle in figure 3.1—it is now the rectangle of size z.[8] Thus, the marginal tax rates on the rich would have to be higher than those indicated by the ideal solution. But this would in turn mean that the rich work less hard and that therefore even less revenue is generated. The alternative, a universalist scheme, would have medium-level marginal tax rates on everybody. The choice is between having a distribution of high marginal tax rates skewed in the direction of the poor, or having a more even spread of marginal tax rates.

Clearly, the final decision depends on the specifics of the case.[9] Kanbur and Keen (1987) provide a general theoretical analysis of the issues. What is needed, however, is detailed country-specific analyses for developing countries. In the past such analysis may have been thought to be problematic because of the lack of adequate microeconomic data. But recent advances in microeconomic data collection make this excuse less plausible. Policy analyses and research programs utilizing these data, and addressing the issue of targeted versus universalist schemes, are now urgently needed.

The political economy of targeting

A purely technocratic approach to the problem of poverty alleviation asks only how the informational, administrative, and other costs can be taken into account. Although useful, this approach neglects issues of distributional and political conflict that lie at the heart of the problem. It is interesting to consider the political support that various types of poverty alleviation programs might enjoy. The ideal solution in figure 3.1 would be rationally supported only by those with incomes below the poverty line. But this group is unlikely to have sufficient political power to prevail against those above the poverty line who have to pay. The universalist scheme in figure 3.5 has the advantage of bringing into the net of beneficiaries some people with incomes above the poverty line. It pits the "middle classes" between z and y in figure 3.5 against those with the highest incomes. This contrasts with the ideal solution.

Tullock (1982) espouses the view that universalist schemes are a way of minimizing net transfers to the poor:

When we consider the political forces which may lead to the expansion (universalization) of a program it is, in general, clear that if people who are interested in expanding the program are trying merely to help the poor, they have chosen an inept way of doing it. Only if they feel that they can trick members of the middle and upper class into voting for a program to help the poor by that indirect method which is more generous than they are willing to give a direct and open way, is it sensible.

Tullock's views are controversial (see Downs 1982). Nevertheless, the considerations that he raises are relevant to the recent debate in developing countries on whether universalist schemes (such as general food subsidies) should be abandoned in favor of targeted schemes (such as food stamps based on income criteria). If a constant budget is maintained, this shift would entail a net loss to the middle- and upper-income classes.[10] The tolerance of political groups then becomes a concern. Bienen and Gersovitz (1985) have analyzed recent attempts to remove food subsidies (as part of a larger stabilization and adjustment program). Their work demonstrates the importance of particular countries' circumstances— the existing configurations of power and the possibilities for power realignment:

> IMF programs may also incorporate cutbacks in subsidies for goods, especially those disproportionately purchased [by the nonpoor]; basic needs programs, it should be noted, benefit urban middle classes. Mexico's middle classes, for example, frequently shop in subsidized retail outlets....But elites are reluctant to make precipitous policy changes that threaten their support....Exceptions include régimes in Sri Lanka (1977), Turkey (1984), and Zimbabwe (1984) that did successfully cut consumer-food subsidies. (Bienen and Gersovitz 1985: 740-41)

But if a universal program is in fact removed and a targeted program substituted, the poor would be isolated in terms of political alliances. The history of food subsidies in Sri Lanka since 1977 (see Anand and Kanbur 1990) is particularly instructive. After targeting with food stamps was introduced, the real value of food stamps was allowed to fall during an ensuing period of inflation, with severe consequences for poverty and undernutrition. With the introduction of targeting, the interests of the middle classes lay elsewhere (maintaining public sector wages, for example), and the poor were to some extent abandoned to their own political devices. General subsidies would have led to important links between the middle classes and the poor—as was the case during the (principally urban) agitation to maintain food subsidies in Zambia in 1984, and in Sri Lanka on several occasions before 1977, although at substantial (and poorly targeted) public expense.

In his fascinating account of the targeting of social programs in Brazil, Macedo (1987) has also highlighted political aspects of poverty alleviation strategies. He concludes that "if policy changes were introduced at the highest levels of decision-making in Brazil, then many changes would follow at the level of programs, both in their design and management."

The political equilibrium is a significant determinant of the types of poverty alleviation program that may be sustained. Proper consideration of it might lead policymakers away from programs that give benefits only to those with incomes below z and toward those that are more universal and a source of political cohesion.

Targeting using indicators

Because of the informational and administrative difficulties of implementing the ideal solution, poverty alleviation programs whose targeting is based on key indicators (a household's region or the age distribution of its members) may be profitable. In developing countries in which income is very difficult to measure, this solution may be particularly appropriate. Such targeting may also be more widely relevant (see Deaton and Stern 1985; and Akerlof 1978). A World Bank study (1986a) discusses the use of geographical area for targeting. Under such a scheme, all individuals *within* an area are treated identically—as with the universalist scheme depicted in figures 3.3 and 3.4—but only certain areas are chosen to receive benefits. These are the low-income neighborhoods, which are easier to identify than individual persons with low incomes. The general aim is to find an indicator that is less costly to identify but that is sufficiently correlated with income to be useful for poverty alleviation. Although there is bound to be some leakage, because no indicator is perfectly correlated with income, it is hoped that any leakage of benefits to those who are not in poverty is much less expensive than administering the cumbersome ideal solution.

Household income and expenditure surveys can be used to evaluate the poverty characteristics of regions as finely as sample size will allow.[11] How can this information be used to develop a priority ranking of regions? This problem has been analyzed in Kanbur (1986). The answer depends on the precise objectives of the government, and how the expenditure devoted to each group translates into individual incomes.[12] If the government's objective is to have as big an impact as possible on the national poverty gap,[13] the relevant regional ranking would be by incidence of poverty in each region (*not* by the regional poverty gap). An intuitive account of this result follows from considering the "poverty alleviation efficiency" of a uniform transfer to a region. If every income in a region is increased by $1, the cost is $1 times the total number of people; the increase in the incomes of the poor is $1 times the number of *poor* people in that region. The poverty alleviation efficiency is simply the ratio of the latter to the former, which is the incidence of poverty in that region.

This argument from Kanbur (1986) can apply to any method—not just regional—of classifying the population. Household size and composition could be used to condition payments if these were felt to be easy to monitor. For example, the number of children might be chosen as an indicator. Or combinations of region, residence, and household characteristics could be used, as in Colombia:

In Colombia areas of poverty were identified as part of the national development plan. Targets of food subsidies were then narrowed to households with children under five years old or a pregnant or lactating woman. This reduced the number of possible beneficiaries and thus lowered administrative and fiscal costs. Little leakage or fraudulent coupon use was apparent. (World Bank 1986a: 35)

If the number of indicators is pushed to the limit, we would be back to a case in which every unit was being identified separately. The beauty of using just a few indicators is that administrative costs are kept low while leakage is less than it would be under a universalist scheme, so that more poverty alleviation could be achieved with the same resources. This suggests a focus for future research on developing countries that quantifies the impact of targeting according to different characteristics. In fact, there are three important decision variables to which data should speak:

- Given a set of partitions of characteristics (for example, regional boundaries), what levels of benefit are appropriate?
- Where should the divisions be made between different groups—that is, where should boundaries be drawn if, for example, targeting is according to age?
- How many partitions should there be—for example, how many age bands or regional areas?

These questions provide exciting possibilities for both theoretical and empirical work.[14] As more and more categories are introduced, the targeting achieved by indicators becomes finer and poverty is reduced. On the other hand, the addition of more categories raises administrative costs (a further justification for the position depicted in figure 3.7). The optimal policy equates the marginal reduction in poverty that can be achieved using an additional indicator with the marginal administrative cost of adding the indicator. This is illustrated in figure 3.9, where n denotes the number of indicators, $C(n)$ is the marginal cost of more indicators, and $P(n)$ is the marginal gain in alleviating poverty as a function of the number of indicators. The optimal number of indicators is n^*.

Interesting empirical work has already begun in this area. Ravallion and Chao (1989) illustrate how the benefits of region-based targeting can be quantified. They first calculate, for a given budget, the poverty level that could be achieved with optimal use of regional poverty information, following the analysis of Kanbur (1986 and 1987a). The gain from targeting is then defined as the amount by which an untargeted budget would have to increase in order to achieve the poverty level attained through targeting. They call this the "equivalent gain from targeting." They present

Figure 3.9 Optimal number of partitions

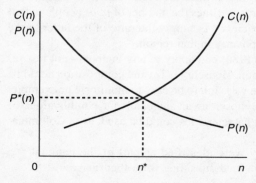

evidence for Bangladesh and the Philippines, for which they distinguish between the urban and rural sectors, and for Sri Lanka, for which they consider urban, rural, and estate sectors. Their illustrative exercises show that the gains from indicator-based targeting vary greatly from country to country, ranging from almost 40 percent in the Philippines to about 2 percent in Bangladesh. Another interesting conclusion is that the percentage gains from targeting are greater the smaller is the budget.

A sidelight on these results appears in the chapter by Datt and Ravallion in this volume (chapter 4), which shows surprisingly small improvements to the poverty indicators from even perfect interregional (but no intraregional) income redistribution in India. As the authors point out, the improvements are larger in Indonesia. Also, they obviously increase in any country if regions are more finely specified (for example, districts rather than states in India). That also applies to direct regional targeting—and, in both cases, at considerable extra administrative cost.

A more detailed analysis of targeting using indicators is provided in Ravallion (1989), which focuses on land-contingent transfers—transfers of income that are given contingent on land ownership. This is attractive because land ownership is often observable where income is not. Such transfers are almost always a feature of policy discussion about poverty alleviation, particularly in Asia and Latin America. For Bangladesh, Ravallion concludes that "the equivalent gain from targeting with unrestricted land-contingent tax powers is only slightly more than 10 percent of mean income for rural Bangladesh or 20 percent of mean poverty deficit of the poor." These gains have to be set against the administrative costs of land-contingent policies. This suggests a further case for studying the administrative costs of poverty alleviation programs, as we outlined above.

Glewwe (1990a) implements a model of statistical targeting for Côte d'Ivoire. He argues that transfers based on such indicators as education and the ownership of land and durable goods can come close to achieving the same result (if they were feasible) as could be achieved by transfers based on income.

To date, however, much of the literature has not explored the incentive consequences of choosing manipulable characteristics as a basis for statistical targeting. Landholdings, ownership of durable goods, and even family composition could be manipulated by individuals attempting to receive greater transfers. Allowing for this is an important topic for future research.

Another type of targeting based on indicators is the subsidizing of certain foods thought to be consumed primarily by the poor. Besley and Kanbur (1988) distinguish between two types of food subsidy program: (1) one in which a fixed quantity of food is provided at below-market prices and (2) one in which the market price is subsidized for every unit that is purchased. If the resale of rations cannot be prevented, the first type of program is equivalent to an income transfer to all those eligible for the program. The size of the transfer is equal to the quantity of the ration times the unit subsidy. The central question then becomes the criterion according to which ration shops are located in particular areas, or according to which ration cards are issued within an area. The second type of food subsidy program benefits consumers in proportion to their consumption of the commodity in question. Thus, in absolute terms, the rich gain more than the poor if the commodity is not an inferior good. Besley and Kanbur (1988) show that, if the objective is to minimize the aggregate poverty gap at the national level, the appropriate indicator to use is the ratio of the quantity consumed by the poor to the total quantity consumed. Commodities should be ranked according to this ratio, and those highest on the list should be prime candidates for protection during a period of retrenchment on the food subsidy.[15]

Notice that the above ratio can be calculated using households' income, and expenditure surveys. Indeed, this is done in Kanbur (1990b) to argue that rice in Côte d'Ivoire is not a prime candidate for subsidy. The importance of this ratio has indeed been grasped in the policy literature. A World Bank study notes that:

> The main determinant of food's suitability for subsidy is the share of it that goes to the target population. If a food is consumed exclusively by the target group, the subsidy will be very efficient; a dollar's worth of subsidy will provide almost a dollar of added income to the target group. But if the target population consumes only 30 percent of a subsidized food, the subsidy is much less efficient. (World Bank 1986a: 35)

It can be shown (see Besley and Kanbur 1988), however, that the use of the "consumption by poor" ratio is strictly valid only when the objective is to minimize the aggregate poverty gap. Different rules come into play if the poverty alleviation objective pays special attention, for example, to the poorest of the poor and when Engel curves for food show significant nonlinearity.

Finally, we take up the case in which individuals respond to targeted poverty alleviation programs by shifting between the categories being used for targeting. For example, families may relocate to areas in which there are ration shops, or increase their family size. Roberts (1984) provides a general theoretical analysis of such problems. Clearly, if individuals can respond to the use of nonincome indicators by manipulating their characteristics to advantage, the policymaker should take this into account. The central question is whether the incentives of poorer families to do so are greater than those of the richer families. For example, if migration costs are smaller as a percentage of richer households' income, the "wrong" households may move in response to the setting up of a ration shop in a distant area. Once again, detailed research is needed to quantify the tradeoffs involved. If these responses are sufficiently adverse, even the use of nonincome indicators for targeting comes into question—creating another argument in favor of more universalist schemes.

Self-targeting

An alternative approach to targeting is to design schemes based on self-regulatory tests that only the truly poor would pass. We refer to such schemes as "self-targeting." In general, programs of this kind involve an agent either making a nonmonetary payment to receive an income transfer or receiving a payment in kind rather than in cash. We first discuss two paradigmatic examples of such schemes and then draw some general conclusions about their design.

Workfare

A workfare scheme operates by making a claimant of poor relief give up labor time in exchange for an income transfer. There are two main incentive-related arguments for doing so: a screening argument and a deterrent argument.[16] The screening argument says that a work requirement may be used to discourage the nonneedy from claiming poor relief in a world in which they cannot otherwise be identified. It rests on the possibility that those who are poor have a lower opportunity cost of labor time relative to others and, hence, for a given income transfer, are prepared to give up more labor time. Such a test of eligibility has figured centrally in Indian famine relief policy (Drèze 1990a). Its efficacy depends crucially on the assumption that the opportunity cost of time is lower for target groups. If we hold other things equal, that seems likely. If, however, poorer families have greater household commitments—for example, to child-rearing activities—willingness to "afford the time" to obtain labor income would be a poor criterion for targeting workfare to the poor. The problem is related to that of using "waiting in line" as an allocation mechanism (Barzel 1974).[17]

Workfare schemes in the form of rural public works projects in India have also been widely studied. Much of the literature is discussed in the survey paper by Ravallion (1991). One important practical example of a workfare scheme is Maharastra's Employment Guarantee Scheme. Ravallion finds evidence that participants in the scheme came from households with lower income, on average, than nonparticipants. The claim that as many as 90 percent of those who participate in rural public works projects come from households initially below the poverty line does not seem unreasonable in the light of the evidence. This speaks favorably of their targeting efficiency.

It is not unambiguously true, however, even in theory, that workfare should be preferred to a scheme of unconditional cash handouts, even if workfare is more effective in targeting the poor. For, although screening has benefits, it may also have a cost in terms of the forgone earnings of participants. Thus, the screening gains from workfare must be weighed against the earnings losses. Achieving a proper cost-benefit appraisal of such programs requires a comparison of the fraction of the population screened out by workfare schemes (a measure of cost savings) with the opportunity cost of a unit of labor to the poor (as measured, say, by their marginal product of labor). This comparison is developed in detail in Besley and Coate (1992).

One might also consider the effects of such schemes on the wage rate earned by laborers, as has been done empirically by Ravallion (1991). If workfare schemes raise the wage by reducing the private sector labor supply, they may have a further beneficial effect on poverty alleviation.

The deterrent argument says that imposing a work requirement may encourage certain kinds of behavior. It may encourage agents to invest in skill formation that makes it less likely that they will require poor relief in the future. This argument has historically been very important in policy discussions. It is vital to an understanding of the preoccupations that led to England's 1834 Poor Law Amendment Act, and to the establishment of possibly the most notorious workfare system in history, in which the poor were forced into workhouses explicitly designed to offer conditions (not just wage rates) less pleasant than the worst obtainable on the labor market. Whether work requirements can deter poor people from "underinvesting"—in a job search or in self-improvement—depends on whether there is a link between such investment decisions and the availability, and nature, of poor relief. In the United States this issue is controversial (see, for example, Murray 1984). But there seems to be little research on the issue in the context of developing countries. Even in theory it is again ambiguous whether workfare makes sense in this role. One still has to consider the losses of output that it may entail. These must now be weighed against any favorable incentive effects, as measured by the fraction of the poor population making poverty-reducing investments.

More generally, this suggests the need to study the dynamics of poverty alleviation programs in greater detail. Only in this way could one make proper sense of, for example, the widespread advocacy of subsidized credit programs, the promotion of human capital formation, and the greater coverage by social insurance schemes. Understanding the link between poverty alleviation programs and life cycle and other dynamic choices remains an important topic for future empirical and theoretical research.

Transfers in kind

Another way to target groups is through transfers in kind, a point first clearly explained by Nichols and Zeckhauser (1982). Consider, for example, a good that is demanded discretely, such as an educational qualification or a course of medical treatment (see Besley and Coate 1991 for a detailed analysis of this problem). Such goods are typically available at different levels of quality. If the state provides a certain level of quality free of charge, then a consumer must choose between public and private provision, weighing the cost of buying the good in the private market. If the government can find a level of quality such that the demand for the publicly provided good is only from the poor, then quality choice provides a self-regulating test, on the basis of which the poor can be targeted even if the government knows nothing else about the poor population (or about who is poor). There are three main principles behind this argument.

First, quality must be a normal good. If variation in taste is also considered, the argument is a little more complex. Consider, for example, the role of religious affiliations; they can create a difference in taste that may in turn be an important determinant of a consumer's propensity to use certain kinds of medical services. The correlation between tastes for quality and incomes then becomes important (for example, poor people of religion A may be less inclined to use a "poverty-oriented" medical facility than rich people of religion B); the story overlaps with the statistical targeting story of the last section.

Second, there must be a private market for the publicly provided good at the higher level of quality. This requirement limits the applicability of this sort of targeting in developing countries because often the only private sector alternatives are typically of a kind that only those individuals with very high incomes can afford.

Third, one must be able to find a level of quality at which only some fraction of the population makes use of the publicly provided good. Otherwise, in-kind transfers are dominated by transfers of cash of the same value. That is because transfers in kind carry a deadweight loss, since cash can be spent on whatever a consumer—poor or not—wishes, normally yielding that consumer more extra welfare and thus constituting a more efficient use of the funds. In general, this deadweight loss can be tolerated only if there is a gain from targeting particular groups—for example, the poor.

Both kinds of self-targeting schemes that we have discussed require the effective prohibition of a secondary market in the publicly provided good. For example, it must be impossible for a rich consumer A to get a poor consumer B to undertake A's work requirement in order for B to get A's benefit. Similarly, those who do not wish to consume public education should be unable to sell their right to a school place to another. In practice, there are many commodities for which this restriction can be enforced. But this requirement suggests that, in general, food will *not* be an acceptable commodity for a self-targeting scheme. Typically, it would be impossible to prevent unwanted food allocations from being claimed, and then sold, by consumers who were not poor. Hence, the gains from the program would cease to be targeted. An important exception is the subsidizing of a high-weight "inferior" food, such as cassava; the transactions costs of resale could in some circumstances be prohibitively high. By contrast, however, the good "meals" has more potential. A person who consumes a meal of a particular quality at a particular time would not also consume another meal right away. Hence, there is imperfect substitution between publicly and privately provided meals.

A little-explored transfer in kind is agricultural research. A long-standing idea is that such research should be directed at upgrading product quality or reducing the proportion of less tasty grains. But this may have an effect opposite to that desired for purposes of targeting because the benefits of such research accrue predominantly to the less poor. This contradiction in policies matters, because many of the products involved, cassava again being a good example, loom large in poor people's budgets and have high transactions costs in trading—products that would be ideal for subsidy in other respects.[18]

When considering the effects of in-kind transfers, it is also very important to bear in mind the general equilibrium consequences. These have been analyzed in detail for food transfers by Coate (1989), who shows that the decision to offer food aid or cash aid will depend on the extent to which food aid has harmful effects through lowering the price of food. Typically, there are poor producers of goods that may be provided publicly, and an increase in public provision of these goods will tend to depress their market price. This may also have unfortunate consequences for laborers employed in such sectors. If there are rents in such markets, public provision may allow them to be captured and transferred to the poor.

Although for analytical purposes we have identified two different types of targeting under limited information—targeting using indicators, and self-targeting—they are best viewed as complementary possibilities. In practice, both may be important in policy design. For example, a rural public works project located in a particular region relies on both statistical indicators and self-targeting. We believe that many thoughtfully designed targeting schemes will similarly combine the two types of targeting strategy.

Conclusion

In the wake of recent calls for finer targeting of poverty alleviation expenditure in developing countries, we have investigated some of the principles of targeting. We posited an "ideal solution," in which transfers went to the poor and only to the poor, as the benchmark for discussion and as the rationale for current trends in the policy debate. But the ideal solution fails to take into account three crucial aspects of the real world: (1) administrative and informational costs of implementation, (2) individual responses and incentive effects, and (3) the political economy of the problem. It has been argued that each of these militates against the ideal solution. The optimal strategy will probably lie somewhere between the two extremes of the ideal solution and complete universalism, mediated by each of the three considerations above.

All of the above suggests the need for more country-specific research that quantifies the costs and benefits of targeting, using the variety of micro-level data that have become increasingly available for many developing countries. Such research needs to be sensitive to the political feasibilities of alternative paths of reform.

Appendix   Principles of targeting for a class of poverty measures

Consider the poverty index suggested by Foster, Greer, and Thorbecke (1984) given by

$$(A1) \qquad P_\alpha(z) = \int_0^z \left[\frac{z-y}{z} \right]^\alpha dF(y) \qquad \alpha \geq 0.$$

We refer to Kakwani (chapter 2 in this volume) for further detail.

This form of poverty indicator provides a convenient way of modeling the impact of policies oriented toward the alleviation of poverty. For our purposes it also has the useful property of decomposability. Specifically,

$$(A2) \qquad P_\alpha(z) = \sum_i \gamma_i P_\alpha^i(z),$$

where γ_i is the population share and $P_\alpha^i(z)$ is the poverty index of the ith group in poverty.

The ideal solution

If y is observable before intervention or, equivalently, the government has enough information to calculate what an individual's y would have been without intervention, then the ideal solution gives every agent a transfer of $z - y$ so that after intervention, each has an income equal to at least z and no matter what α is chosen, $P_\alpha(z)$ is zero—that is, there is no poverty. The revenue required to effect such a policy is

(A3)
$$(z - \mu^p) F(z) = P_1(z),$$

and all of this revenue goes to the poor.

A universal transfer scheme

Under a universal transfer scheme, a benefit that we denote by b is given to rich and poor alike. In this case poverty is given by

(A4)
$$P_\alpha(z, b) \equiv \int_0^{z-b} \left[\frac{z - y - b}{z} \right]^\alpha dF(y).$$

Note that the limit of integration is altered because all those with incomes greater than $z - b$ will have left poverty completely. Those remaining in poverty receive post-transfer incomes of $y + b$. If the universal benefit were set at z, then all agents will have left poverty under this scheme also. But the revenue costs of poverty alleviation would be z (normalizing population size at one). Hence, the reduction in revenue requirements from having a perfectly targeted scheme is

(A5)
$$z - (z - \mu^p)F(z) = (1 - H)z + H\mu^p,$$

where H is the head count ratio $F(z)$. This amount is increasing in z and μ^p, and decreasing in H. This required revenue difference is a weighted sum of the poverty line and the mean income of the poor.

The effects of costly take-up

This class of poverty indicators can be used to model the effects of costly take-up.[19] Imagine that although all other conditions of the ideal solution are met, individuals face a cost c of claiming that is not recouped from the transfer program. In this instance all of those with incomes less than $z - c$ will claim, and those with incomes above will not. Residual poverty among the nonclaiming group is then

(A6)
$$P_\alpha^r(z, c) \equiv \int_z^{z-c} \left[\frac{z - y}{z} \right]^\alpha dF(y),$$

and the cost of the scheme is reduced to

(A7)
$$(z - \mu^m)F(z - c),$$

where

$$\mu^m \equiv \int_z^{z-c} y \, \frac{dF(y)}{F(z-c)}$$

is the mean income of those who continue to claim the benefit offered. The amount in equation A7 could alternatively be given in the form of a universal benefit b. We might ask how high c must then be before so few people claim that a universal benefit leads to less poverty than with the "ideal solution" with take-up costs. Besley (1990) shows that when $\alpha = 1$, this value of costs is given by

(A8) $$c = \frac{H^u}{H^m}\left[(1 - H^m)(z - \mu^m) - (\mu^u - \mu^m)\right] - \frac{H^r}{H^m}(z - \mu^r),$$

where

$$H^u \equiv \int_0^{z-b} dF(y),$$

$$H^r \equiv \int_{z-c}^z dF(y),$$

$$H^m \equiv \int_0^{z-c} dF(y),$$

$$\mu^u \equiv \int_0^{z-b} y + b \, \frac{dF(y)}{F(z-b)}, \text{ and}$$

$$\mu^r \equiv \int_{z-c}^z y \, \frac{dF(y)}{F(z)F(z-c)}.$$

This "critical" cost has three components. The first,

(A9)
$$(1 - H^m)(z - \mu^m),$$

gives the proportion of the previously finely targeted benefit that now goes to other individuals. This measures the leakage from a previously targeted benefit to those who did not claim and those who are not poor. The critical cost rises with this, as one might have anticipated. The second component,

(A10)
$$(\mu^u - \mu^m),$$

is the difference in mean income between the universalist scheme and the ideal solution with take-up costs. The larger the difference in mean incomes between a means-tested and a universalist scheme, the smaller the critical cost. The third component is

(A11)
$$(z - \mu^r),$$

the extent of poverty in the group that does not claim any benefit because it is too costly to be worthwhile. If $\alpha = 2$ were chosen, the critical cost would also depend on indicators of the distribution of income among the poor. The greater the poverty in the group that does not claim in the means-tested program, the smaller is the critical cost above which universal provision is preferred. Further results for the case in which $\alpha = 2$, and some simulations assuming a lognormal income distribution, are given in Besley (1990).

Budgetary rules for targeted groups

Consider splitting the population into mutually exclusive groups according to some observable characteristic (age or region of residence).[20] We will label these groups 1 and 2. Aggregate poverty is

(A12)
$$P_\alpha(z) = x_1 P_{1,\alpha}(z) + x_2 P_{2,\alpha}(z),$$

where x_i is the population share of the ith group. Suppose now that the state has a budget B to dispense among the two groups and that it can give different additive transfers of income to those in groups 1 and 2 respectively. What rules should it pursue in doing this? The government's budget constraint is given by

(A13)
$$x_1 b_1 + x_2 b_2 = B.$$

Minimizing equation A12 subject to equation A13 yields

(A14)
$$P_{i,\alpha-1} = \lambda \quad \text{(a constant)} \quad i = 1, 2,$$

that is, the optimal budgetary rule equates the $P_{\alpha-1}$ indices of the two groups. Hence, if the income gap measure of poverty is used ($P_1(x)$), the optimal budgetary rule equates the head count over the two groups. To get some grasp on the difference between the transfer given on a targeted basis and that given on an untargeted basis, we expand the equality

(A15)
$$P_{1,\alpha-1} = P_{2,\alpha-2}$$

to the first order around the untargeted benefit outcome to obtain

(A16)
$$\gamma_i = \left[\frac{P_{1,\alpha-1} - P_{2,\alpha-1}}{(a_1 + a_2)} \right],$$

where $\gamma_i > b_i + x_iB$. This is the difference between the share of government expenditure that goes to the ith group under targeting and that in the nontargeting situation and $a_i > P_{i,\alpha-2}/x_i$. Since $\gamma_1 + \gamma_2 = 0$ if the budget is the same in both cases, the expression for γ_2 is easily obtained. The highest benefit will go to the group with the highest $P_{\alpha-1}$ in the untargeted state.

Equation A16 can be used to give an expression for the gain in poverty alleviation from targeting. Using a linear expansion around the untargeted point yields[21]

$$(A17) \qquad P_\alpha^T - P_\alpha^{NT} = -(\frac{\alpha}{z}) \frac{(P_{1,\alpha-1} - P_{2,\alpha-1})^2}{(a_1 + a_2)},$$

which is proportional to the squared difference between the $P_{\alpha-1}$ index of the two groups now being targeted. This gives us a measure of the gain that can be obtained by targeting using the type of budgetary rule described in equation A14.

Measures of the fineness of targeting can be obtained by examining what proportion of the benefits go to the poor. For the untargeted case

$$(A18) \qquad F^u = H,$$

and for the targeted case

$$(A19) \qquad F^T = \frac{H_1 b_1 + H_2 b_2}{b}$$

$$= H + \frac{H_1 \gamma_1 + H_2 \gamma_2}{b}.$$

Using equation A16,

$$(A20) \qquad H_1\gamma_1 + H_2\gamma_2 = \frac{(H_1 - H_2)(P_{1,\alpha-1} - P_{2,\alpha-1})}{(\alpha_1 + \alpha_2)}.$$

If $\alpha = 2$, this is always positive since the term in the numerator of equation A20 is $(H_1 - H_2)^2$.

Food subsidies and poverty alleviation

To represent the impact of food subsidies we use the consumer's equivalent income function, which is defined implicitly from

$$(A21) \qquad u(p, y^E) = u(q, y),$$

where $u(\bullet, \bullet)$ is the consumer's indirect utility function, p is a set of reference prices, q is actual prices, y is actual income, and y^E is equivalent income.[22] When utility is monotonically increasing in income,[23] we use equation A21 to give the function

(A22)
$$y^E = g(p, q, y).$$

We can then specify the poverty line in equivalent income space and denote it by z^E, which then implies a cutoff in income space defined by the z, which satisfies

(A23)
$$g(p, q, z) = z^E.$$

In this instance, our poverty indicator is given by

(A24)
$$P_\alpha^e(z) = \int_0^z \left[\frac{z^E - y^E}{z^E} \right]^\alpha dF(y),$$

where z is a function of p, q, and z^E. The poverty indicator is now directly a function of the prices faced by the consumer, and we can consider changes in such prices and their effect on poverty. Differentiating with respect to q_i and evaluating the outcome at $q = p$, where y^E and y and z^E and z are the same, we have[24]

(A25)
$$\left. \frac{\partial P_\alpha^e(z)}{\partial q_i} \right|_{q=p} = \frac{\alpha}{z} \int_0^z \left[\frac{z-y}{z} \right]^{\alpha-1} x_i(q, y) dF(y).$$

This is a weighted sum of the demands in which weights are derived from the P_α class of poverty measures. Consider now the choice between increasing the subsidy to two goods. Let s_1 and s_2 denote their respective subsidies and

(A26)
$$s_1 \int x_1(q, y) dF(y) + s_2 \int x_2(q, y) dF(y) = B$$

denote the government's budget constraint. Differentiating equation A26 to impose a condition of a balanced budget, we find that the effect of a subsidy to good 1, financed by a tax on good 2, aimed at reducing poverty, is given by

(A27)
$$\left. \frac{dP_\alpha^e(z)}{dq_1} \right|_{q=p} = \frac{\alpha}{z} \bar{x}_1 \int_0^z \left[\frac{z-y}{z} \right]^{\alpha-1} \left[\frac{x_1}{\bar{x}_1} - \frac{x_2}{\bar{x}_2} \right] dF(y),$$

where $\bar{x}_i = \int x_i(q, y) dF(y)$ is the mean demand for good i on an economywide basis. The ratio $x_i/\bar{x}_i$ is the demand for good i by a particular poor person in relation to the average demand. The rule in equation A27 says that subsidizing good 1 and taxing good 2 reduces poverty if the weighted sum of $x_1/\bar{x}_1$ exceeds that of $x_2/\bar{x}_2$. In the case in which $\alpha = 1$, equation A27 becomes

(A28)
$$\frac{dP_\alpha^e(z)}{dq_1} > 0 \leftrightarrow \left[\frac{\bar{x}_1^p}{\bar{x}_1} - \frac{\bar{x}_2^p}{\bar{x}_2} \right] > 0,$$

where

$$\bar{x}_i^P \equiv \int_0^z x_i(q, y)\, dF(y)/F(z)$$

is the mean consumption of good i by the poor. This confirms the World Bank view that one should target the subsidy toward the good that has the highest ratio of demand by the poor to mean demand. Other simple rules can be obtained from equation A27 if preferences are restricted.

If

(A29) $$x_i(q, y) = \gamma_i(q) + \beta_i(q)y,$$

that is, if Engel curves are affine in income,[25] then

(A30) $$\left.\frac{dP_\alpha^\epsilon(z)}{dq_1}\right|_{q=p} = \frac{\alpha}{z}\bar{x}_1\left[\left(\frac{\gamma_1}{x_1} - \frac{\gamma_2}{x_2}\right)P_{\alpha-1} + \left(\frac{\beta_1}{x_1} - \frac{\beta_2}{x_2}\right)z(P_{\alpha-1} - P_\alpha)\right].$$

Now, whether a subsidy on good 1 financed by a tax on good 2 reduces poverty depends on weighted differences in demand coefficients where weights are P_α indices. Further generalizations are given in Besley and Kanbur (1988). For practical purposes, rules of the kind given in equation A27 may be implementable. Most estimated demand functions can be written in their P_α form, since almost all lie in the class

(A31) $$x_i(q, y) = [\gamma_i(q) + \beta_i(q)y + \theta_i(q)]f(y)$$

for some function $f(y)$. Which foods should be targeted in this framework depends on the shape of the Engel curve and the various P_α indices.

Other food subsidy schemes are of the ration shop variety, in which a fixed amount of subsidy is given below the market price. If the resale of any unwanted food is permissible, then we are effectively back to the type of targeting scheme using key indicators, as discussed in the text, without targeting subgroups (unless different subsidies are given to different groups, for example, by strategically locating shops and allowing only residents of surrounding areas to shop there). An intermediate scheme is one in which resale is not permitted. If the good being sold through a ration shop is normal, then there will be some income level y, say, at which take-up is complete and the food subsidy is just like an income transfer. For incomes below y, it will be just like the marginal food subsidy discussed above. Under such a scheme, poverty is given by

(A32) $$\int_0^y \left[\frac{z^E - y^E(q, p, y)}{z^E}\right]^\alpha dF(y) + \int_y^{z-m_i} \left[\frac{z^E - y^E(q, p, y+m_i)}{z^E}\right]^\alpha dF(y),$$

where $m_i \equiv (q_i - p_i)x_i^R$, and where x_i^R is the quantity available from a ration shop. The effect on poverty of a change in the subsidy now has two components that are like the food subsidy rule in equation A28 for those with incomes less than y and an additive transfer to those with incomes above y. This suggests the importance of modeling behavior vis-à-vis the take-up of unwanted food in a ration shop scheme.

Notes

An earlier version of this chapter was presented to the World Bank symposium on Poverty and Adjustment, April 11-13, 1988. An earlier, shorter version of the chapter appeared in *Current Issues in Development Economics,* edited by Sanjaya Lall and V. N. Balasubramanyam. Copyright 1991 Macmillan. Copyright 1991 St. Martin's Press. Reprinted with permission of Macmillan Press Ltd. and St. Martin's Press Incorporated. We are grateful to Stephen Coate, Michael Lipton, and Martin Ravallion for comments, and to Anne Hendry for assistance in preparing the final version.

1. See the contributions in Garfinkel (1982).
2. Kanbur (1987c) reviews the issues in the light of recent U.S. and U.K. policy.
3. On these issues see Atkinson (1987b) and Kanbur (1987a).
4. It requires the state to have perfect information about individuals' tastes and characteristics so that individuals are prevented from "pretending" to have incomes below the poverty line in order to claim a transfer.
5. For industrial countries there has been some collation of evidence. Kesselman (1982) classified several programs as "universal" or "tested." Of the seven U.K. programs considered, two were universal and five tested. Administrative costs as a percentage of benefits were 3.8 percent and 3.5 percent for the universal programs, and they ranged from 5.2 percent to 15.4 percent for the tested programs. In the United States the old-age, survivors', disability, and health insurance program (a universal program) had administrative costs of 2.5 percent of benefits; for public assistance and unemployment insurance (tested programs), the administrative costs were 12.1 percent and 11.8 percent. The veterans' welfare program, a tested program, had an incredible administrative cost–benefits ratio of 95.2 percent. What seems to be needed is systematic compilation and analysis of such data for developing countries.
6. The latter has been much discussed in the literature on poverty in industrial countries (see, for example, Moffitt 1983), but very little, if anything, has been written on it in the developing country context.
7. This is the motivation for the analyses of optimal income tax problems, initially by Mirrlees (1971).
8. Besley (1990) provides simulations that suggest that means testing is still very often preferable to a universalist program despite these effects.
9. Much work has been done in the industrial country context. In a recent exercise based on data for the United States, Sadka, Garfinkel, and Moreland (1982) conclude that "the results presented in this paper are sufficient to call into question the consensus among economic experts that transfer programs which provide benefits only to those with low incomes are more efficient than those which provide benefits to all regardless of income."
10. A theoretical analysis of the impact of political economy constraints on the analysis of price reform is provided in Braverman and Kanbur (1987).

11. Such surveys are being conducted with World Bank support in Côte d'Ivoire, Ghana, Mauritania, and Peru.

12. Those interested in the details should consult Kanbur (1986 and 1987a).

13. The national poverty gap is the aggregate of individual shortfalls of income from the poverty line for poor people.

14. For an overview of how the available published evidence for Latin America might be used, see Kanbur (1990a).

15. Besley and Kanbur (1988) also present generalizations of this rule.

16. For further discussion, see Besley and Coate (1992).

17. This is used in practice for a variety of public services and in public food distribution schemes; for these, Alderman (1987a) presents evidence on the effect of having to wait in line for food distributions in Egypt. He suggests that it does indeed discourage many consumers. But he questions the view that a "rationing-by-waiting" method of allocating food benefits the poor disproportionately.

18. We owe this point to Michael Lipton.

19. This section is based on Besley (1990).

20. This section is based on Kanbur (1990b).

21. See Besley and Kanbur (1988) for details and the generalization of this argument.

22. See Besley and Kanbur (1988).

23. This section is based on Besley and Kanbur (1988).

24. The derivative of the equivalent income function is obtained from equation A24 using Roy's identity.

25. Preferences are quasi-homothetic.

Regional Disparities, Targeting, and Poverty in India

4

Gaurav Datt
Martin Ravallion

Disparities in living standards among regions and between urban and rural sectors have long raised concern in India, a concern motivated in part by the desire to alleviate poverty.[1] For example, India's Finance Commissions have used a poverty criterion for allocating public revenues to the states.[2] The World Bank has recently discussed possible changes in the central government's revenue-sharing arrangements that would direct resources to poorer states as part of an overall poverty alleviation strategy (World Bank 1990a). And advocates of policy reforms favoring the agricultural sector have often pointed to the fact that poverty is generally more severe in rural areas than in urban areas.

Directing development resources to poorer regions or sectors has seemed an attractive policy option in India, as elsewhere. This partly reflects the informational constraints facing policymakers in developing countries when attempting to identify and reach the poor.[3] But it also clearly reflects the political constraints that limit the possibilities of redistribution *within* regions or sectors. Given these constraints, the question remains: How much impact can manipulating the distribution of income between regions or sectors have on aggregate poverty?

The answer is far from obvious. It can be argued that because of constraints on policy changes, the costs (to donor regions) and benefits (to recipient regions) of policies to redistribute income *among* regions will tend to be widely distributed *within* regions. Some leakages are probably unavoidable: the nonpoor in recipient regions will receive some benefits and the poor in donor regions will bear some costs. Clearly, the existing constraints on redistribution in most developing countries will diminish the effectiveness of direct policy intervention for alleviating poverty. But even the *qualitative* effect of regional and sectoral policies is not clear. Take, for example, reforms aimed at giving a pro-rural emphasis to sectoral policies. Granted, the rural population is, as a rule, poorer on average. But the intersectoral redistribution associated with the policy reform may impose a heavier burden on the urban poor than the gains to the rural poor can justify. If we are unable to limit the costs of policy reform for the urban poor and effectively target the benefits to the rural poor, we may find that a pro-rural bias actually *increases* aggregate poverty.

Our aim in this chapter is to explore the implications of regional and sectoral disparities for national poverty, and to examine the case for interregional redistributive policies. We address the following questions:

- How much do disparities in average living standards between states and the urban and rural sectors contribute to national poverty in India?
- Under what conditions can national poverty be reduced by transfers aimed at reducing disparities in average living standards between states or sectors?
- Are those conditions plausible for India, and if so, how much reduction in poverty can be expected from this type of policy intervention?

The chapter's objectives are modest in several ways, and the following caveats should be kept in mind in considering the policy implications of the analysis. First, we are concerned only with the *direct* or *first-round* effects of regional redistribution. Thus, for instance, we do not consider the possible effects that redistribution might have through its influence on households' decisions to relocate. Migration is likely to reduce the poverty alleviation effect if, as seems likely, the nonpoor are in a better position to evade regional redistribution by migration than are the poor. Similarly, our analysis does not consider general equilibrium effects on incomes and prices within regions.[4] It is unclear in what direction this would affect our results.

Second, the impact of interregional redistribution on poverty depends in part on the size of the regions. Our study focuses on interstate and urban-rural redistribution. Clearly, a greater effect would be possible if smaller units, such as districts, could be targeted for redistribution; in that case, poor districts within rich states might gain from redistribution, and rich districts within poor states could provide extra resources. But redistribution seems more likely to be politically and administratively feasible at the larger state or provincial level.

Third, the analysis ignores some of the constraints on regional redistribution that may become binding in practice. Most important, perhaps, we do not consider political economy constraints on the central government's power to effect redistribution among regions. For example, it may be politically infeasible to levy taxes on a region beyond a certain point. Not taking into account the effects of such constraints may lead us to err on the side of overestimating the potential of regional redistribution to alleviate poverty. The omission of political economy constraints is probably less worrying when discussing reforms that call for limited redistribution (when the constraints may rarely be binding), however, than it is when examining optimal redistribution policies that may involve large transfers.

Finally, a further limitation of the study is that we analyze only a single cross-section. Our analysis will thus be *static*. We do not consider possible effects of combining spatial and temporal redistributions; for example, transfers from the urban sector to the rural sector during lean seasons or poor crop years can be expected to have a greater impact on aggregate poverty than transfers at other times.[5]

Before turning to the data on India, we show how the contribution of regional disparities in average living standards to aggregate poverty can be quantified. We also consider the effects of certain stylized redistributions from "rich" to "poor" regions or sectors on aggregate poverty. We discuss how the case for regional redistribution to alleviate poverty depends on intraregional distributions and how they are affected by interregional transfers.

Next, we turn to the empirical results. We examine what India's 38th Round National Sample Survey for 1983 shows about regional disparities and the regional profiles of poverty. We then present our simulations of the effects on national poverty of existing regional disparities and of removing them through purely *regional* redistribution; here, we draw on the theoretical results that are discussed earlier.

Regional disparities and national poverty

This section presents the theoretical results needed to answer the three questions posed at the beginning of this chapter. We first consider the contribution of regional disparities in average living standards to aggregate poverty and how that may be measured. We then ask the comparative static question: Will small reductions in those disparities (with the national average living standard unchanged) reduce aggregate poverty? Finally, we consider the question of how much reduction in aggregate poverty can be expected from reducing or eliminating those disparities.

The national poverty level can be thought of as a function of three factors: regional disparities in average living standards, intraregional inequalities, and the national mean income or living standard. The contribution of regional disparities alone can be measured by estimating the national poverty level that would obtain if mean income levels were fully equalized across regions while the national mean and intraregional distributions were held constant. We call this "the *partial* contribution of regional disparities" to emphasize that the last two factors are held constant.

If we express poverty in region j (P_j) as a function of the mean income (μ_j) and the parameters of the Lorenz curve for region j (the vector $\mathbf{L}_j$), initial aggregate national poverty P is

(4.1)
$$P = \sum_{j=1}^{m} w_j P(\mu_j, \mathbf{L}_j),$$

where w_j is the share of region j in the total population of m regions. (We follow recent literature in assuming a class of additively separable and population-weighted poverty measures. Specific examples are discussed later.) If all regional income means are equalized, while the national mean and intraregional distributions remain unchanged, then national poverty becomes P^*, where

(4.2)
$$P^* = \sum_{j=1}^{m} w_j P(\bar{\mu}, \mathbf{L}_j),$$

and

(4.3)
$$\bar{\mu} = \sum_{j=1}^{m} w_j \mu_j.$$

The partial contribution of regional disparities in average living standards to aggregate national poverty is then $(P - P^*)/P$. This is estimated for India in a later section.

There are a number of reasons to be cautious in drawing policy implications from such an experiment. For example, an enforced equalization of regional means may entail some reduction in national mean income (to the extent that resources are constrained from flowing to regions of higher productivity). We do not consider that possibility. Regional equalization may also involve substantial burdens in some regions; we consider more modest transfers below. Nor is it likely that the central government has the detailed information needed for equalizing regional means, holding intraregional inequalities constant; effecting the multiplicative transfers needed for such pure regional redistribution would require the government to know every person's income. We therefore consider alternative assumptions. Nonetheless, quantifying the partial contribution of regional disparities to national poverty is the obvious first step in quantifying their contribution under more realistic assumptions about the induced effects of other determinants of aggregate poverty.

Rather than equalizing regional means, consider instead the effect of small reductions in regional disparities on aggregate poverty. Again, this depends in part on how regional redistribution alters intraregional inequalities, which, in turn, depends on how the redistribution is achieved. For example, lump-sum transfers to or from all residents of each region would reduce inequality in recipient regions and raise it in donor regions. But the overall outcome for the poor remains unclear even if one considers a "pure" form of regional redistribution based on multiplicatively absorbed transfers that do not alter relative inequalities within other regions. Poverty will decrease in recipient regions and increase in donor regions. The aggregate outcome then depends on whether the first effect outweighs the second. This, in turn, depends on the initial value in donor and recipient regions of the chosen poverty measure—that is, on initial regional disparities in average standards of living and in intraregional inequalities.

Consider a situation in which regional disparities are reduced through lump-sum transfers uniformly levied on or received by everyone in a given region. This is termed *additive absorption*. The transfer paid or received by an individual is determined solely by region of residence. Additive transfers are attractive because they do not assume that the government knows anything more than each person's region of residence. It is thus *informationally* feasible for the central government. But multiplicative transfers may be *politically* more feasible at the local levels for two reasons. First, multiplicative transfers do not involve any change in intraregional inequalities. And second, the same local political economy factors (distribution of endowments, local tax powers, the social preferences of governments) that determined initial intraregional distributions tend to operate persistently to preserve those distributions. Thus, there are good arguments for considering both additive and multiplicative absorption.

The outcome also depends on how poverty is measured. We will consider various members of the Foster-Greer-Thorbecke (FGT) class of measures (Foster, Greer, and Thorbecke 1984). The level of poverty in the ith region is denoted

$P_{\alpha i}$ for the parameter $\alpha \geq 0$. The well-known *head count index of poverty* (the proportion of people who are poor) is the FGT measure for $\alpha = 0$. For $\alpha = 1$, we obtain the FGT version of the *poverty gap measure* (mean income shortfall as a proportion of the poverty line). A recently popular *distributionally sensitive* measure of poverty is obtained by setting $\alpha = 2$. We prefer the last measure because it satisfies Sen's (1976) transfer axiom (transfers from a poor person to someone who is poorer will reduce measured poverty). An advantage of the FGT class of measures in this context is that they are additively separable, so that national poverty is simply the population-weighted mean of the regional poverty levels. (This does not hold for Sen's own index.)

We will now make these observations more precise, so as to allow an analytically tractable characterization of the conditions under which regional disparities can be said to contribute to aggregate poverty.

The necessary and sufficient conditions for determining the effect on poverty of additively absorbed lump-sum transfers between regions can be summarized as follows:[6]

Proposition 1 (additive absorption). The head count index ($\alpha = 0$) will decrease when a small, additively absorbed transfer is made from region j to region k if and only if $f_j(z) < f_k(z)$, where $f_i(z)$ denotes the probability density function of income in region $i = j, k$ as evaluated at the poverty line z. Other poverty measures in the FGT class ($\alpha \geq 1$) will indicate a decrease in poverty if and only if $P_{\alpha-1j} < P_{\alpha-1k}$.

Figure 4.1 illustrates how the national head count index of poverty is affected by additively absorbed transfers between hypothetical urban and rural sectors, which we assume (for convenience in diagramming only) to be of equal size. Each person in the rural sector receives an amount x, which is transferred from each person in the urban sector. Distribution functions are thus displaced horizontally (to the right for rural areas, to the left for urban) by an equal distance at all points. Rather than draw this explicitly, we can imagine shifting the poverty line; for example, if a proportion $F(z)$ of the rural population was poor initially, it will fall to $F(z - x)$ when each person receives x.

In figure 4.1 the income distribution functions are drawn convex from below, implying that (for the usual unimodal density) the mode is above the poverty line. (This is not essential.)

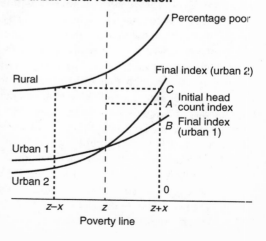

Figure 4.1 Effects on aggregate poverty of urban-rural redistribution

Two possible "urban" distributions are considered; these generate the same initial poverty level, but different final levels. Compared with the rural distribution, the "urban 1" distribution is flatter at the poverty line (implying a lower density), and therefore the aggregate head count index falls (from $0A$ to $0B$) as a result of the redistribution in favor of the rural sector, as claimed in Proposition 1. By contrast, the "urban 2" distribution is steeper than the rural distribution around the poverty line, with the consequence that redistribution in favor of the rural sector now *increases* aggregate poverty as measured by the head count index (from $0A$ to $0C$).

To illustrate the importance of the precise way in which regional redistribution is effected, we consider instead a "pure" regional redistribution in which transfers do not alter intraregional inequalities; specifically, we assume that the Lorenz curve of each region's income distribution remains unaffected by the transfers. In this case, all transfers paid or received are directly proportional to household income per capita and the proportion transferred varies solely by region. In a manner analogous to Proposition 1, we can summarize the necessary and sufficient conditions for such multiplicative regional transfers to alleviate poverty as follows:

> *Proposition 2 (multiplicative absorption).* Small transfers from j to k that preserve intraregional inequalities will reduce the aggregate head count index of poverty if and only if $f_j(z)/\mu_j < f_k(z)/\mu_k$, where μ_i denotes mean income in region $i = j, k$. For other poverty measures ($\alpha \geq 1$), the necessary and sufficient condition is that $(P_{\alpha-1j} - P_{\alpha j})/\mu_j < (P_{\alpha-1k} - P_{\alpha k})/\mu_k$.

When the donor region has the higher mean, and a less dense distribution at the poverty line, the aggregate head count index will fall. Thus, for example, assuming that the urban mean income is higher than the rural mean, transfers from the "urban 1" sector to the rural sector in figure 4.1 would still reduce aggregate poverty. It is no longer clear, however, that transfers from the "urban 2" sector will increase poverty; if the disparity in mean income is high enough (more precisely, if $\mu_j/\mu_k > f_j/f_k$), poverty will fall.

Another way to understand this result is by noting that the head count index is strictly convex in the mean, holding the Lorenz curve constant. This is proved in the appendix, where it is also shown to be true of the FGT measures for $\alpha = 1$ and 2. Thus, aggregate poverty is a strictly quasi-convex function of the vector of regional means, though that function is symmetric only if Lorenz curves are everywhere the same. By well-known properties of such functions, a reduction in regional disparities will reduce aggregate poverty if those disparities are initially large enough. Equalization will not, however, be optimal as a rule; and there can still be transfers from rich to poor regions that increase overall poverty.

This discussion has focused on the theoretical case for redistributing income across regions when that case is to be judged by the *direction* of the effects on aggregate poverty. Also of interest is quantifying optimal regional targeting for minimizing poverty. Of course, the sense in which poverty-minimizing regional allocations are "optimal" is quite restrictive. Poverty alleviation is unlikely to be the sole criterion for judging such regional allocation policies, and there are bound to be tradeoffs against other policy objectives. But we are still interested in knowing the poverty-minimizing allocation because this is the appropriate benchmark of evaluating the *potential* of regional redistribution, as it allows us to estimate the maximum effect that this type of policy could have on poverty. For example, considering that regional redistribution is a form of targeting under imperfect information and that region of residence may be a highly imperfect indicator of poverty, the potential of such redistribution for alleviating poverty may be modest. That potential can be determined with precision only by calculating the optimal (poverty-minimizing) allocation.

Drawing on recent work, we can readily characterize and calculate the optimal allocation of uniform lump-sum transfers for P_2, the distributionally sensitive poverty measure.[7] A necessary condition for minimizing the nationwide value of P_2 is that P_{1i} is equalized across all regions, at a given national income per person (Kanbur 1987a). It is also useful to have a monetary measure of the gain from optimal regional redistribution. For this purpose, the *equivalent gain from targeting* is defined as the uniform increase in all individual incomes (regardless of region) needed to achieve the same reduction in national poverty as would be attainable under optimal regional redistribution (Ravallion and Chao 1989). We calculate the equivalent gain from regional targeting in India later in this chapter.

Average consumption levels, inequality and poverty in India

Our main source of data is the National Sample Survey (NSS) thirty-eighth round survey on consumer expenditure for 1983 (NSSO 1986). The survey gives the size distribution of monthly consumption expenditure per capita in urban and rural areas of different states and union territories. Our analysis relates to forty "regions" in India—the urban and rural sectors of twenty states (see table 4.1). These regions account for 98.4 percent of India's total population (RGCCI 1982).[8] Many of the following calculations were also performed on the data for the twenty states without splitting them into urban and rural sectors. The poverty reduction attainable through regional redistribution will generally increase with finer regional detail in targeting.

Price deflators

The survey data on consumption expenditure are, of course, in current local prices. To make consistent comparisons across regions and to evaluate aggregate poverty, we need to adjust the nominal data for regional variations in the cost of living. We use the following two price indices to express all regional expenditures in 1983 all-India rural prices:

The *rural price index* (RPI) for state j is defined as

$$(4.4) \quad RPI_j = RPR_j \cdot \frac{CPIAL_j(1983)}{CPIAL_j(1973-74)} \cdot \frac{CPIAL_{AI}(1973-74)}{CPIAL_{AI}(1983)},$$

where RPR is the ratio of rural prices in state j to all-India rural prices (rural interstate price relatives) for 1973-74. The RPRs are based on the Fisher regional price indices constructed by Bhattacharya, Joshi, and Roychoudhury (1980, table 3a).[9] CPIAL is the Consumer Price Index for Agricultural Laborers for state j and all-India (AI), as tabulated by the Labor Bureau, Ministry of Labor. This proposed price index simply updates the rural interstate price relatives for 1973-74 to 1983, using the CPIAL as the rural price deflator.

The *urban price index* (UPI) for state j is defined analogously as

$$(4.5) \qquad UPI_j = URPR \cdot UPR_j \cdot \frac{CPIIW_j(1983)}{CPIIW_j(1973-74)} \cdot \frac{CPIAL_{AI}(1973-74)}{CPIAL_{AI}(1983)},$$

where UPRs are the urban interstate price relatives (analogous to RPRs) and URPR is the all-India urban-to-rural price relative for 1973-74. Both UPR and URPR are derived from Bhattacharya, Joshi, and Roychoudhury (1980, tables 3b and 4). CPIIWs are the Consumer Price Indices for Industrial Workers (Labor Bureau, Ministry of Labour); CPIIWs are constructed as state-specific simple averages over urban centers in each state and over months during the relevant periods.[10]

Mean consumption levels and regional inequality

Table 4.1 summarizes the relevant data. The following observations can be made:

- The national mean consumption expenditure for 1983 is about 116 rupees (Rs) per capita per month at 1983 all-India rural prices. At the state level, average consumption ranges from Rs 90 in Bihar to Rs 163 in Punjab. Intraregional inequality, as measured by the Gini coefficient, is low to moderate for most regions, ranging from about 0.18 in urban Manipur to about 0.39 in urban Kerala.
- Mean per capita consumption is generally higher in urban areas than in rural areas, even after allowing for differences in the cost of living. At the all-India level, the difference in mean consumption is about 11 percent of the rural mean consumption. Regional variation in mean consumption is greater among the rural areas than among the urban areas.
- The Gini coefficient of per capita consumption is generally higher in urban areas than in rural areas, and it is significantly correlated with the mean ($r = 0.37$; t-statistic = 2.5) across the forty regions.

Regional and sectoral profiles of poverty

Tables 4.2 and 4.3 give the FGT poverty measures for $\alpha = 0, 1, 2$ for the urban and rural sectors of each state. (The appendix outlines how these poverty measures are calculated from the published grouped data.) The measures are evaluated at two poverty lines—monthly per capita expenditures of Rs 76.65 (table 4.2) and Rs 89.00 (table 4.3) at 1983 all-India rural prices. The lower poverty

Table 4.1 Regional disparities in monthly per capita consumption, India, 1983

State	Urban			Rural			Total		
	Population share (percent)	Mean consumption (rupees) [a]	Gini coefficient	Population share (percent)	Mean consumption (rupees) [a]	Gini coefficient	Population share (percent)	Mean consumption (rupees) [a]	
Andhra Pradesh	1.92	137.46	0.310	6.01	134.84	0.296	7.92	135.47	
Assam	0.32	121.37	0.259	2.67	102.90	0.201	2.99	104.86	
Bihar	1.35	107.29	0.304	9.01	87.59	0.260	10.36	90.16	
Gujarat	1.61	116.62	0.271	3.47	108.85	0.259	5.08	111.32	
Haryana	0.44	147.33	0.315	1.49	150.38	0.276	1.93	149.68	
Himachal Pradesh	0.05	191.22	0.355	0.58	131.59	0.277	0.63	136.21	
Jammu and Kashmir	0.19	113.73	0.247	0.70	145.77	0.230	0.90	138.86	
Karnataka	1.65	129.99	0.339	3.88	107.82	0.304	5.53	114.44	
Kerala	0.72	144.00	0.387	3.02	130.42	0.338	3.74	133.04	
Madhya Pradesh	1.64	118.40	0.298	6.11	117.17	0.297	7.75	117.43	
Maharashtra	3.34	130.16	0.342	5.97	102.96	0.286	9.31	112.71	
Manipur	0.07	103.63	0.176	0.15	112.51	0.187	0.22	109.86	
Meghalaya	0.04	172.05	0.269	0.16	110.05	0.299	0.20	121.73	
Orissa	0.49	125.46	0.303	3.40	91.92	0.271	3.89	96.15	
Punjab	0.71	145.63	0.335	1.78	170.13	0.289	2.49	163.14	
Rajasthan	1.12	124.38	0.307	4.03	145.05	0.346	5.15	140.55	
Tamil Nadu	2.38	119.20	0.356	4.72	103.06	0.328	7.09	108.47	
Tripura	0.03	140.13	0.331	0.27	119.16	0.256	0.31	121.49	
Uttar Pradesh	3.10	116.77	0.315	13.37	118.05	0.295	16.47	117.81	
West Bengal	2.16	126.12	0.338	5.91	89.22	0.289	8.07	99.12	
All-India	23.32	125.12	—	76.68	112.86	—	100.00	115.72	
Population-weighted coefficient of variation		8.23			17.35			14.32	

— Not available.

a. Rupees are at 1983 all-India rural prices.

Source: Authors' calculations based on NSSO (1986).

Table 4.2 Poverty in India at lower poverty line, 1983

(percent; poverty line = Rs 76.65)

State	Urban			Rural			Total		
	P_0	P_1	P_2	P_0	P_1	P_2	P_0	P_1	P_2
Andhra Pradesh	20.93	4.53	1.52	20.36	4.28	1.40	20.50	4.34	1.43
Assam	22.27	3.97	1.06	26.24	4.26	1.08	25.82	4.23	1.07
Bihar	38.27	9.86	3.46	49.43	13.13	4.80	47.98	12.71	4.62
Gujarat	26.76	4.81	1.27	30.49	5.89	1.68	29.31	5.55	1.55
Haryana	17.40	3.32	0.99	11.56	1.94	0.55	12.89	2.26	0.65
Himachal Pradesh	11.08	2.21	0.72	17.88	2.86	0.72	17.36	2.81	0.72
Jammu and Kashmir	24.85	3.75	0.84	5.57	0.65	0.14	9.73	1.32	0.29
Karnataka	29.36	7.67	2.82	37.13	10.01	3.75	34.81	9.31	3.47
Kerala	27.87	6.80	2.42	27.87	6.03	1.91	27.87	6.18	2.01
Madhya Pradesh	30.22	6.25	1.82	30.50	6.95	2.26	30.44	6.81	2.17
Maharashtra	29.83	8.03	3.02	38.97	9.83	3.42	35.69	9.18	3.28
Manipur	17.18	4.15	2.58	17.48	2.56	0.59	17.39	3.04	1.19
Meghalaya	5.10	0.73	0.19	35.28	10.06	3.89	29.59	8.30	3.19
Orissa	26.31	5.60	1.74	45.06	12.35	4.80	42.69	11.50	4.41
Punjab	21.54	4.49	1.37	7.67	1.13	0.29	11.62	2.09	0.60
Rajasthan	27.05	6.17	2.09	23.23	5.33	1.79	24.06	5.51	1.86
Tamil Nadu	36.11	9.80	3.81	43.08	12.50	5.04	40.74	11.59	4.63
Tripura	22.94	5.27	1.81	23.07	4.21	1.16	23.06	4.33	1.24
Uttar Pradesh	32.95	7.90	2.70	29.51	6.61	2.14	30.15	6.85	2.25
West Bengal	30.63	7.66	2.73	47.96	15.01	6.52	43.31	13.04	5.51
All-India	29.48	7.10	2.48	33.61	8.39	3.03	32.65	8.09	2.90
Population-weighted coefficient of variation	17.15	25.75	32.97	32.76	45.56	56.30	28.80	40.40	49.78

Note: P_0 is the head count index of poverty, P_1 is the poverty gap measure (mean income shortfall as a proportion of the poverty line), and P_2 is a distributionally sensitive poverty measure. All are members of the Foster-Greer-Thorbecke class of measures.

Source: Authors' calculations based on data from NSSO (1986).

Table 4.3 Poverty in India at higher poverty line, 1983
(percent; poverty line = Rs 89.00)

State	Urban			Rural			Total		
	P_0	P_1	P_2	P_0	P_1	P_2	P_0	P_1	P_2
Andhra Pradesh	30.81	7.49	2.68	30.32	7.20	2.52	30.44	7.27	2.56
Assam	34.29	7.34	2.24	42.44	8.44	2.43	41.58	8.32	2.41
Bihar	49.28	14.58	5.73	62.48	19.10	7.74	60.76	18.52	7.48
Gujarat	40.05	8.79	2.70	44.43	10.28	3.33	43.04	9.81	3.13
Haryana	26.93	5.93	1.92	20.14	3.86	1.15	21.69	4.33	1.32
Himachal Pradesh	17.58	3.89	1.32	29.79	5.77	1.64	28.85	5.62	1.62
Jammu and Kashmir	39.78	7.73	2.10	14.00	1.87	0.42	19.56	3.14	0.78
Karnataka	38.61	11.33	4.55	47.88	14.53	5.96	45.11	13.57	5.54
Kerala	37.76	10.42	4.02	39.07	9.85	3.47	38.82	9.96	3.58
Madhya Pradesh	42.06	10.41	3.50	41.71	11.01	4.00	41.78	10.88	3.90
Maharashtra	38.82	11.68	4.79	50.71	14.70	5.72	46.45	13.62	5.38
Manipur	31.79	6.91	3.32	30.56	5.53	1.47	30.93	5.94	2.02
Meghalaya	11.09	1.72	0.45	44.79	14.23	6.03	38.44	11.87	4.98
Orissa	37.29	9.24	3.21	57.74	17.79	7.46	55.16	16.71	6.93
Punjab	30.96	7.51	2.57	14.72	2.51	0.67	19.35	3.94	1.21
Rajasthan	37.90	9.83	3.62	32.37	8.45	3.11	33.58	8.75	3.22
Tamil Nadu	46.80	14.21	5.94	54.06	17.52	7.63	51.63	16.41	7.06
Tripura	32.39	8.38	3.11	35.33	7.68	2.39	35.01	7.76	2.47
Uttar Pradesh	44.19	12.17	4.60	40.85	10.58	3.81	41.48	10.88	3.96
West Bengal	40.82	11.56	4.51	59.34	20.39	9.42	54.37	18.02	8.11
All-India	40.03	10.94	4.17	45.07	12.70	4.97	43.90	12.29	4.79
Population-weighted coefficient of variation	13.46	20.47	26.92	26.46	38.21	47.85	23.05	33.68	42.28

Note: P_0 is the head count index of poverty, P_1 is the poverty gap measure (mean income shortfall as a proportion of the poverty line), and P_2 is a distributionally sensitive poverty measure. All are members of the Foster-Greer-Thorbecke class of measures.
Source: Authors' calculations based on data from NSSO (1986).

line corresponds to the widely used Dandekar-Rath poverty line of Rs 15 per capita at 1960-61 all-India rural prices, updated by the all-India CPIAL for 1983. The higher poverty line is obtained by updating the Sixth Plan poverty line of Rs 49.09 at 1973-74 rural prices by the consumer price index for the middle three consumption deciles of the rural population, developed by Minhas and others (1987).

The reason for using two poverty lines is not to compare the merits of alternative poverty lines or consumer price indices, but simply to examine whether the conclusions of our analysis are sensitive to the exact cutoff point used to define poverty. Our range of poverty lines appears to encompass the range of opinion on this issue.[11]

The following observations can be made on the results in tables 4.2 and 4.3:

- When the lower poverty line is used, about 33 percent of the national population in 1983 are considered poor. About 44 percent are considered poor when the higher poverty line is used. For the lower poverty line, the 1983 poverty gap per capita (P_1) represents 8.1 percent of the poverty line, equivalent to Rs 6.20 per person in India per month, or about 5.4 percent of India's mean consumption per capita in that year. The poverty gap rises to 12.3 percent, or about 8.1 percent of mean consumption, when the higher poverty line is used.
- The incidence of poverty is generally higher in rural areas. The rural sector accounts for about 80 percent of aggregate poverty regardless of the poverty line or poverty measure used. The difference between urban and rural areas in P_1 is due mainly to the difference in P_0; the average poverty gap of the rural poor (obtained as P_1/P_0) in 1983—not a bad year for agriculture—is only slightly higher than that of the urban poor (25 percent compared with 24 percent for the lower poverty line and 28 percent compared with 27 percent for the higher one).
- In terms of the preferred FGT measure, $\alpha = 2$, the ten poorest regions (in order of decreasing poverty) for the lower poverty line are rural West Bengal, rural Tamil Nadu, rural Bihar, rural Orissa, rural Meghalaya, urban Tamil Nadu, rural Karnataka, urban Bihar, rural Maharashtra, and urban Maharashtra. The same ten regions are also the poorest when the higher poverty line is used (although there is some reranking).[12] These ten regions account for 62.5 percent of aggregate P_2 for the lower poverty line and 59.1 percent for the higher one; in contrast, their share in total population is about 40 percent, and their share in the total number of poor is 52.2 percent for the lower poverty line and 49.4 percent for the higher one.
- The poverty ranking of different regions is found to be quite insensitive to the choice of the poverty measure or poverty line. The rank correlation coefficients between corresponding poverty measures at the two poverty lines are 0.97 for P_0, 0.98 for P_1, and 0.98 for P_2. For a given poverty line (z), the rank correlations are also highly significant across the three poverty measures:

	Rank correlation coefficient	
	$z = Rs\ 76.65$	$z = Rs\ 89.00$
(P_0, P_1)	0.96	0.94
(P_1, P_2)	0.97	0.97
(P_0, P_2)	0.90	0.88

- For all three measures, the interregional variation in poverty is greater than that in mean consumption (compare the coefficients of variation in the last rows of tables 4.1, 4.2, and 4.3). Governments' inability to alter income distribution *within regions* (as we assume, in the next section, to be true) is therefore likely to weaken considerably the capacity of income redistribution *between regions* to reduce poverty. It is also notable (though not surprising) that regional disparities in poverty (as measured by the population-weighted coefficient of variation) increase with higher values of α for a given poverty line. For any given α, however, regional poverty variation is lower for the higher poverty line.

- As one would expect, the regional profiles of poverty are strongly correlated with average consumption (negatively) and Gini coefficients (positively) across regions. An ordinary least squares regression of the logit of the head count index against the mean consumption and the Gini coefficients in table 4.1 give the following results:[13]

$$\log[P_0/(1 - P_0)]_i = 0.0115 - 0.0303\ \text{mean}_i + 8.78\ \text{Gini}_i$$

(4.6)
$$\qquad\qquad (0.65)\quad (26.5)\qquad\qquad (15.6)$$
$$\qquad\qquad\qquad\quad [2.78]\qquad\qquad [1.89]$$
$$R^2 = 0.953,\quad n = 40$$

for the lower poverty line, and

$$\log[P_0/(1 - P_0)]_i = 1.05 - 0.0268\ \text{mean}_i + 5.96\ \text{Gini}_i$$

(4.7)
$$\qquad\qquad (7.61)\ (29.8)\qquad\qquad (13.5)$$
$$\qquad\qquad\qquad\ [2.10]\qquad\qquad [1.09]$$
$$R^2 = 0.960,\quad n = 40$$

for the higher poverty line. The corresponding absolute elasticities of P_0 with respect to both variables evaluated at mean points are given in square brackets below the absolute t-ratios, which are in parentheses.

Regional disparities and redistribution: Some implications for poverty

As we saw earlier in this chapter, there can be no theoretical presumption that transfers from rich to poor regions will reduce the proportion of the national population that is poor, or indeed will result in an improvement in any of the other measures of poverty. Whether such transfers do so or not is an empirical question to which we now turn.

The qualitative effect on national poverty of reducing regional disparities

We have tested the necessary and sufficient conditions for desirable redistributions between pairs of regions (Propositions 1 and 2) for each of the 780 possible binary combinations of the forty regions. Table 4.4 summarizes the results for each of the three poverty measures ($\alpha = 0, 1, 2$) and for both additive absorption (Proposition 1) and multiplicative absorption (Proposition 2). The table gives the number of cases in which poverty is reduced by a small transfer from a donor region with a higher mean consumption to a recipient region with a lower mean consumption. We find that at least 74 percent of additive redistributions and at least 81 percent of multiplicative redistributions would reduce aggregate poverty.

There is considerable overlap between cases in which additive and multiplicative redistributions would reduce poverty. In at least 73 percent of the cases, regional redistribution would reduce aggregate poverty irrespective of whether transfers are additively or multiplicatively absorbed within regions, or partially absorbed in both ways. These are cases in which the necessary and sufficient conditions of Propositions 1 and 2 are simultaneously satisfied for any given poverty measure.

We also tested the effect of transfers from the urban to the rural sector in each of the twenty states. The results are also summarized in table 4.4. Reducing urban-rural disparities in mean consumption would reduce aggregate poverty in at least seventeen of the twenty states through both additive and multiplicative absorption. In at least sixteen of those states, urban-to-rural transfers reduce poverty whether they are additively or multiplicatively absorbed, or partially absorbed both ways. The exceptions are found mainly in Andhra Pradesh, Madhya Pradesh, and Manipur.

Despite the exceptions, the overall qualitative result is clear—redistribution from India's rich states or sectors (those with higher mean consumption) to its poor states or sectors (those with lower mean consumption) does generally contribute to the alleviation of aggregate poverty. The question remains: How much can poverty be alleviated by such means? To answer this, we first consider the contribution of regional disparities in mean consumption to aggregate poverty in India.

The contribution of regional disparities to national poverty

Using the methodology outlined in the the section on theoretical results, we evaluated the contribution of regional disparities in mean consumption to aggregate poverty in India (table 4.5). We found that such disparities account for at most 11 percent of aggregate poverty, using the poverty gap measure and the lower poverty line. Given the existing intraregional distributions of consumption, even removing *all* regional disparities in mean consumption per capita (through proportional transfers) would achieve only a modest reduction of less than two percentage points in the proportion of the population deemed poor at either poverty line. For example, in 1983 about 32.7 percent of India's population was below the lower poverty line; removing all regional disparities in mean consumption reduces that

Table 4.4 Effects of regional redistribution on aggregate poverty

Poverty measure (P_α)	Redistribution across all states and sectors		Redistribution from urban to rural sectors	
	Decreases poverty	*Increases poverty*	*Decreases poverty*	*Increases poverty*
Additively absorbed redistribution				
z = Rs 76.65				
Head count index (P_0)	664 (85)	116 (15)	18	2
Poverty gap (P_1)	619 (79)	161 (21)	18	2
Preferred measure (P_2)	576 (74)	204 (26)	17	3
z = Rs 89.00				
Head count index (P_0)	594 (76)	186 (24)	18	2
Poverty gap (P_1)	658 (84)	122 (16)	18	2
Preferred measure (P_2)	600 (77)	180 (23)	17	3
Multiplicatively absorbed redistribution				
z = Rs 76.65				
Head count index (P_0)	725 (93)	55 (7)	19	1
Poverty gap (P_1)	675 (87)	105 (13)	17	3
Preferred measure (P_2)	629 (81)	151 (19)	18	2
z = Rs 89.00				
Head count index (P_0)	690 (88)	90 (12)	18	2
Poverty gap (P_1)	727 (93)	53 (7)	19	1
Preferred measure (P_2)	659 (84)	121 (16)	18	2
Additively or multiplicatively absorbed redistribution				
z = Rs 76.65				
Head count index (P_0)	664 (85)	116 (15)	18	2
Poverty gap (P_1)	617 (79)	163 (21)	17	3
Preferred measure (P_2)	571 (73)	209 (27)	16	4
z = Rs 89.00				
Head count index (P_0)	594 (76)	186 (24)	18	2
Poverty gap (P_1)	656 (84)	124 (16)	18	2
Preferred measure (P_2)	598 (77)	182 (23)	16	4

Note: The table gives the number of pairs between which small transfers from the region with higher mean consumption to the region with lower mean consumption will decrease or increase aggregate poverty. It shows those results also for transfers from urban to rural sectors in the twenty states. Corresponding percentages are given in parentheses.
Source: Authors' calculations.

figure by only 5.3 percent, to 30.9 percent. The response for the aggregate poverty gap measure is somewhat greater: eliminating the disparities in regional means would reduce the measure by about 11 percent at the lower poverty line and about 8 percent at the higher poverty line. But the contribution of regional disparities to the aggregate P_2, the preferred FGT measure of poverty, is virtually zero for both poverty lines. Other things being equal, complete equalization among regions of mean consumption per capita would thus have a negligible effect on the *severity* of aggregate poverty in India, as measured by P_2.

Table 4.5 Contribution of regional disparities in mean consumption to aggregate poverty

Poverty measure (P_α)	Poverty line (z) (rupees)	Actual poverty (P) (percent)	Simulated poverty with equal means (P*) (percent)	Contribution of unequal means to poverty (1 – P*/P) x 100
Head count	76.65	32.65	30.91	5.33
index ($\alpha = 0$)	89.00	43.90	42.26	3.74
Poverty	76.65	8.09	7.16	11.12
gap ($\alpha = 1$)	89.00	12.29	11.28	8.22
Preferred	76.65	2.90	2.90	0.07
measure ($\alpha = 2$)	89.00	4.79	4.79	0.01

Source: Authors' calculations.

The quantitative effect on national poverty of reducing regional disparities

Since full equalization of regional mean consumption need not minimize poverty, how much *more* could poverty be alleviated through more flexible regional transfer policies that do not necessarily resort to full equalization? To give some indication of likely magnitudes, we will consider additive absorption of regional transfers aimed at minimizing aggregate poverty as measured by P_2, the FGT measure for $\alpha = 2$. As discussed earlier in the chapter, such transfers are informationally feasible. The poverty-minimizing transfer allocation can be calculated using the algorithm proposed by Ravallion and Chao (1989). Again, we are not prescribing such an allocation; rather, it is a natural benchmark for measuring the *potential* for alleviating poverty by regional redistribution in a way that is informationally feasible. That allocation is given in table 4.6 for both poverty lines. The table also presents summary data on the aggregate effects of regional redistribution on poverty.

A number of observations can be made on the results:
- Among the forty urban and rural sectors, only thirteen would be recipients under the poverty-minimizing allocation of transfers for the lower poverty line. In decreasing size of the optimal transfer per capita, the recipients are rural West Bengal, rural Tamil Nadu, rural Bihar, rural Orissa, rural Meghalaya, rural Karnataka, urban Tamil Nadu, urban Bihar, rural Maharashtra, urban Maharashtra, urban Uttar Pradesh, urban Karnataka, and urban West Bengal. For the higher poverty line, there are eleven recipient regions, all of which are also recipients for the lower line; in decreasing size of optimal transfer per capita, the recipients are rural West Bengal, rural Bihar, rural Tamil Nadu, rural Orissa, rural Maharashtra, rural Karnataka, urban Bihar, rural Meghalaya, urban Tamil Nadu, urban Uttar Pradesh, and urban Maharashtra.
- The burden of an optimal redistribution would thus be spread over more than two-thirds of the regions. Nonetheless, the burden reaches a fairly high proportion of average consumption in a few regions, notably urban

Meghalaya, rural Jammu and Kashmir, rural Punjab, rural Haryana, and urban Himachal Pradesh. It is unlikely, for political reasons, that such tax burdens could be implemented. Imposing limits on the tax burdens associated with regional redistribution will further reduce its effect on national poverty.

- Nonetheless, the potential for alleviating aggregate poverty through even "unrestricted" regional redistribution seems quite modest. Such redistribution would lead to a 10 to 14 percent drop in national poverty using the P_2 measure; however, this result is difficult to interpret. A more useful indicator is probably the equivalent gain from targeting; recall that this is the uniform increase in individual consumption for all regions that would achieve the same reduction in aggregate poverty as that attainable through optimal redistribution across regions. This is given in the last row of table 4.6. We find that the maximum reduction in national poverty attainable through such regional redistribution is equivalent to giving every

Table 4.6 Poverty-minimizing regional redistributions
(rupees per person per month)

State	Poverty line = Rs 76.65		Poverty line = Rs 89.00	
	Urban	Rural	Urban	Rural
Andhra Pradesh	-9.01	-9.86	-10.42	-11.19
Assam	-9.77	-7.71	-9.70	-6.04
Bihar	5.25	10.12	5.70	11.87
Gujarat	-6.57	-3.59	-5.78	-2.52
Haryana	-13.82	-21.83	-15.32	-23.68
Himachal Pradesh	-23.16	-14.14	-27.21	-14.17
Jammu and Kashmir	-9.20	-30.61	-7.77	-31.08
Karnataka	0.68	5.77	-0.57	5.77
Kerala	-1.65	-3.58	-2.67	-3.78
Madhya Pradesh	-2.83	-1.13	-2.42	-1.20
Maharashtra	1.61	5.90	0.24	5.78
Manipur	-10.73	-14.74	-10.52	-14.09
Meghalaya	-35.13	6.18	-37.79	5.51
Orissa	-4.87	9.54	-5.26	10.52
Punjab	-8.97	-29.39	-10.40	-32.05
Rajasthan	-3.34	-6.25	-3.94	-7.91
Tamil Nadu	5.45	10.24	5.24	10.69
Tripura	-6.46	-8.92	-8.05	-8.77
Uttar Pradesh	1.15	-2.02	1.20	-2.12
West Bengal	0.62	14.34	-0.04	14.92
Actual poverty	2.90		4.79	
Minimum poverty	2.48		4.29	
Equivalent gain	1.99		1.81	

Note: The table gives the gain or loss to each region that minimizes aggregate poverty such that population-weighted aggregate gains match losses. All allocations and the equivalent gains are in rupees per capita per month at 1983 all-India rural prices. The poverty measure used is P_2.
Source: Authors' calculations.

person in India an extra Rs 1.8 to Rs 2.0 per month, equal to a little over 1.5 percent of mean consumption in 1983 (and only about 2.5 percent of the lower poverty line of Rs 76.65 per month).

These results offer little encouragement to proponents of regional or sectoral redistribution as a means of alleviating poverty in India; in terms of the direct effects on poverty, the *best* that could be achieved through this means alone is modest. To the extent that the information constraint can be overcome to allow the use of other policy instruments and, hence, to permit greater progressivity in the distribution of transfer payments and receipts, the poverty alleviation effect would be greater. Yet, in practice, regional redistribution will be further constrained by other economic and political considerations. The net additional effect of these considerations on poverty remains uncertain. The above results read in conjunction with those presented in table 4.5 suggest, however, that the immediate potential for poverty alleviation in India through regional redistribution is likely to be small, *unless* such redistribution also significantly alters intraregional distributions in specific ways.

To illustrate this point, we consider another simulation exercise in which existing regional mean consumption levels are kept unchanged, but intraregional transfers bring about a 5 percent drop in the Gini coefficient in each region (table 4.7). In particular, per capita consumption of any household h in any region j changes by 5 percent of the difference between mean consumption per capita in region j and the per capita consumption of h. Of course, such redistribution implies a change in region j's Lorenz function. If the new Lorenz parameter vector is denoted L_j^*, then aggregate poverty P^{**} in table 4.7 is defined (using notation introduced in the section on theoretical results) as

$$(4.8) \qquad P^{**} = \sum_{j=1}^{m} w_j P(\mu_j, L_j^*).$$

It is obvious from the results in table 4.7 that the simulated 5 percent reduction in regional Gini coefficients has a greater impact on poverty than a full equalization of regional means (table 4.4). The difference is particularly striking

Table 4.7 Effects on aggregate poverty of reducing intraregional inequalities

Poverty measure (P_α)	Poverty line (z) (rupees)	Actual poverty (P) (percent)	Simulated poverty with 5% reduction in Ginis (P^{**}) (percent)	Percentage reduction in poverty $(1 - P^{**}/P) \times 100$
Head count	76.65	32.65	30.85	5.51
index ($\alpha = 0$)	89.00	43.90	42.73	2.67
Poverty	76.65	8.09	7.00	13.47
gap ($\alpha = 1$)	89.00	12.29	11.14	9.36
Preferred	76.65	2.90	2.31	20.20
measure ($\alpha = 2$)	89.00	4.79	4.06	15.20

Source: Authors' calculations.

for the preferred measure P_2: a 15 to 20 percent decline in poverty with the reduction in Gini coefficients, as compared with a near zero impact with full equalization. The poverty reduction possible through a 5 percent drop in Gini coefficients is also greater than the best achievable through lump-sum (informationally feasible) transfers (table 4.6).

Conclusion

Even if we limit consideration of the effects of regional redistribution to direct ones, the effect of regional redistribution on national poverty is far from obvious. Whether redistribution from regions with higher average living standards to those with lower ones alleviates aggregate poverty depends on the precise form of redistribution and on the nature of existing intraregional consumption distributions. For example, if intraregional inequalities cannot be altered, the complete equalization of regional consumption means is optimal for alleviating national poverty only if the underlying intraregional distributions are identical. More generally, regional variations in those distributions moderate (and may even reverse) the case for regional equalization. How regional redistribution affects national poverty is ultimately an empirical question.

Our empirical results for India indicate that small transfers from a donor region with a higher mean consumption than the recipient region will generally (though not always) lead to a reduction in national poverty. This holds for 73 percent or more of the possible pairs of regions, defined as the urban or rural sectors of each of twenty states. Transfers from the urban to the rural sector will reduce aggregate poverty in at least sixteen of those states.

But our simulations also suggest that the *quantitative* potential for alleviating poverty through this type of policy intervention in India is quite modest. For example, even in the extreme (and unlikely) case of politically unrestricted, though informationally feasible, redistribution among states and between urban and rural sectors of India using lump-sum transfers, the *maximum* impact on poverty is no more than could be achieved by simply giving all persons a uniform (untargeted) windfall gain equivalent to about 1.5 percent of India's mean consumption. This is not a general finding, but one that pertains specifically to India. Ravallion (1993) demonstrates a larger potential for poverty alleviation through such regional redistribution in Indonesia, equivalent to 4 percent of national mean consumption.

In practice, it may be possible to relax the information constraint somewhat, such as through finer regional targeting based on districts within states. But political restrictions on the central government's redistributive powers across states—let alone districts—and the behavioral responses of households (particularly through migration) are likely to limit even more the effect on poverty of this type of policy. Any adverse growth effects of regional redistribution on the national mean consumption will further reduce the aggregate poverty alleviation effect.

In summary, our results indicate that redistributive measures that primarily address disparities in regional mean consumption levels, without any significant reduction of existing intraregional disparities, are unlikely to have more than a slight effect on aggregate poverty in India. Greater alleviation of poverty will require supplementary interventions that reach the poor *within* regions, by reducing the costs borne by the poor in donor regions and increasing the benefits to the poor in recipient regions.

Appendix   Relevant analytical results

This appendix first summarizes the analytical properties of FGT poverty measures used in the section on theoretical results. Most of these properties are known from recent work (Kanbur 1987a; Ravallion and Chao 1989; Kakwani 1990c; and Thorbecke and Berrian 1989). However, we will elaborate on results for first and second derivatives of poverty measures with respect to additive and multiplicative transfers. The appendix then shows how the FGT poverty measures can be calculated from parameterized Lorenz curves, thus allowing the various simulations reported in the chapter.

Derivatives of poverty measures

Consider the FGT class of poverty measures whereby poverty in the ith region is

$$(A1) \qquad P_{\alpha i} = \int_0^z (1 - y/z)^\alpha f_i(y)\,dy \quad \alpha \geq 0,$$

where $f_i(y)$ denotes the probability density of (pretransfer) income y in region i, and z is the poverty line. For additively absorbed transfers, x_i, the post-transfer head count index of poverty ($\alpha = 0$) in region i is simply

$$(A2) \qquad P_{0i}(x_i) = \int_0^{z-x_i} f_i(y)\,dy,$$

for which

$$(A3) \qquad P_{0i}'(x_i) = -f_i(z - x_i) < 0$$

and

$$(A4) \qquad P_{0i}''(x_i) = f_i'(z - x_i),$$

which may be positive or negative. Similar to equation A2,

$$(A5) \qquad P_{\alpha i}(x_i) = \int_0^{z-x_i} \left[\frac{z - y - x_i}{z} \right]^\alpha f_i(y)\,dy \quad \text{(for } \alpha \geq 0),$$

and so

(A6) $$P'_{\alpha i}(x_i) = -\frac{\alpha}{z} P_{\alpha-1 i} < 0 \qquad \text{(for } \alpha \geq 1)$$

$$P''_{\alpha i}(x_i) = \frac{\alpha(\alpha-1)}{z^2} P_{\alpha-2 i} > 0 \qquad \text{(for } \alpha \geq 2)$$

(A7) $$= f_i(z - x_i)/z > 0 \qquad \text{(for } \alpha = 1).$$

Consider instead the multiplicative case in which the Lorenz curve is held constant. Poverty in each region can be thought of as a function of that region's mean income, μ_i. The marginal effect of a change in the mean is then given by

$$P'_{\alpha i}(\mu_i) = -z f_i(z)/\mu_i < 0 \qquad \text{(for } \alpha = 0)$$

(A8) $$= (P_{\alpha i} - P_{\alpha-1 i})\alpha/\mu_i < 0 \qquad \text{(for } \alpha \geq 1).$$

The second derivative is

(A9) $$P''_{\alpha i}(\mu_i) = z f_i(z)/\mu_i^2 > 0 \qquad \text{(for } \alpha = 0)$$

$$P''_{\alpha i}(\mu_i) = \left[(P'_{\alpha i} - P'_{\alpha-1 i})\mu_i - P_{\alpha i} + P_{\alpha-1 i} \right] \alpha/\mu_i^2$$

(A10) $$= \left[P_{\alpha i} - 2 P_{\alpha-1 i} + P_{\alpha-2 i} \right] \alpha(\alpha-1)/\mu_i^2 > 0 \qquad \text{(for } \alpha \geq 1).$$

P_α is itself a convex function of α, and $P_{\alpha i}(\mu_i)$ is strictly convex in μ_i for all α. Thus, aggregate poverty $\Sigma w_i P_{\alpha i}$ (where w_i is the population share of the ith region) is a strictly *quasi-convex* function of the vector of means $(\mu_1,...,\mu_m)$. It follows that the necessary and sufficient conditions for desirable regional redistributions discussed in the section on theoretical results can also be used to characterize optimal regional targeting. It can be shown that a similar result holds for additively absorbed transfers for FGT poverty measures with $\alpha \geq 1$.

Simulations of poverty measures

Because, like most researchers, we do not have access to the unit record data from the NSS, we need to simulate distributions in order to estimate poverty measures from the published grouped data. Simulated distributions are also required for the policy simulations. For these purposes we have used Kakwani's (1990c) parameterization of the Lorenz curve:

(A11) $$L(p) = p - ap^\gamma(1-p)^\delta e^\varepsilon \qquad 0 \leq p \leq 1,$$

where $L(p)$ is the cumulative proportion of total income or consumption of the poorest p proportion of the population. The parameters a, γ, and δ are positive, and ε is a random error. The fact that the parameters γ and δ do not exceed unity is *sufficient* to ensure convexity of the Lorenz curve. The Lorenz parameters themselves are estimated by ordinary least squares regression for each state and sector from the following regression:

(A12) $$\ln[p - L(p)] = \ln a + \gamma \ln p + \delta \ln(1 - p) + \varepsilon.$$

All simulations are at $E(\varepsilon) = 0$. Given the mean and Lorenz function, the distribution function is fully characterized. Note that the slope of the generalized Lorenz curve, $L'(p)\mu = x$, is simply the inverse of the distribution function $p = F(x)$. In earlier work on Indonesian data, the Kakwani parameterization was found to give a better fit than some obvious alternatives (the original Kakwani-Podder specification and elliptical Lorenz curves), at least in the crucial lower half of the distribution (Ravallion and Huppi 1989).

We have then calculated the poverty measures as follows: Since $L'(p_0) = z/\mu$, equation A11 implies that

(A13) $$1 - aP_0^{\gamma}(1 - P_0)^{\delta}\left[\frac{\gamma}{P_0} - \frac{\delta}{1 - P_0}\right] = \frac{z}{\mu},$$

which is solved numerically for P_0 (we used Newton's method). The poverty gap measure P_1 can be written as

(A14) $$P_1 = \int_0^{P_0}[1 - (\mu/z)L'(p)]dp$$

$$= P_0 - (\mu/z)L(P_0).$$

The FGT measure for $\alpha = 2$ is evaluated as follows. From the definition of P_2, we know that

$$P_2 = \int_0^{P_0}[1 - (\mu/z)L'(p)]^2 dp$$

$$= (1 - \mu/z)^2 P_0 + 2(\mu/z)(1 - \mu/z)P_1$$

(A15) $$+ (\mu/z)^2 \int_0^{P_0} a^2 p^{2\gamma}(1-p)^{2\delta}\left[\frac{\gamma^2}{p^2} - \frac{2\gamma\delta}{p(1-p)} + \frac{\delta^2}{(1-p)^2}\right]dp$$

$$= (1 - \mu/z)^2 P_0 + 2(\mu/z)(1 - \mu/z)P_1$$

$$+ (a\mu/z)^2 [\gamma^2 B(P_0, 2\gamma - 1, 2\delta + 1) - 2\gamma\delta B(P_0, 2\gamma, 2\delta)$$

$$+ \delta^2 B(P_0, 2\gamma + 1, 2\delta - 1)],$$

where

$$B(k, m, n) = \int_0^k p^{m-1}(1 - p)^{n-1}dp.$$

(Several software packages allow one to evaluate this using incomplete beta functions.) Thus, given (μ, a, γ, δ) for any region, the FGT poverty measures for any poverty line are calculated from equations A13, A14, and A15. The probability densities at the poverty line (as required by Propositions 1 and 2) are readily estimated using the relation $f(z) = 1/[\mu L''(P_0)]$.

Notes

This paper was presented at the IFPRI/World Bank Poverty Research Conference in October 1989. The paper draws on results of a World Bank research project "Policy Analysis and Poverty: Applicable Methods and Case Studies" (675-04). The authors wish to thank Michael Lipton, Eric Thorbecke, and conference participants for useful comments. The views expressed here are those of the authors, and should not be attributed to the World Bank.

1. For recent discussions, see Mishra (1985), Bhattacharya, Chatterjee, and Pal (1988), Sundrum (1987), Dev (1988), Jain, Sundaram, and Tendulkar (1988), Sundaram and Tendulkar (1988), and Prasad (1988). On sectoral policies and their implications for the poor, see Lipton (1977).

2. See India, Finance Commission (1988). The specific formula used by the Finance Commission is somewhat contentious; see, for example, Arun (1989).

3. This had been a theme of recent analytical work on poverty alleviation policies; for further discussion and empirical examples, see Kanbur (1987a), Besley and Kanbur (chapter 3 in this volume), Ravallion and Chao (1989), Ravallion (1989 and 1993) and Glewwe (1990a). Ravallion (1993) has examined the potential for poverty alleviation through regional targeting in Indonesia, recognizing explicitly that the policymaker is constrained by often highly imperfect information on individual incomes.

4. Ravallion (1993) discusses how the present methodology can be adapted to incorporate effects on pretransfer incomes, though empirical implementation looks difficult. The possibilities for adverse general equilibrium effects on incomes of the rural poor arising from attempts to redistribute incomes from the urban to the rural sector are discussed in Ravallion (1984). For an interesting approach to this problem using social accounting matrices, see Thorbecke and Berrian (1989).

5. Using the panel data for three villages in India's semi-arid tropics, Ravallion (1988) finds that variability in income over time (particularly in crop and labor incomes) is an important factor in poverty in the long run, as measured by the expected value of distributionally sensitive Foster-Greer-Thorbecke (FGT) measures (though the contribution to the expected value of the head count index is small). Intersectoral transfers, by reducing income variability in the rural sector, may thus be one way to alleviate aggregate poverty. Indeed, this is arguably an important function of Maharashtra's famous Employment Guarantee Scheme, which finances agricultural work in lean seasons through taxes on that state's urban sector (Ravallion 1991).

6. The results for $\alpha \geq 1$ used in Propositions 1 and 2 can be found in recent literature, particularly following Kanbur (1987a). The appendix summarizes relevant

analytical results from which these propositions can be readily proved, including the properties claimed here for $\alpha = 0$.

7. The quantitative approach follows Ravallion and Chao (1989). Also see Ravallion (1993) for further discussion.

8. Data for states disaggregated beyond the urban-rural split are not available (the most recent such distributional data available from the NSS appear to be for 1973-74). But state-level analysis is probably of greater interest in this context, since state-level disbursements are the central government's main policy instrument for regional redistribution. A few states and union territories were excluded because of gaps in the data or because of their extremely small share of national population.

9. Some researchers have preferred to use the interstate price deflator estimated by Bardhan (1974a). This has some disadvantages for our purpose, however: Bardhan's data are for the early 1960s, and they cover only rural areas, and not even those for all states. Rural price indices for 1983 based on Bardhan's data do, however, turn out to be quite strongly correlated with those based on Bhattacharya, Joshi, and Roychoudhury (1980) when both are updated by the CPIAL ($r = 0.83$ across the fifteen comparable states). The interstate variability in real mean consumption is higher using the deflator based on Bardhan's study, though the difference is small (a population-weighted coefficient of variation of 4.2 percent, versus 3.7 percent when based on Bhattacharya, Joshi, and Roychoudhury 1980). Final poverty estimates for some individual states may, however, be very different, depending on the interstate price deflator used.

10. The appropriateness of CPIAL and CPIIW as price deflators for poverty analysis has been questioned recently by Minhas and others (1987, 1989, and 1990), who also develop alternative price indices for the rural and urban middle three consumption deciles as well as for the total rural and urban population. But it is not obvious that their price indices are more appropriate than the deflators used here. See Kakwani and Subbarao (1991) for an appraisal of the price indices in Minhas and others.

11. The Minhas price index applied to the Dandekar-Rath line gives a 1983 poverty line within our range.

12. The poverty estimates for rural Jammu and Kashmir are lower than would be expected a priori; the state is relatively poor according to several socioeconomic indicators, such as the rates of literacy or infant mortality. The lower poverty estimates are largely the result of a "high" value of *real* mean consumption: 29.2 percent higher than mean consumption for rural India at 1983 all-India rural prices. But even in terms of current prices, mean consumption for rural Jammu and Kashmir is 14.5 percent higher than that for rural India. The rest is, of course, accounted for by the difference between rural Jammu and Kashmir prices and rural India prices. It could well be that the interstate price relative constructed by Bhattacharya, Joshi, and Roychoudhury (1980), which we use in this study, underestimates prices in rural Jammu and Kashmir relative to those in other regions. However, as other studies of interstate price variation have a much smaller regional coverage, we are unable to address this issue further.

13. These regressions should be interpreted as simplified representations of the underlying statistical relationship between these variables: all three variables (poverty measure, mean, and Gini) are of course derived from the same distribution. A dummy variable for urban areas was also tested but proved highly insignificant. Note that the logit transform avoids the truncation that arises in using P_0 as the dependent variable (being bounded in the 0, 1 interval). This specification comfortably passed a Ramsey RESET test on functional form.

New Research on Poverty and Malnutrition: What Are the Implications for Policy?

5 *Harold Alderman*

Many economists maintain that a household's welfare is unambiguously indicated by its income per adult equivalent. Planners and government officials, however, often consider health and nutritional status or energy intake as additional indicators of social welfare. This reflects both the expectation of externalities from improvements in health and societies' specific aversion to malnutrition (Tobin 1970). These concerns have led researchers to devote considerable attention to elucidating the pathways from economic policies to nutritional status.

These pathways are often income-mediated, through increases in food consumption and subsequent improvements in nutrition. Recent studies, however, have questioned whether either the links between income and nutrient consumption[1] or the links between food intake and nutritional status are substantial.[2] Clearly, if the first links are weak, many interventions, such as income transfer programs, will be ineffective in raising nutrient intakes. And if the second links are modest, food policy is at best only an indirect means of achieving nutrition goals. Moreover, a weak overall link between income and nutrition implies that nutrition is, to a fair degree, buffered from the effects of an economic downswing or restructuring. That would undercut some of the rationale for complementing macroeconomic adjustment programs with intervention programs aimed at protecting nutrient intake.

Bearing these policy implications in mind, this chapter reviews recent evidence on the relation between income and nutrition, beginning with a discussion of recent econometric evidence on the link between income and demand for calories—in brief, on *elasticity*.[3] This is a point of entry, although calories are of particular concern mainly insofar as they are an input into the production of nutrition and health. A number of sound econometric studies indicate that changes in household incomes and food consumption have comparatively small effects on malnutrition, at least at the margin and in the short run. This departure from conventional understanding obviously needs elaboration and clarification to determine to what degree these studies reflect special circumstances—such as short periods of survey, or observations at the mean, where the pressures of hunger are less than at very low incomes—and to what degree they can be generalized.

The chapter next discusses the evidence on inputs that are alternative or complementary to food consumption in the production of household health and nutrition. It closes by reviewing the implications of current knowledge for research and nutrition policy.

Income and nutrient demand

Understanding the relation between income and nutrition requires an understanding of how nutrients produce nutritional status or other measures of health. The standard model of individual utility maximization, in which home-produced goods (including nutritional status) contribute to utility, provides the basis for most empirical studies of nutrient consumption or nutritional outcome. These models are now well known,[4] and only a few features need to be discussed here. Of particular importance is that food enters the utility function both directly as a consumer good and indirectly as an input in the production of health. Consequently, the demand for food is both the demand for a productive input and the demand for certain taste and other characteristics that provide utility. It is generally not possible to distinguish between these two roles.[5]

Estimates of income elasticities of demand for calories and proteins vary widely in the literature (Bouis and Haddad 1992; and Alderman 1986). The differences may reflect differences in approaches to estimations and choice of variables as much as differences in time and place that lead to behavioral differences for each sample population.

Recent studies that reach different estimated income elasticities within a single population when they use different econometric approaches can be particularly instructive. Bouis and Haddad (1992), for example, indicate the potential for bias in estimation due to measurement error. As accurate data on income are difficult to collect, total household expenditure is often used as a proxy for permanent or long-run income. This causes a bias in measuring calorie elasticity, because errors in reported food acquisition and in total expenditures are correlated.[6] This bias, first pointed out thirty years ago by Liviatan (1961), is generally ignored when the total budget comprises many commodities. Bouis and Haddad, however, reported that the use of an instrumental variable for expenditures reduced the average income elasticity for their sample from the Philippines from 0.41 to 0.25. Similarly, Alderman (1989), in a panel study of five districts in Pakistan, found that using total expenditures in period $t - 1$ as an instrument for expenditures for period t reduced calorie elasticities by an average of one-third. Behrman and Deolalikar (1990), however, did not find substantially different estimates when using instrumental variables.

In a related vein, Behrman and Wolfe (1984) argue that income elasticities are often biased upward because of missing variable biases; higher income is often associated with higher energy consumption not only because one causes the other, but because both of them are associated with better schooling for women. When such information is available, it should of course be used, but often such biases can be controlled for by using community or household fixed effects estimation. When Bouis and Haddad (1992) and Alderman (1987b) estimated calorie demand with household panel data, however, they found that such fixed effects estimations had very little effect on the income response. Although fixed effects estimations do not eliminate errors in variables,[7] these results support the view that estimates of income elasticities are not seriously biased by the inability to include all household characteristics. But the absence of an omitted variable bias does not imply that the excluded variable is unimportant in its own right. For example, disease incidence may well influence household energy consumption at a given household income, even if estimates of the effect of income (or expenditure) on energy consumption are not biased when the effect of disease incidence is excluded.

These two categories of potential bias in estimates of calorie-income elasticities—correlated measurement errors and, to a smaller extent, missing variables—have some empirical importance and potential policy relevance. But a potentially more important source of bias is indicated by the marked difference between elasticity estimates using quantities imputed from food expenditures and those based on data provided by individuals on the food they consumed in the previous twenty-four hours (Bouis and Haddad 1992; and Behrman and Deolalikar 1987). In the Bouis and Haddad study, conducted in a poor rural region of the Philippines, elasticities drop from 0.26 to 0.05 when twenty-four-hour food recall data are substituted for data derived from monthly expenditures using the same panel technique. In the Behrman and Deolalikar study, conducted in six very poor villages of rural south-central India, elasticities fall from a range of 0.77 to 1.18 to a range of 0.17 to 0.37 with the same substitution of data. Bouis and Haddad's lower estimates imply that transfer programs or income growth have a very small effect on nutrition. Behrman and Deolalikar's results imply a greater scope for such income-mediated nutrition programs, although the parameters are estimated imprecisely and the authors emphasize that the elasticities are considerably smaller than earlier estimates.

Two explanations have been offered for the appreciably smaller nutrient elasticities estimated using twenty-four-hour food recall data compared with those derived from expenditure data. Bouis and Haddad suggest that there is a data problem. Data on food expenditure, even when data on quantities of food are also available, often include purchases for guests or laborers. These purchases for nonfamily consumption correlate with income and, hence, lead to an upward bias. Although one round of twenty-four-hour recall data can be shown to be inaccurate relative to repeated recall information, there is less evidence that such inaccuracy varies systematically with income.[8] Lipton (1983c), however, points out that if twenty-four-hour food recall data compress the extremes (as studies that he cites from both India and the United States suggest), they may well bias elasticities downward.

Behrman and Deolalikar attribute the much smaller elasticities derived from twenty-four-hour food recall data to a behavioral source: with rising income, households increase expenditure on food at a much faster rate than they increase the quantity purchased. This means that an increase in expenditure on, say, cereals would lead to an overestimate of the increase in calories from cereals—because the higher expenditure reflects in part the improved quality of cereals purchased (and hence fewer kilograms per unit of spending). This effect was seen in Prais and Houthakker's (1955) decomposition of expenditure elasticities into quality and quantity elasticities. Alderman (1986) presents evidence that more than half of total food expenditure elasticities may reflect such quality effects. Behrman and Deolalikar's results, however, are based on disaggregated commodity groupings and imply significant within-group quality effects—in the above example, as income increased significant shifts occurred from, say, coarser to finer (and costlier) rice, and not only from coarse grains to rice and wheat, as income increased. This finding is in contrast to most other results in the literature (Deaton 1987; Case 1987; and Alderman 1989). Moreover, many of the within-group quality effects in the South Indian communities studied pertain to grains from home production, for which quality effects are not expected to be as pronounced as for goods obtained from the market; if production decisions and consumption decisions are separable—if, as seems likely, transactions costs are not large in most grain markets in rural India—the variety of grain grown should reflect ecological considerations and not consumer preferences. These concerns cast some doubt on the interpretation offered by Behrman and Deolalikar.

The two interpretations are not mutually exclusive, however, and the potential policy implications come as much from the magnitude of the income response observed as from the interpretation. Do these recent results, then, actually suggest that earlier expectations for income responses—that is, that reducing poverty will swiftly and substantially improve energy intake—are inappropriate? Behrman and Deolalikar's warning about deriving nutrient responses using expenditures, although useful, does not invalidate the many previous studies based on quantities, not expenditures (Alderman 1986; Pinstrup-Andersen and Caicedo 1978; and Sahn 1988). The data problems reported by Bouis and Haddad counsel caution, but there are too few other studies that have explored how robust Bouis and Haddad's results are to alternative estimates and variables to assess how general the results are.

The surprising aspect of Behrman and Deolalikar's results is not the average value of the elasticity—even the lowest estimate of 0.17 is not especially low, measured at the mean income of a population—but the finding that there is little difference between the average elasticity and the elasticity for the poorest members of a poor community. This finding differs sufficiently from that in a number of studies that have found marked nonlinearities in the income response to raise questions about any generalizations from Behrman and Deolalikar's results.

Strauss and Thomas (1990), for example, find appreciable curvature in the calorie-expenditure curve using both parametric and nonparametric techniques. They find that the curve is virtually flat for the top seven income deciles, but that the expenditure elasticity for households in the lowest income-per-person decile is 0.26—eight times higher than that in the top decile.[9] Likewise, Ravallion (1990) finds appreciable curvature in an Engel curve estimated for Indonesia. Moreover, Ravallion adds the important new observation that, in his sample, the observed calorie intakes are densely clustered around normal requirements, so that the income elasticity of the probability of meeting those requirements is far higher than the income elasticity of demand for calories.[10] Similarly, Pinstrup-Andersen and Caicedo (1978) find nutrient elasticities for the poorest quintile in

Cali, Colombia, to be three times those of the wealthiest quintile, and Alderman (1986) finds that calorie elasticities from eleven data sets average 0.48 at incomes that correspond to the average income of populations consuming 1,750 to 2,000 calories per capita per day.

To be sure, many of these earlier studies do not use instrumented variables to control for errors in variables or for endogeneity of income due to labor supply choices. Nevertheless, there is enough variability in the literature regarding such instruments, and enough doubt about twenty-four-hour recall data, so that it would be rash to exclude these earlier studies in forming our expectations about the response of the poor to extra income. Behrman and Deolalikar (1987) and Bouis and Haddad (1992), among others, indicate important methodological improvements, but their results are not necessarily representative of a wide range of socioeconomic conditions.

Engel curve estimation is not a new field of econometrics, yet there are enough uncertainties remaining and new techniques available to allow studies of the range of income responses over populations and over income groups within a population to continue yielding important results.[11] There is still work to be done in, for example, estimating the response of those at the lowest tail of the income distribution to changes in income. They are likely to benefit most from programs to improve nutrition—or other health interventions—yet their response to changes in income is the most difficult to estimate. They are likely to be underrepresented in surveys; even when present, they will have few assets or transfer incomes that provide information for constructing instruments for income. Furthermore, many techniques for constructing such instruments reduce the variability of the income variable, and hence the probability of measuring significant curvature in Engel estimates even when it exists.

In circumstances such as famines, marginal increases in incomes may have an important effect on the quantity of food consumed. In a similar manner, a particularly harsh "hungry season" or an unanticipated employment shock may increase a household's calorie-income elasticity. The behavior of households in famines or following shocks may differ from that of households in chronic poverty. There are still few sound empirical studies on the short-term response to famine conditions or employment shocks.

Short-term responses may differ from the long-term response typically measured with cross-sectional data, in part because credit constraints and asymmetries in savings and dissavings possibilities are likely to be more pronounced among low-income households. Consequently, such households may be less able to maintain their level of calorie consumption in the face of transitory shocks than when there is a permanent change in the level of income, as indicated by average returns to physical and human capital or similar instrumental variables.

Short-term and long-term changes in food consumption in response to changes in income may also differ because current demand reflects past investments. Calorie consumption reflects in part the size of the individuals in the household. Measurement issues aside, change in physical size should make the long-run response to a change in income greater than that in the short run. But as household assets, including education, increase, the labor intensity of work usually decreases. Over the long term, or over a cross-section, increased income will be associated with occupations (and perhaps work days) that tend to reduce the demand for energy, thus making the calorie-income curve somewhat flatter. In the short term, however, a reduction in, say, real wages or crop yields is unlikely to affect the energy intensity of work. In such situations—with work input largely given—an income transfer or food subsidy might well have a larger effect on individual and household food intake than a similar increment to income stemming from, say, a move from manual to managerial work.

A broader issue remains, however: Do the policy implications of the more recent studies actually differ much from policies widely advocated? Behrman, Deolalikar, and Wolfe (1988), for example, challenge the view expressed in *World Development Report 1980* that

> malnutrition is largely a reflection of poverty: people do not have income for food. Given the slow income growth that is likely for the poorest people in the foreseeable future, large numbers will remain malnourished for decades to come....The most efficient long-term policies are those that raise the income of the poor. (World Bank 1980: 59)

Although it is difficult to assess efficiency with the data available, Behrman and his colleagues are clearly correct in saying that unrealistic expectations would be raised if income elasticities for nutrients are assumed to be closer to one than to zero. Overambitious predictions often lead to disillusionment, which could discourage policymakers from pursuing income-mediated nutrition programs.

Nevertheless, the realization that calorie-income elasticities are moderate, on average, does not in itself invalidate the proposition that income-mediated nutrition policies are an important means of reducing malnutrition. Indeed, the view cited above from *World Development Report 1980* is based largely on conclusions reached by Reutlinger and Selowsky (1976), who *assumed* an income elasticity for calories of 0.15 at a level of intake equal to calorie requirements reported by the World Health Organization at the time[12]—well within the range of "low" estimates now proposed by the findings of Behrman and Deolalikar (1987). This assumption was used to explore the distribution of caloric inadequacy over income distributions and the likely change in undernutrition with income growth. Because of the income disparities found in most populations—as well as in most data sets from which estimates are derived—a much larger income elasticity would not be consistent with known distributions of food intakes. Upper-income groups often have incomes five to ten times higher than those of the poorest groups in the population, and the ratio of the two groups' calorie intakes cannot be more than two or three to one.[13] It is important to note, however, that the increase in energy intake that occurs as income rises might be compressed into the lower end of the range of incomes.

Reutlinger and Selowsky demonstrated that normal income growth neutrally distributed would have only a moderate effect on energy intake, and hence on malnutrition, in the short run. They therefore argued that a policy goal of reducing malnutrition would require targeted nonmarginal income transfers and other nutritional programs. Behrman and Deolalikar's recent results, then, do not negate these conclusions; they merely keep expectations in perspective.

Production of health and nutrition

Reutlinger and Selowsky, like many other economists concerned with nutrition, focused primarily on hunger or underconsumption of nutrients relative to requirements.[14] Despite the emphasis on nutrient intake in much of the economic analysis of nutrition, however, levels of food consumption are not necessarily precise indicators of nutritional status. As mentioned above, food has two roles in the household: as a consumer good and—the focus of this chapter—as an input in the production of health. The chapter next considers what is an appropriate measure of the outcome of this process of production.

Measurement of nutritional outcome

Clearly, one important measure is the production of survival—that is, the avoidance of childhood mortality. Another is the avoidance of disease. Because disease incidence and severity are difficult to measure with a cross-sectional survey, studies often take the growth or stature of individuals as a direct measure of their health. These studies express the outcome variable in terms of such anthropometric measurements as height and weight, alone or in combination. These indicators can be shown to be strongly correlated with the probability of mortality, but generally in a nonlinear manner (Chen, Chowdhury, and Huffman 1980; and Smedman and others 1987). Although severe malnutrition is linked with higher probabilities of childhood mortality, moderate levels of growth retardation are not strongly associated with mortality.

There has been a fair amount of debate, however, on whether stunting or smallness is actually an indicator of poor health. For example, Seckler (1982) argues that small stature may increase long-term survival of the family. But there is some evidence that size is positively associated with work productivity.[15] And women's size may also indicate fitness in the biological sense of survival of offspring (Martorell and Gonzalez-Cossio 1987; and Thomas, Strauss, and Henriques 1990). In other contexts, however, such as in studies of the relation between malnutrition and learning, it is often difficult to trace lasting harm due to smallness—as opposed to the factors that created smallness.

Therefore, nutritionists increasingly see the damage that has been associated with smallness as due to the process of becoming small (growth faltering)—which is strongly associated with other indicators of poor health—rather than to smallness per se, except at extremes (Beaton 1989; and Payne and Lipton 1991). This faltering generally occurs between six months and two years of age. The timing of growth faltering has particular importance for monitoring the growth of individuals as well as for nutritional surveillance of communities and the evaluation of nutritional interventions. It is also important for studies of the determinants of malnutrition. Although a stunted child may have some catch-up growth, for the most part a child whose growth has faltered in the first two years of life will be on a different growth trajectory during the rest of his or her life. Consequently, over much of any sample of children observed in a cross-sectional survey, some nutritional outcome variables indicate more about past conditions than about current ones. Information about independent variables in the study that are not time-invariant is often not obtainable for analysis. This, then, counsels caution when analysis is conducted in environments in which incomes, prices, or infrastructure are rapidly changing.[16]

The research discussed above has been concerned primarily with nutrition as a direct indicator of health or as a correlate of other indicators of individual and family welfare. In other contexts, however, researchers are interested in nutrition primarily as an input into a further process—the production of health. These two perspectives do differ, and failure to distinguish between them occasionally causes confusion.

Income and the production of health and nutritional well-being

The effect of a policy intervention—say, an income transfer—on health or nutritional status depends not only on the *demand* for nutrients or other inputs but also on the magnitude of the *response* of household health and children's birth weight, for example, to such inputs in the health production function. Ideally, that pathway could be traced using simultaneously estimated production functions and input demands. Rosenzweig and Schultz (1983), for example, use Cobb-Douglas and translog production functions for birth weight in the United States. Guilkey and others (1989) use a similar model to examine the effect of prenatal care on birth outcomes in the Philippines, and Alderman and Garcia (forthcoming) present a model for Pakistan.

These approaches are data-intensive and often prone to identification problems. An alternative approach is to use a reduced-form model. As is well known, such models do not reveal the full structure of the causal pathways—in this case, the marginal effects of various inputs—but they do indicate the potential response to policy interventions.

Often the magnitude, and even the sign, of the coefficients of various inputs into health change when the variables are considered as choice variables—that is, as endogenous. The study by Behrman and Wolfe (1987) of the effects of instrumented energy and protein intake, sanitation, and use of medical care on child health in Nicaragua illustrates the sensitivity of results to alternative specifications. Their base model shows that income has a significant influence on the demand for these three inputs and that energy and protein intake and sanitation have significant marginal effects on health. Income has a much smaller effect on demand for inputs when community effects and the mother's childhood endowments are controlled for. Moreover, there are no variables that significantly influence child health in Behrman and Wolfe's complete model; hence, their findings are primarily negative.[17]

The study by Pitt and Rosenzweig (1985) of the demand for and the impact of inputs into health in Indonesia also indicates the sensitivity of models to the choice of variables presumed exogenous. They estimate the probability of individual illness as a function of predicted household nutrient intake. Using coeffi-cients in the nutrient demand equations that they report, one can calculate the effect of a change in the wage of the household head on the probability of illness. The total effect calculated in this manner indicates that an increase in wages increases the intake of some nutrients and, subsequently, reduces the probability of illness. The effect is seven times larger when calculated using the two-stage tobit than when calculated with an ordinary tobit model. The study also indicates the sensitivity of the choice of instruments for income. The estimated impact of farm profits on nutrient demand, and therefore on health, is consistently less than the impact of wages. This is interpreted as indicating greater impact at lower income, although an instrumented variable for profits was noted to increase the coefficients of profits slightly.

Thomas, Strauss, and Henriques (1991) compared alternative specifications of income and instrumented income in their study of the impact of the mother's education on child height in northeastern Brazil. They find a significant income effect only in the rural areas. The effect remains when income is instrumented but drops when community covariates are included. Moreover, in the fixed-effects model, it no longer differs significantly from zero. The authors interpret this result as an indication that the income effect works mainly through choice of residence.

The studies cited above provide new perspectives on the long-run impact of income on health and nutrition by indicating alternative interpretations of the correlations. Particularly noteworthy is their challenge to prior expectations. But a number of studies that make similar efforts to consider the potential endogeneity of income or errors in variables also confirm the existence of a significant in-come response. That these more conventional results are also noteworthy may therefore indicate a general shift of expectations.

One such study is Thomas, Strauss, and Henriques (1990). This study indi-cates that in most regions of Brazil, improvements in household income (indi-cated by various measures) increase the probability of children's surviving. The doubling of income, measured either by instrumented expenditure or unearned income, has an effect of the same magnitude as that of maternal literacy. Income is not robust in equations predicting child height, however; its significance de-pends critically on the choice of instruments.

Sahn's results (1990) from Côte d'Ivoire show that instrumented income had a significant impact on children's standardized height for age, although education did not. Strauss (1990) explored the same Côte d'Ivoire data set, using both fixed-effects models (with different children in the same household) and random effects. Assets and wages, both proxies for earnings,[18] are positively associated with weight for height in his study. Unlike the cross-sectional ap-proach used by Sahn, however, Strauss's fixed-effects model indicates that the father's education has a strong effect on weight for height. The coefficients of education in Strauss's community effects model are not significant, however.

Pitt, Rosenzweig, and Hassan (1990) look at how the distribution of food is influenced by the gender and the health endowment of family members in Bangladesh.[19] Weight for height is shown to increase with calorie consumption, with the coefficient increasing fourfold when this consumption is instrumented. Moreover, the income elasticity for calorie consumption, when the weight-for-height endowment is controlled for, doubles to 0.12 when endowments are instrumented. The elasticity could well be greater at lower levels of income per person; the study did not investigate whether the coefficients of income, nutrients, or endowments changed as the level of the variables increased.

There are also several studies by nutritionists that—although their statistical techniques differ from the econometrically innovative models discussed above—help bracket expectations about the production of nutritional status. In particular, these studies find that the link between household or even individual food intake and stature or growth is modest (Kennedy 1989; Calloway, Murphy, and Beaton 1988; and Gershoff and others 1988). But income may have a larger effect than that mediated by food consumption (Kennedy 1989). This relatively larger role of income is consistent with the view that other inputs into health also increase with income. These reviews present relatively little evidence, however, on which household choice variables, other than food, are influenced by income and what their subsequent effect on stature is.

The demand for inputs in the production of nutrition is also influenced by the price of those inputs. There is, of course, a large body of literature on the price responsiveness of demand for various food items. The literature on the price responsiveness of demand for nutrients is more limited. The distinction between these subsets of the demand literature is that substitution between food commodities often moderates the effect of a price change on the aggregate demand for nutrients. Pitt (1983) indicates, for example, that both own-price response and cross-price responses in Bangladesh are appreciable for various food items. Consequently, the net effect of a single price rise is small and often positive for some nutrients. But this is not logically necessary. Alderman (1986) reviews a number of cases in which the net effect of a price rise on nutrient consumption is negative and substantial. Moreover, price effects, even income-compensated price effects, are often larger for low-income households.

Most studies of the effects of price on nutrient consumption look at the effect of a single price movement in isolation. But commodity prices often move in parallel. The study of the cross-responsiveness of demand and supply in Cali, Colombia (Pinstrup-Andersen, de Londono, and Hoover 1976), is one of the few models of nutrient intake in interrelated markets. In this study the indirect effects of a change in price for either rice or maize added to the direct effect on calorie consumption rather than moderating it. Although the study used supply shifts due to changes in technology as a point of departure, the approach may also be valid—depending on the nature of international trade—for price shifts due to subsidies, taxes, or movements in exchange rates.

Pitt and Rosenzweig's (1985) reduced-form model of the probability of adult illness also indicates some appreciable net price effects on nutrient consumption, although no consistent patterns emerged. Few other models of health or nutritional status have food prices in the reduced form.

Not only is nutrition an important input into health, it is in turn influenced by aspects of health—the incidence of disease and the use of health care. The price of health care therefore has the potential to affect nutritional status through its effect on the demand for such services. A number of studies indicate substantial price responsiveness for curative health care, particularly among the poor (Gertler, Locay, and Sanderson 1987; and Gertler and van der Gaag 1990). In such cases, however, cross-price responses may also mitigate own-price responses; shifts away from public health care providers may sometimes be shifts to private providers (Alderman and Gertler 1989).

A household's production of health reflects not only the levels of inputs but also the production technology chosen. Many studies have investigated this by exploring the role of parents' education. There is no issue of endogeneity in such studies, but interpretation must separate the role of education in raising incomes from its role—at both individual and household levels—in determining the amounts of inputs used in the health production function (nutrients, health care), and in determining the health production technology through which such inputs influence indicators of health (Thomas, Strauss, and Henriques 1991).

Human capital also influences nutrition through the physical stature of parents. Since studies generally find the effect of the mother's height to be greater than that of the father's height (Thomas, Strauss, and Henriques 1990; Sahn 1990; and Alderman 1990), this effect is not purely genetic.[20] Both parents' education and mothers' size are generally less in low-income populations, which accounts for some of the observed correlation between malnutrition and poverty. It also suggests that the long-run effects of interventions and of income growth on health could exceed their short-run effects.

Behrman and Wolfe (1987) and Wolfe and Behrman (1987) have studied such intergenerational determinants of nutrition, arguing that a mother's education may be a proxy for other aspects of her endowment. As mentioned above, few of the variables in these studies turn out to be statistically significant. Consequently, it is not clear which aspects of the maternal endowment influence the child's health or nutrition. The influence may work through maternal stature, but which factors influence education and stature remains a question for research. In particular, if there are factors that influence one generation's health through the previous one's endowment, one would expect that the current generation's endowment would also be affected by current inputs. In a related vein, Thomas, Strauss, and Henriques (1990) find that the inclusion of maternal height, which may be considered a proxy for maternal endowment, does not reduce the additional effect of education on child survival. The coefficient of education was, however, appreciably reduced in equations explaining children's height, though it retained statistical significance.

Also assumed to affect the production of health is the availability of health infrastructure. To a degree, variables indicating that availability are analogous to price variables. For example, the distance to a clinic affects a family's resource allocation in a manner analogous to prices (Gertler, Locay, and Sanderson 1987). Because these "prices" often are higher for low-income households, they have a distributional impact similar to that of price discrimination.

Moreover, variables for the quality of health services, as well as measures of a community's production of health—such as the prevalence of disease—are often found to influence nutritional status (Strauss 1990). Similarly, Castañeda (1985) found that the most important variable in explaining the reduction of infant mortality in Chile between 1975 and 1982 was the increase in urban coverage of sewerage and potable water. Differences in such coverage were found to be more important than the positive impact of nutrition programs aimed at mothers, which in turn appeared to have more impact than child-oriented programs.

In most countries there is a positive association between the average income of a region or neighborhood and the availability of services there. As indicated in a number of the studies cited above, the failure to include such infrastructure in a model can bias upward the apparent effect of *individual* income on nutrition and health—entirely if higher-income individuals tend to (choose to) live in, or move to, places with better infrastructure—although the model may nevertheless accurately depict the long-term effect of reduced poverty on health and nutrition.

Also important is the question of the potential interactions of infrastructure variables and income. If the use of health care services is an input into a production function, community factors and household variables can be modeled through the input demand equations. But this is a less satisfactory approach for sanitation and other public health goods, where the reduction in the prevalence of infection vectors has clear externalities beyond a household's demand for services. Burger and Esrey (1989) found, for example, that improved sanitation has a greater impact on poor households than it does on comparatively well-off households. Similar interactions between the health effects of water quality and quantity, and between those of education and public health, are also found; these interactions too may depend on income levels. Burger and Esrey's review does not, however, discuss a household's demand for and utilization of such services from the perspective of individual or family constraints and preferences.

Thomas, Strauss, and Henriques (1991) show that maternal education is a complement, in producing health, to some goods (sewerage) and a substitute for others (health care).[21] They also note a strong interaction between education and access to information: the availability of radio and television enhances the effect of education on nutritional status. Indeed, the positive effects on children's growth of literacy, and even of schooling, appear in their study to depend almost entirely on the interaction of education with communications media. The study can be interpreted to imply that the value that schooling provides stems less from the information acquired than from the skills acquired for processing information later in life. Increased income may enhance the contribution of education to family nutrition and health, for example, because information is costly to acquire.

Conclusion

Much of the evidence reviewed in this chapter implies that the short-run elasticity of demand for dietary energy, at the mean income of most populations, is modest. Similarly, many direct relations expected between physical stature or health and various inputs prove less substantial, on the whole, when simultaneity of decisions or heterogeneity in community endowments are considered. Nevertheless, there remains a fair amount of leeway in interpreting such results.

Although blaming data or econometric agnosticism is not particularly constructive, identification conditions for a full household production model (with unbiased estimates) are genuinely demanding. There is often a tradeoff between bias and the efficiency of estimates. When, for example, breastfeeding or disease incidence is made endogenous, bias (and, thus, possibly spurious results) are eliminated, but at a cost: real information must be sacrificed. One consequence of eliminating bias by selecting poor instruments is relatively imprecise, although unbiased, parameters.

Another consequence of the relatively stringent criteria for production models is that adequate data sets are relatively difficult to find and analyze. With increased availability of panel data as well as clever application of family and community fixed-effects or instrument models, however, replication of the types of results discussed here may increase confidence in the range and conditions of such parameters. There is a particular need, for example, to explore such models in settings such as Africa, where levels of absolute poverty are high and infrastructure limited and where marginal impacts may be relatively large.

Similarly, the choice of a model is important if it is suspected that a generally low response for a population may mask comparatively large responses in subsets of the population. Although some of the techniques discussed here reduce the variability of the right-hand-side variables in the model—and hence the ability to model nonlinearities—other techniques considered, such as nonparametric models, are well suited for such exploration. As mentioned, the relation of stature to the probability of mortality has been shown to be nonlinear. The relation of food consumption to nutritional status may similarly vary over the range of observed intakes. To date, however, most nutrition and health production models have focused on the average response (on elasticities measured at the mean of all variables) and have not addressed the question of nonlinearities.

A better understanding of these nonlinear relations may help in promoting targeted programs, both by improving the precision of resource allocation and by refining the arguments of advocates. If transfer programs and other policies aimed at poverty alleviation are promoted as likely to have important effects on nutrition, support for such programs will be undermined if the response is more modest than expected. By moderating expectations about the average response, recent studies help focus community resources on the portion of the population with the least personal resources.

Accurate expectations of response are important in implementing policy as well as in formulating it. Even if it is doubtful that nonlinearities in response can be used for screening programs, they may help gauge the prevalence of undernutrition (Lipton 1983c). More important, proper design of targeted programs requires a knowledge of the probable response of the target group as well as of the difference between the target group's expected response and that of the general population.

In a related vein, certain subpopulations are known to be more vulnerable to the effects of poor nutrition. For example, growth faltering is most likely in a relatively narrow age bracket. Because of this narrow age bracket, only limited socioeconomic data sets are available for studies of this issue. The design of socioeconomic studies of pregnancy and lactation is likewise made difficult by the limited availability of data. Similarly, because maternal death rates, which vary greatly across populations, are far lower than infant mortality rates, few data sets are large enough to study the relation between household and community variables and the probability of successful birth outcomes for both mother and child. As mentioned above, it may be misleading to predict the results of programs targeted to subpopulations on the basis of the response of a broader population.

It has been noted that the apparent effects of household and individual characteristics on health and nutrition vary according to the availability of health and sanitation infrastructure.[22] At times, community variables may be complements to income or education; at other times, they may be substitutes. Only a few studies that quantify such interactions are currently available. Clearly, an understanding of the relation between income or other household assets (including education) and the efficacy of investment in health and sanitation infrastructure is important for program design. For example, if illiterate or poorer households use public facilities less than their neighbors do, synergism between poverty alleviation programs and health care investment might be expected. In such a case, the income effect will be reinforced by the price effect implicit in the increased availability or improved quality of public health care provision. On the other hand, if public investment in sanitation or clean water enhances health only where households are too poor to acquire private substitutes, synergism between programs is less likely.

Some of the most successful nutrition intervention programs have implicitly recognized the complementarity of inputs and have linked food supplements to the provision of health care (Berg 1987; and Castañeda 1985). Such linkage has been shown to increase the economic efficiency of recurring administrative costs in the Narangwal study in the Indian Punjab (Kielmann, Taylor, and Parker 1978). Moreover, the linkages reduce the unit costs for participants, because the costs often include a large time investment in travel that is fixed for each visit and not variable per service obtained.

The degree to which inputs are substitutes or complements also has an important bearing on the design of programs to mitigate the short-run effects of economic shocks. Research results indicating that coefficients of income in health production are a partial proxy for community infrastructure variables should increase the concern about simultaneous reductions in public health services and in poor people's private incomes. Which programs can be safely cut back when government revenues fall depends in part on which programs are utilized by the households facing a decline in income. Such decisions also depend on which publicly provided inputs are most effective when other inputs are reduced. These decisions should reflect equity and efficiency criteria.

Schiff and Valdés (1990), in discussing the complementarity of inputs, recognize that the second derivatives in health production—the derivatives of the effects of privately provided inputs with respect to the level of publicly provided inputs and vice versa—are crucial and largely unknown. Even when such effects are known, the choice among welfare policies depends on the costs of providing services as well as on the production responses. For example, it may be easier to make a nonmarginal impact on incomes in a rural community through a variety of agricultural policies and programs than it is appreciably to increase the provision of sewerage or of health care services.

Finally, it is useful to consider long-run as well as short-run health and nutritional responses to income growth. Investment in health care or in privately owned complementary inputs is often—but not always—held constant in studies of health production. In the long run, however, such investment surely rises with income. Education for the next generation's care providers is also virtually always positively associated with income. Similarly, to the degree that income affects a mother's stature, that impact has a second-generation effect through birth weights and subsequently improved life expectancy.

A generation ago, T. W. Schultz's suggestion that farmers are poor but efficient, constrained more by resources than by ignorance, had an important influence on agricultural development strategy. Although agricultural production is not strictly analogous to health production—budget constraints enter into farm production only through credit rationing or risk avoidance—nutrition policy needs to address a similar set of issues. How much of apparent malnutrition reflects household preferences that depart from what planners feel they should be, particularly in regard to intrahousehold allocations? How much reflects a poor understanding of efficient means of resource allocation and health production? And how much reflects resource constraints that public policy can shift? Dramatic results from policy measures may seldom be observed—in part because dramatic programs are seldom ventured—but moderate responses to moderate changes are still quite different from nonresponsiveness.

Notes

1. An example is found in Behrman, Deolalikar, and Wolfe (1988).

2. Such links might be weak if nutritional status is affected much more by early infections than by food intake in children. They might also be weak because adults' food intake, even at very low levels, responds rapidly to changes in daily requirements, or, more controversially, because people with lower intake levels may permanently have, or be able temporarily to acquire, higher "conversion efficiency" of nutrients into work.

3. In this chapter, unless otherwise stated, this is the elasticity of household *dietary energy (calorie) intake,* per day, per adult equivalent (or per person when independent variables are included to estimate effects of household composition), with respect to *household income,* or to expenditure as a proxy for permanent income.

4. Pitt and Rosenzweig (1985) and Rosenzweig and Schultz (1983) describe such a model for the household production of health.

5. Moreover, it is not a straightforward procedure to go from individual utility maximization to household behavior. See Thomas (1990) and the references contained in that paper for further discussion.

6. The direction of bias when using such a variable cannot always be determined from theory. For example, when the dependent variable is a measure of (or derived from) food expenditures, the bias of the coefficient of total expenditures comprises both the

standard-errors-in-variables bias toward zero and an upward bias due to positive correlation between measurement error in the dependent and independent variables.

7. Indeed, fixed effects estimations may increase the problem. See Ashenfelter, Deaton, and Solon (1985).

8. One useful exercise would be to estimate income elasticities for expenditures implicit in twenty-four-hour recall data. The South Indian data do not currently contain information to estimate quantity elasticities from the monthly purchases or expenditure elasticities from the daily food consumption, but other data sets with twenty-four-hour recalls should have this information. Since the weighted sum of all income elasticities must be one, we can use such results to assess the twenty-four-hour recall data. Another exercise would be to plot estimated elasticities against the degree of aggregation—that is, the number of food groups.

9. Nutrients were estimated by weighing food consumed daily over seven days. Moreover, the results change little when expenditure is instrumented. The study is therefore not susceptible to the two sources of errors that are the focus of Bouis and Haddad's study.

10. The sensitivity of this result to alternative assumptions about requirements is an area that could be profitably explored.

11. For example, nonparametric techniques, such as kernel estimation, may assist in locating nonlinearities.

12. They assumed an elasticity that varied inversely with calorie intake.

13. Kakwani (1977) illustrates the formal relation between Engel curves and elasticities.

14. In general, the focus is on calories. This reflects the prevailing opinion that energy is the limiting nutrient in poor populations; most households that consume adequate calories also consume adequate protein. For a different perspective, see Graham and others (1981).

15. Even in this case, the evidence is clearer in clinical studies than in studies that account for household and individual allocation of resources. See Strauss (1989) and Haddad and Bouis (1991). There is a clear physiological relationship between body size and work *potential,* but not always between potential and work *performance* (see Payne and Lipton 1991).

16. Note, however, that income or expenditure in period $t + 1$ may in some cases be a valid instrument for the variable in period t.

17. This may reflect data limitations; few data sets can hold up to such scrutiny. In any case, "negative" does not imply "useless." Bertrand Russell was once confronted by a student who complained that the professor had destroyed the student's beliefs without replacing them. Russell reportedly referred to the labors of Hercules, who was assigned to clean the Augean stables without, however, being required to refill them.

18. Wages may also influence substitution, but it is unlikely that an increase in the price of leisure for males would have a strong positive effect on the height of children.

19. Pitt, Rosenzweig, and Hassan (1990) indicate that the direction of bias in the endowment effects estimated using ordinary least squares cannot generally be determined a priori. There are both potential missing variable and measurement error biases.

20. Although the genetic contribution of both parents is equal, the mother also has an effect through the environment of the womb. As one does not observe the genotype but only the phenotype, the estimated importance (as an influence on child health) of the genetic pathway is biased downward by errors in variables, while that of the environmental pathway is not.

21. Barrera (1990) also indicates that education can substitute for some community infrastructure and complement others.

22. Absence of health and sanitation infrastructure may partially explain low income elasticities for food and apparent biased intrahousehold distribution. Illness influences the marginal productivity of food and, hence, its optimal level. Households rendered prone to illness (for example, by lack of medical infrastructure) may correctly perceive little benefit in using extra income to obtain more calories. On the sale of food stamps by very poor women to buy medical services, see Gulati (1977).

Part II
Events Affecting the Poor

Living Conditions in Developing Countries

N. Kakwani
Elene Makonnen
Jacques van der Gaag

6

For many developing countries the 1980s were the most difficult period since the depression of the 1930s. They faced severe new tests—soaring energy prices, reduced demand for exports, rising real interest rates, deteriorating terms of trade, and abrupt reductions in the supply of external finance. Because of external events like these, scores of countries could not cope without extra help from such international institutions as the International Monetary Fund (IMF) and the World Bank.

Yet during the 1980s developing countries as a group experienced negative net financial flows from both the IMF and the World Bank. This occurred despite World Bank disbursements almost doubling between 1980 and 1990. Perhaps even more important than this increase in disbursements was the new set of conditionalities that accompanied the new disbursements. The IMF provided credit tied to stabilization programs, negotiated with the recipient governments, that were intended to correct imbalances in domestic demand to bring it into line with domestic supply. The programs generally focused on fiscal austerity, monetary tightness, wage restraint, and currency devaluation.

The World Bank developed structural adjustment loans (SALs), the first of which was signed in 1980. This rapidly disbursing lending instrument increased to 25 percent of the Bank's portfolio by the mid-1980s. The adjustment programs supported by SALs were intended to increase economic efficiency through changes in pricing and trade policies and through reforms in the public sector.

The stabilization and adjustment programs became controversial. In the view of some economists, the conditions accompanying the loans were likely to damage developing countries in a variety of ways. The conditions would raise food prices (through devaluation), contract the demand for labor (and thus reduce real wages), raise interest rates, and possibly increase tax rates. Fiscal austerity would lead to reduced government spending, and public sector retrenchment would increase unemployment. Curtailed consumer subsidies would further increase the price of staple foods, which account for a large part of the expenditures of the poor. This would lead to a marked drop in living standards among the poor.

There is still little theoretical guidance for judging the effect of complex adjustment measures. But concern about the poor has been growing. A UNICEF study advocating efforts to protect poor people during adjustment—*Adjustment with a Human Face* (Cornia, Jolly, and Stewart 1987)—drew attention to the deteriorating social conditions of the poor. The study sought to raise the consciousness of the development community about the possible social implications of policies that seemed to focus solely on macroeconomic indicators. In 1989 UNICEF's *State of the World's Children* estimated that at least half a million young children had died within twelve months as a result of the slowing or reversal of progress in the developing world; it did not, of course, imply that this was all due to stabilization and adjustment programs.

Other work suggests that UNICEF may have overstated the case, however. In a critical review of the UNICEF study *Adjustment with a Human Face*, Preston (1986) notes that country data show continuous improvements in infant and child mortality, nutritional indicators, and school enrollment. A recent internal World Bank report assesses the analytical base for the UNICEF case study of Jamaica. It concludes that, although adjustment programs can in principle lead to negative effects on health and nutrition, the evidence for this has been unconvincing because of confusion among levels, trends, and deviations from the trends, and because of questionable interpretations of data. Hill and Pebley (1989) evaluate available evidence on trends in child mortality for countries with reliable data. They conclude that the decline in child mortality accelerated in Sub-Saharan Africa in the 1980s, despite the poor economic performance of many countries.

There are at least three factors that explain why such contradictory conclusions have been drawn from essentially the same evidence:

- Data on the living conditions of the poor in developing countries are scarce and often of dubious quality. This is especially true of internationally comparable data over a long period. Even the best of such data are usually a mix of accurate data for a few years, many interpolations, and some extrapolations. On the basis of these data, it is difficult to judge trends.
- Adjustment policies are a relatively new phenomenon. Their effect on such basic social indicators as child mortality and life expectancy may be slow. Long time lags may prevent some analysts from detecting any impact in a short time series; other analysts may give more weight to theoretically plausible implications and partial or anecdotal evidence.
- A particularly intractable problem is the difficulty of establishing causality. Large and persistent budgetary or balance of payments deficits are normally caused by external shocks or policy errors, not by subsequent adjustment. The deficits need to be corrected, and, in the short run, any correction will tend to reduce employment, domestic incomes, and net subsidies. If countries had adopted policies other than those supported by the IMF and the World Bank, would they have done better or worse? Would the living conditions of the poor have improved or deteriorated?

Answering these questions would require separating the effects of SAL policies on living conditions from the many other influences operating before and after the adjustment period.[1] This would demand an elaborate general equilibrium model for the world economy and its linkages with specific countries. Such a model would incorporate changes in the world economy that occurred long before the crisis period.

In this chapter we do not answer the hypothetical question of whether living standards would have been better under alternative adjustment strategies. Rather, we reassess evidence on socioeconomic trends in developing countries during the 1980s. We compare this evidence with that for the 1970s. We then assess whether the recent period was indeed "the lost decade for development"—and in particular for the poor.

Most of our results are aggregates for eighty-eight developing countries. Virtually all comparative analyses were compiled from the Bank's economic and social data bases (BESD) and the International Economics Department's retrieval, analysis, and reporting system (ANDREX). The BESD includes more than twenty data bases from the World Bank, the IMF, the United Nations, UNESCO, the United Nations Industrial Development Organization, and the Food and Agriculture Organization. When additional information was available for one or a few countries, the sources of the data are indicated.

Growth performance: Comparison of the 1970s and 1980s

The world economy grew rapidly during the 1950s and 1960s. But the 1970s brought dramatic change. The decade's most severe shock was the 1973-74 rise in oil prices, which fueled inflation and led to a sharp decline in economic growth. Developing countries either adjusted remarkably well to the new, adverse conditions, or continued to grow at the cost of increasing balance of payments deficits, and increased borrowing or inflationary financing—or both. As a group they maintained an average annual growth rate of 5 percent during 1973-80. Low-income economies suffered more than those in the middle-income range, however. The group's annual growth rate was pulled up by a few very successful middle-income countries.

The world economy was just beginning to show signs of recovery when it encountered new shocks. These included the Iranian revolution, the Iran-Iraq war, and OPEC price hikes of more than 170 percent during 1979-81. In response to the crisis, industrial countries adopted tight monetary and fiscal policies. Unemployment was allowed to rise while attention was focused on tackling inflation. The Keynesian policies of fiscal stimulus to escape recession fell out of fashion. Monetary restraint in the United States caused a sharp rise in interest rates and the deepest, most sustained recession in half a century.

The growth performance of many developing countries deteriorated rapidly in the 1980s (table 6.1). The growth rate of total real GDP of all developing countries declined from 4.9 percent in 1971-79 to 2.8 percent in 1980-87. Several features of the growth performance stand out. First, real GDP growth declined faster among middle-income countries than among low-income countries, except in Africa. Second, from 1971-79 to 1980-87, the yearly growth rate of total real GDP of low-income Asian countries increased from 4.6 percent to 5.7 percent. Third, the rate of growth of total real GDP dropped faster in

Table 6.1 Growth rates of real GDP, developing countries, 1971-87
(percent)

Country group	Number of countries	1971-79	1980-84	1985-87	1980-87
Low-income	35	3.4	2.0	3.2	2.5
Africa	28	3.2	1.2	2.9	1.9
Asia	6	4.6	5.9	5.2	5.7
Latin America and the Caribbean	1	4.0	0.5	0.4	0.5
Middle-income	46	6.0	3.0	2.9	3.0
Africa	8	7.3	5.9	3.4	5.0
Asia	4	7.8	5.0	4.2	4.7
Europe, the Middle East, and North Africa	13	7.0	4.8	3.3	4.2
Latin America and the Caribbean	21	4.6	0.4	2.3	1.1
Low-income manufacturer	7	3.6	4.7	3.8	4.4
Middle-income manufacturer	21	6.0	3.0	3.6	3.2
Low-income primary	26	3.1	1.4	3.1	2.0
Middle-income primary	14	5.1	1.5	3.4	2.2
Oil exporting	13	7.2	4.3	1.3	3.2
Highly indebted	17	5.1	0.3	2.7	1.2
All developing countries	81	4.9	2.6	3.1	2.8

Note: The averages for groups of countries are weighted by population. See Kakwani (1990a).
Source: Authors' calculations, using World Bank data for individual countries and years.

Latin American countries than in Europe, the Middle East, and North Africa or even in Africa. Fourth, the highly indebted countries performed worst, achieving a growth rate of only 0.3 percent in 1980-84; these countries were most severely affected by a steep rise in interest rates in the early 1980s. Fifth, growth in oil-exporting countries slowed in 1985-87 because of a huge fall in oil prices. Finally, most groups of developing countries performed better during 1980-84.

The paragraphs that follow look at other variables that could have influenced the growth performance of developing countries. Trends during the 1980s in key variables affecting growth rates appear in table 6.2. The data are averages for all developing countries. It is important to bear in mind that such averages are aggregates of the growth performance of countries at different income levels.

Terms of trade

Changes in terms of trade can have a considerable impact on a country's economic growth. For developing countries, the terms of trade on average deteriorated during the 1980s, though the change was not large. Of eighty-four countries for which data are available, forty-five experienced a worsening of their terms of trade during both 1981-84 and 1985-87. The deterioration was larger in 1985-87 than in 1980-84 despite the later period's higher growth rate of GDP. Oil-exporting countries—Egypt, Mexico, Nigeria, Oman, Trinidad and Tobago, and Venezuela—suffered the greatest deterioration during 1985-87.

Table 6.2 Change in variables related to growth rates for all developing countries, 1980-87

(percent)

Variable	1980-84	1985-87
Terms of trade	-0.4	-1.8
Exchange rate depreciation	9.6	1.8
Current account balance	-6.8	-4.5
Resource balance	-9.6	-6.6
Inflation rate	25.8	76.7
Domestic saving–GDP ratio	8.8	13.2
Domestic investment–GDP ratio	18.0	19.4
Growth rates of imports	-1.7	3.0
Growth rates of exports	2.4	3.9
Government consumption–GDP ratio	12.0	15.0

Note: These figures are simple averages for eighty-four developing countries.
Source: Authors' calculations based on World Bank data for individual countries and years.

Exchange rate depreciation and current account balance

Most of the SAL packages required countries to devalue their currency. Developing countries on average devalued their currencies in real terms by 9.6 percent from 1980 to 1984 (table 6.2). But the rate of currency depreciation declined substantially in 1985-87. Of eighty-seven countries, only eight appreciated their currency in real terms during 1980-84; thirty-seven did so during 1985-87.

The main objective of devaluation is to provide incentives to firms to shift productive resources toward tradables (exports and import substitutes), and thus improve the current account balance. Developing countries as a group did improve their current account balance during 1985-87. Yet the record of trends in real exchange rate depreciation suggests that this improvement cannot be attributed entirely to the currency depreciation of 1980-87. And the record of growth rates of developing countries' imports and exports during the 1980s suggests that many countries must have restructured their economies, providing greater incentives to the tradable sector.

In attempting to assess the effect of policies that shift a country's resources from nontradables to tradables, we must ask where the poor are employed and what they consume. If most of the poor produce tradables, such policies would have benefited them. But many of the poorest work in the informal nontradable services sector, which often provides a "reserve occupation" in time of need. The *security* of the poor may thus suffer when incentives shift toward tradable production, even if their average income increases. In consumption, the poor may lose if their purchases are largely tradable at market rates (wheat, rice, or maize). But they may gain if they buy mainly staples that are largely nontradable (root crops, in areas with bad transport). In addition, government expenditure cuts to offset the expansionary effects of devaluation may negatively affect the poor.

Investment and saving

One of the essential requirements for improving economic growth is to increase domestic investment. Such investment can be financed from domestic saving or from foreign borrowing. A nation can increase domestic saving through taxation or reduced government expenditure. During recession, when incomes are falling, both routes to higher saving become tougher. People's propensity to save falls as per capita incomes fluctuate downward. The government's capacity to increase taxes is also considerably reduced during recession, for two reasons. First, progressive income taxes (and all profit taxes) fall more than in proportion to the fall in GNP. And second, because many developing countries collect much of their tax revenue from indirect taxes, especially import duties, foreign exchange shortages that lead to sharp cuts in imports can often result in a decline in government tax revenue. That in turn can lead to a decline in public investment.

In the 1970s many middle-income countries, particularly those in Latin America, maintained high investment through foreign borrowing. But the unexpected global crisis of 1980-84 led to huge cuts in foreign borrowing and a sharp rise in debt service payments for these countries. At the same time, their domestic savings were low. Government resources were further strained by the steep rise in debt, in real interest rates, and in the dollar's value: debt servicing rose from about 6 percent of central government expenditures for developing countries in the mid-1960s to about 17 percent in the mid-1980s. As a result of the constriction in both domestic and foreign financing, the countries' investment declined relative to GDP in 1980-84. During 1985-87, however, developing countries—including middle-income ones—increased their domestic saving and investment. This was partly responsible for the developing countries' considerably higher economic growth in 1985-87 (3.1 percent) than in 1980-84 (2.6 percent).

Government consumption

One of the important aims of adjustment was to reduce government expenditure in order to bring aggregate demand into line with aggregate supply. But average government consumption *increased* in the 1980s as a proportion of GDP for developing countries as a group. The main reason was higher payments of interest by governments. A standard recommendation is to defer investment in crises and let consumption avoid the adjustment. Yet what took place during the 1980s may not have benefited the poor. Later in this chapter we analyze the expenditures that have direct effects on the welfare of the poor.

Per capita GDP growth rates

The GDP growth rates of country groups presented in table 6.1 were not adjusted for growth in population. Population growth is probably little affected by adjustment policies, at least in the short run. Still, the per capita GDP growth rate is a better indicator of change in a country's economic state and in its living conditions.

**Table 6.3 Frequency distribution of developing countries according to
growth rate of per capita GDP, 1970-87**

Percentage growth in per capita GDP	1970-79	1980-84	1985-87	1980-87
Negative	19	47	41	44
0-1	12	17	9	15
1-2	8	7	12	8
2-3	13	2	9	6
3-4	11	5	9	8
Above 4	23	10	8	5
Total	86	88	88	86

Source: World Bank data.

Table 6.3 presents the frequency distribution of average growth rates of per capita GDP for eighty-eight countries. Nineteen countries registered negative per capita growth in 1970-79. This number rose to forty-four in 1980-87—half the developing countries with usable data (though containing much less than half the population). Twenty-three countries had an average per capita growth rate of more than 4 percent in 1970-79; this number fell to five in 1980-87. Notably, though, the two largest developing countries, China and India, improved their growth performance in the 1980s.

To explore the implications of growth performance for poverty, we need to contrast countries grouped by such socioeconomic criteria as region, overall development status, indebtedness, and so on. In the World Bank's preparation of data on growth for the *World Development Report*, each country's GDP is converted to U.S. dollars and aggregated across regions or groups through the construction of a weighted average, with the weights based on the countries' output. Growth rates are based on these aggregates. This procedure is sensible for looking at some aspects of growth in tradable output, but it has two drawbacks when used to assess the change in the living conditions in developing countries. First, the method depends on official exchange rates, which seldom accurately measure the ratios between national currencies. Second, the procedure gives greater weight to the growth rates of richer countries, regardless of the size of their population. But from a welfare point of view, we want to see not how the average (or total) GNP of developing countries performed, but how the average or the poorer *person* in these countries fared.

In this section we calculate aggregate growth rates in a way more suitable for welfare comparisons. Growth rates for individual countries are calculated in local currency (after adjusting for inflation but without having to correct for exchange rate differences). The average for a group of countries is obtained by weighting the growth rates by the size of the population.[2] The numerical results for several country classifications appear in table 6.4.

In 1980-87 the overall population-weighted growth performance of eighty-six developing countries was not as dismal as the erroneous impression of welfare trends given by the output-weighted figures. Per capita GDP grew at an average annual rate of 3.3 percent. But growth performance varied among the

Table 6.4 Growth rates of per capita GDP, developing countries, 1971-87
(percent; population-weighted averages)

Country group	Number of countries	1971-79	1980-84	1985-87	1980-87
Africa	37	0.7	-2.3	-0.9	-1.7
Europe, the Middle East, and North Africa	14	5.2	1.2	1.6	1.4
Asia	12	2.5	5.0	5.0	5.0
Latin America and the Caribbean	23	3.6	-0.7	1.3	0.1
Low-income	39	2.1	4.0	4.3	4.1
Middle-income	47	4.1	0.5	1.5	0.9
All developing countries	86	2.6	3.2	3.6	3.3

Source: World Bank data.

different groups of countries. Low-income countries showed an impressive performance, with 4.1 percent annual growth. Clearly, the growth record in China and India dominates the aggregate result. Middle-income countries, on the other hand, suffered a large drop in growth rates in the decade. Most of these countries are in Europe, the Middle East, and North Africa or the Latin American regions. The per capita growth rate in Africa was very low even in the 1970s and became negative in the 1980s. Developing countries in Asia performed better as a group during 1980-87 than those in Africa and Latin America. The Philippines was the only Asian country with a large negative growth rate.

Price-adjusted per capita GDP

Although average GDP growth rates of countries can perhaps be compared by the above method, actual GDP levels cannot be. That is because national accounting systems estimate GDP in domestic currency; conversion into a single currency (for example, U.S. dollars at the official rates) ignores the fact that such rates do not reflect purchasing power parity (PPP) rates. We have used the PPP rates for 1980 provided by Summers and Heston (1988) to convert per capita GDP of all developing countries to U.S. dollars. The per capita GDP values we obtained (table 6.5) are comparable over time as well as across countries.

The aggregation of adjusted per capita GDP over time was done by simple arithmetic averaging. As with the weighted growth rates of local currency GDP per capita in table 6.4, the levels and growth of PPP per capita GDP are aggregated by weighting each country's per capita GDP by the size of its population. The last two columns in table 6.5 give the percentage change in welfare as measured in per capita GDP in 1980 PPP dollars between the relevant time periods. Note that the calculations of the percentage change in welfare do not require the use of the PPP rates (assuming these stay roughly at 1980 levels). These estimates are independent of the conversion rate.

According to the measure of per capita GDP in PPP dollars, the countries in Africa with the lowest levels of welfare in 1970-79 suffered further deterioration in economic conditions during 1980-87. The welfare of the average person in

Table 6.5 Per capita GDP in 1980 PPP dollars for developing countries, and percentage change, 1970-87

Country group	1970-79	1980-84	1985-87	1980-87	1980-84 to 1985-87	1970-79 to 1980-87
					Percentage change	
Low-income	816	994	1,173	1,059	18.0	30.0
Middle-income	2,016	2,535	2,601	2,560	2.6	27.0
Africa	521	497	457	482	-8.1	-7.5
Europe, the Middle East, and North Africa	1,662	2,408	2,536	2,454	5.3	47.6
Asia	910	1,171	1,441	1,266	23.1	39.0
Latin America and the Caribbean	2,675	3,050	3,035	3,045	-0.5	13.8
All developing countries	1,006	1,248	1,425	1,312	14.0	30.4

Source: Authors' calculations based on World Bank data on individual countries for each year.

Africa was 8 percent lower in 1980-87 than in 1970-79. But the welfare of the average member of the population of all developing countries was 30 percent higher in 1980-87. Latin American and Caribbean countries saw a modest 13.8 percent improvement despite a considerable slowing of their economic growth; countries in Europe, the Middle East, and North Africa managed to raise the welfare of their average citizen by more than 47 percent in the 1980s. This demonstrates, among other things, that the growth rate of income per capita *over an entire period* is not necessarily a good indicator of a country's performance in improving the welfare of an average citizen.[3]

In the aggregate, the low-income countries improved their average per capita welfare by 30 percent in the 1980s. This impressive performance results in part from the record of India and China, which offset the poor performance of low-income African countries.

This aggregate picture gives cause for modest optimism. But it is a sad commentary on the 1980s that many countries that were among the poorest to begin with saw their conditions further eroded. Although the period was not a lost decade for all developing countries, it brought declining real purchasing power to the average African.

Growth rates in private consumption

Per capita GDP and related income measures are widely used to appraise the economic performance of individual countries. But these measures are less satisfactory for measuring standards of living. A preferred measure is per capita private consumption, excluding purchases of dwellings (but ideally including imputed rent for owner-occupied dwellings, though this is not feasible in practice). For this chapter, real consumption was aggregated across countries and weighted by population. Its growth was calculated by deflating total consumption by the consumer price index. For all developing countries as a group, real per capita consumption grew at an average rate of 2.6 percent in 1980-87, an

Table 6.6 Growth rates of real per capita private consumption, developing countries, 1971-87
(percent)

Country group	1971-79	1980-84	1985-87	1980-87
Low-income	1.4	4.4	1.3	3.2
Middle-income	4.0	0.3	1.1	0.6
Africa	0.8	-1.1	-1.3	-1.2
Europe, the Middle East, and North Africa	5.3	0.6	0.9	0.7
Asia	1.7	5.1	1.7	3.8
Latin America and the Caribbean	3.7	-0.8	1.4	0.6
All developing countries	2.0	3.3	1.3	2.6

Source: World Bank data.

improvement of 0.6 percentage point over 1971-79 (table 6.6). Most of this improvement can be attributed to the good performance of the Asian countries. But real per capita consumption in Africa clearly declined.

Table 6.7 presents per capita private consumption in 1980 PPP dollars. The last two columns show the percentage change in average per capita consumption. The average person in Africa consumes less than the average person in Asia, but the difference is smaller than the difference between the two regions' per capita GDP. Except for Africa, all regions have improved their per capita real consumption. For all developing countries as a group, per capita consumption in the 1980s was 14.4 percent higher than it was in the 1970s. These results are broadly consistent with the results for GDP, reflecting global progress on average, with considerable variation within regions. The most notable example of this variation is the steady decline in consumption levels in many of the African countries that can least afford it.

To what extent is this picture reflected by other variables that measure welfare? The following sections discuss government expenditure on welfare programs and look at more direct measures of living conditions—life expectancy at birth, food security, and access to education.

Social welfare expenditures

In most developing countries the public sector plays the dominant role in financing social welfare programs. The public sector grew rapidly in almost all developing countries in the 1970s and continued to grow in the 1980s. Still, the share of central government spending in GNP in these countries remains below that of industrial countries (World Bank 1988). This is mainly because industrial countries have higher levels of transfers for social security and welfare programs. The low levels of social services in many developing countries often generate demand for more public social spending. But many of these countries are engaged in programs aimed at reducing fiscal imbalances that require a mixture of revenue expansion and expenditure reduction measures. Although stabilization and adjustment programs are not always explicit in specifying the focus for cuts

Table 6.7 Per capita consumption in 1980 PPP dollars for developing countries, and percentage change, 1970-87

					Percentage change	
Country group	*1970-79*	*1980-84*	*1985-87*	*1980-87*	*1980-84 to 1985-87*	*1970-79 to 1980-87*
Low-income	373	421	441	427	4.8	14.5
Middle-income	1,290	1,541	1,550	1,545	0.6	19.8
Africa	350	345	322	336	-6.7	-4.0
Europe, the Middle East, and North Africa	895	1,142	1,188	1,159	4.0	29.5
Asia	433	516	559	531	8.3	22.6
Latin America and the Caribbean	1,785	2,038	1,988	2,021	-2.5	13.2
All developing countries	570	646	671	652	3.9	14.4

Source: Authors' calculations based on World Bank data on individual countries for each year.

in expenditure, it is generally believed that the social sectors suffer the most from these cuts. There is therefore growing concern that reducing government expenditures may severely and adversely affect the most vulnerable population groups.

This section looks at two questions. The first is whether government spending as a proportion of GDP dropped in the 1980s in developing nations. The second is whether the proportion of government expenditure for health, education, and other welfare programs changed between 1975-80 and 1980-86.

The government expenditure data reported in this section were obtained from the IMF's *Yearbook of Government Finance Statistics*. The data are for central governments only (reliable data for spending by state and local governments are scarce). Expenditure includes all nonrepayable payments by government for current or capital purposes. Current expenditure includes that for goods and services, interest payments and subsidies, and other current transfers. Capital expenditure includes the acquisition of fixed capital assets that will be used for productive purposes for more than a year.

We have classified the data into three categories related to welfare: education services, health services, and other welfare expenditures. The last category includes social security and welfare services, housing and community services, and recreational, cultural, and religious services. For comparison, we also look at the budget for defense. We were able to compare these data for a sufficiently long period for only thirty-four countries.

Between 1975 and 1986 total government spending as a proportion of GDP increased for the thirty-four countries as a group (table 6.8). The increase was smaller in 1980-86 than in 1975-80. The ratio remained more or less the same between 1980 and 1986 in countries producing primary commodities in Asia and in Europe, the Middle East, and North Africa.

In examining data on individual countries, we found that the ratio of government expenditure to GDP grew sharply in Bolivia and Mexico, fell sharply in Tanzania, and declined modestly in Chile, Morocco, and the Republic of Korea

Table 6.8 Welfare and defense as percentage of total government expenditure, developing countries, 1975, 1980, and 1986

Country group	Number of countries	Education 1975	Education 1980	Education 1986	Health 1975	Health 1980	Health 1986	Other welfare 1980	Other welfare 1986	Defense 1975	Defense 1980	Defense 1986	Total government expenditure as percentage of GDP 1975	Total government expenditure as percentage of GDP 1980	Total government expenditure as percentage of GDP 1986
Low-income countries	11	11.2	10.0	10.1	5.4	4.1	3.9	7.3	7.3	17.6	13.1	13.3	18.9	22.6	24.1
Middle-income countries	23	14.1	13.7	12.9	4.6	5.9	5.1	16.9	17.5	15.2	15.8	13.7	23.0	26.8	28.6
Africa	8	14.9	14.5	13.7	6.8	5.4	5.0	10.2	9.1	12.7	10.6	9.8	21.8	25.0	26.8
Europe, the Middle East, and North Africa	8	11.9	10.2	12.2	3.2	3.4	3.6	12.0	11.0	24.0	22.9	22.1	31.3	39.1	39.5
Asia	8	10.1	9.6	10.6	3.7	3.1	3.4	6.8	7.8	20.5	18.8	17.2	16.0	20.1	20.6
Latin America and the Caribbean	10	15.1	15.0	11.5	5.4	8.5	6.3	23.6	26.1	9.4	9.0	6.8	19.4	19.1	22.8
Highly indebted	9	15.8	15.8	11.8	5.3	8.4	6.0	23.3	24.6	9.4	9.8	7.0	22.0	22.0	26.5
Oil exporters	7	11.2	11.1	11.5	3.8	3.5	3.6	11.8	10.2	19.5	18.7	17.7	26.8	29.1	33.3
Manufacturing	11	14.5	14.2	12.3	6.1	5.9	4.6	14.8	16.2	15.1	12.2	10.8	20.1	20.9	23.5
Primary producers	16	13.1	12.0	11.9	4.4	5.7	5.2	13.9	14.7	15.0	15.2	13.7	20.4	27.0	26.9
All developing countries	34	13.2	12.5	12.0	4.8	5.3	4.7	13.8	14.2	16.0	15.0	13.6	21.7	25.4	27.1

Source: Based on data from IMF, *Yearbook of Government Finance Statistics,* various years.

(appendix table A.1). In 1986 Hungary and Oman had the highest ratio of public expenditure to GDP among the thirty-four countries.

On average for all developing countries, the shares of total public spending on education, health, and defense dropped in the 1980s in both low- and middle-income countries. Notably, Korea showed an upward trend in the share of spending on health and education during the entire period of 1975-86. Mexico, Tanzania, and Turkey all registered declines. The average share of expenditure on other welfare programs grew in the thirty-four nations during the 1980s. This was due mainly to increased spending in Bolivia, Chile, Costa Rica, Pakistan, and Paraguay. In Brazil and Mexico the share of spending for other welfare dropped substantially in 1980-86.

Costa Rica is an interesting case. Both health and education expenditure shrank between 1980 and 1986, while other welfare expenditure nearly tripled. Much of the increase took place in social security payments. Costa Rica's reallocation of public resources has implications for the poor that depend, of course, on whether social security spreads to the rural and informal sectors; this needs to be explored. In Mexico, by contrast, *all* welfare spending ratios declined substantially in 1980-86. At the same time, central government outlay rose enormously as a share of GDP because of Mexico's exploding burden of interest payments.

Because total government expenditure varies over time, ratios of spending on welfare to total spending do not indicate whether real per capita welfare expenditures are growing or shrinking. To shed light on this issue, we constructed appendix table A.2 by first deflating nominal welfare expenditures by the consumer price index. To make cross-country comparisons, we converted all spending to U.S. dollars by the 1980 PPP conversion rates. The figures in appendix table A.2 are per capita welfare expenditures in 1980 U.S. dollars, comparable over time as well as across countries. Table 6.9 shows average per capita welfare expenditures, weighted by population size, for various country groups.

In real terms, per capita government expenditure grew significantly in many developing countries. The increase was considerably larger in middle-income countries than in low-income ones. The countries in Europe, the Middle East, and North Africa almost doubled their average per capita spending in the 1980s. The highly indebted and manufacturing exporting countries, however, reduced real per capita public expenditure. Their cuts were made by slashing per capita expenditure on education, health, and defense.

Despite the severe economic crisis in the 1980s, many developing countries managed to increase their real per capita spending on defense. Among these countries were Cameroon, Egypt, India, Korea, Mali, Oman, Pakistan, Sri Lanka, Thailand, and Tunisia. But other developing countries reduced their real per capita expenditure on defense. They included Argentina, Bolivia, Chile, Mexico, Morocco, Turkey, Uruguay, Yemen Arab Republic, and Zimbabwe.

From this overview, the only conclusion can be that no discernible pattern emerges in spending by developing countries in the 1980s, either by region or by income group. A 1989 study by the Pan American Health Organization (PAHO) on the effect of economic crisis on public health expenditures reached a similar

Table 6.9 Per capita welfare and defense expenditure in 1980 PPP dollars, developing countries, 1980 and 1986

Country group	Number of countries	Total per capita expenditure		Education		Health		Other welfare		Defense	
		1980	1986	1980	1986	1980	1986	1980	1986	1980	1986
Low-income countries	11	158.6	174.4	14.6	15.9	6.6	5.7	13.9	14.0	16.6	22.5
Middle-income countries	23	641.2	909.5	75.7	93.8	35.5	46.0	110.1	155.7	124.7	176.8
Africa	8	182.9	198.6	28.1	28.7	10.7	10.8	23.2	23.4	18.5	15.5
Europe, the Middle East, and North Africa	8	827.7	1,589.0	63.3	139.1	22.2	64.8	59.7	184.6	248.5	415.6
Asia	8	232.8	288.8	25.9	35.5	7.4	9.0	18.6	22.5	42.6	54.1
Latin America	10	673.1	622.5	96.3	70.8	56.7	44.4	187.3	189.0	57.6	43.3
Highly indebted	9	735.2	694.4	107.6	81.0	60.3	47.7	201.9	204.3	66.7	50.6
Oil exporters	7	828.8	1,241.6	77.3	136.0	27.2	57.1	79.1	82.4	251.0	417.1
Manufacturing	11	314.9	302.2	42.5	36.4	18.4	13.4	83.1	83.9	36.9	28.9
Primary producers	16	439.0	676.3	55.8	61.3	31.0	35.9	76.1	139.7	55.6	67.3
All developing countries	34	480.3	671.7	55.9	68.6	26.1	33.0	79.0	109.8	89.8	126.9

Source: Based on data from IMF, *Yearbook of Government Finance Statistics*, various years.

conclusion. It revealed great differences in health expenditure patterns among Brazil, Ecuador, Honduras, Mexico, and Uruguay. The study says:

> These five national experiences confirm that there definitely was a crisis of resources for health at the central government level and that, in the typical case, the pre-crisis expenditure per capita had still not been regained in 1986. However, one cannot conclude from this that the health sector suffered discrimination on account of the crisis. It neither systematically suffered a reduction of its relative share of the reduced total product nor was it revealed as not having priority for the national governments. (PAHO 1989: 35)

In sum, trends in government expenditure do not seem to suggest an overall reduction in real welfare spending per person in the 1980s. Some countries showed declines, but many managed to increase government budgets for welfare programs. Many nations reallocated funds among welfare programs. Against this background of government efforts in the social sectors, we turn next to trends in indicators of living conditions.

Life expectancy, infant and child mortality, and immunization

Life expectancy is perhaps the single most comprehensive indicator of a population's health status. It results from many variable inputs—nutrition, water supply, educational attainment, sanitation, and access to medical facilities. Country performance in this indicator is often measured by the absolute change in years of life or by the percentage increase. But as Sen (1981b) notes, as longevity increases, it becomes more of an achievement to raise it further.

This chapter uses a performance index developed by Kakwani (1990b) that gives greater weight to the performance of countries with greater life expectancy. The index is given by $K(L_0, L_1) = 100 [\log_e(M - L_0) - \log_e(M - L_1)]$, where L_0 is the life expectancy at birth at the beginning of the period, L_1 the life expectancy at the end of the period, and M the maximum life expectancy that can be achieved. Thus, the index K measures the logarithmic difference between life expectancy in year 1 and that in year 0, relative to the maximum attainable, M. We took the value of M to be eighty years. With this index, if life expectancy increases from fifty to fifty-five years (10 percent), $K = 18$. A similar five-year increase from fifty-five to sixty years (9.16 percent) gives $K = 22$, indicating a greater achievement. K is negative if life expectancy decreases.

The average life expectancy and performance indicators for females and males, for different country groups, appear in tables 6.10 and 6.11. The indicators for the groups were calculated by means of averages weighted in proportion to each country's population. The life expectancy for females improved far more than that for males in all periods. Although life expectancy for males in low-income Asian countries was still slightly higher than that for females in the 1970s and early 1980s, the data for 1987 show females living longer than males in all country groups.

Table 6.10 Life expectancy at birth for females and performance index, developing countries, 1972-87

Country group	Number of countries	Actual life expectancy (years) 1972	1977	1982	1987	Performance index 1972-77	1977-82	1982-87
Low-income	37	47.7	50.6	53.4	56.5	9.7	10.6	13.3
Africa	28	45.7	47.5	49.2	51.9	5.4	5.5	9.0
Asia	7	48.3	51.5	54.6	57.9	10.9	12.0	14.6
Europe, the Middle East, and North Africa	1	44.3	47.1	49.9	52.4	8.2	8.9	8.8
Latin America and the Caribbean	1	50.0	52.2	54.4	56.4	7.8	8.0	8.3
Middle-income	46	61.9	64.1	66.0	67.7	14.7	14.3	15.8
Africa	8	54.4	56.3	58.3	60.6	8.6	9.3	12.3
Asia	4	61.8	64.5	66.5	68.0	17.6	15.4	13.3
Europe, the Middle East, and North Africa	12	61.6	63.6	65.4	67.3	12.8	10.5	20.7
Latin America and the Caribbean	22	63.3	65.5	67.6	69.1	15.7	17.0	14.1
Low-income primary	30	46.9	48.7	50.3	53.0	5.8	6.0	8.4
Middle-income primary	15	61.8	63.7	65.6	67.1	14.2	16.4	13.5
Low-income manufacturer	8	47.6	50.8	53.8	57.1	10.4	11.5	13.6
Middle-income manufacturer	22	62.6	64.6	66.3	68.0	13.7	12.4	16.6
Oil exporting	13	53.6	56.8	59.6	62.4	14.0	14.6	15.8
Highly indebted	17	60.1	62.2	64.0	65.7	13.3	14.2	13.8
All developing countries	83	52.8	55.5	57.9	60.5	11.5	11.9	14.2

Source: Based on World Bank data.

Progress has been steady; there is no evidence of deteriorating longevity in the 1980s. Indeed, the data indicate a slightly better performance than in the 1970s.

Progress in life expectancy appears to have a momentum of its own that is not quickly affected by broad fluctuations in the world economy, severe recessions in many countries, or other external economic shocks (barring, of course, major famines). This is not surprising. Life expectancy is the result of many inputs that affect it in complex and little understood ways. Some inputs, such as adult literacy, do not respond to fluctuations in living conditions in the short run. Other inputs, however, may be more dependent on current economic conditions—for example, funds for immunization programs. If infant and child mortality depend more than adult mortality on the availability of such inputs, as is plausible, the first indicator is likely to be more sensitive than the second to economic fluctuations.

Infant mortality is a measure of the number of infants per thousand live births who, in a given year, die before reaching their first birthday. The population-weighted averages of the infant mortality rates for various country groups show that, in all countries, the infant mortality rate declined during 1972-87 (table 6.12).

Table 6.11 Life expectancy at birth for males and performance index, developing countries, 1972-87

Country group	Number of countries	Actual life expectancy (years)				Performance index		
		1972	1977	1982	1987	1972-77	1977-82	1982-87
Low-income	37	47.5	50.3	52.8	55.3	9.2	9.5	10.1
Africa	28	42.9	44.7	46.0	48.6	4.9	3.8	7.8
Asia	7	48.8	51.8	54.8	57.3	10.5	11.2	10.7
Europe, the Middle East, and North Africa	1	42.5	44.7	46.9	49.4	6.0	6.4	7.9
Latin America and the Caribbean	1	47.1	49.2	51.2	53.1	6.5	6.7	7.1
Middle-income	46	57.6	59.5	61.2	62.8	8.9	9.0	9.2
Africa	8	49.7	51.6	53.4	55.7	6.8	7.0	9.5
Asia	4	58.0	60.2	62.1	63.6	11.0	10.5	9.2
Europe, the Middle East, and North Africa	12	57.6	59.3	61.1	62.9	7.5	8.7	10.8
Latin America and the Caribbean	22	58.8	60.6	62.2	63.6	9.3	8.9	8.2
Low-income primary	30	44.2	46.0	47.1	49.7	5.2	3.9	8.1
Middle-income primary	15	57.5	58.9	60.6	62.2	7.7	9.8	9.2
Low-income manufacturer	8	48.8	51.8	54.7	57.0	8.4	11.2	9.5
Middle-income manufacturer	22	58.1	9.9	61.5	63.0	10.3	8.4	9.3
Oil exporting	13	50.3	53.1	55.5	58.2	10.0	9.7	12.1
Highly indebted	17	55.9	57.7	59.2	60.7	8.3	8.0	8.3
All developing countries	83	51.2	53.6	55.8	57.9	9.1	9.4	9.8

Source: Based on World Bank data.

To reflect the fact that past success makes future progress harder, we calculate the performance index as follows: $P(M_0, M_1) = 100 [\log_e M_0 - \log_e M_1]$, where M_0 is the infant mortality rate at the beginning of the period, and M_1 the rate at the end of the period. The positive (negative) value of P indicates an improvement (deterioration) in performance.[4]

The performance index values for infant mortality, in the last three columns of table 6.12, are similar to those for life expectancy, reflecting steady progress in all periods, with the pace of progress apparently increasing over time. The decline in the absolute value of the infant mortality rate is eleven points in each five-year period.

Some demographers prefer to use the child mortality rate as a measure of living conditions. This rate is the number of children per thousand live births who die before the age of five. Hill and Pebley (1989) examined UN child mortality data and eliminated "fillers" and other data of dubious quality. We used their data only for the twenty-two countries for which at least the change in child mortality from 1975-80 to 1980-85 could be calculated (table 6.13). Of these twenty-two countries, nine showed a faster pace of improvement in the 1980s than in the 1970s. Costa Rica, Mexico, and the Philippines continued to

Table 6.12 Infant mortality rate and performance index, developing countries, 1972-87

Country group	Number of countries	Infant mortality rate (per thousand)				Performance index		
		1972	1977	1982	1987	1972-77	1977-82	1982-87
Low-income	37	134	125	112	101	7.0	11.0	10.3
Africa	28	146	133	125	115	9.3	6.2	8.3
Asia	7	131	122	108	96	7.1	12.2	11.8
Europe, the Middle East, and North Africa	1	168	150	135	120	11.3	10.5	11.8
Latin America and the Caribbean	1	155	139	128	117	10.9	8.2	9.0
Middle-income	46	90	77	66	58	15.6	15.4	12.9
Africa	8	110	98	88	80	11.6	10.8	9.5
Asia	4	58	48	43	36	18.9	11.0	17.8
Europe, the Middle East, and North Africa	12	135	114	93	78	16.9	20.4	17.6
Latin America and the Caribbean	22	80	69	61	54	14.8	12.3	12.2
Low-income primary	30	138	129	122	112	6.7	5.6	8.6
Middle-income primary	15	82	72	63	56	13.0	13.4	11.8
Low-income manufacturer	8	135	127	112	101	6.1	12.6	10.3
Middle-income manufacturer	22	88	75	65	57	16.0	14.3	13.1
Oil exporting	13	115	100	87	75	14.0	13.9	14.8
Highly indebted	17	93	80	72	65	15.1	10.5	10.2
All developing countries	83	119	108	97	86	9.7	10.7	12.0

Source: Based on World Bank data.

show reduced child mortality, but the pace of progress slowed. In Bangladesh, improvement is slow, slowing, and badly needed.

The picture was also troubling in Haiti, Liberia, Mali, and Senegal. But only Ghana showed an increase in child mortality. Ghana's deep recession and two consecutive years of drought caused rising malnutrition (Alderman 1990; and United Nations 1989).

The newest, and probably the most reliable, data on life expectancy are from the Demographic and Health Surveys (DHS).[5] Table 6.14 shows infant mortality rates calculated by the DHS and the World Bank for selected countries. The rates reported by the DHS are generally much lower than those published in *World Development Report 1989* (World Bank 1989b), suggesting faster progress. Moreover, the decline in infant mortality appears to be large and to have continued during the 1980s for all countries shown.

If living conditions in some developing countries worsened during the 1980s to the point of threatening the life of newborns, this is not reflected in the DHS data. Yet there is still great reason for concern. The excess mortality of newborns in most low-income countries is appalling, given the low-cost technologies available—immunization and oral rehydration. Steady progress in the use of these

Table 6.13 Change in child mortality, selected developing countries, 1960-85
(percent)

Country	1960-65 to 1965-70	1965-70 to 1970-75	1970-75 to 1975-80	1975-80 to 1980-85	Child mortality rate 1980-85
Argentina	5.6	14.7	17.2	12.5	42
Bangladesh	—	0.0	3.1	2.7	215
Brazil	8.6	10.7	16.8	19.6	86
Chile	17.6	29.5	34.2	46.2	28
Colombia	11.9	25.2	28.1	34.4	42
Costa Rica	21.4	27.3	45.3	37.7	24
Dominican Republic	—	—	25.8	10.2	88
Egypt	—	14.3	18.3	15.3	166
Ghana	10.1	11.2	13.8	-6.7	160
Haiti	—	—	10.8	8.7	189
India	—	—	8.7	16.1	167
Liberia	5.1	1.4	11.6	9.5	220
Malaysia	20.9	13.9	25.8	10.9	41
Mali	7.1	9.9	272.0	—	—
Mexico	11.0	11.5	13.0	11.5	77
Panama	15.5	17.1	30.9	21.3	37
Peru	11.0	18.0	7.6	23.8	112
Philippines	10.9	11.4	11.9	6.7	83
Senegal	10.0	2.5	12.0	13.2	210
Sri Lanka	13.9	9.2	16.5	39.4	40
Trinidad and Tobago	5.7	26.0	13.5	12.5	28
Uruguay	-1.9	3.7	5.8	30.6	34

— Not available.
Source: Hill and Pebley 1989.

techniques lies behind observed achievements. In a 1989 press release, the World Health Organization (WHO) reports that:

> For the first time in history, immunization coverage for the world has reached the two-thirds mark (67 percent) for a third dose of polio vaccine for children reaching their first year of life....Other good news is contained in the global immunization figures...third dose coverage of diphtheria, pertussis, and tetanus (DPT) stands at 66 percent, coverage for the vaccine used against tuberculosis (BCG) has reached 71 percent and measles vaccine coverage is 61 percent.

WHO warned that great effort would be needed to sustain these achievements and to improve on them. Widespread deterioration in incomes, particularly in Africa, is likely to slow progress. Most countries increased their immunization coverage for measles and polio in the 1980s (table 6.15). But there are countries in every group that have already seen their progress eroded; coverage remains low in Bangladesh, the Central African Republic, Chad, Ethiopia, Gua-

Table 6.14 Infant mortality rates, selected developing countries, 1971-75 and 1981-86

(per thousand)

Country	1971-75		1981-86	
	DHS[a]	WB[b]	DHS[a]	WB[c]
Burundi	100	132	75	115
Dominican Republic	80	88	68	51
Ecuador	97	87	58	50
Guatemala	92	87	73	66
Liberia	192	112	144	89
Mali	170	196	108	133
Morocco	104	115	73	93
Senegal	120	157	86	124
Sri Lanka	40	37	25	29
Thailand	55	60	35	51
Trinidad and Tobago	47	28	26	29

a. Sometimes covers 1972-76 or 1972-77.
b. Refers to 1975.
c. Refers to any year between 1981 and 1986.
Source: Based on World Bank data and data from Demographic Health Surveys (DHS).

temala, Guinea, Indonesia, Niger, Sierra Leone, Sudan, and Uganda. At the same time, Côte d'Ivoire, Mexico, and the Philippines showed significant improvements despite severe economic setbacks.

These data send a variety of signals. They suggest that the positive correlation between economic development (as measured by growth in GDP per capita) and social progress (as measured by increasing life expectancy or decreasing infant mortality) does not hold during recessions. Short of such disasters as famine, mortality is probably affected only in the long run, due to long time lags. Furthermore, the increased availability of affordable and simple life-saving interventions makes progress possible even during periods of recession.

Food production, undernutrition, and protein intake

The growth in global food production outpaced the growth in world population over the past three decades. Yet vast population groups throughout the developing world continue to suffer from hunger and malnutrition. An overwhelming majority of persons in at-risk groups are concentrated in Asia and Africa. Two sets of indicators—undernutrition and malnutrition—are used to identify and monitor at-risk population groups. Undernutrition relates to deficiency in one or more essential nutrients in the daily diet, and malnutrition refers to such anthropometric measures as weight for height or height for age.

Food production

The number of countries with negative per capita growth in food production varies widely between years (table 6.16). This variability may be due, at least in part,

Table 6.15 Immunization coverage, selected developing countries, 1981-84 and 1986-88

(percent)

Country	Measles			Polio		
	1981-84	1986-88	Difference	1981-84	1986-88	Difference
Algeria	17	59	—	46	63	—
Argentina	76	78	2	64	78	14
Bangladesh	1	5	4	1	7	6
Benin	24	39	15	17	46	29
Bolivia	17	17	0	56	35	-21
Botswana	75	86	11	77	84	7
Brazil	80	58	-22	89	88	-1
Burkina Faso	94	53	-41	2	23	21
Burundi	30	47	17	6	41	35
Cameroon	47	31	-16	6	35	29
Central African Republic	19	24	5	21	20	-1
Chad	8	16	8	1	13	12
Chile	77	91	14	86	90	4
Colombia	53	56	3	61	61	0
Congo	49	63	14	42	67	25
Costa Rica	83	75	-8	84	86	2
Côte d'Ivoire	28	85	57	34	71	37
Dominican Republic	19	40	21	99	36	-63
Ecuador	40	50	10	36	47	11
Egypt	41	79	38	67	88	11
El Salvador	41	57	16	44	60	26
Ethiopia	8	13	5	7	7	0
Gabon	35	56	21	48	46	-2
The Gambia	70	81	11	70	65	-5
Guatemala	27	31	4	53	31	-22
Guinea	44	9	-35	—	—	—
Guinea-Bissau	33	43	10	14	28	14
Guyana	33	45	12	41	74	33
Haiti	13	22	9	12	22	10
Honduras	51	60	7	84	62	-22
India	—	30	—	37	49	12
Indonesia	7	39	32	7	31	24
Jamaica	60	54	-6	56	71	15
Jordan	30	78	48	41	90	49
Kenya	55	62	7	57	74	17
Lesotho	63	75	12	64	79	15
Liberia	83	37	-46	23	12	-11
Madagascar	—	—	—	7	18	11
Malawi	64	57	-7	68	52	-16
Malaysia	—	35	—	55	64	9
Mali	—	—	—	10	6	-4
Mauritania	55	66	11	21	48	27
Mauritius	53	70	17	88	84	-4
Mexico	30	59	29	49	87	38

Table 6.15 Immunization coverage, selected developing countries, 1981-84 and 1986-88 (cont.)
(percent)

Country	Measles			Polio		
	1981-84	*1986-88*	*Difference*	*1981-84*	*1986-88*	*Difference*
Nepal	2	56	54	65	31	-34
Nicaragua	30	51	21	73	81	8
Niger	16	19	3	5	6	1
Nigeria	20	21	1	24	16	-8
Oman	47	72	25	40	70	30
Papua New Guinea	—	32	—	27	38	11
Panama	72	70	-2	70	80	10
Paraguay	53	49	-4	59	96	37
Peru	32	43	11	26	47	21
Philippines	30	59	29	8	40	32
Rwanda	48	77	29	26	83	57
Senegal	67	60	-7	57	53	-4
Sierra Leone	23	31	8	9	16	7
Somalia	16	30	14	81	24	-57
Sri Lanka	2	42	40	65	75	10
Sudan	3	17	14	4	22	18
Syrian Arab Republic	39	41	2	41	49	8
Tanzania	50	76	26	53	60	7
Thailand	7	34	27	55	57	2
Trinidad and Tobago	10	47	37	65	75	10
Tunisia	55	75	20	61	83	22
Uganda	10	31	21	2	25	23
Uruguay	17	79	62	63	70	7
Venezuela	25	54	29	59	64	5
Yemen, PDR	8	28	20	7	19	12
Yemen Arab Republic	18	37	19	8	40	32
Zaire	29	39	10	42	34	-8
Zambia	55	55	0	44	57	13
Zimbabwe	43	68	25	46	74	28

— Not available.
Source: Data were obtained from WHO. We are grateful to Mark Gallagher for providing them.

to the poor quality of the data, especially for Africa. Of eighty-eight developing countries considered here, forty-two had negative growth in per capita food production in 1981 and sixty-five had negative growth in 1987. Table 6.17 gives the average per capita food production indexes for different country groups, weighted in proportion to each country's population. The index is set equal to 100 in 1980. For the eighty-seven developing countries as a group, the per capita food production index increased gradually to 114 in 1986 and then dropped to 110 in 1987. Most of this improvement can be attributed to the performance of low-income Asian countries. The African countries suffered a loss in per capita food production, especially during 1983-84. Latin American countries have barely kept their food production in line with their population increase. The conclusions from tables

6.16 and 6.17 differ because the drop in per capita food production in many small countries was outweighed by the large increases in a few populous countries.

Undernutrition

A 1987 UN report on world nutrition (United Nations 1987) reveals the unacceptably large proportions of population suffering from undernutrition. Based on estimates of the proportion of undernourished population by region (table 6.18), the report concluded that during 1960-85, malnutrition increased in much of Africa, remained stable in South America, and decreased in Asia and Central America. Although estimates on the undernourished population in China are not given in table 6.18, other indicators suggest improvements in nutritional status in China. For instance, per capita food production increased by 75 percent over the past twenty-five years.

Improvements in the populous regions of Asia suggest an overall decline in the proportion of the world population suffering from undernutrition. But focusing only on proportions masks the overwhelming magnitude of the world's nutrition problem. The absolute number of the undernourished increased in Sub-Saharan Africa from 60 million at the end of the 1960s to 80 million at the end of the 1970s, and to 100 million by the mid-1980s. Despite improvements in nutritional status in South Asia, the region still has about 170 million undernourished persons, or almost half the world's undernourished population. Finally, the growth in population in South America was likely accompanied by an increase in the number of undernourished in that region.

Table 6.16 Number of developing countries with negative rates of growth in per capita food production, 1981-87

Country group	Number of countries	1981	1982	1983	1984	1985	1986	1987
Low-income	40	19	23	23	28	15	19	33
Africa	30	15	17	22	21	10	12	26
Asia	8	2	4	1	5	3	5	6
Europe, the Middle East, and North Africa	1	1	1	0	1	1	1	1
Latin America and the Caribbean	1	1	1	0	1	1	1	1
Middle-income	48	23	25	34	22	20	25	32
Africa	8	1	5	7	5	2	4	6
Asia	4	1	2	3	1	0	3	3
Europe, the Middle East, and North Africa	14	11	4	10	6	3	5	8
Latin America and the Caribbean	22	10	14	14	10	15	13	15
All developing countries	88	42	48	57	50	35	44	65

Source: Based on World Bank data.

Malnutrition

Two sets of data are used to assess the prevalence of malnutrition: (1) child anthropometric measurements of weight for age, weight for height, and height for age, and (2) data on dietary deficiencies in energy (calories), protein, and micronutrients. Weight for age is used as an indicator of overall malnutrition (underweight), weight for height as an indicator of acute malnutrition (wasting), and height for age as an indicator of chronic malnutrition (stunting). These conditions reflect infection history and genetics at least as much as they do previous food intake, however, and, except for wasting in small children, bear almost no relation to very recent or current food intake.

A recent assessment of child malnutrition in seventy-six countries (Carlson and Wardlaw 1990) found that during 1980-84 the prevalence of underweight children increased in most Sub-Saharan African countries, remained the same in Latin America, and decreased in Asia. About 36 percent, or 150 million, of the children under age five in the developing world, excluding China, were underweight; 39 percent, or 163 million, were stunted; and 8 percent, or 35 million, were wasted. By all accounts about two-thirds of the malnourished children in the world live in Asia.

To supplement these findings, we looked at the evidence on protein deficiency and micronutrient deficiencies, though neither of these problems are necessarily correlated with poverty. Assuming that many poor households are likely to shift their consumption to inferior food items that contain less protein but more calories during periods of falling income, we examine briefly the evidence suggested by the protein intake data available in the BESD. The ratio of protein

Table 6.17 Per capita food production index, developing countries, 1980-87
(1980 = 100)

Country group	Number of countries	1981	1982	1983	1984	1985	1986	1987
Low-income	40	103	105	111	114	115	118	113
Africa	30	100	100	96	92	99	101	95
Asia	8	103	106	114	117	117	121	116
Europe, the Middle East, and North Africa	1	99	91	92	90	89	89	86
Latin America and the Caribbean	1	98	96	98	98	98	96	97
Middle-income	47	101	102	98	100	102	101	100
Africa	8	111	98	84	99	97	96	91
Asia	4	103	102	101	103	104	102	99
Europe, the Middle East, and North Africa	13	97	102	99	100	102	106	103
Latin America and the Caribbean	22	101	102	98	100	101	98	100
All developing countries	87	102	104	108	110	111	114	110

Source: Based on World Bank data.

Table 6.18 Undernourished population by region, 1969 and 1983
(percent)

Region	1969[a]	1983[b]
Sub-Saharan Africa	24	26
South Asia	21	17
Southeast Asia	18	8
Central America and Caribbean	20	15
South America	9	8
Near East and North Africa	15	5

Note: Country groups used in this table exclude China and differ from those used throughout this report.
a. Some of the data in this column are for 1971.
b. Some of the data in this column are for 1985.
Source: United Nations, ACC/SCN, 1987, table 3.

intake to calorie intake during 1980-86 for all developing countries remained stable, with a close relation between calorie and protein intakes. We therefore concluded that the protein consumption pattern of countries did not change at the aggregate level during the 1980s. This conclusion has to be weighed against the observation that "protein consumption is an unreliable indicator of malnutrition because generally applicable standards of requirements are more difficult to define" (Reutlinger and Selowsky 1976: 9).

The most important micronutrients in terms of their nutritional consequences and the number of people affected are iodine, iron, and vitamin A. Iodine deficiency is prevalent in the Andes of Latin America, the Himalayas of Asia, and the mountainous areas of Sub-Saharan Africa. Of the estimated 800 million people at risk of iodine deficiency, 85 percent are in Asia. The remainder are distributed equally between Africa and Latin America.

In summary, although the food production data show, in the aggregate, some modest improvement in per capita production over time, the data on undernutrition clearly indicate that this progress is insufficient. Moreover, an increasing number of countries show an actual decline in per capita food production. This decline does not fully offset the progress in other countries, but it is cause for great concern in those countries in which malnutrition is already a severe problem. The degree of undernutrition and malnutrition worsened in more than one-third of the Sub-Saharan African countries and improved in Asia. An overwhelming majority of the malnourished children continue to live in Asia.

School enrollment

In this section we present net enrollment ratios for primary education as an indicator of a country's achievement in providing its population with the necessary human capital to escape poverty.

Enrollment ratios vary widely among countries. In Burkina Faso, Ethiopia, Guinea, Mali, Niger, and Somalia, only 20 to 30 percent of children are enrolled in primary school. Tanzania had a good educational performance during the

Table 6.19 Rate of growth in number of children in primary school and net enrollment ratio, developing countries, 1965-85

(percent)

Country group	Number of countries	Annual growth rate			Net enrollment ratio				
		1965-75	1975-80	1980-85	1965	1970	1975	1980	1985
Low-income	38	6.2	6.3	3.4	36	40	46	53	55
Africa	28	6.5	7.0	3.2	31	35	41	48	48
Europe, the Middle East, and North Africa	1	14.6	0.9	3.7	25	50	75	69	72
Asia	8	4.0	4.8	3.2	56	57	59	69	77
Latin America and the Caribbean	1	5.6	4.3	9.4	30	34	39	37	55
Middle-income	47	3.7	3.1	2.9	73	75	81	85	89
Africa	8	4.9	4.0	3.8	67	74	80	85	92
Europe, the Middle East, and North Africa	14	2.8	3.8	4.5	66	66	74	78	85
Asia	4	2.6	1.6	0.3	93	94	96	100	99
Latin America and the Caribbean	21	4.0	2.7	2.0	75	78	82	86	89
All developing countries	85	4.8	4.5	3.1	56	60	65	71	74

Source: Based on World Bank data.

1960s and 1970s, but between 1980 and 1985 its gross enrollment ratio dropped precipitously, from 93 percent to 72 percent; its real per capita government expenditure on education also declined. During 1965-85 Zimbabwe made significant progress in improving its gross primary enrollment ratio, and its government spending on education rose sharply during 1975-86. Oman's improved record reflected growing per capita government expenditure—from $114.70 in 1980 to $560.00 in 1986.

Developing nations as a group increased their net enrollment ratio (table 6.19). But the growth rates for children age six to eleven declined monotonically between 1965-75 and 1980-85. This suggests that the improvement in the net enrollment ratio resulted in part from falling growth rates in the total number of children.

Net enrollment in low-income Africa remained stagnant between 1980 and 1985; low-income Asian and Latin American countries made substantial gains in that period.

It may be argued that recession affects the quality of education rather than the quantity indicated by the enrollment ratio. As a proxy for the quality of education, the student-teacher ratio can be useful. The average student-teacher ratio varies widely among country groups (table 6.20). Between 1965 and 1985, it was substantially lower among middle-income countries than among low-income countries. Between 1980 and 1985, the ratio fell in both these groups.

The student-teacher ratio depends on both the number of enrolled students and the number of teachers. The rate of growth in the number of teachers is likely to have declined following the cuts in expenditure on education in many countries in recent years; this is evident in the four right-hand columns of table 6.20. The rate of growth in the number of teachers in all developing countries as a group slowed from 5.2 percent in 1975-80 to 4.3 percent in 1980-85. During that period, however, the growth in the number of students enrolled slowed even more. The result was an improvement in the student-teacher ratio.

Conclusions

Economic growth in India and China, where most of the world's poor live, was stronger in the 1980s than previously. It was even stronger in Indonesia, Thailand, and other East Asian countries. In these areas, poverty retreated. Elsewhere, however, the recession of the 1980s undermined the living conditions of millions of people. Negative growth rates in per capita GDP and in private consumption, where they occurred, surely led to a rise in poverty. In this chapter we have attempted to assess the extent to which economic shocks resulted in deterioration of key social indicators. Our chief findings are these:

- Although developing countries as a group showed continued growth in GDP, despite the shocks of the 1970s, the growth performance of many individual countries greatly deteriorated during the 1980s. On average, developing countries' per capita GDP grew faster in the 1980s than in the previous decade, mainly because of the impressive performance of Asian

Table 6.20 Student-teacher ratio and rate of growth in number of primary school teachers, developing countries, 1965-85

Country group	Number of countries	Number of students per teacher					Rate of growth in primary school teachers (percent)			
		1965	1970	1975	1980	1985	1965-70	1970-75	1975-80	1980-85
Low-income	38	43.8	42.5	44.8	43.4	41.8	6.0	5.5	6.6	4.9
Africa	28	45.5	44.7	47.3	46.2	43.9	5.8	6.0	7.5	4.7
Europe, the Middle East, and North Africa	1	31.0	31.0	34.0	27.0	26.0	21.9	9.3	8.6	4.0
Asia	8	38.9	35.6	37.8	35.4	36.9	4.6	3.0	3.1	5.5
Latin America and the Caribbean	1	46.0	47.0	41.0	44.0	38.0	4.7	8.6	4.4	9.7
Middle-income	47	36.7	36.6	34.1	32.1	30.9	4.5	6.4	4.1	3.7
Africa	8	43.6	44.9	41.3	39.1	39.0	4.1	6.4	5.3	4.7
Europe, the Middle East, and North Africa	14	35.9	34.1	31.0	28.1	27.0	4.7	10.5	5.2	5.5
Asia	4	39.3	38.0	35.3	32.3	28.0	4.1	3.1	3.4	2.4
Latin America and the Caribbean	21	34.2	34.9	33.2	32.0	30.9	4.6	4.3	3.1	2.4
Low-income primary	28	46.2	45.1	48.0	46.5	43.7	6.7	5.7	7.1	5.1
Middle-income primary	14	33.9	35.3	34.4	33.4	32.1	4.5	5.0	4.1	3.1
Low-income manufacturer	8	36.9	36.0	36.8	34.5	37.0	3.0	4.3	3.5	5.2
Middle-income manufacturer	22	37.8	35.7	31.0	29.4	28.0	4.0	5.6	3.1	3.5
Oil exporting	13	38.0	38.8	38.6	35.7	34.8	5.8	9.5	6.8	4.5
Highly indebted	17	35.2	33.9	32.1	31.1	30.2	5.3	4.6	3.9	1.7
All developing countries	85	39.9	39.2	38.9	37.1	35.8	5.1	6.0	5.2	4.3

Source: Based on World Bank data.

countries. But the number of countries with negative per capita GDP growth rates rose from nineteen in 1970-79 to forty-four in 1980-87.

- Welfare, as measured in PPP dollars of GDP per capita, averaged 30 percent higher in 1980-87 than in 1970-79 for developing countries as a group. In Africa, however, welfare was 7.5 percent lower. The results were similar in direction of change—but not in magnitude—when per capita private consumption in PPP dollars was used as the welfare indicator: welfare for all developing countries as a group was 14.4 percent higher in 1980-87 than in 1970-79, but it was 4 percent lower in Africa alone.

- Average per capita real government expenditure on education and health increased in many countries. For the nations for which we could obtain data, public outlay for education and health averaged $82 per capita in 1980 and $101.60 in 1986. Average per capita real public expenditure on other welfare programs—social security, housing, community affairs, and so on—grew from $79 in 1980 to $109 in 1986. Some countries appeared to have shifted public funds from health and education to other welfare programs.

- For all developing countries, life expectancy at birth for both females and males continued to rise steadily throughout the 1970s and 1980s, with slightly better performance in the second decade. In both decades, infant mortality continued to drop.

- Developing countries as a group enjoyed improvements in nutritional status. Yet the magnitude of the global nutritional problem continues to be staggering, with massive increases in the number of undernourished in Sub-Saharan Africa—from 60 million at the end of the 1960s to 100 million by the mid-1980s. Despite the impressive improvements in nutritional status in Asia, about 170 million undernourished people—or almost half the world's undernourished population—continue to live in this region.

- In education, the net enrollment ratio of children in primary schools improved steadily for developing countries as a group throughout the 1970s and 1980s. This improvement came in part because of falling growth rates in the number of children between the ages of six and eleven. Significantly, however, thirty-two countries showed a declining net enrollment ratio between 1980 and 1985.

These findings do not confirm the fears that the economic problems and adjustment programs of the 1980s irreparably damaged living conditions in the developing world. Two points deserve particular attention.

1. The improvements in social indicators for developing nations as a group conceal very great differences among nations and regions. Indicators show that progress was often least in countries that need it most, and that problems are of staggering proportions in those countries. In 1987, for example, the African region had negative economic growth, the lowest life expectancy at birth, very high infant mortality rates, and the lowest primary school enrollment ratios. Undernutrition in low-income African countries remained very high.

2. As we have shown, some measures of social progress have had greater momentum and have remained more resilient than others in the face of economic

shocks. We have also given examples of poor countries with very favorable social conditions and of countries that have managed to protect their achievements despite new constraints. Taken together, these findings suggest that much can be done to improve social conditions even during periods of stabilization and adjustment. Progress will depend on sound short- and long-term policy judgments and on the best use of funds, programs, and technology.

Notes

1. A review of the Bank's structural and sectoral adjustment projects (SALs and SECALs) showed that they specify an average of 40 conditionalities each. The links between these conditionalities and the standard of living are in some cases positive, in other cases negative, and—most commonly—ambiguous. Therefore, the best one can do is to measure the impact of various components of adjustment programs on poverty. Such attempts have been made by, for example, Glewwe and de Tray (1988 and 1989), Kakwani (1990d), Kanbur (1988), and Laraki (1989).

2. For a welfare justification of this procedure see Kakwani (1990a).

3. For instance, consider two situations: (1) the growth rate of 5 percent in the first period and –5 percent in the second period; (2) the growth rate of –5 percent in the first period and 5 percent in the second period. Although the two situations give exactly the same average growth rate for the two periods, the average levels of welfare in both situations will be quite different. The first situation is clearly preferred to the second situation.

4. Note the similarity of this performance index to the one used for life expectancy. In the case of mortality, the maximum achievable value is zero.

5. DHS data are produced from surveys by the Institute for Resource Development, Columbia, Maryland. DHS infant mortality rates are generally much lower than those published in the World Bank's *World Development Report*.

Table A.1 Welfare and defense as percentage of total government expenditure, selected developing countries, 1975, 1980, and 1986

Region/country	Education 1975	Education 1980	Education 1986	Health 1975	Health 1980	Health 1986	Other welfare 1975	Other welfare 1980	Other welfare 1986	Defense 1975	Defense 1980	Defense 1986	Total expenditure as a percentage of GDP 1975	1980	1986
Africa															
Burkina Faso	17.1	15.5	19.0	6.6	5.8	5.8	9.0	9.9	4.9	23.8	17.0	17.3	12.2	16.4	17.4
Cameroon	15.7	12.4	11.8	4.8	5.1	3.4		11.2	12.9	9.1	9.1	6.9	16.8	14.1	20.9
Liberia	12.8	11.9	14.2	9.3	5.2	5.7		7.8	4.4	4.7	5.8	7.7	16.5	25.2	25.2
Mali	25.1	13.0	9.1	7.0	3.1	1.7		4.0	7.0	19.2	11.0	8.1	12.8	21.3	34.9
Mauritius	11.7	17.6	13.9	8.2	7.5	7.8		22.2	21.1	0.6	0.8	0.8	21.0	27.2	22.6
Tanzania	12.5	13.3	8.3	7.0	6.0	5.7		4.8	4.1	12.0	9.2	15.8	32.0	28.7	19.2
Togo	8.8	16.7	13.1	4.7	5.3	3.8		13.7	11.2	16.3	7.2	7.6	38.0	32.6	39.3
Zimbabwe	15.2	15.8	20.3	6.9	5.4	6.1		8.3	6.8	16.1	25.0	14.2	24.8	34.8	34.7
Europe, the Middle East, and North Africa															
Egypt	9.0	8.6	10.9	2.7	2.2	2.3		22.6	21.6	10.6	13.5	17.7	5.8	45.6	45.8
Hungary	—	1.8	2.3	—	2.7	3.6		24.3	25.3	—	4.4	4.0	—	56.2	57.2
Morocco	14.9	17.3	16.9	3.6	3.4	2.9		7.6	7.5	13.5	17.9	14.5	34.1	35.0	33.3
Oman	2.0	4.8	10.1	3.2	2.9	5.0		2.7	3.8	51.7	50.8	41.9	64.4	38.5	56.7
Syrian Arab Republic	7.8	5.5	9.4	0.8	0.8	1.4		12.9	8.1	33.9	35.8	38.9	47.0	48.2	36.9
Tunisia	21.1	17.0	14.3	6.2	7.2	6.5		16.6	15.0	4.5	12.2	17.9	29.1	31.6	39.1
Turkey	23.1	14.2	11.9	3.0	3.6	2.2		6.2	3.9	15.9	15.2	13.5	21.7	25.8	21.9
Yemen Arab Republic	5.4	12.6	21.7	2.7	4.0	4.5		3.4	2.6	37.7	33.2	28.5	16.9	31.9	25.4
Asia															
India	2.3	1.9	2.0	2.4	1.6	1.9		4.3	6.0	25.3	19.8	18.5	12.6	13.3	17.7
Indonesia	8.9	8.3	9.8	2.0	2.5	1.5		2.8	2.4	19.1	13.5	10.7	19.4	22.1	23.0
Korea, Rep. of	14.0	17.1	18.1	1.0	1.2	1.5		8.3	8.4	29.0	34.3	29.0	15.7	17.3	15.0
Myanmar	13.5	10.1	11.7	6.6	5.3	6.6		11.4	11.6	28.5	21.9	17.4	12.7	15.8	16.7

Table A.1 Welfare and defense as percentage of total government expenditure, selected developing countries, 1975, 1980, and 1986 (cont.)

Region/country	Education			Health			Other welfare		Defense			Total expenditure as a percentage of GDP		
	1975	1980	1986	1975	1980	1986	1980	1986	1975	1980	1986	1975	1980	1986
Nepal	10.4	9.9	12.1	5.9	3.9	5.0	2.3	7.4	6.5	6.7	6.2	9.0	14.3	18.6
Pakistan	1.1	2.7	2.6	1.5	1.5	0.9	6.0	10.1	35.4	30.6	29.5	17.4	17.5	21.9
Sri Lanka	10.5	6.7	8.8	6.1	4.9	3.9	13.4	11.0	2.9	1.7	7.6	25.3	41.4	31.3
Thailand	20.1	19.8	19.5	3.7	4.1	6.1	5.5	5.2	17.5	21.7	19.0	15.9	18.9	20.2
Latin America														
Argentina	10.7	8.9	9.5	0.0	1.7	1.8	36.6	38.9	7.1	11.9	8.8	19.6	19.0	16.8
Bolivia	23.2	26.6	12.2	8.9	11.9	1.5	2.8	5.5	17.9	18.1	5.4	12.8	14.4	37.1
Brazil	6.5	3.4	3.0	6.5	6.6	6.4	33.6	23.9	6.0	3.5	3.1	18.3	19.7	21.8
Chile	12.1	14.5	12.9	7.0	7.4	6.0	38.0	43.2	13.4	12.4	10.7	34.3	28.0	30.0
Costa Rica	28.8	24.6	16.2	4.5	28.7	19.3	11.3	29.9	3.1	2.6	2.2	20.1	25.0	26.9
Dominican Republic	10.3	12.6	12.8	6.8	9.3	9.0	14.6	14.6	8.7	7.8	8.1	18.9	18.2	14.2
Mexico	18.2	17.9	9.1	4.2	2.4	1.3	19.4	9.8	3.7	2.3	2.0	14.4	16.8	28.7
Paraguay	13.3	12.9	12.2	2.8	3.6	3.1	19.6	32.5	14.0	12.4	12.1	11.1	9.8	7.9
Uruguay	11.5	8.8	7.1	3.9	4.9	4.8	49.3	50.5	11.6	13.4	10.2	24.2	21.8	22.9
Venezuela	16.5	19.9	19.6	9.1	8.8	10.0	10.9	12.6	8.3	5.8	5.8	19.8	18.7	21.3

— Not available.

Source: Based on data from IMF, *Yearbook of Government Finance Statistics*, various years.

Table A.2 Per capita welfare and defense expenditure in 1980 PPP dollars, selected developing countries, 1980 and 1986

Region/country	Total per capita expenditure		Education		Health		Other welfare		Defense	
	1980	1986	1980	1986	1980	1986	1980	1986	1980	1986
Africa										
Burkina Faso	58.7	76.7	9.1	14.6	3.4	4.5	5.8	3.8	10.0	13.3
Cameroon	123.4	243.5	15.3	28.7	6.3	8.3	13.8	31.4	11.2	16.8
Liberia	171.4	126.3	20.4	17.9	8.9	7.2	13.4	5.6	9.9	9.7
Mali	77.1	135.4	10.0	12.3	2.4	2.3	3.1	9.5	8.5	11.0
Mauritius	403.6	433.2	71.0	60.2	30.3	33.8	89.6	91.4	3.2	3.5
Tanzania	101.3	59.3	13.5	4.9	6.1	3.4	4.9	2.4	9.3	9.4
Zimbabwe	323.6	323.1	50.2	65.6	17.5	19.7	26.9	22.0	80.9	45.9
Europe, the Middle East, and North Africa										
Egypt	453.7	550.5	39.0	60.0	10.0	12.7	102.5	118.9	61.3	97.4
Hungary	—	3,513.2	55.7	80.8	83.6	126.5	752.2	888.8	136.2	140.5
Morocco	419.7	414.9	72.6	70.1	14.3	12.0	31.9	31.1	75.1	60.2
Oman	2,390.0	5,544.1	114.7	560.0	69.3	277.2	64.5	210.7	1,214.4	2,323.0
Syrian Arab Rep.	1,044.0	1,035.0	81.4	97.3	11.8	14.5	190.9	83.8	529.9	402.6
Tunisia	583.0	748.0	99.1	107.0	42.0	48.6	96.8	112.2	71.1	59.1
Turkey	598.3	604.9	85.0	72.0	21.5	13.3	37.1	23.6	90.9	81.7
Yemen Arab Rep.	305.3	301.2	38.5	65.4	12.2	13.6	10.4	7.8	101.4	86.8
Asia										
India	81.7	132.9	1.6	2.7	1.3	2.5	3.5	8.0	16.2	25.9
Indonesia	234.9	269.6	19.5	26.4	5.9	4.0	6.6	6.5	31.7	28.8
Korea, Rep. of	409.8	563.5	70.1	102.0	4.9	8.5	34.0	47.3	140.6	163.4
Myanmar	76.3	91.7	7.7	10.7	4.0	6.1	9.7	10.6	16.7	16.0
Nepal	70.1	104.5	6.9	12.6	2.7	5.2	1.6	7.7	4.7	6.5
Pakistan	173.1	266.5	4.7	6.9	2.6	2.4	10.4	26.9	53.0	78.6

Table A.2 Per capita welfare and defense expenditure in 1980 PPP dollars, selected developing countries, 1980 and 1986 (cont.)

Region/country	Total per capita expenditure		Education		Health		Other welfare		Defense	
	1980	1986	1980	1986	1980	1986	1980	1986	1980	1986
Sri Lanka	496.4	464.5	33.3	40.9	24.3	18.1	66.5	51.1	8.4	35.3
Thailand	320.2	417.3	63.4	81.4	13.1	25.5	17.6	21.7	69.5	79.3
Latin America										
Argentina	825.0	631.7	73.4	60.0	14.0	11.4	301.9	245.7	98.2	55.6
Bolivia	220.2	420.7	58.6	51.3	26.2	6.3	6.2	23.1	39.9	22.7
Brazil	661.1	858.1	22.5	25.7	43.6	54.9	222.1	205.1	23.1	26.6
Chile	1,196.0	1,200.3	173.4	154.8	88.5	72.0	454.4	518.5	148.3	128.4
Costa Rica	757.8	755.1	186.4	122.3	217.5	145.7	85.6	225.8	19.7	16.6
Dominican Rep.	340.0	248.9	42.8	31.9	31.6	22.4	49.6	36.3	26.5	20.2
Mexico	727.9	1,154.6	130.3	105.1	17.5	15.0	141.2	113.2	16.7	23.1
Paraguay	193.9	142.0	25.0	17.3	7.0	4.4	38.0	46.2	24.0	17.2
Uruguay	981.4	919.7	86.4	65.3	48.1	44.1	483.8	464.4	131.5	93.8
Venezuela	827.3	799.8	164.6	156.8	72.8	80.0	90.2	100.8	48.0	46.4

— Not available.
Source: Based on data from IMF, *Yearbook of Government Finance Statistics*, various years.

Technological Change and Commercialization in Agriculture: Impact on the Poor

7

Hans P. Binswanger
Joachim von Braun

There are conflicting views on how technological change and commercialization can affect the poor.[1] The optimistic view emphasizes the economic gains from commercialization and technology reaching the poor. An extrapolation from this view is that through "social engineering," technology and commercialization can be used in targeted poverty alleviation. The pessimistic view emphasizes institutional and market failure induced by technological change and commercialization.

In the economists' optimistic perspective, technical change can be viewed as the ultimate source of growth. As Mellor points out, "one of the most important theoretical and empirical findings in analysis of western economic growth is the identification of technological change as a major source of growth" (1986: 76). General growth does not guarantee growth in the income of the poor, although there is a good chance of that. But other scenarios can be constructed in which the poor would lose.

Commercialization can be viewed as part of the expansion of domestic and international trade. Specialization normally arises out of the use of such trade, based on comparative advantages and economies of scale, to raise incomes. Again, while there is no guarantee that commercialization will increase the income of the poor, especially in the short run—some regions or nations (though seldom the poorest) may displace unskilled labor and specialize in capital-intensive products—the presumption is that commercialization, by raising over-all output, will usually improve poor people's incomes and thus their food consumption.

Some critics reject this presumption because they believe that the poor in low-income countries are subsistence-oriented, unlikely to be much affected by changing crop technology, and little integrated into market transactions. That notion is incorrect. The poor are usually well integrated into the rural labor market; whether as hired workers or small farmers, they participate in the exchange economy and, although the share of their income allocated to food is large, their cropping patterns and crop-livestock mixes show high involvement in markets.

Although the critical roles of technology and commercialization in stimulating agricultural growth accompanied by poverty alleviation are now widely accepted, there is also a tradition of allegations that both technology and commercialization have adverse consequences for the poorest.[2] During the green revolution in Asia, pessimists feared that the poor would be unable to participate in the adoption of new technologies or that poor farm workers would be displaced by machinery. Pessimists also worry about commercialization. They fear that the food consumption of the poor who produce for markets will decline. For example, pessimists alleged that milk-marketing schemes in India induced milk-producing households to sell their milk rather than feed it to their children. They fear that households that produce cash crops will not have access to purchased foods if their cash crops fail, or if cash crop prices collapse.

Proponents of the optimistic view—that there are opportunities for the poor in technological change and commercialization—have advocated "engineering" technology and commercialization in such a way that the poor can easily adopt technologies and participate in the growth. They argue that technology must target crops produced and consumed by the poor; that technology must be easy for the poor to adopt; and that rural development projects must provide targeted market assistance and credit to smallholders and poor farmers so that they can more easily participate in commercialization.

This chapter first discusses the optimistic view. The focus is on the open-economy model. Second, it explores scenarios under which the poor might lose absolutely or relatively. This discussion focuses on price effects and other second round effects. Third, it discusses the opportunities for targeting the poor with technology and commercialization.

The key messages are:

- Technology and commercialization normally improve agricultural growth and employment, and expand food supply, all of which are central to poverty alleviation.
- The pessimists are mostly wrong. Where technology or commercialization has been blamed for the decline of the poor's income, other antipoor interventions or policies, not necessarily linked to technology or commercialization, have usually been responsible for the adverse effects.
- Although the optimistic views are mostly right, there are indeed cases in which some of the poor do not benefit from technical progress and commercialization, or they may even lose. These adverse situations are usually due to inelastic demand or unfavorable institutional features or policies.
- The scope for narrowly targeting benefits from technology and commercialization toward the poor is limited.

The favorable effects of technological change and commercialization

This section discusses conditions under which technical change and commercialization, or a combination of the two, have positive effects on income distribution, and provides real-world examples of where these positive effects have materialized.

Technology taking the lead

Because of the increasingly limited availability of land, growth in agriculture depends more and more on yield-increasing technological change.[3] When a new technology, such as a green revolution crop variety, is introduced into a region, higher farm profits initially accrue to all producers who adopt it, including poor farmers. If demand is elastic, a supply response to the higher profits will usually lead to an expansion of production sufficient to cause an increase in the demand for agricultural labor. Demand for purchased inputs and marketing and transport services will lead indirectly to an expansion of employment. Consumer spending out of the higher profits will fuel demand for rural household goods and also expand demand for labor. Rural wages will rise, and workers may migrate from poorer areas to take advantage of the expanded opportunities.

The green revolution expanded farm output, nonfarm output, employment, wages, and immigration in, for example, the Punjab in India, the Muda irrigation scheme in Malaysia, and the Laguna province of the Philippines. Much of the employment effect of new technology in agriculture is indirect. The direct effects —on the labor used per hectare in crop production—appear to have declined in the second phase of green revolution technology, after large initial employment creation in the first phase. Kikuchi, Huysman, and Res (1983) show this pattern for rice-producing villages in the Philippines (see also Jayasuriya and Shand 1986).

It is now widely accepted that technology plays a key role in leading poverty-alleviating growth. But commercialization may also take the lead. Normally, favorable complementary effects exist between the two, and these effects can be stimulated by policy.

Commercialization taking the lead

Regions in the developing world that produce commercial crops for domestic or export markets tend to be better off than regions that produce subsistence crops. The poor in the commercial regions frequently earn higher wages and have more stable employment. But opposite findings are also reported. Comparisons of sugarcane-growing areas with other rural areas in Kenya, for instance, seem to imply that cash cropping has an adverse effect on nutrition. In Sri Lanka, Zimbabwe, and elsewhere, health indicators on plantations are usually reported as worse than those on smallholdings. Such simple interregional comparisons are not sufficient, however, to establish a causal link between commercialization and poverty.[4] The greater wealth of the commercial regions could be the result of a more favorable climate for agriculture rather than of a causal relation between commercial production and lower poverty levels. Examples of positive effects of commercialization observed over time provide more convincing evidence of a causal link.

In Guatemala the opening up of new export marketing channels for vegetables resulted in the expansion of high-value, labor-intensive crops. Favorable agroecological conditions, basic infrastructure (roads), cooperative arrangements, and farmers' know-how in traditional vegetable production helped create a success story. Income gains to small farmers (with farms averaging 0.7 hectare) from specialization were large, and employment in agriculture increased by 45 percent (von Braun, Hotchkiss, and Immink 1989). The small farmers who joined the commercialization process also adopted yield-increasing technology on their now reduced maize and bean fields. In this environment of risky output and factor markets, and without insurance markets, farmers insure against risks to their food supply by maintaining some self-sufficiency in food production. Thus, they may fail to capture the maximum short-term gains from specialization.

Another example of commercialization taking the lead can be seen in the rapid expansion of cassava production in northeastern Thailand. Production increased in response to new, policy-induced trade opportunities with the European Community in the 1970s and 1980s (Konjing 1989).

The complementarity between commercialization and technical change

Low-income countries that shift their crop mix toward marketed and (internationally) traded crops were found to be more successful in increasing yields per unit of land in staple food crops (von Braun and Kennedy 1986). Although this success may be due to policies that favor all crops in such countries, and although different crops do compete for scarce resources, there are causal chains through which cash cropping can stimulate staple food production; input supply and output marketing channels may be opened up, and rural financial institutions improved, in connection with cash crops. Such complementarities between commercialization and technological progress in staple food production were strong in Sub-Saharan Africa (Lele, van de Walle, and Gbetibouo 1990). The other side of the coin is that hindering commercialization also hinders the technological change that advances food crop production frontiers.

Poverty is alleviated by exploiting the complementarities between yield-increasing technological change in staple foods and commercialization of agriculture. Specialization in labor-intensive cash crops, which promotes the adoption of technology in staple food production, can lead to employment creation, greater food security, and lower food prices. The employment generated by labor-intensive cash crops can benefit the landless. Household food security is maintained not only because of the income effects of cash crops, but also because farm households, as they adopt cash crops, improve their technologies in staple food production. This in turn can dampen potential increases in local food prices.

The example of export vegetables in Guatemala referred to earlier revealed precisely this pattern of complementarity (von Braun, Hotchkiss, and Immink 1989). Similarly, in the Philippines, following an expansion in sugarcane production, sugar farmers had higher maize yields on the reduced maize crop area and continued to produce significant amounts of maize for subsistence. But their consumption of maize was much lower than that of maize farmers, as sugarcane-producing households preferred to purchase more rice in the market instead (Bouis and Haddad 1990). In an area in Kenya with expanded sugarcane production, many of the sugarcane farmers expanded their maize crops into fallow land at constant yields to maintain subsistence (Kennedy and Cogill 1987)—clearly an employment-generating sequence.

Real income gains from technical change and commercialization translate into increased food consumption for the poor and improved nutritional welfare for children. In three areas of the Gambia, Guatemala, and Rwanda, a 10 percent increase in annual per capita income from a level of US$100 translated into a 3.5 to 4.9 percent increase in households' calorie consumption. The calorie consumption per adult equivalent of a large proportion of the households below the US$100 cutoff point falls below accepted levels, so this increase matters: indeed, it led to a 1.1 to 2.5 percent increase in anthropometric measures of the nutritional status of children (table 7.1). As Alderman (chapter 5 in this voume) shows, the response of calorie intake to increases in income, and of children's anthropometric measures to calorie intake, is much smaller in other rural areas (Kenya, Nicaragua, the Philippines) where initial poverty is less.

Scenarios in which the poor might lose absolutely or relatively

It is easy to construct hypothetical scenarios of technological change and commercialization in which the poor might lose absolutely or relatively. We discuss eight such scenarios below and confront them with empirical research. The scenarios range from inherent consequences of technological change and commercialization of which policymakers must be aware (such as the agricultural treadmill effect) to policy failure (for example, coerced production).

Consumers versus producers: The agricultural treadmill

There has been much debate about the distribution of gains between agricultural producers and consumers. The basic conclusion of partial equilibrium models is that, under perfectly elastic demand, producers can capture all the gains from

Table 7.1 Effect of increase in income on food consumption and nutritional welfare in three areas of the Gambia, Guatemala, and Rwanda

Location of study area	Focus of technology and commercialization	Percentage change as the result of a 10 percent increase in income [a]	
		Calorie consumption of households	*Weight for age of children* [b]
The Gambia	Irrigated rice	4.9	1.9
Guatemala	Export vegetables	3.5	1.1
Rwanda	Potatoes	4.7	2.5

a. Total expenditure including value of home-produced foods approximating permanent income is used in the respective models. All percentage changes computed for annual per capita income of US$100.
b. Z-score values of weight for age.
Source: von Braun 1989.

technology, but if demand is inelastic, consumers gain and producers may either gain or lose. Because price elasticities for many agricultural commodities are low, farmers have been viewed as working a treadmill on which gains from improved technology forever elude them and are transferred instead to consumers.

Producers of a crop faced with declining prices can cushion the impact on farm profits by moving into other crops—a substitution or diversification response. For consumers, a fall in the real price of a staple food crop leads to a progressive impact on income distribution, especially in the nonfarm sector. Poor people spend a large part of their budget on food, so the proportional gain in their real income from a decline in food prices is larger than the gain of the rich. Even in rural areas the poor may benefit from the price decline as consumers, but they may lose farm profits in their role as producers. Poor workers and poor farmers are also affected by the impact of technology on their employment and wages in the labor market.

Although substitution and consumption effects may dampen treadmill effects, they will not eliminate them. Once substitution effects, consumer effects, and employment effects are introduced, more complex methods are required to assess the quantitative impact of technical change on incomes. Quizon and Binswanger (1986b) used a general equilibrium model that includes these three effects. They computed a reference path of the real incomes of rural and urban income groups in India from 1960-61 to 1980-81 (table 7.2). Agricultural production grew rapidly during the beginning of the green revolution (1965-66 to 1970-71, even allowing for the very bad harvests in 1965-66) and again from

Table 7.2 Simulated indexes of income distribution and income sources, India, 1960-61 to 1980-81
(1970-71 = 100)

Endogenous variables	Agricultural year				
	1960-61	*1965-66*	*1973-74*	*1975-76*	*1980-81*
Total actual agricultural output	79.3	81.2	99.4	107.1	119.6
Actual prices = agricultural/ nonagricultural goods	89.8	97.2	97.7	91.6	76.3
Real residual farm profits	64.2	67.9	86.0	85.1	76.4
Agricultural employment	98.2	100.1	112.3	118.8	118.5
Real agricultural wage bill	91.2	95.3	101.4	104.9	105.4
Rural per capita income, by quartile					
First (poorest)	101.0	99.0	95.9	97.4	107.0
Second	96.9	95.8	94.6	94.8	99.9
Third	93.8	93.5	93.8	93.3	96.3
Fourth (richest)	88.5	88.6	92.4	90.7	88.8
Aggregate	92.9	92.4	93.6	92.9	94.9
Urban per capita income, by quartile					
First (poorest)	91.9	100.4	98.1	100.7	136.0
Second	90.9	102.8	99.3	102.6	141.9
Third	90.2	102.7	99.7	102.5	139.3
Fourth (richest)	87.6	102.3	99.8	102.2	133.5
Aggregate	89.4	102.3	99.4	102.2	136.7

Source: Quizon and Binswanger 1986b.

1973-74 onward. Agricultural terms of trade rose prior to the green revolution, stayed fairly constant until 1973-74, and then dropped substantially by 1980-81. Using the model, Quizon and Binswanger estimated that:

- Farm profits were seriously depressed between 1960-61 and 1965-66, but then moved dramatically upward by 1970-71 as a result of technical change and improved terms of trade during the first period of the green revolution (1965-66 to 1970-71). There were also substantial gains during the same period in rural income. The production gains were associated with rising prices, especially for wheat, because the government used the gains largely to build stocks and to replace imports. But once self-sufficiency in food production was assured, the surplus grain production had to be absorbed domestically. Therefore, the rapid gains in production during the late 1970s were not translated into further increases in income for producers, but transmitted to consumers through declining prices. (The model allows for the resulting higher real wage rates, increasing labor supply, and subsequent slight *decline* in nominal and real wage rates.) By 1973-74 farm profits had declined to 85 percent of their 1970-71 level, and by 1980-81 to 76 percent of the 1970-71 level.
- Employment in agriculture grew by about 20 percent during the period. Because real wages declined by about 5 percent, the total real wage bill for the period rose about 15 percent.
- In the late 1970s the combination of rapid nonagricultural growth and declining agricultural terms of trade greatly benefited urban groups.
- During the late 1970s the rural poor gained as well, because their gains as consumers outweighed their losses in producer and wage incomes. Despite a drastic shift in the distribution of rural income from wages to profits in the late 1960s, rural income distribution was remarkably stable for the period as a whole. The effect of adverse wage trends on the rural poor was alleviated in part by the increase in agricultural employment and by their gains from the growth in farm profits. They also had substantial gains in nonagricultural income.
- In the early 1980s large farmers, the fourth rural income quartile, had per capita incomes at about the same level as in the early 1960s, as their production and income gains of the late 1960s and early 1970s were lost to population growth and urban groups.
- None of the rural groups experienced losses in real per capita income as a result of the green revolution.

Treadmill effects on poor regions

Can technical change hurt the poor if it is adopted in only one region? Technical change is often confined to certain regions because of favorable environmental or economic conditions. For example, the green revolution has been confined largely to irrigated zones with good water control. These tend initially to be areas of higher average income, smaller annual fluctuations in income, and hence less poverty (Rao, Ray, and Subbarao 1988).

Partial equilibrium analysis of the distributional consequences of unequal regional access usually describes two regions supplying an inelastic demand in a national market. If region A increases supply because of technical change, prices will drop. Region B will lose because its production is no greater, input costs remain the same, but the selling price has fallen.

The gains in region A will be distributed among landowners and workers. In region B farmers will lose, and both wages and demand for labor will fall. The largest share of the losses will be borne by the factors in most inelastic supply— the immobile factors of production. Land prices will decline more than wage rates if some labor can migrate to the gaining region (and contain the rise in the wage rate there).

This partial equilibrium model ignores consumer gains, however—even in region B—and cannot quantitatively assess the effect of labor mobility. Moreover, it ignores the ability of farmers in region B to take up the production of crops that are displaced in region A by the technologically dynamic crops (Lipton with Longhurst 1989).

Quizon and Binswanger (1986a) extended the general equilibrium model for India discussed above to include regional effects and to allow for migration responses to regional differences in wages. Four regions supplying the same national market were analyzed. Two regions adopted the green revolution technology—and benefited massively; the other two were less able to adopt the technology because of either poor water control or lack of rain.

Quizon and Binswanger simulated the increases in rice yields in the two regions that adopted green revolution technology. Based on the results of their simulation, they estimated that large farmers in the regions that did not adopt technology lost as the price of rice fell and their farm costs and yields remained the same. But in the same regions, those in the poorest two quartiles of the rural income distribution gained at least as much from lower food prices as they lost in farm profits, ending up with an overall gain, or at least no net loss.

When they simulated increases in both wheat and rice yields, Quizon and Binswanger found that urban groups and net purchasers of food in rural areas benefited. Farm profits rose in the two technology-adopting regions, but fell in the other two regions. Despite this fall, the poor in those regions gained because of lower food prices.

Thus, scenarios can be modeled in which the poor can lose due to technological change. But the advantages of falling food prices often outweigh the disadvantages of falling farm profits. If treadmill effects arise, diversification to and commercialization of other crops is usually advocated. In addition, where export barriers still exist, price changes can be limited by eliminating or reducing export restrictions.

Worldwide treadmill effects

A region or country can partially or fully escape the treadmill effect by removing policy constraints on export markets or investing in infrastructure to reduce export costs, but worldwide demand constraints cannot be avoided. World prices for agricultural commodities have followed a declining secular trend associated with expanded production capacity, the main source of which has been technical change; world cereal prices have been falling by about 0.4 percent a year (with marked fluctuations) for four decades.

The principal way for a country to avoid losses imposed by more rapid cost reduction or technical change in other countries is to accelerate its own technical change beyond the rate of cost reduction elsewhere. If it does not do so, its resulting loss of cost-competitiveness leads to increased pressure on its balance of payments and faster depreciation (or slower appreciation) of its exchange rate. This mechanism implies that the income losses associated with loss of competitiveness do not fall only on the producers of the commodity but will be widely shared among consumers of tradable commodities.

If worldwide technical change occurs rapidly in the production of commodities consumed widely by the poor in the developing world—such as rice, wheat, and maize—poor consumers would benefit from the resulting decline in real prices. But they would not benefit if the country in which they live reacts to a loss of competitive advantage by increasing the protection of domestically produced staples, as low-income countries often do.[5]

Not available to the poor, or available to only a very limited extent, is the consumer benefit arising from technical change in the production of such commodities as tropical beverages, whose final demand is inelastic and whose consumption benefits are concentrated in the industrial world. Developing country producers impose losses on each other by expanding production. International commodity agreements—such as the international coffee agreement—have been mostly unsuccessful in controlling output.

Where competitive advantage in a crop is reduced, substitution or diversification of crops provides an avenue for avoiding some of the losses. The extent to which this option is available depends on agroclimatic conditions, the costs of diversification (high if beverage crops or other tree crops are involved), and the quality of infrastructure for production, marketing, and trade in the alternative commodities.

Commercialization of nonfoods driving up local food prices

Technological change can have adverse effects on revenues in regions that do not adopt the technology, as we showed in the second scenario above. The adoption of a cash crop can raise food prices both in regions that adopt the crop and in those that do not. In a region in which staple food crops for local consumption are displaced by nonfood cash crops, net food exports of the region may decline, or the region may even switch from being a net exporter to being a net importer. The resulting increases in prices, as the region moves from free on board (f.o.b.) to cost, insurance, and freight (c.i.f.) payments, will be larger, the more deficient the transport infrastructure is. If income gains resulting from the switch do not accrue to the local poor, they may lose to the extent that they are net purchasers of food, as most of the poor are, even in rural Africa. Price effects for other regions depend on market infrastructure, and possibly on the trade policy response.

With free trade, imports of food can substitute for domestic production. Thus, food prices will not rise beyond the c.i.f. price plus internal distribution costs. But if trade in an export crop is controlled and foreign exchange is channeled through a system of government controls, the allocation of foreign exchange for food imports may be constrained, resulting in higher food prices and consequent adverse effects on the poor.

In Benin, von Oppen (1989) shows, expanded cotton production in the north reduced food crop exports from the north to the south. Under such circumstances, effective household demand, and appropriate government response, are required to translate part of the increased export earnings from cotton into food imports, and thus to prevent a decline in the food available to households and to the country as a whole. There are no case studies that evaluate how policy has actually responded in such situations. Therefore, this scenario, although potentially relevant, remains hypothetical.

Late adoption

The speed at which tenants and small farmers—who form a large share of the poor in many countries—adopt new technologies has been studied intensively since the green revolution. An early review of the literature on the adoption of high-yielding seed varieties suggested that neither farm size nor farm tenure has been a serious constraint on the adoption of new high-yielding grain varieties (Ruttan and Binswanger 1978). Although rates of adoption were found to differ by farm size and tenure, the available data implied that, within a few years of introduction, such differences usually disappeared. Of course, those that did not adopt high-yielding varieties have forgone gains that could have resulted from early adoption and may have already suffered as a consequence. These conclusions have not been altered by more recent research.

Unlike the cost of seeds, the cost of fertilizers, herbicides, and other yield-increasing inputs can be a serious impediment to their adoption by small farmers. Typically, small farmers use less of these inputs per unit of labor than do large farmers. Small farmers may or may not use less of these inputs per unit of land, however, depending on the steepness of the inverse farm size-productivity relationship.

The effect on the poor of adopting such inputs depends not only on factor ratios, however, but also on the overall efficiency of use, and the relative speed of production growth, for different farm sizes. A survey by Berry and Cline (1979) shows that small farmers use inputs at least as efficiently as large farmers do. Econometric evidence from the Indian Punjab (Sidhu 1972) indicates that new wheat technology was not strongly biased in either a labor-saving or a capital-saving direction. Small and large farmers achieved approximately equal gains in efficiency. Data from the Pakistan Punjab and the Philippines indicate that, although small farmers face more constraints in obtaining irrigation and credit than do large farmers, the constraints are not large enough to cause any significant differences in yields between the two groups (Ruttan and Binswanger 1978: 388).

The pattern of later adoption by smallholders of cash crops and new market channels is similar to that for new production technology and staple foods. Among the smallholders in Guatemala who adopted the new production technology for export vegetables, the larger farms (more than 1.5 hectares) are disproportionately represented among the early adopters, and the smallest trail behind. Similarly, in Kenya and the Philippines significantly fewer smallholders moved into sugarcane production, compared with larger farmers (Kennedy and Cogill 1988; and Bouis and Haddad 1990).

Trailing behind in the adoption process is not necessarily a problem for efficient resource allocation and income security for the poor. And it permits small farmers to avoid the risks of early adoption. A problem arises, however, when waiting too long to adopt new opportunities results in being shut out when market channels have organizational or capacity-related bottlenecks. The capacity of an established sugar mill, for instance, may be filled rapidly by the (bigger) early adopters. The export vegetable cooperative in Guatemala has effectively stopped enrolling new members because of concerns about bottlenecks in handling and cold storage capacities.

The instruments usually advocated for speeding adoption by small farmers are extension and credit. There may be scope for targeting extension and credit policies, but much would already be achieved if they did not discriminate against the poor, as they frequently do, enhancing the adverse effects of scale economies in technology utilization.

Committed expenses

Committing capital to perennial crops or other long-term investment—such as dairy cattle or housing—reduces one's capacity to adjust to technological breakdown, price risk, or market disruption. When returns to capital do not materialize, the fixed capital resources cannot be switched to new productive tasks. For the poor these risks weigh more heavily than they do for better-off producers. Examples are investments in tea bushes or coffee trees. Investment in irrigation infrastructure is also sometimes crop-specific. But empirical evidence shows that the poor do not specialize completely. Smallholders in Guatemala, for instance, maintained about half of their cropland for staples. Similar behavior was found among smallholder sugarcane-producing households in Kenya.

Related to the committed expenses trap is the case in which a project introducing technological change and commercialization attracts households to a new project area, and then collapses. The collapse of a rice irrigation project in the Gambia, for example, led to disinvestment in housing and community services, and even to increased divorce rates (Webb 1989).

Gender issues

New production technology in agriculture and new market opportunities can have profound implications for the control of resources and the division of labor in rural households. Evaluations of the effects of technology and commercialization for households on an aggregate basis fail to capture possible differences in those effects among household members and between genders. Both the burdens and the benefits of technological change and commercialization need to be assessed at the household level to judge differences in how they affect males and females; a focus both on gender issues and on child welfare is important in such assessments (Leslie and Paolisso 1989). For poor women the effects will be more complex and dramatic, as they tend to face a sharper division by gender of labor and labor markets, and a greater separation of control between female-managed and male-managed farm resources, than do wealthier, educated, or peri-urban women.

A comparative analysis of commercialization in five cases studies in the Gambia, Guatemala, Kenya, the Philippines, and Rwanda showed that women had a much reduced role in the new technologies or commercialized crops, even if they had been important decisionmakers in the farm production program before the change (von Braun, Kennedy, and Bouis 1989). Two examples highlight conflicts and tradeoffs. These argue, contrary to the new conventional wisdom, that there is considerable income pooling within the household, so that women gain, though proportionately less than men, when "male-managed" sources of income expand.

First, in the Gambia it was found that women's access to new rice irrigation technology was hampered by their limited access to hired labor. Their work burden increased relative to that of men. Technological change resulted in increased household income, despite women's relative—and in some subgroups, absolute—loss of personal income (von Braun, Puetz, and Webb 1989). The increased household income led to increased calorie consumption and smaller seasonal weight fluctuations for women.

Second, in the Guatemalan export vegetable cooperative, households' food consumption—including women's—improved despite the men's predominant control of incremental income. But the growth in employment led to seasonal increases in the use of child labor, to such an extent that local communities became concerned about school attendance and changed the school and vacation schedules. It was the income effects of the commercialization, however, that had permitted communities to invest in schooling and in improving child welfare under a cooperative system (von Braun, Hotchkiss, and Immink 1989).

Eviction of tenants and effects for land markets

The profitability of new crops or of crops grown with improved technology may increase the incentive to evict tenants and induce a shift to owner operation of farms. An example of this—fostered by an administrative ruling—is found in a Philippine study area in which contracts for growing sugarcane were given not to tenants but only to landowners. The ruling led to an increase in landlessness and the deterioration of tenancy status in the area around the sugar mill (Bouis and Haddad 1990).

In Pakistan the green revolution made farming more profitable. This was followed by an increase in cultivation by landowners and in farm size, and a sharp decline in tenant cultivation. Between the 1960 and the 1980 censuses, the number of tenant farmers declined from 2.0 million to 1.1 million, and the area they farmed from 19 million acres to 10 million acres. This shift toward cultivation by landowners and away from cultivation by tenant farmers may have been triggered in part by a possible failure of land rents to adjust immediately to higher profits.

Two other factors accelerated the decline of tenant farming in Pakistan. First, generous subsidies for mechanization increased purchases of tractors and other technology.[6] The increase in tractors made large farms less dependent on bullock drivers and tenants. The largest decrease in tenant labor hours is reported by McInerney and Donaldson (1975) in a before-and-after study of tractorization. The World Bank financed loans for the purchase of large tractors at substantial subsidies to farmers. Land ceilings or tenancy laws in Pakistan did not exist or were ineffective, and the 202 farms surveyed grew, on average, from 18.2 to 44 hectares. The farms acquired the additional land through reduction in land rented out (32.3 percent), increased renting (28.6 percent), reclamation and improvement (26.2 percent), and purchases (13 percent). For each tractor acquired, an average 4.5 tenants were displaced.

Second, as the result of changes in 1959 and 1972, land tenancy laws became increasingly adverse to landowners (Nabi, Hamid, and Zahid 1986), and it became riskier and less profitable for landowners to rent out their land. The decline in tenancy in Pakistan resulted from a combination of technology-related factors and bad policy. It is difficult to tell how much each contributed to that decline, however.

It is easier in two examples of tenant eviction in Africa to pinpoint a single cause. In the first example, in the Sudan, extensive eviction of land users was a direct effect of the promotion of large-scale mechanized sorghum production (Elhassan 1988). A policy decision was made to allocate large areas of land to farmers prepared to invest in mechanized farming. A rural population newly dependent on wages emerged in an environment of declining employment, with little opportunity to provide for household or community food security. This seems to have most adversely affected the poorest: child malnutrition rates in the areas affected by the evictions were found to be significantly higher than those in the traditional rainfed sector (Sudan 1988). This case of eviction *before* new technology was adopted could be considered a case of bad policy.

In the second example, in Ethiopia, tenants were evicted *after* new technology was adopted. The Chilalo Agricultural Development Unit (CADU) project, launched in the late 1960s in Chilalo, Ethiopia, to promote improved agricultural inputs and integrated markets, led to almost complete eviction of tenants in project areas once the new technology was disseminated to large producers and landowners (Cohen 1975). Tenants had not been provided access to technology, and tenancy rights had not been protected in these areas. The CADU project thus represents a case in which good supplementary policies were lacking.

Coerced production or forced procurement

One of the worst outcomes of commercialization is associated with coerced production. An example of this is an attempt by government, or powerful monopsonistic procurement partners in contractual arrangements, to shift losses resulting from an ill-designed scheme for commercialization to farm producers. Another example is an attempt by the monopsonistic procurement agent to capture excessive profits. As the poor usually have little political power, they may be particularly vulnerable to such perverse policy.

A case of coerced production evolved in an unsuccessful tea scheme in northwest Rwanda (there are several successful schemes in the country). Smallholders were talked into converting to tea production, which did not turn out to be profitable for them. Supply was therefore not forthcoming, and established processing capacities were underutilized. To increase capacity utilization, the parastatal tea factory then expanded its tea plantation by expropriating small farmers near the factory (von Braun, de Haen, and Blanken 1991).

Area allotment schemes with procurement regulations that lead to coerced production are widespread. Examples include cotton and rice in Egypt, cereals in parts of China, and persistent localized insistence on *cultures imposées* in Zaire.

The opposite of enforced production is exclusion from production opportunities. During the colonial period, bans on cash crop production by local small farmers were widespread. Export crops were reserved for settler farmers in Kenya, Tanzania, and other East African colonies. Even where cultivation of cash crops was not explicitly prohibited, extension, credit, and marketing services were not available to the native smallholder. In Zimbabwe, for example, these services were confined to the large-scale (white) sector. Independence swept away most of these constraints, opening up the opportunities to all farmers and resulting in big increases in smallholder maize production and marketing. But the vestiges of constraints on smallholder participation in commercial crops remain, as new regulations are passed by indigenous elites. For example, in Malawi burley tobacco production is reserved for the estate sector; small farmers can participate in the lucrative tobacco economy only under contractual arrangements with estate owners (Lele, van de Walle, and Gbetibouo 1990). The consequences of this for the poor are discussed by Sahn and Arulpragasam in chapter 13 in this volume.

Targeting technological change and commercialization

An optimistic view of the effects of technology and commercialization for the poor, or the conclusion that most adverse effects are due to bad policy and can thus be rectified by appropriate policy, leads to the "social engineering" concept: technology and commercialization as tools for targeted poverty alleviation. Before we review the potentials and limitations of specific targeting criteria, three basic problems of social engineering need to be emphasized.

First, research to develop poverty-targeted technology may have opportunity costs. Targeting introduces constraints into purely growth-oriented R&D investments, which may result in forgone growth. The hypothetical tradeoff, then, is between untargeted, but possibly higher, agricultural growth—which may offer more for poverty alleviation—and poverty-targeted technology development and dissemination.

Second, poverty-targeted technology and market development cannot be assessed in isolation. Alternative instruments for targeted poverty alleviation may (or may not) exist for specific economic and ecological environments and poverty structures. (Alternative instruments are discussed in other chapters in this volume.) But comparing instruments is not always easy. The specific nature of poverty, agroclimatic conditions, and institutional conditions determine whether technology and commercialization are ranked high among instruments for poverty alleviation.

Third, no country—especially one that is poor and small—can determine its own technologies entirely. World demand for research comes mainly from rich countries, and technologies that increase employment are seldom a high priority for them. Some of the implications are briefly discussed in the introduction to this volume.

In discussing six alternative targeting criteria below, we deal with only a subset of the first two of these three issues.

Targeting by agroclimatic potential

Green revolution technology reduced poverty in the favorably endowed regions in which it could be adopted (Hossain 1988b), and commercialization did the same in areas with known or hidden potential. It is therefore tempting to direct research or other programs that accelerate technological change and commercialization toward agroclimatically poor regions in order to reach the poor. The developing countries and the donor community have made research and project efforts to replicate the green revolution's success in low-potential areas, such as the Sahel, the semiarid zones in India, and the humid tropics of Africa. The complex environmental constraints in these zones cannot be easily overcome, however, and the efforts have not yet achieved widespread results. Yet there have been noteworthy successes in sorghum, ragi, and, perhaps, millet breeding in India and in hybrid maize in East Africa. In high-potential areas, research for wheat and rice could build on a long history of research for technological change. The costs of adaptive research, per unit of value added achieved, still tend to be lower in high-potential ecologies with a high degree of water control. It is possible that regional-level research has not yet reached sufficient scale, and that the research is still too immature to tap the (hidden) potentials of low-potential areas.

Targeting foods consumed by the poor

The poor consume many staple foods that are considered inferior. Research targeting roots, tubers, and coarse grains is one possible avenue for exploiting the treadmill effect in favor of poor consumers. Compared with research on wheat and rice, the history of research on these crops is rather short, and the jury is still out on whether the approach is effective. Moreover, such targeting may become less powerful, even if it were successful. Increasingly, evidence suggests that low-income households are shifting into new staple foods—not mainly in response to advertising or subsidies, but because the preparation of such foods requires less time, and thus frees up more for income-earning purposes. One example is the increasing rice consumption among the urban and rural poor in West Africa (Delgado 1989); another is the increased wheat consumption of low-income households in Sri Lanka (Senauer, Sahn, and Alderman 1986). The cost of women's time appears to be a key factor in these changes.

A large percentage of the poor still consume a lot of what they produce, however. When technical change occurs for crops produced and consumed by the same households, the treadmill effect is largely irrelevant, as is the potential conflict between net buyers and sellers. Greater and more stable yields of subsistence crops promise to mitigate both the chronic and the transitory food insecurity of the subsistence household. Increased population pressure rapidly raises demand for yield-increasing technology in subsistence crops, especially where food and labor markets are risky. For instance, in Rwanda sweet potato production rises rapidly when man-land ratios increase (von Braun, de Haen, and Blanken 1991). The drought sequence of the 1980s in many parts of the Sahel led to a rapid shift from sorghum into early millet, which has lower mean yields but higher resistance to drought, to counter transitory food insecurity. Efforts by the Consultative Group on International Agricultural Research (CGIAR) and national research systems to raise the productivity of sweet potatoes and to improve the drought resistance of coarse grains remain important.

Targeting nutrients and diet components

Two types of effort have been pursued in the domain of targeting nutrients and other components of diet: nutritional targeting by plant breeding and nutritional targeting in rural development. Based on the conventional wisdom of the nature of malnutrition in the 1960s and 1970s, many efforts were made to increase cereals' content of protein and of certain amino acids, such as lysine. The International Agricultural Research Centers (IARCs) and many national programs took part in these efforts. By the early 1980s most of these breeding activities with explicit nutrient goals had been abandoned. The nutritional traits had low heritability, and there were tradeoffs between these traits and other attributes, such as higher yield and resistance to disease and pests.[7] Nutritionists shifted emphasis from the protein gap to energy deficiency, not least because they came to see the nutritional characteristics of commodities in the context of the total diet of the poor. The diversity of their diet has frequently been underestimated; the diets of very few of the undernourished poor would be protein-deficient if their calorie consumption were increased to adequate levels, even by traditional, unenriched cereals alone.

Plant breeding by IARCs now focuses mainly on minimum standards of nutrient content and on consumption and processing characteristics (palatability, preparation requirements, storage characteristics). Meeting the poor's specific resource constraints (including time, cooking fuel, absorbability by young children) may be more important than a commodity's nutrient content, and may offer some scope for targeting (Lipton with Longhurst 1989: ch. 5).

An example of nutritional targeting in rural development is dairy development schemes. It has been claimed that these schemes contribute directly to
improving the nutrition of dairy producers by making more milk available for
home consumption. In most instances, however, the effects on consumption and
nutrition are more indirect. Poor dairy smallholders sell expensive calories (milk)
and increase their net purchases of cheap calories, thereby improving food consumption (Alderman, Mergos, and Slade 1987). Thus, the favorable effects on
nutrition arise from the commercialization-income link, rather than directly from
the technology-production effect. This distinction is not merely academic. It
implies a need to facilitate poor milk producers' access to market outlets, not just
to better technology, if they are to enjoy substantial nutritional benefits.

Speeding adoption

We have noted that poorer people's tendency to adopt both technology and
market opportunities later is an inherent problem of change in agriculture. The
implications for poor people's prospects of capturing income opportunities are
clear. Treadmill effects tend to lower prices, and late adopters forgo the early
rent of technology and commercialization.[8] And with commercialization, late
adopters may miss opportunities because of closing-door effects in procurement
and processing lines. This suggests a need for policy that would help speed
adoption by the poor.

Extension and credit, usually advocated as instruments for overcoming the
disadvantages of smallholders and the poor, have been mentioned before. Another key instrument is the marketing cooperative. Early cooperative marketing
arrangements can be powerful and sustainable tools for targeting market opportunities to the poor. The Guatemalan export vegetable cooperative and the Indian
dairy cooperative system are good examples.

Targeting poor producers

Targeting the poor frequently means targeting farm households with high labor-
land ratios and low capital-labor ratios. Such households are more subject to
credit constraints than large farmers. It follows that poor farmers would more
easily adopt technologies that do not require high capital-input ratios. They
would more readily adopt disease-resistant varieties, for example, than pesticides to combat the diseases. Emphasis in breeding on resistance to and tolerance
for pests, diseases, and moisture stress would therefore be especially beneficial
to poor farmers.

Much attention has been given to the issue of whether green revolution
varieties are superior to traditional varieties at low doses of fertilizer or only at
high doses. If they require high doses of fertilizer, it would be more difficult for
poor farmers to adopt them. Most results of experiment station research in which
the environment is held constant suggest that high-yielding varieties yield more
than traditional varieties at both high and low doses of fertilizer. Moreover,
rental markets, credit markets, and tied contracts allow the poor to rent out labor

and obtain cash for fixed and working capital.[9] If a small tenant farmer can get the landlord to pay for fertilizer, he may still adopt the optimal dose. Resource allocation will be efficient, although the landlord can usually extract some of the benefit of the fertilizer from the tenant by choosing the terms of the rental contract accordingly. This produces efficiency gains, just as if the technology had been neutral (or even targeted to the small, labor-intensive farmers), but it does not, of course, solve the equity issue.

Even where the poor specialize in an enterprise, targeting that enterprise in technology development may not benefit them if richer farmers respond to the enhanced profitability by moving into the enterprise. Jodha's (1985) intensive surveys of Rajasthan villages illustrate the problem. Raising sheep and goats had been a traditional occupation of the local, seminomadic tribal group in Rajasthan. But following the land reform in Rajasthan in 1952, the profitability of raising sheep and goats increased sharply because households no longer had to pay land revenue to feudal landowners or fees for the use of common property resources. Prices developed favorably, too. As a result, Jodha (1985) found, by 1963-64 many high-caste households in his study villages were engaged in sheep and goat production; in 1955 no higher-caste households had invested in these enterprises. Researchers who thought in 1950 that research on sheep and goats would have benefited only the poorer households in the community would have been disappointed.

Targeting by gender

Because of the disadvantages that women face in many rural areas of the developing world, development organizations and research institutes have given increased attention to targeting technology and the benefits of commercialization to women.

Experience with an irrigated rice development program specifically targeted toward women, who are the traditional rice growers in the Gambia, underlines the difficulties of this strategy. The program promoted rice in the belief that better technology for this crop would directly benefit poor women. The outcome was different than expected, however, because men responded to the increased profits available from growing rice. A strong inverse relationship between the level of technology and women's control over the newly improved crop resulted (table 7.3). The reason was that the technology changed the very nature of the cropping arrangements and induced or required a large shift in men's labor from communal agriculture into the newly developed rice perimeters to overcome labor bottlenecks. Constraints in the credit program and the inability of women to hire more labor also contributed to the results (von Braun, Puetz, and Webb 1989). This example does not make a case in principle against targeting by gender, but it does suggest that the full range of constraints under which women operate, and the interplay of the new, targeted technology with these constraints, need to be understood when such targeting is attempted.

It is also worthwhile to consider ex ante implications of untargeted new technology for poor women in rural areas. In semiarid India almost all hand

Table 7.3 Rice technologies and women farmers in the Gambia, wet season, 1985

	Project pump-irrigated rice	*Project-improved rainfed rice*	*Traditional rice*
Fields under women's control (percent)	10.0	77.0	91.0
Yields per hectare (wet season, in tons)	5.9	2.5	1.3
Input cost per hectare[a] (US$)[b]	294.0	154.0	20.0
Labor input by women (percentage of unpaid family labor)	29.0	60.0	77.0

a. Variable input cost (seed, fertilizer, irrigation, hired labor, transportation, mechanized land preparation).
b. Converted at parallel exchange rate (US$1 = 6 dalasi).
Source: Survey by the International Food Policy Research Institute, Washington, D.C., and Programming, Planning, and Monitoring Unit, the Gambia, 1985-86.

weeding is done by hired women, and earnings from hand weeding comprise significant shares of women's wage income. Thus, any reduction in this task made possible by herbicides would primarily reduce work and income opportunities for the most disfavored labor group—female agricultural laborers. The development of technology that would make herbicide use more cost-effective would certainly have adverse effects on female laborers (Binswanger and Shetty 1977).

Concluding remarks

How then do the optimistic and the pessimistic viewpoints fare? Even with well-functioning factor and product markets, it is easy to construct scenarios in which poor producers lose from technical change. Most of these scenarios depend on highly inelastic demand. Commercialization, on the other hand, is usually induced when demand is elastic. Often commercialization and specialization in new commodities are used to circumvent the problem of inelastic demand for traditional commodities; therefore, it is not easy to construct adverse scenarios of commercialization without explicitly introducing institutional, policy, or market failure.

Discussed in an earlier section of the chapter were scenarios in which the poor might lose. Such scenarios most often have adverse effects for the poor when several of them coincide. Moreover, most of the adverse effects arise from bad policy alongside—rather than inherent features of—technological change or commercialization.

- The agricultural treadmill effect has an important regional and international dimension. In considering its adverse impact on small nonadopters, however, we should bear in mind how treadmill effects can benefit consumers. Most of the poor are net purchasers of food. Once one includes that fact or moves to even broader general equilibrium models, the treadmill effects are usually diffused. The favorable consumer benefits for the poor, however, do not arise with commodities—such as coffee—that are largely consumed in the industrial countries; and these benefits are smaller for products with highly income-elastic demand, such as most meats, dairy products, fruits, and vegetables.

- When late adoption of new technology occurs in conjunction with treadmill effects, adverse consequences for the profits of poor farmers are likely.
- The issue of closing doors in marketing and processing argues for policies that facilitate capacity expansion in marketing and processing, and for credit and extension facilities, which often are needlessly biased against the poor, that make rapid adoption of commercialization possible.

These inherent problems of technological change and commercialization can be either worsened or mitigated by policy. Adverse tenancy policies, constraints in trade, or coercion in production may prevent the realization of favorable potentials. The wrong conclusion would be to slow technological change and commercialization because of the related risks (Nerlove 1988). The appropriate conclusion is to face up to potential problems in specific settings for the poor, and to implement appropriate mitigating or safeguarding policies.

This conclusion assumes that the policy and institutional response can be exogenous and independent of the technology or the expanded commercialization. In some cases, however, institutional changes and policy responses are not exogenous but reflect existing conflict among social groups. The perverse responses then are logical outcomes of these conflicts and cannot be altered by benevolent policy advice. The evictions of tenants discussed above fall partly into this category. This type of endogeneity of institutional and policy responses leads to much more pessimistic conclusions about the benefits of technology and commercialization for poor, politically weak groups. An important empirical issue for further research, therefore, is how endogenous these responses are (de Janvry and Sadoulet 1988).

In considering the case studies discussed in this chapter, we find little foundation for the pessimistic view, or for the excessively optimistic view—that it is feasible to target technological progress and commercialization for poverty alleviation. We are thus back to the view that technological change and commercialization do expand opportunities, with large general benefits whose very complex distributional implications are hard to predict precisely. Targeting is difficult not only because distributional implications are hard to predict, but also because technological tradeoffs or agroclimatic constraints limit the potential success of the technologies or commercialization strategies attempted.

Limited opportunities for targeting do, of course, exist, and they should be seized wherever possible. But at least as important is the elimination of policies and interventions that alone, or in combination with technical change and commercialization, harm the poor, and that may needlessly bias the availability of productive support services against them.

Notes

1. *Poor* refers to the absolute poor—households and individuals unable to achieve income levels high enough to provide sufficient food and meet other basic needs.

2. For a comprehensive review of this literature related to technological change in cereals, see Lipton with Longhurst (1989); and on the critique of literature on the adverse effects of commercialization of subsistence agriculture, see von Braun and Kennedy (1986).

3. Increased output per hectare contributed 70 percent of the increase in production of major food crops in developing countries in the 1960s. Its contribution rose to 80 percent in the 1970s and further increased in the 1980s (Paulino 1986).

4. For a comprehensive analysis of the issue that finds no adverse effects for nutrition from sugarcane growing, see Kennedy and Cogill (1987).

5. The poor may also fail to benefit if the country is a net exporter of the food staple, so that a real exchange rate depreciation (harmful to poor people producing tradables) results from the international price declines.

6. Certain forms of mechanization, especially when heavily subsidized, have a detrimental impact on the poor's labor income. The effects of mechanical technology are not considered in this chapter. For a review, see World Bank (1987).

7. For a review of the experience, see Pinstrup-Andersen, Berg, and Foreman (1984); for other proposals, see Lipton with Longhurst (1989).

8. If a policy were adopted that enabled the poor to speed up their adoption, the poor would also carry the greater risk associated with early adoption. It is these greater risks that the innovators' rents reward.

9. Thus, even if endowment ratios differ strongly among farmers' groups, factor use ratios are often much closer (Ryan and Rathore 1980).

Farm-Nonfarm Growth Linkages and the Welfare of the Poor

8

Peter Hazell
Steven Haggblade

The welfare of the poor in most developing countries is linked closely to agriculture. Most of the poor live in rural areas, and they depend on agriculture for their incomes—directly, in the case of farmers and agricultural workers, or indirectly, in the case of self-employed persons and workers engaged in trade, services, agro-processing, and other nonfarm activities that cater largely to rural demands.

Several studies have shown that technology-driven agricultural growth can contribute significantly to growth in national income (Adelman 1984; Rangarajan 1982; Cavallo and Mundlak 1982; and Byerlee 1973). A large, if more contentious, body of literature discusses the poverty-reducing effect of technological change (Pinstrup-Andersen and Hazell 1985; Lipton with Longhurst 1989; and Hazell and Ramasamy 1991).

Nonfarm linkages generated by technical change in agriculture can enhance both growth and its poverty-reducing effect. A growing agricultural sector demands nonfarm production inputs, and supplies raw materials to transport, processing, and marketing firms. Likewise, increases in farm income lead to greater demand for consumer goods and services. Besides stimulating national economic growth, these production and consumption linkages affect poverty and spatial growth patterns, particularly when agricultural growth is concentrated on small and medium-size farms (Johnston and Kilby 1975; Mellor 1976; and Mellor and Johnston 1984). Because much of the resulting growth in nonfarm activity occurs in rural areas and small towns, it can help contain rural-to-urban migration. Moreover, the kinds of nonfarm goods and services demanded by small and medium-size farms are often those produced by small, labor-intensive enterprises, whose growth can contribute to increased employment and income-earning opportunities for the poor. For these reasons, any book on poverty issues would be incomplete without adequate consideration of the indirect, or downstream, benefits of agricultural growth.

Importance of the rural nonfarm economy

Nonfarm activity occupies an important place in rural economies throughout the developing world, particularly in Asia and Latin America. Nonfarm enterprises account for only 14 percent of full-time employment in rural Africa, but for 26 percent in Asia and 28 percent in Latin America (table 8.1). When rural towns are included, shares of nonfarm employment increase appreciably, rising to 19 percent in Africa, 36 percent in Asia, and 47 percent in Latin America. The employment densities in table 8.1 confirm the weaker pattern of nonfarm employment in rural Africa.

Income shares—which, unlike employment data, include earnings from part-time and seasonal activity—underscore the importance of rural nonfarm activity. They show nonfarm earnings contributing 25 to 30 percent of income in rural Africa and 30 to 40 percent in Asia and Latin America, and sometimes more when rural towns are included (Chuta and Liedholm 1979; Phongpaichit 1982; Islam 1984; Haggblade, Hazell, and Brown 1989; and Luzuriaga and Zuvekas 1983).

The rural nonfarm economy is especially important to the rural poor. Landless and near-landless households everywhere depend on nonfarm earnings; those with less than 0.5 hectare typically earn more than one-third of their income from nonfarm sources (table 8.2). Low-investment manufacturing and services—

Table 8.1 Share of the rural labor force employed primarily in nonfarm activities, Africa, Asia, and Latin America, various years

Type of locality	Africa	Asia	Latin America
	(percent)		
Rural settlements[a]	14	26	28
Rural towns[b]	59	81	85
Rural settlements plus rural towns			
Total	19	36	47
Male[c]	16	37	36
Female[d]	19	34	79
	(employment density per 1,000 population)		
Rural settlements[a]	50	83	79
Rural towns[b]	187	238	245
Rural settlements plus rural towns			
Total	65	121	129
Male[c]	35	90	87
Female[d]	30	31	42

Note: Includes all nonagricultural activity except mining—that is, International Standard Industrial Classification activities 3-9.

a. Rural settlements vary in size with individual countries' census definitions. Generally, rural settlements in Africa and Asia are those with populations less than 5,000. In Latin America, the cutoff is normally 2,000 or 2,500.

b. Rural towns do not exceed 250,000 in population.

c. Male nonfarm employment divided, for percentages, by total male employment; for densities, by total population.

d. Female nonfarm employment divided, for percentages, by total female employment; for densities, by total population.

Source: Population censuses for forty-three countries (fourteen in Africa, fourteen in Asia, and fifteen in Latin America); they include all those for which employment data could be broken out by locality, size of settlement, and sex. The censuses were conducted in various years during the 1960s, the 1970s, and the 1980s.

including weaving, pottery, gathering, food preparation and processing, domestic and personal services, and unskilled nonfarm wage labor—typically account for a greater share of income for the rural poor than for the wealthy.[1] The reverse is true of transport, commerce, and such manufacturing activities as milling and metal fabrication, which require sizable investments. Women, relatively more active than males in nonfarm activities in Africa and Latin America (table 8.1),

Table 8.2 Share of nonfarm income in total household income, by size of landholding, selected developing countries, various years

Country or region/year	*Size of holding (hectares)*	*Nonfarm income as a share of total household income*[a] *(percent)*
Korea, Republic of (1986)	0-0.5	73
	0.5-1.0	49
	1.0-1.5	35
	1.5-2.0	26
	2.0+	19
Taiwan (China) (1979)	0-0.5	67
	0.5-1.0	58
	1.0-1.5	48
	1.5-2.0	40
	2.0+	33
Ecuador (1974)	0-1.0	40
	1.0-2.0	22
	2.0-10.0	14
	10.0-100.0	10
	100+	9
India (1970-71)	landless	62
	0-1.0	34
	1.0-4.5	21
	4.5-10.5	11
	10.5+	3
North Arcot, India (1982-83)	0-0.1	35
	0.1-1.0	23
	1.0+	20
Northern Nigeria (1974)	0-0.99	55
	1.0-1.99	29
	2.0-2.99	24
	3.0-3.99	14
	4.0-4.99	17
	5.0+	26

a. Nonfarm income was estimated by deducting agricultural wage income (1.8 percent of total earnings) from reported "off-farm" income.
Source: Korea: Korea 1987; Taiwan (China): Ho 1986; Ecuador: Luzuriaga and Zuvekas 1983; India: National Council of Applied Economic Research 1975; North Arcot, India: Hazell and Ramasamy 1991; and Nigeria: Matlon and others 1979.

dominate many of the equity-enhancing subsectors, such as weaving, gathering, food processing, personal services, beverage preparation, and selling of prepared snack foods (Haggblade, Hazell, and Brown 1989).

Factors affecting change in the rural nonfarm economy

The density and composition of rural nonfarm activity vary considerably across continents (table 8.1), across countries, and even within nations. But the overwhelming importance of commerce and service activities is clear, in both rural villages and rural towns (Haggblade, Hazell, and Brown 1989; and Hazell and Haggblade 1991). Manufacturing typically accounts for one-third or less of total nonfarm employment, with household manufacturing more important in the villages and nonhousehold manufacturing more important in the rural towns.

Why does nonfarm activity vary over time and across regions? Certainly resource endowments, location, ethnicity, historical happenstance, and government policy all play a role. Yet agriculture, because of its size, must be added to the list of key suspects.

Agriculture can influence nonfarm activity in at least three ways: through production, through consumption, and through labor market linkages. On the production side, a growing agricultural sector requires inputs—of fertilizer, seeds, herbicides, pumps, sprayers, equipment, and repair services—either produced or distributed by nonfarm enterprises. Moreover, increased agricultural output stimulates forward production linkages by providing raw materials that require milling, processing, and distribution by nonfarm firms. Consumption linkages arise when growing farm incomes boost demand for basic consumer goods; these linkages typically increase over time as rising per capita income induces diversification of consumption spending into products other than food. Much of the overall increase in demand—for inputs, services, distribution, and many basic consumer goods—can be met by firms in rural areas and rural towns. But the heavy production inputs and consumer durables are more likely to be produced in large cities or abroad.

Although production and consumption linkages attracted most of the initial interest in research on agricultural growth linkages (Mellor and Lele 1973; and Johnston and Kilby 1975), more recent investigations highlight a third important link: the labor market interactions. A growing agricultural sector can raise agricultural wages, and these in turn raise the opportunity cost of labor in nonfarm activities. This induces a shift in the composition of nonfarm activity out of very labor-intensive, low-return activities and into more skilled, higher-investment, high-return activities (Hossain 1988b; and Ahmed and Hossain 1990). Thus, rising agricultural productivity may be instrumental in inducing a structural transformation of the rural nonfarm economy.

Effects of agricultural growth on the rural nonfarm economy

A small but growing array of empirical work has begun exploring the relation between changes in agriculture and changes in the rural nonfarm economy. The cross-country data in figure 8.1 depict a strong positive correlation between agricultural income and the share of the nonfarm economy in rural employment. Charting the increasing importance of rural nonfarm activity as one moves from Africa to Asia to Latin America, figure 8.1 also documents the close connection between nonfarm activity and the development of rural towns. As the contrast between panels A and B reveals, a much stronger nonfarm spinoff from agricul-

Figure 8.1 Rural nonfarm employment as a function of agricultural income, Africa, Asia, and Latin America, various years

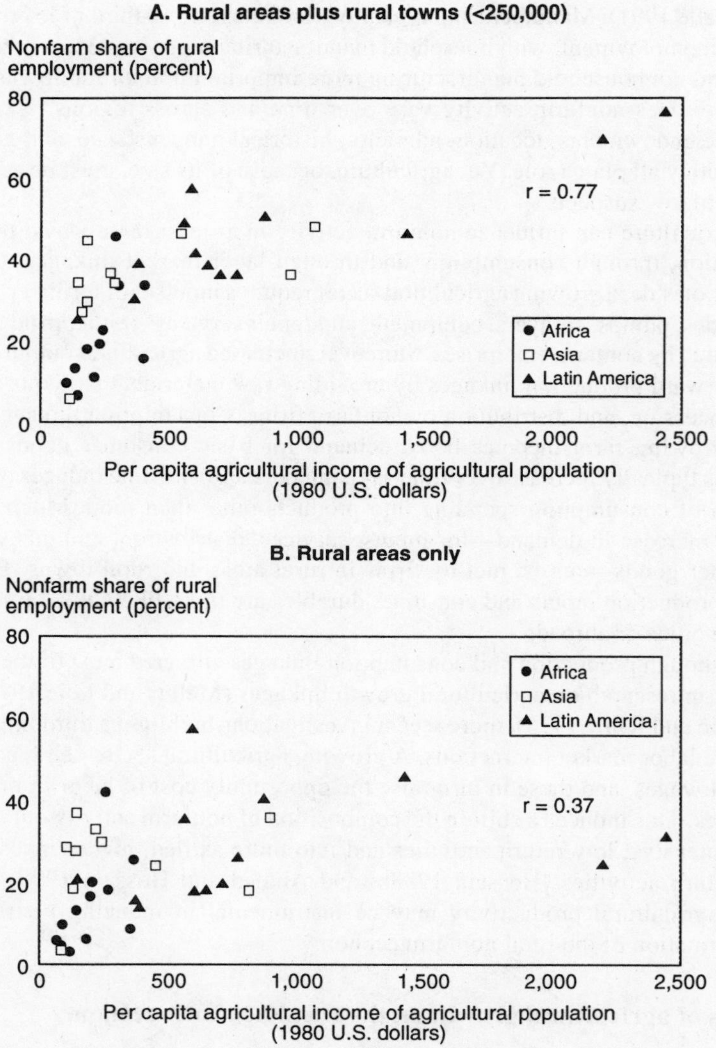

A. Rural areas plus rural towns (<250,000)

Nonfarm share of rural
employment (percent)

r = 0.77

● Africa
□ Asia
▲ Latin America

Per capita agricultural income of agricultural population
(1980 U.S. dollars)

B. Rural areas only

Nonfarm share of rural
employment (percent)

● Africa
□ Asia
▲ Latin America

r = 0.37

Per capita agricultural income of agricultural population
(1980 U.S. dollars)

Source: Census data for various years in the 1960s, 1970s, and 1980s; see table 8.1.

tural growth is observed if we include the effects of the many people who work in rural towns (see also Gibb 1974; World Bank 1978b; and Haggblade, Hazell, and Brown 1989). These correlations are consistent with the notion that growth in agricultural income leads to a diversification of consumption into nonfoods, many of which can be supplied by rural firms. Yet one cannot necessarily infer causality from these associations, since investments in infrastructure, introduction of improved agricultural technologies, growth in rural incomes, and increases in rural nonfarm incomes all frequently move in tight parallel.

Estimating agriculture's growth multiplier effects on the nonfarm economy requires more formal analysis. Most of the multiplier estimates available in the literature to date (see the review in Haggblade, Hammer, and Hazell 1991) are Keynesian demand-driven multipliers computed from input-output models, economic base models (Richardson 1985), or semi-input-output models. All assume fixed-coefficient Leontief technology and a perfectly elastic supply of rural nontradables—hence their constant price.

Within these assumptions, agricultural income multipliers range from 1.2 to 4.3. That is, a $1 increase in agricultural income, induced by technological change, generates an additional $0.20 to $3.30 of income in other sectors of the rural economy (Bell, Hazell, and Slade 1982; Krishna 1975; Haggblade, Hazell, and Brown 1989; Haggblade and Hazell 1989; and Hazell and Ramasamy 1991). If the input-output estimates, which are based on the unrealistic assumption that agricultural output is perfectly elastic, are ignored, the multipliers are consistently less than 2.0. Haggblade and Hazell (1989) use a semi-input-output model to show how the multipliers vary across different types of farming systems, ranging from about 1.3 for hoe-cultivating smallholders in rainfed areas of Africa and Latin America to about 1.8 for irrigated rice farming in Asia.

Recognizing the limitations of the fixed-price models, Haggblade, Hammer, and Hazell (1991) recently developed a price-endogenous extension that explicitly allows for input substitution as well as for a less than perfectly elastic supply of rural nontradables. An upward-sloping labor supply function for nontradables can arise from two sources. One stems from an upward-sloping labor supply curve facing a region. As the demand for nontradables grows and their production increases, the regional demand for labor also increases, raising the nominal wage rate and the average cost of nontradables. The other source of price increase arises from the possibility that capacity constraints and fixed factors in the short run lead to diminishing returns in variable inputs and hence to rising average cost as output increases.

When applied to regional data, the results from the price-endogenous model lead to more tempered multiplier estimates, generally in the range of 70 to 90 percent of the levels projected by fixed-price models. The magnitude of the dampening varies considerably by type of region, and corrections are most needed for labor-tight regions, such as may be found in parts of Africa. But the fixed-price models provide reasonable approximations of the multiplier for labor-surplus regions in Asia.

A consistent finding of all the multiplier studies is the relatively greater importance of household consumption linkages compared with the production (interindustry) linkages. The consumption linkages typically account for some 60 to 90 percent of the total multiplier.

An alternative approach to estimating the multipliers is through econometric analysis of country data across time and across regions. We have recently undertaken such work, and table 8.3 reports our estimated multipliers for India (Hazell and Haggblade 1991).

As with the semi-input-output approach, the model used to estimate these multipliers assumes that agricultural output is constrained by technology, land, and agroclimate, but that rural nonfarm activity is constrained by demand. Improved agricultural technology increases farm output and hence the demand for nonfarm inputs and consumer goods. Since agricultural output varies across regions, the following relationship allows a rough estimate of the growth multiplier:

$$(8.1) \qquad RNFY = a + bAGY,$$

where RNFY is rural nonfarm income, AGY is agricultural income, and $b = dRNFY/dAGY$ is the agricultural growth multiplier.

Of course, factors other than agricultural income vary across regions, and they too may affect the size of the nonfarm economy. Different types of agriculture may generate different linkages since input intensity and processing requirements vary across cropping systems. In the nonfarm sector analysts generally single out infrastructure, population density, and per capita income as the candidates most likely to increase growth multipliers. Infrastructure facilitates com-

Table 8.3 Rural income multipliers across states with different agricultural incomes, India, 1981

Region/agricultural income[a]	Rural areas 2SLS-PH[b]	Rural towns[c] 2SLS[d]	Rural areas plus rural towns[e]
All-India average (Rs 1,100)			
No feedback	1.21	1.16	1.37
With feedback	1.32	1.22	1.54
Punjab/Haryana (Rs 2,560)			
No feedback	1.34	1.24	1.58
With feedback	1.54	1.36	1.90
Karnataka/Gujarat (Rs 1,130)			
No feedback	1.19	1.16	1.34
With feedback	1.28	1.23	1.51
Madhya Pradesh/Bihar (Rs 730)			
No feedback	1.12	1.11	1.22
With feedback	1.17	1.16	1.33

Note: The multipliers are calculated using the same national regression coefficients, but using the sample means of the explanation variables for each of the geographic regions indicated.
a. Per capita 1982/83 agricultural income of the agricultural population.
b. Two-stage least squares with the Prais-Houthakker adjustment for heteroskedasticity.
c. Rural towns are localities with populations between 5,000 and 100,000.
d. Two-stage least squares.
e. Calculated as the sum of the separate multipliers for rural areas and rural towns.
Source: Hazell and Haggblade 1991.

munication, transport, and credit flows and should improve the responsiveness of the nonfarm economy to increases in demand from agriculture. Likewise, population density, especially in rural areas, may reduce the catchment area necessary to achieve minimum efficient scales of production and reduce transport costs, and thereby improve the prospects of rural responses. And higher agricultural income per capita should lead farm families to diversify their consumption, and thus to increase their incremental expenditure on nonfoods.

To take account of these other influences on the growth linkages, we elaborated the model as follows:

$$(8.2) \quad \text{RNFY} = a + b\text{AGY} + c\text{AGY} \times \text{INFR} + d\text{AGY} \times \text{POPDEN} + e\text{AGY} \times \text{AGYCAP} + f\text{AGY} \times \text{IRRIG},$$

where INFR is infrastructure, POPDEN is rural population density, AGYCAP is the per capita agricultural income of the agricultural population, and IRRIG is the share of total cropped area under irrigation. Irrigation is used as a proxy for the intensity of input use across agricultural zones. The four ancillary variables are included as multiplicative interaction terms because in this form the growth multiplier becomes

$$(8.3) \quad \partial \text{RNFY}/\partial \text{AGY} = b + c\text{INFR} + d\text{POPDEN} + 2e\text{AGYCAP} + f\text{IRRIG}.$$

That is, infrastructure, population density, per capita agricultural income, and the intensity of input use in agriculture affect the multiplier itself (the slope), rather than merely the level of nonfarm activity (the y-intercept).[2]

An element missing from this simple model is the possible feedback effect of growth in the rural nonfarm economy on agriculture. The urban growth pole literature has stressed the role of rural towns in stimulating agricultural growth. Rural towns may stimulate such growth because they lead to more readily available, or cheaper, supplies of inputs, easier access to markets, or more readily available credit. Moreover, rural towns may stimulate demand for perishable horticultural and livestock products, and thus promote agricultural expansion. To capture these effects, we expand the model to include a structural equation for agricultural output:

$$(8.4) \quad \text{AGY} = \alpha + \beta \text{RNFY} + \gamma' \text{X},$$

where **X** is a vector of farm input and agroclimatic variables.

When allowance is made for the feedback effect of RNFY on agriculture, the income multiplier becomes more complex than the one defined in equation 8.3. Solving equations 8.2 and 8.4, and noting that, since AGY is now endogenous to the model, the multiplier must be defined with respect to a shift in the intercept (α) of the agricultural income equation 8.4, we obtain the revised multiplier as

$$(8.5) \quad \partial \text{RNFY}/\partial \alpha = B/(1 - \beta B),$$

where $B = b + c\,\text{INFR} + d\text{POPDEN} + 2e\text{AGYCAP} + f\text{IRRIG}$ is the derivative of equation 8.2 with respect to α.[3]

Incorporating this feedback increases the size of the multiplier. Since both B and ß are likely to be positive, equation 8.5 should give a larger multiplier than equation 8.3, the right-hand side of which equals B.

The data base for our analyses was based on the same sample of eighty-five districts used by Binswanger, Khandker, and Rosenzweig (1989) and Khandker (1989). It is a representative, India-wide sample that includes districts from Andhra Pradesh, Bihar, Gujarat, Haryana, Jammu and Kashmir, Karnataka, Madhya Pradesh, Maharashtra, Punjab, Rajasthan, Tamil Nadu, and Uttar Pradesh. Because income data are not available at the district level, we estimated both farm and nonfarm income from employment, wage, and wage share data.[4]

We estimated the RNFY equation separately for rural areas (RNFY) and rural towns (RTNFY). In estimating equations 8.2 and 8.4, it was necessary to correct for endogeneity problems both because of the simultaneous relation between AGY and RNFY and because of possible endogeneity problems with some of the other right-hand-side variables. For example, it could be argued that population and infrastructure are concentrated in regions with higher agricultural potential, which would lead to selectivity bias problems (Binswanger, Khandker, and Rosenzweig 1989). To purge the model of any biases from these effects, we used two-stage least squares. In the first round, we used agroclimatic instruments for fitting reduced-form equations for AGY and other endogenous variables. Then we regressed the fitted values of these variables on RNFY and AGY in the second round.

The econometric estimates for the RNFY equation are reported in table 8.4. Because of multicollinearity problems, the irrigation variable was never significant, so we dropped it from the final runs. The Breusch-Pagan test revealed heteroskedasticity in the district data, so all regressions were run using the Prais-Houthakker adjustment in an attempt to correct the problem.

The regression for agricultural income (equation 8.4) was satisfactory, and we were able to include for each district variables measuring fertilizer use, the size of the agricultural labor force, irrigation potential, total cropped area, annual rainfall, length of the rainy season, soil moisture capacity index, number of months of excess rain, number of cold months, and the area subject to flooding (these variables are defined in Binswanger, Khandker, and Rosenzweig 1989). To save space, we do not report the full results here. The key parameter for our multiplier calculations is ß, and this has an estimated value of 0.336. However, with a t-statistic of only 0.5, the feedback effect of RNFY on AGY is not statistically significant.

In addition to national multipliers in table 8.3, we have also estimated the multipliers for high-, medium-, and low-income states to show how differences in local infrastructure, population density, and per capita agricultural income affect the multiplier. To calculate these multipliers, we used the parameters from the national regression and the means of the variables for the selected states.

The income multipliers in table 8.3 suggest five major conclusions. First, on average, an increase of 100 rupees (Rs) in agricultural income will generate an additional Rs 37 to Rs 54 in rural nonfarm income, with the amount of the addi-

Table 8.4 Regression coefficients for estimating income multipliers, India, 1981

Type of locality and estimation method	AGY	AR	AP	AU	AY	R^2	F	X^2
Rural areas								
2SLS[a]	-0.245	0.025	0.005	0.005	0.033	0.88	121.7	84.0
	(3.2)	(6.2)	(0.5)	(0.3)	(3.2)			
2SLS - PH[b]	-0.072	0.012	0.001	0.006	0.019	0.55	21.3	12.6
	(1.5)	(3.2)	(0.2)	(1.1)	(2.6)			
Rural towns								
2SLS[a]	-0.013	-0.002	0.002	0.005	0.016	0.34	9.4	70.0
	(0.2)	(0.8)	(0.2)	(0.5)	(2.1)			
2 SLS - PH[b]	-0.124	0.016	0.006	0.007	0.017	0.51	17.8	43.6
	(2.6)	(5.0)	(0.9)	(0.9)	(1.6)			

Note: AGY = agricultural income in each district; AR = AGY x road density (kilometers of roads per square kilometer of area); AP = AGY x population density (people per square kilometer); AU = AGY x urban distance (kilometers to one of eight major urban centers); AY = AGY x daily agricultural wage rate (used as an alternative to per capita agricultural income for the agricultural population); and RNFY = rural nonfarm income. The sample size is eighty-three observations. The absolute values of the t-ratios are listed in parentheses under the regression parameters.
a. Two-stage least squares estimate.
b. Two-stage least squares with the Prais-Houthakker adjustment for heteroskedasticity.
Source: Authors' calculations.

tional income depending on the strength of the feedback effect of rural nonfarm activity on agricultural income. The absence of a statistically significant ß coefficient suggests some caution in accepting the higher multiplier figure.

Second, these econometric estimates indeed project lower indirect effects than those obtained through semi-input-output modeling. Without feedbacks, the econometric estimates of indirect effects range between Rs 37 and Rs 53, compared with the Rs 80 that is more typical in semi-input-output modeling of similar economies (Hazell and Ramasamy 1991; and Bell, Hazell, and Slade 1982). This suggests that realized multipliers may lie in the range of 45 to 65 percent of the levels predicted by the fixed-price, input-output-type models (see also Haggblade, Hammer, and Hazell 1991).

Third, the multiplier effect is stronger in rural areas than in rural towns, by a ratio of about 2 to 1.

Fourth, all the ancillary factors—infrastructure, population density, and per capita agricultural income—increase the agricultural growth multiplier. Take roads as an example, because policymakers can most easily influence infrastructure. Given our estimated parameters for the model without feedback, a 20 percent increase in the density of roads will increase the indirect income increment of rural areas plus rural towns by 3 percent, resulting in a multiplier of 1.38.[5]

Fifth, because infrastructure, population density, and per capita agricultural income differ so markedly across states, the multipliers are far stronger in some states than in others. While Rs 100 of agricultural income will generate Rs 58 in nonfarm income in rural areas plus rural towns in Punjab and Haryana, it will support only Rs 22 of nonfarm income in Bihar and Madhya Pradesh. Higher consumption linkages and higher input intensity in agriculture account for the substantially higher linkages in the high-productivity agricultural states.

The estimated model can also be used to derive the nonfarm employment generated by agricultural growth (Hazell and Haggblade 1991). Assuming a continuation of current growth rates of 2.4 percent a year for agricultural income and 2.2 percent a year for population, the model predicts that, without feedback effects, nonfarm income in rural areas and rural towns will grow by 2.3 percent a year and nonfarm employment by 2.1 percent. This corresponds to an employment elasticity of 0.9. That is, each 1 percent increase in agricultural income leads to 0.9 percent additional employment in the nonfarm sector. This is very close to Gibb's (1974) finding for Central Luzon in the Philippines. He observed a compound growth rate of 7 to 8 percent in nonfarm employment between 1967 and 1971, and an 8 percent growth rate for agricultural income. These rates imply an employment elasticity of about unity.

The indirect benefits and the poor

So far we have shown only that the total increase in rural nonfarm income emanating from agricultural growth can be substantial; we have yet to show that an important part of this benefit accrues to the poor.

An expectation that the poor do gain is based on the importance of household consumption linkages in determining the multiplier. Contrary to Hymer and Resnick's (1969) expectation, detailed household expenditure studies have shown that rural households have positive income elasticities—sometimes above unity— for many rurally produced, non-food-grain goods and services (King and Byerlee 1978; and Hazell and Roell 1983). Many of these goods and services are important to the rural poor because of their labor-intensive production and consequent effect on employment and wages. They include food processing—in which women play a major role—and service and manufacturing activities with low investment requirements.

The expectation that the poor gain is confirmed by detailed analysis of changes in household incomes in the Muda River irrigation region in Malaysia, and in the North Arcot district in Tamil Nadu, India. Results of detailed semi-input-output models of these two regions track the changes in per capita income, by household type, induced by large increases in agricultural output (table 8.5). In the Muda region the change in output was induced by a large irrigation project (Bell, Hazell, and Slade 1982). In North Arcot the change stemmed from a decade of agricultural growth during the era of the green revolution; the data are normalized to simulate average weather conditions (Hazell and Ramasamy 1991).

In both regions the landless agricultural workers are the poorest household group, but these workers gained proportionally more income than any other

Table 8.5 Project-induced changes in per capita income in two regions, by household type

Household group	Preproject income per capita[a]			Ratio of post- to preproject income	Percentage of income increase	
	Agri-cultural	Nonagri-cultural	Total		Due to preagri-cultural sources	Due to nonagri-cultural sources
Muda irrigation region, Malaysia, 1972						
(Malaysian dollars)						
Landless paddy workers	65	68	133	1.71	89.4	10.6
Small paddy farms	138	71	209	1.59	88.7	11.3
Large paddy farms	250	92	342	1.64	91.3	8.7
Nonproject farms	116	269	385	1.06	50.0	50.0
Nonfarm households	17	896	913	1.14	17.5	82.5
North Arcot, India, 1982						
(rupees)						
Rural villages[b]						
Landless laborers	295	118	413	1.33	85.5	14.5
Nonfarm households	49	592	641	1.20	15.0	85.0
Small farms	457	309	766	1.32	70.9	29.1
Large farms	1,246	347	1,593	1.32	89.1	10.9
Urban villages[b]						
Agriculturally dependent	648	384	1,032	1.28	82.2	17.8
Employed nonagricultural	40	1,282	1,322	1.15	8.0	92.0
Self-employed nonagricultural	55	2,684	2,739	1.18	4.5	95.5
Towns[b]						
Agriculturally dependent	616	556	1,172	1.30	64.3	35.7
Employed nonagricultural	22	1,366	1,388	1.18	3.6	96.4
Self-employed nonagricultural	4	4,191	4,195	1.27	0.1	99.9

a. For the Muda region, the "project" is the irrigation scheme; for North Arcot, it is a decade of growth induced by the green revolution.
b. The classification of rural villages, urban villages, and towns is based on census definitions. Rural villages have populations of fewer than 5,000 people.
Source: Muda: Bell, Hazell, and Slade 1982; and North Arcot: Hazell and Ramasamy 1991.

group as a result of the growth in agriculture. An overwhelming share of their gain in income came from an increase in agricultural wage earnings, but 10 to 15 percent of their total gain was still derived from nonagricultural sources. Small farms also had significant increases in nonagricultural income; it accounted for 29 percent of the increase in total income for small farms in North Arcot. Large farmers gained relatively little from nonagricultural sources in both regions. The real gains from the growth linkages accrued to the specialized, nonagricultural households, especially those in urban areas.

These results demonstrate that the rural poor do gain in absolute terms from the growth linkage multipliers. But it is also clear that, because the nonpoor gain even more, the indirect effects of agricultural growth are unlikely to improve the relative distribution of income within rural regions.

Conclusions

Technological change in agriculture not only has powerful direct effects on rural incomes and employment. It sets in motion important second-round growth effects in the rural nonfarm economy. Although estimated income multipliers vary across regions with the type of agricultural growth and with the methodology used, they seem to cluster around 1.6. That is, each dollar of additional value added generated in agriculture generates about $0.60 of value added in the rural nonfarm economy. These multiplier effects provide an important supplement to many of the poorer household groups in rural regions, accounting for 10 to 30 percent of their total gains in income when agriculture is growing.

To enhance these multiplier effects, policymakers need to focus on the following:

- The discrimination in investment codes and related legislation against small, rural nonfarm firms, together with historic urban policy biases, will need to be redressed if rural nonfarm enterprises are to achieve their potential in generating income and in contributing to economic decentralization.

- The historical focus on manufacturing, by both policymakers and researchers, should be redirected. Spatial, time-series, and consumption data uniformly point not to manufacturing, but to commerce and services (including housing construction) as key growth sectors over the course of rural structural transformation. Services and commercial enterprises should not be excluded from assistance programs, as has frequently been the practice in the past.

- Rural towns emerge as focal points in the development of the rural nonfarm economy. Cross-sectional data consistently show much higher densities of nonfarm activity in rural towns than in dispersed rural settlements. By providing larger markets, rural towns offer nonfarm enterprises the opportunity to exploit economies of scale. The possibilities of sharing equipment and the emergence of repair and support facilities encourage entrepreneurs to establish enterprises in rural towns. Moreover, rural towns enable policymakers to provide necessary productive infrastructure at a lower cost than would be possible under widely dispersed settlement patterns.

- For rural towns to play their role in a balanced rural development process, adequate economic and social infrastructure to support nascent modern nonfarm activities must be provided. Physical infrastructure will undoubtedly play a key role. Anecdotal evidence on the rise of secondary cities in developing countries identifies ground transportation—roads and railroads—as necessary initial infrastructural investments (Rondinelli and Ruddle 1978; and Rondinelli 1983). The consumption data from Africa and Asia reinforce this notion, highlighting the importance of road access to rural towns in stimulating agricultural consumption linkages. Beyond that, the spotty record of rural electrification programs alone in fostering industrialization (Fluitmen 1983; and Okelo 1973) suggests a need to review evidence on complementarities, sequencing, and other conditions necessary for ensuring that infrastructural investments are productive. Institutional infrastructure will also be essential in fostering the transition to a more specialized, productive rural economy. Efficient rural financial markets will be particularly important. It appears that improvements on this front will require integrating the existing informal credit markets with the formal banking system. Labor markets are also essential, and their efficiency will increase as communication and transport infrastructure improve.

- Because much current writing emphasizes the need for investment in infrastructure, policymakers can all too easily overlook the corresponding need for investment in people. Because services will be among the most rapidly growing rural nonfarm activities, investment in human capital will likely be essential for realizing those potential gains. Services depend more on skilled people than on equipment and infrastructure.

- Many programs of direct assistance to rural nonfarm enterprises, although by no means all, have been cost-effective. The record of technical assistance and projects providing modern workshop facilities has been checkered; two-thirds of seventeen recent project evaluations have found benefit-cost ratios below one (Haggblade 1982; and Kilby 1979). Credit projects, especially those supplying working capital, have enjoyed greater success. A recent evaluation of seven small-enterprise credit projects found that all have benefit-cost ratios in excess of one (Kilby and D'Zmura 1985). Overall, as Kilby (1979) originally suggested and subsequent appraisals have confirmed, programs that aim to provide a complete package of financial, technical, and management assistance—nursery industrial estates, for example—are generally less effective than programs that identify and provide a single missing ingredient necessary for enterprise success.

- Women dominate many of the nonfarm activities that will grow most rapidly during structural transformation—such activities as trading, tailoring, many services, and food processing and preparation. They also dominate many of the declining rural nonfarm occupations—weaving, ceramics, mat making, and basket making. Consequently, women will be key actors in the economic transition of rural developing economies. Facilitating their contribution to an accelerated rural transformation will require that assistance agencies and governments explicitly recognize the central role that they will play.

Notes

1. Lipton (1984a) has analyzed the unique features of family modes of production (fungibility in resource use, complementarity with activities related to household consumption, and so on) that explain this concentration of nonfarm activity.

2. Note that since AGYCAP = AGY/POP, then $\partial(e\text{AGY} \times \text{AGYCAP})/\partial\text{AGY} = \partial(e\text{AGY}^2/\text{POP})/\partial\text{AGY} = 2e\text{AGYCAP}$.

3. In this feedback model, the shift in α also has a multiplier effect on agricultural output itself, and the full regional income multiplier is:

$$\frac{\partial Y}{\partial \alpha} = \frac{\partial \text{RNFY}}{\partial \alpha} + \frac{d\text{AGY}}{\partial \alpha}$$

$$= \frac{B}{1 - ßB} + \frac{1}{1 - ßB}$$

$$= \frac{1 + B}{1 - ßB}$$

4. We estimate income (Y) as a function of employment (L), the wage rate (W), and wage share of income (S_w) as follows: $Y = L \times W/S_w$. We take wage rates as equal in agriculture and rural nonfarm activities. From Hazell and Ramasamy (1991), we estimate S_w as 0.58 in agriculture and 0.70 in nonfarm pursuits.

5. This does not mean that building more roads will necessarily guarantee higher nonfarm growth linkages. Since all infrastructure variables are highly correlated, it is not possible to separate out the effects of roads from those of banks, electricity, or telephones, at least not with these cross-sectional data. Rerunning the model using the density of banks rather than the density of roads, for example, produces virtually identical parameters. So, to achieve the 3 percent increase in multipliers, it will probably be necessary to increase infrastructure across the board by 20 percent. Khandker (1989) is more successful in isolating the separate contributions of different kinds of rural infrastructure, but he has access to pooled time-series, cross-sectional data for the same districts.

Population Growth, Externalities, and Poverty

9

Nancy Birdsall
Charles Griffin

Rapid population growth in developing countries is at the root of a number of concerns that have been raised in both popular and scholarly literature. Some of these concerns are:

- That rapid population growth reduces the rate of growth of real per capita income by, for example, reducing per capita investment in human and physical capital[1]
- That rapid population growth has negative externalities,[2] leading in some scenarios to the degradation of countries' natural resources or contributing to such environmental problems as global warming
- That rapid population growth has undesirable "pecuniary" externalities— that is, that it reduces the incomes of some groups, particularly the poor, compared with those of other, better-off groups, and therefore exacerbates poverty in developing countries.

The first concern has been amply explored for at least two decades. But its merits are difficult to address empirically, and because of the lack of compelling evidence, it remains controversial.[3] Economists have recently noted, in any event, that in the absence of externalities, a negative effect of rapid population growth on economic growth need not in itself be of great concern. Parents may fully realize that children are costly to them (and to society), and yet prefer to have more children rather than higher consumption of other costly things.[4] If so, rapid population growth may be socially optimal even if it impedes economic growth. There are some countervailing arguments, however. Some recent approaches to growth theory emphasize that investment in human resources may make a more important contribution to growth than previously believed, and that there may be positive externalities associated with such investment. To the extent that rapid population growth inhibits such investment, its effects on growth may not be socially optimal.[5]

We do not consider this first concern further in this chapter. Instead, we concentrate on the policy implications of the other two concerns: the negative externalities of rapid population growth and its effects on income distribution (and thus on poverty).[6] We are concerned in particular with the implications for the poor of the various approaches to population policy that arise from these two concerns. We begin by briefly setting out the two concerns, using simple graphs to illustrate how each can be translated into a rationale for some sort of population policy. We note that the two concerns suggest policy approaches that would affect the poor in a virtually identical manner. We then discuss the implications of these two concerns for the structure and content of programs to reduce fertility. In this context we review education, health, and family planning programs; the effects of family planning on women's welfare; the expansion of contraceptive choices; and the use of incentives to reduce fertility. We conclude by assessing the importance of an essentially redistributive approach to population policy—an approach in which one segment of society (the relatively rich) offers another segment (the relatively poor) additional resources—to the future success of fertility reduction efforts, irrespective of the specific rationale for the policy.

The externality and income distribution approaches

Negative environmental externalities

Negative externalities to childbearing arise if the private costs of having children diverge from the social costs—that is, if one couple's childbearing decisions impose costs on other families.[7] In a recent paper Lee and Miller (1991) set out a framework for considering such externalities empirically. They conclude (with great caution—they note that the numbers are rough and the exercise is experimental) that the externalities are neither great nor always in the expected direction—they are not always negative for developing countries. As the authors themselves point out, however, they do not include any estimate to account for externalities arising from damage to such common property resources as air and water quality (what we will refer to crudely as environmental externalities).[8] In addition, since they use countries as the unit of analysis, they are unable to take into account environmental externalities (possibly negative) from one nation's population growth that accrue to other nations or to the global commons.

Yet negative environmental externalities, at both global and national levels, are increasingly alluded to as a rationale for efforts to slow population growth in developing countries. On a per capita basis, industrial countries produce far more of the fossil fuel emissions that may contribute to global warming. But developing countries will likely have far higher rates of increase in income and in population, rates implying that their contribution to global emissions could rise from about 20 percent today to 50 percent by the middle of the next century. At the national level, the combination of poverty and rapid population growth is often cited as contributing to environmental degradation. For example, population pressure can lead to the farming of hillsides and other marginal areas (causing soil erosion) or the heavy cutting of forests for fuel (causing damage to watersheds and hence to agriculture, and contributing to possibly irreversible reductions in biodiversity).

Figure 9.1 illustrates how these externalities (and we are assuming their existence at this point) can justify a policy to reduce fertility and thus population growth. The figure shows a production possibilities frontier in a two-good world that produces environmental services and food. Greater food production comes at an increasing cost to the environment in this simple world, as environmental services are traded for more food.

A country may find itself pushed inside the frontier, to a point such as *M*, because of rapid population growth that threatens both the production of food and the production of environmental services. A program to reduce fertility may be justified if a developing country is inside the frontier because parents (especially poor parents, an issue we explore further below) are having more children than is optimal for the country as a whole. In this example, parents are not taking into account the economic costs to their country associated with high fertility, population pressure, and the resulting environmental degradation.[9]

If such a country could, through a population program, induce parents to have fewer children, that country could move out to a point such as *N* on the production possibilities frontier. With smaller families, output would rise and the country as a whole would be better-off.[10] Analogously, if industrial countries could induce developing countries to reduce their fertility levels, global welfare could increase.

The question then is how to induce people to have fewer children. We assume for the moment that people are having the number of children they wish—that there is no excess or unwanted fertility, even among the poor. With the population problem rooted solely in these environmental externalities, inducing lower fertility requires that the external costs of children be somehow imposed on parents (reducing their demand for children), or, to put it another way, that the constraints parents face be somehow altered in a manner that raises the cost of children to them.

There are several ways to do this. A tax on children[11] would reduce the demand for children, and a tax-financed incentive to forgo having more children would have the same effect. Although taxes or cash incentives have been used in some countries to reduce fertility (Singapore and Bangladesh, for example),[12] they are politically unpalatable in many countries.[13] Moreover, incentives designed to correct for negative externalities, which could in principle be structured to be less regressive than taxes, raise other problems, such as entrapment.[14]

Figure 9.1 The externality argument

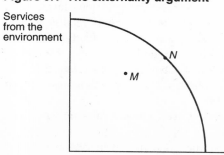

More often discussed are interventions that, in the presence of negative externalities, governments may use to alter individuals' reproductive behavior—particularly that of the poor, who tend to have more children than the nonpoor, especially in developing countries. Successful interventions tend to involve improvements in the situation of the poor: expanded opportunities for women, better health for their children, ready access to family planning, education programs that attract children into school and keep them there, and programs that help parents to substitute for the income-earning capabilities of children, reducing the value of children as a source of immediate income and old-age security. These changes in the parents' situation affect the demand for children by raising the "price" of children to parents.[15] All such programs are essentially investments in the human capital of mothers and children, or poverty alleviation activities.

These programs tend to have the same effect as taxes on children, but they work indirectly and have the desirable characteristic of succeeding by raising the "quality" of children. They do need to be financed, presumably through taxes. The rich, who would presumably bear the tax burden of these programs, are likely to be willing to do so because they can also gain. The lower average fertility would permit the society to move from point M in figure 9.1 to the frontier, generating additional output and environmental services.

The fundamental point, to which we will return, is that a change in the reproductive behavior of the poor requires a change in their situation—that is, a change in the relative prices they face. The poor will voluntarily choose to have fewer children only if the change in their situation makes them at least as well-off as they are currently.[16] Any other approach would have to include an element of compulsion; otherwise, the poor have no reason to alter their reproductive behavior (and to help society to move away from the suboptimal point M in figure 9.1).

Similarly, a change in the fertility rate of poor countries is unlikely unless there is a change in the circumstances that induce high fertility in those countries. Thus, it may be in the interests of the citizens of rich countries to "purchase" lower fertility in poor countries by financing such changes as an increase in the educational opportunities in poor countries. To the extent that these changes move the global society from point M to point N, all countries can be better-off.[17]

Income distribution and poverty

In this section we assume away the pure externalities referred to above and consider only the problem of "pecuniary" externalities—the negative effect of rapid population growth on income equality and thus on the poor. Rapid population growth can worsen the distribution of income in developing countries, and it probably exacerbates the problems of the poor. At the aggregate level, rapid population growth increases the supply of labor in an economy relative to land and physical capital, reducing the real wage rate.[18] This is likely to worsen inequality and hurt the poor, who are more reliant on labor income. Moreover, there is evidence that unskilled, but not skilled, laborers suffer a relative decline in wages if they are members of a large cohort; this has been demonstrated for males in Brazil (Behrman and Birdsall 1988b).

At the family level, poverty and high fertility seem to form a vicious circle. As we show elsewhere (Birdsall and Griffin 1988), high fertility contributes to poverty. It strains the budgets of poor families, reducing available resources to feed, educate, and provide health care to children. A study of households classified by per capita income in Brazil, Colombia, Malaysia, and rural India, using data from the 1970s, found that the ratio of income per child in the richest quintile of households to that in the poorest quintile ranges from about 12 in rural India to more than 100 in Brazil (Birdsall 1988). A study of families with twins in India found that the additional unexpected child represented by twins reduced the likelihood of enrollment of children in the household (Rosenzweig and Wolpin 1980). Estimates based on Malaysian data show that couples with a higher biological propensity to have births have lower schooling attainment for their children (Rosenzweig and Schultz 1987).

At the same time, a massive body of literature has shown repeatedly that many characteristics of poor households contribute to high fertility—high infant mortality, lack of education for women, too little family income to "invest" in children, and inaccessibility of family planning services.[19]

Why do poor parents persist in having many children if it tends to exacerbate their problems? For simplicity, the answer can be divided into two categories.

Unwanted fertility. First is the simplest explanation: that some fertility of the poor is unwanted. In many countries a significant proportion of women say that they would like to limit their fertility, yet do not do so. This condition of "unmet need" (as defined and measured by demographers) characterizes a quarter of married, fecund women in Bangladesh, one-fifth in Nepal, and one-eighth in Egypt (Boulier 1985). The phenomenon of "unmet need" does not imply that parents are acting irrationally, however. Chomitz and Birdsall (1991) set out a number of market failures, including those of credit, insurance, and information markets, that explain why individuals may fail to use contraception even when they want no more children; these market failures are all possible barriers to the optimal use of contraception from an individual's or a couple's point of view. In fact, demographers use the term "unmet need" to indicate the demand for contraception if its price were zero (including psychic as well as monetary costs). Yet the price of contraception is never, of course, zero. The credit, information, and other constraints that keep the price well above zero tend to affect the poor more than the rich; and even the direct costs of contraception for the poor represent a larger fraction of the total resources, both human and financial, available to them.

The implication of unwanted fertility for population policy is obvious: subsidized family planning services targeted to the poor. Just as in our discussion of negative externalities, so with pecuniary externalities: social "excess" fertility, like unwanted fertility, is likely to persist unless there are changes in the situation of the poor, and hence in the incentives and constraints affecting the decision to have another child. These changes are likely to involve not only better access to family planning, but improvements in access to capital, to information, and to such complementary services as health and education. In short, even assuming that there is "unmet need," a change in the reproductive behavior of the poor still requires a change in their circumstances—including, at the least, better access to family planning services.[20]

Endogenous altruism and the welfare of children. Our second explanation for the high fertility of the poor is based on the possibility of a distinction between the welfare of parents and the welfare of children. We noted in a different context above that parents may reasonably trade off higher consumption of other costly things in favor of more children. Consequently, even if high fertility impedes economic growth, it may still be socially optimal because lower fertility would reduce the utility of parents. But what if this tradeoff is chosen by poor parents without full information about the costs of this high fertility for their children? Suppose parents trade off more children against more education per child—unaware that the returns to education are rising? Suppose parents "choose" additional pregnancies because they fear that some of their children will die— unaware that child mortality is rapidly falling?

Or suppose that the degree of parents' altruism toward their children is in fact endogenous, for example, that altruism toward children is itself a positive function of income—a luxury only the relatively well-off can afford?[21] Desperately poor parents may choose to have more children because children seem critical to their own survival—in the process trading off some small measure of additional welfare for the children they already have. This decision would seem likely, even necessary, for parents with three or four daughters in a society in which only a son can provide them with reasonable security in old age.[22] In short, though the high fertility of a poor couple worsens the situation of society (the global environmental externality) and even the situation of poor families as a group (the pecuniary externality—that the wages of unskilled labor fall), each such couple might well be better-off with many children—who can earn more than they consume and provide their parents some security in old age—even though the children themselves are not better-off.

Figure 9.2 illustrates the case in which the problem of externalities does not arise. The figure shows the distribution of welfare in a two-person society in which, in the absence of externalities, the society is on its production frontier (at a point such as N in figure 9.1). We are treating the two people as composite populations of the rich and the poor. The rich are assumed to prefer smaller families (including smaller families for the poor), and the poor are assumed to prefer larger families. The two utility possibilities frontiers (UPF_1 and UPF_2) correspond to two different policy regimes: UPF_1, with no social programs for the poor, favoring utility of the rich, and UPF_2, with social programs for the poor, favoring utility of the poor. Each utility frontier shows all possible utility distributions associated with some point on a production possibilities frontier.

Suppose that UPF_1, with no service programs, is the current situation, and the current distribution of goods is shown by point X_1, corresponding to U_1^P utility for the poor and U_1^R for

Figure 9.2 The social welfare argument

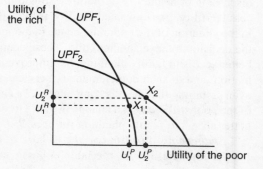

the rich (presumably the rich are a much smaller group). Suppose a social program—for example, education or family planning—is proposed that will lead the poor to have fewer children while maintaining them at no less than the utility they achieve now, with their larger families. The social program is financed by taxing the rich.[23] Such a reallocation corresponds to UPF_2, where the rich are willing to finance the new program, requiring society to produce a bundle of goods that reduces the *potential* maximum utility of the rich and increases the *potential* maximum utility of the poor.[24]

Suppose that the social program moves society from X_1 to X_2. Both the rich and the poor would enjoy an unambiguous increase in *actual* welfare (from U_1^P to U_2^P for the poor and from U_1^R to U_2^R for the rich). The rich secure higher utility for themselves, given that they prefer smaller families among the poor, by financing the social programs through taxes.[25]

All this approach tells us is that, in the absence of true externalities, noncoercive programs that reduce fertility are essentially income redistribution programs.[26] In practice, this is the same result as would be obtained if noncoercive policies were pursued in an environment with externalities, as discussed in the previous section.

From theory to practice

Whether the fundamental problem is one of externalities, unwanted fertility among the poor, or endogenous altruism, the implication is the same. Reducing the population growth rate requires policies designed to keep the poor at least as well-off as they are now, but with fewer children. This welfare approach puts three issues into perspective:

- If there is a divergence between the world's actual population growth rate and its desired population growth rate, noncoercive policies can move us closer to the optimum.
- A population policy will impose a short-run cost on someone (if there are externalities, the long-run benefits will outweigh the costs). One option consistent with the externality approach in figure 9.1 is to tax children, implicitly or explicitly. But such a tax would be regressive, and difficult to collect from the poor. The alternative is to introduce programs and policies that will improve the situation of the poor. The rich are likely to pay through taxes for these programs.
- Difficulty in justifying population programs on the basis of negative externalities to rapid population growth does not mean that the programs cannot be justified on other grounds. There may be redistributive social programs that would improve overall welfare and—through their effect on the fertility of the poor—the welfare of the rich, who would therefore be willing to finance the programs (figure 9.2). In short, in an extension of the ideas and literature discussed in an earlier article (Birdsall and Griffin 1988), we believe that valid arguments can be made based on either the externality or the income distribution approach for programs whose fundamental purpose is to reduce fertility by improving the lives of the poor.

What are the implications of this view for the structure and content of programs to reduce fertility?

Incentives and fertility reduction

A cash-based tax or subsidy program would be an economist's first choice as an approach for reducing fertility under either negative environmental or negative pecuniary externalities.[27] It should be clear that taxes on children or cash incentives to forgo having children are mechanisms through which society assures that parents internalize any negative externality associated with high fertility (figure 9.1). It should also be clear that a program that uses cash or near-cash compensation—such as health insurance, direct cash transfers, a retirement annuity, or a guaranteed opportunity of college for two or three children—to maintain the poor parents' welfare is consistent with the compensation principle implicit in figure 9.2.

Such subsidies or compensation are more typically tied to specific goods and services, such as social services, however. Cash and near-cash payments to reduce fertility are often impracticable, and in most societies it is difficult to design a payment policy that is ethically acceptable (one that avoids penalizing children with high birth orders for their parents' decision not to respond to an antinatalist incentive, for example). Therefore, we consider only redistribution through social programs.

Targeted social programs

A large body of evidence summarized in Birdsall and Griffin (1988) confirms that high infant mortality, lack of education for mothers, low educational opportunities for children, and poor access to family planning services all contribute to high fertility, both directly and indirectly.

When high infant mortality rates fall, mothers are able, for the first time, to choose how many children to bear. In a high-mortality, traditional agricultural environment, a risk-averse couple must produce children almost continually during its reproductive years to guarantee an adequate number of surviving children (particularly if the sex of children is a concern to parents) to provide farm labor and security in old age. As infant mortality drops, the probability that investments in higher-quality children will be lost through death also falls, allowing the price of children to begin rising. The lag in parents' response to these changes may be several years, but they do respond.

More education for women delays marriage, increases the likelihood that contraceptives will be used (and used effectively), helps women to gain more control over the decisions that affect fertility, and boosts the probability that babies will survive and be healthy. It also raises female labor force participation (hence creating further economic opportunities for women) and endows women with the ability to purchase more education for their children. Each of these effects, as the analyses following the World Fertility Survey have abundantly confirmed, tends to lower fertility rates.

More education for children raises their cost to parents and also increases the quality of surviving children. This is true not only if schooling is paid for directly by parents, but also if it is provided free by the state; in the latter case the household, by sending children to school, loses economic services that they would otherwise provide. The direct costs of education, which are substantial in developing country households even if it is provided by the state, are multiplied by the number of children, so the cost (of education or quality) to a family rises in a multiplicative, not additive, fashion as more children are born. Education costs alone can create large incentives for poorer parents to raise fewer children.

Availability of family planning services of reasonable quality lowers the cost of fertility control, making such control easier, if all other things are unchanged. But a family planning program appended to a social welfare system that delivers few if any health or education services to the poor is unlikely to produce meaningful results once the problem of "unwanted births" is eliminated. A combination of family planning services and effective health and education services has been shown to be more successful in reducing fertility than either of the two alone (Wheeler 1985).

The implication is obvious. Health and education programs targeted to the poor in developing countries are one way to reduce fertility. Complementing these with targeted family services assures that the poor can translate reduced demand for large families into fewer births. The effect of the combined programs will exceed the sum of the programs' individual effects because of the known complementarities among the three services. A package of services is an effective and eminently sensible method for compensating poor families in a way that results in lower fertility.

In the same spirit, family planning programs could be reconstituted to strengthen their welfare-enhancing aspects. A family planning program designed to enhance the welfare of the poor client would then be redesigned as part of a set of services to improve the mother's health, the safety of the birth process, and the health of her children. Nutritional supplements would almost certainly be provided to poorer women (and their babies), who are the main targets of such programs. Helping mothers to space or delay births would be integrated with these other services. Contrast this approach with one, common until recently in South Asia, in which a family planning worker's success was measured by increases in the number of sterilizations performed, new acceptors recruited, or contraceptives distributed. Such a worker had every incentive to avoid pregnant women, for example, who would be a prime target of a welfare-enhancing program.

Broader contraceptive choice

Probably the most pressing welfare issue in the design of family planning systems is the narrow focus of some programs on sterilization, particularly in South Asia. This narrow focus is the result of the long period during which family planning programs in South Asia were designed with demographic targets in mind—and thus without a clear welfare objective.

In India, for example, the rate of contraceptive use for all methods increased from 14 percent in 1970 to 35 percent in 1980. Almost the entire increase was accounted for by sterilizations, condoms, and traditional methods. In 60 percent of couples using some method of contraception, at least one partner was sterilized. Less than 5 percent used intrauterine devices (IUDs) or birth control pills, and the remaining couples used less effective methods. In fact, the proportion of those using IUDs and pills fell over the decade.

Older women at the end of their childbearing years request sterilization more often than younger women; consequently, the impact on fertility of permanent methods, although initially large, may be small over the long run for the investment required. In India in 1980, according to an internal World Bank report, 38 percent of married women between the ages of 35 and 39 were sterilized, compared with 4.5 percent of those between 20 and 24, and 18 percent of those between 25 and 29. In contrast, the highest rate of condom and pill use was among the two younger groups, although in absolute terms it was minuscule even among them—less than 2 percent. About 40 percent of women with four children were sterilized, compared with 16 percent of those with one child— another indicator that women are careful to use permanent methods late in their reproductive lives.

Without good access to temporary methods, younger women cannot benefit from the possibility of planning the timing as well as the number of births, nor from the larger welfare benefits associated with reduced uncertainty in their lives. A program oriented to younger women would also deliver services valuable to older women; the converse of that statement is less likely to be true, however.

Women's welfare and the timing of births

As the above illustrates, a population program aimed at enhancing welfare as well as reducing fertility is more likely to be shaped by the particular needs of important groups of clients. The most obvious such group is women.

Access to effective fertility control methods allows women to make reproduction predictable and thus to approach economic life on a more level playing field with men. Birdsall and Chester (1987) argue, for example, that the relatively low status of women in Japan compared with that of women in other industrial countries results in part from their heavy reliance on condoms and abortion to control fertility. The reason for their low status is not high fertility itself—Japan's fertility rate is among the lowest in the world—but the probability of unplanned pregnancies, which is higher for women in Japan than for women in other countries at similar levels of development who use more reliable means of control. Birdsall and Chester argue that family planning programs, while perhaps dependent for success on women's status, are also likely to enhance women's status substantially.

This positive and independent effect of family planning on the welfare of women is not simply a rationale for offering family planning programs. It is also the basis for a program strategy oriented toward improving control over the timing of births. Such an orientation implies a contraceptive mix aimed less at meeting state targets for births averted and more at increasing a woman's ability to manage the number and frequency of births that she experiences.

Moreover, a strategy designed to meet targets would not necessarily result in fewer births than one designed to help women manage their births. A program aimed at helping women to space births, or to delay the first birth, could be a cost-effective way to reach a given population growth target; more important, it is much more likely to contribute to a fundamental change in society's views of the entire reproduction process and in the long run, therefore, to a large decline in fertility rates.

Conclusion

We have tried to suggest that, regardless of the reason for one's interest in population programs, the only reasonable way to view them is as activities in which one segment of society (the rich) is offering another segment (the poor) compensation in order to elicit a change in behavior. Where there are true externalities (figure 9.1), the rich may also end up at least as well-off, even in income, as before; everyone can benefit from the overall gain in efficiency. Where there are no true externalities (figure 9.2), only the poor are made better-off in real income, but the rich can gain in utility, because they value the socio-environmental benefits to them from a smaller total population more than the tax costs to them of financing the necessary social programs. Any other approach is, by definition, either coercive or ultimately ineffective. There is thus a fundamental logic in treating population programs as both client-oriented social services and poverty programs.

Underlying this approach is the idea that fertility is endogenous: it is the outcome of a rational decision by households, given their opportunities and constraints. If that is so, policymakers—if they want to elicit changes in behavior among the poor (whose fertility tends to be higher than that of the rich)—must treat them as clients, and must give them sufficient incentives to change.

The principle that parents who want more children must be compensated for not having them is at the core of welfare economics. It matters little whether the rationale for a population program is based on externalities, unwanted fertility, or income distribution. Such programs in the end must involve compensation, either directly or indirectly. A necessary condition for a well-designed program is that it keep the poor at least as well-off, in their own eyes, *after* they choose to have fewer children as they were prior to the program, when they chose otherwise.

We should carefully rethink whether the resources devoted to these programs are adequate and whether the programs are designed with the clients' welfare in mind. The critical question for any population program or policy when welfare concerns are brought to the forefront is: Will the program help the poor to improve their lives after they have smaller families?

Notes

The authors thank Jere Behrman, Ken Chomitz, Harry Cross, Ronald Lee, Michael Lipton, Marc Nerlove, Steven Sinding, J. P. Tan, and participants in the 1989 Poverty Research Conference organized by the International Food Policy Research Institute and the World Bank for helpful comments.

1. The classic presentation of the argument is that of Coale and Hoover (1958). See Birdsall (1988) for a review of the literature on the economic consequences of rapid population growth in developing countries.

2. Some argue that population growth may have positive externalities. While we do not dismiss that possibility, in this chapter we are concerned with the implications of possible negative externalities.

3. In addition to the citations in note 1, see Kelley (1988), World Bank (1984), and National Research Council (1986), which in turn cite hundreds of earlier studies and reviews.

4. Lee and Miller (1990) set out this point clearly. They note that Demeny, in 1972, pointed out that to decry such a decision by parents would be like decrying people's decision not to work on Sundays on the grounds that it reduces their incomes.

5. See Romer (1986) and Azariadis and Drazen (1990) on sources of growth, including such externalities to human resource investments.

6. Some readers may find the distinction between the negative externality argument and the income distribution argument, as each is characterized in this chapter, somewhat artificial, since both concerns point to the need to improve social welfare through population programs. But we believe that it is useful to understand the differing motivation and meaning of the two arguments as well as the fact that they lead to the same end.

7. The World Bank's *World Development Report 1984* argued that this divergence between private and social costs provided an important justification for government programs to reduce fertility.

8. Lee and Miller also assume that the population is homogeneous—that is, that all members have the same constraints and preferences (thus not taking into account, for example, the possibility that differences in the tax burden and the incidence of public expenditures imply transfers from one portion of the population to another).

9. There may be other reasons why poor parents are having "too many" children. Some of these we discuss below. Here we concentrate on the simple example of a negative environmental externality.

10. Total output, not just output per person, would rise. In this example, it is probably more accurate to say that the present discounted value of long-run output would increase. Short-run output could decrease while environmental problems are addressed.

11. That is, a Pigovian tax to address the specific source of externality-inducing behavior.

12. Payments in Bangladesh, however, are provided only for permanent methods of contraception and are very low, designed to compensate for the time and discomfort of the procedure itself.

13. Subsidies or positive incentives to encourage high fertility are more common, having been used in France and parts of Eastern Europe, and are obviously a politically acceptable incentive.

14. Entrapment occurs if an individual is induced—for example, because of myopia or desperate poverty—to take an irreversible step that he or she later regrets. It has been

discussed in the context of cash payments to persons who are sterilized. Chomitz and Birdsall (1991) discuss the justification for and welfare implications of incentives to reduce fertility, as well as of child taxes and child quotas. They conclude that incentives to correct for failures in the market for information about contraception could be effective in many developing countries, but that incentives to correct for externalities are harder to justify, would probably involve larger financial amounts, and raise a number of difficult ethical issues.

15. For a discussion of these policies as interventions to reduce fertility, see World Bank (1984). Although it may be counterintuitive, it is easily demonstrated that interventions that would improve the lives of people, such as education and programs that lower mortality, will increase the "price" of the quantity of children by raising the cost of inputs required to rear children, such as the opportunity cost of parents' time; see Becker and Lewis (1974).

16. Note that the definition of the "welfare" of poor (or other) persons is what *they* think makes them better-off, not what others believe should make them better-off. A compulsory population program that is imposed on the poor and that provides no compensation to them gives little weight to their perception of what makes them better-off.

17. It should be noted that figure 9.1 contains no information about the distribution of output gains between rich and poor if a society (or the world) succeeds in moving from M to N.

18. Note that although wages are depressed in this scenario, rents and profits are boosted. High fertility is therefore potentially Pareto-superior to low fertility, assuming that there is a mechanism for redistributing some of the rents of landlords and capitalists (Ng 1986; and Willis 1987).

19. Studies on the determinants of fertility are reviewed in Birdsall (1988). See also World Bank (1984). Birdsall and Griffin (1988) review the evidence that reduced fertility, including among the poor, is associated with lower infant mortality, more educated mothers, better educational opportunities for children, and better access to family planning services.

20. Family planning services, if of reasonable quality, have certainly contributed to lower fertility, though they are most effective where women are reasonably well educated. In Bangladesh, where women's education is low, contraceptive use rose from 14 to 31 percent in the 1980s, and the total fertility rate fell from 6.3 to 4.6 (Ahmed 1987).

21. Nerlove, Razin, and Sadka (1987) show that, if parents do not care about their children, an intergenerational externality will not exist. In the more likely case that parents do care about their children, an intergenerational externality can arise because their altruism drives a wedge between the private and social costs of additional children. Altruism of parents (or caring about their progeny) enters through the utility function and is consequently subject to the usual concavity restrictions. People with higher incomes can afford to be more altruistic because the amount of altruism "purchased" depends on income, just as purchases of other goods would.

22. A second type of argument, based on the quantity-quality tradeoff, leads to the same conclusion. Higher-quality (healthier, better educated) children may be valued by parents, but they are costly. In developing countries, children enter the budget constraint on both the expenditure and the income sides because they can add to family income. At low levels of family income it is possible that, even though the quality of children is an important consideration, families are so constrained by their low income that short-term survival leads them to place greater weight on children's incomes, however low, than on

spending for children's quality. Thus, the fact that parents care about their children may not cause them to behave in a way that is entirely in the long-term interests of the children. Poor parents must make difficult choices as they juggle a number of conflicting objectives.

23. We assume here that the burden of taxes is borne by the rich. This is more obvious if we consider transfers through international aid programs as taxes on the rich countries.

24. We make a distinction between potential and actual utility. The maximum potential utility of the rich drops as we move from UPF_1 to UPF_2, which is seen in the drop in the y-intercept. The converse is true for the poor, as seen in the increase of the x-intercept between the two regimes. The reason is that society, through the social programs we have posited, has chosen to give up some goods that the rich would enjoy consuming in order to provide basic services needed by the poor. *Actual* utility is shown by the X's in the graph. The rich give up potential utility because doing so increases their actual utility, from X_1 to X_2 (or X_3). Actual utility increases because, in this example, the poor have fewer children as a result of the social programs, an outcome that is valued by the rich. It is almost inevitable that a noncoercive approach to social policy means that society must move northeast from X_1 into a region where both the rich and the poor are at least as well-off as before the program is instituted.

25. For example, taxpayers in industrial countries finance, through bilateral aid, programs in Africa or South Asia to reduce fertility.

26. Note also that society may care about income distribution and poverty per se, and prefer a more to a less equal distribution and less poverty to more poverty. If this is so, it strengthens the argument for fertility reduction programs, defined in the broad sense, that we have used. Reducing the fertility of the poor as a means of reducing poverty may be preferable to direct income transfers, and it may be less likely to introduce perverse incentives (for example, for labor supply). But the argument that the maximum point of social welfare depends on equity as well as efficiency is a problematic one. There is no consensus on whether a social welfare function could be identified for a specific society, what information it would convey to us in a practical sense, whether it is possible to aggregate individual preferences regarding equity to arrive at any consensus about income distribution, and what types of interpersonal comparisons of welfare could be defended and acted upon through public policy. Of course, despite these reservations, income distribution decisions lie at the base of most public policy decisions, which are made all the time. Nor does anybody *really* doubt that some socially desirable outcome is achieved when food is transferred from the table of a replete person to the hands of a starving person.

27. See Chomitz and Birdsall (1991) for a formal discussion of incentives and fertility reduction.

Poverty, Policy, and Industrialization in the Past

10

Ben Polak
Jeffrey G. Williamson

Does industrialization increase or decrease poverty? There has been much debate among development economists on this question of late. Debate on the same question attracted even more attention as the first industrial revolution unfolded in Britain in the early nineteenth century. Pessimists say it increased poverty; optimists say it didn't. An outside observer might well be puzzled that there is a debate at all. After all, what's the counterfactual? Are the pessimists really arguing that things would have been better for the poor without an industrial revolution? Can any pessimist really believe that slower growth is better for the poor than faster growth? Of course not. What the pessimists are really saying is this: just how much poverty is eradicated by industrialization depends on the form that industrialization takes. The better we understand that historical moral, the better we will be equipped to understand how contemporary economic growth in the developing world can aid or impede progress in eradicating poverty.

This chapter poses two questions. First, what happened to the share of the population in poverty, and to the living standards of the poor, during nineteenth-century industrial revolutions? Second, why did poverty statistics behave the way they did? The first question is easier, and we start there.

Morris and Adelman (1988) assert that poverty was worse in those countries in which industrialization was more rapid, such as Belgium and Britain, than in countries in which industrialization was slower, such as France and Switzerland. They base their assertions on qualitative evidence, however, and they may have confused awareness of poverty with prevalence of poverty. There are no data that permit a comparison of the numbers in poverty across nations in the nineteenth century, let alone the living standards of the poor. Thus, this chapter will limit its coverage of changes in poverty to two situations in which comparative judgments are more tractable. We can get some impression of the trends in and composition of poverty in Britain and the United States in the nineteenth century: what little we know about other countries does not appear to conflict with this experience.

The second question is harder. Do industrialization and modern economic growth diminish poverty? On the face of it, the answer seems obvious. If by growth we mean an increase in per capita income, *and if there is no change in the distribution of that income,* then by definition the incomes of the poor will rise along with everything else; people will escape from poverty. This trickle-down theory suggests that it is not possible to discuss the effect of growth on poverty without discussing its effect on distribution. Did inequality rise so sharply during past industrialization that the share in poverty could have risen, or the average living standards of the poor have fallen? That would have required severe trends indeed; but it is important to understand that the forces driving inequality are similar to the forces driving poverty. Although increasing inequality need not imply increasing poverty, it may well imply a slow rate of escape from poverty.

Modern economic growth can affect poverty both directly and indirectly. The direct influence has already been stated: if incomes of the poor rise along with average incomes, then poverty declines. The indirect influence takes account of the fact that much of the poverty that we observe both in the nineteenth century and today occurs at predictable stages in an individual's life cycle. The incidence of poverty is greatest among those who do not earn full incomes, such as the aged, or among those subject to crisis, such as the sick or widowed. It is a mistake to infer that higher incomes have no indirect effect on such individuals even if they are cut off from the market economy. After all, those who receive higher incomes, including the working poor, should be better able to save for crises and old age. And the growth of, and wider access to, financial institutions for saving, credit, and insurance should help even poor individuals to spread their lifetime incomes over their lifetime needs. Furthermore, a richer society can be expected to be willing and able to transfer more resources to those in need, whether through state intervention, private charity, or transfers between family members. As it turns out, however, none of these potential indirect connections between higher incomes and poverty helped the poor very much in nineteenth-century Britain and the United States.

There are four ways that poverty might fail to fall early in industrial revolutions:

- Earnings of the working poor may lag behind in response to technological events driving industrial revolutions.
- The cost of living facing the poor may rise for the same reasons, eroding their living standards in ways that conventional income statistics may fail to capture.
- Early industrial revolutions may undermine both the earnings potential of secondary unskilled workers and the secondary earning sources of primary unskilled workers.
- Modern economic growth may erode nonmarket entitlements that serve as safety nets in preindustrial societies.

1.   The most important way that early industrialization might raise poverty, or at least inhibit its eradication, is if it generates rising inequality: the left arm of Kuznets's inverted U-curve. There is some evidence that this occurred in the nineteenth century (Lindert and Williamson 1985; and Williamson 1985). Inequality seems to have been driven by unskilled-labor-saving technical change,

a phenomenon emphasized by Marx and explored at length by development economists in the 1960s and 1970s. The derived demand for unskilled labor does not share equally in the boom for other primary inputs—such as land, skills, and capital—during early industrial revolutions. And if the working poor suffer, those in extreme poverty suffer more.

There is a tendency, in writing about poverty, to associate it with low-wage jobs, and to reach the empty conclusion that low pay harmed the poor. It is surely a mistake to blame the existence of poverty on the existence of low-wage jobs in what in the nineteenth century was called the sweated trades or casual employment and what is now called the informal sector. After all, how would the poor have been affected if such low-wage jobs were unavailable? Instead, we should try to isolate the forces of demand and supply for unskilled labor that resulted in such low wages. The next section will identify some historical cases in which unskilled-labor-saving technological progress tended to retard the growth in the demand for unskilled labor. These cases suggest that the poor failed to share fully in economic progress.

2.   There is a second, and directly related, way that early industrial revolutions can inhibit poverty eradication. Technical change during the early industrial revolutions was slowest in the production of those goods and services that were most important to the poor—in particular, food and housing. The shares of family income spent on both food and housing were larger for the poor than for higher-income classes. Therefore, relative price increases in food and housing affected the poor disproportionately. We do not measure the effects of high food prices and bad housing very well, but they seem to have been manifested by a decline in nutritional status and physical well-being during the early industrial revolutions (Fogel 1989).

In England the terms of trade between farm and nonfarm goods rose through most of the nineteenth century, driven by unbalanced productivity advance favoring nonfarm sectors and by inelastic land supplies. The relative cost of urban housing rose even more, again driven by relatively slow technical progress and scarce land. Rising rents encouraged the poor to crowd into (and drive up the rents of) lower-quality housing. Overcrowding increased the mortality and morbidity of the poor, and reduced their ability to work. The poor tended to concentrate in the core of nineteenth-century cities, rather than at the periphery as in the squatter developments in developing countries today. This, plus government neglect of urban infrastructure, heightened the environmental deterioration surrounding the urban poor in the early nineteenth century. The quality of urban life then was even lower than that observed in the worst cities in the developing world today.

Of course, not all sectoral price changes are bad for the poor. In the late nineteenth century, relaxation of the land constraints in both housing and agriculture led to relative cost reductions that helped the poor. The urban transport revolution gradually increased the distances that people could travel to work, enabling some to escape the worst slums to the benign periphery. The scarcity of agricultural land in Europe was overcome by importing cheap food from the

New World. This was facilitated in part by technical progress in rail and sea freight and in part by the lowering of tariffs protecting domestic agriculture (O'Rourke and Williamson 1992).

In the early stages of the industrial revolution, however, the same forces that tended to cause the income of the working poor to lag behind also tended to raise their relative cost of living. In short, the pattern of technical change across sectors lowered the prices of the goods that the poor produced relative to those of the goods that the poor consumed.

3.   Before moving on to the other forces that may have contributed to the slowing of progress in eradicating poverty early in the industrial revolution, we should reiterate that beneath the working poor were the extreme poor. These included disproportionate numbers of old and sick people, large families, and female-headed households. This chapter therefore considers how technical change affected the demand for the labor of women, children, and the elderly. A definitive historical answer is not yet within our grasp, but a key part of the answer depends on the fate of cottage, or domestic, industries. These were and are very important to the economic status of the poor. They were and are intensive in their use of the labor of women, children, and the elderly, and hence are important income sources for vulnerable groups. They often required little strength and could be undertaken alongside child care in the home, where the pace of production was self-regulated. Moreover, these industries were often an important secondary source of income for the family, a source that took on extra importance during slack agricultural seasons and periods of low market employment or food shortages. The rise of the factory and the development of integrated commodity markets may have tended to eliminate these cottage industries. That fact is much stressed by pessimists in the standard-of-living debate; we return to it later.

4.   The other chief way in which early industrialization might increase distress among the poor is by eroding traditional means of support and nonmarket entitlements. Many reasons have been cited for this erosion, including the breakdown of the village "moral economy" (Scott 1976), and the increased importance of migration generating "child default" on parental investment (Williamson 1986). The greatest danger to the poor arises during the lag between the destruction of older support systems and their replacement by modern government transfer mechanisms (Sen 1981a). Lindert (1989), for example, argues that modern transfer systems were not introduced in the first industrial countries until the twentieth century, and only then in response to the fact that slowly improving economic conditions of the poor had increased their political voice.

Others have pointed out, however, that a large part of the responsibility for poor relief in preindustrial societies was in fact borne by local government, in the form of both entitlements and price intervention. The erosion of these traditional support mechanisms was the direct result of the laissez-faire government policies that tended to accompany industrialization.

Of course, safety nets were not the only government policy that affected the poor. In this chapter we also discuss policy designed to twist the relative prices of food and manufactures, and policy on urban infrastructure. We chose these for two reasons. First, as we have already emphasized, food and urban amenities were of particular importance to the poor. Second, these policies appear to follow patterns that are replicated in the developing world today.

Having suggested four main ways in which early industrialization might inhibit poverty eradication, we return to a central theme of this chapter: few people really believe that economic growth per se makes the poor poorer; most believe instead that the processes and policies associated with various growth regimes might do so. This suggests that the arguments sometimes put forward by the optimists are simply not relevant to the claims put forward by the pessimists. For example, in a recent survey Fields (1989b) compares changes in the proportion of the population that is poor in developing countries exhibiting rapid growth with changes in the proportion of poor in those exhibiting stagnation. He concludes that the poor did better during periods of rapid growth. Similarly, the Council of Economic Advisers found in 1964 that the share in poverty in the United States declined more rapidly in periods of rapid growth. But few have denied that rapid growth is better than slow growth for eradicating poverty, *given the economic structure and policy environment.* The question is how changes in that structure and policy environment—perhaps themselves causes or effects of growth—affect the poor.

This is an ambitious set of questions to ask with regard to nineteenth-century experience. Despite the attention that historians have paid to these questions since Britain started the first industrial revolution, history yields the answers only with great reluctance. Yet a survey of what we do know may still help place the contemporary debate in perspective. What, then, does nineteenth-century experience tell us about the connection among industrialization, mediating policies, and resulting changes in the well-being of the poor?

Inequality during past industrial revolutions

The pessimists' argument that economic growth coincides with increasing poverty rests on the claim that the poor's share of income falls sharply as average incomes rise. This section argues that the interaction between growth, inequality, and poverty is conditioned by the way in which development shapes the rewards to unskilled labor relative to capital, land, and skills. When we understand what forces condition the demand and supply for unskilled labor relative to other factors, we will have learned much about the most important determinant of poverty eradication: the path of real unskilled wages. This section reviews what history tells us about those forces.

Labor-saving technological change

Technological progress tends to economize on some factors of production while favoring the use of others. An unskilled-labor-saving bias can widen income gaps by worsening job prospects and wages for the unskilled while bidding up the returns to skills, capital, and perhaps even land. Economic history provides some support for this case. We know, for example, that U.S. growth in the nineteenth century was heavily unskilled-labor-saving; the same seems to have been true of Britain prior to 1860, and, most would argue, of the developing world since 1950.

Did the high rates of unskilled-labor saving abate as the early industrializing countries approached maturity? The best evidence is from the United States, where several studies have found a strong aggregate labor-saving bias from about 1900 to 1929, followed by a switch to either neutrality or a labor-using bias until the Korean War. Labor saving meant unskilled-labor saving, and thus was especially important for the wages of the near-poor. Thus, the downswing of the Kuznets curve, which starts in the late nineteenth century in Britain and after 1929 in the United States, may have been due to a switch in the bias of aggregate technological progress away from unskilled-labor saving.

What do we mean by unskilled-labor saving? It can appear in the historical data for any of three reasons: a labor-saving bias within industries; shifts in the output mix away from labor-intensive sectors, notably agriculture; and relatively rapid technological advance in capital- and skill-intensive industries, raising relative demand for these factors provided the industries face price-elastic demands for their output. The first source—labor saving at the industry level—was a favorite subject of econometric analysis two decades or so ago, but nothing in that literature establishes any historical pattern, Kuznetsian or otherwise. The second and third sources appear more promising.

The classic example of changes in the output mix during development is the transition from an agrarian base toward industry. If land ownership is highly concentrated, this shift can have an egalitarian effect on *overall* income distribution. But for the poor, the net effect of industrialization on the demand for unskilled labor is more relevant. Thus, as unskilled-labor-intensive agriculture undergoes a relative decline, so does the demand for the services of the working poor. Such changes in output mix are not in general exogenous. They can be the direct consequence of growth, through Engel effects. They can also be the consequence of foreign demand, or they can be induced by an urban bias in government policy, a topic that we discuss in a later section. And they can be caused by the unbalanced technical advance favoring capital- and skill-intensive sectors that seems to have characterized the early stages of development in both Britain and the United States. In both countries the timing of the switch to more balanced productivity advance seems to have coincided with a historic peak in the Kuznets curve.

Capital goods production and accumulation

The capital goods sector deserves special attention for three reasons. First, its rapid growth characterizes nineteenth-century industrialization. Second, the production of capital goods tends to be capital- and skill-intensive. Third, when used as inputs to production downstream, capital goods tend to be skill complements and unskilled labor substitutes. The growth of this sector thus shifted relative factor demand away from unskilled labor.

Why did the production of capital goods grow so fast? History offers three explanations: (1) labor-saving and capital-using development created a strong demand downstream; (2) technical change in the capital goods sector itself lowered supply prices and encouraged increased capital-intensity downstream; and (3) an increase in the savings rate augmented the demand for capital assets.

What were the effects of capital accumulation on poverty? The answer cannot rely solely on simple capital-deepening stories. Capital accumulation—to the extent that it was driven by technical changes that increased capital's productivity downstream or decreased the cost of producing capital goods upstream— decreased the relative demand for unskilled labor. To the extent that it was driven by increased saving, the effect on the relative income of unskilled labor is ambiguous. As capital supplies increased, quasi-rents on skills rose, but rents on capital fell. Overall, early capital deepening seems to have increased inequality, and to have had only modest effects in eradicating poverty, but we should interpret this as a consequence of biased technical change, not of the increase in the supply of savings.

Labor supply: Flooding the bottom

So much for the demand for unskilled labor; what about supply? It has become common in the historical literature to associate the demographic transition with labor surplus, poverty, and inequality. The argument develops as follows. Modern economic growth begins on a traditional agrarian base characterized by elastic labor supplies, better known as surplus unskilled labor. Accelerating rates of capital accumulation thus fail to generate rising wages among the unskilled until the surplus labor pool is exhausted. This turning point can be postponed if the forces of either demographic transition or immigration continually replenish the pool. Indeed, these forces could even depress real wages among the poor.

Increased fertility and immigration associated with the industrial revolution foster poverty in two ways. First, they glut labor markets with young and unskilled new entrants, causing massive changes in the age distribution of the population and the labor force. Such changes in the age distribution can create poverty even if factor prices and the structure of incomes are unaffected, because there will be more people at the bottom of the distribution than before (Kuznets 1976; and Morley 1981). Second, the glut lowers the relative wage of the unskilled poor, while raising the returns to skills and conventional capital. It also follows that countries that were beset with immigration during their industrial revolutions are more likely to exhibit rising inequality and poverty (as in the New World). Similarly, countries that underwent significant emigration during their industrial revolutions are more likely to have avoided such problems (as in the Old World). And countries that underwent more dramatic demographic transitions are far more likely to trace out unambiguous Kuznets curves in their historical data than those that did not (such as France and Japan).

What about the expenditure side?

While the poor experienced lagging income in nineteenth-century Britain and the United States, they also suffered on the expenditure side, as the relative price of their consumption bundles rose sharply. That is, the same forces that caused the wages of the poor to lag behind also raised the poor's living costs—by lowering the prices of the goods that they produced relative to those of the goods they consumed. Most critical among these forces were unbalanced productivity advance, inelastic land supplies, and an antipoor regime of state intervention.

The relative prices of food and housing are crucial to the story, since both loomed so large in the budgets of the poor, especially the urban poor. For the extreme poor, these relative prices were even more important; the poorer the household, the larger the share of the budget devoted to food and shelter. Both relative prices increased during periods of rising income inequality. Technological advance was fast in industry, but slow in agriculture and urban housing, thus increasing the relative price of the two wage goods most important to the poor. These technological forces were reinforced by inelastic supplies of land, which were, of course, more important inputs to agriculture and urban housing than to manufacturing. To make matters even worse for the poor, domestic price policies biased against agriculture often raised the cost of food even more, and inadequate public investment in urban infrastructure, especially in poor districts, aggravated the effect of crowding on the poor. These policies are explored in a later section.

We first establish the assertion that food and housing were the key wage goods of the poor in the nineteenth century. We focus here on the urban poor,

Table 10.1 Expenditure shares of urban poor in the nineteenth century, Britain and the United States

	Share in expenditure (percent)		
	---	---	---
Group	Food	Rent, fuel, and lighting	Clothing
Massachusetts, unskilled urban poor, 1875	68.9	20.6	4.1
London, unskilled urban poor, 1795-1845	63.8	23.2	13.0
Late nineteenth-century Northampton, England			
Income group (shillings earned per week)			
< 10	—	44	—
10-15	—	40	—
15-20	—	23	—
20-25	—	20	—
25-30	—	20	—
30-35	—	20	—
35-40	—	17	—
40-45	—	15	—
45-50	—	14	—
50-55	—	13	—
55-60	—	10	—
60+	—	8	—

— Not available.

Source: For Massachusetts, Williamson and Lindert 1980; for London, Williamson 1985; and for Northampton, Bowley and Burnett-Hurst 1915.

who were increasing as a share of the total poor as the century progressed. For the urban poor in Massachusetts in 1875, 89.5 percent of expenditure was on food and rent: 68.9 percent went toward food and 20.6 percent toward rent (table 10.1). Similar shares were typical of London's poor in the early nineteenth century. In Northampton, England, the share of expenditure on rent varied dramatically among income classes at the end of the nineteenth century, from 44 percent among the extreme poor to only 8 percent among the richest.

What happened to the prices of these key wage goods? Three pieces of evidence confirm that the relative price of these wage goods rose during the first half of the nineteenth century. First, in eastern U.S. cities the ratio of the living costs of the poor to those of the rich rose by about 10 percent over the first two decades of rapid industrialization (1820-39), driven by the terms-of-trade forces outlined above. This estimated rise in the relative cost of living for the urban poor was driven by the increase in the relative price of food (Williamson 1976) and is understated because it excludes rents.

Second, the relative price of food in England also rose during the first industrial revolution. Between 1820 and 1840 the terms of trade between food (accounting for 63.8 percent of expenditures by the poor) and textiles (accounting for only 13 percent of those expenditures) almost tripled (Lindert and Williamson 1983). And third, the relative price of housing for the urban poor (23 to 44 percent of their budgets) also increased dramatically, at 2 to 3 percent a year through 1800-40 (table 10.2). Real rents may therefore have increased by as much as 30 percent—eroding the urban poor's living standards by 7 to 13 percent—*each decade*.

Thus, the poor suffered on two counts: employment and expenditure. Increasingly expensive food and housing forced them to economize on both, leading to poorer nutrition and overcrowding in slum dwellings, where they were exposed to greater health hazards. The result was far higher mortality and morbidity rates in the cities (table 10.3), where an increasing share of the poor lived as the industrial revolution wore on. These high rates persisted throughout Europe and the United States until late in the century, when the state began to allocate more resources to the expensive task of cleaning up the urban environment.

Table 10.2 Trends in urban rents, England, 1790-1840
(annual percentage growth)

Item	1790 to 1839-40	1790 to 1839-42	1800-40
Black Country town rents	—	—	1.7
Leeds rents			
Demand-side estimate	2.0	—	—
Supply-side estimate	3.6	—	—
Average	2.8	—	—
Trentham (Staffordshire) rents	—	2.9	—
Cost of living	0.3	0.3	-0.9
Rents relative to cost of living	2.5	2.6	2.6

— Not available.
Source: Williamson 1990a, table 9.1.

Table 10.3 Infant mortality rates in England's cities and countryside, 1841, 1871, and 1906
(deaths per thousand)

Region	1841	1871	1906
North			
Benign countryside	114.8	156.1	145.3
Ugly cities	174.5	212.1	148.8
Difference	+59.7	+56.0	+3.5
Yorkshire			
Benign countryside	138.3	163.5	138.9
Ugly cities	171.7	189.4	149.5
Difference	+33.4	+25.9	+10.6
Lancashire-Cheshire			
Benign countryside	154.7	172.3	143.4
Ugly cities	198.2	195.6	164.1
Difference	+43.5	+23.3	+20.7
Midlands			
Benign countryside	137.0	124.9	116.8
Ugly cities	190.2	193.2	145.4
Difference	+53.2	+68.3	+28.6
East and South			
Benign countryside	129.8	154.3	110.5
Ugly cities	173.2	170.9	133.0
Difference	+43.4	+16.6	+22.5

Source: Williamson 1990a, table 9.3.

What about the living standards of the poor?

Increasing inequality between the rich and the poor need not preclude improvements in poor people's absolute standard of living. The best information documenting such improvements during nineteenth-century industrial revolutions concerns England, and is summarized in figure 10.1. Four occupational groups are presented there: two represent the poor—farm laborers and the urban unskilled (middle group), one the more skilled urban workers (artisans), and one the most skilled and literate (white collar).

Until 1819 there was almost no increase in the living standards of the poor. Between 1819 and 1851 their living standards rose, but by less than those of skilled workers; farm laborers lagged furthest behind, as the wage gap between city and countryside opened up. Indeed, the nominal gap in England reached 73 percent by the 1830s, a gap greater even than that in the United States in the late nineteenth-century or that in much of today's developing world (Williamson 1987). Furthermore, these real wage gains among the poor would look even more modest if we could adjust for the declining quality of life associated with cities' high mortality rates and poor amenities. Only in late nineteenth-century Britain did the growth of real unskilled wages accelerate. In the very long run industrialization *did* pull people out of poverty, but progress was slow, and its start was delayed.

Figure 10.1 Average full-time earnings for adult male workers, Britain, 1781–1851
(constant prices)

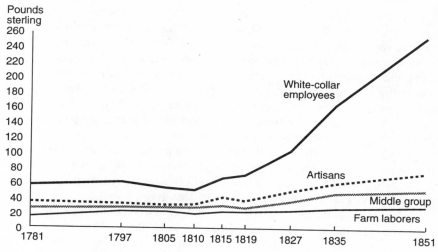

Source: Lindert and Williamson 1983: 12–13.

So far we have shown that, due to technical and demographic changes associated with growth, the benefits of nineteenth-century industrialization were slow to trickle down to real unskilled wages and hence to the living standards of the near-poor. In the next section we identify the extremely poor, and show that improvement was probably even slower for them.

What about poverty?

What can we say about the evolution of poverty in countries undergoing industrialization in the nineteenth century? Adelman and Morris (1978) and Morris and Adelman (1988) have used a wide range of sources to compare poverty across countries in the nineteenth century. The evidence leads them to pessimistic conclusions: "at low levels of development any kind of structural change such as industrialization or expanded commercialization tends to increase poverty among the poorest members of the population" (1978: 256). But much of their evidence is qualitative and impressionistic. There are dangers in using such evidence. For example, there was an increase in writing about the poor in the nineteenth century, but that does not necessarily mean that there was an increase in poverty. Upper classes may have been made more aware of poverty by changes in its location: rapid urbanization brought with it an increase in residential crowding—the most obvious and outward sign of poverty—near the doorsteps of the urban middle classes. The impression that this squalor made on Engels, Carlyle, Mayhew, and Dickens is important in its own right: it has shaped the popular image of poverty during the industrial revolution. But such evidence will not easily support claims that there was more poverty in rapidly industrializing

England than in slowly industrializing France, where more of the poor were rural and out of sight.

Ideally, we would like to have household survey data of the kind favored by Fields (1989b) in his recent survey of poverty and economic growth in the developing world. But no such data exist for most of the nineteenth century. Only toward the end of the century was there a series of detailed investigations of urban poverty that can be seen as the precursors of the kind of household surveys that Fields favors. For earlier periods, we must rely on data generated by local administrators providing poor relief to "paupers" in Britain and America. *Paupers* refers to those on relief, not to those in poverty, and the difference between the two will widen or narrow as public generosity changes. So, how good are data on paupers in documenting trends in poverty?

Figure 10.2 tests the claim that statistics on paupers can be used as a proxy for poverty. It is based on a survey of the incomes of people over age sixty-five in twenty-eight places in England in 1899. The horizontal axis shows the proportion of old people with known incomes of less than 10 shillings a week. The vertical axis shows the proportion of old people who were, or had been, receiving outside poor relief (that is, relief outside the workhouse). There is a clear, if imperfect, relation between the two proportions, which becomes even stronger when we control for policy.

Does economic growth reduce poverty?

Having established that pauperism can be used as an imperfect proxy for poverty, what can we say about long-term trends? In figure 10.3 there appears, at first sight, to be a clear downward trend from the late 1840s to World War I. But a closer look reveals that it is outdoor relief that declined. Some have concluded that the overall decline is evidence of the authorities' success in limiting access to outdoor relief rather than of an improvement in the standard of living of the extreme poor. But the decline in the share of paupers in the population after the 1840s is nonetheless consistent with wage trends for the working poor.

So far, we have discussed trends in poverty after the late 1840s. What about early industrialization—a period of greater interest to contemporary analysts of problems in the developing world? Here we are on

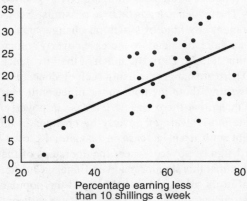

Figure 10.2 Old age poor and old age pauperism, England and Wales, 1899

Adjusted sample, outside pauper rate (percent)

Percentage earning less than 10 shillings a week

Source: United Kingdom, Parliament 1900.

Figure 10.3 Paupers per 1,000 people, England, 1840–1939

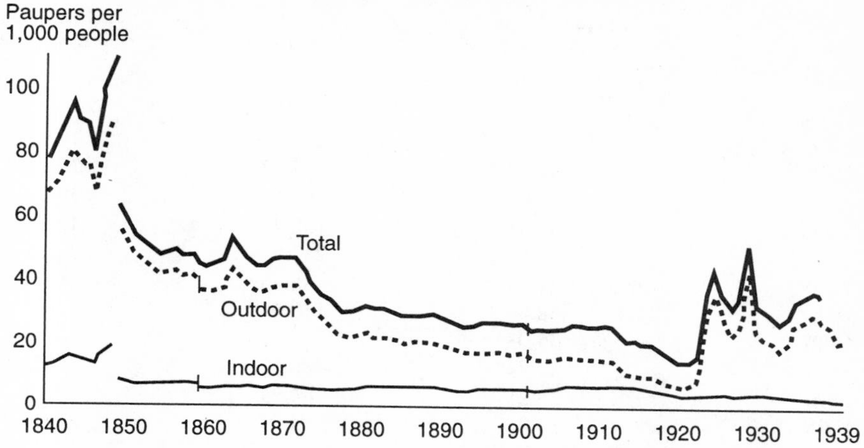

Source: Williams 1981: 164.

even shakier ground. The original social tables by Gregory King (1688), Joseph Massie (1759), Patrick Colquhoun (1801-03, 1812), and Dudley Baxter (1868) took very different approaches to estimating pauperism, but they did supply some well-informed guesses. The revised social tables show the following trend in the share of the population in poverty in Britain (Williamson 1985): in 1759, 12.5 percent; in 1801-03, 19.9 percent; in 1812, 14.8 percent; in 1850, 10 percent; and in 1867, 6.2 percent. The share of the population in poverty increased in the late eighteenth century, a period of stable real wages for the poor. Between 1812 and 1850 that share declined slowly at a rate of 0.3 percent per decade; the real wages of the unskilled had begun to rise, although at a rate that lagged behind increases in wages for other groups. The rate of reduction of the share in poverty accelerated thereafter to 2.2 percent per decade—a result consistent with figure 10.3 and with the previous section. Of course, changes in the supply of relief may have influenced those estimates; the supply probably grew until the early nineteenth century but then fell until 1850. These trends must therefore be treated with caution, but they support the view that economic growth reduces poverty, although at a rate that can vary considerably.

Table 10.4 reports rates of pauperism for New York State at five-year intervals from 1835 to 1895. Pauperism (and poverty) rose throughout the antebellum period, and Hannon (1986) views these trends as evidence of an increase in the demand for poor relief and thus in the distress of the poor. The big gains in poverty reduction in the United States, according to such proxies, came after 1865 as industrialization hit full stride, much as in Britain.

Regional variation in poverty: Industrialization and urbanization

We might get a better impression of the aggregate effect on the poor of long-term economic development by comparing rates of pauperism in agricultural and

Table 10.4 Local relief recipients, New York State, 1835-95
(per thousand)

Year	New York State	New York City	Rest of state
1835	18.69	84.03	8.73
1840	25.17	88.11	15.27
1846[a]	38.51	146.43	18.93
1850	42.26	97.47	29.13
1855	65.04	160.61	39.73
1860	65.93	138.42	42.33
1865	81.10	233.98	39.95
1870	51.50	85.43	40.96
1874[b]	68.49	130.68	47.77
1880	55.03	124.79	28.79
1885	39.84	86.72	22.42
1890	35.21	64.74	21.59
1895	35.07	54.03	26.96

a. There is no figure for 1845.
b. The figures for 1875 are out of line with the neighboring years. They are 101.43, 253.40, and 53.38, respectively.
Source: Hannon 1986, appendix A.

industrial counties. Table 10.5 gives such rates for the early stages of the British industrial revolution, 1803-04. Excluding London, as in the last two rows, reveals no obvious difference between agricultural and industrial counties in the generosity of relief policy (as measured by the proportion of paupers forced into the workhouse, with low proportions implying generous relief policy). But in the agricultural counties, despite the high agricultural prices caused by the Napoleonic Wars, a far higher proportion were on relief. This suggests that poverty was either more widespread in agricultural areas or more widespread in those areas (in the South) most distant from new industrial job opportunities (in the North). The scanty data suggest the latter. Among the agricultural counties for which data are available, the two northernmost (Lincoln and Rutland) had the smallest shares of paupers. Among the ten industrial counties, three of the four with rates of pauperism over 13 percent are southern, and five of the six with rates under 10 percent are northern.

It appears that during the British industrial revolution the poor fared better in the regions that underwent industrialization. Indeed, the effect on poverty of the better earning opportunities generated by industrialization in the North spilled over into the agricultural areas within the region. The rural poor could and did move to urban areas, with the result that higher wages and less poverty prevailed throughout the North.

While regions that grew fast and that industrialized tended to have lower poverty rates, the effect of urbanization per se is ambiguous. Statistical studies from both sides of the Atlantic found that town size made almost no difference to the proportion of the population who were paupers, after other factors were controlled for (Hannon 1984b; MacKinnon 1986; and United Kingdom, Parliament 1910, vol. LIII, p. 390). The new earning opportunities for the poor in the

Table 10.5 County paupers, England and Wales, 1803-04
(percent)

Region	Paupers as share of population	Indoor paupers as share of total
England and Wales	11.4	8.0
Industrial counties	9.5	10.9
Agricultural counties	16.1	7.7
Industrial counties, excluding Middlesex and Surrey (London)	9.8	7.2

Note: Agricultural and *industrial* are as defined in the original *Parliamentary Papers.*
Source: Williams 1981.

towns were perhaps roughly balanced by the influx of unskilled labor to the towns, leaving the proportion in poverty unchanged. Nineteenth-century England and America saw a relocation of the poor (as well as the nonpoor) to the towns. As table 10.3 suggests, however, the living conditions of the poor were worse in the towns. We return below to the policy problems posed by the urbanization of the poor.

Who were the poor and who were the paupers?

The question of who were the poor and who were the paupers is important for two reasons. First, economic development may affect different groups in different ways. If we can identify the groups that are poor, we may be able to say something more useful about the relation of poverty to growth. Second, there may be differences between the composition of the poor and that of the paupers. The poor were largely in households of low-wage, unskilled workers; hence, the main forces driving changes in their well-being were those discussed earlier: the introduction of labor-saving production methods and adverse shifts in terms of trade. The paupers, on the other hand, represent the *extreme* poor. Their well-being may be less directly related to the wages of the unskilled.

The number of male, able-bodied paupers fell over the nineteenth century in England; by 1901 this group had shrunk to approximately 7 percent of its size a century earlier (Williams 1981). One reason for the decrease was the conscious decision by British authorities to refuse outdoor relief to healthy adult males. The other cause was market-related—rising wages, driven by market forces already discussed.

By the end of the century, however, we must look beyond the adult male work force when discussing pauperism and extreme poverty. Then, as now, the elderly, the sick, widows, children of single parents, and those in large families were much more likely to be very poor. Poverty follows the life cycle. This is illustrated in figure 10.4, which shows rates of pauperism by age group in England and Wales in 1906. The rates rise steeply in old age: almost one in five of the population over 65 and almost one in four of those over 70 were receiving poor relief.

People over 65 constituted 28.3 percent of all paupers in the 1906 census and 35.3 percent of those in the workhouses. There are no data on the ages of outdoor paupers before 1890, but the percentage of paupers listed as "not able-bodied" (of which 80 percent were over age 60 in 1906) rises from 38.9 percent in 1850 to a peak of 49.2 percent in 1900. The percentage of indoor paupers over age 65 rose in the same period from 19.8 percent to 36.5 percent of the workhouse population (Williams 1981). For both groups, the rise was due in part to the decision in the 1870s to restrict outdoor relief to the elderly. The trends continue until 1900, however, suggesting that government policy is not the only driving force.

Three conclusions seem warranted by the data. First, the economic position of the elderly was falling behind that of the rest of the working class in the late nineteenth century. Second, English poor relief was becoming less generous to the elderly over the same period. Third, this older and more vulnerable age group increased as a share of paupers, a result driven in part by the forces of industrialization, and in part by demographic events. (The role of demographic forces sends an important warning about "the greying of poverty" for Asian countries, which face an unprecedentedly rapid aging of their populations in 1990-2010.) The demographic influence became increasingly strong as Britain began to move along the downside of the demographic transition and the elderly increased as a share of the population. An increasing number of aged were left behind by their children, who migrated in increasing numbers to cities in Britain and the Americas. The high incidence of pauperism among the elderly suggests that we should pay special attention to the effects of industrialization on this group.

Figure 10.4 reveals a "hump" in rates of pauperism during childhood; the rates peaked for those age ten to fourteen and then fell rapidly for teenagers, as they entered the labor market. By the end of the nineteenth century only a minority of child paupers were in two-parent families. More than half were in households headed by women, especially widows; the economic circumstances of women and children were closely related. Through early adult life, the proportion of women who were paupers rose relative to the proportion of men, peaking between the ages of thirty-five and forty-five, and then falling. The upswing coincides with the childbearing

Figure 10.4 Indoor and total paupers as a percentage of population, by age group, England and Wales, March 1906

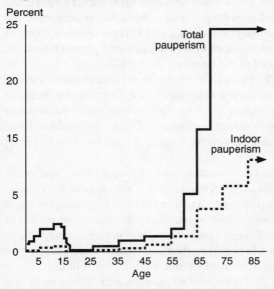

Source: United Kingdom, Parliament 1910.

years and seems to be due to the special burdens of parenthood on single or widowed mothers. The downswing may reflect a greater tendency for older women than for men to have been supported in their children's homes.

The vulnerability of widows to pauperism is a familiar problem in modern developing countries, and did not originate with industrialization. The evidence we have for preindustrial England suggests that it was far harder for a widow to remarry than for a widower, especially for a widow with dependent children. Supporting a family as a single parent was difficult then, as it is now. Consequently, almost 40 percent of widow-headed households in eighteenth-century England were on relief (Smith 1984).

Although still high, the proportion of all paupers who were widows and children and the proportion of widow-headed families that were paupers was declining in late nineteenth-century England (Williams 1981). Once again, these trends can be explained in part by government policy. Outdoor relief to these groups, as to the elderly, was systematically cut in the 1870s. The decline continues beyond that period, however, up to the eve of World War I. This is probably due to the accelerated decline in fertility after the 1880s (MacKinnon 1986; and Boyer and Williamson 1989). As the number of dependents declined, more single parents were able to get by without being driven into pauperism. These dependency rate effects should have played a symmetric role when poverty rates were rising in the late eighteenth and early nineteenth centuries on the upswing of the English demographic transition, which yields peak rates of population growth between 1820 and 1840. That is, a large share of the rise in poverty up to 1820 or 1840 is likely to have been driven by rising fertility and increasing dependency rates. The opposite seems to have been true in the late nineteenth century.

How did the composition of English poverty differ from that of English pauperism? Table 10.6 gives a breakdown of the proximate causes of urban poverty at the end of the century reported in the investigations of Rowntree and Bowley. Most of the poverty was associated with low wages or large families. Thus, widow-headed households, the elderly, and the sick made up a far smaller proportion of the poor than of the extreme poor—that is, of paupers. And although most pauperism among children was explained by single-wage families, most child poverty occurred in large families in which the chief wage earner received low pay. The proximate causes of poverty in the United States differed little from those in England (Hannon 1986).

Seasons, cycles, and secondary activities

Secondary occupations are jobs typically undertaken either by secondary wage earners in a household or by the primary wage earner as a secondary source of income. Before and during early industrialization, households often supplemented their main source of income with earnings from rural domestic, household, or cottage industries, such as spinning and weaving. Later in the industrial revolution, secondary earners worked in sweated trades—such as clothes-making shops—most notably in such large cities as London and New York. Throughout

Table 10.6 Immediate causes of poverty in five towns, England, selected years, 1899-1914

(percentage of poor households below Rowntree's poverty line)

Immediate cause	Northampton 1913	Warrington 1913	Bolton 1914	Reading 1913	York 1899
Chief wage earner					
Dead	21	6	35	14	27
Ill or old	14	1	17	11	10
Unemployed	—	3	3	2	3
Irregularly employed	—	3	6	4	3
Chief wage earner regularly employed,					
but wages insufficient for 3 children					
Families of 3 children or less	21	22	20	33	
Families of 4 children or more	9	38	9	15	
Chief wage earner regularly employed					57[a]
and wages sufficient for 3 children					
Families of 4 children or more	35	27	10	21	
Total	100	100	100	100	100

— Not available.
a. This figure applies to the last three categories combined.
Source: Bowley and Burnett-Hurst 1915; and Bowley and Hogg 1925.

the period people engaged in occupations now associated with the informal sector in developing countries, such as cleaning or street hawking.

Domestic manufacturing was hardly the only secondary occupation important in rural areas. Small farmers, whether owner-occupiers or tenants, often practiced a variety of land uses in addition to raising their main crop. Households whose main source of income was wage labor often cultivated a small plot on which they grew crops either for their own consumption or for the local market. Even landless households in preindustrial England kept their own livestock, using the commons for grazing, and urban workers often kept pigs and chickens.

Such secondary activities were especially important to the poor, and they formed part of the safety net against extreme poverty. At times of crisis, the secondary occupations became the primary source of income. Because they often had a different seasonal cycle from primary occupations—even where their long-run success was linked to that of nearby agriculture (see Hazell and Haggblade, chapter 8, this volume)—they smoothed demands on household labor and thus the household income. Outlets for the products of secondary industries were often local and hence were also less subject to macroeconomic fluctuations in demand. Varied sources of household income spread market and other risks. Furthermore, these activities typically employed a high proportion of women, children, and the elderly, groups most vulnerable to extreme poverty. These secondary activities can thus have an important effect on poverty during industrialization, and their role in modern industrializing countries differs little from their role in the nineteenth century.

Why do we find the most vulnerable groups—the elderly, women, and children—employed in domestic industries? Two explanations are the low strength requirements of most domestic tasks and the easy access to such tasks. In addition, domestic workers could, to a large degree, arrange the demands on their labor to accommodate the supply, determined by child rearing and outside labor demands. Work in domestic industries was especially convenient for women with children and for older people, because it was located in the home and flexibly paced and timed.

Thus, domestic or household industries and small land allotments probably reduced pauperism. They provided alternative income streams that became essential if the chief wage earner fell ill, or if the market demand for the primary occupation collapsed; they smoothed out seasonal fluctuations in income and provided employment for secondary workers and for groups most vulnerable to poverty. Late eighteenth-century English experts on poverty and the rural economy agreed that the erosion of allotments and domestic industries in the South was a primary cause of pauperism. Similarly, in her study of pauperism in New York State in the second quarter of the nineteenth century, Hannon (1984a, 1984b, and 1986) found that household production was negatively correlated with pauperism.

While contemporaries recognized the benefits of allotments and of domestic industry for the poor, they disapproved of the newer, urban secondary occupations. The fact that the urban poor were often employed in sweatshops or in the informal trades led many commentators to blame these industries for the existence of nineteenth-century poverty. In fact, life for the poor would have been worse without these occupations. When northern factories undermined traditional manufacturing in London, sweated trades grew up to absorb the displaced poor. Immigrants were similarly absorbed in the eastern seaboard cities of the United States. Workers for whom these trades had become the primary source of family income, such as widows, had to compete with workers for whom this was supplementary family income. With an abundant supply of unskilled labor, informal sector pay was often low and work conditions in the sweatshops were often ugly. But these industries did not cause poverty; they were a symptom of it. Had they not existed, the poor would have had to find work on an even lower demand curve.

Many studies have documented the effect of the demise of particular household industries on employment opportunities for women and the elderly. The studies often show that the demise is related to two key processes of economic development—market expansion and new technology. The story seems to be the same whether it is early nineteenth-century New England, where the cotton textile factories wiped out domestic spinning almost overnight, or late eighteenth- and early nineteenth-century Ireland, where factory competition from the Lancashire mills in England did the same.

But it would be a mistake to imply that industrialization always displaces secondary activities. It can also create them. A good historical example is offered by the evolution of technologies using cotton and wool. In the late eighteenth century, new factory spinning technologies destroyed the household hand-spinning industry, but the cheaper thread it produced led to a boom in the household weaving industry; the number of handloom weavers in Britain increased fivefold between 1780 and 1810. In the early nineteenth century, however, new factory weaving technologies undercut the handloom weavers, and by 1851 their number had returned to its 1780 level. Nor was this the end of the process. The new cheaper cloth played a role in the emergence of new sweated clothes-making industries. These industries also benefited from such technical changes as the invention of the sewing machine. By the end of the century, however, even the sweated trades were being displaced by factory production.

That the factory technologies that displaced one domestic industry often created another should not, however, lead us to the false conclusion that the extreme poor were on balance unaffected. The elderly poor were often least able to adjust to new technology. Furthermore, the new industries were often distant from those they replaced, and it was often most difficult for the elderly poor to migrate. A typical pattern was for the children of displaced workers to migrate while the old stayed put, suffering the falling wages and pauperism that accompanied the collapse in demand for their particular skills.

How did industrialization affect seasonal fluctuations in the demand for labor? This is an important question because seasonality in labor demand produced seasonality in pauperism, especially among able-bodied men. We have already noted that secondary activities tended to smooth the seasonal demand for labor either because they had different peaks than primary activities or because of their inherent flexibility in time demands. The factory-induced demise of cottage industry was one reason for the more pronounced seasonal income cycles in eighteenth-century England. Increased crop specialization, driven by rising grain prices and enclosures, was another (Snell 1985). A similar process occurred in the United States, where specialization in grain production increased as western agriculture became more closely linked to world markets.

The forces that made the rural poor more vulnerable to seasonal cycles in agriculture were not typical of the net effect of development on seasonality. Even within agriculture such new crops as turnips spread labor demands over the year. And although many industrial activities—such as construction—remained seasonal, as development shifted employment away from agriculture, it eventually led to a reduction in the importance of seasonal fluctuations in labor demand. This was clearly the main force at work. Indeed, MacKinnon (1986) shows that the difference between summer and winter rates of pauperism declined in England during the late nineteenth century.

Development increased the problem of market-oriented macroeconomic shocks, however. MacKinnon (1986 and 1987) has compared the rate of indoor pauperism among able-bodied, adult males with male unemployment rates in three areas of England from 1860 to 1910. She found a strong relationship, especially in the North, where industrialization had proceeded furthest, with pauperism lagging slightly behind unemployment. Hannon (1986) argues that the changing structure of pauperism in the United States in the first half of the nineteenth century was also due to greater reliance on the market. Short-term unemployment became a more important cause of distress as households became more dependent on specialized wage labor and as domestic employment declined.

In short, poverty became more subject to market fluctuations in the late nineteenth century as technology, market development, and the division of labor led economic agents to become more dependent on the market, and as secondary activities were undermined. These activities had been important as sources of income to supplement primary household incomes (especially under seasonally slack labor demand, and when macroeconomic shocks caused unemployment), and as primary sources of income for groups at greater risk of pauperism. One lesson of the nineteenth century is that it was the elderly and the women with children who found it hardest to adapt to economic events that diminished access to secondary employment.

Poverty and policy

Two issues hold our attention for the remainder of this chapter: the effect of macroeconomic policy on poverty and the response of policy to poverty. The literature on both is enormous, so some selectivity is necessary. We discuss only one influence of macroeconomic policy on the poor: its effect on the terms of trade between foodstuffs and manufactures. These price-twisting policies are important—first, because they hurt the poor, and second, because they follow a historical pattern. With regard to policy responses to poverty, we consider two important cases: social infrastructure investment in the cities and safety nets.

Policy intervention and price twist

Every development economist is aware that the economic policies of modern developing countries often exhibit an urban bias (Lipton 1977). Policies that twist the relative prices between (often imported) manufactures and (often exported) food and raw materials tend to be detrimental to the poor. Such policies are not new; they follow patterns established in earlier industrial revolutions.

In a recent paper Lindert (1989) has shown that most economies undergoing an industrial revolution gradually shift from policies that (implicitly or explicitly) tax agriculture to ones that (implicitly or explicitly) subsidize it. Symmetrically, the bias toward manufacturing lessens with development. Agriculture is usually the export sector and manufacturing is usually the import-competing sector. The policy switches toward the export sector tend to coincide with increases in fiscal progressivity. And these fiscal trends, in turn, tend to move with egalitarian trends in pretax market incomes. In short, antiagricultural policies, regressive fiscal policy, and market income inequality go hand in hand as countries enter their newly industrializing stage.

This pattern is evident in U.S. history. In the first half of the nineteenth century manufacturing received only modest protection. Agricultural producers in the South were well aware that policies protective of manufacturing would constitute a tax on their exports, and had the political clout to resist. The Civil

War eliminated that clout, however, and ushered in a period of antiagricultural price-twist policies that persisted until the 1930s. Since then, agriculture has been favored not only by price supports, but by explicit transfers. Similar tales can be told for France, Germany, and Japan, taking into account both direct taxation and price-twist policies. Industrial protection persisted in the nineteenth century, but was eroded in the face of agricultural interests in the twentieth century; aggressive protection of agriculture arrived in the 1930s and was reinforced by subsidies in the postwar period.

In Britain, the first nation to industrialize, the story is a bit more complex. Britain's main export good on the eve of its industrialization was manufactures, and its import-competing sector was agriculture. Nevertheless, the historical pattern is still evident. The import-competing sector (agriculture) was heavily protected during the early decades of industrialization, before 1820. Protection was gradually eroded under increasing fire from the export sector (manufacturing) lobbies. Finally, with the repeal of the Corn Laws in 1846, Britain opted for free trade.

Because they have been so intensely examined, the Corn Laws present a useful case study of the effect of price-twist policies on the poor. It is clear that agricultural protection benefited landlords and hurt capitalists in manufacturing. But the effect on unskilled labor, the near-poor, is less obvious. On the one hand, workers were forced to pay an implicit "bread tax." On the other, agriculture was intensive in its use of unskilled labor.

Williamson (1990b) uses a general equilibrium model to weigh these two effects. He estimates that early repeal of the Corn Laws would have led a fifth of the agricultural labor force to have fled toward manufacturing. But so important was food in the consumption bundle of the working poor that the agricultural price effect dominates. In net, early repeal of the Corn Laws would have raised unskilled real wages by more than a fifth. It follows that the rising inequality and lagging living standards of the poor during the first industrial revolution can in large part be attributed to price-twist policies.

Allocation of public goods: Social infrastructure in the cities

We have seen that urban rents rose dramatically during the early industrial revolutions and that this had a damaging effect on the urban poor. Expensive housing led the poor to crowd into relatively cheaper, densely packed districts. The pollution generated by crowding transformed the rapidly growing cities into health hazards. Engels (1971) called them killers. By contrast, today's cities in the developing world are relatively benign. In 1960 developing countries' urban mortality rates were on average 6.3 per thousand lower than rural mortality rates. In Britain in 1841 urban mortality rates were 5.6 per thousand higher than those in the countryside. Conditions were similar on the Continent and in America. Increased death and sickness fell most heavily on the poor, those least able to escape the ugliest urban environments.

Sickness and mortality are, of course, always correlated with poverty, but public policy can make a difference. During the nineteenth-century industrial revolutions, governments failed to react to the problems posed by urbanization. How was this failure manifested?

We begin with an apparently extraneous, but in fact central, observation. Britain recorded very modest investment as a share of national income by the standards of later industrializing countries (Williamson 1984). One of the chief reasons why total investment was so low during the first industrial revolution was that Britain failed to commit resources to those investment activities that make industrialization such a costly venture today. Investment in urban social infrastructure failed to keep pace with the rest of the economy. The stock of capital in residential housing plus public works actually fell in per capita terms in late-eighteenth-century Britain (Williamson 1990a). Thereafter, per capita stocks in public works continued to decline while those in dwellings rose only slowly. By 1830 Britain had accumulated an enormous deficit in its social infrastructure stocks by pursuing seventy years of industrialization on the cheap.

The contrast with modern industrializers highlights the point. Lewis (1978) wrote that "the difference between the cost of urban and rural development does not turn on comparing the capital required for factories and that required for farms....The difference turns on infrastructure." When infrastructure is added to direct capital requirements, the capital-labor ratio in India's cities is 4.5 times that in its rural areas (Becker, Williamson, and Mills 1992). In mid-nineteenth-century Britain, urban and rural capital-labor ratios were about the same.

Low investment in urban infrastructure contributed to the ugly environment of nineteenth-century cities and hence to the excess mortality and morbidity of the urban poor. But to say that investment was low does not in itself imply that there was *underinvestment.* To clinch the case for public intervention, we need to show that the social rate of return from infrastructure investments would have exceeded that on actual private investment. The case can indeed be clinched. Meeker (1974) quantified the social cost of excess mortality and morbidity and the impact that public investment had at the margin. He estimated that the social rate of return on investment in public health in American cities from 1880 to 1910 was between 6 and 16 percent, far greater than private market rates at that time. The social rates of return on such investments in mid-nineteenth-century British cities would have been even higher (Wohl 1983; and Williamson 1990a). This is evidence of massive capital market failure coupled with a failure of the public sector to respond.

A lesson from nineteenth-century industrial revolutions is that particular growth strategies (in this case, low investment in urban infrastructure) can contribute to a deterioration in the life of the poor. There is sometimes room for public intervention to alleviate these problems.

Safety nets

Safety nets—resources provided by the family, the community, or the state to support individuals during crisis—matter most to the poor. Without safety nets, fluctuations in their incomes (or in their consumption capacity) will lead to high mortality and social disruption.

There is a commonly held myth about the historical evolution of safety nets. The myth has two parts. First, during early modern economic growth, industrialization and the emergence of markets undermine a traditional agrarian society in which the poor, the sick, and the elderly had been supported by extended families and the local village community; the state played no active role. Second, late in the industrialization process, formal institutions invented by modern governments, such as social security, replace the traditional functions of family and charity in caring for the poor. In between lies an intermediate phase of development, in which the dependence "on the market increases sharply (given the breakdown of the traditional peasant economy) and in which guaranteed entitlements in the form of social security benefits have yet to emerge" (Sen 1977: 56).

Support for the second stage of this mythical evolution of safety nets appears to be provided by Lindert's (1989) recent analysis of state-induced post-fisc redistributions, the key examples being the rise of twentieth-century welfare programs in Europe and North America. Lindert is correct in pointing out an increase in state support of the poor during the first two-thirds of this century. But this is only half the story. If we accept the myth of a simple two-stage path from traditional to modern safety nets, we will miss a key lesson of history.

The first big error embedded in the myth is its romanticized image of traditional society. The considerable efforts of demographic historians over the past three decades have made it clear that extended family systems were never the norm in northwestern Europe (Hajnal 1982), where the industrial revolution began. Far from undermining the extended family, industrialization may actually have strengthened it. Michael Anderson's (1972) studies of nineteenth-century Lancashire found more old people living with their married children in industrial Preston than in nearby rural areas. The same has been found to have been true in industrializing Massachusetts in the nineteenth century. Other studies of household structure may not provide a clear verdict on whether the extended family strengthened or declined during the nineteenth century, but they do make it clear that the family was not the typical safety net in preindustrial Britain. That is hardly surprising. Most parents did not live long enough to be a burden on their children, anyway. As mortality rates fell during the industrial revolution, parents lived longer. And their children, enjoying higher incomes, were better equipped to support them. But children could also better escape those responsibilities and default on their parents' investment in them by migrating to labor markets in distant towns at home or abroad.

There was, however, a safety net in preindustrial Britain and the United States that was threatened by nineteenth-century industrialization in both countries, and it was provided by the state. From the seventeenth to the nineteenth century, "the collectivity rather than the family was the source of security for the individual over the life course" (Laslett 1985: 360). The text of the famous Elizabethan Poor Law Act of 1601 explicitly confirms the responsibility of the state to support the same kind of individuals who were supported by poor relief in the late nineteenth century: the elderly, the disabled, widows, orphans, and large families (R. Smith 1981). Evidence from four English communities suggests that one of every five households received some kind of relief in the eighteenth century (J. Smith 1984). State old-age pensions, relative to the market wage of the working poor, were in 1834 twice what they were in 1984 (Thomson 1984). New York State relief programs at the start of the nineteenth century, just before the industrial revolution, were as large a share of the state budget as federal welfare programs are in the U.S. budget today (Hannon 1986). So much for the myth that state welfare programs are an invention of modern governments. And so much for the myth that the industrial revolution displaced traditional family safety nets.

The existence of preindustrial state support systems is explained in part by the absence of extended family networks. Nuclear family systems bring with them nuclear family risks. Formal state relief systems were a means of spreading those risks. But not all the poverty relieved by the state intervention in preindustrial England was attributable to the life cycle of nuclear families. Nor was the intervention restricted to poor relief. Fogel (1989) has shown that food price controls were regularly used by the early modern state in England to prevent famine. Like Sen's work on India, Fogel shifted our attention away from food shortage as a cause of famine, toward low price elasticity of total demand for food, especially in local grain markets linked only poorly to national markets. With only a small decline in supply, food prices rose sharply to eliminate excess demand; in the absence of relief, poor net consumers of food could be forced into starvation. Price intervention muted local famines in preindustrial England. And in 1795, when food prices soared during the Napoleonic Wars, the Speenhamland system was created to supplement wages of the poor.

This sympathetic attitude toward poverty and the generous safety nets for the poor did not persist after the Napoleonic Wars when the industrial revolution gathered steam. And we see roughly the same swing in attitude and policy in the United States.

The most recurrent argument against poor relief on both sides of the Atlantic was that the poor were to blame for their fate, and that charity and relief merely removed the will to work. These arguments were not new even then. The same debates about who were and who were not the "deserving poor" are to be found in medieval writing. Many nineteenth-century writers called for poor relief to be restricted to the workhouse in order to discourage shirkers. More generous relief was believed to cause not only idleness, but intemperance, extravagance, gambling, and prostitution. But there were also more subtle arguments. The most important opponent of poor relief in the early nineteenth century was Malthus. He agreed that society had an obligation to support the neediest, especially the elderly, but he believed that poor relief, by supporting large families, encouraged population growth and thus depressed wages.

A similar argument has recently surfaced about English and American nineteenth-century poor laws (Boyer 1990; and Hannon 1986). In the modern argument, labor migration takes the place of fertility and mortality, and implicit contract theory takes the place of Malthusian demographics. But the story is familiar. Offering poor relief to seasonally and cyclically idle farm laborers reduced out-migration and made labor locally available for the seasonal and cyclical peaks. Without such poor relief, employers who needed labor at times of peak demand would have had to offer higher wages and long-term contracts. Boyer and Hannon argue that early-nineteenth-century poor relief in Britain and America allowed employers to shift part of the cost of their implicit contracts with their workers onto the state.

Two other arguments used against generous poor relief should be familiar to those who follow contemporary debate on welfare reform. Opponents of outdoor relief worried that relief reduced incentives to work and save. Victorian opponents of poor relief argued that it undercut family and charitable responsibility. Nineteenth-century writers believed the myth that the family supplied support for the needy in the preindustrial age and thought that cutting poor relief would resurrect the mythical golden age. The myth that poor relief was a recent substitute for family support, private charity, and personal thrift enabled opponents of state intervention to argue that benefits were not a traditional entitlement of the poor or a right, like that to trial by jury. At times, however, the poor themselves seem to have recognized that laissez-faire policies often entailed transfers of entitlements from the poor to the rich (Thomson 1971).

The main swings in attitude toward poor relief and poverty during the industrial revolution were as follows. In response to heightened seasonal unemployment (following enclosure and changes in the crop mix) and to high food prices (during the Napoleonic Wars), poor relief became more generous by the end of the eighteenth century. In the first part of the nineteenth century, however, an increasing concern emerged about outdoor relief to the able-bodied as well as the generosity of that relief. The debate became heated on both sides of the Atlantic. It culminated with the passage of a tougher New York State poor law in 1824 and a tougher New Poor Law in England in 1834. Both laws aimed to restrict outdoor relief. In the 1870s, again on both sides of the Atlantic, there was a crusade against outdoor relief. During this period, outdoor relief was cut for many disadvantaged groups, including widows and the elderly. Late in the century, we see some loosening up and an increased interest in the poor among social reformers, the most famous being Booth and Rowntree. Although both attributed a great deal of poverty to the actions of the poor, they found much more "innocent" poverty than others had believed existed.

The first decade of this century is often seen as laying the foundation of modern welfarism. By 1914, England had old-age pensions, some public "make-work" schemes, and less harsh attitudes toward the poor. This liberal surge before World War I ushered in what Lindert (1989) identifies as a widespread shift in attitudes among the newly industrializing countries of that time, as evidenced by the rise of redistributive schemes that had a significant impact on post-fisc income distributions. We should not forget, however, that the rise of the twentieth-century welfare state represents a return to the more liberal attitudes toward the poor of preindustrial Europe and America. It was only during the interim that nineteenth-century industrializing nations retreated from those liberal attitudes.

What was the effect of the reductions in poor relief? For many of the poor, it is hard to say. We can be fairly sure, however, that the elderly in Victorian England were made much worse off. Thomson (1984) shows that the ratio of old-age pensions to average wages fell sharply in the late 1860s, enough to imply an absolute fall in the income of the elderly. Indeed, there was a marked increase in the proportion of those over sixty-five in the workhouse during the 1870s and a similar increase in the ratio of indoor to total non-able-bodied paupers (a group that includes the elderly) in the same period. MacKinnon (1987) calculates that, had there been no crusade against outdoor relief, 200,000 more old people would have received it in 1900, and the average working-class old person's income would have been 8 percent higher. Although policy had a powerful negative impact on the elderly poor in the 1870s, it had an equally powerful positive impact in the early twentieth century. Two years after the introduction of old-age pensions in 1911, outdoor pauperism among the elderly had fallen to 5 percent of its 1906 level.

What have we learned about safety nets? Although it may be convenient to think otherwise, the poor in preindustrial European and North American societies typically were *not* supported by the family and private institutions. In most leading nineteenth-century industrializing countries, a large part of the responsibility lay with the state and other formal, state-like institutions. These bodies intervened in food markets, and their interventions mattered to the living standards of the poor. Where laissez-faire policies were adopted during the industrial revolution, as in the United States and England, many of the poor were big losers. The removal of traditional preindustrial safety nets by laissez-fair-driven nineteenth-century industrial revolutions was viewed by many as the theft of what had come to be seen as a property right. We do not yet know how much this "theft" hurt the poor, but it clearly mattered to those in extreme poverty at the bottom of the income distribution.

Note

This revised background paper for *World Development Report 1990* was delivered at the Poverty Research Conference organized by the International Food Policy Research Institute and the World Bank at Airlie House in Virginia, October 25-28, 1989. We acknowledge with gratitude the help given by George Boyer, Gary Fields, Joan Hannon, Michael Lipton, Mary MacKinnon, Cynthia Taft Morris, Lyn Squire, Jacques van der Gaag, and participants at Airlie.

Part III
Remedies for Poverty

Rural Development in Latin America: Relinking Poverty Reduction to Growth

Alain de Janvry
Elisabeth Sadoulet

The crisis affecting Latin America since mid-1982 has had severe economic and welfare costs. Real gross domestic product (GDP) per capita in 1990 was still below the level achieved a decade earlier; open and hidden unemployment has risen sharply and real wages have fallen; and there has been a general deterioration in the provision of social services.

Like all crises, however, this one offers an opportunity to redefine development strategies and political regimes. The conditions of the 1970s, characterized by Dutch disease and large government budgets resulting from oil and debt booms, reinforced old structural and policy biases and allowed postponement of necessary reforms (Husain 1989). They led to growing inefficiencies in investment (evidenced by sharply rising incremental capital-output ratios); the preservation of noncompetitive, domestic-market-oriented industries; excessive growth of government and large budget deficits; permanent trade distortions and antiagriculture biases; inefficient and ineffective tax systems; and a distribution of benefits from extensive welfare state expenditures that gave the poor disproportionately few.

There have been important reforms in economic policy since the onset of the crisis. The real exchange rate has been sharply depreciated in all countries. Reductions have been made in government expenditure, in industrial protectionism, in quasi-fiscal deficits associated with inefficient public enterprises, and in antiagriculture biases. With the reduction in social welfare expenditures, there have been efforts at targeting the remaining subsidies to the poor. Despite the continuation of the crisis, due to the debt overhang, the structure of the economies has been altered, with a shift in economic activity toward the tradable goods sectors—agriculture in particular—and toward informal sector production.

There have also been reforms in political regimes, with a general return to democratic forms of government—although a precarious one because of the frustrations stemming from the lack of economic growth and the social costs of economic stabilization. Greater political participation and the multiplication of new social movements and grassroots organizations have opened channels through which the demands of the poorer groups can be voiced more openly. Thus, even within the present economic and political context, interesting new avenues have been opened that could allow an attack on rural poverty through a growth-centered strategy and a new division of labor between public and private sectors. If the debt burden can be alleviated, international protectionism for agriculture reduced, and democratic regimes preserved, this embryonic new development strategy could become an important element of both a long-overdue recovery of the Latin American economies and a strategy to reduce rural poverty with minimal recourse to the welfare state.

It is this thesis that we defend in this chapter. We start by briefly reviewing the performance of agriculture within the crisis, the positive and negative determinants of this performance, and the future prospects for agricultural growth. We then review the effect of the crisis on rural welfare and identify the causes of differences in the welfare effects for different segments of the rural population. We discuss the prospects for poverty reduction, and propose a strategy to relink poverty to growth. We then turn to the microeconomic analysis of several recent experiences that demonstrate the potential for rural poverty alleviation alongside growth. This potential exists in the production of agroexports, and of staple foods for import substitution, in employment creation in commercial agriculture and in rural nonagricultural activities linked to agriculture and based in either farm households or rural towns, and in improved access to land through a new approach to redistributive land reform. Finally, we advance a set of concrete guidelines for the implementation, in the context of structural adjustment, of a strategy of rural development that reduces poverty. They concern in particular the relative roles of the state and grassroots organizations, ways to increase income for highly differentiated rural households, and the possibility of combining environmental protection with poverty alleviation in a context of taxable externalities. The success of this strategy depends upon a set of internal and external conditions, which we identify.

Agriculture in the crisis and adjustment

The 1970s saw rapid economic growth for the Latin American economies, with GDP increasing at an average annual rate of 5.3 percent (table 11.1). In 1965-70 growth was remarkably rapid in several countries: 9 percent in Brazil, 8.7 percent in Ecuador, 7.3 percent in the Dominican Republic, 6.5 percent in Mexico, and 6.2 percent in Costa Rica. This growth occurred in the context of import-substituting industrialization, booms in exports of primary commodities, and the rapid accumulation of debt. The subsequent crisis reduced the growth of GDP to an average annual rate of 1.3 percent between 1980 and 1987; several countries (including Argentina and Venezuela) experienced negative growth, and virtually all countries had negative per capita growth.

The economic adjustments induced by the crisis have created some important reversals in the sectoral structure of growth. Agriculture lagged in the 1970s, with average annual growth of 2.7 percent compared with 5.3 percent for GDP. But under adjustment, agriculture became the most dynamic sector, with growth of 1.8 percent compared with 1.3 percent for GDP, even though its growth rate fell by a third, to less than the rate of population growth. As a result, the contribu-

**Table 11.1 Economic and agricultural performance,
Latin America, 1970-87**
(average annual percentage growth rates or averages)

Indicator	1970-80	1980-87
Growth		
GDP	5.3	1.3
Agriculture	2.7	1.8
Agriculture/GDP	-2.5	0.5
Contributions to GDP growth (percent)		
Contribution of agriculture	6.8	13.7
Contribution of industry	37.3	22.7
Contribution of services	55.9	63.6
Real effective exchange rate	0.4	-6.3
Trade		
Export volume (percentage growth)	-1.1	3.6
Import volume (percentage growth)	4.6	-2.1
Agricultural trade		
Export volume	4.4	1.6
Unit value	11.6	-2.1
Value (millions of US$)	17.1	-0.3
Import volume	7.7	-2.6
Unit value	9.7	-3.5
Value (millions of US$)	19.1	-5.6
Exports/imports	3.0	2.7

Source: IDB 1988; and FAO, *Trade Yearbook,* various years.

tion of agriculture to growth in GDP rose from an average of 6.7 percent in the 1970s to 14.3 percent in the 1980s and to 23.1 percent in 1987. The share of agriculture in the total value of exports, which had declined steadily from 50.7 percent in 1960 to 44.3 percent in 1970 and to 25.2 percent in 1982, had bounced back to 31.3 percent by 1987 (ECLAC 1988).

The performance of agriculture has been highly uneven across countries and over the years, however, due to particularly erratic weather and to policy instability (for example, in Argentina and Peru), and its overall performance has been clearly inadequate. But the truly remarkable acceleration of growth in some countries and in some agricultural activities indicates the potential that agriculture can offer under proper policy management. In Chile, Ecuador, and Peru agricultural growth rates in the 1980s exceeded those in the 1970s (table 11.2). Livestock, with a high income elasticity that makes it vulnerable to downturns in income, stagnated, but the cereals sector grew rapidly, taking advantage of opportunities offered by import substitution in Chile (where the average annual growth rate was 10.6 percent in 1980-87), Peru (8.5 percent), Venezuela (6.7 percent), Ecuador (4.4 percent), and Brazil (4 percent).

The main positive determinant of this short-run growth, which occurred despite falling international commodity prices for temperate goods, was the

Table 11.2 Average annual growth in agricultural production, selected Latin American countries, 1970-87
(percent)

Country and sector	1970-80	1980-87
Argentina		
Total	3.0	1.2
Crops	3.2	1.8
Food crops	3.0	1.3
Cereals	0.7	1.2
Livestock	3.5	0.1
Brazil		
Total	3.4	2.9
Crops	3.0	3.6
Food crops	4.4	2.9
Cereals	2.9	4.0
Livestock	4.9	1.2
Chile		
Total	2.3	2.3
Crops	1.9	4.0
Food crops	1.9	2.3
Cereals	0.1	10.6
Livestock	4.0	-0.4
Ecuador		
Total	2.3	3.0
Crops	0.7	2.4
Food crops	2.4	2.7
Cereals	-0.3	4.4
Livestock	4.7	4.2
Mexico		
Total	3.3	1.2
Crops	2.4	0.9
Food crops	3.8	1.3
Cereals	3.3	0.5
Livestock	5.8	1.5
Peru		
Total	-0.1	2.3
Crops	-0.8	3.3
Food crops	-0.4	2.6
Cereals	-1.1	8.5
Livestock	1.4	2.1
Venezuela		
Total	3.0	1.9
Crops	3.3	3.1
Food crops	3.2	1.8
Cereals	8,1	6.7
Livestock	5.1	2.5
Latin America		
Total	2.7	1.8
Crops	3.0	2.4
Food crops	3.6	2.0
Cereals	2.7	2.4
Livestock	4.2	1.1

Source: FAO, *Production Yearbook,* various years.

depreciation of the real exchange rate resulting from reduced ability to borrow and trade liberalization. The effective real exchange rate, almost constant during the 1970s (with an average annual growth rate of 0.4 percent between 1970 and 1980), depreciated rapidly between 1980 and 1987 at an average annual rate of 6.3 percent (table 11.1).

On the negative side, agricultural production was hurt by rising interest rates; by credit constraints; and by imperfectly competitive marketing structures, which resulted in part of the gains from higher relative prices for tradables accruing to traders rather than to producers. Production was also hurt by rising prices for imported inputs, and, in some cases, by a higher tax burden. And a sharp fall in public expenditure on research, extension, infrastructure, and social services severely damaged the potential for long-term growth (Garramón 1988; and Twomey 1988).

Agriculture's strong showing in 1987 (a growth rate of 6.4 percent), despite these negative conditions, indicates its resilience. This resilience was particularly evident in nontraditional exports, such as fruits and vegetables (Brazil, Chile, and Mexico), edible oils (Argentina and Brazil), and fish and seafood (Ecuador and Mexico), in which Latin American agriculture has international comparative advantages. Cereals performed strongly in import substitution, reducing the import gap that had been created by appreciating real exchange rates in the 1970s. This performance was due in part to favorable weather, but it was also made possible by important adjustments in economic policy that reduced antiagriculture biases in price formation, and by greater stress on relaxing the nonprice constraints on the elasticity of aggregate supply, such as the availability of credit (IDB 1988).

Price incentives

The agricultural terms of trade have been affected by changes in the exchange rate, in trade policies, and in international prices. In general, there had been a strong tendency since the beginning of the debt crisis for the effective exchange rate to depreciate (table 11.3). After appreciating 1.6 percent a year between 1970 and 1982, on average, for sixteen Latin American countries, it depreciated an average 3.4 percent annually between 1982 and 1988. Of these sixteen countries, eleven had a depreciating effective exchange rate during that period.

Trade liberalization generally has been implemented as a complement to stabilization policies since 1982, often as part of loan conditionality. This has benefited agriculture both through reduced export taxes (or higher differential exchange rates) and through reduced protectionism on industrial inputs.

International prices for agricultural commodities fell sharply after 1980, with some rebound in 1988. Between 1980 and 1988 the price of wheat fell by 36 percent in nominal terms, the price of corn by 36 percent, the price of rice by 30 percent, and the price of sugar by 64 percent. Some tropical commodities fared better (the price of bananas increased by 20 percent); the price of coffee fell by 26 percent, however, and that of cocoa by 39 percent. There is thus a question as to whether the decline in international agricultural prices outweighed

Table 11.3 Average annual changes in index of effective exchange rates, Latin American countries, 1970-88

Country	1970-82	1982-88
Argentina	-1.7	1.0
Bolivia	-2.4	6.5
Brazil	0.8	-2.7
Chile	-4.1	4.1
Colombia	-3.0	7.0
Costa Rica	0.4	0.8
Ecuador	-2.1	12.5
El Salvador	-3.4	-1.8
Guatemala	-1.1	10.4
Mexico	0.3	0.9
Honduras	0.7	-3.4
Panama	-2.1	5.1
Paraguay	-5.2	5.6
Peru	3.1	-6.9
Uruguay	-2.2	-0.4
Venezuela	-1.3	4.0
Average	-1.6	3.4

Note: The effective exchange rate is the nominal exchange rate multiplied by the ratio of the U.S. wholesale price index (WPI) to the domestic WPI.
Source: IMF, *International Financial Statistics,* various years.

the positive effect for agriculture of the depreciation of the effective exchange rate. The data in table 11.4 show that this generally was not the case and that the domestic terms of trade for agriculture have in fact improved since 1982. For export crops, the terms of trade, which had declined at an average annual rate of 0.8 percent between 1970 and 1982, improved at the rate of 0.8 percent between 1982 and 1988. For import substitutes, agricultural terms of trade, which had declined by 2 percent annually during the first period, improved by 2 percent annually from their level at the beginning of the crisis. Thus, despite falling international prices, agriculture has benefited from real exchange rate adjustments, which provided the price incentives for supply response. The intensity of supply response also depends on a number of nonprice factors, related to the availability of public goods, which condition the ability of farmers to take advantage of price incentives.

Nonprice factors

There are few detailed empirical analyses of the effect of stabilization and structural adjustment policies on agriculture, but it is clear from past studies of supply response that nonprice factors play a key complementary role to price incentives in explaining agricultural output (Binswanger and others 1987; and Commander 1989). Price response requires shifts in production between nontradables and tradables, and shifts in factor use and in the choice of techniques. Some of the key nonprice factors that assist such shifts are availability of credit, greater

Table 11.4 Average annual changes in index of potential terms of trade for agriculture, selected Latin American countries, 1970-82

Agricultural terms of trade for export crops based on international prices *(price index for exports times exchange rate/WPI)*		
	1970-82	*1982-88*
Argentina	-3.6	-1.1
Brazil	0.8	-4.2
Colombia	-0.7	5.1
Costa Rica	1.5	0.0
Ecuador	0.3	1.5
El Salvador	-1.5	-2.6
Guatemala	0.1	8.2
Honduras	1.4	-6.2
Mexico	1.0	-1.7
Panama	-2.2	5.0
Uruguay	-4.1	0.9
Average	-0.8	0.8

Agricultural terms of trade for all crops based on international prices *(price index for production times exchange rate/WPI)*		
	1970-82	*1982-88*
Argentina	-4.0	-0.7
Bolivia	-3.2	5.1
Brazil	0.4	-4.4
Chile	-5.9	2.3
Colombia	-2.1	5.4
Costa Rica	1.0	-0.2
Ecuador	-0.8	10.9
El Salvador	-2.3	-3.7
Guatemala	-0.1	8.4
Honduras	1.7	-4.4
Mexico	-0.2	-1.4
Panama	-2.5	4.5
Paraguay	-6.7	3.5
Peru	3.2	-8.9
Uruguay	-4.5	-0.8
Venezuela	-1.1	2.5
Average	-2.0	2.0

Note: Potential terms of trade with perfect substitution between domestic and foreign goods.
Source: Authors' calculations.

efficiency in marketing, and public investment in infrastructure and technology. In general, although the terms of trade for agriculture have improved, the incentives that this represents have not been adequately supported by nonprice factors, limiting the potential positive effects on agriculture and seriously compromising long-term growth.

The main victim of the debt crisis and fiscal austerity has been public investment. Falling foreign borrowing and rising interest payments on accumulated debt have reduced both current expenditure (other than repayment of debt) and public investment by a disproportionate amount. For Latin America as a whole, the share of government expenditure on debt rose from 4.9 percent in 1975 to 6.9 percent in 1980 and to 15.5 percent in 1985. Total public investment fell from 21 percent of government expenditure in 1975 to 19 percent in 1980 and to 13 percent in 1985. Total gross domestic investment also fell sharply. After increasing at an average annual rate of 7.5 percent between 1960 and 1980, it fell 4.7 percent between 1980 and 1986 (IDB 1988). Agriculture apparently fared even worse. For Latin America as a whole, the share of agriculture in government expenditure fell from 8.1 percent in 1975 to 4.7 percent in 1985. In Mexico public investment in agriculture fell from US$1,824 million in 1982 to US$500 million in 1987 (Knudsen and Nash 1989). In Brazil the real value of agricultural credit was halved between 1980 and 1985 (Fagundes 1988).

The prospects for continued growth of agriculture are contingent upon overcoming a number of external and internal constraints, which we discuss at the end of this chapter. If these constraints can be either relaxed or avoided, agriculture could play a key role in the region's economic growth, at least in the early phases of economic recovery. This role could, in turn, serve as the basis for a new strategy of rural poverty reduction.

The social costs of the crisis and adjustment

Any characterization of the social costs of the crisis and adjustment must start from the observation that rural poverty had remained widespread in Latin America before the crisis, despite rapid economic growth and substantial improvement in the provision of basic amenities in the 1970s, a decade of large government budgets. The improvement between 1970 and 1980 in meeting basic needs is indicated by the increase in life expectancy from sixty to sixty-four years, the fall in the infant mortality rate from eighty-one to sixty-four per thousand (IDB 1988), and the increase in per capita daily calorie supply from 2,516 to 2,673 (FAO 1988). These indicators provide important evidence on overall welfare and show that the growth of the 1970s had brought about considerable improvements. But in countries with high inequalities, there is only a weak correlation between these indicators and the welfare of the poor.

Because of the rapid economic growth during the 1970s and the sustained migration to the urban areas (with the agricultural labor force growing at only 0.6 percent annually, compared to 4.6 percent for the urban labor force), it is likely that absolute poverty in the rural sector declined. Data for Brazil, for instance, indicate that, although rural income inequality increased sharply in all ten regions (with a Gini coefficient for the rural sector rising from 0.44 in 1970 to 0.54 in 1980), absolute poverty fell (Denslow and Tyler 1983)—a pair of trends also seen in Pakistan (see chapter 20 in this volume). For Brazil as a whole, the share of households with incomes below the poverty line declined from 39 percent in 1960 to 38 percent in 1970 and to 22 percent in 1980 (Fields 1989a). Yet it is likely that the trickle-down effect of growth on rural poverty was weak, and that rural poverty was extensive by the early 1980s, because of conditions that were biased toward larger farms—and against small farms and rural laborers. Landownership became increasingly concentrated, and the average size of peasant farms fell. Peasants lacked access to credit while larger farms received substantial subsidies in the form of negative real interest rates (in Brazil credit subsidies in the 1970s equaled 21 percent of the total value of agricultural output; farms of less than 10 hectares received only 4 percent of institutional credit). The benefits from rapidly growing export crops were concentrated in the larger farms. Mechanization and the widespread displacement of labor-intensive crops by extensive livestock operations resulted in slow or negative employment creation in commercial agriculture. Import substitution industrialization policies and exchange rate distortions limited opportunities for migration toward the urban sector. Between 1960 and 1980 employment in commercial agriculture increased by only 16 percent; during the same period labor absorption in the peasant sector, which served as a refuge for surplus populations, increased by 41 percent (de Janvry, Sadoulet, and Wilcox 1989).

Because rural poverty is highly differentiated socially, the distribution of the social costs of the crisis is inevitably also unequal. There are no observations over time at the household level that can be used to measure directly the real income effects of the crisis. Thus, to characterize its social impact, we rely on aggregate welfare indicators and on simulations in a computable general equilibrium model for Ecuador.

Aggregate welfare indicators

Open urban unemployment in Latin America as a whole rose from an average of 7.9 percent in 1975-82 to 10.8 percent in 1982-87 (IDB 1988, table 5). In addition, real wages fell by 11 percent between 1980 and 1986. In Mexico real wages in industry fell by 40 percent between 1982 and 1987, and the share of workers earning the minimum wage or less increased from 13 percent in 1982 to 38 percent in 1985 (Lustig 1986). It is, of course, almost inconceivable that living standards fell that fast; surplus labor was absorbed in part by the informal sector, but probably in lower-productivity work. Employment in that sector had increased rapidly, from 13 percent of the economically active population in 1950 to 19.3 percent in 1980 (de Janvry, Sadoulet, and Wilcox 1989). During the 1980s the informal sector showed explosive growth in such cities as Bogota, Lima, Mexico City, and São Paulo. While employment in the urban formal sector increased by 0.7 percent annually between 1980 and 1985 (an unweighted average for Argentina, Brazil, Chile, Colombia, Mexico, Peru, and Venezuela), it increased by 5.2 percent in the urban informal sector (Pinstrup-Andersen 1989). One of the consequences of this growth has been the creation of a class of new social actors able to assume an increasingly defined role in national politics.

Rising unemployment and falling real wages have led to a sharp increase in the population below the poverty line, from 130 million in 1981 to 150 million in 1986 (CASAR 1986). Food prices have in general risen faster than nonfood prices, leading to a sharp deterioration in the nutritional status of the poor (Pinstrup-Andersen 1989). In Peru the share of the population with insufficient income to cover a minimum food basket rose from 51 percent in 1972 to 70 percent in 1984. In Mexico the cost of a basic diet for a family of five increased from 43 percent of a minimum wage in 1982 to 65 percent in 1986 (Lustig 1986).

Public expenditure in education and health has been reduced by fiscal austerity policies. An unweighted average for seven countries (table 11.5) indicates that per capita expenditure on education had increased by 4.6 percent annually between 1970 and 1981, only to fall by 3 percent annually between 1981 and 1985. In health the corresponding figures are 6.2 percent and 5.9 percent. Food subsidy programs have also been severely reduced, particularly in Brazil and Mexico. Despite improved targeting, it is likely that the calorie consumption of the poor has fallen.

The scattered data reported here indicate that the economic crisis and the types of stabilization policy followed have had a negative effect on the welfare of the poor: real wages have fallen while unemployment has risen, the price of food has increased while food subsidies have declined, and the availability of health and education services has decreased. The urban poor have been the principal victims, but the rural poor who are net buyers of food and heavily dependent on employment in the services sector (particularly construction) have also been hurt by the crisis and the stabilization policies.

Some effects are already apparent. Infant mortality rates, which had declined significantly during the 1970s, have increased in Bolivia, Brazil (particularly in the poorer northern and northeastern states), Mexico, and Uruguay, and have stopped declining in Costa Rica. Only in Chile, which has continued a very effective nutrition surveillance program managed by a powerful medical profession, has the infant mortality rate continued to decline despite falling calorie consumption among the poor (Pinstrup-Andersen 1989). The time lags between falling inputs and worsening welfare consequences are usually long, however. Kakwani, Makkonen, and van der Gaag (chapter 6 in this volume) put together evidence of continued improvement during the 1980s in several key indicators of welfare—literacy rates, life expectancy—in much of Latin America (and even in the few African countries with reliable data).

General equilibrium analysis

The question has often been raised as to whether the negative effects of the crisis on the welfare of some social groups came from the foreign sector shock itself (represented here by a 75 percent decline in foreign borrowing) or from the stabilization policies implemented in response to the crisis (see, for example, Pinstrup-Andersen 1989). To disentangle these effects, we use a computable general equilibrium model for Ecuador (Kouwenaar 1988; and de Janvry and Sadoulet 1989) to simulate the effects of both a shock without adjustment in the level of government expenditure and fiscal policies that freeze the government deficit at the precrisis level, either by cutting current expenditure or by cutting proportionately both current and investment expenditure (table 11.6). The welfare effects on households of alternative policies are measured by adding to the

Table 11.5 Social indicators, selected Latin American countries, 1970-87
(average annual percentage growth rates, unless otherwise indicated)

Latin America	1970-82	1982-87
Open urban unemployment (average annual percentage)	7.9	10.8
Real minimum wage (1980 = 100)	96.0	89.4
Argentina	*1970-81*	*1981-87*
GDP	2.0	0.7
Population	1.8	1.6
Share of expenditure on education in GDP (percent)	1.4	1.6
Per capita education expenditure	6.4	-1.4
Share of expenditure on health in GDP (percent)	0.5	0.5
Per capita health expenditure	3.5	9.7
Brazil	*1970-82*	*1982-86*
GDP	7.0	5.4
Population	2.7	2.2
Share of expenditure on education in GDP (percent)	1.0	1.0
Per capita education expenditure	0.7	17.8
Share of expenditure on health in GDP (percent)	1.3	1.6
Per capita health expenditure	6.8	-6.8
Chile	*1970-81*	*1981-85*
GDP	2.1	1.7
Population	1.8	1.7
Share of expenditure on education in GDP (percent)	4.4	3.5
Per capita education expenditure	-1.4	-4.8
Share of expenditure on health in GDP (percent)	2.4	3.0
Per capita health expenditure	-0.8	-5.7
Ecuador	*1970-81*	*1981-86*
GDP	8.6	1.4
Population	3.1	2.9
Share of expenditure on education in GDP (percent)	3.9	4.5
Per capita education expenditure	11.5	-7.5
Share of expenditure on health in GDP (percent)	1.1	1.7
Per capita health expenditure	24.8	-15.0
Mexico	*1971-81*	*1981-85*
GDP	6.6	-0.3
Population	3.1	2.2
Share of expenditure on education in GDP (percent)	2.7	2.9
Per capita education expenditure	11.8	-11.4
Share of expenditure on health in GDP (percent)	0.4	0.3
Per capita health expenditure	7.1	-12.0
Peru	*1971-81*	*1981-85*
GDP	3.1	-0.9
Population	2.7	2.6
Share of expenditure on education in GDP (percent)	3.2	2.8
Per capita education expenditure	-1.4	-8.3
Share of expenditure on health in GDP (percent)	1.0	1.0
Per capita health expenditure	2.3	-5.3
Venezuela	*1971-81*	*1981-86*
GDP	4.4	-0.8
Population	4.0	2.8
Share of expenditure on education in GDP (percent)	4.0	4.7
Per capita education expenditure	4.3	-5.1
Share of expenditure on health in GDP (percent)	1.4	1.3
Per capita health expenditure	-0.6	-6.3

Source: World Bank, *World Tables,* various years; and IDB 1988.

Table 11.6 Simulated effects of debt crisis and stabilization policies, Ecuador

(effect of a 75 percent decrease in foreign borrowing with alternative government budget adjustments)

Item	Base values, 1980	Short run			Long run [a]		
		Constant expenditure N	Constant deficit and cut in current expenditure C_c	Constant deficit and proportional cut in current and investment expenditure C_i	Constant expenditure N	Constant deficit and cut in current expenditure C_c	Constant deficit and proportional cut in current and investment expenditure C_i
	(millions of sucres)	(percentage change over base values)					
GDP at market prices	293,341	-1.4	-3.3	-2.9	-2.1	-0.4	-1.0
Exchange rate index	100	10.2	11.3	11.6	10.5	13.4	13.2
Government							
Deficit	8,963	-24.7	-114.9	-114.8	-36.7	-113.9	-114.0
Current expenditure	42,562	0.0	-19.6	-13.0	0.0	-4.5	-4.2
Investment	18,646	0.0	0.0	-13.0	0.0	0.0	-4.2
Private investment	57,984	-17.5	-6.9	-6.2	-16.8	-5.4	-5.7
Utility per capita	(US$)	(percentage change over base values)					
Rural							
Small farm	612.5	-3.0	-4.7	-4.6	3.3	-1.8	-2.4
Medium-size farm	753.1	-1.0	-2.2	-2.0	-1.3	0.9	0.3
Large farm	1,410.3	-0.3	-1.8	-1.3	-0.7	1.7	1.1
Rural nonagricultural	1,504.6	-4.0	-7.3	-6.8	-4.5	-3.4	-4.0
Urban							
Urban poor	1,250.4	-4.4	-7.4	-7.0	-4.9	-4.0	-4.6
Urban middle-income	2,532.8	-3.7	-8.1	-7.1	-5.6	-7.4	-7.7
Urban rich	4,826.0	-2.9	-8.8	-7.1	-7.3	-13.9	-13.8

a. In the long run, both public and private investment create growth in total factor productivity.
Source: Authors' simulation, using a computable general equilibrium model.

changes in real per capita income the changes in the per capita real dollar amount of public goods and services to which each class of households has access. This measure is called utility.

The results obtained in table 11.6 are summarized qualitatively in the following table. In the table, N denotes no intervention other than exchange rate devaluation—that is, constant government expenditure at the precrisis level; C_c denotes a situation in which the deficit is maintained at the precrisis level by cutting current expenditure; C_I denotes a situation in which the deficit is maintained at the precrisis level by cutting both investment and current expenditure proportionately; and > means "is preferred to."

	Short run		Long run
Growth	$N > C_I > C_c$		$C_c > C_I > N$
Rural households	$N > C_I > C_c$		$C_c > C_I > N$
Urban households	$N > C_I > C_c$	Poor	$C_c > C_I > N$
		Middle-income	$N > C_c > C_I$
		Rich	$N > C_I > C_c$

We see that avoiding fiscal contraction is tempting in the short run for the sake of economic growth as well as for the welfare of all social groups because contractionary policies worsen the crisis. That is because fiscal contraction implies the loss of the Keynesian multipliers with the withdrawal of some of the effective demand created by government expenditure. But failure to impose fiscal austerity is detrimental to growth in the long run, because constant public expenditure crowds out private investment through a rising government deficit that requires extensive public borrowing. As expected, all social classes lose in the short run compared with the precrisis levels of welfare. Medium-size and large farmers lose least because of exchange rate devaluation that benefits tradables.

Fiscal austerity policies to prevent a rising government deficit can be directed at either current or investment expenditure. For political reasons, most Latin American economies have chosen to reduce both (simulated in our model by a proportional cut in current and investment expenditure), rather than to shelter investment and put the burden of fiscal austerity on current expenditure only (Pfeffermann 1986). In the short run investment expenditure does not create productivity gains, and cutting it is akin to reducing absorption. In the long run, however, investment creates productivity gains, and a cut in investment has a double cost: reduced absorption and a loss of potential productivity gains. Cutting current expenditure, by contrast, leads not only to a decline in absorption but also to a loss in the utility derived from the consumption of publicly provided social welfare services. It is the tradeoffs among these three effects—absorption, utility, and productivity—that we seek to capture in table 11.6.

We see that, in the short run, the choice of cutting investment expenditure is preferred to that of cutting current expenditure. For growth, that is because current expenditure has a lower import content than investment expenditure, and thus a larger domestic multiplier effect. For welfare, it is because investment expenditure is less labor-intensive and does not create utility gains in the form of public services. Yet in the short run all classes incur losses from this policy choice, particularly urban classes, who are seriously penalized by losses in public employment, losses in access to public services, and rising prices for tradable staple goods.

In the long run maximizing economic growth requires fiscal policies that reduce current expenditure and preserve public investment. And the restoration of growth is critical for the reduction of poverty, both rural and urban. It is only the urban rich who would prefer a strategy of constant expenditure, which would allow the preservation of civil service employment and public benefits. Their dominance of policymaking would thus result in policies (constant expenditure) that have a high opportunity cost for both economic growth and the welfare of the poor. Yet even policies that minimize losses in growth leave the poor with losses in welfare, particularly the urban poor.

The main losers from fiscal policies that reduce current expenditure are the urban middle-income and rich households. The main gainers from such fiscal policies are, by contrast, medium-size and large farmers, who benefit from exchange rate devaluation and from the maximum protection of growth.

Medium-size farmers, who are net sellers of food, benefit because of the positive effects of adjustment on agricultural tradables. This indicates that a strategy of rural development directed at extending these benefits from medium-size to small farmers, as producers of a marketed surplus, has a real potential to relink rural poverty alleviation to growth. The potential is increased by small farmers' normally higher ratio of nontradable inputs (labor, buffaloes, and manure) to tradable inputs (tractors and fertilizers). This potential may be realized in the production either of (normally nontraditional) export crops or of tradable staples for import substitution. For the landless and marginal farmers, employment in commercial agriculture is the principal source of income, and the employment effects of agricultural growth need to be carefully nurtured by the proper policy incentives.

Access to land is the main instrument for reducing rural poverty. With the phase of large-scale land reform virtually ended, less adversarial strategies can be explored. These could include enhancement of the land rental market, market purchases of land mediated by local authorities, titling of squatters, and carefully managed frontier settlements. And because access to land and employment in commercial agriculture generally cannot suffice to eliminate rural poverty, also necessary is a complementary strategy of agriculture-led regional development, with employment in nonagricultural activities linked to agriculture (see chapter 8 in this volume by Hazell and Haggblade). We explore in the following section some recent Latin American experiences with these five strategies. Their very existence suggests the possibility of using them as the building blocks of a systematic, growth-based strategy of rural poverty reduction.

Linking rural to agricultural development

The volume of agricultural exports increased rapidly between 1980 and 1987 (table 11.1 reports average annual growth at 3.6 percent). The growth was particularly strong between 1982 and 1985 (6 percent), before declining because of bad weather in 1986. Temperate exports have been harmed by agricultural protectionism in industrial countries, and tropical products benefit from generally favorable but unstable markets. Nontraditional lines of exports, however, have gained substantial momentum in recent years, and have benefited strongly from the devaluations of the real exchange rate brought about by the crisis. Between 1982 and 1986 the value of fruit and vegetable exports from Mexico increased 12.8 percent annually, and from Chile, 22.4 percent. The strength of Latin America's comparative advantages in these labor-intensive crops has been demonstrated in several recent studies (Moulton and Runsten 1986). Consequently, it is not surprising that the area planted in vegetables and fruits for export has expanded rapidly in Mexico and in several other Latin American countries.

Production for exports

Although growth in the production of these export crops could serve as the basis for linking rural with agricultural development, this generally has not occurred. In Chile and Mexico most of the production for export originates on medium-size and large farms, which are generally linked with transnational corporations for access to markets and technology. That this need not be the case is well demonstrated where small farmers have effectively entered these activities and, with the appropriate institutional support, proved competitive. A scheme in Guatemala, the Alimentos Congelados Monte Bello (ALCOSA), illustrates the potential for small farmers in producing for export.

ALCOSA was started by the Latin American Agribusiness Development Corporation, with funding from the U.S. Agency for International Development. Its goal was to export frozen cauliflower, broccoli, and brussels sprouts. At first, the company leased land to grow its own crops (Kusterer, Estrada, and Xuya Cuxil 1981; von Braun, Hotchkiss, and Immink 1989; and de Janvry and others 1989). Because this proved uneconomical, ALCOSA turned to contracting with local, medium-size commercial farmers. This too was unsatisfactory. The farmers had little experience with vegetable production; they were often absent, attending to nonfarm business interests; and the contracts led to disputes over grading and pricing, with the firm acting as a monopsonist. Consequently, ALCOSA increasingly turned to smallholders in the highlands as a source of supply; 2,000 small farmers produced 90 percent of the firm's procurement by 1980.

The arrangement proved satisfactory for both the processing firm and the peasants. Through the scheme, the peasants gained access to new crops, credit, and new chemicals and fertilizers, and increased their knowledge of and sophistication in marketing opportunities. Although there was competition for land between food and cash crops, food production also increased; the reduction in food crop area (as it was switched to cash crops) was more than offset by the higher yields achieved when the modern inputs applied to cash crops spilled over to food crops. The organization of a cooperative and assistance from nongovernmental organizations (NGOs) helped peasants gain further access to credit and strengthen their bargaining positions with the agribusiness company. By 1987 five companies other than ALCOSA also processed frozen vegetables, and six other companies were processing dried vegetables for export. The cooperative started its own freezing and drying facilities and was exporting to U.S., European, and Central American markets. The production and processing markedly increased the demand for labor, leading to a rise in local wages.

Similar export activities in the Bajio region of Mexico were dominated by medium-size and large farmers, although ejidatarios could have produced at a lower cost (Moulton and Runsten 1986). The transactions costs of contracting with small farmers were apparently perceived to be too high by multinational corporations and Mexican exporters. Unlike the Guatemala case study, the Bajio export activities did not include cooperative organizations of smallholders, access to credit for *ejidatarios*, and the delivery of technology.

The experience of ALCOSA shows that rural development can be effectively linked to labor-intensive agroexport activities, which have found a new competitive edge in the context of the adjustment to the crisis. Needed for success are local organizations, a good infrastructure in irrigation and transportation, access to credit and technology, and subcontracting with transnational or domestic agroexport companies for access to markets.

Production for import substitution

Production of temperate goods for export (cereals, meat and dairy products, sugar, and oilseeds) is hampered by the trade distortions that prevail on international markets. And penetrating these markets requires marketing and credit facilities that many marginal exporters do not have. But real exchange rate depreciations have opened up important opportunities in import substitution for these products. Import dependency increased sharply in the 1970s because of appreciated real exchange rates, and this market window can now be recaptured. In many countries this has occurred. The production of cereals has increased very rapidly in Brazil, Chile, Ecuador, Peru, and Venezuela (table 11.2). In Chile wheat production increased by 22.3 percent annually between 1982 and 1987, allowing a reduction in import dependency from 61 percent to only 1 percent. In Brazil wheat production increased by 6.2 percent annually, and import dependency fell from 70 percent to 33 percent.

The salience of small farmers in production for import substitution varies greatly across countries. In Brazil wheat is produced principally on large farms. In Chile, while the bulk of production also comes from large farms, wheat is an important traditional crop for the Mapuche Indians. In general, there has been an important shift in the production systems of small farmers away from autarky toward the production of a marketed surplus. This is evident in a set of projects promoted by grassroots organizations following an agroecological approach (Altieri and Yurjevic 1989).

In the 1970s most of the agroecology projects were motivated by an ideology of self-sufficiency. The projects attempted to apply modern science to technologies used by peasants for generations to produce basic foods while reducing the use of purchased inputs. For that reason, organic farming and other low-input techniques were promoted. Under the conditions of Dutch disease in the 1970s, with strongly appreciated real exchange rates, this strategy was correct: the terms of trade for tradable agricultural goods were highly unfavorable. Even though the prices of tradable inputs were held low, withdrawal from the market on the product side implied the need to withdraw from the market on the factor side also, because of the lack of cash to acquire inputs.

Extrapolating that strategy beyond the 1970s would be erroneous, however. Depreciation of the real exchange rate has made production of a marketed surplus or of cash crops more attractive. On the factor side, the strategy remains valid because it promotes the substitution for tradable inputs of nontradable factors, many of which are captive within the household—for example, family labor. Both global and national adjustment policies have led to substantially higher rural real interest rates, however, diminishing substantially the general incentive to invest for the distant future rather than for short-run returns. International donors and NGOs that have been supporting the agroecology movement, with its autarkic objectives, need to recognize this new reality and to continue their support in the context of a growing market orientation.

Several agroecology projects have successfully promoted the production of a marketed surplus for import substitution. Servicios Multiples de Tecnologias Apropriadas in Bolivia assists in the production of potatoes, and of vegetables in greenhouses; Centro de Educación y Tecnologiá in Chile promotes the production of strawberries and milk; Centro Andino de Acción Popular in Ecuador helps in the production of onions; Centro de Investigaciones, Educación y Desarrollo in Peru promotes animal husbandry as a source of cash income; and Centro de Promoción Campesina de la Cordillera in Paraguay assists in the production of citrus, vegetables, and honey.

Recent evaluations of more conventional rural development projects, such as PRODERO in Honduras, observed that the projects have increased food self-sufficiency on small peasant farms. But failure to focus more explicitly on cash crops (such as fruits, vegetables, tobacco, coffee where possible, and basic grains) has left monetary incomes and credit repayment capacity unimproved. This has led the International Fund for Agricultural Development (IFAD), in a significant revision of its original strategy defined in the food crisis of the 1970s, pragmatically to redesign its rural development projects (in the Northern Zone of Costa Rica, the Paracentral Region in El Salvador, and Zacapa and Chiquimula in Guatemala) away from concentration on food crops for home consumption, and more broadly toward crops with domestic or export market opportunities.

Employment creation in commercial agriculture

The welfare of rural inhabitants depends heavily on employment opportunities in agriculture. This is true not only for the landless but also for many marginal farmers. It is likely that two-thirds of the farm households in Latin America derive more than half of their income from off-farm sources, principally agricultural employment.

Important changes have occurred in the Latin American agricultural labor market. Permanent workers are being replaced by temporary workers, the urban and agricultural labor markets are becoming increasingly integrated, and labor contractors are playing a growing role in mediating the supply and demand for labor (de Janvry, Sadoulet and Wilcox 1989). As a result, increasingly fewer agricultural workers are recruited from surplus labor on family farms and more from households in small towns and cities. In 1986 in the Central Valley of Chile, for instance, 52 percent of the temporary agricultural workers came from urban areas (Gomez and Echenique 1988). Farm-based workers are increasingly finding principal employment in the nonagricultural sector; this is the case for 23 percent of the rural economically active population in Brazil, 26 percent in Ecuador, 41 percent in Costa Rica, and 42 percent in Mexico.

Employment creation in commercial agriculture has been highly unsatisfactory during the last two decades, and it is not clear that the revival of growth will by itself lead to greater employment opportunities. Between 1950 and 1980 agricultural output increased by 85 percent, but this led to an increase in employment in modern agriculture of only 19 percent. As a result, the share of the economically active agricultural population working in commercial agriculture declined from 39 percent in 1950 to 35 percent in 1980. In some countries faster growth was associated with rapidly expanding employment opportunities; elsewhere it was associated with an absolute loss in employment. The principal causes for the poor performance of modern agriculture in creating employment, despite eventually rapid growth until 1980, were mechanization, often promoted by overvalued exchange rates, subsidized credit, and generous tax write-offs; land concentration that eliminated labor-intensive forms of farming; and displacement of crops (cereals in particular) by extensive livestock operations. The displacement of crops has occurred as a result of the income effects of rapid growth, which displaced demand toward the more income-elastic animal products; the effects of real exchange rate appreciation, since animal products tend to be less tradable than cereals; and the effects of agricultural protectionism in industrial countries, which discourages the production of cereals.

In the 1990s the employment effects of the growth of commercial agriculture could be potentially more significant. Most subsidies to mechanization have been eliminated as part of the fiscal austerity programs; depreciations of the real exchange rate favor nontradable inputs, particularly labor, over imported inputs; and the production of livestock has fallen relative to that of crops. Success in the General Agreement on Tariffs and Trade (GATT) negotiations on agriculture could further reinforce this effect.

In several areas of labor-intensive agroexports, real wages have risen. This was the case in Chile in the late 1980s, after a decade of massive surplus labor despite rapid growth of the export sector. Agricultural unemployment, 18 percent in 1982-83, fell to 5 percent in 1986-87. In the Bajio region of Mexico, however, employment gains in the production of vegetables for export have been fully erased by rapid expansion in the production of sorghum for feed, a highly mechanized crop that displaced labor-intensive production of corn (Wilcox 1987).

Access to land: Toward a less adversarial land reform strategy?

Land reform in Latin America has occurred in two phases. The first, in Bolivia and Mexico, was pushed by revolutionary forces in the first half of the 1900s, and the second, in virtually every other country, by legislated changes induced by the pressures created by the 1959 Cuban revolution. Although some of the land redistributions have been extensive (particularly in Chile before 1973, Ecuador, El Salvador, Mexico, Nicaragua, and Peru), they have in general failed to reduce rural poverty. Land reform ground to a halt in the early 1970s except in El Salvador and Nicaragua, where the reforms continued through the 1980s. The by-product of the reforms has in many situations been to induce large farmers to increase the intensity of land use to avoid expropriation. The issue of land reform remains on the political agenda, but the political strength to manage orderly land reform is lacking. In Brazil the extensive land reform promised by the new democratic government was only minimally implemented.

There are less adversarial avenues through which access to land can be gained, however, and they all started to play significant roles in the 1980s. One avenue is through reactivation of the land rental market. An important contrast exists here between Latin America and Asia. In Asia the rental market and the agricultural ladders that it permits have been important avenues for landless households to gain access to land. Thus, because much of the peasantry is already in place as tenants before the land reform, it is less difficult to implement in Asia. Reform mainly redistributes the land rent from landlords to peasants. In Latin America, by contrast, the rental market had never been important; what market existed was weakened by land reform, which either gave land rights to tenants (inducing their eviction or rapid turnover) or made rental illegal. Thus, Latin American land reforms must not only redistribute rent but also settle peasants on the land, at a high cost in infrastructure, institutional reorganization, and managerial training.

In recent years, however, the rental market has been reactivated. In Mexico *ejido* lands, which had for years been illegally rented out, can now be leased legally. As a result, ejidatarios have become both wage and rent earners, because the land is rented by large farmers with better access to credit and economies of scale in machinery and marketing (a similar situation has emerged in the Indian Punjab). In Argentina, Brazil, and Chile rent contracts have also become increasingly widespread. In many countries, however, important gains are still to be achieved, both in efficiency and in poverty reduction, through promotion and rationalization of the land rental market.

A second less adversarial avenue of increasing access to land is through decentralized arrangements between local administrative authorities and landlords to transfer land to peasants though advantageous purchases and compensation. A key requirement is that the land be sold at a price that does not fully internalize, to the (wealthy) seller, the potential productivity gains that land redistribution will permit for the (poorer and more labor-intensive) buyer. In a number of instances mayors of rural towns and grassroots organizations have been the intermediaries in these transactions. Local authorities may see the transactions as a way of mobilizing political support and reducing the cost of welfare programs (Tendler 1988). Credit lines for this type of transaction should be made available by international lending and bilateral organizations.

Finally, a third avenue for increasing access to land has been made possible by frontier settlements in the lowland tropics. Although such settlements have often resulted in both ecological disasters and ethnic conflicts, there are also properly managed settlements, adequately supported by credit, legal titling, infrastructure services, and technological research and extension. Because spontaneous land settlement is difficult to restrain, experiments with alternative technologies and institutions are urgently needed.

With access to land still the main determinant of rural income levels, redistributive land reform should remain high on the political agenda. While collective organization of production in Chile and Peru has generally failed, farming by individuals supported by service cooperatives has proved effective in the Dominican Republic and, more recently, in Peru (Carter and Alvarez 1989). The new opportunities to manage the politics of land reform through less adversarial approaches and to capitalize on the revitalization of viable family farms are consequently important elements in a strategy of poverty reduction with growth. In chapter 12 in this volume, Carter and Mesbah chart the changing approaches in three Latin American land reforms.

Employment creation in rural nonagricultural activities

Even extensive land reform and successful farm-oriented rural development are unlikely to suffice to erase rural poverty. Employment creation in rural nonagricultural activities is therefore a necessary component of a strategy of rural development. Indeed, throughout Latin America the share of the rural labor force engaged in nonagricultural activities has risen rapidly.

Rural nonfarm enterprises are concentrated in food processing, textiles and apparel, furniture and carpentry, and metalworking, including the making of tools and equipment (World Bank 1978a). Successful rural microenterprise programs have been observed in the POLONORDESTE program in Brazil and in the CREA (Centro de Reconversión Económica del Azuay, Cañar y Morona Santiago) program in Ecuador. Many of these activities are linked to agriculture or to consumption by farm households. Good transport and communications infrastructure, as well as labor skills, are preconditions for the success of these activities in rural areas (Scott 1988). But the administrative apparatus has generally neglected to adequately support microenterprises because they are not regarded as falling under the sphere of either rural development or industrial promotion agencies.

In the Asian countries the strongest linkage that agriculture provides to rural nonagricultural activities is through final demand for consumer goods (Mellor 1986; see also Hazell and Haggblade's chapter 8 in this volume). There is no similar strong linkage in Latin America. This difference is probably due in part to the fact that the distribution of rural income is less unequal in most of Asia, because of redistributive land reforms or an active land rental market, than in most of Latin America. In Latin America the high concentration of landownership and the weakness of the land rental markets imply that a few landlords benefit from the bulk of the income effects of agricultural growth. Many are absentee landowners (which reduces their demand for local services), and the level of their incomes creates a demand for luxury items that is more likely to be met by urban industries or imports. As a result, unless industrialization in the rural areas is preceded by redistributive land reforms, much of it would have to aim at servicing a demand that originates in broader markets outside the rural areas. This raises an important question: How can the rural areas acquire comparative advantages for the location of these industries?

Large, traditional mass production industries are able to move to rural areas if they rely on few linkages and cheap, unskilled or narrowly skilled labor. This type of industry has created a high level of instability in local employment because such firms can relocate easily if they discover cheaper sources of labor elsewhere.

In recent years this traditional model of industry for mass production has given way to another approach that has much greater potential for the decentralization of industrial activities to the rural areas. This new system of subcontracting with a large number of small, decentralized workshops (*maquilas*) and household units is well adapted to the 1990s' environment of market uncertainties and the tremendous growth during the 1980s of the informal economy. The system of "flexible specialization" allows the production of specialized products with broadly skilled and weakly specialized resources (Sabel 1987). This approach also characterizes the Japanese *kanban*, in which many small suppliers and subcontractors are clustered around a large firm, and the northern Italian system of regional clusters of small firms. In this system, products can be easily changed to accommodate uncertain demand and shifting market niches.

The Latin American strategy of import-substituting industrialization, based on large-scale mass production firms, played an important role in initiating rapid industrialization after the Great Depression. The debt crisis and the need to liberalize trade have placed limits on the sustainability of this strategy, however. This, in turn, opens up the possibility of rethinking the entire industrialization strategy. In many countries small-scale enterprises in the informal sector exploded in number during the 1970s and the 1980s. Wood products, textiles and clothing, and shoes and leather goods are commonly produced under subcontract by such enterprises. The shoe industries around Nova Hamburgo in Brazil (Sabel 1987) and León in Mexico (de Janvry and others 1989) are organized on that basis, with many subcontracting workshops and households located in the surrounding rural areas.

Support to these enterprises in the form of credit, infrastructure, simple technology, and the development of skills may be one of the most effective ways of promoting the revival of competitive industries and their location in the rural areas. Once this institutional and technological support has been provided, these industries will be largely demand-led. The Mexican shoe industry produces nontradables under heavy protection; its growth therefore depends on growth in domestic effective demand. The industry has grown an average 2.3 percent a

year between 1970 and 1984. The Brazilian shoe industry, by contrast, by cater-
ing to the international market, has been able to increase exports 31 percent a
year during the same period.

Conditions for success

In the 1980s the role of the welfare state declined for both economic reasons
(fiscal austerity in stabilization) and ideological reasons (the rise of liberalism on
a world scale). As a result, an attack on poverty needs to be more explicitly
located within an economic growth strategy than it was in the 1970s. For such a
strategy to succeed, the rate of economic growth must increase in both the economy
at large and in agriculture, and the style of economic growth must be one that
incorporates the poor as productive agents. We identify below the conditions
necessary to achieve these two results. Public investment in health and education
is essential to permit the poor to contribute to growth. Also necessary, as complements to a growth-based antipoverty strategy, are direct income transfers of a
limited magnitude—to compensate those who lose during the transition, on
grounds of either preventing absolute poverty or achieving political acceptabil-
ity, and to ensure that the basic needs of the unemployable and those unable to
help themselves are met.

Conditions for overall economic growth

Both external and internal conditions are necessary for the revival of the growth
of the Latin American economies. External conditions include (1) a recovery of
growth in the international economy, following the recession in the early 1980s
and sustained but sluggish growth in the rest of the decade; (2) trade liberalization in the industrial countries to allow access to markets for industrial goods
produced in the developing countries; and (3) reduction of the debt burden,
access to new international sources of loans, and an increase in foreign direct
investment. These conditions have been extensively discussed elsewhere (for
example, IDB 1988), and we do not elaborate on them here.

Internal conditions are economic and political. On the economic side, policies must aim at promoting economic efficiency and comparative advantages,
not solely the rise of new industries under protectionism. Significant policy
mistakes in the past were made not in promoting import substitution as an initial
phase of industrialization, but in extending protectionism in response to rent-
seeking pressures and in abruptly shifting from protectionism to trade liberalization before ensuring that national industry was competitive. Indeed, trade
liberalization on the basis of ideological views (Chile) or in response to external
pressures (policy conditionality) often led to massive imports and the liquidation
of domestic industry, rapidly increasing indebtedness while it was possible, and
then precipitating a prolonged unemployment crisis.

Also needed is policy continuity to establish credibility with regard to the
real exchange rate. Some credibility has come with the recent bureaucratization
of Latin American governments, particularly in Brazil, Chile, and Mexico. Policy

continuity is dependent on political stability. There has been a remarkable return to democracy in Latin America since the beginning of the 1980s, although the regimes remain fragile because of the lack of economic growth. The result is an inability to satisfy electoral promises and to finance the necessary reforms. In several countries frustration with extended austerity has led either to the rise of civil strife (Colombia, Peru) or to a turn toward populist regimes with a reduced ability to impose unpopular policy reform. Nevertheless, bureaucratization, redemocratization, the widespread acceptance of new ideas about development strategies (in particular, on the role of trade and of the real exchange rate and the contributions of agriculture to economic growth during recovery from debt), and the emergence of new social actors and of a multiplicity of grassroots organizations all enhance the possibility of a growth strategy with a strong component of rural development.

Conditions for agricultural growth

Although agriculture performed better in the 1980s than the rest of the economy in Latin American countries, with remarkable expansion in some countries and subsectors, its overall rate of growth has been insufficient to support any significant attack on poverty. With an overall population growth rate of 2.2 percent, the growth of agriculture has been negative on a per capita basis. A precondition for relinking poverty reduction to growth is thus the acceleration of agricultural growth. For that, again, there are external and internal conditions that need to be satisfied.

Externally, the level of prices on the international market has been depressed, and their instability increased, by agricultural protectionism in the industrial countries. In the short run more Latin American countries would lose than would gain from a rise in international prices resulting from trade liberalization in the European Community and the United States, but the continent as a whole would benefit (CEPAL 1989b). In the longer run Latin America has strong comparative advantages in the production of many of the temperate goods and tropical substitutes that would be affected by trade liberalization by the industrial countries. The result should be to stimulate the growth of agriculture and thus to allow agriculture to play a greater role in economic growth. Success in the GATT negotiations on agriculture is thus an important external condition for the acceleration of agricultural growth.

Internally, the priority that economic policy has long given to urban areas must give way to a priority for agricultural investment, at least during recovery from the debt crisis, to ensure that nonprice factors complement the price incentives resulting from adjustment. Recent studies on aggregate supply response have clearly shown the key role that public investment in irrigation, transportation infrastructure, and technology play in price response (Binswanger and others 1987; Cavallo and Mundlak 1982; Lele and Mellor 1988; and de Janvry and Subbarao 1986). Success in structural adjustment has also been linked to the strengthening of the nonprice determinants of supply response (Commander 1989). Yet in recent years not only has public investment been cut disproportionately to protect current expenditure, but the share of agriculture in public invest-ment has fallen.

Declining investment in infrastructure, irrigation, research, and human capi-tal formation is bound to have serious consequences on factor productivity in agriculture, thus compromising future growth. With the technological advances of the green revolution relatively exhausted, delaying the reorganization of the university and public research systems for research on biotechnology is danger-ous. New patent systems need to be defined, and contractual arrangements made between public and private sectors, between nations in the region, and between regional and transnational corporations (de Janvry, Runsten, and Sadoulet 1987). The time that it will take for these investments to yield benefits implies that any further delays will have costs over an extended period and will compromise the potential role that agriculture can play in economic recovery. This need not be the case; fiscal austerity need not imply a fall in public investment in agriculture. The funds released from reductions in input and food subsidies and in quasi-fiscal deficits should be reallocated at least in part to agricultural investment. In addition, user fees can be levied on commercial agriculture to recover the costs of both public services and capital investments.

Finally, policy reforms that benefit agriculture will achieve the expected long-term results only if they are sustained. As the success of Chile's agricultural growth demonstrates, policy reforms need to be sustained over some five to ten years to yield visible results, and the road to agricultural response can pass through considerable instability and unemployment. In the short run achieving that sustainability first requires establishing its credibility. In turn, achieving credibility requires not only that the reforms be politically acceptable to those with the power to derail programs, but that they be institutionalized to guarantee continuity. Administrative and legal reforms are needed for that purpose, and to ensure that after the fiscal emergency there is no recurrence of the rent-seeking pressures that had created the initial distortions. These reforms include disman-tling the control agencies and the legal regulatory framework that were imple-menting the former urban-biased policies. Privatizing some of the parastatals and public commercial operations and acquiring membership in the GATT (and hence agreeing to submit to the sanctions that trade distortions imply) are some of the essential signals of reform.

Conditions for rural development

There have been some nineteen years of experience with rural development projects in Latin America. That experience has been mixed, and often explicitly criticized. It suffers from the lack of a new generation of ideas capitalizing on lessons learned from past successes and failures, in part because there has been no systematic economic evaluation of past projects. The present context of struc-tural adjustment, improved terms of trade for agriculture, democratic forms of government, and explosion in the number of NGOs and grassroots organizations is one that allows experimentation with a new strategy of rural development. As we will argue, the success of this strategy depends importantly on maintaining an active role for the state in agriculture, rather than the massive withdrawal observed in Africa (Commander 1989). We outline here some of the salient features of this strategy.

A new division of labor between public and private sectors. In the 1970s' strategy of rural development, integrated projects were designed in which a public agency was to coordinate the delivery of public goods and services to the targeted segment of the peasantry (Leonard 1984). In this top-down strategy institutional coordination proved difficult to achieve. Public agencies with no tradition of working together were supposed to be coordinated by one central institution with little presence in the field, or by a specialized agency with little tradition of work in the many areas involved. Alternative approaches that placed projects in semiautonomous regional corporations (following the Tennessee Valley Authority model)—such as the Cauca Valley Corporation in Colombia, Plan Sierra in the Dominican Republic, and CREA in Ecuador—or in the universities (Piaui Project in Brazil) have sometimes been more successful. They have been constrained, however, by eventual conflicts with or lack of support by national policymakers and budget allocators, by weak access to supportive national programs, and by lack of coordination with other public or private organizations operating in the same geographical area.

Several important social and political changes have occurred in Latin America during the last two decades that create a possibility of redefining the strategy of rural development introduced in the 1970s. These are the following:

- The emergence on the political scene of a set of new social actors who are quantitatively (with the growing relative importance of the urban and rural informal sectors), qualitatively (with better health, education, and information due to success in the provision of basic needs), and economically (with ownership of assets in the informal sectors) different from the traditional popular sectors (represented by labor unions, political parties, and corporatist organizations).
- The emergence of a multiplicity of new social movements, many of which started in the 1960s, as governments turned to authoritarianism and the welfare state failed, with the assistance of the church and of international organizations. The institutions created by these movements include NGOs, intermediate organizations, and a wide variety of grassroots organizations. This rich web of decentralized institutions has an important role to play with the withdrawal of the state from many economic and social functions.
- A return to democracy in nearly all Latin American countries. The result has been to make policy less clientelistic, as politicians need to mobilize popular support directly rather than through the traditional mediation of landlords and political bosses. With the economic crisis limiting the possibility of economic concessions by governments to their constituencies (in contrast to the generous distribution of economic rents in the 1970s), they have to turn to political concessions. This opens important new channels of access to power for the new social actors.
- A growing bureaucratization of governments, forced in large part by the constraints imposed by the economic crisis, which to some extent

depoliticizes and thus also stabilizes the management of economic policy. Declining subsidies limit the scope for rent seeking. In addition, fiscal austerity compels a search for more efficient forms of administration, leading to bureaucratic decentralization and the promotion of self-help organizations to relieve fiscal budgets (producer and user associations such as the CREA groups in Argentina).

These changes should permit a redefinition of the relative roles of the state and civil organizations, based on their comparative advantages, in a new approach to rural development. Past experiences have shown that projects' macroeconomic and institutional context is critical to their success. It is the responsibility of the state to manage this environment in a way that is supportive of rural development. This requires a macroeconomic and sectoral policy that removes the price distortions against agriculture, both indirect (exchange rate overvaluation and industrial protectionism) and direct (agricultural trade policies and direct interventions in the pricing of agricultural commodities). It requires increasing the share of agriculture in public investment at least during the recovery from the debt crisis, and increasing the efficiency of public sector operations. And it requires eliminating the historical antipeasant biases in access to markets, credit, and public goods and services. Rural development projects that have been managed at a decentralized level (by regional corporations, universities, and grassroots organizations) have often been seriously hampered by the lack of a supportive policy, of public goods, and of an appropriate institutional environment; defining these is the unique responsibility of the state. In order for the depreciation of the real exchange rate to favor agriculture and provide a favorable context in which to link poverty reduction to growth, it is essential that price incentives not be undermined by state contraction (Lipton 1989). Far from weakening the role of the state, this division of labor between the public and private sectors should relegitimize the state in the functions that it should efficiently perform in a post-welfare-state era.

Regional development corporations, NGOs, and grassroots organizations should be the ones to manage the implementation of projects because of their comparative advantages in organizing rural communities and in tailoring services to the clientele. For the same reason, they should also be the ones that mediate access to state institutions, in a clear departure from the top-down strategy of the 1970s. These decentralized organizations need access to public resources, to credit, and to technology, and their initiatives need to be coordinated both among themselves and with public programs. Important new avenues of state-NGO cooperation have been introduced in Brazil, Ecuador, and Mexico (de Janvry and others 1989). In Brazil the government abolished the POLONORDESTE Project in 1985 and replaced it with the equally ambitious Projeto Nordeste, with its Program of Support for Small Rural Producers (community-initiated projects and investments), in the largest such reversal in strategy away from integrated rural development (Chaloult 1988). Where grassroots organizations do not exist or where they prefer not to cooperate with government agencies, state-managed integrated rural development should remain, but with decentralized management and sources of revenue.

From unique to diversified, flexible, and policy-robust projects. With poverty highly differentiated socially (according to region, access to assets, and source of income), and with the welfare effect of the crisis correspondingly highly uneven across social groups, rural development strategies must be equally varied. A serious error in the strategy of the 1970s was the belief that the rural poor were mainly small farmers and that poverty alleviation required mainly increasing the productivity of their resources. This led to a focus on agricultural technology (the roles of CIMMYT, CIAT, and CIP), institutional changes to improve access to credit and modern inputs (Plan Puebla in Mexico), and infrastructure investment (PIDER in Mexico). As subsequent detailed observations of the causes and dynamics of poverty have shown, this focus was a serious error. Only a small fraction of rural poverty is found among viable small farmers, and a large share of the rural poor cannot be helped by production-oriented rural development projects (de Janvry 1981).

A comprehensive approach to rural development therefore requires defining a portfolio of approaches that correspond to the specific determinants of poverty for each social group and region. These approaches include:

- Farm-oriented rural development directed at a clientele of viable family farms in relatively well-endowed regions. These projects need to have well-defined sequential priorities (as opposed to a broad integration of services), including, according to specific instances, credit, technology, irrigation, and marketing. This decentralized or grassroots-based approach with well-defined priorities is the one that derives most directly from the 1970s' strategy of rural development. As illustrated above, adjustment to the crisis has given these projects a renewed opportunity to be effective in increasing the production of export crops or of a marketed surplus of staples for import substitution.
- Household-oriented rural development, directed at subfamily farms, which promotes a multiplicity of home-based activities, including animals and nonagricultural activities, and stresses the key role of women and the importance of human capital formation.
- Access to land and security of access through redistributive land reform when possible, the titling of squatters, revival of the land rental market, and minimal or carefully monitored colonization of the tropical lowlands.
- Agricultural employment creation through the elimination of policy biases favoring mechanization and extensive livestock operations, and through the promotion of such labor-intensive activities as producing fruits and vegetables for export.
- Regional nonagricultural development through incentives and support to microenterprises either linked to agriculture, particularly on the final demand side, or export-oriented and based on the principles of flexible specialization and subcontracting.

Because relative prices are highly uncertain in the context of recovery from the economic crisis and with the current turbulence in the international market, projects must be organized as learning processes. Project evaluation and monitoring, and participation in evaluation and redesign not only by project personnel, but also by the organized communities, should thus be integral components of project design. This will increase the ability to adjust projects to shifting market opportunities, and increase policy robustness in the typical Latin American context of weak democracies and political instability.

From welfare to bankable projects and resource conservation. Adjustments in the real exchange rate allow a shift in the strategy of rural development from a set of antipoverty projects to an investment strategy with social rates of return competitive with other projects. Removing the institutional biases that have historically undermined the profitability of investment in rural development would permit the expansion of this set of bankable projects. The rising cost of the negative externalities created by rural poverty further adds to the possibility of shifting toward bankable projects: it becomes profitable to devise projects that provide poor people with productive alternatives to degrading the environment. These negative externalities include soil erosion in the watersheds, desertification of collective lands, depletion of underground water tables, settlement in the tropical frontiers and deforestation, and congestion costs following rapid migration to the cities. In Latin America a significant share of environmental degradation can be traced to the failure to address poverty; thus, reducing rural poverty would lower the costs of solving these environmental problems, an external benefit of effective rural development (de Janvry and Garcia 1988).

Soil erosion in the watersheds provides a good illustration of the opportunity to make rural development economically bankable. The soil erosion is caused by peasants farming in the highlands. The silt deposited in the reservoirs as a result compromises hydroelectrical and irrigation projects for the lowlands. With real exchange rate depreciation, the opportunity cost of importing oil and foods increases sharply (but so do interest and discount rates that play in the opposite direction). An optimum solution would be a scheme of downstream taxes and upstream subsidies that would transfer resources to rural development programs that address watershed stabilization. These subsidies could be used to induce peasants to reforest or to produce crops in ways that cause less erosion when these activities are not privately profitable. Through such schemes, the set of bankable antipoverty programs would be increased and poverty reduction would be linked to economic growth. The examples of the Cauca Valley Corporation in Colombia and Plan Sierra in the Dominican Republic demonstrate how this can be done.

Preserving an incipient welfare state. Shifting toward bankable programs in order to relink poverty reduction to growth cannot eradicate all rural poverty. Indeed, many of the poorest of the poor are simply not bankable, even after internalization of all the externalities created by poverty.

For many rural areas with no absolute advantages, the best solution to poverty is to assist emigration. In addition, the scarcity of fiscal resources under austerity requires targeting resources for maximum efficiency gains—and thus focusing first on the best, not the marginal areas (unless they are marginal only because of past neglect in providing public goods, for example, agricultural research). For the poor in other marginal areas, education programs to assist migration is the most cost-effective approach.

Turning to bankable rural development projects would still leave a need for the welfare state to assume coverage of the basic needs of the populations most at risk, particularly the unemployable and those temporarily affected by adjustments in the economy. For that purpose, effectively targeted subsidies programs remain essential. But the magnitude of these programs can be significantly reduced by a growth strategy that stresses the role of agriculture and gives an explicit productive function to peasant and rural households.

Note

We are indebted to Michael Lipton for his many constructive questions and suggestions.

State-Mandated and Market-Mediated Land Reform in Latin America

12 *Michael R. Carter*
Dina Mesbah

Reports of land reform's death in Latin America are, to pinch a phrase from Mark Twain, greatly exaggerated. El Salvador and Nicaragua are in the midst of major land reform programs. Land reform is firmly entered into the political debate in Brazil and, more recently, in Paraguay. Honduras is somewhere between debate and action. Elsewhere, land reform remains alive in the sense that problematic, socially destabilizing patterns of growth in agriculture continue to create a demand for it, though one that is not always politically effective.

This chapter offers a theoretical review of land reform in Ecuador, Nicaragua, and Peru, with particular emphasis on the constraints, real and imagined, that limited the scope and effectiveness of those reforms as antipoverty programs.[1] The focus of the review is decidedly forward-looking, rather than historical. The review is intended to inform two contemporary policy debates. The first is the debate over the possibilities and prospects for conventional land reform programs using state intervention to redefine and reallocate property rights. The second debate concerns *new wave* policies, which propose to utilize market-based mechanisms to achieve the land reform goal of linking agricultural growth to poverty reduction and social stability. New wave policies are particularly important in those countries in which economic and political constraints have driven land reform off the agenda of realpolitik. The likely effects of such policies ultimately depend, it will be argued, on the same factors that shape and constrain land reform.

Land reform

The distribution of agricultural landownership in Latin America is highly unequal compared with that in other developing regions.[2] The agricultural sector in almost every country in the region has historically been dominated by large farm units that operate hundreds, sometimes thousands, of hectares. The stratum of the large farm typically controls the majority of agricultural resources, although its members constitute only a tiny minority of farm and rural households. The coexistence of large farms with vast numbers of smallholdings and landless families creates what has come to be known as a bimodal agrarian structure. The stark contrasts of this structure, and the accumulated evidence of low-intensity land use and high capital-labor ratios on large farms,[3] lend credibility to the interpretation that agricultural growth in Latin America (in the large-farm stratum) has displaced small farmers, absorbed little labor, and heightened inequality, in contrast with the experience in South Asia and elsewhere.[4]

This agrarian structure, and the fact that the rural sector accounts for 20 to 70 percent of the population—and a higher share of total poverty—in the countries of Latin America, make a compelling case for land redistribution as an antipoverty program. Lipton assembles the arithmetic of asset redistribution in an informative way:

> Calories are less unequally distributed than food, food than consumption, consumption than income, and income than assets...[T]he richest decile can well be, at most, four times better placed than the poorest to meet calorie requirements for a full and active life—yet three hundred times better placed in respect of asset ownership....This latter vast discrepancy naturally focuses, upon asset redistribution, the attention of fighters of wars against poverty. (1985: 4)

Writing of the world as a whole, Roy Prosterman and Jeffrey Riedinger argue that large-scale programs of land reform would, among other things, preclude "100 million or more of the hunger- and health-related deaths that would otherwise occur between now and 2000...[and] literally hundreds of millions more such deaths during the first quarter of the coming century" (1987: 1-2).

The effect of any change in landownership on the poor depends at least as much on what it does to the employment and wage rate of hired workers as on what it does to the income of beneficiary farmers. Later sections of this chapter consider the total labor absorption of different land reform models. The effect of reform on the poor also depends on the distribution of the total labor absorption and employment opportunities. Small units of land, which may absorb a lot of labor, may also be very exclusionary if they absorb only family labor at full-time levels; the landless, if excluded from direct access to reform land, may find themselves out of the labor market.

What is the regional record of land reform as an antipoverty program in Latin America? The political debate and, to a lesser extent, the political practice of land reform have long, often prominent, histories in Latin America. In later sections this chapter reviews land reform programs in Ecuador, Nicaragua, and Peru—three countries that have undertaken land reform under different domestic and international political circumstances. Of these three reforms, Ecuador's had the most modest quantitative impact, affecting 9 percent of the agricultural land and 15 percent of rural households. Some of those households may have been negatively affected by aspects of the reform that helped large farmers to displace resident laborers by assigning the laborers less desirable plots.

The Peruvian and Nicaraguan reforms led to greater quantitative effects. Peru's reform affected 40 to 50 percent of the farmed area, Nicaragua's 30 to 40 percent. Peru's reform directly benefited 25 to 30 percent of the rural population,

Nicaragua's 15 to 20 percent. The structure of the reform in both Peru and Nicaragua reduced the income of the largest landowners, but it also tilted the distribution of benefits toward relatively well-off segments of society. For Peru Figueroa (1975) estimates that land reform redistributed 1 to 2 percent of national income to those in the top 40 percent of rural income distribution.

With the possible exception of some beneficiaries of land reform in Ecuador, those who benefited from reform in the three countries gained notable increases in income, access to social services, and economic security. What is perhaps surprising is the rather large number of rural poor left out of the more ambitious reforms of Nicaragua and Peru. Peru's reform excluded from direct benefit the 20 percent of the rural population who were landless—probably including most of the poorest. Nicaragua's reform also failed to directly benefit the landless, who constitute about one-third of the rural population. Although it is unfair to measure these experiences against the buoyant expectations of Prosterman and Riedinger, neither these reforms nor others in Latin America have measured up to the expectations of their proponents (Thiesenhusen 1977). What explains this gap between the promise and the reality of land reform as an antipoverty program?

There are two proximate answers to this question. They concern the *scope* and the *organizational model* of the agrarian reforms. The scope of reform may seem to be a simple matter of political will. In a limited sense, it is. Yet, as will be argued later, economic tradeoffs and constraints, real and imagined, define the political costs of executing a land reform of a given scope.

At its simplest, *organizational model* refers to the choice between collectivist and distributist reform.[5] In both Nicaragua and Peru land reform initially relied primarily on forms of collective property that maintained large-scale production. In addition, land reform benefits were often assigned to the preexisting permanent work forces of large farms. This froze the existing pattern of inequality between permanent and temporary workers, and excluded large numbers of landless poor from directly benefiting from agrarian reform.

These choices of scope and form provide the proximate explanation of the gap between the expectation and the reality of reform. They also motivate the deeper question to which this chapter is primarily addressed: What explains the choices, particularly of organizational model, that structured and ultimately limited land reform in these countries? This chapter takes the perspective that these choices were not random, or simply woodenheaded, but reflected economic constraints that the reformers perceived as restricting the feasible scope and models of land reform.

To understand the perception and the reality of these constraints—and hence, ultimately, the gap between the expectation and the reality of land reform—this chapter relies on a mix of theoretical argument and empirical case study. The following section argues that the conventional case for distributist land reform is not airtight—particularly its stronger versions, which imply that land reform faces neither economic nor political constraints of model and scope. The section poses a legitimate and important question with respect to the conventional case for land reform: If redistribution of land to smallholders promises net social benefits, why have market processes failed autonomously to allocate land to smallholders? The answer to this question, it is argued, determines how sharply constrained land reform is in both scope and form.

Subsequent sections of the chapter harness the land reform experience of Ecuador, Nicaragua, and Peru to evaluate the constraints that structure and limit land reform. The chapter lays the groundwork for the case study analysis by describing the nature of land reform in the three countries. It then focuses on the constraints that policymakers in the three countries *perceived* as limiting the choice of organizational form. It draws on the country-specific evidence to reflect on the political limits to the scope of land reform, and argues that these limits depend on the underlying perceived economic constraints as well as on the political power and independence of the reform coalition. The chapter goes on to present evidence on the accuracy of those perceptions, as revealed by the performance of the initial reforms in the countries, and by the decollectivization that later followed in Peru and, to a lesser extent, in Nicaragua. Finally, the chapter concludes by arguing that land reform in Latin America is not ancient history, and focuses on contemporary policy debate of the issues and evidence that it has presented.

The case for distributist land reform

Berry and Cline (1979) offer an impressive set of evidence confirming the generality of an inverse relationship between farm size and productivity per hectare. The inverse relationship forms the microeconomic core of the conventional case for distributist land reform, as articulated by Dorner and Kanel (1971). Confirmation of this relationship would seem to indicate that land reform, and the goal of social equity, can be pursued without economic constraint, and in harmony with the pursuit of agricultural productivity. Indeed, the greater the scope of land reform, and the greater the number of people among whom the land is divided, the greater would seem to be the beneficial effects on productivity.[6]

If, then, there is no productivity tradeoff or constraint, land reform should be *politically* achievable for two reasons. First, as Cline (1975) argues, land reform can be self-financing under this circumstance. The added farm production achieved by smallholders should suffice to buy off the acquiescence of large landowners to reform (without recourse to taxpayers) while still leaving a margin of improved living standard for the new smallholders. Second, a relatively low-productivity large-farm sector should be perceived as an unnecessary brake on other sectors of the economy, and a coalition between urban industrial interests and peasants motivated by this perception would have the potential politically to overwhelm the large-farm class.

The spirit of this economic case for distributist land reform is well captured by an open letter to the Chilean landlord class written by Peter Dorner in 1965. Quoted at length by Castillo and Lehmann (1983: 240), the letter offers with remarkable clarity a series of propositions about the economic and political prospects for land reform. With respect to microeconomics, the letter foresees no productivity problems in the reform sector. With respect to macroeconomics, it forecasts a pattern of agricultural-demand-led industrialization and accumulation. And with respect to politics, it confronts the landlord class with a transcendent national interest in land reform, or at least a politically insurmountable capitalist-peasant political alliance that can, out of self-interest, overcome all opposition to realize a land reform program.

Missing land market transactions and the Chicago question

There is a puzzling aspect to the case for land reform based on the inverse relationship: If there are strong Pareto-improving gains to be had by shifting land from large to small units, why is land reform necessary? That is, why does the economy fail autonomously to achieve the requisite reallocation and agrarian structural change? We call this query the *Chicago question* because it is one that would occur to an individual schooled in the belief that markets naturally exhaust possibilities for mutually beneficial exchange.

There is a series of responses to the Chicago question, some of which preserve intact the economic case for distributist land reform. Under other responses, the case begins to evaporate, and economic and political constraints to land reform mount in unison. The prospects for new wave market-mediated resolutions to the land problem also fade under these answers. The answers to the Chicago question considered below are:

1. *Feudal hypothesis:* Large-scale agriculture is a remnant of feudal lack of interest in profit maximization.[7]

2. *Land market imperfections hypothesis:* The absence of, or severe transactions costs or imperfections in, the land market inhibit the requisite transactions.[8]

3. *Price distortions hypothesis:* Distorted price policy lends an artificial competitive advantage to large-scale agriculture.

4. *Inadequate small-farm savings hypothesis:* Despite (or because of) the socially desirable labor intensity of small-farm production, these units cannot generate sufficient surplus over subsistence to participate in land markets.

5. *Countervailing capital constraints hypothesis:* Quantity-rationed access to capital constrains the ability of the small-farm sector to absorb land, and, more generally, offsets the benefits of the small farm's access to cheap on-farm labor.[9] A final explanation of the missing land market transactions would simply be that the inverse relationship is incorrect, and that there are no economic incentives for these transactions. In the language of the Latin American debate on the evolution of agrarian structure, this perspective is consistent with the view that agriculture, driven by technical scale economies, develops down a large-farm, "Junker path."[10]

Explanations of missing land market transactions

Central to any answer to the Chicago question is the underlying explanation for the inverse relationship and its persistence in the economy. One possible explanation is the *feudal hypothesis* that the inverse relationship reflects the fact that low-productivity, large-farm agriculture is a remnant of a feudal lack of interest in profit maximization. The economic incentives to reallocate land (through either rentals or sales) to small units have no more effect on large farms than do the incentives to maximize profits in current production, which the large farms also ignore. Under this hypothesis the case for distributist land reform maintains its full force. The politics and economics of land reform are easy. Both Lehmann (1978) and de Janvry (1981) describe important episodes of land reform in Latin America in these terms. But the very success of those reforms, both in achieving redistribution and in shaking large-scale agriculture out of its feudal torpor, spells the end of land reform under this scenario.

The empirical literature has found the inverse relationship to extend well beyond circumstances in which larger farms could reasonably be described as feudalistic, however. Carter (1984a), for example, evaluates econometrically a series of explanations that could, at least in partial equilibrium, explain the inverse relationship between farm productivity and size. Like most of the literature, Carter finds no evidence of decreasing returns to scale, or of differences in technical efficiency that favor the productivity of smaller units. Instead, huge doses of labor explain the higher productivity per hectare of smaller units. In a fashion consistent with a Chayanovian peasant household logic, smaller farm units treat the effective cost or shadow price of labor as if it were only a fraction of the market wage. It is the market wage that seems to guide large farms' resource allocation, and, in conformity with the dictates of conventional profit maximization, results in their lower labor absorption. Strictly speaking, the low opportunity cost of family labor can result from high marginal utility of consumption (many mouths to feed) *and* imperfect marketability of family labor,[11] or from the costs of recruiting and supervising hired labor, which increase effective wage rates.

As Sen (1966), Feder (1985), and Eswaran and Kotwal (1986) make clear, however, this partial equilibrium, imperfect labor market explanation of the inverse relationship does not suffice to explain its persistence in general equilibrium. If the labor market cannot realize the transfer of cheap labor to abundant land, what prevents the transfer of abundant land to cheap labor? That is, as we asked earlier, why does a competitive market mechanism fail to achieve the redistribution of farm operatorship that is the goal of land reform?

One possible explanation is the *land market imperfections hypothesis* that land market operation is inhibited, perhaps by transactions costs.[12] In Latin America the distribution of landownership is so highly concentrated that hundreds of land rental or sales transactions would be required to reduce a single large farm unit to holdings small enough to achieve high productivity. If transactions costs discourage these exchanges, or if for some other reason the land market does not operate, the inverse relationship would persist in general equilibrium. Land reform through redistribution would simply circumvent transactions costs (or, more accurately, externalize them as a cost of reform). Under this explanation of the market's inability to achieve land redistribution, the economic case for distributist land reform persists.

The *price distortions hypothesis* suggests that large farms' profitability is artificially maintained by capital subsidies. Thus, although land transactions would indeed reshape the size structure toward smaller farms if economic activity were valued at shadow prices, price distortions preempt them. There are, under this hypothesis, no intrinsic market failures that ultimately limit market efficiency.[13] This hypothesis, which is a Chicago answer to the Chicago question, can be considered the agrarian structure component of what de Janvry (1981) calls the "monetarist" explanation of agricultural crisis in Latin America. Under this hypothesis, price reform can bring about the same reallocation of land through private incentive as land reform is supposed to do through state action.[14]

The *inadequate savings hypothesis* offers another land-market-related explanation for the market's inability autonomously to shift the land distribution: the smallholder's inability to generate an economic surplus over subsistence requirements. As noted, the inverse relationship is rooted in massive labor inputs on smallholdings. Although these labor inputs carry a low *marginal* opportunity cost, the people who embody that labor present a much higher (*average*) subsistence claim on realized production. Put differently, savings cannot be generated without threatening the subsistence of the labor that generates high output per hectare. The poor will, for the same reason, be unable to use credit at the market rate of interest to purchase land at market prices without reducing consumption to levels below subsistence (Binswanger 1987).[15] This is what Binswanger (1987) has labeled the "fundamental financing problem of poor people."

Binswanger and Elgin (1988) use this logic to evaluate the feasibility of land reform. Under the inadequate savings hypothesis, distributist land reform would be expected to yield higher agricultural production. But two important constraints emerge that dampen the economic desirability and political feasibility of distributist reform. First, individuals who could not finance land purchases on the market also could not underwrite the self-financing land reform, described by Cline (1975), that makes land available at near-market prices and market interest rates. Second—and this is not discussed by Binswanger and Elgin (1988)— agricultural savings might well decline following the land reform. This would present an important constraint on macroeconomic accumulation for the government carrying out land reform. Although these problems could be ameliorated by increasing the size of the landholdings transferred under land reform, that would mean the loss of an important degree of freedom needed to maximize land reform's effect as an antipoverty program.

A final explanation of the lack of market-based transfers to the small-farm sector, the *capital constraints hypothesis*, rests on the effect of capital constraints on the small-farm sector's ability to absorb land, through either rental or sales transactions. Central to this explanation is the notion that access to capital is, in equilibrium, quantity-rationed. Stiglitz and Weiss (1981) develop a general theoretical rationale for capital rationing, and Carter (1988) extends their theory to suggest that capital rationing in low-income agriculture will systematically tend to ration smallholders out of the market.[16] Feder (1985) and Eswaran and Kotwal (1986) theoretically show that when access to capital varies according to size of farm, otherwise uninhibited land rental markets are unable to reallocate land with sufficient agility to eliminate differences among holdings in factor productivity.

The capital constraints explanation carries with it the implication that the high shadow price of capital on smallholdings potentially has countervailing effects on farm productivity. Feder (1985) and Carter and Kalfayan (1989) develop the argument that capital constraints weaken the inverse relationship. In agriculture, capital is needed not only for land market transactions, but also to finance the working capital costs of a seasonal production process in which output comes at the end of a seasonal cultivation period. Therefore, in an environment of imperfect capital markets, the strength of the inverse relationship dissipates, even in the face of very cheap marginal labor. As Carter and Kalfayan stress, even own labor requires up-front financing (in the form of subsistence costs because of the time by which farm input precedes output). Without that financing, the cheap labor household may find it necessary to pursue low-return, off-farm opportunities whose only virtue is payment of wages before harvest.

Carter and Kalfayan (1989) show that the interaction of labor and capital market imperfections creates a *skewed-U-shaped* relationship between farm productivity per hectare and farm size. *Skewed-U* describes a conventional inverse farm productivity-size relationship for very small farm units that is abruptly reversed at the farm size at which external credit becomes available. After this turning point, productivity *increases* with farm size to an inflection point beyond which the productivity-size relationship levels out.[17] This theoretical prediction accords well with some empirical evidence (Villa 1977; and Carter, Wiebe, and Blarel 1989), and with the more general stylized fact of low-productivity semiproletarian agriculture in Mexico and Central America.[18]

The capital constraints hypothesis thus introduces further ambiguities into the conventional case for land reform. It raises the possibility that small farms are not the most productive in some structural and capital market environments,[19] and suggests that this possibility increases as technical change increases the working capital requirements of agricultural production. Thus, it identifies yet more economic and, consequently, political costs and constraints to a broadly distributist, poverty-reducing land reform.

Finally, the capital constraints hypothesis raises important questions about the longer-term evolution of agrarian structure through competitive market processes. Using a computable general equilibrium model,[20] Carter and Kalfayan (1989) explore the effects of the interaction of labor and capital market imperfections on production and agrarian structure. They identify a stratum of medium-size farms that are best positioned to mediate the countervailing labor and capital market imperfections. Farms in this stratum employ relatively little nonfamily labor and have low average (but high marginal) labor costs, and they are large enough to have access to quantity-rationed capital markets. Highly productive and profitable per hectare, this stratum of farms is best positioned economically to expand through land rental and, especially, land sales markets. This type of farm unit corresponds well to the *capitalized family farm* identified by some empirically oriented literature as the emerging dominant agricultural form in Latin America (see, for example, Lehmann 1986a and 1986b; and Scott 1985). The capitalized family farm operates with substantial fixed and working capital and uses little hired labor from outside the household.[21] And it is characterized by increasing capital-land and capital-labor ratios (Lehmann 1982). The Carter-Kalfayan model similarly presents this type of producer as the least labor-absorbing of the competing modes of production. The expansion of this stratum may thus have perverse effects on labor absorption. As later sections discuss, understanding the stratum of capitalized family farms and its welfare implications is crucial for evaluating the future of both land reform and market-oriented distributist policies.

The record of land reform in Nicaragua, Peru, and Ecuador

The historical record of land reform in Nicaragua, Peru, and Ecuador, three very different countries, shows that the political and economic circumstances that greeted and conditioned their reforms are likewise very different. But reform in all three countries reflected a shared understanding of the economic constraints that bind choices of scope and model of agrarian reform.

Nicaragua: The three stages of land reform

Like the rest of Central America, Nicaragua before the mid-1970s was characterized by extreme inequality of land distribution and heavy dependence on exports of agricultural products. In 1971, 44 percent of rural families owned only 2.2 percent of the land, and 6 percent of rural households owned 63 percent (table 12.1). Immediately after the revolution, the Sandinistas launched their agrarian reform to redress this imbalance, "not at first, however, in the most obvious way, by redistributing land. The Sandinistas instead focused on redistributing rights of access to the fruits of agricultural labor, rather than on restructuring access to the means of production per se" (Luz 1989: 29).

During the 1979-90 period of Sandinista government, agricultural and land reform policy in Nicaragua fell rather neatly into three phases:

Phase 1, 1979-82: Emphasis on the establishment of state farms
Phase 2, 1983-84: Emphasis on the establishment of production cooperatives
Phase 3, 1985-90: Redistributive alliance with the peasantry and possible shift toward capitalized family farms.

Since the 1990 electoral defeat of the Sandinistas, agrarian reform policy—indeed, the fate of the agrarian reform sector—has been unclear. Table 12.1 illustrates this evolution of land reform policy through its effect on agrarian structure.

During phase 1 the 23 percent of the national agricultural and grazing land that had been controlled by the deposed dictator Somoza and his client group was shifted to a state farm sector called the *Area de Propiedad del Pueblo*, the People's Property Area (APP). During phase 2 the focus of land policy shifted to production cooperatives. By the end of this phase in 1984, production cooperatives, called *Cooperativas Agrarias Sandinistas* (CAS), contained about 10 percent of the national cultivated area. A large portion of this area was land transferred from the APP sector, with a smaller portion coming from the expropriation of large private properties under the terms of the 1981 agrarian reform law. During this period the CAS and APP enterprises received a disproportionate share of state services, credit, and capital.

In phase 3 the focus of land policy shifted to the redistribution of land as small parcels to individuals. Land expropriations became bolder and more common under the land reform law as revised in 1986. Although it is difficult to develop consistent time-series data, it appears that another 10 percent of the national area was redistributed, with perhaps 8 percent as small individual parcels. In addition, the production cooperative sector simultaneously underwent at least a partial decollectivization (Carter and Luz 1990; and Bastiansen 1988).

With respect to poverty alleviation, the land reform strategy pursued in phases 1 and 2 must be given mixed marks. The strategy scores well in the provision of social services to the rural population.[22] This was made possible largely by international donations and soft loans (Kaimowitz 1986). But the strategy largely failed in its attempt to provide secure wage employment for the majority of the rural population. Although the state farm sector had a land base that peaked at 23 percent, it never employed more than about 31,000 workers on a full-time basis (8 percent of the economically active rural population) and

Table 12.1 Evolution of landownership structure, Nicaragua, 1963-88
(percentage of total)

| | Prereform | | | | Reform era (by area) | | |
| | 1963 | | 1971 | | | | |
Unit	By units	By area	By units	By area	1982	1984	1988
Nonreform sector							
> 350 ha	5	59	6	63	14	13	6
140-350 ha					13	13	9
35-140 ha	17	26	19	24	30	30	17
7-35 ha	27	11	32	11	7	7	12
< 7 ha	51	4	44	2	1	1	2
Reform sector							
State farms (APP)					23	19	12
Production cooperatives (CAS)					2	10	11
Other cooperatives					10	7	3
Individually titled					0	0	3
Secured tenure					0	0	18
Abandoned area					0	0	6

Note: Before the publication of CIERA (1989), agrarian reform categories did not include the *Titulos Especiales* figures reported here as secured tenure. In 1984-86, a number of tenants with insecure tenure were given property titles, especially in war zones. Prior to CIERA (1989), these individuals were apparently counted in the category of other cooperatives and nonreform sectors.

Source: Data for 1963 and 1971 are agricultural census data reported in Peek (1983). Data for 1982 and 1984 are government figures reported in CAHI (1985). The 1988 figures are from a government publication (CIERA 1989).

another 26,000 on a part-time, seasonal basis (Fitzgerald 1985, table 2). Employment stagnated early in this sector, and by 1982 large private farmers were generating about 13 percent more employment per hectare than the state farms (Kaimowitz 1986: 171).[23] In addition, much of the new permanent employment on state farms did not go to the poorest stratum of the rural population, but to semipermanent workers in the capitalist agroexport regions (Kaimowitz 1986: 150-51). Moreover, concern about inflation led policymakers to restrain unskilled agricultural wages, particularly harvest wages (Fitzgerald 1985: 218; and Kaimowitz 1986: 173).

Phase 2 extended permanent employment and employment security to some 44,000 workers who became members of production and other types of cooperatives. But because a large percentage of the area cultivated by the cooperatives came from the breakup of state farms, it is difficult to know how many of these 44,000 are not part of the permanent state farm work force. The incomes of those who became members of cooperatives, 10 percent or so of the economically active rural population, were estimated by a 1985 government study of agrarian reform to be twice those of average semiproletarian families (cited in Kaimowitz 1986: 202).

In the abstract there seems little reason to think that state farms would pursue more labor-absorptive strategies than would large private farms. Indeed, there are several reasons to predict the opposite. Work discipline on a state farm is likely to be weaker than that on a private farm, raising the efficiency wage even further above its social opportunity cost. Cooperatives face disincentives to employ labor, as doing so increases the membership among which rent is distributed (Ward 1958). For these reasons, phase 1 and 2 policies were ultimately limited in their ability to address rural poverty.

Peru: Ambitious production-minded reform

The self-described "military revolutionary government" of General Juan Velasco took power in Peru in 1968. In 1969 it initiated an ambitious program of agrarian reform that, by 1980, had expropriated 40 to 50 percent of the agricultural and grazing land in Peru. Before the reform, land ownership had been extremely concentrated (table 12.2). In its first land reform action, the military government occupied literally overnight the very heart of large-scale capitalist agriculture on the Peruvian coast, the twelve agroindustrial sugar complexes. Centralized management of these complexes continued but was reorganized under a cooperative form. The expropriation of these units alone affected nearly 130,000 hectares of land and 28,000 workers (table 12.3). The reform was then steadily extended to other areas of the country.

As more and more area was brought into the reform, it was adjudicated primarily to large-scale cooperative or associative units of various types. On the coast the Agricultural Production Cooperative (CAP) was the main vehicle employed. In the highland sierra nearly 3 million hectares (one-third of the unweighted total area affected) were adjudicated to Agrarian Social Interest

Table 12.2 Number and area of farm units by size class, Peru, 1961

Size group (hectares)	Percentage of units	Percentage of hectares
< 5	83.2	5.5
5-20	12.6	4.7
20-100	2.9	5.2
100-500	0.9	8.7
500-2,500	0.3	15.0
> 2,500	0.1	60.9

Source: Barraclough 1973: 253, table 11-1.

Societies (SAIS). Land redistributions to individuals accounted for only 8 percent of the affected area and 11 percent of the beneficiaries.

The military's decision to maintain preexisting production units and pursue a collectivist reform effectively excluded large numbers of people from directly benefiting from the reform. In the highlands the government established SAIS on the large estates that had expanded at the expense of surrounding indigenous communities, and thus ignored the communities' historical claims to that land. On the coast it assigned the ownership of the cooperatives largely to the preexisting permanent work force, thus excluding former tenants of the coastal estates who had been expelled during the years leading up to the reform (see Alberts 1983) as well as the many individuals traditionally employed as seasonal workers.[24] The reform's collectivist organizational model thus created a situation in which nearly half the national agricultural area was affected but only about 25 percent of the rural population—permanent workers who were already relatively well-off—benefited.

The beneficiaries experienced an improvement in their living standards, principally in increased wage incomes and access to social services provided by

Table 12.3 Distribution of land by type of adjudicatory unit, Peru, 1969-79

Unit	Adjudicated land Hectares	Adjudicated land Percent	Percentage of agri-cultural area	Direct beneficiaries Number	Direct beneficiaries Percent	Percentage of rural economically active population
Agricultural Production Cooperatives	2,428,800	28.2	13.0	80,943	21.6	5.1
Agroindustrial complexes	128,566	1.5	0.7	27,783	7.4	1.8
Agrarian Social Interest Societies	2,805,048	32.6	15.0	60,954	16.2	3.9
Peasant groups	1,685,382	19.6	8.9	45,561	12.1	2.9
Peasant communities	889,364	10.3	4.7	117,710	31.5	7.5
Independent peasants	662,093	7.7	4.6	42,295	11.2	2.7
Total	8,599,253	100.0	46.9	375,246	100.0	24.0

Note: Percentages may not add to totals because of rounding.
Source: Matos Mar and Mejia 1980, table 23.

the reform enterprises (see Carter 1984b). They should also have benefited from year-end profit distributions. But because of the productivity and profitability problems that plagued the cooperatives in the late 1970s and the 1980s, these distributions did not materialize.

The cooperatives' worsening economic situation in the late 1970s and the early 1980s occurred because of problems intrinsic to the cooperative organizational model[25] and external problems related to a macroeconomic environment unfavorable to agriculture (see Carter and Alvarez 1989). Melmed (1987) argues that the two types of problems interacted in a way that severely weakened the cooperatives: as profitability declined because of macroeconomic events, labor discipline problems within the cooperatives worsened.

Ironically, given the preoccupation with productivity that drove the initial choice of the organizational model of reform, productivity problems on the cooperatives seemed to play an important role in the decision of members, in the early and mid-1980s, to subdivide their enterprises into family parcels. In 1981 new agrarian reform legislation was passed that legalized decollectivization (or *parcelación*, as it is known in Peru). This "reform of the reform" has dramatically reduced the scale of production in the coastal sector, establishing a large stratum of 4- to 5-hectare farms. Thus, with more than 75 percent of Peru's coastal cooperatives "parcelized," the type of redistributive agrarian reform that the military government had studiously avoided was launched in Peru in the early 1980s.

Ecuador: Complementing agricultural capitalism with land reform

Before Ecuador initiated its agrarian reform program, its agricultural sector was characterized by an extreme inequality of land distribution (table 12.4). It was also characterized by a variety of production relations. Capitalist labor and ten-

Table 12.4 Distribution of agricultural production units and farmland by farm size, Ecuador, 1954 and 1974

(percent)

Size category (hectares)	Percentage of units		Change in number of units 1954-74	Percentage of farmland		Change in hectares 1954-74
	1954	1974		1954	1974	
< 5	73.1	69.5	36.3	7.2	7.7	22.9
5-9.9	10.5	10.7	46.1	4.5	5.3	34.3
10-99.9	14.2	17.9	80.0	23.9	36.6	74.8
100-499.9	1.7	1.6	36.2	19.3	20.7	22.5
500-999.9	0.2	0.2	10.6	7.7	7.4	9.1
> 1,000	0.2	0.1	-14.3	37.4	22.1	-32.6
Total	100.0	100.0	43.5	100.0	100.0	13.9

Note: For both years, the data exclude the jungle and refer only to the highlands and the coast. Columns may not add to totals because of rounding.
Source: Based on the agricultural censuses of 1954 and 1974, as reported in Barsky (1984).

ant relations were entrenched much more deeply on the coast than in the highlands. Landless wage laborers accounted for 52 percent of the coastal agrarian work force in 1954; precapitalist relations of production continued to dominate on the traditional haciendas of the Andean highlands. Landless wage laborers constituted only 2 percent of the highland agrarian work force.[26]

Ecuador's agrarian reform since the 1960s has aimed to modernize agriculture and to establish the dominance of capitalist relations in that sector. Two state interventions have contributed significantly to the elimination of precapitalist relations in Ecuadoran agriculture. First, the Agrarian Reform Law of 1964, implemented in the Andean highlands, proscribed precapitalist (noncash) landlord-tenant arrangements referred to under the generic name of *precarismo*. *Precaristas* were to receive formal title to land, with their payment to the landlord—if any—depending on the number of years that they had worked on the hacienda. The Reform Law also aimed to encourage capitalism by establishing maximum size limits for landholdings.[27] The ceilings for private landholdings were too high, however, to affect either the coastal landowning elite or the modernizing highland *hacendados*; thus, they affected only the most inefficiently run—and politically ineffective—southern Andean estates, where precapitalist labor relations prevailed. Second, Decree 1001, promulgated in 1970, proscribed *precarismo* in the coastal rice zones. The rice estates were declared "of public utility" and subject to expropriation and immediate occupation by *precaristas*, who, nevertheless, had to pay for the land.

The evidence suggests that neither Decree 1001 nor the 1964 reform before it brought about a major redistribution of land, whether in the highlands or in the coastal rice zone. From 1964 to 1983, about 9 percent of all agricultural land in the country (808,692 hectares) was adjudicated through land reform to an estimated 15 percent of the country's farm families (table 12.5).[28] A comparison of data from the 1954 agricultural census with data from the 1974 census reveals the modest scope of land redistribution achieved through the two reforms

Table 12.5 Land adjudicated and number of families benefiting through land reform and colonization, Ecuador, 1964-83

| | Land reform | | | | | | Colonization | |
| | Sierra | | Coast | | Total | | | |
Period	Hectares	Families	Hectares	Families	Hectares	Families	Hectares	Families
1964-70	125,232	27,087	34,405	1,982	159,637	29,069	461,324	12,929
1971-79	268,646	24,410	213,276	20,541[a]	481,922	44,951[a]	1,069,593	22,946
1980-83	104,284	7,329	62,193	4,727[a]	166,477	12,056[a]	654,632	12,613
1964-83	498,162	58,826	309,874	27,250[a]	808,036	86,076[a]	2,185,549	48,488

a. No information is available on the number of the beneficiaries of Decree 1001 (through which some 90,000 hectares were adjudicated to cooperatives in the rice zone). The figures presented here include estimates of the potential number of beneficiaries from Decree 1001 as reported in Redclift (1978: 128).
Source: Based on Instituto Ecuatoriano de Reforma Agraria y Colonización (IERAC) statistics reported in Barsky (1984).

(table 12.4). The most dramatic change in the land distribution pattern during the intercensal period was the diminished role of the largest *latifundia*. The data in table 12.4 show, however, that those benefiting most from the decline in the dominance of *latifundia* were the medium-size farmers with 10 to 100 hectares.[29]

The effect of the reforms on poverty has been subject to much debate. Landless laborers, 22 percent of the economically active rural population, were completely bypassed by the reforms. In fact, Redclift (1978) claims, the agrarian reform may have led to the creation of a class of landless laborers, both on the coast and in the highlands, as the landed elite evicted tenants from their estates in an attempt to avoid expropriation.

Among the direct beneficiaries of the reform, the precapitalist tenant farmers in the highlands are generally believed to have suffered economically. The modernization of the *haciendas* in the highlands has taken place at the cost of increasing still further the number of *minifundistas* (Redclift 1978). Beneficiaries were adjudicated land in small plots averaging about 3.5 hectares—below the minimum figure of 5 hectares specified by the law—that were generally of much lower quality than the plots they had been cultivating before the reform. Moreover, because of the change in their status from tenants to owners, beneficiaries had to forfeit their traditional water, pasture, and firewood rights (Blankstein and Zuvekas 1973). And the amount of credit and technical assistance that they received was negligible.

The former rice *precaristas* (who had had the lowest status among the coastal peasants) have benefited more directly from the agrarian reform. First, rice tenants received title to the plots that they had been working before the reform. These holdings averaged nearly 10 hectares—far larger than those in the highlands—and were located on good-quality terrain. In addition, their change of status entitled them to immediate credit and technical assistance from the state. These factors, combined with a favorable price policy, enabled many rice-producing peasants to increase their output and to accumulate capital after the 1970 reform (Zevallos 1989). Such gains have been limited to a small minority of the coastal peasants, however.

Constraints to reform in Nicaragua, Peru, and Ecuador

The land reforms of Nicaragua, Peru, and Ecuador have taken place in very different political environments. Nicaragua's reform followed a revolutionary change in power, Peru's was executed by a self-styled military revolutionary government that took power in a bloodless coup, and Ecuador's took place within the relatively tame confines of Alliance for Progress politics. This section argues that policymakers in all three countries perceived constraints and tradeoffs that invalidated the strong case for distributist land reform. In Nicaragua and Peru, where policymakers enjoyed substantial political power, these constraints expressed themselves most visibly in the choice of organizational model. In Ecuador, where the government had less political power, these constraints are most obviously expressed in the reform's limited scope.

Economic constraints in the land reforms of Nicaragua and Peru

From 1950 through the mid-1970s agriculture in Nicaragua grew at a brisk average rate of 7 percent a year, powered by growth in agricultural exports of 11 percent a year (Williams 1986). Landownership probably became more concentrated during this period of remarkable growth, as the share of land operated by the large-farm stratum grew from 59 to 63 percent between 1963 and 1971 (table 12.1). The available data—from a time series shorter than would be desirable—show no sign of the transfer of land from large to small units that would be anticipated by the Chicago question.[30] Moreover, coming at the end of this period of rapid agricultural growth was the Sandinista revolution, which was fueled by discontent with the way in which growth had occurred.

A casual reading of Nicaragua's agrarian history (Deere and Marchetti 1981; Williams 1986; and CIERA 1984) suggests that three structural changes characterized its agricultural growth during this period:

1. *Dispossession:* The distribution of landownership became more concentrated as increases in the returns to large-farm agriculture were followed by large farms gaining property rights to lands previously held under different forms of communal rights.

2. *Expulsion:* Farm operatorship became more concentrated as large farm units shed their permanent laborers, who often farmed plots within the large farm units, and shifted to pure wage labor relations of production.

3. *Mechanization:* Substantial mechanization took place and the seasonality of labor demand became more pronounced even as the wage labor force grew as a result of the dispossession and expulsion.

Freedom became just another name for nothing left to lose for the increasingly proletarianized labor force, "freed" of its direct access to land and yet lacking secure and stable employment.[31]

This history suggests that Nicaraguan agriculture was firmly on a large-scale, or Junker, path to agrarian development and that the years of growth in agroexports had gone far toward creating a proletarianized rural society. According to this interpretation, Nicaragua's Junker path development—although it took place in a Keynesian world,[32] creating social and human casualties and ultimately fomenting revolution[33]—reflected an intrinsic economic logic and the competitive advantage of larger-scale production.

The second column of table 12.6 presents an agnostically empiricist definition of rural social structure developed by the Centro de Investigaciones y Estudios de la Reforma Agraria (CIERA 1985b). Following the analysis of Kaimowitz (1986), the left-most column aggregates the CIERA data to present a view of class structure consistent with the Junker path interpretation. Although this interpretation recognizes that a substantial portion of the rural population has direct access to some land, that access was presumed to be transitory as the economy marched down its Junker path. Table 12.6 represents this view by lumping most of the rural population into a proletariat/incipient proletariat category. Production by these

Table 12.6 Nicaraguan class structure and beneficiaries of agrarian reform

Polarized class structure as seen by phase 1 and 2 policy		Actual decomposition of agricultural labor force, 1982		Peasant capitalism view of class structure		Agrarian reform beneficiaries, 1979-88		
Class	Percentage of total	Class[a]	Percentage of total	Class	Percentage of total	Group	Number of workers	Percentage of total
Capitalists	9	Latifundistas	0.1	Large-farm capitalists	1	State farms (APP)[b]		
Small commercial	13	Agrarian bourgeoisie	0.2	Capitalized family farmers and incipient capitalized family farmers	32	Permanent	15,500	3.5
Proletariat and incipient proletariat	78	Agrarian petty bourgeoisie	3.0			Part-time	13,000	2.9
		Family labor	1.5			Production co-ops (CAS)	30,999	6.9
		Self-employed peasants	9.6	Marginalized semiproletariat	37	Other co-ops	13,772	3.1
		Peasant family labor	12	Proletariat	30	Individually titled	6,519	1.5
		Semiproletariat	36			Secured tenure	31,335	7.0
		Permanent workers	20			Total	111,125	24.7[c]
		Seasonal workers	17					

a. Based on the number of hectares devoted to specific crops, as follows:

	Latifundistas and agrarian bourgeoisie	Agrarian petty bourgeoisie	Peasant farmers
Basic grains	>350	35-350	<35
Coffee	>45	10-45	<10
Cotton	>140	35-140	<35
Grazing	>700	140-700	<140

b. The figures reported for state farm workers are only half of peak employment levels on these enterprises; it is assumed that the other half were absorbed into other land reform categories as the state farms broke up.

c. Column may not add to total due to rounding.

Source: The figures in the second column are from CIERA (1985b), reprinted in Fitzgerald (1985). The first and third columns are based on Kaimowitz (1986). The fourth column is based on CIERA (1989) and Fitzgerald (1985).

individuals is seen as marginal and of minimal economic importance. Correspondingly, this interpretation imputes tremendous economic importance (and thus political bargaining power) to large-scale agrarian capitalist producers, who are perceived as being at the front line of agricultural growth and development.

Fitzgerald (1985: 213) bluntly expresses the implications of this interpretation for land reform policy when he writes that "division of land, particularly on the agroexport estates, would [have] limit[ed] the future potential for accumulation, productivity growth and social transformation." This statement refers to two constraints to land reform stemming from the economics of small-scale agriculture. The first constraint is the productive potential of small-scale agriculture. This interpretation calls into question the validity of the inverse relationship in Nicaragua—a proposition for which there is some support. The second constraint concerns the state's ability to mobilize a surplus out of small-scale agriculture. If these perceived constraints were valid, a distributist land reform would have been costly in direct economic terms. It would also have been costly politically because a small-scale sector was deemed incapable of buying out large-scale producers.

In summary, the policy for phase 1 land reform in Nicaragua, the phase in which state farms were established, was guided by the notion that the country had little choice but to follow the old patterns of production, accumulation, and foreign exchange generation. With a marginalized and unproductive peasantry, the perception was that the only feasible land reform organizational model was one that maintained large-farm agriculture. The shift away from state farms and the redistribution of private lands to production cooperatives in phase 2 (see table 12.1) can be safely interpreted as a pragmatic response to limited state competence to manage state farms and a political response to growing pressure for greater redistribution of access to means of production.[34] As Luz (1989) documents, the cooperatives established in this phase were to play the same role as state farms in the first phase.

Production cooperatives in Peru's land reform, like those in Nicaragua, were seen as vehicles for redistributing property rights while maintaining a scale of production appropriate for perceived technological scale economies and for state control of the agricultural surplus. Although the debate and language surrounding Peru's reform contain many more references to the "feudal oligarchy" than does the debate on Nicaragua's agrarian reform, it would be misleading to portray Peru's large-farm sector as a low-productivity backwater. Paige (1975) relates the rising tide of social protest in the Peruvian highlands in the 1960s to the *expansion* of the large-farm sector, rather than to its continued stagnation. In the coastal zone, the reform unambiguously confronted a capital-intensive, high-technology large-scale agriculture.

An explanation of the decision to aggressively pursue collectivist reform and to retain the preexisting scale of production is suggested by the SAIS model established in the sierra. Highland agriculture was burdened by a history of expansion of large-scale estates at the expense of surrounding indigenous communities. Yet, rather than respond to the communities' demand for the land they felt was rightly theirs, SAIS were created as a compromise. The core of each of the SAIS was a production cooperative established on the land of the prereform farm unit and assigned as collective property to the unit's permanent work force. Surrounding communities were integrated into the SAIS through a scheme in which they were to share in the profits of the production cooperative. Perhaps better than anything, this decision not to change the scale of production in the highlands (despite a politically powerful case to do so) symbolizes the military government's concern with productivity issues and economic tradeoffs.

Interaction of politics, economics, and scope of land reform

Ecuador's land reform was limited in scope compared with Nicaragua's and Peru's land reforms, two of the most politically empowered reforms in Latin American rural history. Its limited scope may be interpreted as a simple matter of constrained political power and will. The government was unable to bear the political cost of a radical distributist land reform.

The debate surrounding the Ecuadoran reform (de Janvry 1981; and Zevallos 1989) concerns primarily the degree to which the reform prodded large-scale producers onto a capitalist path of growth, or whether they were already well along that path. Missing from the discussion is any concern about the productivity of the reform's beneficiaries. Their productive potential seems, in retrospect, not to have been taken at all seriously. Also not taken seriously was the possibility that distributist land reform could positively contribute to the national economy in the way anticipated by the economic case for distributist land reform.

Judging the reality of perceived constraints to land reform

The previous section argued that the scope and the organizational models of land reform in Nicaragua, Peru, and Ecuador have been shaped by perceptions of the economics of agrarian structure—perceptions at odds with the analysis underlying the economic case for distributist land reform. The effect of these reforms on rural poverty (which, although significant, has been modest relative to expectations) has been importantly shaped by these perceptions. The perceived constraints help explain the particular histories of these reforms, but were the perceptions in fact accurate? Have events borne them out? Answering these questions is clearly important for the design of both state-mandated and market-mediated reform policies.

Decollectivization and "capitalized family farm revisionism"

In Peru the production cooperatives were in severe economic crisis by the early 1980s. Decollectivization, once legalized, took hold rapidly, and within five years most coastal cooperatives had been parceled into smallholdings.[35] In Nicaragua the evidence on the performance of production cooperatives is thin and mixed. CIERA's (1985a) case study documents problems, but Carter and Luz (1990) find no statistical evidence of microeconomic productivity problems of the sort that signaled intrinsic difficulties on the Peruvian cooperatives. The ongoing autonomous process of decollectivization in Nicaragua has received much speculative attention, but the data in Carter and Luz (1990) show that the decollectivization is limited.

The problems of cooperative production in Peru, and perhaps in Nicaragua, obviously say something about the desirability of the collectivist model chosen.[36] They do not, however, permit inference about the accuracy of the constraints that were perceived to limit smaller-scale agriculture and that drove distributist reform off the agenda. Some inferences can be garnered from the post-decollectivization experience of these countries, which is reviewed below. To help place that evidence in context, it is useful first to examine the revisionist view of the economics of structural evolution that emerged in Nicaragua and helped reshape phase 3 land reform policy.

Kaimowitz (1988) and others attribute the shift from phase 2 to phase 3 land reform policy largely to short-term political and military considerations. Kaimowitz calls it a "strategic alliance with the peasantry" undertaken in the context of the "survival economy." The implication is that the worsening military and economic situation necessitated sacrifice of the productivity and growth goals that had guided (and constrained) earlier land reform policy. Yet behind this shift, and legitimizing it at least in part, has been the Baumeister (1985) critique of the Junker path interpretation of Nicaraguan agrarian history. This critique, which Kaimowitz (1986) labels the peasant capitalism interpretation, challenges the Junker path interpretation's portrayal of the degree to which rural society had been polarized into proletarians and large-scale capitalists. The third column of table 12.6 portrays the peasant capitalism interpretation of Nicaragua's agrarian structure as one with a significant agrarian middle class—the capitalized family farmers. Baumeister and other advocates of the peasant capitalism interpretation show that capitalized family farms produce a substantial part of some export crops and behave in a "normal," price-responsive way. If nothing else, this view of agrarian class structure, which downplays the economic preponderance of large-scale producers, creates a political opening for bolder redistributive measures.

In addition, the peasant capitalism interpretation duplicates the claim of Lehmann (1982) and others that growth *can* be centered on moderately sized family farms. Peasants, broadly defined, can be reached in their role as direct producers. This interpretation implies that a more distributist approach to land reform does not require forsaking productivity and accumulation goals—indeed, it implies that they can be aggressively pursued through a family farm strategy.

The peasant capitalism interpretation moves us closer to an analysis of the economics of agrarian structure that is consistent with the strong case for distributist reform. But it may be misleading to associate the peasant capitalist farms with the small-scale units (and their factor proportions) that would be implied by a poverty-oriented distributist reform. Baumeister, in documenting the degree to which smaller-scale agriculture actively participates in export production, uses a very elastic definition of the moderately sized farm: the peasant capitalist stratum in table 12.6 includes farms of up to 145 hectares. More generally, as Carter and Kalfayan (1989) analyze theoretically, and as Lehmann (1986a) argues empirically, the competitive advantage of medium-size units is rooted in their ability to mediate multiple market failures by *economizing on labor* and obtaining access to rationed capital. As the discussion above on the capital constraints hypothesis indicates, this analysis of the economic viability and strength of medium-size farms does not support the economic case for distributist land reform. Nor does the capitalized family farm revisionism taking root in Nicaragua unambiguously predict economic stability and success for the decollectivized land reform farms.

Where will decollectivized agriculture go?

Peru is not the first Latin American country to decollectivize agriculture after agrarian reform. Decollectivization was pursued with a vengeance in Chile following the military coup of Pinochet in 1973. Following decollectivization, a variety of market and nonmarket processes rapidly restructured Chile's agrarian reform sector. Jarvis (1989) estimates that, over the period 1973-86, the farm area controlled by the Chilean large-farm sector grew from 3 percent to 25 or 30 percent. (Prior to the land reforms of Frei and Allende in the 1960s and 1970s, the large-farm sector had controlled 55 percent of the cultivated area.) Subjected to a variety of economic pressures, and unable to exploit new and profitable production niches, fully half of those who had received parcels, of 10 standard irrigated hectares each, through decollectivization (*parceleros*) sold out over this same period. In an interpretation that differs slightly from Jarvis's, Castillo and Lehmann (1983) describe Chilean decollectivization as a process in which many *parceleros* sold out to a new class of medium-size, structurally stable, capitalized farms of 40 to 50 standard irrigated hectares. Both interpretations support an analysis of the economics of structural evolution that is closer to the hypothesis of countervailing capital constraints than it is to the economics of the economic case for distributist reform.

The changes that followed decollectivization in Chile occurred under a variety of exceptional circumstances that make it difficult to draw inferences about the causes. What seems to have driven the shifts in the agrarian structure are the more favorable returns to land on large holdings compared with those on smallholdings. Is there evidence that decollectivization in Peru has been driven by similar forces? There have been no comparisons of total annual production by *parceleros* and that of the cooperatives that preceded them, both using the same resource base. But the general conclusion of several single-crop studies in Peru is that crop yields have remained more or less constant since decollectivization, with changes ranging between approximately −5 percent and +5 percent (Gols 1985; Auzemery and Eresue 1986; Chavez 1988; and Melmed 1987).

Declines in yield following decollectivization clearly would have provided negative evidence about the economic viability of the new smallholdings. But the main claims of the inverse relationship are based on crop mix and cropping intensity (extent of double cropping) on smallholdings, *not* on significantly higher yields for the same crop in the same season. Although informative, simple yield comparisons are inadequate for assessing the static production efficiency effects of decollectivization and the existence of an inverse farm size-productivity relation. In some of the more ambitious statistical analysis undertaken to date, Melmed (1987) and Melmed-Sanjak and Carter (1991) have found, on the basis of stochastic production frontiers estimated for a sample of decollectivized parcels and the cooperatives of which they had been part, that the actual technical efficiency of production of the *parceleros* exceeds that of the cooperatives. At the same time, the estimated *potential* efficiency of the cooperatives exceeds that of the *parceleros*. This finding suggests that neither the fully collectivized nor the fully decollectivized reform model is the optimal institutional choice. More telling evidence on the economic incentives for land concentration will have to await a more complete comparison of the economic performance of the decollectivized parcels with that of larger-scale private agriculture.

Will Peru see land transactions driven by the sort of differentiation among *parceleros* that Castillo and Lehmann describe for Chile? Carter (1990) uses simulation analysis to investigate the potential for differentiation among the Peruvian *parceleros*. The analysis is based on econometrically estimated efficiency differentials and empirical estimates of the nature of the stochastic environment in which the *parceleros* produce. According to the simulation analysis, the least technically efficient decile of producers would sell out at a price that is one-twentieth of the reservation purchase price of the most efficient producers. Moreover, stochastic shocks confront the lowest-decile producers, who face economic disaster nearly once every five years. The median producer at the fiftieth percentile of the estimated technical efficiency distribution is sufficiently productive to be immune from stochastically induced disaster. Yet even the median producer has a reservation selling price half that of the most efficient producers.

To what extent has this potential for differentiation been played out? For Peru, the evidence to date shows little indication that such a process is under way. Neither Figallo (1990) nor Melmed (1987) find much land market activity among *parceleros*. But Auzemery and Eresue (1986) suggest, though without supporting data, that there has been substantial differentiation. Torre's (1985) study of the Lambayeque Valley shows that 564 hectares, of a total of 10,190 hectares that had been parceled, were subsequently sold. Torre suggests that such transactions could underlie the emergence of a new stratum of medium-size (50- to 100-hectare) holdings.

Unlike in Chile, where the agrarian structure changed rapidly after cooperatives had been parceled, legal restrictions in Peru hamper land transactions by *parceleros*. (These restrictions may also hamper collection of data about such transactions.) In addition, the development of new agroexports in Chile undoubtedly stimulated great interest in agricultural investment; in Peru profitability in agriculture is depressed. The combination of these two conditions (together with a weak labor market, which discourages sales) may have sufficed to prevent the realization of the potential for differentiation that the simulation indicates exists in Peru. It may also be that Chile is an exceptional case, that small-scale production can indeed be viable, and that for this reason land concentration has not taken place in Peru. The discussions of Guatemalan vegetable cooperatives, which combine small farming with large-scale marketing, by Binswanger and von Braun (chapter 7 in this volume) and by de Janvry and Sadoulet (chapter 11 in this volume) may illustrate similar prospects.

Research on Nicaragua and Ecuador yields some additional evidence on the problems and prospects for smaller-scale agriculture in contemporary Latin America. The econometric analysis in Carter and Luz (1990) indicates favorable prospects for the more decollectivized forms of production emerging on the Nicaraguan production cooperatives. As Carter and Luz emphasize, these forms of production are best described as semicollective because substantial linkages are maintained between the fully collective and the more individualized sectors of production.

In Ecuador there is some evidence that transactions shifting land from large to small units are occurring, as anticipated by the Chicago question. Since the 1970s an increasing amount of land has been transferred to the peasant sector through private sales, as some of the larger estates were broken up through inheritance, as pressure for modernization and reform increased, and as urban investment became increasingly attractive (Zevallos 1989; and Forster 1989). Although these market transfers cannot be quantified becuase of the lack of data after 1974, they are documented in a number of case studies. Haney and Haney (1989) report a significant increase in the Chimborazo province in the number and prominence of medium-size farms in 1980 compared with 1974, an increase related to a sharp decline in the size of the largest holdings. Barsky's (1984) and Lehmann's (1986a) studies in the province of Carchi have documented the decline of the great estate and the tendency of peasant farms to capitalize and purchase land, evolving into capitalized family farms.

The prospects for transfers of land to the rural poor

The effect on the rural poor of land reform in Latin America appears to have been limited by the choices made on the scope and organizational model of that reform. The interpretation offered here is that limits were imposed on land reform because *perceived* economic constraints indicated that it would be very costly to do otherwise—economically and, therefore, politically. Prejudice against peasant production and a fallacious belief in the superiority of "factories in the field" may partly explain the perceived constraints and the choices made. Yet the agrarian history of Latin America can be interpreted as indicating that the complex economics of agrarian structure do not fully support the economic case for distributist land reform. Microeconomic analysis built around insights on intrinsically and informationally imperfect labor and capital markets gives that complexity theoretical voice, and may imply that holdings small enough to produce a significant effect on poverty are economically handicapped, at least when the distribution of land is as inegalitarian as it is in Latin America.

So what is to be done, given that the antipoverty case for asset redistribution remains strong in Latin America and elsewhere? Three points should be considered. First, and most obvious, the positive effect reform has had on rural poverty should not be overlooked, even if it has fallen short of expectations. Second, there is a need to escape the conundrum that reduces the choice of the organizational model for agrarian reform to the two poles of what is really a continuum of models, ranging from fully collectivized to fully individualized. The Israeli *moshav*, the associative model in the Dominican Republic (see Meyer 1989), different forms of semicollective production in Nicaragua, and models from Eastern Europe and China are all examples of intermediate forms of production that resolve some of the problems confronting completely individualized and completely collectivized production. Carter (1985 and 1987) discusses these models in more detail.

The final point, and perhaps the most important given the current international environment, concerns the new wave of policies based on the argument that a market-oriented development strategy, unencumbered with price distortions, can be used successfully to mediate the transfer of opportunities and resources to the rural poor. The strength of such policies is that they do not require state intervention. They are "bankable," to use de Janvry and Sadoulet's (chapter 11 in this volume) language, and therefore possible in the current environment in which, in many places, state-mandated reform is unlikely to occur, primarily because it is perceived to be costly.

As this chapter has stressed, however, the very economic factors and constraints that make state-mandated reform costly also tend to block market-mediated transfers of land to smallholders. With the important exception of the price distortions hypothesis, the hypotheses discussed in this chapter indicate that the new wave of market-oriented policies is problematic because of the underlying expectation that smallholdings can emerge from the existing agrarian structure in Latin America and be competitive.

The evidence to distinguish among the competing hypotheses is incomplete.[37] The experiments under way in decollectivization and market-oriented policies will yield substantially more evidence over the next few years. The evidence now available makes it appear unlikely that new wave policies will supplant or otherwise bring about the death of land reform. For reducing rural poverty, the challenge will remain to do land reform right in a world of binding political and economic constraints.

Notes

1. These three countries were chosen because of their interesting and active experience with agrarian reform. Much of the analysis that follows considers the politics and economics of carrying out agrarian reform in the face of a commercialized large-farm sector. How representative are Peru, Nicaragua, and Ecuador of Latin America's three big countries, Brazil, Mexico, and Argentina? In Brazil, at least in the Northeast, these constraints may be less binding, and reform easier, although Thiesenhusen and Melmed-Sanjak (1990) find evidence that Brazilian agriculture is modernizing rapidly. In Mexico Sanderson (1986) describes many of the same constraints and tradeoffs between large and small farms discussed here. Argentina, a highly urbanized country, probably faces economic constraints of another realm.

2. Tables 12.1, 12.2, and 12.4 give farm size distribution data for Nicaragua, Ecuador, and Peru. Barraclough and Domike's (1966) compilation of data for Latin America as a whole remains the classic one.

3. Thiesenhusen and Melmed-Sanjak (1990) show that this stylized characterization of the differences in factor use between small and large farms continues to describe contemporary Brazil.

4. Williams (1986) and de Janvry and Sadoulet (chapter 11 in this volume) summarize evidence on the problematic nature of agricultural growth in Latin America.

5. As later sections of this chapter argue, however, it is critically important to step beyond this polarized view of organizational alternatives.

6. It is important to note that the inverse relationship refers to *operated* holdings, whereas distributist land reform typically changes the *ownership* of holdings. Where large ownership units are operated by multiple tenants, distributist land reform that gives tenants ownership rights over plots that they had been cultivating prior to the reform may not affect operated holdings sufficiently to benefit much from any inverse relationship that does exist. This is less of an issue in Latin America, where large estates are actually operated as large production units.

7. An echo from Asia is the argument that large, semifeudal landowners in eastern India make more money by operating in interlocking markets—by underfarming their own land or by having it sharecropped—than they could by efficient production (for instance, with fixed rental to small operational farm tenants) that maximizes total profits on the farmland. Such landowners, it is argued, can also lend to "captive" tenants and laborers at usurious rates of interest, an option that would disappear if they behaved as efficient farmers (Bhaduri 1973; for a contrary view and evidence, see Braverman and Stiglitz 1982).

8. In fact, if big landowners are precluded from adopting the more "efficient" labor-intensive methods associated with small operational farms, there must be imperfections both in land markets (discouraging tenancy) and in labor markets (discouraging managerial subdivision or labor hire—see Binswanger and Rosenzweig 1986). It is the labor market imperfections that seem to drive the inverse relationship (see, for example, Carter 1984a).

9. These constraints may become more important during agricultural growth and modernization because the share of inputs in the total growth of farm output (for the best technique) tends to increase.

10. See Carter and Walker (1989) for further review of the literature on structural evolution in Latin America.

11. Chayanov (1967) analyzed a world without an off-farm labor market. Subsequent neoclassical renditions (for example, Singh, Squire, and Strauss 1986) have clarified the dependence of the Chayanovian logic on labor market characteristics that drive a wedge between cheap on-farm labor cost and the off-farm purchase price of efficiency labor.

12. Alain de Janvry suggested this explanation, which we have not seen otherwise developed.

13. The labor market failures or transactions costs that underlie the inverse relationship could exist, but multiple market failures are necessary for resource allocation to deviate from a first-best allocation in a model with multiple inputs.

14. This proposition might be hard to test, because the governments that carry out price reform are often undoing past land reforms, so that the distribution of land at the end of the exercise might be less equal than at the beginning despite the improvement in incentives to private distribution.

15. Even given a perfect market situation in which the value of land reflects capitalized agricultural profits, a poor farmer financing a land purchase at the market price with a mortgage at the market rate of interest will need the entire increment in his agricultural income from the extra unit of land to finance the interest charges on the loan. The poor farmer's consumption expenditure *as well as* his repayment installments on the loan will

therefore have to come entirely out of his imputed family income (valued at the market wage—Binswanger 1987). But to the extent that subsistence and other living costs of family members approach the market wage, consumption may thus be curtailed below subsistence levels.

16. Carter's argument is that credit rationing is an intrinsic property of laissez faire competitive equilibrium. As he and other authors (see the review in Adams and Graham 1981) show, the credit rationing results hold, a fortiori, in the presence of binding government-imposed interest rate restrictions.

17. Productivity per hectare is highest for an intermediate stratum of medium-scale producers, whom Carter and Kalfayan (1989) identify as "capitalized family farmers," defined below.

18. The degree to which the standard literature on the inverse relationship has looked for skewed-U-shaped relationships is not known. Preliminarily, it might be theorized that the skewed-U appears only in inegalitarian structural environments such as those found in Latin America and the commercialized area of Kenya studied by Carter, Wiebe, and Blarel (1989). It may be that the pattern of capital rationing that drives the skewed-U can emerge only in those structural environments. In more equal agrarian structures composed primarily of small farms, the *equilibrium* expected rate of return achievable by lenders may fall, and, in accordance with the predictions of the Carter (1988) model, small farmers would have access to capital.

19. To the extent that credit rationing is based on real costs of information, simply willing into existence a credit program for small farms does not resolve the issue, as expected returns would always remain higher on loans to larger farm units.

20. The computable general equilibrium simulation model developed by Carter and Kalfayan (1989) starts from the assumption that all agricultural agents, differentiated only by their land endowment, maximize household income. The model goes on to show that optimizing agents, arrayed according to their wealth, will in competitive equilibrium endogenously differentiate themselves into a class structure defined by the shared behavioral strategies of the individuals within each class.

21. The defining characteristic of the capitalized family farm is not size. The emphasis is instead on family. According to Lehmann (1986b: 611), the size criterion "can be adduced with the explicit proviso that its specification be left to the circumstances of each case," because the size of unit that can be operated without recourse to nonfamily labor will clearly depend on circumstances.

22. Peek (1983) and Kaimowitz (1986) document the increases in the provision of social services that occurred.

23. Because of the deteriorating economic situation of the state farms after 1981, the farms—which were expected to finance better working conditions, more social services, and greater employment—had to be subsidized through government deficits and foreign savings (Kaimowitz 1986).

24. McClintock (1981: 61) calculates that approximately 250,000 landless workers were excluded from directly benefiting from the reform—a number equal to 60 percent of those who did benefit. Later efforts by the government to formally incorporate more individuals into the CAPs as full members met with considerable opposition (see the discussion in Carter 1984b). Ward (1958) presents the basic economics of the labor-managed, or "Illyrian," firm that result in members' opposition to the incorporation of additional individuals.

25. Cooperatives responded to their internal labor discipline problems by hiring nonmember labor to replace the work effort (but duplicate the work hours) of CAP

members. This strategy led to the emergence of a new category of "permanent temporary workers" (*eventuales permanentes*). Calculations reported in Carter and Alvarez (1989) indicate that treating this new class of workers as a type of second-class agrarian reform beneficiary probably increases the number of families that benefited from the coastal reform by at least 25 percent.

26. Most of the rural households in the sierra were either *minifundistas* or precapitalist tenants (known as *huasipungueros*, *arrimados*, and so on) who secured usufruct of a plot (or the use of pasture and infrastructure) through virtually unpaid labor on the landlord's own operational holdings.

27. The size limit was set at 2,500 hectares on the coast and 800 in the sierra, plus 1,000 hectares of pastureland in both regions.

28. The two reforms contributed mainly to the "enfranchisement" of the *campesino* tenant, whose status was changed from tenant to owner-occupier, and to the elimination of nonwage forms of employment in highland and coastal enterprises.

29. The breakup of many of these large estates into medium-size units is attributed mainly to subdivision through inheritance and some private sales carried out in an attempt to circumvent the reforms.

30. Barraclough (1982) argues that these figures *overstate* the relative access of those with smaller farms to resources, because the growth had increasingly pushed smallholders off better land and onto marginal land.

31. Peek (1983) summarizes data on the rural poverty and income inequality that attended this dispossession, displacement, and mechanization: The rural labor force was fully employed for only four months of the year. For the other eight months, unemployment ranged from 15 to 40 percent (1975-78 estimates). The richest 3.5 percent of the economically active rural population received 63 percent of the income; the poorest 50 percent received only 7.5 percent (1971 data). The average annual income of the poorest 50 percent of the rural population was only about $35 per capita in 1972. Members of this same population group consumed on average only 79 percent of the minimum intake of 2,244 calories (1976 data). Only 20 percent of the rural population had access to schools, 8.4 percent had access to health facilities, and 16 percent had electric power (1976 data).

32. *Keynesian* is used here in the restricted sense that there was involuntary unemployment. It is unemployment, and sluggish agricultural and industrial labor absorption, that makes the Junker path in the contemporary developing world problematic in a way not considered by Lenin (1974) in his writings on this path of agrarian development.

33. Deere and Marchetti (1981) describe the agrarian history and roots of the Sandinista revolution. It would not be correct, however, to describe the Sandinista revolution as exclusively, or even primarily, a rural-based movement.

34. The other policy shift in phase 2 was an explicit reduction in the ancillary programs designed to support food production. This shift emerged from the swirl of a debate over whether phase 1 support to food production had damaged export production by inducing former semiproletarian producers to "peasantize" and withdraw from the agroexport labor market. Peek (1983) describes the tradeoffs that emerged when policy supported both the food and nonfood sectors. In the terms of the Junker path interpretation, the state faced a choice between backward peasant food production and modernized export agriculture and decisively chose the latter.

35. Although decollectivization reduced the scale of production, it did not increase the size of the population that directly benefits from land reform. Indeed, as Carter and Alvarez (1989) indicate, decollectivization has de facto expropriated a second class of

reform beneficiaries, the *eventuales permanentes*, who had secured permanent employment on the cooperatives that had trouble in mobilizing members' labor.

36. The cooperative members' decision to subdivide their enterprises into individual family parcels, given their restricted choice between two polar alternatives, is of course not the same as saying that the individual small farm dominates all forms of production in a market sense.

37. The decollectivization experience of Chile (Jarvis 1989) and the literature on an emerging medium-size farm sector in Latin America (Scott 1985; Lehmann 1986a and 1986b; and Carter and Walker 1989) bring into question the efficacy of new wave policies as a substitute for land reform's efforts to better link growth with poverty reduction. The case study work on Ecuador (in the section above on the scope and organizational model of land reform) predicts the success of these new policy efforts. Von Braun, Hotchkiss, and Immink (1989) report that the incorporation of smallholders into new agroexport development in Guatemala has had favorable results. But drawing general inferences from their report is difficult because they studied only producers affiliated with a showcase marketing cooperative. In new work now under way, Carter, Barham, and Katz are constructing a broader sample of the industry, motivated in part by reports in Katz (1989) that large-scale direct production is reappearing and displacing the contracting system that extends opportunities to smallholders.

Land Tenure, Dualism, and Poverty in Malawi

13

David E. Sahn
Jehan Arulpragasam

Land policy, linked inextricably with marketing and pricing policy, is the corner-stone of Malawi's dualistic agricultural system and thus of the nation's entire economy. Inherited from a colonial past, this dualistic system was designed and justified as a system to propel growth through agriculture. Estate-based, export-oriented agriculture was to be the national growth pole.

Malawi's early economic growth record was viewed as testimony to the success of this strategy. With agriculture accounting for more than 40 percent of the country's gross domestic product (GDP) and directly generating more than 70 percent of its export revenues, its per capita growth reached 3.9 percent a year in the 1970s. By contrast, the Africa region's mean per capita growth rate was 1.1 percent during this period. Malawi ranked seventh in per capita growth among the thirty countries for which such data are available.

The 1980s cast a shadow on this record, however, and raised some troubling questions. Malawi's average annual growth in GDP per capita fell to –1.5 percent. This ranked Malawi only twenty-fifth among thirty-six Sub-Saharan African countries in growth performance over the past decade (table 13.1), with growth slower than the mean regional rate of –0.5 percent a year. Consequently, Malawi remains one of the poorest countries in the region. With an annual per capita GDP of only $176, Malawi ranks thirty-fourth among the thirty-eight countries in Sub-Saharan Africa.[1] The general constraints of low aggregate incomes are compounded by the inequality of the income distribution (Pryor 1988). Poverty not only persists, but is pervasive.

The issue in Malawi is not whether the land and associated agricultural policies have meant an inherent tradeoff between growth and poverty reduction. Rather, it is whether this policy set has compromised both growth and poverty reduction. This chapter argues that the poverty problem in Malawi has been critically defined by the dualistic tenurial structure inherited from the colonial era and reinforced by government policies. Land and related agricultural policies have played a crucial role in determining both aggregate economic performance and the livelihood of the poor rural population in Malawi. Moreover, the structural duality of agriculture, imposed by the rules and regulations regarding land use, continues to constrain poverty alleviation, productivity, and growth itself.

In developing this argument, we discuss in the next section the history and the dualistic nature of Malawi's agricultural sector. We then examine the characteristics and causes of poverty among smallholders, estate workers, and tenant farmers, and look at how policy has contributed to stagnating productivity and limited equity. We conclude by commenting on the potential role of policy in improving Malawi's economic performance and in raising its living standards.

Table 13.1 Selected economic and social indicators, Malawi

| | | *African* | *Values* | |
| | *Malawi's* | *countries* | | *Mean for* |
Indicator	*rank*	*ranked*	*Malawi*	*Africa*
GDP, 1987 (millions of US$)	25	43	1,307	3,151
Average annual percentage change in GDP, 1971-79	7	40	7.50	3.90
Average annual percentage change in GDP, 1980-87	23	36	1.54	2.47
GDP per capita, 1987 (US$)	34	38	175.72	513.8
Average annual percentage change in GDP per capita, 1971-79	7	39	3.89	1.08
Average annual percentage change in GDP per capita, 1980-87	25	36	-1.50	-0.52
Population, 1987 (thousands)	18	40	7,438	11,375.9
Average annual percentage change in population, 1971-79	11	40	3.06	2.68
Average annual percentage change in population, 1980-87	18	40	3.08	3.00
Population density, 1987 (people per square kilometer)	8	40	63.03	11.24
Infant mortality rate, 1985 (per 1,000)	29	32	163	119.8
Percentage change in infant mortality rate, 1975-85	14	32	-14.44	-14.50
Calories consumed per capita, 1985	9	43	2,415	2,158
Percentage change in calories consumed, 1970-80	15	43	5.83	2.92
Percentage change in calories consumed, 1980-85	24	43	-1.51	-1.11
Average annual percentage change in calories consumed, 1971-79	11	43	0.78	0.27
Average annual percentage change in calories consumed, 1980-85	29	43	-0.42	-0.05
Illiteracy rate, 1985 (percent)	17	29	59	54
Gross enrollment ratio, 1985 (percent)	17	28	64	75
Percentage change in gross enrollment ratio, 1980-85	12	28	4.29	7.28

Note: For the infant mortality rate and the illiteracy rate, countries are ranked in ascending order, with 1 indicating the lowest rates. For change in infant mortality, countries are ranked in descending order, with 1 indicating the greatest rate of decrease.
Source: UNDP and World Bank 1989; and World Bank 1989a.

The history and nature of dualism in Malawi

The evolution of policy in Malawi since before independence has fostered a sectoral duality in agriculture, with agricultural land falling into two major categories.[2] The first is the customary land that existed prior to independence. It is viewed as belonging to the entire community, "to the living, the dead, and the unborn" (Mkandawire and Phiri 1987: 10). Community residents obtain access to land through the village headperson, who has the right, as custodian of communal land, to allocate holdings.[3] Through this channel, village residents attain usufruct and occupation rights only.[4] They are not vested with ownership rights. Customary land, therefore, cannot be alienated, namely assigned, charged, or mortgaged. Nevertheless, rights of use and occupation can be transferred between generations.[5] Residence and use are generally sufficient to maintain use rights on land from generation to generation.

The colonial era introduced the estate sector, distinguished by its system of tenure that incorporates freehold and leasehold titles. By 1920 an estimated 193,472 acres of land had been designated as freehold and an additional 118,504 as leasehold, almost all of which was claimed by Europeans. The new estate sector fulfilled the British objective of rapid and controlled export of primary commodities from its colony to fuel the industrial expansion at home and the demands born of it.[6]

The institutionalization of dualism: The postindependence era

Land policy in postcolonial Malawi perpetuated the dualistic agricultural sector, and production, marketing, and pricing policy have reinforced it. Export-producing estates were reaffirmed as the engine of growth while the customary sector effectively remained a handmaiden to growth, supplying the estate sector with labor and food.

Several facts help illustrate how Malawi's land policy in the decade after independence largely institutionalized the tenurial system inherited from its colonial era. First, there was no large-scale land reform or land redistribution upon independence. The Customary Land Act of 1967 recognized and maintained the land tenure structure existing during colonial times.[7] Second, postcolonial land policy maintained, if not increased, the state's ultimate control of and access to land. In this regard, Malawi has conformed to a pattern common throughout Sub-Saharan Africa (Noronha 1985). Third, land legislation since independence has clearly been structured to promote stated policy and growth objectives by expanding the area of land under the individually tenured estate sector and restricting the area of land under the customary tenured sector. The Land Act gave the Ministry of Lands the authority to grant a lease on customary land to an estate for a period of up to ninety-nine years. Land policy introduced after independence has thus maintained policies that facilitated conversion of customary into private leasehold land and permitted the growth in estate lands of the past two decades.

Although smallholders cultivating customary land may apply to convert their land to leasehold estates, under the Customary Land Act of 1967, this practice was fairly uncommon in the 1970s. More recently, however, a large set of graduated smallholders has come into existence—progressive smallholders who attained leases during the 1980s either for their individual smallholdings or for consolidated family holdings (Mkandawire, Jaffee, and Bertoli 1990). But the vast majority of farmers in the smallholder sector have not converted the land they cultivate into leaseholds.[8]

In addition to the Customary Land Act permitting conversion of customary land into leasehold estate land, the newly independent government also instituted legislation that would permit smallholders to acquire individual (freehold) land rights to their customary holdings—the Registered Land Act of 1965. The Act embodied the government's stated belief that individual tenure was more conducive to development than customary tenure. Although these acts were designed in theory to permit the large-scale conversion of smallholder plots from customary to individual tenure, in practice they have been implemented on only a limited and experimental basis.[9]

In a reflection of the binding land constraint on smallholders, informal markets in land have also developed in Malawi. This follows a pattern, observed elsewhere, in which the increased scarcity value of land appears to generate informal markets even where formal markets are illegal (Feder and Noronha 1987).[10]

Malawi's dualistic agricultural sector, perpetuated by land policy, has been reinforced by production, marketing, and pricing policy. First, on the production side, the Special Crop Act has prohibited the cultivation on customary land of tea, sugar, and burley and flue-cured tobacco, effectively giving a monopoly on these crops to the estate sector.[11] As a result, the main crops grown by smallholders are rice, maize, cotton, pulses, sorghum, cassava, and a restricted variety of tobaccos (sun- and air-cured, fire-cured, and oriental).[12]

Second, just as the segmentation of production over the past two decades has been legally mandated, so too has an enforceable separation of marketing channels. Smallholder produce channeled through the state marketing agency, ADMARC, is heavily taxed, but estate produce is auctioned privately, offering growers high world prices. The separation of marketing channels, therefore, has both permitted the application of different pricing rules to the two subsectors and facilitated the enforcement of crop production restrictions on customary land by smallholders. As we discuss in greater detail below, these factors, in combination, have had important implications for income inequality and poverty in Malawi.

In addition, under the policies of the commercial banks, credit was directed to estate agriculture. Any individual who could secure a lease on customary land was able to procure a loan upon meeting certain minimum conditions.[13] Little credit was available to smallholders except through informal channels.[14]

Together, therefore, land tenure policy, agricultural production policy, and agricultural marketing and pricing policy have defined and strengthened the dualism in Malawi's agriculture. They go far toward explaining the nature of economic growth since independence, and the estate sector's important role in that growth. Indeed, agricultural products dominated the export sector, and estate crops were dominant among these. Tobacco, tea, and sugar accounted for 60 percent of all exports in 1968. By 1988 their share had risen to 85 percent, with tobacco alone accounting for 64 percent of export revenues (table 13.2). That agricultural growth in the aggregate has relied on the estate sector is also clear. The share of estate production in agricultural GDP has steadily increased, from 13 percent in 1973 to 23 percent in 1988 (table 13.3). Similarly, gross crop production data reveal a fourfold increase in estate sector production during the 1970s, while smallholder crop production grew by only 33 percent.

The impressive increase in production by the estate sector through the 1970s and into the 1980s is a result not so much of its relative productivity or intensity of production, but of the expansion of land under the estate sector in general, and burley tobacco in particular. There has been large-scale appropriation of customary land by the estate sector over the past twenty-five years. Although figures regarding actual changes in the amount of land under leasehold vary from one source to the next, all available information points in the same direction. According to the most conservative estimates (Mkandawire and Phiri 1987), the number of estates increased from 111 in 1967 to 1,150 in 1986; the land under leasehold

Table 13.2 Commodity exports as a percentage of total exports, Malawi, 1964-88

Year	Tobacco	Tea	Sugar	Groundnuts	Cotton	Other
1964	36.7	29.0	—	9.7	8.4	16.2
1965	37.9	27.8	—	12.1	8.0	14.2
1966	32.7	32.2	—	9.3	7.8	18.0
1967	25.5	27.1	—	20.7	4.2	22.4
1968	31.5	28.9	0.0	13.8	3.8	22.0
1969	34.6	26.0	0.4	15.3	4.7	19.0
1970	40.9	26.9	0.4	10.5	6.8	14.5
1971	44.5	24.0	0.6	11.9	5.1	13.8
1972	45.3	21.8	0.7	12.9	4.7	14.7
1973	44.0	19.9	4.8	8.6	2.8	19.9
1974	43.9	19.2	10.3	5.8	3.0	17.8
1975	48.1	20.4	11.6	6.1	1.8	12.0
1976	46.0	18.7	16.5	8.0	1.7	9.1
1977	50.4	24.2	8.7	5.2	1.4	10.2
1978	57.9	19.6	8.2	3.1	0.5	10.7
1979	55.7	17.3	10.1	5.0	0.5	11.4
1980	45.3	13.4	17.0	7.2	2.0	15.2
1981	42.7	13.1	24.3	4.6	0.6	14.7
1982	58.5	18.2	9.7	1.9	0.1	11.5
1983	51.6	21.1	10.2	1.1	0.0	16.1
1984	52.9	26.0	6.7	0.2	0.5	13.7
1985	44.7	21.8	10.6	1.4	3.1	18.9
1986	54.7	15.3	9.0	3.6	0.5	17.0
1987	62.0	10.1	10.5	2.2	0.1	15.0
1988	64.4	10.6	9.8	3.3	0.0	12.1

— Not available.
Source: Reserve Bank of Malawi 1987 and 1988.

Table 13.3 Shares of estate and smallholder sectors in agricultural GDP, Malawi, 1973-88

Year	Agricultural GDP (millions of kwacha)	Estate share (percent)	Smallholder share (percent)
1973	223.6	0.13	0.87
1974	228.2	0.14	0.86
1975	230.3	0.17	0.83
1976	257.6	0.15	0.85
1977	286.5	0.17	0.83
1978	294.9	0.17	0.84
1979	304.1	0.17	0.83
1980	284.2	0.19	0.81
1981	261.0	0.19	0.81
1982	277.6	0.22	0.78
1983	289.9	0.23	0.77
1984	306.5	0.21	0.79
1985	307.4	0.21	0.79
1986	308.0	0.21	0.79
1987	310.9	0.22	0.78
1988	331.9	0.23	0.77

Source: Reserve Bank of Malawi 1987 and 1988.

also increased dramatically, from 79,000 hectares in 1970 to 308,000 hectares in 1985. Other estimates, however, reveal a much larger expansion. An internal World Bank report put estate acreage in 1985 at 691,000 hectares. The most recent estimates suggest that the number of estates (freehold and leasehold) increased from about 1,200 in 1979 to about 14,700 in 1990, and the area covered by estates from about 300,000 hectares to about 843,000 hectares (Mkandawire, Jaffee, and Bertoli 1990).[15]

Several factors explain this dramatic growth in estate land area and estate production, but it is the nature of the growth that is of consequence to employment and income generation in rural Malawi. How the growth in area of the estate sector has affected the utilization of land, access to land, and land tenure among rural households is what tells much of the poverty story in Malawi. It is to these issues that we now turn.

Promoting productivity and equity

Malawi's export agriculture-based development strategy is predicated on the notion that there is a need to develop a productive subsector that departs from the rules and practices of the low-input, low-productivity, customary land tenure. Such a strategy, if it enhanced productivity and growth, would also be a vehicle for poverty alleviation. The employment and income generated in the estate sector have been implicitly relied upon to provide the resources necessary for poverty alleviation in rural Malawi.

Whether Malawian rural households would have been better off with no estates at all is a question that we do not explicitly address in this chapter.[16]

What we do argue, however, is that productivity and equity both have been compromised by the rules that specifically dictate duality in Malawi. In other words, not only does agricultural productivity stand to gain through reforms that work to remove many of the policies that originated and perpetuated this dualistic system, but Malawi's poor stand to gain, in both employment and income opportunities.

The smallholder sector

The prospects for economic growth and poverty reduction in the largely subsistence smallholder sector is limited by land. The population growth rate of 3.7 percent a year between 1977 and 1987 (Malawi 1987), together with the alienation of customary land in the central and southern regions, increased the pressure on land available to smallholders. This is not to say that the conversion of customary land to leasehold land has forced peasants off their land. It has not.[17] But by appropriating previously uncultivated customary land, estate expansion reduces the land area available for the future expansion of smallholder cultivation in the face of an expanding rural population.

The resultant land pressure on smallholders is evident in the statistics. The number of households with less than 2 hectares of land increased between 1968-69 and 1980-81 from 29 to 81 percent. Even more troubling is that more than half of all smallholders had less than 1.0 hectare in 1980-81 (figure 13.1). No recent survey data are available, but extrapolating these trends suggests that Malawi is facing the prospect of a significant number of landless and near-landless peasants who rely for income on agricultural work on estates and on other smallholder plots, as well as on nonfarm sources of income (Christiansen and Kydd 1987).[18]

Employment and incomes in the smallholder sector

The resource constraints that smallholders face are reflected in data on employment and incomes. The smallholder sector, which employs 72.0 percent of the labor force and generates 34.2 percent of value added, is also the lowest-paid sector. Income per worker is just over half that in the estate sector and only 8.6 and 5.8 percent that in the government and manufacturing sectors (table 13.4). This pattern of a low value added per smallholder in absolute and relative terms has not changed during the

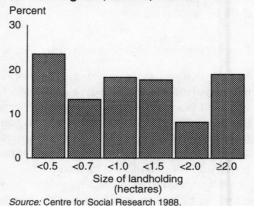

Figure 13.1 Percentage of households by landholding size, Malawi, 1980–81

Percent

Source: Centre for Social Research 1988.

past decade. In fact, the evidence suggests that the real value added per worker has only increased from 131 to 138 kwacha (Mk) between 1978 and 1987.

Low value added as a result of low productivity has important implications for food security. These implications are especially serious in conjunction with the shrinking size of landholdings. Calculations indicate that, given present technology and yields, the average smallholder household with a holding of less than one hectare would produce each day, on average, the equivalent of 1,231 calories per capita (Sahn, Arulpragasam, and Merid 1990). This is clearly inadequate to meet normal calorie requirements.[19] Moreover, data from the 1980/81 National Sample Survey of Agriculture (NSSA) reveal that 83 percent of the households with holdings of less than 0.7 hectare depleted their food stocks by February, before the harvest. Seventy-two percent of households with 0.7 to 1.49 hectares and 51 percent of those with more than 1.5 hectares depleted their stocks before February (Quinn, Chiligo, and Gittinger 1988). Similarly, survey data from 1989/90 indicate that 60 percent of farmers ran out of food in December in Salima Agricultural Development District, and 85 percent of farmers in Kasungu and Ngabu Agricultural Development Districts depleted their food stocks by February (Babu, Ayoade, and Bisika 1990).

The obvious need to increase incomes in the smallholder sector is inextricably linked with the need to increase production. The evidence indicates an extremely low level of productivity on customary holdings in Malawi and a general failure to innovate. Yields of maize barely rose through the 1980s, and the increase, from 1.07 metric tons per hectare in 1982/83 to 1.19 metric tons per hectare in 1988/89, was due in part to weather (table 13.5). Similarly, yields of most smallholder export crops have stagnated or declined. Between 1978/79 and 1987/88, yields of southern dark-fired (SDF) tobacco fell 59.1 percent, yields of sun- and air-cured tobacco fell 31.8 percent, and yields of oriental tobacco fell 14.4 percent. Cotton yields dropped 14 percent between 1978/79 and 1986/87.

Toward greater productivity and equity in the smallholder sector

The means to improving both agricultural productivity and rural incomes lie in addressing a number of the distortions that characterize dualistic agriculture in Malawi. A primary need is to improve incentives to smallholders. Smallholder producer prices for export crops, set by the government, have traditionally been associated with high levels of implicit taxation. Nominal protection coefficients (NPCs) reveal that producer prices have been well below border prices.[20] In 1977, for example, the nominal protection coefficient for smallholder rice at the official exchange rate was calculated at 0.57, that of groundnuts at 0.36, and that of smallholder tobacco at 0.17 (table 13.6).[21] Smallholders have been further taxed by the misalignment of the exchange rate. At the shadow exchange rate, the 1977 nominal protection coefficient for smallholder rice was 0.36, that for groundnuts 0.23, and that for tobacco 0.11.[22] The pricing policy for maize does not seem to involve similarly high levels of taxation on smallholder production. Nevertheless, real, official producer prices of maize declined between 1982 and 1987.

Table 13.4 Labor force, functional distribution of income, and income per worker, by sector, Malawi, 1968, 1978, and 1987

Sector	Labor force (age 15–64) (thousands)			Functional distribution of income (percentage of value added)		Income per worker (current Mk)		Income per worker (1978 Mk)	
	1968	1978	1987	1978	1987	1978	1987	1978	1987
Smallholder	1,497.3	1,768.7	2,138.6	31.1	34.2	131	398	131	138
Estate agriculture[a]	64.5	207.5	266.4	6.4	7.2	234	704	234	244
Government[b]	31.6	36.6	52.6	8.3	9.3	1,760	4,625	1,760	1,606
Manufacturing and other industries[b]	82.6	133.8	176.4	53.6	48.5	2,976	6,840	2,976	2,375
Informal sector	44.9	87.4	121.0	—	—	—	—	—	—
Unemployed	—	48.0	197.0	—	—	—	—	—	—

— Not available.
Note: The table does not ascribe a portion of the value added to the labor force in the informal sector. To what extent its contribution to GDP is captured in the figures of other sectors is unknown.
a. Includes wage and nonwage employees; nonwage employees include tenant households.
b. Includes wage and nonwage employees.
Source: World Bank 1989b; and World Bank data.

Table 13.5 Crop yields, Malawi, 1978-89
(kilograms per hectare)

Year	Estate crops						Smallholder crops					
	Flue-cured tobacco	Burley tobacco	NDF[a] tobacco	SDF[b] tobacco	Sun/air tobacco	Oriental tobacco	Cotton	Rice	Local maize	Composite maize	Hybrid maize	Total maize
1978	1,189	969	—	—	—	—	491	—	—	—	—	—
1979	1,325	1,080	286	548	286	561	720	—	—	—	—	—
1980	1,402	1,206	289	450	304	437	633	—	—	—	—	—
1981	1,324	1,176	388	468	295	235	594	—	—	—	—	—
1982	1,624	1,184	345	161	272	87	496	—	—	—	—	—
1983	1,576	1,055	202	243	157	61	410	—	—	—	—	1,070
1984	1,637	1,113	467	482	241	97	629	—	1,040	1,790	2,760	1,190
1985	1,376	964	301	361	100	233	515	1,610	1,030	1,750	3,110	1,180
1986	1,321	1,069	267	118	191	445	405	1,640	960	1,730	2,940	1,080
1987	1,457	1,066	250	183	188	129	619	1,490	950	1,640	2,710	1,020
1988	1,237	878	428	224	195	480	—	1,520	1,090	1,200	2,670	1,170
1989[c]	—	—	—	—	—	—	—	—	1,060	1,770	2,800	1,190

— Not available.

a. NDF tobacco is Northern District fire-cured tobacco.

b. SDF tobacco is southern dark-fired tobacco.

c. Estimate.

Source: Malawi Ministry of Agriculture data; Malawi 1978; Malawi, Ministry of Agriculture 1988; and Dickerman and Bloch 1989.

The suppression of smallholder earnings through the tax on agricultural production has two distinct effects. First, the high rate of implicit taxation of smallholder production is a disincentive for undertaking investment, adopting improved technology, and utilizing agricultural inputs. Better incentives may be expected to increase incomes by increasing productivity and production. Similarly, ending the quantity rationing of fertilizer and the credit constraints that have restricted fertilizer application by many smallholders is also necessary, even if it is at the expense of a lower rate of subsidy for this input.[23]

Second, the suppression of smallholder earnings helps keep agricultural wages low. Raising producer prices for smallholders would raise the average reservation wage in agriculture and thus exert upward pressure on the wage rate offered by larger farmers for casual labor. Such employment, called *ganyu*, is relied upon by many households with relatively smaller holdings as well as by the growing number of near-landless.[24] Increased producer prices, by raising the opportunity cost of labor, would also raise the wage rate that must be offered by the parallel estate sector in order to engage labor.

Increasing the price to labor is especially important in Malawi. The meager prospects for earning a livelihood solely from one's smallholding reveals itself in the important share of smallholder income derived from off-farm sources. Such income, albeit low, is quite significant for most smallholder households, particularly for those with smaller holdings. Off-farm sources of income account for 51.4 percent of the total earnings of households with less than 0.5 hectare of land and 25.8 percent of the total income of those with more than 3 hectares of land (table 13.7). Distinct from productivity considerations, therefore, raising

Table 13.6 Nominal protection coefficients for selected smallholder crops, Malawi, 1975-88

Year	Rice		Groundnuts		Tobacco	
	Official rate	Shadow rate	Official rate	Shadow rate	Official rate	Shadow rate
1975	—	—	1.96	1.41	0.17	0.13
1976	0.32	0.21	0.48	0.33	0.17	0.12
1977	0.57	0.36	0.36	0.23	0.17	0.11
1978	0.41	0.30	0.33	0.25	0.52	0.38
1979	0.34	0.25	0.54	0.40	0.52	0.38
1980	0.36	0.25	0.56	0.39	0.46	0.32
1981	0.28	0.18	0.37	0.25	0.31	0.20
1982	0.20	0.13	0.88	0.58	0.17	0.12
1983	0.30	0.20	0.92	0.60	0.34	0.22
1984	0.29	0.18	0.92	0.57	0.39	0.24
1985	0.39	0.24	1.42	0.88	0.89	0.55
1986	0.23	0.15	0.84	0.53	0.49	0.31
1987	0.21	0.14	1.05	0.70	0.35	0.24
1988	0.20	—	1.02	—	0.26	—

— Not available.
Source: Sahn, Arulpragasam, and Merid 1990.

the implicit wage to agricultural labor by removing taxes on such labor is essential for reducing rural poverty.

Recent efforts at market liberalization in the smallholder sector have focused on maize. But there is also a need to ensure that smallholders receive higher prices for cash crops. Smallholder incomes and national agricultural productivity both stand to gain from the removal of the ban on smallholder production of such export crops as burley tobacco. The auction price of burley tobacco exceeded the auction price of sun- and air-cured tobacco by 32 percent in 1988. And it exceeded the smallholder producer price of sun- and air-cured tobacco by 207 percent, or by 354 tambala per kilogram, equivalent to the value of enough maize to meet an adult's subsistence requirement for more than three-fourths of a month in 1988.[25] Thus, permitting smallholders to produce burley and flue-cured tobacco, like raising smallholder producer prices, would raise the implicit wage in the smallholder sector and drive up the competitive wage rate in the estate sector.

The removal of production restrictions would also have positive effects on national growth and smallholder incomes by increasing productivity.[26] It has been shown that the domestic resource costs of producing burley and flue-cured tobacco are lower for smallholders than they are for estates (Lele and Agarwal 1990). This is also true of production valued—appropriately—at international prices.[27] And it is even true for production on smaller farms. Carr (1988) indicates that smallholder production of burley tobacco is technically and economically feasible on holdings as small as 0.5 hectare. Lifting the restriction on smallholder production will, besides increasing smallholder incomes, thus raise the value of marginal product on most of Malawi's landholdings and possibly increase Malawi's foreign exchange earnings.

The reasons for the stagnation of smallholder productivity go beyond distortions in incentives. One important reason has been the failure of government extension services and agricultural research to make significant inroads in improving smallholder productivity over the past two decades (Kydd 1990). The causes of this failure require greater study, including a determination of the extent to which the provision of these services has been biased toward the estate

Table 13.7 Per capita income and expenditure by size of landholding, Zomba district, Malawi, November 1986 to August 1987
(Malawian kwacha)

Item	Landholder group by hectares cultivated					
	< 0.5	0.5-1.0	1.0-1.5	1.5-2.0	2.0-3.0	> 3.0
Total per capita expenditure	79.11	62.30	75.30	68.10	84.80	155.10
Total per capita income	76.62	61.29	77.65	74.50	78.65	156.85
Home consumption	18.20	15.19	22.10	22.00	28.24	57.46
Agricultural sales	16.18	18.06	27.37	23.66	22.05	44.80
Nonfarm earnings	17.03	4.67	11.46	12.41	8.69	4.30
Transfers, remittances, and others	15.17	12.22	12.24	13.99	17.81	48.84
Agricultural wages	10.04	11.15	4.48	2.44	1.86	1.45

Source: Peters and Herrera 1989.

sector. Efforts that should be made include developing food security policies to help farmers avert the higher risk for hybrid maize of crop failure; addressing, through both agricultural and agroindustrial research, the poor taste, processing, and storage characteristics of hybrid maize; and exploring other low-risk and high-yield crops, such as finger millet and hybrid sorghum, while recognizing the limitations on the viability and speed of adoption due to social and cultural factors.

Another cause of the lagging productivity and income in the smallholder sector is the virtual lack of credit to smallholders, which has constrained the level of investment and technology in the sector. It may be argued that this is in large part because commercial banks do not view usufructuary rights as sufficient collateral for lending. The demand for funds from the parallel leasehold sector has also contributed to the diversion of credit from the smallholder sector. But the lack of collateral among smallholders need not be an argument for the increased individualization of tenure; rather, it could be an argument for the development of appropriate credit institutions. Over the past two decades there has been little investment in the development of rural banking institutions geared to the smallholder in Malawi. Even with the registration of smallholdings in Lilongwe under the Customary Land Development Act, little credit has been forthcoming. This could be in part because registration of land is permitted to families and not to individuals, a factor that may need to be addressed. But it is in large part because of the lack of an appropriate and extensive rural credit system targeted at smallholders.

Further contributing to the low productivity of labor and land in the smallholder sector in Malawi is poverty itself. The combination of increased land scarcity and commercialization of agriculture has meant a greater reliance on the wage labor market and nonfarm incomes to feed poorer households during the preharvest season. In Malawi this has had serious consequences. Forced to rely on *ganyu* income by the depletion of their stocks well before the next harvest, smallholders neglect preharvest preparation on their own small landholdings, seriously compromising their harvest for the next year. Poverty decreases labor productivity in a more fundamental way as well. Data from other countries suggest that reduced food intake among poor farmers will likely mean lower energy expenditure and lower productivity among these farmers (Strauss 1989; Deolalikar 1988; and Sahn and Alderman 1988). Increased incomes to smallholder agriculture will thus have secondary effects on productivity.

Finally, the poor productivity of the smallholder sector raises the important question as to what extent this may be attributable to the inefficiencies inherent in customary tenure. It has been argued that the insecurity of tenure on customary land impedes development because it acts as a disincentive to investment on the land. At the same time, the lack of ownership rights accounts for farmers' difficulty in acquiring credit. It has also been suggested that customary tenure is impeding the efficient economic mobility of an important factor of production and income.

Customary tenure may indeed restrain productivity among smallholders, but there is reason to question its significance in Malawi. First, most smallholders in

Malawi—like smallholders elsewhere in Africa (Noronha 1985)—are secure in the historically based notion that they will not lose their land. And usufructuary rights are by and large inheritable, assuring the transfer of land to offspring. Furthermore, although smallholders do not avail themselves of the right to sell and rent land (and consequently to recover any improvements to the land other than directly through its cultivation), the importance of this aspect of security should be questioned. Because land remains the sole means of economic security for most rural households, most households are not interested in selling. And because of the slow pace of expansion of the nonfarm economy and thus of nonfarm employment, this is likely to be the case for the medium term, and land is likely to remain the key to sustained economic growth and equity in the long term.

Second, it is unclear that the conversion of customary land into private land would improve tenure security, equity, and productivity. Attempts at such conversion often increase the insecurity of tenure for those remaining on customary land because of the inherent insecurity "that flows from frequent amendment of formal laws and the absence of any ability to forecast what might happen next" (Noronha 1985: 207). The changes inherent in a move toward registration may especially affect the tenurial security of women. The increasing pressure on land appears to be altering the rules of succession from that of a matrilineal system to that of a patrilineal one (Pervis 1984). As such cases as Kenya show, this particularly affects the security of land access for single women, separated women, and widows (Davison 1988).

Third, a related argument against land registration and privatization, on the grounds of either productivity or equity, is that improving the efficiency of land mobility fosters increased concentration of land ownership, and possibly of incomes. This has been the case in Kenya, for example (Collier and Lal 1980; and Shipton 1987). Following from this is the argument that individualization of tenure contributes to landlessness: villagers could lose their rights to cultivate their ancestral land. In Chimanimani, Zimbabwe, for example, families went from being farmers, to being tenants, to being landless refugees in Red Cross camps (*African Business,* August 1989). As Swynnerton, the architect of Kenyan land policy, recognized: "Energetic or rich Africans will be able to acquire more land and bad or poor farmers less, creating a landed and a landless class" (1954: 10). He viewed this as "a normal step in the evolution of a country," but others have contested it on equity and poverty grounds. Still others have pointed to the fact that "rich Africans" are not necessarily better farmers. Many are urbanites with no farming or managerial experience who have invested in land as an asset. Thus, efficiency of land mobility would not necessarily translate into efficiency of land use.[28]

Fourth, and perhaps most important, experience reveals that, in practice, land registration is no quick panacea for smallholders, either in Malawi or elsewhere in Africa. The realities of political economy, the strain on limited bureaucratic capabilities, and just plain bad implementation have left a sad record. In Kenya the initial enthusiasm about the prospects of individualizing tenure has been replaced by creeping doubt after forty years of slow implementation (Shipton

1987; and Noronha 1985). Registration of land was to have been a major prong of land policy in Malawi, but because of the lack of political commitment, among other reasons, it has made little progress. In the Lilongwe Agricultural Development District, where registration has been under way since the early 1970s, there is little evidence that credit has become more widely available, that the trend toward smaller landholdings has abated, that land improvements are more widespread, that yields are increasing more rapidly, or that a vibrant market in land has evolved.[29]

This poor track record may be due in part to problems of implementation in practice. But practice matters. Even if the individualization of tenure is beneficial for long-term development, the ability of a government to undertake the administrative requirements of such a task, and the political will to continue it, must be considered. The process of registering and titling is an expensive one, requiring trained professionals and sound institutions. The costs of introducing a new system could well outweigh the gains in efficiency (Feder and Noronha 1987).

The potential role of registration in addressing the productivity concerns within the smallholder sector requires further study. In Malawi at least, it cannot be looked to as the solution to the urgent problems of the lagging subsistence sector. Rather, the constraints represented by the other aspects of Malawi's dualistic agricultural sector should probably be addressed first. The welfare and productivity of smallholders depends critically on removing the constraints they face with regard to choice of crops, access to inputs, and opportunities to market a surplus. Thus, immediate concerns should revolve around improving rural infrastructure, credit institutions, input supply, product markets, and agricultural extension.

A strategy for poverty alleviation therefore calls for a two-pronged approach. First, there must be an emphasis on increasing smallholder productivity and incomes. This will increase smallholders' welfare in general and directly counter poverty among subsistence farmers. And increasing the implicit wage rate within the smallholder sector has an indirect effect, leading to an increase in the price paid to labor in the estate sector. Second, then, is the need to increase the wages and amount of labor employed by estates. We turn to this issue next.

The estate sector

The justification for the reliance on the estate sector as both an engine of national growth and a provider of resources for the alleviation of poverty depends crucially on the supposition that the sector is efficient, highly productive, and labor absorptive. In practice, there are indications that the estate sector has not lived up to any of these counts, despite the advantages it has been provided.

Employment and incomes in the estate sector

The number of those employed in the estate sector—both wage earners and tenants—has grown dramatically, although they still remain a small fraction of those employed in agriculture. The number of wage earners in the estate sector increased almost 400 percent between 1969 and 1987, to an estimated 157,200 (table 13.8).[30] In the more densely populated South, and especially in the Zomba district, where surplus labor is plentiful, estates rely almost exclusively on wage labor; no sharecropping has been observed there. Yet, despite the large increase in estate laborers since 1969, they still represent just over 7 percent of the number of smallholders.

Much of the estate production, especially on burley tobacco estates in the central part of the country, is carried out by tenants. One estimate puts the number of tenants nationally at 105,000 in 1989, up dramatically from 21,000 in 1980 (Duncan 1990). This growth reflects the recent expansion of estates; most of the new lands are cultivated by tenants rather than by wage laborers. The number of tenants, although it has grown more rapidly over the past decade than that of wage laborers, still remains smaller.

Together with these data on employment, an understanding of earnings helps to assess the estate sector's contribution to aggregate agricultural incomes. There is evidence, in a number of forms, that the earnings of wage laborers are

Table 13.8 Wage and salary employment in commercial (estate) agriculture and tenants on burley estates in Malawi, 1969-89
(thousands of people)

Year	Tea estates	Tobacco estates	Other private commercial agriculture	Total wage and salary employment	Tenants
1969	30.1	8.1	4.5	42.6	—
1970	30.7	13.1	4.8	48.6	—
1971	32.6	15.9	5.2	53.7	—
1972	32.5	20.2	6.8	59.5	—
1973	35.2	24.6	11.5	71.4	—
1974	35.2	22.5	17.1	74.8	—
1975	36.8	20.5	28.8	86.1	—
1976	36.7	30.6	28.5	95.8	—
1977	39.6	71.7[a]	21.5	132.8	—
1978	39.0	87.5	21.8	148.3	—
1979	—	—	—	—	—
1980	—	—	—	—	21.0
1981	—	—	—	—	24.0
1982	—	—	—	—	35.0
1983	63.7	85.3	23.3	172.3	59.0
1984	49.6	80.6	25.0	155.2	40.0
1985	47.3	89.7	28.7	165.7	47.0
1986	—	—	—	162.3	42.0
1987	—	—	—	157.2	52.0
1988	—	—	—	—	78.0
1989	—	—	—	—	105.0

— Not available.
a. Before 1977, only firms employing more than 20 employees were included in wage or salary employment numbers. After 1977, all firms were included. Figures for 1977 and 1978 include about 18,300 workers not previously counted.
Source: Malawi, *Reported Employment and Earnings Annual Report*, various years, and official sources; and Duncan 1990.

low.[31] First, an examination of the value added per estate worker indicates that it is approximately 75 percent higher than that in the smallholder sector (see table 13.4). But this does not take into account that income per worker is highly skewed in the estate sector, which includes wealthy estate owners and managers as well as tenants and wage laborers. Thus, assuming, for example, that the estate owners and managers represent 5 percent of those engaged in the estate sector, and receive 50 percent of the income (probably a conservative estimate), the average value added for the rest of those employed in the estate sector would have been Mk370 a year in 1987. This is less than that of smallholders.

Second, data on average earnings by sector indicate that estate workers' wages have corresponded almost exactly to the minimum wage since 1980; before that year it was higher than the legislated floor (figure 13.2).[32] The monthly real agricultural wage was Mk9.54 in 1987, down from Mk16.95 in 1975 and the peak level of Mk17.92 in 1982. More important, estate workers are paid markedly less than any other classification of workers (although other workers also experienced a declining real wage during the 1980s). For example, in 1987 the earnings of agricultural estate workers were just over one-third those of construction workers, the next lowest-paid category, and less than one-fifth those of workers in manufacturing. But more interesting is that, even if the estate worker is employed twelve months a year, his or her annual earnings would have been Mk252, less than the optimistic estimate above, which we expected to overstate the welfare of those engaged as estate workers.

Third, survey data (Mkandawire and Phiri 1987) indicate that estate wages ranged from 70 to 90 tambala a day. Assuming that the workers were employed 26 days a month, this gives an income of between Mk18.20 and Mk23.40. In constant 1980 kwacha, the upper bound is extremely close to the estimates found in figure 13.2. More recent 1990 data reveal that approximately 50 percent of adult male permanent workers were paid less than the statutory minimum

Figure 13.2 Monthly average earnings, by private sector, Malawi, 1975–87

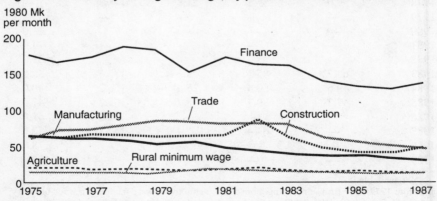

Note: Assumes thirty days work at minimum wage.
Source: 1971–75: Malawi, *Reported Employment and Earnings Annual Report, 1975*; 1976: World Bank data; 1977–78, 1983–87: Malawi, *Monthly Statistical Bulletin,* various issues; 1979–81: Malawi, *Reported Employment and Earnings Annual Report, 1979–81*; 1982: World Bank data.

wage, and 32 percent were paid less than nominal Mk30 a month (Mkandawire, Jaffee, and Bertoli 1990).[33]

This evidence on estate workers' wages shows that they did not keep pace with administered consumer prices for maize over the period 1982-88. As a result, while it would have taken the head of a rural household without any other source of income fifteen days of work a month at the average agricultural wage to feed a family of five in 1982, he or she would have had to work twenty-two days a month to sustain the family in 1987 (figure 13.3).[34]

Figure 13.3 Days of work at average agricultural wage required to buy subsistence quantity of maize for a month for a family of five, Malawi, 1975–87

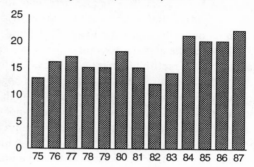

Source: Ministry of Agriculture data; 1971–75: Malawi, *Reported Employment and Earnings Annual Report, 1975*; 1976: World Bank data; 1977–78, 1983–87: Malawi, *Monthly Statistical Bulletin*, various issues; 1982: World Bank data.

For tenants, mean earnings are somewhat better. The figures on tenants' incomes from various studies reveal that mean earnings compare favorably with the minimum wage, although they vary considerably. Vaughan and Chipande (1986) found that most tenants' annual profits were between Mk200 and Mk300 in 1985; Nankumba (1985) cites an average annual net return to tenants in 1989 of Mk476.[35] Another study reports that the mean profits of tobacco tenants in 1989 were Mk396 (Nyanda and Shively 1989), although when non-estate income was added, total household income rose to more than Mk600. A more recent survey showed mean reported tenant cash income at Mk621, with smaller estates paying lower wages (Mkandawire, Jaffee, and Bertoli 1990). All these figures compare favorably with an annual minimum wage rate of Mk281 from 1987 to 1989,[36] which corresponds closely to the average agricultural wage. This observation is tempered by the revelation of a high degree of skewness in tenant incomes, however. A large number of tenants receive no income at all, and a few account for a large share of receipts (Mkandawire, Jaffee, and Bertoli 1990).

Toward greater productivity and equity in the estate sector

Although estates have been growing in land area, the laborers and tenants are still extremely poor and have benefited little from that expansion. The reason for this appears to be market failures, which restrain the productivity of both land and labor. They also restrain labor demand and wages in the estate sector, both of which are of crucial and increasing importance to rural households.

Of particular concern is the observed underutilization of leased land. The concern is especially acute in light of the rapid conversion of customary land into leasehold land and the associated land pressure on smallholders. There are no national land use surveys, but studies such as that by Mkandawire and Phiri

(1987) support the contention that large tracts of leasehold land lie idle while many smallholders are nearly landless. On the large estates (greater than 100 hectares) cropping intensities average 23 percent, and more than one-third of these estates cultivate less than 15 percent of their land (Mkandawire, Jaffee, and Bertoli 1990).[37] Increasing the utilization of this idle land should increase the potential of estate expansion to absorb labor.

Most of the explanations for the observed phenomenon of unutilized estate lands point to rectifiable market failures.[38] In theory, assigning a rental value to land is the most direct means of raising the opportunity cost of holding land and inducing its productive use. In practice, though, land rental values in Malawi are not related to land productivity. Land rents not only lie well below the economic value of land, but also do not vary with the productivity of land. Fixed at Mk10 per hectare regardless of the land's quality and potential returns, these rents are often not even collected, according to an internal World Bank report. Designing and then enforcing an appropriate land rent or land tax structure for the estate sector is necessary to prevent land from being viewed as a costless asset. Charging land rents would encourage land utilization and raise labor requirements, and thus help reduce rural poverty.

A second reason for the underutilization of estates is slow start-up, due in part to the slow pace at which lease applications are reviewed and capital for estate development is procured. One justification for converting customary land to leasehold land was to direct land rights toward those with the financial capacity to maximize productivity. But in Malawi many leases, especially in the 1970s, were issued to civil servants and others who had enough money to obtain a lease, but not enough financial or managerial capacity to do anything with it. Thus, contrary to the theory that underutilization of estates may be due simply to a lack of labor, it may be due instead to the problems associated with absentee landlords and the lack of managerial capacity.[39] In a recent estate survey very few managers reported having had any managerial experience before their present job (Mkandawire, Jaffee, and Bertoli 1990).

The differences between regions in population density may shed light on why there might be underutilization of estate lands in the central region. Unlike the South, where near-landless farmers form a pool of surplus labor, there appears to be a labor shortage on estates in the central region.[40] The solution to any possible labor shortage on estates lies in making labor markets clear. To begin with, there is a need for information and infrastructure to lower job search and related transactions costs. At present these are quite high because workers rarely relocate permanently and travel is expensive. This pattern of seasonal migration reflects such factors as the limited growing season for tobacco, the inaccessibility of estate land for subsistence maize cultivation, the risk of losing one's own customary holding because of prolonged absence, and the generally poor working conditions and lack of long-term contracts. Labor mobility would be increased and job search costs reduced by such solutions as the diversification of estate cultivation to allow for maize production on unused land, the registration of smallholdings, and the construction of housing on estates to help smallholders resettle in the central part of the country. Here, too, tenancy contracts that are better defined and less exploitative, and higher wages, would make estates more attractive to potential migrants.

A concern related to the high rates of underutilization revolves around the productivity of estate crops during the past decade (table 13.5). The data in table 13.5 appear to reveal substantially higher yields by estates, but a simple comparison of burley and flue-cured yields with those of smallholder tobacco is of limited meaning. The differences in yields are a function of the type of tobacco grown, and smallholders are prohibited from growing burley and flue-cured crops. And, unlike estate managers, smallholders growing sun- and air-cured tobaccos do not generally apply fertilizer, for the reasons alluded to earlier.

Nevertheless, several reasons continue to be cited as to why the estate sector may be expected to have a theoretical advantage in yield over the smallholder sector. First, as discussed, the estate sector has better access to higher output prices, to credit, to cheap labor, and to larger landholdings. Second, though this is less well substantiated, labor inputs for smallholder production are lower than for estate production, including on the few smallholder farms producing burley (Lele and Agarwal 1990).[41] Third, in theory, the ratio of product to input prices is higher for estates than for smallholders, compelling estates to be relatively more input-intensive. Fourth, under the hypothesis perhaps most difficult to substantiate, even if crops were comparable, and input usage the same, estates would appear to be more productive because they are in fact cultivating better land.

Estates may hold these advantages in theory, but in practice the empirical evidence presented above on domestic resource costs reveals that the smallholder sector holds the productivity edge. In fact, the evidence of the stagnating productivity of estates in Malawi (see table 13.5), frequently observed elsewhere in Africa as well, would also refute the argument that estate production should be favored over smallholder production on efficiency grounds. There are several reasons for the estate sector's failure to achieve productivity gains. First, the low productivity on estate land may stem from insecurity of long-term tenure; this may limit investment on some estates. Many estates are under leases of only twenty-one years, a time horizon that appears too short to encourage extensive investment in the land. An internal World Bank report suggests that, if there is a problem with poor land utilization, it seems to be concentrated on mid-sized estates with short, twenty-one-year leases. The optimal economic solution would be the conversion of leasehold to freehold land in conjunction with the introduction of a market in land. But this is politically unlikely, and, therefore, the lengthening of lease terms is recommended.

Second, the low investment and consequent low productivity on estate land may be associated with the insecurity of tenure of tenants rather than that of the leaseholder. Under tenancy relationships in Malawi, the burden of risk invariably falls on the tenant. In the event of a crop failure or a fall in the price of the crop, the tenant must bear the uncompensated costs incurred during production, including the value of food and inputs provided on credit.[42] This distribution of risk, although evidently one of the primary attractions of tenant labor over wage labor for estate managers, is not conducive to technological change. A more equitable sharecropping arrangement could thus be expected to result in productivity gains.

Third, the limits set by the allocated tobacco quotas, as well as capital shortages and transportation constraints, are also cited by estate owners as reasons for low productivity and low levels of land utilization. The detrimental effect of tobacco quotas on land utilization is evident in the fact that several estate owners admitted to registering land as estates simply to obtain an additional quota, with no intention of developing the estate (Mkandawire, Jaffee, and Bertoli 1990).

Fourth, there are several elements of the contractual relationship between tenants and landlords that help explain the low productivity. The frequently exploitative contractual relationships contribute to the high rate of turnover among tenants. This problem has been identified as serious by both owners and managers (Nankumba 1990).[43] The turnover rate among tenants was recently estimated at more than 30 percent a year (Mkandawire, Jaffee, and Bertoli 1990).

The price paid to tenants is set by the government, not the market, on the basis of recommendations received by the producers' organization, the Tobacco Association of Malawi (Mtawali 1989). As a result, the price paid to the tenant is low relative to the auction price, ranging over the past decade from a low of 19 percent of the auction price in 1988 to a high of 41 percent in 1983. The price that is set is a maximum rather than a minimum price; this would in theory tend to hold down the price paid to tenants, rather than support a reasonable price. Moreover, estates frequently pay less than this maximum price; and this is often done less directly, by undergrading tobacco purchased from tenants, delaying payment until after the auction, and paying in installments (Nankumba 1990).

The cost at which credit is made available to tenants by landlords appears to be extremely high. Data show that the interest paid on credit for fertilizer is as high as 140 percent and that on hoes 45 percent (Mtawali 1989). The interest on the maize ration is as high as 40 percent, significantly increasing the price of a subsistence diet. Debt repayment substantially reduces actual tenant incomes.[44] On the Chilanga estate, for example, as much as 90 percent of the value of the crop is designated for repayment of debt accrued that year, under contracts specifying that tenants will receive only 10 percent of the value of the crop in cash (Nankumba 1990).

Other elements of the contractual arrangement between landlord and tenant are also unfavorable to tenants and may partly explain their high turnover rate. Generally, holdings are contracted by estates to married men, who work the land with their families. Estate managers see this as a way of reducing the turnover rate, and as a cost-effective way of increasing the size of the labor force, as a married man presumably brings his wife and grown children to work his plot with him. Holdings among tenants are small, averaging 0.4 hectare (Mtawali 1989).[45] Under the contract, the tenant must cultivate a specific crop, predominantly burley tobacco, which the tenant then must sell solely to the estate. Only occasionally are tenants provided with an extra plot of land for the cultivation of crops for their subsistence needs (Nyanda 1989; and Vaughan and Chipande 1986).[46] Estate managers prefer to provide a food ration on credit, an arrangement that may leave some tenants at nutritional risk. The food ration, which varies by estate, typically consists of one tin of maize and 3 kilograms of beans per household per week, regardless of household size (Mtawali 1989). As a result, larger households especially are often short of food. And landlords do not always adhere to the food distribution arrangement. They frequently run short of maize and extend the ration distribution period from once every week to up to once every two weeks (Mtawali 1989). In addition, once the tobacco crop is planted after January, landlords are observed to pay less attention to agreed upon food rations since they know that tenants are now bound by debt and investment until harvest.[47]

In sum, the landlord-tenant relationship is characterized by ambiguity. The tenancy contracts are essentially unenforceable. Often negotiated orally rather than in writing, such contracts have generally been biased in favor of landlords. Most contracts lack clauses that would protect tenant interests, and unwritten contracts encourage breaches of contract. As a result, disputes frequently arise regarding such conditions as the cost of credit and the provision of food and of social services. More often than not, these disputes are resolved in favor of the more powerful estate managers (Nankumba 1990).

The low pay, high cost of credit, and other unfavorable aspects of the contractual relationship may thus contribute to lower productivity by driving the high turnover rate among tenants. The transactions costs of the associated job search pose a threat to the household's welfare, and the estate manager bears indirect costs because of the frequent lack of a reliable, experienced work force. In addition, these factors serve as disincentives for tenants to cultivate intensively or to invest in their tenancy holdings. A clearer definition of tenancy contracts and the removal of certain exploitative provisions can be expected not only to increase estate productivity, but also to improve the welfare of tenants.

In the estate sector, then, strategies need to focus on increasing the utilization of both land and labor, essential for generating higher levels of rural employment and income. In improving productivity, these strategies will enhance the capacity of the estate sector to absorb labor and pay higher wages. In so doing, they would provide the rural poor with much-needed access to a source of cash income as well as to land. In a two-sector agricultural economy, this is the only way that an estate sector can be justified—either in terms of promoting a strategy for national growth or in terms of promoting a strategy for the alleviation of poverty.

Conclusions

This chapter has examined the effect of land and related agricultural policies on economic development and poverty in Malawi. The focus has been on Malawi's decision to channel resources to the estate sector, a policy that is predicated on the notion that smallholder agriculture, based on customary land, was not an appropriate engine of growth. Rather, the smallholder subsector was viewed as a source of cheap labor and wage goods to support the estate sector in generating needed revenues and foreign exchange.

It remains debatable whether, and to what extent, the favoritism accorded estate leaseholders has limited Malawi's ability to attain the aggregate growth objective. Marketing arrangements and support services that favor the estate sector have encouraged dramatic expansion since independence, especially in tobacco. But the low levels of land utilization and the stagnating productivity of estates, coupled with the increasing number of estates unable to repay commercial bank loans, is strong evidence of the failures that have beset Malawi's growth strategy.

Less contentious is the point that the land policies have failed to be conducive to poverty alleviation, for several reasons. First, policy has contributed to the failure of the smallholder sector to raise household incomes and welfare. The combination of shrinking holding sizes (due to population growth and alienation of land to estates) and lack of technological innovation have contributed to widespread household food insecurity. This is especially so in the more densely populated regions of the country, where productivity growth in maize has lagged far behind population growth. In addition, export crop production by smallholders cultivating customary lands has not proven very profitable because of a combination of restrictions on crops produced, high levels of taxation, and shortages of credit, extension, and other public inputs into agriculture.

Second, the estate sector has failed to generate remunerative employment. Although the number of agricultural wage laborers has risen substantially during the past two decades, wages have not. This reflects a combination of factors, including the failure to raise estate productivity, explicit wage policies that have tended to maintain minimum wages at barely subsistence levels, and the taxation of smallholder production that reduces the smallholder reservation wage. In addition, government policies toward tenants working on estates can be characterized as benign neglect at best. Virtually nothing has been done to protect tenants' rights and to avoid exploitation of workers. Indirect efforts to improve tenant welfare, such as removing barriers to migration, have not been implemented.

Third, the mechanism for applying for and receiving leases encourages rent-seeking behavior and factor price distortions, both of which contribute to inefficiencies. Fourth, there is little evidence that surpluses generated from agriculture have been reinvested in agriculture in a way that addresses the large income differentials between agriculture and other sectors, such as manufacturing and government. The profits that accrued to ADMARC from taxing the smallholders were used for an array of activities, many of which involved transferring the surpluses out of rural areas altogether.

Throughout this chapter we have discussed the types of changes in land policy and other agricultural policy that will facilitate more rapid and equitable growth: raising leasehold land rents; enforcing land covenants; imposing a moratorium on land alienation; reducing the taxation of smallholder export crops; eliminating restrictions barring production of profitable export crops on customary land; promoting written and equitable contracts for tenants working on estates; investing in rural credit and related infrastructure to serve smallholders; and imposing greater penalties on estate holders who default on loans.

A common thread runs through these recommendations. Specifically, policy must address the inequities and inefficiencies that result from suppression of the costs of local factor inputs (land, labor, and capital) to estates. Providing an opportunity for factor use to reflect the factors' scarcity value will improve equity in the distribution of agricultural value added. It will remove the rents that accrue to the privileged estate owners who have access to low-priced land alienated from the customary sector, to low-priced labor because of the high level of taxation of smallholders, and to cheap credit because of the negative real interest rates that have prevailed. This, coupled with increased public investment in agriculture, will foster more efficient production methods and greater equity. Malawi's factor ratios at independence, with scarce capital and abundant land, may have justified a policy direction promoting expansion of large-scale estates at that time, but present circumstances warrant a different tack. The land scarcity in densely populated regions of Malawi today contributes to rural poverty and draws into question the appropriateness of current policies.

The policy implications of much of the material in this chapter have been clear, but lessening the differences between the estate and smallholder sectors presents a new set of challenges. Thus, while removing the distortions and institutional discrimination that have reinforced agriculture's duality, it is important to carefully consider appropriate changes in the structure of the smallholder and estate sectors. In particular, there is a need to end the constraints to smallholder production and marketing while increasing smallholder producer prices, thereby placing "competitive" pressure on the estate sector in order to raise rural incomes. This is the most politically feasible and realistic approach to tackling the distortions and poverty induced by the dualism in Malawi.

Notes

1. There has also been an increasing awareness of Malawi's low living standards. The illiteracy rate of 59 percent is higher than the average for Sub-Saharan Africa of 54 percent, ranking Malawi seventeenth among twenty-nine countries for which data are available. With an infant mortality rate of 163 per thousand in 1985, Malawi's performance is among the worst; the region's average is 120. Furthermore, by 1986, results of the 1980/81 National Sample Survey of Agriculture began to reveal the extremely weak nutritional status of Malawi's rural population. More than 55 percent of preschool-age children in the smallholder sector suffer from long-term, chronic malnutrition (stunting), a figure considerably higher than that for every other country in Africa for which data are available.

2. A third category, public land, is addressed later in the chapter.

3. Use of village land has traditionally been contingent on residence in the village, a verbal agreement with the headperson regarding terms of use, the payment of an annual tax by the smallholder to the headperson, and the presentation of an annual gift by the smallholder to the headman. The presence of witnesses at these events ensures that the implicit contract is binding. Such rights, once allocated, are lost only if the landholding is abandoned or if the farmer in question is expelled from the village. This occurs only if the smallholder is accused of a serious offense, such as witchery, or treachery toward the village chief.

4. Use rights, furthermore, allow the cutting of trees for firewood that were not planted privately and the grazing of livestock on the village commons and on agricultural land in the off-season.

5. Use rights are transferred between generations in accordance with the inheritance rules of the ethnic group in question. In Malawi the majority of the population, residing in the more densely populated southern and central parts of the country, follow matrilineal rules of inheritance. Land is passed on to a group of consanguine sisters (a sorority), and their husbands move to live on the wives' land (uxorilocal residence). Some northern ethnic groups follow a patrilineal pattern. For more details, see Riddell (1985).

6. For a more detailed discussion of how dualism was introduced during the colonial period, see Sahn and Arulpragasam (1991).

7. *Customary land*, cultivated by smallholders, was defined by the Act as all land under customary law (not including public land) and corresponded to the African Trust Land classification of the preindependence era. *Public land* was defined as all land occupied, used, or acquired by the government and any other land that is not customary or private land. It corresponds to what was British Crown land prior to independence. *Private land* is defined as all land that is owned, held, or occupied under a freehold title, a leasehold title, or a certificate of claim. In other words it incorporates the estate sector.

8. A number of factors may limit the acquisition of leases by smallholders. Stipulations on land utilization inherent in the granting of leases would compromise a risk-averse farmer's ability to cultivate an adequate quantity of maize for subsistence. These same stipulations may require more capital or credit than the farmer has access to. Furthermore, the farmer may simply be unaware of his rights to leasehold land or of the process required to procure a lease. In addition, the nature of tribal relationships would make it difficult for a farmer to get the chief's approval (needed for the conversion of customary to leasehold land), and the farmer may be unable to afford the gifts needed to facilitate such a transaction.

9. The Registered Land Act of 1965 and Customary Land Act of 1967 became operational when the first land registry was opened in 1972 to delineate land titles within the area of over one million acres of customary land covered by the Lilongwe Land Development Programme. Registration has proceeded slowly, however, and appears to have stalled. By 1981 only a little more than a quarter of the designated area had been registered. Furthermore, although application of the acts was extended to the capital city area, registration has not proceeded beyond the Lilongwe district.

10. Other strategies to cope with the land shortage are also apparent. Common lands are often encroached upon without the consent of the village chief. According to an internal World Bank report, encroachment of smallholders onto leased land is also commonplace and constitutes a continuing source of dispute.

11. To the extent that smallholders "cheat" by illegally producing restricted crops, this monopoly is weakened. There are some indications that such illegal production does in fact occur (Duncan 1990).

12. There are also restrictions on the area of smallholder land on which these varieties of tobacco can be cultivated. In 1990-91 a pilot program was scheduled to begin in eight rural development projects to eliminate the prohibition of smallholder production of burley. But the importance of this is limited; the permission to plant burley applies only to smallholders with less than two hectares, and the permitted area of burley cultivation is restricted to 20 percent of the farmer's holding.

13. As a result, by 1980 more than 50 percent of commercial bank advances were to estates, and mainly for the cultivation of tobacco (Mkandawire and Phiri 1987). The estates were also disproportionately favored to the extent that this credit was subsidized (as revealed by the negative real rates of interest in Malawi).

14. A revolving credit fund administered through the National Rural Development Programme (NRDP) covered much of the country by 1984, but is reported to favor better-off farmers.

15. In the 1970s many of the new estates were larger and belonged to corporate entities, businessmen, and civil servants. The 1980s, though, were characterized by the registration of much smaller estates, and in greater numbers. There are new indications that many of these small estates of less than 30 hectares, registered in the 1980s, belong to progressive smallholders (Mkandawire, Jaffee, and Bertoli 1990). These estates differ from most of those registered in the first decade after independence in that they generally lack salaried managers, a permanent work force, or even a concentration in cash crops.

16. Moreover, with respect to policy prescription, the question is moot. In the current political economy and policy environment in Malawi, the prospect of wholesale land reform and the elimination of the estate sector is improbable at best.

17. In fact, the amount of land actually planted by smallholders has recently increased, even if only slightly. It reportedly rose from 1.29 million hectares in 1964-65 (Pryor 1988) to 1.58 million in 1982-83 and to 1.77 million hectares in 1986-87 (Malawi Ministry of Agriculture data). Much of this and other nonrecorded land newly brought into cultivation likely is on the many hilly slopes.

18. The data on the declining size of landholdings have some important regional dimensions. Population densities vary widely, reflecting partly the fertility and arability of the land. The South, with 50 percent of the national population, has a population density of 125 per square kilometer. Population density in the central region, with 39 percent of the total population, is 83 people per square kilometer. The North, with the least fertile land and 11 percent of the population, has 11 people per square kilometer. Mzuzu Agricultural Development District, where most smallholders reside, registers only 26.5 percent of households holding less than 0.15 hectare per capita. The fact that the comparable figure for Karonga is 40 percent illustrates that smallholdings are a function not only of population density, but also of the quantity of arable land, land quality, and the proximity of a market to sell the surplus.

19. The average holding size for households with less than one hectare is 0.55 hectare. The average household has 4.2 members. It is assumed here that 100 percent of the holding is cultivated with local maize. These data and average yield data are from the 1984/85 Annual Survey of Agriculture and do not take into account variations in land quality. Similarly, the figures do not address whether, if the households planted their landholding in hybrid or composite maize, they would be likely to fulfill their food energy needs, even on smaller holdings. Most smallholders, however, grow local maize to meet their subsistence needs because of considerations of taste, fertilizer requirements, and storage. Furthermore, it is noteworthy that this stylized fact about the inadequacy of own production potential is supported by a study completed by the Liwonde Agricultural Development District in 1982, which reveals that up to 63 percent of households with less than 0.5 hectare could not provide for their own basic food requirements (Mtawali 1989).

20. The subsidy on smallholder fertilizer mitigates the degree of taxation. Because of the low levels of uptake, however, the fertilizer subsidy would not contribute to a great divergence between effective and nominal rates of protection.

21. The recent move liberalizing the production and sale of burley among smallholders, if sustained, should go a long way toward raising the nominal protection coefficient of tobacco for smallholders.

22. Some reduction in the level of implicit taxation has been noted since the initiation of the Malawian structural adjustment program, but this can be attributed largely to the

falling world prices of Malawian exports and to increased transportation costs (Sahn, Arulpragasam, and Merid 1990).

23. Unlike estates that purchase their fertilizer through Optichem, a commercial enterprise that sells fertilizer at market prices, smallholders rely on ADMARC, which sells fertilizer at a subsidized price. The Smallholder Farmer's Fertilizer Revolving Fund has provided fertilizer at a subsidy rate that has ranged between 20 and 30 percent during the past few years. Demand is constrained by a combination of the farmer's inability to procure credit and the quantity rationing at the subsidized price.

24. There are two major classes of *ganyu* labor. Laborers on farms are called *ganyu-olima* (farm *ganyu*) and those involved in other types of labor are called *ganyu-kumanga*. This work, mainly in construction and transportation, is relatively limited in rural areas.

25. This calculation was based on the assumption of a daily subsistence requirement of 2,200 calories and a conversion factor of 3,570 calories per kilogram of maize. The smallholder producer price for sun- and air-cured tobacco is an average of the producer price of the five highest grades of this variety as reported in Malawi (1989).

26. Arguments are frequently raised that restriction of smallholder production is required to control the reliability and quality of exported tobacco and to exercise Malawi's market power in dictating international price. But there is no reason that tobacco grown by smallholders could not pass through quality control, as other crops do in other countries. Another option is for smallholders to organize around a "nucleus" estate that could control quality. Examples include rubber and palm plantations in Guinea and tobacco in Sri Lanka. Quantity could be controlled through the auctioning of licenses. The rents now received by estate producers would instead accrue to the Treasury as revenue from the sale of licenses.

27. The smallholder domestic resource costs for burley and flue-cured tobacco in 1986 have been calculated at 0.55 and 0.49, and those for the estate sector at 0.61 and 0.53 (Lele and Agarwal 1990).

28. Bates (1981, cited in Feder and Noronha 1987: 33) points to cases in a number of countries in which the urban elite and large farmers have utilized their knowledge of the law to acquire additional land. Similarly, studies in Kenya show that civil servants and other influential individuals tend to have gained land at the expense of poorer, less influential and less knowledgeable individuals. Analogous observations have been made in Botswana, Nigeria, and Senegal (see Feder and Noronha 1987 for an extensive review).

29. Some of these failures may well be due to imperfect policy implementation. For example, the low level of credit growth has been attributed to the fact that the process of titling allows the registration of land to households and families rather than just to individuals, posing a collateral problem to creditors.

30. These figures should be interpreted with caution, however; even among the "permanent" wage earners on estates, employment is highly seasonal, peaking in January and February precisely when the demand for maize cultivation is at its highest.

31. Low wage rates were achieved through two means. The first is through low (barely subsistence) minimum wage policies. The second is through the taxation of smallholder crops, which lowered the returns to farming customary lands and, consequently, the opportunity costs of being a wage laborer or tenant. This cheap labor, of course, has fueled the expansion of leaseholds and contributed to the growth in employment on estates.

32. It should be noted that the minimum wage increased markedly in 1989. It is unclear whether average agricultural earnings rose in parallel with this jump.

33. As many as 75 percent of adult male permanent workers were paid less than the minimum wage on estates under 15 hectares, according to the same study. Children were

almost universally paid below the minimum wage. The large number of refugees from Mozambique is hypothesized to be exerting a downward influence on rural wages.

34. These calculations assume that all household calories are from maize, and that 70 percent of the budget is allocated to food; and they assume a minimum requirement of 2,200 calories per day per person and a standard content factor of 3,570 calories per kilogram of maize. In other words, the calculations assume a requirement of 92 kilograms of maize to satisfy the subsistence requirements for a family of five. These calculations use the official consumer price for maize. Actual retail prices for maize are generally higher even in rural areas; thus, at these prices more days of work would be required to meet minimum subsistence requirements.

35. Caution should be taken in interpreting these returns, however, since there are a number of costs that should be subtracted in these calculations that often are not. For example, the Nankumba study subtracts only production expenses for which tenants received advances from landlords. It does not take into account rental value, if any, on housing. Furthermore, it is unlikely, for example, that tenants' migration costs are subtracted in calculating their net returns. It is also likely that the value of the food ration provided and of the implicit interest rate for such food are not taken into account.

36. The sharp increase in the minimum wage in 1989, however, permits an annual income of Mk635 for a laborer who works every day of the year.

37. In the past it was estimated that 86 to 92 percent of estate land lay idle; the recent estate survey found that close to 70 percent of estate lands were uncultivated. This percentage was found to vary by estate size; much land on larger estates remains uncultivated, but cropping intensities on estates of less than 30 hectares approached 50 percent. Cropping intensities also differ by region, varying, for example from 20.6 percent in Rumphi to 42 percent in Lilongwe.

38. There may also be technical reasons for the underutilization of estate lands. For example, the optimal fallow period for tobacco ranges from two to three years. And woodlots may occupy a significant portion of land, especially where critical for the drying of tobacco.

39. The most recent estate survey found absentee ownership of estates less pervasive than claimed in the past. This is probably due in part to the increase in the number of leases extended to "graduated smallholders" during the past decade. Approximately 60 percent of sampled estates are now found to be managed by a resident owner (Mkandawire, Jaffee, and Bertoli 1990).

40. A recent internal World Bank report suggests that there is little evidence of "land hunger" in the Kusunga, Mchinj, and Salina tobacco-growing areas. This contrasts with densely populated areas of the South, such as Blantyre and Chirdzulu, where population densities are 292 and 275 persons per square kilometer. Low utilization of land on some estates may thus simply reflect the lower ratios of labor to land in those districts.

41. To the extent that this assertion is correct, it is in conflict with the observations from land-scarce Asia that labor inputs are inversely proportional to holding size. One possible reason for this divergence is that there are seasonal labor shortages likely during transplanting and harvesting which may induce smallholders to neglect their own holdings in search of high seasonal wages that are offered during the period when stocks of maize have been depleted.

42. This sometimes leads to tenants remaining on the estate after the crop season to perform casual labor as a method of repayment.

43. Of the 90 tenants interviewed on tobacco estates in 1989, for example, only 46 had been there for two or more years. Such turnover is a reflection of tenant discontentment and welfare.

44. These charges are subtracted from the value of the final tobacco sale, which obfuscates a determination of the extent to which low sales revenue is actually due to low prices on output rather than high credit costs of inputs.

45. Holdings of tenants on nontobacco estates are apparently larger. An internal World Bank report states that the average amount of land under cultivation by tenants was 0.32 hectare on tobacco estates, 0.68 hectare on tea estates, and 1.54 hectares on sugar estates.

46. Estate managers are aware that allowing the cultivation of subsistence crops, besides reducing the amount of land that could be used to produce highly remunerative export crops, diverts tenant labor and other inputs, such as fertilizer, from producing tobacco.

47. These factors certainly play an important role in explaining the relatively high rate of malnutrition on estates. A recent study on nutritional status in the estate sector found the degree of malnutrition to be higher on estates than among smallholders or wage laborers (Mtawali 1989).

Efficiency and Equity in Social Spending: How and Why Governments Misbehave

14 Nancy Birdsall
Estelle James

An important issue in development economics concerns the appropriate degree of reliance on the private sector for the provision of health, education, and other social services, and the use of private finance within the public sector. Proponents of privatization and user charges claim that these will conserve scarce public funds and promote efficiency in the sense of cost-effectiveness and responsiveness to consumer preferences (Psacharopoulos, Tan, and Jimenez 1986; Akin, Birdsall, and de Ferranti 1987; and Jimenez 1987). Opponents retort that privatization and user charges, because of their reliance on ability to pay as a rationing criterion, will have negative distributional effects that are likely to outweigh any efficiency gains (see, for example, Gertler, Locay, and Sanderson 1987, and Gertler and van der Gaag 1990 on user charges for health care in Peru and Côte d'Ivoire). Most of the literature that argues against privatization and user charges implicitly accepts the existence of a tradeoff between efficiency and equity in the allocation of resources for social programs.

In this chapter we argue that in many settings in the developing world this presumption of a tradeoff between efficiency and equity is incorrect. We argue that in many countries greater equity in social spending would also be more efficient (in reducing mortality, for example, or in maximizing social returns to spending on education). Put another way, in these countries there is an identifiable group of potential reallocations that would simultaneously improve efficiency and distribution.[1]

This chapter sets forth the theoretical reasons for predicting that the state will often finance a bundle of social services that is both inefficient and inequitable—inequitable because it will benefit the upper- and middle-income classes disproportionately more than the lower-income groups. It presents a variety of empirical examples, from both industrial and developing countries. And it points out some of the conceptual problems in measuring the distributional effects of social services, problems that in most cases have led us to overestimate the degree to which government spending redistributes to the poor.

The conclusion summarizes the crux of the political economy problem. Because we start with a model in which the degree of efficiency and the degree of redistribution are endogenous, the real difficulty is in determining how we break into the chain of causality and bring about a new equilibrium, more efficient and more redistributive, when—as is made clear by the fact that it has not happened—this was apparently not in the interest of the main actors.

Theory

Welfare theory

Classical welfare theory gives us a *normative* view of what government *should* do, focusing on efficiency rather than distributional considerations. The economic role of government is to correct for market failure by funding public goods, by subsidizing (or taxing) goods that generate positive (or negative) externalities, and by compensating for capital market or insurance market failure—and otherwise simply to set the framework within which private enterprise will function. When efforts of government to correct for market failure in themselves introduce some efficiency losses—because of transactions costs or the distortionary effects of taxes—a second-best world results in which the benefits of intervention must be weighed against the costs. But much of classical welfare theory nevertheless can be depicted as a pursuit of the first best.

With respect to distribution, the "maximum" point of social welfare is acknowledged by most economists to depend on equity as well as on efficiency. But how and how much to take this into account is problematic.[2] For example, opinions vary widely on whether a *social welfare function* exists, what an *equitable* distribution might be, and whether it is possible to aggregate diverse preferences and get a consensus on this matter. Opinions similarly vary on how much the government should intervene to alter the market distribution (see Rawls 1971 and Nozick 1974 for strongly contrasting views). The strongest advocates of redistribution argue that it is justified on efficiency as well as on equity grounds— if people care about the utility of others, or if there is a set of *merit goods* (health, education) about which society does not trust consumers to make the right consumption decisions (Meade 1964; Musgrave 1959; and Hochman and Rodgers 1969). Skeptics point to the lack of consensus on the desired distribution and to the disincentive effects of redistribution. Bourguignon (1991), for example, sets out a model in which the pursuit of equity—through education and health programs that build human capital, or through transfer programs, such as food subsidies for the poor—requires that governments generate tax revenues, which reduce overall efficiency. Despite the ambivalence about the redistributive role of government, however, most economists agree that, if there is to be any redistribution, it should be from the rich to the poor and not vice versa—the "Robin Hood" function of government (Birdsall 1992).

In this chapter we examine the tendency of governments not to play Robin Hood, even where there seems to be no tradeoff—where playing Robin Hood would increase efficiency. We try to explain the causes of this tendency and what could (should) be done to change it. We use the terms *equity* and *perverse redistribution* as shorthand for *redistribution to the poor* and *redistribution to the rich* (while recognizing that these are value-laden terms reflecting value judgments that go beyond the standard use of terms in welfare theory).

Public choice theory

A more recent and less benevolent view of government activities stems from public choice theory, which gives us a *positive* model of what the government *will* do, under the presumption that the chief agents act to maximize individual utility rather than social welfare. According to this theory, politicians do not seek to maximize efficiency but rather to maximize their own chances of staying in power, bureaucrats seek to maximize their budgets, and individuals use governments to augment their real income through the creation of protected market positions and the direct provision of services and transfers.[3]

Politicians and political parties have some discretionary power because of barriers to entry and because they are in a position to both shape and respond to peoples' tastes. At the same time threats from actual or potential competitors limit the scope of their monopoly power. Thus, natural selection operates in political life as well as in economic or biological life. Politicians who survive to make policy are those who correctly assess the tradeoffs for different groups of voters with respect to the entire spectrum of issues and give influential groups what they want on the issues most important to them. A similar process often occurs under nondemocratic regimes because of threats to the government of overthrow by potential rivals (a contestable markets view of politics). But for such governments there are greater discretionary monopoly powers; a dictator may choose to be either a populist or an elitist dictator, so the outcome is more difficult to predict.

Public policies designed to maximize private interests will not necessarily be inefficient. Indeed, politically influential groups would have a potentially larger pie to capture if the Pareto frontier were reached; compensatory mechanisms could then make everyone better-off. To take an extreme example, in an economy with perfect efficiency, poll taxes could be imposed on some (less influential) groups and transferred to others.

The allocation of resources resulting from public choice politics often is inefficient, however, for several reasons.

Veil of ignorance. In a context of imperfect information, people may not know the degree and the direction of the redistribution that is occurring. If well-defined groups know they are losers, they are more likely to mobilize and foment opposition to existing policies; therefore, the gainers benefit from perpetuating a *veil of ignorance.* Suppose that the most efficient form of transfer is also the most obvious (for example, transfers in cash are more transparent than those in kind). In that case efficiency imposes costs on the gainers by reducing the amount that they potentially will be able to extract; they are therefore likely to choose inefficient transfer mechanisms. Most commonly, some private goods may be publicly provided and oversupplied because they benefit a politically influential group of people in a nonobvious way (see Becker 1983 and Borcherding 1985).

This point is illustrated in figure 14.1, which assumes a starting point such as A or A'. A politically strong group wishes to use government to increase its utility to point B on the Pareto frontier, which could be achieved by a direct transfer of endowments (for example, land redistribution or a reduction in its tax share). This transfer would be efficient, but it would also be transparent; because the losers would object strongly, B is not politically feasible. Suppose that, for this reason, B' is the highest efficient point that the strong can reach. If the gain of the strong group can be camouflaged, however—for example, by their securing privileged, subsidized access to superior universities and hospitals—the opposition is muted. Thus, point C, which is inefficient, is politically attainable. Point C is worse for both groups than B, but B is not politically feasible. C is much worse for the weak group than A' or B', but it is better for the strong—who therefore use their influence to convince the public sector to provide these private goods.

Fiscal illusion. Imperfect information and uncertainty also surround the relation between the tax structure and the bundle of public services provided. Although taxes and services may be interdependent components of a long-run political equilibrium (for example, if a group's benefits increase, its tax burden may also increase), they may appear to be independent of each other in the short run—a kind of *fiscal illusion.* Thus, some public or quasi-public goods may be undersupplied because their benefits accrue to dispersed, less influential individuals and it is not clear (to the influential losers) that the tax share of the gainers can be adjusted upward commensurately with their benefits. Similarly, some goods may be oversupplied because their chief beneficiaries are politically powerful, and these groups expect to avoid much of the tax burden (which was implicit in the above example).[4]

Starting again at point A in figure 14.1, suppose that a public program (for example, improved primary schools) is considered that disproportionately benefits weak groups but generates some externalities for the strong. If financed on the basis of preexisting tax shares, this program would put society at point D. If the strong were to bear a slightly smaller share of the tax burden, society would be at point A', which leaves the strong as well-off as they were at A. Point A' is not quite as good for the weak as D, but it is much better than A; thus, the program is clearly Pareto-improving. But the strong doubt that it will be politically feasible to raise the tax share of the weak, fear that society will end up instead at D (which makes them worse-off), and therefore suc-

Figure 14.1 Inefficient public choices

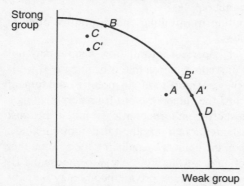

Note: Starting point is *A* or *A'. B* is politically infeasible for the strong group. *D* is politically infeasible for the weak group. *B'* is politically feasible, but the strong prefer *C* or *C'*, which are therefore chosen.

cessfully object to this program. There are compensation mechanisms (in the form of taxes), but influential groups underestimate their existence, regard taxes as independent of benefits, and thus impede Pareto-optimal government actions. The greater this fiscal illusion, the greater is the tendency toward inefficient choices.

High costs of public sector provision. The real costs of publicly produced private goods may be higher than necessary because governments impose bureaucratic rules and red tape (in part as a substitute for the profit motive) and often lack competitive pressures for internal efficiency (perhaps because politicians gain from monopolistic provision). Heads of bureaucratic agencies who wish to maximize their prestige and perks, and have more information than the politicians and citizens they supposedly serve, are often able to argue successfully for budgets larger than needed for least-cost production. In addition, distortionary tax financing also raises the nonprogram costs of publicly produced private goods (Niskanen 1971; Romer and Rosenthal 1978; and Borcherding, Pommerehne, and Schneider 1982).

Program costs may be higher than necessary even when politicians and bureaucrats wish to choose an efficient product and factor mix. The nonprice rationing of publicly funded goods that is often adopted for distributional reasons, and the civil service procedures governing wages, hiring, and firing procedures, which substitute for managerial discretion in the public sector, mean that prices do not serve as a measure of the real costs and benefits of a program, as they do in the private market. So politicians and bureaucrats lack the information needed to minimize costs. In figure 14.1, point C falls to C' as public education and health care costs rise and tax-induced distortions increase.

Rent seeking. The diversion of entrepreneurial energies toward the extraction of a surplus from public agencies and away from productivity-enhancing market activities leads to the misallocation of both public and private resources. This rent seeking thus impedes growth and efficiency in both the public and the private sectors (Krueger 1974; and Buchanan, Tollison, and Tullock 1980).

The resulting distribution of real income is likely to depend on political power as well as on market power. Political power will, of course, vary across societies and over time depending on the size of different producer and consumer groups, the coalitions among them, and the long-run "rules of the game" that have been set up (for example, through constitutions) for allocating voting rights. Because the distribution of voting rights is ordinarily more equal than the distribution of income, political decisionmaking might be expected to be relatively egalitarian.[5] But low-income people often do not vote, and economic power can buy political power through campaign contributions and purchases of media that shape other people's votes. Because producer groups are likely to be more concentrated and better organized than consumer groups, because upper- and middle-income groups are generally more articulate and politically active than poorer groups, and because lines of communication and mobility are often strong between government agencies, their bureaucratic chiefs, and the private industries or professions they supposedly regulate, public choice theory predicts that producer and upper-income groups will benefit disproportionately from government policies (see Stigler 1970 and 1971; Peltzman 1976 and 1980; and Fiorina and Noll 1978).

Public choice in developing countries

How would we expect these divergent forces to sort themselves out in the developing country context? The gulf between the rich and the poor, and the proportion of poor people, are much greater there, so under "one man, one vote" we would expect to find the poor gaining from politically induced redistributions. Indeed, there are examples of countries (Malaysia) in which economically disadvantaged groups are using their political advantage to increase their share of the national income. But differences in education, and thus in organizational and communication skills, are also much greater in developing countries, and democratic institutions are often primitive, limiting the power of the poor. On balance, we would expect these conditions to dominate in most developing countries.

This is not to say that there will be no redistribution to the poorer classes. Even when the rich are in control, we would expect to find some redistribution to the poor on efficiency grounds because it makes everyone better-off; in these circumstances it would be a redistribution of income but not a redistribution of utility. For example, people give to beggars and use the government as an efficient mechanism for giving to disadvantaged groups, in part because extremes of poverty and socioeconomic immobility raise fears of crime or revolution that will ultimately hurt the rich. Historically in industrial countries the provision of certain merit goods to the poor (basic education, and unemployment or medical insurance) has been viewed as an effective way of combating these possibilities.

In addition, in developing countries, where the poor vastly outnumber the rich, the desire to constrain the popularity of opposition groups encourages some distribution to lower-income groups on grounds of expediency. Groups with little power must be appeased by giving them "just enough" to prevent opposition parties from gaining strong support (a contestable market view of political equilibrium). But "just enough" may not be very much. The poor may be given low-cost services (for example, high-quantity, low-quality primary school systems), or limited access to high-cost services that mainly benefit the rich (for example, selective, high-cost universities). In short, in many situations, perverse distributional criteria—rather than efficiency or equity criteria—determine the allocation of government funds in developing countries: these criteria imply large benefits to powerful upper-income groups, combined with small redistributions to the poor.[6]

Public choice and social services

The social services sector is an arena in which these tensions are particularly salient, as it involves a variety of quasi-public goods with different mixes of public and private benefits and different beneficiaries. The frequent designation of social services as *externality-generating goods* or merit goods for the poor provides justification for government intervention along classic welfare theory lines. Yet, once this intervention begins, ostensibly to correct for market imperfections and benefit poor consumers, more influential consumer and producer groups are often able to divert resources to the costly overprovision of "private" services (services that are publicly financed but that provide high private returns) that benefit predominantly the rich (although in a somewhat disguised way, as public choice theory would predict). Although the rhetoric stresses the importance of avoiding price rationing in order to guarantee access for the poor, alternative rationing mechanisms emerge that may be equally income-biased.

Where this is the case, the current starting point is neither equitable nor efficient, as is usually assumed. Turning the provision of private social services over to the private sector (and instituting user charges for private services provided by the public sector) would allow governments to concentrate on financing social services that have a larger public component, simultaneously improving efficiency and combating poverty.

Empirical examples

In this section we cite numerous examples from developed and developing countries that make it clear that allocations within the social services sector often disregard the benevolent prescriptions of welfare theory and instead fulfill the more pessimistic predictions of public choice theory. In these examples the public sector provides services for which there is no strong efficiency rationale and from which upper-income groups disproportionately benefit. (The related question of whether the upper-income groups pay commensurately higher taxes is discussed in the next section.) These examples are not universal, but they are common. We also suggest a set of reallocations, involving a shift of financing to private sources, that would increase efficiency and equity at the same time. Finally, we consider potential pitfalls of these privatization policies and ways of guarding against the pitfalls.

The efficiency and equity criteria discussed in the previous section and used in this section deal mainly with the question of who *finances* quasi-public services. Another set of efficiency considerations deals with the question of who *produces* these services and how much private choice and public controls are involved. (For the distinction and connections between these issues, see Birdsall 1992 and James 1991.) Throughout this chapter we focus on the benefits of shifting some of the financing of quasi-public services to the private sector, irrespective of whether the private or the public sector manages and provides the service. We also abstract from the possible links between financing and provision that can arise in the real world for institutional or political economy reasons (for example, the amount raised through user charges may be greater if the provider retains control over the resources, and public regulations may accompany public subsidies).

Education

Education is a prime example of a quasi-public good, one that yields a combination of private and external (social) benefits. The mix of public and private benefits varies across educational products. External benefits, such as contributions to economic growth, improvements in citizenship, and increases in the cognitive skills and health of future generations, are frequently mentioned; these external benefits are inherently difficult to observe and measure. A stronger case can be made for their presence at the primary and secondary levels, where basic literacy and numeracy skills are developed and values are formed, than at the undergraduate tertiary level. Measures of the social rate of return (based on earnings, and therefore excluding externalities) are generally also higher at the primary and secondary levels (mainly because spending per beneficiary is so much lower at those levels). The average rate of return to education in developing countries has been estimated to be 24 percent at the primary level, 15 percent at the secondary level, and 13 percent at the higher levels (Psacharopoulos, Tan, and Jimenez 1986). The absence of controls for student ability and school quality biases these rates upward (Behrman and Birdsall 1983 and 1987), but the omission of external benefits has the opposite effect. On balance, there is no reason to believe that the inclusion of all these factors would substantially change the ranking of returns to different levels of education; in fact, if externalities are concentrated at the primary and secondary levels, their relative advantage might grow. There is therefore a compelling efficiency rationale for greater spending at these levels.

Yet many countries spend a disproportionate share of their total education budgets at the tertiary level, the level that heavily benefits upper-income groups. Thus, a large expenditure at the tertiary level is concentrated on a small number of advantaged students, in contrast to the smaller expenditure on primary education, which benefits large numbers of the poor (Selowsky 1979; and Meerman 1979).

Public universities typically do not have price barriers to entry; even room and board are often subsidized. But they do impose the cost of forgone earnings, as well as academic barriers to entry. Both of these are more likely to be surmounted by high-income families whose children complete primary school, attend a high-quality secondary school, benefit from after-school tutoring, and are therefore able to pass the entrance examination to public universities (Armitage and Sabot 1990; and James and Benjamin 1987a).

For example, Brazil spends only 9 percent of its public education budget (including spending at the federal, state, and local levels) on secondary education, but 23 percent on higher education (in 1987, US$144 per student at the secondary level and almost US$5,000 per student at higher levels—IPEA/IPLAN 1988). Yet 95 percent of all students at public universities come from middle- and high-income families, according to an internal World Bank report. In Mexico a person from a high-income family is ten to twenty times more likely to attend a public university than one from a low-income family (Winkler 1990). The top income quintile receives more than 50 percent of higher education subsidies and the bottom quintile less than 10 percent in Chile, Costa Rica, the Dominican Republic, and Uruguay (Winkler 1990; and Petrei 1987). In India 19 percent of the total public education budget is spent on colleges and universities, and the majority of rural children do not even finish primary school (Tan 1992). In

Africa 22 percent of the public education budget is spent on universities, which are attended by only 2 percent of the relevant age group (see Psacharopoulos, Tan, and Jimenez 1986; and Winkler 1990). Based on enrollments and cost data for ten African countries, Mingat and Tan (1985) estimate that eliminating stipends for the living expenses of university students would permit a 20 percent increase in primary school enrollments, even if operating costs of universities continue to be covered out of public funds.

One of the most detailed studies of subsidies for education, conducted in Colombia, showed that 60 percent of all higher education subsidies were received by the top income quintile, and only 6 percent went to the bottom two quintiles; these proportions were exactly reversed at the primary level. Overall, the education subsidy per household was approximately the same for all income groups. But the rich received most of their subsidies through attending university, and the poor received their subsidies at the primary level (Selowsky 1979). Similarly, in Malaysia 50 percent of postsecondary subsidies were received by the top quintile and 10 percent by the bottom two quintiles, in a mirror image of the distribution pattern at the primary level (Meerman 1979).

Even within higher education the allocation of resources is more consistent with the predictions under public choice theory based on pressure groups than with the efficiency or equity prescriptions of welfare theory. Within higher education there is an efficiency rationale for public funding of research and graduate training, whether at public or private institutions. Although precise measures do not exist, these activities probably yield externalities for society as a whole that will not be funded privately (Birdsall 1990). In addition, capital market failure may justify public funding for expensive scientific equipment and financial aid for low-income students. But at the undergraduate level, private institutions and public institutions that receive private funding should be able to provide instruction in the less-expensive labor-intensive fields (liberal arts, law, management), especially to middle- and upper-class students, where private benefits predominate and tuition can cover costs.

Yet, in contrast to this prescription based on efficiency, most public funds for higher education are spent on undergraduate instruction at public colleges and universities, and, as just noted, most of the students come from middle- and upper-income families. Expenditures on research and graduate training in most developing countries are minuscule, and only a few countries have student grants and loans targeted specifically toward the poor.[7] The explanation by now is familiar: while the middle class clamors effectively for access to higher education for their children, the beneficiaries of research are widely dispersed, and economically disadvantaged students are also likely to be politically disadvantaged.

A more efficient solution would delegate responsibility for undergraduate instruction to the fee-charging private sector, and impose fees at the small group of public institutions. Public funds could then be reallocated toward the primary and secondary levels, or toward research, scientific equipment, and financial aid for needy students at the higher level. Moreover, these funds could be awarded, on a competitive basis, to both public and private institutions. Indeed, elements of this pattern are found in such countries as Japan and the Republic of Korea, which have achieved high rates of educational attainment at low cost to the public treasury. In Korea only 9 percent of the public education budget is spent at the higher level, but because this public spending is heavily supplemented by private resources from those who receive the private benefits, Korea's aggregate enrollment ratio is one of the highest in the world (see Tan 1992; and James and Benjamin 1987b).

Privatization in higher education: Does it make matters worse?

A shift toward privatized social services might at first seem to threaten the achievement of efficiency and equity goals, rather than to advance these goals. We use higher education to illustrate the nature of these a priori arguments, to present some preliminary evidence for why they are not borne out in fact, and to suggest some further research that is needed on this issue.

The most obvious threat to equity under private provision is that it will lead to enrollments heavily biased toward upper-income groups. It is true that in countries in which private education is the elite, preferred sector (for example, Catholic universities in Ecuador, Mexico, and Peru), private institutions are more income-biased than public institutions (Levy 1986; and Winkler 1990). Typically, these countries rely heavily on public finance of higher education and have opted for quantity over quality in their public systems. As we showed above, they tend to end up with an income-biased public sector; but the bias is much greater in the high-quality private institutions, from which the poor are excluded by both price and academic barriers. In these countries a moderate number of poor students in the public system receive small subsidies, and the rich students in the private system pay their own way.

By contrast, other countries limit government spending in higher education by greatly restricting public sector capacity; in these countries a large privately financed sector often develops to accommodate the excess demand (Japan, Korea, and the Philippines). High academic barriers then keep the poor out of public institutions, and price barriers restrict their access to private institutions. So, on balance, the two sectors are roughly equivalent in degree of income bias.[8] In these countries, a small number of poor students in the public system receive large subsidies, but most students, both rich and poor, are in the private system, where they pay their own way.

From the viewpoint of equity the question is which of these two patterns provides more access and more redistribution to the poor. Their comparative redistributive effects depend largely on the progressivity of the tax structure and the relative share of the poor in the public systems, and we do not yet have a general answer to that question. (But see the discussion of taxes in the following section). But preliminary evidence suggests that the second pattern—restricted public sector capacity and a large private sector—is superior with respect to access, providing much higher overall enrollment ratios and thus higher rates of participation by lower-income groups—surely an important index of equity.

Moreover, the poor have greater access to both the elite and the mass parts of the higher education system, and thus to jobs associated with both elite and mass higher education training, enhancing their chances for intergenerational mobility. In return, they pay a larger share of total higher education costs, largely through fees.

Countries choosing this route can afford the greater expansion in part because costs per student tend to be lower in private than in public sectors, and thus more students can be accommodated for any given share of gross national product (GNP). Even more important, the taxes these countries save on their small public higher education systems can be reallocated to increase the quantity and quality of their primary and secondary schools, thus increasing the potential clientele for tertiary education; this is probably the most effective way to expand the enrollment of low-income groups in higher education.[9] Finally, the problem of affordability for the poorest could be mitigated by using some of the savings in public funds to subsidize grants and loans for disadvantaged students at private universities.

The political feasibility of this first-best solution is, of course, a critical question that requires further investigation, and it probably varies from country to country. But empirical evidence indicates that relying primarily on public finance in higher education is not even second or third best from the viewpoint of equity.

Privatization also raises concerns about efficiency because private institutions will produce a product mix with more private benefits and fewer externalities. For example, the higher cost of public universities is due in part to the fact that they engage in more research, graduate training, and capital-intensive scientific education, for which the social benefits exceed the private.[10]

Does this matter? Not necessarily, because public funds for these public goods need not be cut with privatization. Indeed, they can be increased by a reallocation from teaching to research, and from business to science programs, within the public higher education budget—with both public and private institutions eligible for grants on a competitive basis. The criteria for awarding these funds, and the political feasibility of such a reallocation, are then crucial. Some developing countries are now experimenting with this very process, and it would be worthwhile to evaluate their experience.

Finally, we must acknowledge that the lower costs at private universities may stem from lower quality, which may be below optimal levels if consumers underestimate the returns to quality. In that case private universities will be socially inefficient unless they are heavily regulated—and regulations pose another set of problems. But a vast literature documents the fact that lower inputs into education do not necessarily imply lower outputs or value added.[11]

This issue of the relative quality of the public and private sectors and the relative returns to quantity and quality in higher education is an important one, requiring further research and analysis. But the evidence we have cited strongly suggests that a shift from public responsibility to private within the education sector would improve both efficiency and equity.

Health

In general, efficiency criteria would dictate government expenditures for such programs as immunizations (generating externalities), improved water supply (a public good), monitoring of minimum standards for pharmaceuticals and pesticides, and publicity about lifestyles that promote good health (such as antismoking and pronutrition campaigns) to help consumers make better-informed, utility-maximizing decisions (Birdsall 1989). And the provision of basic medical services to low-income groups and to rural regions that cannot support a private competitive market in medical services is probably warranted if people care about the health of others. Maternal and child health programs are particularly important examples of such services, as these affect the health of entire generations, a result in which there may be a large societal interest.

These basic services and fundamental regulatory and information programs likely would raise health standards and reduce mortality in the most cost-effective way, because they would touch the lives of many people directly and indirectly through the externalities they generate.[12] But because they have characteristics of public goods (and possibly because many of their beneficiaries are poor), they are not likely to be provided by the private market; thus, they are logical candidates for public funding on efficiency grounds.

In most countries, however, we observe relatively little public health money going to these cost-effective programs (where government intervention is warranted because of private market failure). Rather, a large portion of public health budgets is spent on hospitals, usually located in urban areas, even in countries in which the vast majority of the population lives in rural areas and suffers from high mortality rates caused by diseases that need not be treated in hospitals.

In Bangladesh in 1986 hospitals consumed more than 80 percent of recurrent public health spending. In Brazil in 1982, 70 percent of public health funds went to reimbursements for physician and hospital care, including expensive high-technology procedures (kidney dialysis, coronary bypasses, cesarean sections). In Zimbabwe, which has tried to make its health sector more egalitarian, two-thirds of Ministry of Health expenditures are for hospital services; 60 percent of these expenditures were absorbed by four hospitals in Harare. In Tanzania, which has made a special effort to improve rural clinics, 60 percent of the recurrent health budget was nevertheless spent on hospitals in 1983-84.[13]

In developing countries hospitals typically are located in urban centers of population and serve the urban middle classes, and superior public hospitals (for example, armed forces or social security hospitals) serve the elites. Because hospital services are parceled out to patients, they have a large private benefit component and could therefore be financed privately. But once government undertakes the task of financing hospitals, private resources are crowded out and a large share of the public budget is absorbed, in part because of the high cost of modern medical technology.

Suppose instead that many hospitals were turned over to private organizations, with fees to be covered by mandated health insurance (which might be administered by the government but financed by premiums paid by the beneficiaries or their employers). Along similar lines, user charges could be instituted at the remaining public facilities, whose effectiveness might be improved by the existence of competitive and privately managed services. Public funds would then be freed up to provide externality-generating health programs and to subsidize health insurance for the poor—very likely bringing about a net improvement in health indicators.

An increasing number of countries are experimenting with privatization and user fees in the health sector. In Zambia the university hospital at Lusaka is being turned into a parastatal that charges clients for services, releasing public funds to finance new maternal, child health, and family planning services. In Zimbabwe fees have been introduced for patients who bypass lower levels of the health system and for those who want a private hospital room. In the Gambia fees charged for drugs are turned over to village development councils (Akin, Birdsall, and de Ferranti 1987). In Jamaica costs declined when housekeeping and food services at public hospitals were contracted out to private firms (Griffin 1989). And in Chile increased reliance on private hospitals during the past decade was accompanied by a shift toward less expensive medical personnel (more nurses and midwives, fewer doctors), by structural changes to improve incentives, and by the targeting of government services toward primary health care and other services for the poor (Griffin 1989).

Moreover, where reliance on government funds has limited the expansion of hospitals, access to private funds (including insurance reimbursement) may increase the supply of hospital services and thus improve overall access to health services, in a manner analogous to the private sector expansion in higher education described above. In the Philippines in the 1970s, following a policy change allowing private expenditures, the greatest expansion of hospitals occurred in the most poorly served regions (Griffin 1989). Like private universities, private hospitals are sometimes accused of taking actions designed to maximize their profits at the expense of ill-informed clients. For example, they may downgrade quality, refuse to carry out important but costly services, recommend an excessive number of lucrative surgical and laboratory procedures, and deny admission to indigent patients. In any privatization program, considerable thought and research must be given to ways of guarding against these pitfalls. There are several possible alternatives, though each has drawbacks. Regulations could be instituted requiring hospitals to provide crucial services and admit poor patients, although monitoring their compliance may be difficult. Self-regulation and peer review could be used to safeguard quality and reduce excessive surgery, but this may open up possibilities of self-dealing, logrolling, and conflict of interest. There could be a shift from reliance on for-profit hospitals to reliance on nonprofit hospitals; there is little evidence, however, that nonprofit hospitals are more trustworthy than for-profit hospitals, although some economic theories of nonprofits argue that this is the case. And mandatory insurance could be adopted, with premiums subsidized for the poor so that no one is left out of the system; this introduces moral hazard problems, however, discussed below.

Another pitfall to avoid is the possibility that public funds will not be reallocated in an efficient, equitable way, even after private financing and service delivery are introduced. For example, in Brazil about half of health care expenditures are private, there are many private hospitals (70 percent of the total), and health maintenance organizations (HMOs) privately funded by workers and their employers are a rapidly growing urban phenomenon, demonstrating the viability of the market in health care. Nevertheless, most of the public health funds are spent on hospital procedures with a large private benefit component (including public reimbursement of private hospitals) for upper-income groups, according to an internal World Bank report.

The availability of medical insurance generally plays a key role in the scenarios that shift responsibility for hospital care to the private sector. But insurance raises the problem of moral hazard, and thus overspending, which must be addressed to prevent the reduction or even the elimination of the efficiency gains that insurance makes possible. From this point of view, uncontrolled private hospitals and mandatory public medical insurance may be the worst combination (Birdsall 1989). Ways of controlling spending include requiring coinsurance (for example, an annual deductible or a copayment for each treatment, or both), exempting small costs from coverage, paying hospitals on the basis of diagnosis rather than procedure, reviewing recommendations for surgery and unusually high surgical rates, and introducing competition among insurance carriers—all, in general, employing greater reliance on market incentives to contain costs. At the same time, it must be recognized that cost escalation in the health sector is a problem whose first-best solution has not yet been found in any country. Perhaps all that is possible is a second-best solution, in which the burden does not fall disproportionately on the public treasury or on the lowest-income groups.

The reallocation of public funds to public goods just described, together with a shift of responsibility for "private" services to the private sector, aided by privately financed medical insurance, holds the promise of increasing efficiency (achieving greater improvement in health indicators at lower cost) and, at the same time, of improving equity (assuring that health gains are particularly great for the poor). Once again, efficiency and equity seem to be complements rather than substitutes.

Social security and other social programs

Public pension programs may be justified on efficiency grounds if the private discount rate exceeds the social rate, so that many people will not voluntarily save enough for their old age. Society may then make a collective decision requiring people to save, to provide a minimum safety net for all. To permit maximum risk pooling, avoid adverse selection, and provide inflation insurance, compulsory savings may be administered through a public social security program, as they are in most countries.

This is an efficiency rationale for a social security safety net, not an equity rationale, and it dictates broad coverage with benefits above subsistence levels but below wages. The relation between individual contributions and payouts would vary with life span (the insurance function), but the two would otherwise be closely related unless redistribution was an explicit goal. If redistribution was desired, it would presumably be from the rich to the poor and not vice versa.

Nevertheless, the pattern in some countries is quite different. In Brazil about half the population, mainly urban workers, is covered by public pension and disability insurance; a high proportion (28 percent) of total benefits accrues to early retirees, many of whom are from upper-income groups; and initial benefits are almost as high as wages (though the real value of benefits has in the past declined rapidly because of inflation). As a result of these expenditures, according to an internal World Bank report, social security in recent years ran a deficit that had to be covered out of general tax revenues, and it is in danger of doing so again.

This is another instance in which greater reliance on the private sector (personal savings and supplementary optional private pension plans) would relieve the pressure on the public treasury and permit a reallocation of public funds toward safety net coverage for the masses. Such a system would be both more efficient and more equitable.

A similar pattern holds in housing. Public funds are sometimes used to subsidize construction or mortgage loans for middle-income housing, whose benefits are largely private, while housing for the poor remains a major problem and the rental market is distorted by price controls. This is the case in Brazil, according to an internal World Bank report, and in the United States, for example. Reallocating public funds toward more public goods, while letting the private market operate freely to provide private goods—such as middle-class housing and rental housing—is not only preferable on classical efficiency grounds, it would also free up resources that could be used to benefit the poor.

Measurement problems and policy ambiguities

The previous section gave examples of public interventions that seemed unwarranted on efficiency grounds and that seemed to have perverse redistributional effects. Measuring the distributional effects of government spending or its private alternatives poses a host of practical and conceptual problems, however; these will be discussed in this section. Would the story change if these problems were taken into account? We find that some of the measurement problems require corrections that make government spending appear even less equitable; others work in the opposite direction. Overall, our conclusion remains unchanged regarding the prevalence of public programs that are both inefficient and inequitable, and potential policy changes that would simultaneously improve efficiency and equity.

Resource inputs versus willingness to pay

Should we measure the benefits to different groups of consumers according to the real resource inputs into the services they receive, or according to their willingness to pay for these services? In empirical studies of quasi-public goods, real inputs or physical outputs are almost invariably used as the measure of benefits per consumer, since we do not really know people's willingness to pay for goods that are not rationed by price. For example, calculations of the distribution of the benefits of education are typically based on enrollments and cost per student, and those for medical benefits on patient days or types of operations.

But because willingness to pay for normal goods is positively related to income for any given quantity, it understates the consumer surplus received by the rich relative to that received by the poor from publicly provided goods. Environmental conservation is a middle-class political issue for this reason; the working class is relatively more concerned about jobs and income, and the middle class is relatively more concerned about clean air. Because of the positive income elasticity of demand, the rich will benefit more than the poor (in terms of willingness to pay) from each consumption unit of normal goods, and conventional measures of benefit (for example, proportion of enrollments or medical operations or air purity) therefore understate the income bias inherent in public spending and overstate its redistribution toward the poor.

A similar question arises regarding the benefits of publicly financed information programs. Information is a quasi-public good that is consumed differently by (and faces a different effective demand from) upper- and lower-income groups. Wealthier groups have a demonstrated willingness to pay more for information, as evidenced by their consumption of newspapers and books, for example. The poor, who are less educated, are also less likely to gain access to and absorb new information, even when it is presented to them as a free good. For example, the poor may not place a high value on or even be aware of public health campaigns, although they have more to gain in terms of reduced illness or mortality. Thus, their behavior is less likely to change—unless special efforts are made to target information toward low-income communities. Conventional measures of the distribution of benefits from information are unlikely to capture these biases in willingness to pay for and ability to use information.

Consumers versus producers

Redistribution to the poor is overstated for a second reason as well. Some of the benefits of government spending for social services undoubtedly accrue to producers, and the producers are often from higher-income groups than are consumers.

For example, in many countries, increases in public spending on primary and secondary education are captured mainly by middle-class teachers in the form of higher salaries, rather than by the poor in the form of a higher quantity or quality of education. As another example, when subsidies are granted to private schools, teachers' salaries in those schools tend to rise to public school levels; indeed, this is often the raison d'etre for the subsidies (James 1991).

Teachers are an articulate group, better organized than consumers and taxpayers, and their unions are politically skillful at pressing governments to raise spending and salaries. And because publicly financed schools are shielded from market pressures, teachers unions and other professional groups have more power than they would have in competitive private markets. If the higher salaries teachers thereby attain attract a more qualified teaching staff (as may occur over the long run) or provide an incentive for the existing staff to perform more effectively, this represents a real cost of quality, not a transfer or rent. But the eligibility criteria for higher salaries, such as credentials and experience, do not always imply higher teaching productivity. And if teaching productivity does not rise but salaries do, a redistribution has occurred, from society at large to the producers of education. If producers of publicly funded social services receive rents, conventional measures that assume that inputs are being paid their opportunity cost understate the benefits of government spending that accrue to the middle and upper classes and overstate the real resource inputs that accrue to lower-income groups (consumers).

Social insurance versus redistribution

Many programs that look redistributive from an ex post (or transitory income) point of view are really insurance from an ex ante (or permanent income) point of view. For example, unemployment or disability compensation is received by groups with lower temporary income, but much of this transfer is an insurance payoff in exchange for the earlier payment of insurance premiums by these same groups. It represents a smoothing or maintenance rather than a redistribution of expected lifetime income. Redistribution is correctly measured by the difference between premiums paid and expected insurance returns—which may be positive for some and negative for others but is far less than total transfers for all.

We digress for a moment to comment on the relation between social insurance and redistribution. All social insurance programs have some elements of risk pooling and some elements of redistribution, since in a public program premiums are constrained to be relatively uniform and cannot fully reflect the fact that some people are actuarially more vulnerable than others.[14] In homogeneous societies where most people are actuarially similar, the insurance element predominates. In heterogeneous societies, however, definable groups may have large differences in riskiness that are not reflected in differential premiums; thus, the redistributive component is relatively large.

In general, groups that are being "redistributed away from" will oppose a high level of social insurance and favor a private, voluntary system. If these groups are politically influential, heterogeneous societies are likely to have less social insurance. Unfortunately, private insurance markets may also be unsustainable because of adverse selection or insufficient scale for risk pooling (for example, to cover catastrophic risks). These societies may end up with relatively little public or private insurance and with individuals bearing a high degree of risk, as in the United States, for example. It would be useful to test this hypothesis about the inverse relationship between heterogeneity in riskiness among groups and availability of social insurance across a larger set of countries.

The political pressures against social insurance are often mitigated by the fact that, for any given level of insurance, middle- and upper-income groups find ways to get a larger share of benefits than their actual life experience warrants, and low-income groups do not receive all the benefits to which they are entitled (because they do not know all the rules or all the ways around the rules).

In measuring the redistributive effects of these programs, then, one must eliminate the part that represents insurance, in the sense that actuarially fair premiums have been paid on the basis of demographic characteristics, and take account of the fact that some groups systematically receive less than their formal characteristics would suggest. Both these adjustments reduce the degree to which these programs actually provide redistributions to the poor.

The distribution of benefits and redistribution of real income

The appropriate treatment of taxes raises both philosophical and pragmatic issues. If we believe that the distribution of taxes and the distribution of benefits are and should be independent of each other—that taxes are dues that should be distributed according to ability to pay and that everyone should have equal access to the fruits of government expenditure—then benefit shares alone may be said to determine the redistributional effects of a particular program. This was the implicit approach in the section giving empirical examples. But if we believe that taxes constitute, in effect, a user charge, and that higher taxes therefore justify higher use, we must examine both tax shares and benefit shares to determine the net redistributional effect of the program. It is possible that a service will be redistributive even if the rich receive a disproportionate share of benefits, because they pay an even larger share of the tax bill.

Measuring the distribution of the tax burden is difficult for several reasons. One reason is that the marginal distribution may be quite different from the average. Another is that the initial incidence is often quite different from the final impact, once the shifting of the tax burden to consumers and workers is taken into account. Most empirical studies, however, deal only with averages and with initial incidence—and even these cannot be determined with precision (Hansen and Weisbrod 1969). Moreover, taxes earmarked for social services are rare, so we usually must use general tax revenues and assume that each person's tax bill is allocated among different services in the same way.

Using this interpretation of tax shares, and treating taxes as a user charge for services, studies of U.S. and Japanese higher education indicate that benefits are always skewed toward the upper classes, but that taxes are even more skewed. Therefore, higher education is still, in most cases, moderately redistributive. The Japanese public system is more redistributive than most U.S. state university systems because the national income tax system used to finance universities in Japan is more progressive than the state sales and property taxes used to finance higher education in the United States. Most redistributive of all, however, is the community college system in the United States, because its students come disproportionately from low-income groups (James and Benjamin 1987a and 1987b).

Selowsky (1979), in his study of the distribution of health, education, and other social services in Colombia, found that the upper-income groups received larger benefits but that the distribution of benefits was not nearly as skewed as the distribution of income and taxes; thus, the overall effect of government spending and taxation was mildly redistributive toward the poor.

In Brazil the bottom income quintile receives 7 percent of total social benefits and the top quintile 41 percent. This is certainly an income-biased pattern of benefits. If the tax system were progressive or proportional, the net effect would nevertheless be redistributive toward the poor, because income is even more skewed, according to an internal World Bank report. Brazil's tax system is probably regressive, however, because of the preponderance of payroll taxes, the flat rate structure, the poor coverage, and the existence of hidden subsidies and tax credits cited in another Bank report. Therefore, it is not at all clear that the public provision of social services increases the real welfare of the lowest-income groups, on balance.

At the same time, there is probably a redistribution to the poorer regions. For example, social security benefits urban areas more than rural areas, but urban areas are also taxed more regularly and heavily for social security. An internal World Bank study reports that the rich southeastern part of Brazil gets a disproportionate share of social security and medical benefits, but residents of that region pay an even larger share of taxes. On balance, therefore, the system redistributes to the poor Northeast. This is consistent with predictions from public choice theory that some redistribution to poor groups or regions may take place, but in the form of public programs from which influential middle- and upper-income groups disproportionately benefit.

On the whole, taking tax incidence into effect makes social services more redistributive to the poor than otherwise; however, this correction is probably much smaller in developing than in developed countries, since tax systems in developing countries tend to be less progressive.

Life-cycle income shifts

Some programs that appear to be redistributive merely shift income from one stage of the life cycle to another. For example, social security is sometimes thought of as a payment to low-income retirees. But to the extent that it is actuarially fair, it merely represents compulsory savings by the young to finance their consumption when they are old and not working. Thus, it is less redistributive to the poor from a life-cycle point of view than from a static cross-sectional one. Indeed, in some countries people with high lifetime incomes (although relatively low current incomes) receive a disproportionate share of total benefits, so the net redistribution may actually be perverse. In Brazil, for example, the poor are much less likely to benefit from pension benefits since they are less able to demonstrate the necessary minimum years of continuous attachment to the labor force. In 1986, according to an internal World Bank report, 28 percent of benefits were absorbed by early retirees, who represented just 9 percent of all recipients, and relatively few of these were poor.

Another example of a life-cycle effect, one that creates the opposite kind of distortion, concerns the provision of public education. Think of people as paying for public education throughout their working lives but receiving the benefits at particular points in time—a life-cycle shift in real income. Primary school students usually have young parents whose current income understates their life-time income; university students have middle-aged parents whose income is at the life-cycle peak. University education, of course, is much more expensive than primary education. If we examine data based on the population as a whole, it appears that high-income families are receiving disproportionate benefits from public education spending, particularly from high-cost public universities. But this is due in part to the relation between income and age, not just to the access of different groups to education. Distribution figures for higher education that do not adjust for this life-cycle view systematically understate the benefits received by low-income families.

A more appropriate set of data would compare lifetime benefits received by different groups within a given age cohort. This kind of calculation, carried out for public universities in Japan and the United States, showed substantially large lifetime cohort enrollment shares for lower-income groups. This resulted in an income bias in enrollments that was cut in half; the ratio of enrollments from the top quintiles relative to those from the bottom quintiles fell from 5.8 to 2.6 in Japan and from 4.5 to 2.4 in California.[15]

In developing countries, however, income differentials due to life-cycle effects are probably small relative to the large lifetime income differentials found in Japan and the United States. In addition, as noted above, developing countries are more likely than developed countries to have proportional or regressive tax structures. Thus, we would expect these two corrections to have a much smaller equity effect in developing than in developed countries. Because other measurement problems lead to overestimates of benefits to the poor, we believe that on the whole our story of "perverse redistributions" is relatively undisturbed.

Changes in tastes

For completeness we note one other measurement problem, with particularly difficult underlying philosophical problems. Some public programs involve taste change—for example, successful public antismoking or anticholesterol campaigns. If the poor are more resistant to changes in taste, do they benefit less from such programs?[16] If tastes have been changed, do we measure benefits in terms of ex ante or ex post preferences? Or do we impose external, "objective" criteria, contrary to the usual subjective approach in welfare economics?

Political strategies

In this chapter we have argued for a policy that concentrates government funding on public goods and encourages the market to do what it can do best—fund and produce private goods. A drift away from this policy in the social services sector of many developing countries in recent years has had negative distributional and efficiency consequences. Efficiency and equity objectives do not always lead to the same set of actions, but the many examples that we have given suggest that certain actions would advance both objectives in many countries. These actions usually involve increased financial responsibilities for the private sector combined with a reallocation of government funds within the public sector.

But without political change, these shifts will not be easy to accomplish. The "misbehavior" of government—in inefficiently providing private goods that benefit the upper classes—has come about precisely because people with political power gain from these private goods and will resist relinquishing this source of real income. This creates a positive *prediction* problem as well as a normative *change-producing* problem.

The predictive problem is as follows. The present situation in the social services sector is the outcome of a political process, and possibly a political equilibrium, in which each group has tried to maximize the utility it can extract from the system. The payoffs for the rich are selective universities and superior hospitals; those for the poor are primary schools and, sometimes, rural health clinics. If one element of this equilibrium is disturbed or constrained, other elements will change in reaction, so that the end result may be quite different from that sought with the initial step.

For example, suppose that the upper classes feel that they receive fewer benefits after the government shifts from funding private goods to funding public goods—for example, from financing medical operations to financing malaria control and immunization campaigns. They may then lobby successfully for a corresponding tax cut, so that the government has less to spend, or for a shift in the structure of taxes, so that relatively more is collected from the lower classes. (The tax cuts in the United States during the Reagan years could thus be viewed as a reaction to the buildup of poverty programs in the 1960s and early 1970s, beyond those of the New Deal years, though other factors obviously also contributed.)

Along similar lines, suppose that undergraduates from high-income families are charged higher fees for access to superior public universities in an attempt to capture private revenues for the private benefits they receive. They may respond by switching to the private sector and withdrawing their political support from the public facilities. Thus, both the student mix and the resources available to superior public universities may change; and by the time a final equilibrium has been reached, they may no longer be superior. And the upper classes may successfully resist targeting the revenues from university fees for need-based scholarships, so the poor may end up paying more than before for inferior public universities.[17]

Finally, elites may try to recapture their higher real income in other ways—for example, by increasing the bribery and corruption elsewhere in the economy.

In formulating public policy, this chain of responses, leading to a new political equilibrium, must be evaluated and taken into account. Pragmatic choices may have to be made between a smaller public budget targeted toward the poor and a larger public budget with benefits accruing to the rich, and between a benefit pattern that is biased toward the rich but also financed by them through progressive or proportional taxation, and a more egalitarian distribution of services financed by a more regressive tax system.[18]

We move now to the question of how to produce change, in a situation in which government behavior is endogenously inefficient and inequitable.

As discussed in the section on theory, many inefficient and inequitable policies are stimulated and perpetuated by imperfect information. The losers do not always know how much they are losing, and the gainers incur costs to hide information from them. Spreading more accurate information may thus in itself alter the feasible political equilibrium. Along similar lines, politicians do not know with certainty peoples' preferences or the intensity of these preferences, and if their perceptions of preferences are changed, the policies they deem politically optimal will also change. Researchers may play an important role by generating and disseminating new information, and advocacy groups may play an important role by informing disadvantaged groups about the effects of different policies and informing politicians about the preferences of disadvantaged groups. This is the role that nongovernmental organizations (NGOs) play in Sweden, where they are an integral part of the political process (see James 1989a). Information, and the organizations that spread it, can thus help change the balance of political power; this is one reason why some groups support such organizations and why many influential groups oppose them.

Policies, and the distribution of their benefits, should be designed with explicit consideration of the coalitions that might be formed to support them. For example, if service delivery becomes more efficient as a consequence of privatization policies, resources will be freed up that could be used to make many people better-off. If the surplus is distributed in such a way that there are more gainers than losers, including some influential gainers, this could offset political pressure to once again expand the public sector inefficiently. This is one reason for avoiding overtargeting toward the poor and for structuring programs so that the broad middle class also participates in benefits, in order to gain its support.

To minimize the coalition opposed to policy change, the current cohort of consumers should be exempted as much as possible from price-increasing reforms. For example, students currently enrolled in public universities should probably be exempted from large fee increases, and fees should be gradually phased in for new cohorts, to minimize the risk for politicians. As a corollary, rather than withdrawing entirely from a service area (such as higher education or hospitals), governments could simply forgo future expansion, leaving the private sector to meet increases in demand. This too should minimize opposition among consumer groups.[19]

Along similar lines, it is easier not to start than to cut off services because influential groups of consumers and producers would not yet have been identified and mobilized. Therefore, social reformers should pay particular attention to proposed new programs, and should oppose them unless they have a high social rate of return, will not be undertaken by the private market, and do not have perverse distributional effects.

Even where government retains funding responsibility, economies of competition may be attained if production and management responsibilities are shifted to the private sector (as in contracting-out schemes based on competition), or if market approaches are introduced into the public sector (as in voucher schemes in which funds follow students or patients within public institutions). These market elements should reduce rents that often have a perverse distributional effect and generate a surplus that can be spent in a more egalitarian manner. Once these possibilities are put on the agenda, they may generate new constituencies and coalitions (from private sector organizations, for example) that some political entrepreneur could seize upon and use to alter the political equilibrium.

Ultimately, large changes in the distribution of benefits from government spending will occur only if there is a corresponding change in the distribution of political power. For example, as the urban working class grew in size and became enfranchised in nineteenth- and twentieth-century Europe, it acquired greater power to influence government policies. In the United States, enfranchisement of black voters in the South, which accelerated with the Civil Rights Act of 1964, has increased the access of blacks to the benefits of state-sponsored social programs. Changes in the internal power structure can be slow and difficult to achieve. But a temporary change in power can sometimes be multiplied and become permanent if it is used to alter the long-run rules of the game through constitutional change, precedent-setting judicial interpretations, reapportionment, and irreversible extensions of voting rights. All these elements were present in the acquisition of political power by the working class in Europe and by blacks in the United States. Some now argue (Nelson 1989) that redemocratization in Latin America will increase the political power of the urban working poor, who may then use that power to increase their share of social benefits.

Notes

1. For alternative views on whether efficiency and equity conflict in industrial countries, see Okun (1975), Blinder (1987), and Haveman (1989).

2. Thus, a vast literature has developed on the question of whether actual compensation or simply the potential for compensation should be used to compare the relative desirability of two alternative allocations. When the potential for compensation is used, distribution is essentially deemed as irrelevant, and when actual compensation is used, the nature of compensatory mechanisms is crucial.

3. For fuller summaries of public choice theory, see Mueller (1979) and Borcherding (1985).

4. For an early statement of the fiscal illusion argument, see Buchanan (1967); for a more recent review, see Pommerehne and Schneider (1978).

5. Thus, Meltzer and Richard (1978 and 1981) have argued that redistribution is likely to flow to the median voter, whose income is generally lower than average, and Demsetz (1982) ties this tendency to the extension of the franchise.

6. For this result with respect to public expenditure on education in Brazil, see Behrman and Birdsall (1988a).

7. For evidence from the Philippines, Japan, and Latin America, see James (1988), James and Benjamin (1987a), and Levy (1986). For similar evidence from the United States, see Hansen and Weisbrod (1969).

8. For example, in Japan, where 85 percent of all undergraduates are in private colleges and universities, a student from a top quintile family is roughly five times more likely to attend university than one from the bottom quintile in either sector. (This income bias is cut in half in both sectors when adjustments are made for life-cycle effects, discussed in the section on measurement problems and policy ambiguities.)

9. For a more detailed analysis of this effect on access and redistribution in Japan, the United Kingdom, and the United States, see James and Benjamin (1987b). An analysis of higher education enrollment rates across fifteen Asian countries showed these rates to be highest in countries with the largest private sector shares, although their total expenditure on higher education (as a percentage of GNP) is no higher than average. These countries also have relatively low Gini indices of educational inequality (James 1989b; and Tan 1992). Typically in these countries public funds have expanded enrollments at the primary and secondary levels, thereby increasing demand at the tertiary level, which is satisfied mainly in the private sector at a low cost per student. By contrast, countries that have relied on public higher education spend more per student, accommodate fewer students, and have less left over for the lower levels. Thus, the policy of encouraging private universities when public resources are limited seems most conducive to expansion of higher education.

10. Evidence along these lines is presented in James (1988); and James and Benjamin (1987b). Resources for these products are larger in the public sector, although they are small relative to total spending in both sectors.

11. See Hanushek (1986) for a summary of this literature. Also see James, Alsalam, Conaty, and To (1989) for an empirical analysis of American higher education.

12. See Birdsall (1989) and Akin, Birdsall, and de Ferranti (1987) for comparisons of the cost-effectiveness of these relative to that of hospital services in reducing mortality.

13. These examples are from selected years in the 1980s from Griffin (1989) and an internal World Bank report.

14. Indeed, one reason for operating such insurance programs as a public monopoly is to prevent opting-out and adverse selection, thereby inevitably permitting some redistribution to take place.

15. This life-cycle approach also increased the lifetime cohort tax shares of lower-income groups, but by a smaller amount, so, on balance, the correct calculation showed a more equitable sharing of benefits—that is, more redistributive from rich to poor (see James and Benjamin 1987a and 1987b).

16. Above, we noted that the rich are likely to have a higher willingness to pay for information, and thus, in some cases, for change in taste as well.

17. But these public universities, which would have more space for the poor as the rich shift out, may be better and cheaper then the private ones now attended by lower-income groups in many countries.

18. For a discussion of the political equilibrium in Japan and the reactions to educational reform that brought about an unexpected new equilibrium, see James (1986) and James and Benjamin (1987b).

19. Any structural or other major policy change involves transactions and transitional costs. By covering these costs, in projects that are conditioned on efficiency and equity improvements, World Bank loans can help to diminish the resistance to change.

Protecting the Vulnerable: Social Security and Public Policy

15   *Ehtisham Ahmad*

An important objective of public policy is to ensure the maintenance of minimum living standards. This often involves instituting social insurance-type measures designed to protect individuals from the risk of deteriorating standards posed by life-cycle contingencies, such as old age or bereavement, and from exogenous risks, such as unemployment. Commercial insurance is generally unavailable for many of these contingencies, and it excludes those perceived as poor risks, including those whose average incomes put them at or below the poverty threshold. Some contingencies are inherently uninsurable, such as major systemic shocks. These include systemic reforms leading to large-scale unemployment, such as those in the centrally planned economies undergoing the transition toward market-based systems, and large relative price changes caused, for example, by exchange rate realignments. Each of these contingencies may threaten to push people who are above the poverty threshold into poverty, often permanently, and to increase the misery of those who are already poor.

Forms of organization and financing arrangements for social security differ even among industrial countries with established systems. But there has been a common objective in many different types of society; the systems protect against contingencies and risks that are foreseen through contributions or collections drawn from the community at large. In many countries traditional insurance-type measures are generally unable to cope with major natural calamities or economic shocks. Policy instruments that have been used to protect the poor under these circumstances include direct transfers, commodity price interventions of various kinds (food subsidies, rationing, and other variations), and such labor market interventions as public works programs.

The focus of this chapter is on protection against contingencies that, for those affected, pose a risk of becoming poor, of falling further below an acceptable standard of living, or, in the extreme case, of famine. Some of the instruments discussed here may also prove beneficial to those who are already poor. There is no general one-to-one correspondence between a cause of poverty and a remedial approach. Low standards of living or poverty due to the absence of resources, technology, or skills cannot usually be addressed by these protective measures, as there may be a tradeoff. In many centrally planned economies the safety net of guaranteed employment provision has been associated with relatively low living standards, and it is clear that protective measures cannot substitute for the structural adjustments necessary for sustained growth and rising income levels. There may be positive interactions between protective measures and structural adjustment, however. Rising mean incomes can provide the base for financing protective policies that are needed even in industrial countries. And protecting minimum living standards appropriately ensures that opportunities for structural change can be utilized effectively.

The chapter examines more or less permanent social safety nets[1] that are required for contingencies common to all countries. The evolution of social insurance in industrial countries, discussed briefly in the following section (along with some lessons for developing countries), illustrates the wide diversity of experience and outcomes with respect to one set of policy instruments. Among developing and centrally planned economies with a significant organized wage sector, there is considerable scope for appropriately designed formal social security programs. The principles underlying such programs are also reflected in traditional societies, although the forms of organization and the financing mechanisms differ.

The chapter then discusses compensatory commodity price and labor market interventions for coping with the effects of shocks and major changes in price and employment levels. As the current dilemmas in Eastern Europe and the experience of such countries as Sri Lanka testify, commodity and food price subsidies have been enlarged in scope, from measures used to protect consumers to general devices that transfer incomes on a permanent basis. General subsidies depress producer prices, which could generate balance of payments difficulties, or (if not passed on to producers) may result in large budgetary outlays. Attempts to limit expenditures include the appropriate choice of commodity and the choice of delivery mechanisms, such as rationing and more targeted provision. Necessary policy choices relate to degrees of targeting and whether the transfers should be denominated in cash or kind. Similar policy choices arise for compensatory public works programs, which are also discussed.

Permanent measures for social security

One of the earliest objectives of formal social security[2] was to alleviate poverty, and to provide an alternative to charity and the Poor Laws without the stigma attached to them (Beveridge 1942). Other objectives have included the guarantee of minimum living standards and the replacement of income in times of adversity. Social security may also entail a smoothing of consumption or a spreading of income over the life cycle, and the reduction of risk. Often there is a redistribution of income between groups with differing needs. This variety of objectives, and the different configurations of political and interest groups, have led to the different forms that social security has taken in different countries.

An important component common to social security systems is *social insurance*. This entails the financing of benefits through contributions that might be earnings-related or collected through payroll taxes. Unlike *private insurance*, the contributions for social insurance need not fully cover benefits, either for groups (old people might be privately uninsurable but strong candidates for social insurance) or for the total population covered; a fortiori, social insurance need not show an expected (actuarial) positive rate of return. The seeking out of the poor and the coverage of those who are poor risks under social insurance implies an inherent element of redistribution within each generation and among succeeding generations.

Some of the effects of social insurance are similar to those inherent in the tax system; and *tax expenditures*, although not always perceived as social security, address the same objectives. *Targeted expenditures*, which may be either *means-tested* or related to particular categorical indicators of need (such as age, gender, and disability), also meet the criterion of protecting the vulnerable.

The social security system in most countries relies on combinations of these measures. Among the measures there are often substantial interactions; these interactions help to determine whether the basic objective of protecting the vulnerable is achieved. It is thus likely to be misleading to focus solely on one program, such as the public provision of retirement pensions. Evaluating groups of related schemes and their alternatives is difficult, but it is important in many developing countries because of their precarious budgetary positions and the expansion in benefits and in costs of provision. Costs can be expected to escalate in Africa, for example, as the proportion of those under age five continues to increase, and in Asia, as the proportion of elderly people rises.

The concern with targeting benefits effectively is as relevant for industrial countries as it is for developing countries, as the rising costs of provision coincide with growing budget deficits and political sensitivities associated with the "middle-class capture" of benefits (see LeGrand and Winter 1987). Effective targeting means including *all* the target groups, not merely excluding the nontarget population, but there is a tension between these two aims (see also Besley and Kanbur, chapter 3 in this volume). If the budget permits, some inclusion of the nonpoor may not be too worrying. Broad categories of need are met by universal programs with no means testing, such as child allowances in a number of industrial countries. And because of the interaction of the tax and social security systems, it may be possible to "claw back" the provisions to middle-class beneficiaries through taxation. It is thus important to examine the tax and benefit systems as a whole.

The evolution of social security and lessons for developing countries

In a stylized representation the International Labour Office depicted social security as evolving over three stages.

> First was an era of paternalism: private charity and poor relief provided for the poor, being often subject to harsh conditions which impose stigma. Second was an era of *social insurance*: following the precedents of friendly societies and of pensions and sick pay for employees in

public and some private occupations, wider compulsory programs were developed covering more and more occupations and more and more contingencies. In some countries, the occupational origin of social security is still retained in the form of separate funds. In the third stage the concepts of prevention and universality have begun to be incorporated and the range of services is being extended with the aim of *maintaining and enhancing the quality of life*. (ILO 1984: 17)

The characterization of the initial phase is relatively firmly based. Charitable provision, organized largely through the church, remained a mainstay for the poor in Europe for centuries. In England, the workhouse system, which existed for at least a century after the Poor Law Amendment Act of 1834 was passed, is a prime example of self-targeted provision, although the stigma it involved excluded not only the nonpoor, but many of the self-respecting needy. The laws relating to the charitable support of the disadvantaged came to be viewed as inadequate and demeaning, and there was political pressure to adopt more acceptable means of providing support. According to Beveridge (1942), the architect of the modern welfare state, there has been a strong movement against the form and spirit of the old poor law since the beginning of this century.

The identification of life-cycle causes of poverty and deprivation, and widespread readiness to support the victims if they (or their families) could not afford private insurance, led to the development of social insurance as an important policy instrument. Different perceptions of need and vulnerability among industrial countries led to different policies to provide social security. Perceptions of threats to political stability also played a role, as in Bismarck's introduction of social insurance in Germany. Guaranteeing minimum living standards and replacing income during times of hardship were other objectives of social insurance policies pursued in industrial countries. Social security entailed a smoothing of consumption, or a spreading of income over the life cycle, as in compulsory pension plans. The different configurations of political and interest groups influenced the varied directions that social provision has taken in the industrial countries.

In the United Kingdom an old-age pension act was introduced in 1908, followed by National Insurance in 1911 (some years after Bismarck's reform in Germany). National Insurance represented an important change, as it replaced means-tested benefits and assistance with the contributory benefits of social insurance. There were unemployment and sickness benefits for some trades, but it was not until 1934, during the Great Depression, that general assistance to the unemployed was introduced, under the Unemployment Act. Another instance of a public response to changing need occurred after the outbreak of World War II, when supplementary provisions were introduced in Britain for widows, who may never have worked. Formal social security, guaranteeing the replacement of income in times of adversity, constituted a political response to the need for stability.

Beveridge (1942) argued for making the coverage of National Insurance in the United Kingdom universal because of the strong popular objection to any kind of means test. The idea was to reduce dependence on assistance. As a precondition for the success of the reform of the benefits system, Beveridge argued for a set of family allowances, neither social insurance nor means-tested benefits, with the basic benefit for children. At the turn of the century, means-tested programs had comprised 100 percent of publicly provided social protection. The Beveridge proposals envisaged a rise in the share of (non-means-tested) social security to more than 80 percent of total outlays by 1975, with family allowances accounting for another 12 percent, and assistance for the rest.

According to Atkinson (1986 and 1989), although there were increases in the scope of social insurance after 1949, there was a relative decline in the share of social security and allowances over time, and the means-tested National Assistance increased (in 1949 there were 1.1 million payments each week; in 1969-70 there were 2.7 million). Means-tested assistance, which accounted for about 10 percent of social security expenditure in 1969-70, increased to more than 30 percent by 1985 because of new means-tested measures and greater reliance on established tests. Thus, the United Kingdom's experience, which appeared to follow the ILO stylized schema initially, suggests that there is no inevitability about these stages. Rather than progressing toward the third stage, the United Kingdom appears to be regressing toward the first stage.

Atkinson and Hills (1991) describe the social security systems in France, the United Kingdom, and the United States in terms of three main elements. The relief of poverty through assistance is typified in Britain by income support, in France by *minimum vieillesse*, and in the United States by welfare programs. The provision of security and spreading of income over the life cycle by social insurance is illustrated in Britain by National Insurance premiums, unemployment benefits, and invalidity benefits, in France by a similar range of insurance benefits, and in the United States by Old Age, Survivors, Disability, and Health Insurance. Categorical transfers, which are provided to certain types of households on a universal (non-means-tested) basis and directed at redistribution between specific groups, are illustrated by child benefits in the United Kingdom and *allocations familiales* in France, but have no counterpart in the United States.[3] These elements interact with each other and with the tax system (particularly with tax expenditures) in meeting the objectives of social security.

In the industrial countries, where the initial impetus to the development of social security was poverty among the aged and infirm, there is a growing realization that there is now a greater incidence of poverty among families with children (see, for example, Burtless 1986 for a discussion of the United States). Reform of the social security system in the United States in the early 1980s led to increased benefits for the elderly. Estimates suggest that 24 percent of the elderly in the United States were poor in 1979, but this share fell to 12 percent in 1987. Child poverty, however, has remained stagnant despite means-tested benefits, with a fifth of all children classified as poor over this period. In the United Kingdom universal child benefits ensured that only 9 percent of children were poor (Coder, Rainwater, and Smeeding 1989).

It may be possible to transplant a program from an industrial to a developing country, but it is important to "view in entirety all measures which contribute to a particular objective" (Atkinson and Hills 1991: 106). An example of a transplanted strategy is the use of income tax deductions in developing countries for children. Because the value of the deductions increases with the marginal tax rate, the richest taxpayers benefit most, and when those paying income tax are a minority, this concession is likely to be highly regressive, and may offset other, better-targeted transfers directed at children. Thus, governments of developing countries considering the adoption of a measure should carefully examine the circumstances that would determine whether it has any chance of meeting its objectives.

Another lesson from industrial countries is that the interactions between different types of programs might have important implications for the choice of program and for the design of the overall social security system. Thus, a combination of different programs and their financing through earmarked wage and payroll taxes, in conjunction with general (income and commodity) taxation, might result in unexpectedly high marginal tax rates, with undesirable consequences for equity and incentives. Further, the interaction between formal social security and other programs may have important budgetary implications. For example, it may be important to examine whether it would be cheaper to take action to prevent unemployment or sickness, or to pay for unemployment insurance and sickness benefits. This brings into sharp focus the interactions between the social security system, possible labor market interventions, food relief programs, and other education and health programs that are not strictly part of the social security system.

Social security in traditional societies

Public policy to ensure social security should take into account what individuals and households do to protect themselves. Identifying this protective behavior requires an examination of savings behavior and the ability to smooth consumption over time, and of transfers and support mechanisms within the extended family or community. There is evidence, reviewed in this section, that individuals in poor countries can smooth consumption in the face of income fluctuations (due to, for example, changes in weather or agricultural prices) despite their relatively limited access to credit markets and their low incomes, barely above subsistence levels. The scope for smoothing consumption through accumulation and asset liquidation is limited, however, particularly when there are major and repeated shocks.

For life-cycle contingencies such as old age, the extended family remains the principal source of support in societies as diverse as rural China (see Ahmad and Hussain 1991), India, and Sub-Saharan Africa. This typically reinforces the desire and the need for sons, severely limiting the prospects for a reduction in the birthrate. Problems arise when there are no male offspring or there is a breakdown in filial concern, often connected with an inability to provide support in time of need, given the constraints of a spreading nuclear family structure. In many parts of Africa, the term for poor is synonymous with lack of kin or friends (Iliffe 1987).

Support for the indigent who lack sources of family support tends to be based on community-level food security arrangements. For example, in the Gambia deliveries of staple food (based on the precept of *zakat*, discussed below) provide for the needy and the indigent. There is also a system of mutual labor transfers (neighbors provide labor assistance when an able-bodied person is sick, for example), which provides half of the total labor input at the community level (von Braun 1991). Although local provision is effective in identifying the indigent, without wider public support it tends to break down if local risks are highly covariant (for example, in a drought affecting all households in a given locality).

At the community level there are many fairly sophisticated survival strategies equivalent to social security coverage. These are particularly common in communities centered on high-risk occupations, such as traditional fishing communities—among the poorest in many parts of Asia, Latin America, and Sub-Saharan Africa. Not only are fishing incomes subject to abrupt daily variations (production risks are often independent of price risks), but fishermen also face the risk of loss of, or damage to, assets and lives in rough seas or unlucky or poorly executed operations. In addition, the work is so physically demanding that fishermen run a high risk of shortened active working lives.

One strategy for diffusing the high risk in activities such as fishing is immediately manifest in the choice of share contracts in which owners and employees agree to a share of the catch. The high probability of low or zero catches precludes the payment of fixed wages. Households are at risk not only because of potential shortfalls in catch, but also because of abrupt changes in prices. A form of coverage for sickness is also provided, equivalent to one share (or half a share) of the current income of the fishing unit; this phenomenon is often observed in Sub-Saharan African fisheries. Some arrangements also provide for the subsistence needs of old fishermen, or of poor families that have lost all adult income earners. The preempting rights of the indigent resemble an informal tax system designed to finance social security objectives.

Risk pooling also takes the form of interest-free consumption loans among households, as in southern Kerala. Again, because community (local) insurance cannot handle covariant risks, these loans are possible—that is, they can be reciprocated—only if the high risks involved in fishing do not affect all fishermen simultaneously. There is a commitment to reciprocity implicit in the acceptance of free credit, which is enforced by the community.

Another form of risk pooling in fishing communities is the share system of employment and remuneration. Under this system the work force on individual expeditions is expanded to accommodate unemployed fishermen. This strategy for reducing unemployment leads to worker (and, possibly, owner) remuneration that varies inversely with the firm's employment level.[4]

An early example of a formal social security system is the Islamic system for providing for the indigent. In this system only the financing mechanism is formalized; benefits and indigent recipients are determined locally. There is a tax on wealth (*zakat*) and a tithe on land (*ushr*) above an exemption limit fixed in real terms. *Ushr* has aspects of insurance—landowners pay more in good years and less in years with bad harvests—and it combines redistribution with moral suasion. There are also effective information flows regarding payments and eligibility that provide the preconditions for efficient targeting; local administration makes it more likely that the tax will be paid and that only the indigent (widows, orphans, and the elderly) receive payments (see Ahmad and Stern 1991).

The community-based social security instruments described above illustrate fairly sophisticated elements of redistribution and insurance. But coping mechanisms that work relatively well in normal times may fail in times of severe stress; for example, households at the margin of subsistence in normal years will be hard-pressed to protect themselves in the face of consecutive shocks. Such shocks may also lead to a deterioration of the environment, unless measures are taken to prevent famines and hardship for the entire community. These coping mechanisms do not exist in all places, and there is increasing evidence of dissolving family and ethnic ties, and of weakening community support systems in many countries. Moreover, traditional social security mechanisms based on the family encourage population growth, which may itself weaken community-based mechanisms. Thus, more or less formal mechanisms are needed to protect the vulnerable on a consistent basis, and to ensure that the financing needs for these mechanisms are met. And because of the widespread stringent fiscal constraints, there is a need to design effective formal mechanisms that reinforce—rather than supplant—traditional support systems.

Social insurance in developing countries

There has been increasing concern about public provision for the aged and infirm in developing countries. The concern has arisen in part because of a shift in demographic profiles—an aging of the population in large parts of the world, including Latin America, China, and South Asia, in conjunction with growing urbanization—and a weakening of traditional family and community-based social security mechanisms. Several policy options could be pursued in developing countries. A range of contributory policies that could be grouped under social insurance could provide coverage for old age, disability, and health care. Minimum or basic benefits could be targeted to, say, the elderly, or mothers with small children. Means-tested provision, because of the information costs and incentive effects it involves, is likely to be feasible only at the local level,[5] with community participation.

Many Latin American countries have relatively mature programs and aging populations. Most began with full funding of social security through trust funds (Mesa-Lago 1991). These funds have been eroded by forced holdings of government paper at below-market interest rates, inappropriate investments, and a proliferation of benefits conferred when the schemes were in initial surplus. Typically, under a unified system of contingent liabilities and health care, surpluses accrued for pensions are used to cross-subsidize burgeoning expenditures on health care. The schemes have now become mainly pay-as-you-go, and face looming financing crises, notably in Argentina, Brazil, and Mexico. In an inflationary context, contributions that are not indexed, combined with benefits that are, put increasing pressure on general revenues to meet the deficits of formal social security systems (see, for example, Mesa-Lago 1991). Raising the resources necessary to meet the current obligations and projected costs will be difficult because the indirect, income, and payroll tax rates are already high.[6] The combined social security tax rates (on workers and employers, together with contributions from general revenues) are already more than 30 percent of the wage bill in many Latin American countries; thus, further recourse to increasing the payroll tax, in particular, may not be desirable.

The high rates of taxation lead to tax evasion, reducing the base for social security and increasing the incentive to hire workers from the informal sector (who then lack longer-term coverage). In general, the indigent elderly have not been provided for because coverage is limited to the formal—mainly urban—sector. Exceptions are Chile and Costa Rica, where equity was achieved, in large part through an expansion in coverage (Mesa-Lago 1991). Both countries have a well-organized labor force in both the urban and the rural sectors.

Evaluating the distributional consequences of social security provision would require examining the entire system of benefits, funding, and taxes, and the implications for the population as a whole. There is a presumption that Latin American social security systems are regressive, but this is usually based on a simplistic comparison of pensions to poverty-level incomes, and preconceptions about the relative incidence of different tax instruments (see, for example, Mesa-Lago 1991).

A priori, evidence that pensioners are not poor should be taken as an indication that the social security system is successful, and has met the important objective of protecting the aged. That some of the aged outside the system are poor reflects the coverage of the system, not regressivity. The presumption that the Latin American social security system is regressive is based in part on its recourse to general revenues, along with the assumption that such taxes as the value added tax (VAT) are likely to be regressive. But the need to turn to general taxation is strongest when coverage is extended (this, of course, ignores the effects of incompetence or corruption, both of which are possible) to include poorer rural or informal sector workers who have not contributed, or whose contributions may be small relative to benefits. This appears to have happened in Brazil to some extent, for example.

The incidence of indirect taxes in Latin America is an empirical issue, one that has not been addressed in studies of Latin American social security. It is important to note that income and corporate taxes yield twice as much revenue, as a proportion of GDP, as the VAT or sales taxes in the Latin American countries (Tanzi 1987). Direct taxes are more likely to be progressive than indirect taxes, and even in a country such as India indirect taxes have been shown to be mildly progressive (Ahmad and Stern 1987). But generalizations on this issue are not possible; that the net incidence of the tax system is progressive is as likely as that it is regressive. A system of benefits that prevents people from falling into poverty, financed directly by those people and, possibly, through progressive general taxation, cannot, on the basis of a priori reasoning, be described as inherently regressive. Of course, in some countries, there has been a proliferation of benefits to the rich that cannot be financed by contributions, illustrating the need for reform.

Despite the mismanagement of social security trust funds and the poorly targeted operations in some Latin American countries, the need is clearly for reform, rather than abolition, of the formal social security systems. Similarly, it is inappropriate to argue that formal systems are not needed in such low-income countries as India, where formal sector employment is a relatively small proportion of the total labor force. The absence of a formal system of unemployment insurance in India severely constrains the needed adjustments and reforms to highly protected and inefficient public sector enterprises. With respect to other contingencies—aging, for example—the small proportion comprises several tens of millions of people, and the fairly rapid urbanization and the spread of wage-based activities in rural areas increase the prospects for the success of contribution-based social security systems. Because of demographic patterns in India, these systems should soon generate surpluses. Noncontributory assistance schemes are also growing in importance in India, and pension programs for rural widows in several states attest to the importance given to this vulnerable group.[7]

The Indian state of Kerala, whose social indicators have performed exceptionally well, has provided an old-age pension scheme for the informal sector since 1961, but destitution has not been a criterion for eligibility (Guhan 1988). In 1981-82 roughly half the aged in Kerala received pensions (1.43 percent of the population, or more than 300,000 people) at a cost of 2.52 percent of the state budget (India, Economic Administration Reforms Commission 1984). Most other Indian states have been less successful in extending coverage; stringent means tests have restricted eligibility and have been administratively cumbersome.

Social security in centrally planned economies

Many centrally planned economies have met social security objectives essentially through a system of employment guarantees and the provision of consumer goods at artificially low prices, in conjunction with a set of programs nominally classified as social security. But these systems neither prevented poverty nor ensured the availability of consumer items in demand. Rather, they led to a distorted structure of production incentives. The provision by state-owned enterprises of such public goods as housing, medical care, and care for the elderly has contributed in part to a soft budget constraint, which has slowed the transformation of their production to a market-based system. Thus, for the social security systems of centrally planned economies, reform issues include a reevaluation of the existing arrangements, the provision of benefits adequate to remove the responsibility of provision from enterprises (beyond appropriately defined employers' contributions), and the coverage of newly recognized contingencies, such as unemployment.

In the transition period, when the restructuring is likely to lead to widespread, though temporary, unemployment, a normally defined unemployment insurance scheme may not be adequate. There may be substantial start-up costs requiring support from the budget and general revenues. In addition, for the longer-term unemployed, appropriately designed public works could be a targeted and cost-effective means of provision.

Universal coverage remains a contentious issue. In the former USSR there were until recently special arrangements for collective farmers, with lower benefits and different financing mechanisms (see, for example, Madison 1990). In China there is no formal coverage for the rural sector. The extended family has traditionally provided much of the old-age support in rural areas. This form of support has been enshrined in successive constitutions since the creation of the People's Republic, along with a system of basic guarantees (*wu bao*) for the particularly distressed (widows, orphans, or the elderly) who lack family or kin support. Like Victorian poor relief in Britain, *wu bao* emphasizes preventing the nondeserving from receiving relief, rather than ensuring that all the deserving are covered. Thus, there is severe social stigma attached to *wu bao*, which restricts take-up rates. This ensures that rural social security remains anchored to the ability to work, and to reliance on sons in old age.[8] Even with basic local support, the state has had a role to play, particularly in ensuring that grain is supplied to poor areas and to those with grain shortages. The result of these different elements has been an ineffective rural social safety net that has not succeeded in replacing the traditional reliance on able-bodied sons.

The reforms proposed in many centrally planned economies, however, envisage universal coverage for life-cycle contingencies, including pensions for old age. The issues that the proposed reforms raise include the financing of benefit levels, eligibility criteria, and the establishment and identification of individual contributions.[9]

Temporary protective and compensatory measures

The existence of permanent social security institutions can provide a basis for assessing whether short-term or temporary compensatory measures are needed. These institutions can help minimize outlays that may have to be incurred for short-term measures, and indicate groups that might be at risk. Compensatory measures may be needed for a variety of shocks—for example, those arising from the correction of unsustainable budgetary or balance of payments situations. Possible adverse consequences of adjustment include rising prices—particularly for food items, which lead to declining real standards of living for net consumers—and unemployment.

To ensure the availability of cheap food for urban consumers, governments have resorted to widespread controls on production with low prices. Holding agricultural procurement prices substantially below world prices can lead to considerable, inefficient taxation of producers (Ahmad and Stern 1991). And artificially maintained exchange rates can distort the relative prices of tradables. The difficulty is that the taxed producers may be poorer than the consumers of the controlled food items, who usually are found in the urban and formal sectors. Moreover, the controlled prices can distort incentives and stifle both production and marketed output. In extreme situations, such as in Sri Lanka in the 1970s, low prices lead to excess demand that cannot be met because of the stagnating growth in output, and balance of payments difficulties are often exacerbated. Thus, as seen in many developing countries and in Eastern Europe, low procurement prices do not ensure the availability of key consumer goods.

The assurance of appropriate prices to producers is a key element of most adjustment programs. It is likely to benefit poor producers directly, but the short-run costs associated with rapid relative price changes may cause net purchasers to suffer sharp real income losses. Such losses, or "entitlement" failures (Sen 1981a), can lead to famine conditions, even if there has been no aggregate decline in food production. An example is the 1974 famine in Bangladesh, which occurred even though agricultural production was higher than it had been in previous years. The cause of the famine was local shortages associated with speculative hoarding and price increases.

If retail prices for consumers are not adjusted under structural adjustment—even in centrally planned economies—which involves rapid increases in procurement or support prices, budget deficits may be exacerbated because implicit subsidies are transformed into explicit transfers. This occurred in China in the late 1970s and early 1980s, with the abolition of collective agriculture and the introduction of the production responsibility system. A full pass-through of the price changes to consumers depends on the speed at which incomes and transfers (particularly transfers to pensioners and those unable to participate in the labor market) are adjusted,[10] and on the scope for compensatory measures in the interim period. The options for compensatory measures depend on the feasibility of cash or in-kind transfers, usually linked to items of basic consumption,[11] and on income support, through unemployment compensation or public works, for those who became unemployed as a result of major restructuring.

In this section two groups of compensatory instruments are examined: commodity price interventions and public employment provision. In selecting compensatory instruments, there need not be a one-to-one correspondence between a cause of poverty and a remedial approach, and it may be difficult or undesirable to restrict benefits from some instruments. For example, subsidies would provide transfers to those affected by price changes as well as to those made unemployed. It would clearly make little sense, however, to provide support for the elderly through commodity subsidies if pensions and direct transfers are feasible. Similarly, where deep-seated or chronic poverty is due to the absence of resources, technology, or skills, the only viable long-term solution is sustainable investment and growth. Subsidies and employment provision may temporarily assist some of the chronic poor, but they do not provide permanent solutions. Indefinite provision of transfers to the chronic poor, through either commodity price interventions or employment provision, is unlikely to be sustainable in budgetary terms, and may exacerbate the conditions causing their poverty by substituting for needed technological change, or migration, that would pull people out of submarginal existence.

Consider first compensation for major changes in relative prices. The policy issues relating to compensation are whether it should be universal or targeted in some way, whether it should be in cash or in kind, and, for commodity-based transfers, which method should be used to deliver the subsidy. Possible methods for commodity price interventions range from general subsidies to more restricted rations denominated in kind, or cash-equivalent formulations, such as food stamps. Various degrees of targeting are feasible for each option.

Because changes in relative prices lead to gainers as well as to losers, universal compensatory measures are generally not justified. At the other extreme, detailed means testing is likely to be administratively infeasible, and may also lead to high marginal tax rates at the point of withdrawal of the benefit.[12] Nonetheless, a degree of targeting is administratively feasible, and may be desirable. For example, targeting could be regional, with benefits restricted to, say, urban areas, as in China.[13] This still leaves the problem of identifying and providing benefits for net purchasers in rural areas, however (Ahmad and Wang 1991). Other forms of non-means-tested targeting are possible—for example, categorical cash transfers to vulnerable groups, such as children, the unemployed, or the aged. As with other forms of targeting, some vulnerable groups might be inadvertently excluded from these programs.

Whether cash or in-kind provision should be chosen depends on the nature of the risk facing consumers, and the administrative capabilities of the country in question. Cash and in-kind provision would be equivalent if producers are assured border prices for their produce—for example, through appropriate support prices, so that there are no adverse effects on supply—if prices are known with certainty, and if resale is permissible and costless. If price adjustments are uncertain, cash provision leads to higher risks for the consumer than in-kind provision, although its budgetary consequences are known with greater precision. The ability of the government to import food places an outer limit on budgetary outlays, however, and can also influence the variance in market prices faced by consumers. Where low consumer prices affect producer prices and output response, an option under famine conditions is to effect cash transfers to consumers quickly in order to generate purchasing power, support higher prices to discourage hoarding, and induce greater market supplies (Drèze and Sen 1989). This may not be a feasible option if there are genuine supply constraints. Moreover, under supply constraints, the injection of cash would exacerbate inflationary pressures, particularly in the presence of a monetary overhang.

Commodity-based transfers

Food price interventions have been used as a protective measure for several thousand years. In Egypt the state has stored food since Pharaonic times, subsidizing sales and distributing food to the indigent. These functions were seen as the moral responsibility of rulers and played an important role in maintaining social stability. Crises arose because of shortfalls in domestic production, the financing of military requirements, and disruptions of trade, and food riots were reported in the fourteenth and fifteenth centuries (Scobie 1988). In classical Rome a grain or bread ration was also provided free, although the authorities tried to limit the number of recipients. This could be construed as a basic income in kind. The poor were a political force at that time, capable of being aroused against the rulers (Atkinson 1990).

For most governments, undertaking commodity price interventions requires, first, choosing the commodity to subsidize, and second, determining whether the subsidy should be provided for all purchases of the good through a general subsidy, or restricted in some fashion, by rations or food stamps, for example.

Choice of commodity. Commodities chosen as transfer instruments for the poor should ideally be those consumed only by the poor. Coarse grains and unrefined sugar, known as *gur* in India and Pakistan, are good candidates for this reason. But most inferior commodities are not widely marketed. Moreover, encouraging heavier use of certain items—for example, firewood for cooking, used extensively by the poor in such countries as Nepal—would tend to have negative externalities on the environment. Subsidies for more environmentally acceptable alternatives, such as kerosene, might be preferable.

It is in general difficult to identify items that are consumed only by the poor. The alternative is to distinguish marketable commodities that are important in the consumption baskets of *all* the poor, even if they are also consumed by the nonpoor. Examples include such important staples as wheat, maize, and rice. By the same token, commodities not generally consumed by the poor should not be subsidized. Subsidies on imported meat products in Jordan, on frozen meats and macaroni in Egypt, and on sardines, chicken, and salted fish in Jamaica, for example, are inappropriate, because these commodities are not consumed by the poor. The subsidies could be redirected to commodities with more attractive distributional characteristics.

The choice of commodity for intervention, and the form that this might take, are illustrated by the British response to the major disruptions and shortfalls in food supply that occurred after the outbreak of World War II. The interventions were carefully designed by nutritionists and became the prototype for similar policies in areas influenced by the British: the Caribbean, North Africa, and South Asia. Such items as meat,[14] dairy products, and sugar were rationed to ensure that excess demand by the rich would not price them beyond the reach of the poor; this was consistent with the policy's emphasis on balanced diets. Without rationing, real incomes of the poor would have been restricted, and demand would have been diverted to the less nutritious starches and staples: bread and potatoes. Despite reductions in overall food availability, the nutritional status of the poor *improved* during this period. The food rationing and subsidy system was gradually withdrawn after the war.

General subsidies. A state provides a general subsidy for a commodity when it guarantees unlimited supplies of the commodity at a price that is generally below cost. General subsidies can achieve wide coverage, but the associated costs can place unsustainable burdens on the budget or the balance of payments. Moreover, unless there is some targeting through subsidies on inferior goods, general subsidies can be fairly regressive. In Egypt and Sri Lanka the lowest-income groups received less in absolute terms than richer groups through the general subsidy on wheat. As a proportion of incomes, however, the subsidies appear more progressive. The transfers amounted to 8 to 10 percent of the incomes of the poorest urban and rural quartiles in Egypt (Alderman and von Braun 1984) and about 9 percent for the poorest quintile in Sri Lanka; the transfers were 3 to 4 percent of the incomes of the richest groups. A general subsidy may also undermine the establishment of higher support prices for farmers because of the possibilities for arbitrage. Nonetheless, the administrative costs of a general subsidy scheme are likely to be lower than those for such alternatives as rations or targeted schemes, which require the identification of recipients by, say, income status.

Rations. The provision of a fixed quantity of a commodity at the subsidized price can lead to substantial budgetary savings compared with a general subsidy. If quantities subsidized are restricted to amounts consumed by the poorest income groups, the ration will ensure that the poor will be protected from the effects of the price adjustments. Typically, the poorest 10 to 20 percent of the population consume 40 to 50 percent of the average consumption of the main staples; thus, a ration would cost half as much to implement as a general subsidy. In addition, supplying a specific quantity at a given price protects the recipients of rations from unexpected changes in prices, an important issue when there is considerable uncertainty about retail prices. And, if the ration can be resold, the provision is equivalent to a cash transfer. A ration can pose difficulties for the poorest, however, because liquidity constraints may prevent them from purchasing weekly supplies.

Ration programs for staple goods implemented to limit costs and ensure availability, similar to those in the United Kingdom, have been observed in developing countries, such as Egypt (rice, sugar, and oils), India (wheat and rice), Pakistan (sugar and wheat),[15] and Sri Lanka (rice). In Pakistan sugar rationing, which had wide rural and urban coverage, did not invariably involve a subsidy, as domestic prices were kept above world prices for extended periods.[16] When domestic availability improved, the ration was withdrawn. The restriction of the wheat ration in rural parts of India and Pakistan to areas without a wheat surplus was dictated by a desire to protect producers.

The incidence of the ration system appeared to be much more progressive than that of general subsidies in Sri Lanka, with a larger absolute benefit to the poorer groups. In Egypt the ration system led to roughly equal transfers for different income classes. Both systems were progressive because the transfer was more important to the poor (20 percent of the income of the poorest quintile in Sri Lanka) than to the rich.

Distribution of rationed quantities through a public distribution system, if one exists, would minimize leakage. In addition, the special placement of public distribution outlets allows the targeting of rations; school feeding programs and in-kind provision at maternal and child health clinics are examples of methods for targeting. Setting up a public distribution system from scratch may be expensive and time-consuming, however, and such a system may be inappropriate as a compensatory mechanism that needs to be put into place rapidly.

A reform of ration mechanisms that lead to uniform prices for retailers is important in encouraging the development of a market economy. Quantity-based coupons (with the quantity guided by the consumption levels of the poor) could be sold to all or specified households, at a subsidized price, for use in obtaining given commodities. If more of a commodity is required, it would have to be purchased at the open market price. The retailer would face a single price if reimbursed in kind or if reimbursed in cash at the average price over a period. In both cases, a handling fee would be needed. The disadvantage of this system is that it involves administrative costs.

Ration coupons denominated in cash may be attractive from an administrative point of view if there are plenty of private retail outlets. The ration coupon system is less attractive when private retail outlets have yet to be established, as in some centrally planned economies. In addition, because the ration coupons are redeemable at the current market price, the consumer bears the risk of price changes.

Means-tested food stamps. Food stamps are akin to cash-equivalent rations, but they usually involve an element of means testing. Introduced in the United States as a way of reducing the wheat surplus, the food stamp scheme has evolved into a major income transfer program in that country. Yet, despite the administrative capabilities of the United States, the take-up rate for food stamps has been limited to 40 percent of the eligible population because of the stigma attached to them. Jamaica and Sri Lanka are the only two developing countries that have instituted food stamps on a national scale.

In Sri Lanka budgetary outlays fell substantially with the introduction of food stamps, from 14 percent of government expenditure in 1979 to 3 percent in 1984. This was largely because the nominal value of the food stamps was kept constant (kerosene stamps more than doubled in nominal value, however). The net income transferred declined by 1984 to half its 1979 level. Eligibility for food stamps was to be based on self-declared household income, and the stamps were to be provided on an adult-equivalent scale. But the income threshold does not appear to have been taken very seriously, and, despite alleged targeting properties, the coverage of the population in the upper-income deciles did not differ greatly from that of the rice ration. The coverage of the poor, and those nutritionally at risk, was less than complete (Rouse 1990). Furthermore, for several years after 1977, excluded persons could not readily enter the scheme, even if their income fell below the level at which they should have been eligible. Yet the political economy aspects of even *claimed* finer targeting are also evident: middle-class support, though strong and vocal for the subsidized or free food rations before 1977, dwindled for the food stamps.

In Jamaica 50 percent of the aid-financed food stamps were allocated to maternal and child health and nutrition clinics. The rest were to be allocated to the indigent on the basis of a self-declared certification. Although in Sri Lanka the nonpoor did not hesitate to declare incomes below the cut-off point, in Jamaica the certification procedure led to stigma. This largely excluded the nonpoor, but, like the new poor law in Britain after 1834, it also excluded many of the indigent.

Employment provision and public works

The provision of employment has long been an important instrument for preventing famine. There is evidence that it was used as early as the fourth century B.C. in India, and it was an integral element of the Famine Codes developed in British India in the late 1800s. Public works have been undertaken to assist the unemployed in industrial countries—for example, in the United States—as a response to the economic recession and food shortage in the 1930s. This form of provision is less common now, as unemployment benefits have been incorporated into the formal social security system.

In principle, employment provision can play an important role in maintaining the living standards of those affected by temporary economic setbacks. Insurance and credit markets provide little protection against deprivation; labor market interventions, however, can provide both insurance and transfers for income maintenance. Such schemes can provide assistance rapidly, and can be effectively self-targeting if employment is provided at subsistence wages.[17]

For large-scale unemployment that occurs as a result of adjustment—as in some Eastern European countries—appropriately designed public works programs are likely to be more effective in protecting the vulnerable than unemployment insurance as a limited first round of protection. But permanent employment guarantees, through support to industries and sectors that are uncompetitive in an open trading environment, are unlikely to be sustainable, and as the experience in Eastern Europe has shown, they can have stifling effects on incentives and initiative.

Employment in public works at subsistence wages and the distribution of relief remain at the core of the system of famine prevention in contemporary India. One element of the system is the Maharashtra Employment Guarantee Scheme, which had the objective of building up infrastructure as well as preventing famine. An extended drought led to a fall in India's cereal production in 1972/73 to less than 50 percent of 1967/68 levels, indicating drought more severe than those in Sub-Saharan Africa in the early 1980s, which resulted in several severe famines. India's rural population was particularly vulnerable because of limited irrigation, seasonality, and growing environmental degradation. But utilization of a portfolio of projects prevented famine in India, and appeared to be fairly well targeted. Similarly, in Bangladesh, the rural works program proved to be an effective safety net, preventing a famine in 1988 under conditions similar to those that had led to famine in 1974. Public works employment for famine prevention—not relief—has also been strikingly successful, under very difficult conditions, in Africa in the 1980s in such countries as Botswana and Cape Verde (Drèze and Sen 1989).

Chile has one of the oldest and most advanced social insurance systems in Latin America. Nevertheless, self-targeted employment provision played an important role during two major crisis periods—1974-77 and 1982-84—that led to a halving of the real wage rate. By 1976 the Programas de Empleo (EEP) employed about 6 percent of the labor force. At that stage open unemployment was at 16 percent of the labor force. During the second shock a third of the labor force became unemployed, and the EEP was doubled to cover 13 percent of the work force. Because of the self-selecting nature of the EEP, its total budgetary cost was only 1.4 percent of GNP at the height of the crisis in 1983. A survey conducted in 1986-87 suggests that most of the workers in the main schemes of the EEP were in the lowest income quintile.[18] The EEP was gradually phased out as the labor market tightened, and was withdrawn completely in 1988, as open unemployment returned to about 6 percent, or close to 1970 levels (World Bank 1990c).

Employment provision through public works that does not attempt to target through low wages can be fairly expensive. Tunisia ran such a scheme from 1953 until the 1960s. Because wages were high, employment had to be rationed, and individuals were employed in rotation. Most projects were for land development and irrigation. The scheme provided employment for 39 percent of the unemployed, but at its peak it cost as much as 5 percent of GNP.

Chile's experience with self-targeted employment provision illustrates what is possible in the context of short-term shocks. The contrast between Chile's experience and Tunisia's emphasizes the desirability of targeting through low wages; targeting makes it easier to wind the scheme down when it is no longer needed, and limits the overall cost. The experience of Maharashtra and Bangladesh shows the usefulness of such schemes in preventing famine, and in smoothing the effects of seasonal variations in income. It is important to build administrative ability to implement employment programs rapidly. There may be considerable complementarity between employment provision and regular public works programs for asset generation.

Conclusions

Attempts should be made in developing countries to establish institutions and financing mechanisms to assure permanent measures to insure against normal life-cycle contingencies. An additional set of measures may be needed to protect against the effects of shocks and major realignments in relative prices. The standard issues for both permanent and temporary measures are that, if the transfers are adequate to live on, there will be incentive problems, and the tax rate will be high. Efficient targeting of the measures would need to be balanced against the costs of their administration, including the imposition of a means test. For countries considering alternative social insurance measures, the choice should depend on the nature of contingencies experienced and on their administrative and financing capacities.

Notes

This paper was presented at the Poverty Research Conference organized by the International Food Policy Research Institute and the World Bank in October 1989 and at seminars at IFPRI and the World Bank. Particular thanks are due to Tony Atkinson, Robin Burgess, Ke-Young Chu, Jean Drèze, Ravi Kanbur, Michael Lipton, Jean-Philippe Platteau, Nick Stern, Jacques van der Gaag, and Joachim von Braun. Responsibility for the views expressed rests with the author and not the institutions with which he has been associated during this period: the London School of Economics, the World Bank, and the IMF.

1. For a fuller discussion of social security as a "permanent" measure, see Ahmad (1991) or Ahmad and others (1991).

2. For a review of social security and income maintenance in industrial countries, see also Atkinson (1987a).

3. Assistance to single mothers with dependent children is means-tested.

4. The examples on fishing communities are based on work by Platteau (1991).

5. This is also true in industrial countries.

6. In countries with older demographic profiles, the aging of the population puts additional pressure on the schemes. The relevant consideration, however, even with such demographic profiles, is to bring younger groups of workers into the system. In countries with younger demographic profiles, there are likely to be surpluses in the initial stages.

7. Unless widows have grown sons, they are often badly treated by in-laws and generally cannot return to the safety of their own families. They are thus among the most vulnerable, even if their extended families are relatively prosperous (see, for example, Drèze 1990b).

8. See Ahmad and Hussain (1991) for a discussion, and Aimei (1988) for a description, of some experimentation.

9. This involves setting up systems for issuing social security identification numbers, which requires an initial investment in time and resources. Many developing countries now have such identification numbers.

10. This in turn depends on budgetary constraints, since much of the formal employment is in the state-owned sector, and wage increases are felt either as losses of the public sector or as direct outlays for public sector employees (teachers, doctors, administrators, and the like).

11. These are mainly, though not exclusively, food items.

12. This is also known as the poverty trap phenomenon, and its severity depends on the extent of work disincentives that might be created in a particular context.

13. The presumption was that rural areas benefited largely through the increases in procurement prices.

14. Unlike in many developing countries, meat is consumed by all income classes in industrial countries.

15. Far from being a commodity suitable for rationing in Pakistan, wheat is an excellent candidate for taxation because of its consumption patterns and revenue potential (see Ahmad and Stern 1991).

16. The issue price was below the market-clearing scarcity price, however, given limitations of supply.

17. "The problem to be solved is how to avoid the risk of indiscriminate and demoralizing profusion on the one hand, and of insufficient and niggardly assistance on the other....Some safeguards then are essential in the interests of the destitute people no less than of the public treasury, and they are best found in laying down certain broad self-acting tests by which necessity may be proved, and which may, irrespective of any other rule of selection, entitled to relief the person who submits to them....The chief of these tests, and the only one which in our opinion it is ordinarily desirable to enforce, is the demand for labor commensurate in each case with the laborer's powers, in return for a wage sufficient for the purposes of maintenance but not more. The system is applicable of course only to those from whom labor can reasonably be required." Excerpts from India, Famine Commission (1880: para. 111).

18. In the Programa de Empleo Minimo 65.65 percent were from the lowest quintile, and in the Programa de Obras por Jefes Hogares, 56.5 percent.

The Role of Food-Linked Income Transfers in Efforts to Alleviate Malnutrition

16 *Per Pinstrup-Andersen*

Government transfer programs and policies are frequently linked to basic human needs, such as food and housing. Food price subsidies, food stamp programs, and food supplementation schemes are common forms of transfer.

The reasons for linking transfers to food vary among countries and over time. In some cases food is used as a transfer carrier simply because it occupies a large share of the budget of the poor and therefore provides a certain degree of targeting. In other cases government transfers are politically feasible only if linked to basic human needs because that form of transfer is perceived to be more effective than cash transfers in alleviating human misery. In many cases food-linked transfers are an outcome of policies aimed at the maintenance of relatively low wages. Whether intended or not, the value of the transfer may be partially or entirely offset by lower wages among recipients.

Food-linked transfers are often justified on nutritional grounds. Yet efforts are rarely made in designing and implementing such transfers to assure a high degree of cost-effectiveness from a nutritional point of view.

The purpose of this chapter is to place food-linked transfers in the micro-economic context of overall efforts to alleviate malnutrition and explore how they might be more cost-effective in achieving nutrition goals. The most common constraints to good nutrition are (1) insufficient access to food, (2) infectious diseases, (3) lack of knowledge, and (4) high rates of childbirth. Past and present policies and programs have attempted to alleviate one or more of these constraints. This chapter reviews the effectiveness of these programs.

Programs and policies to improve access to food

Food price subsidies, food stamp programs, and food supplementation schemes all fall into the category of programs and policies designed to improve access to food. Income-generating and income transfer programs not aimed specifically at improving nutrition, such as public works—including food-for-work programs—employment generation, social programs, unemployment compensation, and support to small-scale entrepreneurs and farmers, may also be effective in enhancing access to food among the poor and malnourished.

Food price subsidies and food stamps

The real income transfers embodied in food subsidies are frequently large.[1] In several of the fifteen developing countries for which information on this subject is available, 15 to 25 percent of the incomes of the poorest quartile of the population came from food subsidies (Pinstrup-Andersen 1988). This does not necessarily mean that the poor's incomes would have been 15 to 25 percent lower without the subsidies. The net effect is likely to be smaller because of wage adjustments and changes in household expenditure patterns. In all fifteen countries the income elasticity of demand for the subsidized foods was positive and decreasing with increasing income. Thus, with no targeting, the absolute amount of transfer increased with increasing income. The value of the subsidies as a percentage of total income was higher for the poor than for those better-off, however. Some programs, but not all, were heavily biased toward urban consumers. A considerable variation in the size and distribution of benefits from subsidy programs was found across program types and countries (Pinstrup-Andersen 1988).

Although the scarcity of solid empirical evidence prevents an estimate of the extent to which wages are affected by food prices, it is clear that food price subsidies tend to depress wage levels. This is so because food is an important wage good. The empirical evidence on this relationship is clearest in public wages. Thus, the real income embodied in subsidies overestimates the net effect of subsidies on incomes after wage incomes forgone are taken into account. In some cases—for example, in Bangladesh and Egypt—food price subsidies to public sector employees may be viewed as an in-kind wage. Therefore, as illustrated by reductions in food subsidies in Sri Lanka in the late 1970s (Edirisinghe 1988), the net fiscal cost savings associated with a reduction in food subsidies will be less than the amount of the reduction because cash wage compensation to public employees is often a political necessity.

Many food price subsidy schemes—for example, food ration schemes in India—were originally aimed at ensuring households' access to certain food rations at stable prices (George 1988). By providing fixed quantities of rations at fixed prices, these schemes transferred price fluctuations from the recipients to the government or to the rest of the market and reduced both chronic and transitory household food insecurity. Some of these programs—for example, the Sri Lankan ration scheme—have been changed to programs providing a transfer of a fixed nominal value. These programs are less effective in reducing transitory food insecurity in recipient households, and the real value of the transfer decreases over time.

Income transfers are linked to food in part because of a belief that food-linked transfers have a stronger effect on food consumption than the same real income transferred in cash. This is clearly true for extramarginal price subsidies (price subsidies for quantities that exceed those purchased prior to the subsidies) because they lower prices at the margin. The evidence for subsidies limited to intramarginal quantities (subsidies limited to quantities less than those purchased without subsidies) is not as clear, as further discussed below.

Studies of food stamp programs in Colombia (Pinstrup-Andersen 1984), Puerto Rico (Fraker, Devaney, and Cavin 1986), and Sri Lanka (Edirisinghe 1987) found no statistically significant difference in the marginal propensity to consume food with respect to food stamps and cash income. These findings are contradicted by the results of studies of other subsidy programs—for example, that in the Philippines (Garcia and Pinstrup-Andersen 1987) and the U.S. food stamp program (Senauer and Young 1986). These studies found that the marginal propensity to consume food was significantly higher for food-related transfers than for other income. All of the studies controlled for the effect of income level. Senauer and Young (1986) offer four possible explanations of differences among sources of income in the marginal propensity to consume food:

- A sense of gratitude associated with the receipt of food subsidies
- Intrahousehold differences in taste linked with the distribution of budget control among household members for different sources of income
- The operation of the permanent income hypothesis
- Differential cash flows—for example, subsidy income may be more or less lumpy than other income.

Differences in transactions costs, where they exist, may also help explain the differences in the marginal propensity to consume food. More research is needed to explain these conflicting findings.

The marginal propensity to consume food is relatively large for low-income households. Income elasticities for food expenditures are often about 0.6 to 0.8 for households at income levels at which the risk of energy and protein deficiencies is high. The income elasticities for quantity of food expressed in energy are considerably lower, often about one-half of the expenditure elasticities (Alderman 1986).[2] Thus, the percentage increase in household energy consumption resulting from intramarginal food subsidies has been between one-third and one-half of the percentage increase in incomes. Simultaneous shifts toward more expensive diets have resulted in somewhat larger increases in protein consumption.

Direct price elasticities of demand for the foods most commonly subsidized—rice and wheat—among the poor are frequently about –0.5 to –0.8 (Alderman 1986; and Pinstrup-Andersen 1985). Thus, extramarginal subsidies lead to relatively large increases in the consumption of the subsidized commodities. If a commodity is not rationed, explicit (government-financed) subsidies will benefit suppliers, whether domestic or foreign, while significantly increasing fiscal costs.

Some household members (children between six and twenty-four months of age, and pregnant and lactating women) are more likely to be malnourished than others. Thus, how the additional food obtained because of a subsidy is distributed among a household's members is important. In the Philippines a subsidy for rice and cooking oil increased energy consumption among preschool children by 5 percent and total household energy consumption by 7 percent (Garcia and Pinstrup-Andersen 1987). Thus, the distribution of the increase in household energy consumption was biased in favor of adults. In Mexico a milk subsidy resulted in increased milk consumption among preschool children and decreased consumption of other commodities (Kennedy 1987). The net effect on energy and protein consumption by preschool children was positive but smaller than the energy and protein embodied in the subsidy.

Because malnutrition may be a result of both insufficient food intake and infectious diseases, increased food intake may not necessarily improve nutrition. Empirical evidence on the effect of food subsidies on nutritional status is very limited. In a study of food subsidies in Kerala, India, Kumar (1979) found that the weight for age of preschool children in recipient households would have been 8 percent below current levels without the subsidies. Similar results were found for a food subsidy scheme in the Philippines (Garcia and Pinstrup-Andersen 1987). Other recent studies (for example, von Braun, Hotchkiss, and Immink 1989) have shown a statistically significant relationship between increases in household food consumption and the nutritional status of preschool children. Many others have not (for example, Kennedy and Cogill 1988). The explanation for changes in household food consumption significantly affecting the nutritional status of preschool children in some but not all cases is probably to be found in intrahousehold food distribution and in the importance of food deficiencies relative to such non-food-related factors as parasites, poor sanitation, and infectious diseases and related diarrhea.

A key consideration in most explicit food subsidy programs is fiscal cost, which in large part determines the feasibility of a program. Real fiscal costs of explicit food subsidies decreased during the 1980s in many developing countries (Pinstrup-Andersen, Jaramillo, and Stewart 1987). The decrease was due primarily to falling real prices of the food procured by governments, although a few countries—for example, Mexico and Sri Lanka—made explicit policy changes to reduce subsidy costs.

For nutrition, what is important is the cost-effectiveness—the nutrition benefit derived per unit of cost. The cost-effectiveness of most food subsidy schemes is very low, and large cuts in fiscal cost could be made without reducing nutrition benefits if the cuts were accompanied by better targeting and improved program implementation. Alternatively, nutrition benefits could be greatly enhanced at current cost levels.

The cost-effectiveness of food subsidies could be further improved by strengthening primary health care and improving water and sanitation. The associated increases in government expenditures could be met with savings gained from better targeting of food subsidies. But efforts to improve the targeting of food subsidies should take into account the effect on political sustainability. As the Colombian food stamp program showed, it is possible to target a program out of existence simply because the narrower target population has little or no political power. This and other related political economy issues are analyzed in Pinstrup-Andersen (forthcoming) and Hopkins (1988).

Food supplementation

Supplementary feeding programs distribute food through public agencies to infants, preschool children, and pregnant and lactating women. Three types of delivery system are used: on-site feeding, take-home feeding, and nutrition rehabilitation centers. Experience from past programs shows that the degree of success depends on the amount, type, and quality of food delivered to the target group, the duration of feeding, the timing of supplementation, the nutritional status of entrants, and the degree of targeting (Kennedy and Knudsen 1985). The target households' behavior, economic situation, and access to primary health care and to nutrition information are also critical.

Some food supplementation schemes have been associated with greater birth weight, improved growth, decreased morbidity, and improved cognitive development among infants and preschool children. But the benefits are usually small, and many schemes show no effects. One reason for this is that the amount of food made available is so small that the effects cannot be measured. After leakage to other household members and reductions in food acquired from other sources are taken into account, net additions to food consumption typically fill only 10 to 25 percent of the apparent energy gap of the target individuals (Beaton and Ghassemi 1982). Another important reason for the disappointing results is that lack of access to food might not be the most binding constraint.

To be cost-effective, food supplementation schemes must be based on a solid understanding of the existing food-related constraints and integrated with programs that can effectively deal with other binding constraints—for example, lack of knowledge, and infectious diseases. Furthermore, the supplement must be large enough to make a difference to the target individuals after accounting for sharing with other household members and substitution between the supplement and food from other sources.

A recent assessment of food supplementation programs for which valid evaluations of nutritional impact were available shows that the programs had a significant effect on both the nutrient intake and the weight for age of preschool children (Pinstrup-Andersen and others forthcoming). These programs did not suffer from the deficiencies mentioned above.

Food stamp programs and food price subsidies, including subsidized rations to target households, may be preferable to food supplementation because they usually require less administrative capacity. Unless they are well targeted, however, they tend not to be cost-effective. Targeted food stamps or ration cards combined with nutrition education and primary health care could be an effective strategy in countries with sufficient infrastructure and administrative capacity to manage such integrated programs. One successful example of such a strategy was the Colombian food stamp program, which issued food stamps and provided nutrition education to mothers who brought their preschool children to primary health posts (Pinstrup-Andersen 1984).

One of the principal deficiencies of food supplementation and food stamp programs is that they treat the symptoms of malnutrition rather than the causes. Therefore, they are sustainable only as long as they are funded. Unlike some programs that enhance households' income-generating capacity, they do not lead to a situation in which they are no longer needed. The challenge is to design programs that will increase access to food in the short run while creating a capacity within the household to obtain the food independently in the long run. Opportunities for using income and food transfer schemes to create self-sustained income-generating capacity among the poor have not been fully exploited and should be pursued. Such opportunities include the formation of human capital through improved health, nutrition, and education, and the use of food along with technical assistance and credit to facilitate the development of small-scale enterprises and other self-help activities for the large share of the poor who are self-employed. Public works schemes properly focused not only on generating incomes during the life of the scheme, but—equally or more important—on developing infrastructure that will help increase employment for the poor after the scheme ends, offer great promise.

Programs to provide knowledge

Inadequate knowledge undoubtedly has been and still is an important cause of malnutrition. But care should be taken to introduce nutrition education programs only where insufficient knowledge is the most important constraint. The need for nutrition education is greatest where large changes have occurred in the environment and constraints within which household decisions are made (Hornik 1985), such as rural-to-urban migration, shifts from subsistence to cash cropping, and other changes that significantly alter the size and source of household incomes and the availability of food and nonfood commodities. But nutrition education is often promoted in situations in which households are unable to respond because of other constraints. Households with severely malnourished members are frequently deprived of other basic necessities in addition to food, and insufficient incomes are their most important constraint. Nutrition education aimed at reallocating a given amount of real income or food in these households is not likely to be successful. This is illustrated by a recent study in the Philippines that found that nutrition education was most effective in households that also received a food subsidy (Garcia and Pinstrup-Andersen 1987).

Nutrition education may be effective in households in which a significant share of the budget is spent on nonessential goods, the cost of the diet is high due to a lack of emphasis on available low-cost foods, and the allocation of food is biased against members of high-risk groups. Nutrition education focused on behavioral changes related to breastfeeding, feeding of weaning-age children, diarrheal diseases, and sanitary practices has also proved effective in many cases (Hornik 1985). Although, as mentioned above, nutrition education is most likely to be successful when linked with other changes in resources, a recent project in Indonesia illustrates that it may also be successful by itself (Manoff 1985). This project, which was based on mass media communication, led to significant increases in food intake and growth of children at a relatively low cost. Similarly, a recent nutrition education project in the Dominican Republic resulted in significant nutritional improvements (USAID 1988).

Nutrition education programs based on a thorough understanding of the problems, and the constraints within which they must be solved, are more likely to be successful than those based on preconceived ideas about what households and individuals ought to do. And nutrition education that is integrated with other efforts to improve nutrition, such as income enhancement and primary health care, has proved effective in a number of cases (Cerqueira and Olson forthcoming).

Growth monitoring for children deserves particular attention as a source of information for mothers. Precisely because it is a source of information rather than a nutrition intervention, its effectiveness depends on the quality and timeliness of the information as well as its use. Unless the information is used to guide action, even the best growth-monitoring system will have no impact on nutrition. And growth monitoring that provides faulty information is not only useless but may lead to inappropriate action and a waste of resources.

Although good evaluations of growth monitoring are scarce, it appears that much of it either has been poorly implemented or has lacked links with effective action (Ruel forthcoming). The integrated nutrition project in Tamil Nadu, India, for example, has successfully used growth monitoring to guide action to improve the nutritional status of preschool children.

Integrated programs

The critical tailoring of nutrition programs to the constraints and opportunities faced by the target group may require designing an integrated strategy. Because constraints interact, removing one may do little to improve nutrition. In many cases there is a need for several elements: primary health care, more food, better information, and better child spacing.

Several integrated nutrition and health programs have been at least partially successful. One of the most successful of these programs, the integrated nutrition project in Tamil Nadu, India, uses growth monitoring to identify children, age six months to three years, at risk of malnutrition. The program provides food supplements to these children until they reach normal growth, and nutrition education to the parents, along with a series of health services. The impact on participants' nutritional status has been impressive, according to an internal World Bank report and Shekar (forthcoming).

The Iringa project in Tanzania is another example of a successful integrated health and nutrition intervention. Child weighing is used as a source of information for nutrition education and screening. Child feeding and a variety of health services are integral parts of the project, and malnutrition has been reduced considerably over a few years (Yambi, Jonsson, and Ljungqvist 1989; and UNICEF 1989).

A number of other integrated health and nutrition projects were reviewed by Lamptey and Sai (1985). The authors conclude that most of the projects have been successful to varying degrees, but that, because most were pilot projects, it may be difficult to maintain their success if they are scaled up. This is because of several characteristics that the pilot projects share. First, the pilot projects have effective organization and administration; service personnel are carefully selected and trained, well supervised and supported, and given carefully developed and realistic job assignments to carry out for a relatively small population. Second, the projects tend to have highly motivated, dedicated, and, at times, charismatic leaders whose departure may lead to collapse of the projects. Third, most of the projects are of limited duration. And fourth, the projects' continuing evaluation and feedback helps them realistically reorder project activities to more appropriately fit the needs of the children.

Many of these characteristics may not be transferable to larger projects—that is, the success of small projects may be due in large measure to their size. Lamptey and Sai identify many recurring difficulties with integrated programs and projects:

- Planning that requires input from several individuals and agencies may prove difficult to harmonize.
- Collaboration and coordination at all stages can be problematic, in part because of vested interests.
- The traditional governmental organization of line agencies creates peripheral management problems in personnel, budgeting, and many other areas.
- The training of most health workers is too specific and technological to prepare them to be readily adaptable to the broader perspectives required for integrated activities (working with the community as an equal partner is generally too new a concept for health workers).
- Peripheral managerial expertise is often lacking.
- Evaluation is more difficult in these programs than in vertical ones.

According to Lamptey and Sai, successful programs require:

- High-level political commitment
- Administration that ensures decentralization
- Local administrative control
- Community participation.

Ensuring participation of the community means helping it to identify its own needs and to develop its own plans for meeting these needs, recruiting the necessary personnel from within the community, and mobilizing resources from outside the community for funding subactivities.

The emphasis among donors and national governments on the need for scaling-up is exaggerated. A large number of small projects, each reflecting the particular needs and opportunities of the household group it serves, may well be more cost-effective than a few large-scale projects, each attempting to cover many household groups with different constraints. Yet many small projects have been criticized and abandoned because they could not be scaled up successfully, and many attempts to scale up projects have failed. The critical issue is to identify the components of successful projects that can be handled most cost-effectively at a large scale and provide such large-scale support to small-scale projects, rather than attempting to scale up entire projects. Food subsidies, primary health care, and nutrition education may well be components needed in most projects, but the way they should be provided is likely to vary among communities.

The sustainability of nutrition programs and projects is of critical importance. Ideally, they should become self-sustained or unnecessary over time. The use of food-linked transfers to enhance income-generating capacities in the target group could make an important contribution toward meeting the goal of self-sustainability. Programs and projects effectively targeted at the poor and malnourished tend not to be politically sustainable in the longer run if they depend largely or entirely on support from outside the target group—even when they meet their stated goals.

Designing cost-effective targeted nutrition programs

In the foreseeable future, we will not eradicate poverty, make available to all a complete array of primary health care services, information, and education, or ensure individuals' right to self-determination. In this imperfect world, which targeted nutrition programs should be pursued by governments, and how can food-linked income transfers best be utilized? The answer will vary among countries and population groups, and over time. But experience from past and ongoing programs provides at least some general guidelines.

Increased breastfeeding, greater child spacing, and improved weaning practices have resulted in improved infant and child nutrition, and well-designed programs to promote these practices are likely to have a significant impact (Pinstrup-Andersen and others forthcoming). Family planning resulting in more appropriate child spacing, and programs to support the nutritional needs of low-income women in their childbearing years, are likely to be effective in reducing mortality, morbidity, and malnutrition among women, as well as in reducing the prevalence of low birth weight among infants and the associated nutritional risks during the first year of life.

Poverty and the associated lack of access to sufficient food to meet nutritional requirements is clearly a primary cause of malnutrition. Yet programs aimed solely at enhancing incomes have not been as effective in alleviating malnutrition as expected (Behrman 1988). The reasons vary among population groups. Severely malnourished infants and children usually live in an environment that fosters high health risks, including infectious diseases. Under such conditions, additional food may have little effect on nutrition, in part because of lack of appetite and in part because of poor physiological utilization of ingested food. In the longer run, increased incomes are likely to lead to an improved environment, reduced health risks, and improved nutrition. In the short run, however, enhanced access to food will likely have a significant effect on nutrition only if primary health care programs and programs to modify health behavior and improve sanitary conditions and drinking water are introduced.

Another reason that increases in income may not be effective in alleviating malnutrition is that households may be unaware that a nutrition problem exists, or they may lack knowledge and information about how best to use new income to improve nutrition. Competing household priorities are another possible explanation. In such cases growth monitoring or nutrition education, or both, may be needed, along with increased income.

The effects on nutrition of increases in income may also be less than expected if the increases are achieved as a result of women's decisions to allocate more time to income-generating activities and less to child care, cooking, and other nutrition-related activities. In this case programs to increase the productivity of women's time within and outside the household are needed.

A national strategy to alleviate malnutrition may usefully distinguish between policies and programs aimed at maintaining or modifying factors exogenous to the household—for example, the economic environments in which households with malnourished members operate—and programs aimed at alleviating nutrition problems in specific population groups. The first category includes price, income, credit, interest rate, and employment policies, and policies influencing asset ownership and user rights; the second includes targeted nutrition programs. Food-linked income transfers may play a role in both. But because policies that affect exogenous factors are likely to exercise powerful influences over the nutritional status of the poor, the choices and design of targeted programs must take into account existing policies and expected changes in them. For example, economic policies may benefit some poor groups and hurt others, changing the needs and the appropriate targets for nutrition programs. The most appropriate program choice, design, and implementation strategy will depend on existing economic policies, as will opportunities for program financing.

Ideally, the most appropriate government support will be identified through effective participation by communities and target households. With or without such participation, however, the choice, design, and implementation of targeted nutrition programs should be preceded by several steps:
- Identification of the target groups and the constraints to good nutrition with which they are faced, and an assessment of their food acquisition and allocation and their health-seeking behavior
- Assessment of institutional and administrative capabilities for program implementation
- Identification of sources of financing.

Each of these is briefly discussed below.

Identifying target groups, their constraints, and their behavior

Growth monitoring may be useful for identifying individual children needing assistance, but targeting is needed to identify groups of households likely to face a high risk of malnutrition. Several indicators may be used in targeting, including household incomes, asset ownership, geographical location, employment status, and occupation. Geographical targeting, which has been used successfully in several countries, including Colombia and the Philippines, offers great promise in countries in which the poor tend to be concentrated, particularly if it is linked with either growth monitoring or child weighing. The eligibility criteria used in targeting should be simple and easy to verify to increase participation by those most in need and to limit participation by nontarget households.[3]

Assessing institutional and administrative capabilities

Some types of program require more institutional support than others. For example, food stamp schemes and food price subsidies may be based exclusively on private sector distribution. By contrast, food supplementation usually requires separate distribution channels. If a solid primary health care system is in place, food distribution may be linked to the system at a relatively low cost, particularly if there is excess capacity.

Programs that integrate food-related activities with primary health care offer great promise because they address several interacting constraints simultaneously. The drawback of these programs is that they demand substantial administrative and institutional capabilities. For this reason, many integrated programs that succeeded as small pilot schemes fail when extended nationally. This does not mean that no integration should be attempted, but that administrative and institutional capabilities should be assessed before programs are designed and implemented. The distribution of food from health posts has been successful in many programs and should be considered as one of several options. But the logistical problems associated with public food distribution should not be underestimated. These problems can be avoided by issuing food stamps that may be redeemed by private sector retailers, as was done in Colombia and the Philippines.

Identifying sources of funding

How realistic is it to recommend targeted nutrition programs during a period of macroeconomic adjustment that includes severe cuts in government spending? The answer depends on government priorities. Government spending on food subsidies, nutrition, and health could be increased even though total spending is reduced. Furthermore, nutrition and health spending can be reallocated to favor preventive over curative strategies, and recurrent over capital costs, and targeting could be improved.

External funds are becoming available to compensate groups of low-income households expected to suffer short-run losses from macroeconomic adjustments, and to assist countries in making adjustments within specific sectors, including agriculture and health. These funds could be used to support new initiatives for improved nutrition.

Innovative use of external food aid offers another opportunity for funding health and nutrition programs while protecting farmers from food aid's adverse effects. Food aid can be used directly in food supplementation schemes and recipients asked to provide a small payment that in turn could be used to cover the cost of primary health care or other nutrition-related activities. Such a strategy was successful in financing some of the costs of running primary health care clinics in Lesotho, for example. Or the government could sell the food aid and use the local currency revenues to support a variety of nutrition-related activities, including a targeted food stamp or other transfer program.

In addition to partial payment for food or food stamps, target households could be charged user fees for health care services. Selective user fees graduated by ability to pay would be preferable if the necessary administrative capability is available.

Institutional requirements

As illustrated above, the interaction between an intervention and the socioeconomic and cultural environment within which it is introduced, and the interaction among types of interventions, are of paramount importance. This has led to two conclusions:

* Interventions must be tailored to the environment.
* Integrated interventions are more likely to be successful than single ones.

This implies that a great deal must be known about the target group before an intervention is designed. Generating this knowledge is expensive and time-consuming and requires participation by communities and target groups. Furthermore, integrated interventions require institutional and administrative capabilities and infrastructure that are frequently in short supply.

In countries in which the necessary capabilities and infrastructure exist or can be developed as part of the program, integrated health and nutrition programs combined with favorable government policies could be very effective. Each program should be tailored to its particular circumstances, but at the core of most programs should be a combination of growth monitoring; nutrition education emphasizing breastfeeding, child spacing, and weaning practices; financial and technical assistance for the production and distribution of weaning food; food stamps or food price discounts to participating households; and primary health care. Participation by communities and target groups in all aspects of program design and implementation is essential for long-term sustainability, and separate but related efforts to assist target groups in strengthening their income-generating capacity are needed to reduce the need for future external financial support.

In countries with weak institutional and administrative capabilities and poor infrastructure, less complex programs should be undertaken. In areas that have health posts but in which insufficient food intake is a problem, the distribution of food stamps to low-income mothers who bring their preschool children to the posts should be considered. This strategy was successful in urban and rural areas of Colombia and in both remote and less remote rural areas of the Philippines. The use of food stamps rather than the more traditional food supplementation relieves the health system of the role of distributing food—one for which it is ill equipped.

In areas that lack health posts, small-scale ad hoc programs may still be the only viable alternatives. Such programs may be very cost-effective if designed by and for the community target groups with outside support.

Attempts to set up large-scale nutrition programs that exceed the available institutional and administrative capabilities have failed in the past and will fail again. Emphasis should be placed on strengthening these capabilities. Training should be provided at all levels, and nationwide primary health care systems should be built that could become conduits for integrated nutrition and health programs. While capacities are being strengthened, nutrition intervention may have to be limited to only part of the malnourished. Effective programs for some are clearly preferable to ineffective programs for all. This point is amplified by Lipton (1988a). Nutritional improvements should also be pursued through policies and programs that require less infrastructure and administrative and institutional capability. These could include basic training and education, price, incomes, and employment policies, and credit and technical assistance to low-income people.

Conclusions

A variety of nutrition programs have been used to alleviate malnutrition in specific population groups. The record of these programs is mixed. Some have achieved their goals at reasonable cost, others have been excessively costly, and many have failed to achieve any measurable effect on nutrition. Despite many years of experience with targeted nutrition programs and many attempts to determine what works, our understanding of how best to ensure success at reasonable cost is still deficient—although it has been greatly improved by recent experiences in India, Tanzania, and elsewhere.

The causes of malnutrition are complex, and they differ among households and communities and over time. Attempts to alleviate nutrition problems are influenced by the socioeconomic, cultural, and political environments within which they are found, and by household behavior, factors that also differ among communities and over time. Therefore, cost-effective and sustainable solutions must be tailored to particular sets of circumstances. There is no one, cost-effective way to solve nutrition problems globally. This is most obvious for energy and protein deficiencies, but even for micronutrient deficiencies, for which such quick-fix technologies as iodine fortification and vitamin A capsules are available, programs will succeed only if correctly matched to local environments and behavioral patterns. When this point is overlooked, programs fail.

Nutrition programs must be based on a solid understanding of the environment within which they are to operate, and target households and communities should play a major role in identifying and diagnosing the problems, and in designing and implementing programs to address them.

A great deal of lip service has been paid to community participation in primary health care and nutrition programs, but in the vast majority of these programs there has been very little or no real participation by the target households and individuals in decisions affecting design and implementation. The top-down approach is still prevalent, and failures are still more common than successes. Where programs have succeeded—for example, the Tamil Nadu Integrated Nutrition Project in India and the Iringa Project in Tanzania—they have been tailored to the local environment, community participation has been real, and flexibility to modify the programs in response to new knowledge derived locally through the programs has been ensured.

Household and community participation does not reduce the need for government action, it merely changes its nature. Rather than offering predesigned programs to the target groups, the role of the government becomes one of providing support to target groups and their communities in solving their own nutrition problems in the most appropriate—thus most cost-effective—manner. The nature of the support will vary; it may include information, education, primary health care facilities, income support, food, credit, technical assistance, and a variety of other resources and programs. Target groups and communities also need support in becoming effective participants in efforts to diagnose their problems and to identify the most binding constraints and the most appropriate solutions.

In the absence of true community participation in decisionmaking, government agencies should make a special effort to ensure that intervention programs are appropriate for the target groups. Programs should be designed to alleviate the most binding constraints to good nutrition, taking into account the socioeconomic and cultural context, household behavior, and institutional and administrative capabilities. Experience gained from past and ongoing programs provides a point of departure, but not a recipe.

Food-linked income transfers can play an important role both in narrowly focused nutrition programs and in efforts to ensure a favorable socioeconomic environment for the target population within which such programs operate.

Notes

Prepared for the Poverty Research Conference organized by the International Food Policy Research Institute and the World Bank, Airlie House, Virginia, October 25-28, 1989.

1. Results from recent analyses of consumer food subsidies in more than a dozen countries are reported in Pinstrup-Andersen (1988) and a number of research reports listed in that publication. This chapter provides a brief summary of only those findings that are particularly relevant to its topic.

2. As further discussed by Alderman (chapter 5 in this volume), some recent empirical evidence indicates that these estimates are upward-biased (Behrman 1988).

3. Targeting strategies are further discussed in Pinstrup-Andersen (1988).

Poverty Alleviation Policies in India

17

Kirit Parikh
T. N. Srinivasan

India's constitution (Basu 1983) enjoins the state to strive to secure "a social order in which justice, social, economic and political, shall inform all the institutions of national life" and "to minimize inequality in income, status, facilities and opportunities, amongst individuals and groups" (Article 38). It further directs the state to ensure "that the ownership and control of the material resources of the community are so distributed as best to subscribe the common good; that the operation of the economic system does not result in the concentration of wealth and means of production to the common detriment" (Article 39). And it seeks to make effective provision for securing the right to work, to education, and to public assistance for those afflicted by unemployment, disability, or illness (Article 41).

The strongly egalitarian and redistributive thrust of these principles is evident. But from the early days of economic planning, India's policymakers have been concerned that the benefits of growth might not be equally shared.[1] As early as 1960, long before such agencies as the World Bank recognized problems of poverty and income inequality, an official committee began a study of the trends in distribution of income and levels of living in India during the first decade of planning. In addition, a fifteen-year development plan to assure a minimum level of living for the entire Indian population was prepared (though not adopted) by the Planning Commission in 1962.[2] This plan defined for the first time a poverty line, which has formed the basis of all subsequent studies on poverty in India. The minimum level of living included not only a bundle of goods and services expected to be purchased by households from their own resources, the cost of which constituted the poverty line, but also expenditure on health and education, both of which were expected to be provided by the state. The plan explicitly recognized that certain segments of the poor (such as the old, the infirm, and the disabled) that are weakly linked to the income-generating process would not benefit from growth and would have to be provided transfers. The worthwhile elements of the basic needs approach advocated by some international agencies were already anticipated in this fifteen-year plan.

Even though poverty alleviation has been, and continues to be, the overarching objective of all of India's development plans, programs that are specifically poverty-oriented, such as the provision of minimum or basic needs (other than through the public food distribution system), were not formally included until the Fifth Five-Year Plan (1974-79). The Sixth Plan (1979-84) added a number of poverty eradication measures, including programs for rural works and self-employment and schemes for increasing the productivity of small and marginal farmers and rural artisans. The urban poor were already beneficiaries of the public food distribution system that supplied food grains and other basic items of consumption to all urban residents at subsidized prices—a legacy of the food rationing system that the colonial government had introduced. The supplies for the distribution system were obtained in part from imports and in part from domestic procurement at prices that were, until a few years ago, considerably below open market prices. In addition, the Sixth Plan introduced policies to encourage production through the adoption of high-yield, fertilizer-responsive varieties. These were mainly in the form of subsidies on the purchase of such agricultural inputs as fertilizer, fuel, power, and water from public irrigation systems. It was believed that such policies alleviated poverty in two ways—first, by improving the productivity and incomes of small farmers and inducing an outward shift in the demand for agricultural labor, and, second, by moderating any increase in the price of food due to outward shifts in the demand for food stimulated by increases in real incomes. Subsidized credit was made available for working capital and for investment in irrigation and farm equipment.

We propose to compare the effectiveness of some of these types of policy interventions in alleviating poverty. The analytical framework we use for this is an applied general equilibrium (AGE) model of the Indian economy. After a discussion of the distinguishing characteristics of AGE models and the rationale for their use in policy analysis, we briefly describe the features as well as the strengths and weaknesses of our AGE model for India. The policy analysis proceeds with a comparison of a base or reference scenario with a number of counterfactual scenarios representing alternative policies. The reference scenario is meant to portray the outcome of the continuation of policies (in a broad sense) that were in place in 1980 in the simulation period 1980-2000. The policy alternatives considered include variants of the existing urban public food distribution system, ranging from its abolition to the provision of 100 kilograms of food grains free to every Indian, the introduction of a rural public works program in which the poor are employed in slack agricultural seasons for wages paid in food grains, the abolition of the existing subsidy on the use of fertilizers, and various investments of the resources saved.

Applied general equilibrium model

In a mixed economy in which market transactions are dominant, such as India's, the welfare of individuals depends on the quantities and prices of the goods and factor services they sell (or buy) in the market and on any income transfers they receive from others, including the government. Government fiscal policies (other than income transfer policies) affect the welfare of all, including the poor, through their direct effects on prices and incomes. Income transfer policies affect prices indirectly through their effects on demand.

It is self-evident that in an economy with a fairly complex structure, such as India's, any economic policy is likely to affect market prices, and thus will affect the welfare of the poor, although for many policies this effect is likely to be negligible. Policies that explicitly target the poor can, in principle, be expected to have significant effects. But governments are unlikely to have a single, well-defined objective—such as poverty alleviation—and to choose a consistent set of policies to achieve that objective. They are much more likely to have several objectives and choose policies that promote some objectives over others. The combined effect of the mix of policies—on the economy in general and the poor in particular—is sometimes difficult, if not impossible, to assess without an empirical model that incorporates the important feedback effects.

No real economy is likely to remain in a static or steady-state equilibrium. Thus, the dynamic or intertemporal effects of policies are important. A frequently discussed tradeoff, mistakenly described by some as that between growth and equity, is that between more equity (or less poverty) in the present and less equity (or more poverty) than otherwise in the future. This tradeoff is inherent in policies that finance present poverty alleviation through reductions in growth-promoting investments. For example, shifting resources from subsidizing the food consumption of the poor to investing in increasing the quantity and productivity of assets owned by the poor will obviously reduce the present welfare of the poor but improve their future incomes. These considerations suggest that the analytical framework must be capable of evaluating the combined effects of several policy interventions on different socioeconomic groups over time. A natural framework satisfying these conditions is the dynamic applied general equilibrium model.

An applied general equilibrium model that is Walrasian in spirit assumes that all agents recognized in the model behave rationally—that each has a consistent set of preferences with respect to the outcomes of his or her actions and chooses from among all feasible actions the one that has the most preferred outcome. Typically, a consumer's preferences are assumed to be represented by a utility function whose argument is the vector of his consumption of various goods and services. An action as well as its outcome is a particular choice of the consumption vector. And the feasible set of actions simply comprises those within his budget; it is the set of all consumption vectors that cost no more at the prices he faces (over which he is assumed to have no influence) than the value of his endowment of commodities and factors and his share of the net profits of firms. In principle, the utility function and the budget constraint can extend over several periods, incorporating the consumer's savings and portfolio choices. Consumer choices, aggregated over all consumers, yield the consumer demand for commodities, supplies of factor services, and demand for equities and debentures in firms. A firm's action is a vector of outputs it produces and inputs it purchases. Feasible action vectors are those permitted by the technology available to the firm for transforming inputs into outputs. This set is the firm's production set. Firms are assumed to maximize net revenue—the difference between the value of output and the cost of inputs at the prices they face over their production sets. Firms' choices, aggregated over all firms, result in the supply of goods and the demand for factors. Once again, when actions are defined as extending over several periods, investment activities can be accommodated, with the finance for investment stemming from the sale of equities and the issue of debentures. The price vectors that ensure that markets for goods, factors, and equities clear are equilibrium price vectors. Government is most naturally modeled in this setup as an agent that sets commodity and factor taxes, tariffs, and so on, makes transfers, and supplies some goods and services and demands others. Its expenditures are restricted to what it can finance through tax revenues and borrowing from the public at home and abroad. Although real-world governments also have the option of using the inflation tax mechanism of fiat money creation for financing their expenditures, there is no theoretically satisfactory way of introducing it in a "real" model of the Walrasian type. Of course, the market clearance requirement will take into account government demand and supply as well.

The task of empirically specifying such a model is demanding in terms of the required data, the need to specify functional forms for utility functions, production functions, and so on, and the required estimates of the relevant parameters. And it will inevitably involve compromises, dictated by the available data and econometric knowledge, that are unsatisfactory from a theoretical perspective. Nevertheless, this framework, or something akin to it, is absolutely essential if the various feedback effects of several policies are to be analyzed consistently. Most important, it ensures that there are no hidden sources for meeting excess demand, or black holes into which excess supplies disappear and in which subsidies must be financed and tax revenues spent. For example, it will require that the introduction of, say, a subsidy on the food consumption of the poor is accompanied by a specification of the mode of its financing so that both the direct effect of the subsidy on the welfare of the poor and the indirect effect arising from the particular way in which it is financed are fully reflected in the equilibrium.

Features of the applied general equilibrium model for India

The analytical model we use is of the sequential applied general equilibrium type in which an equilibrium price vector is computed for each year in succession. Unlike in similar models, a number of behavioral functions relating to demand and supply have been econometrically estimated, with data mostly from the period 1950-51 to 1973-75. In running the model for the period up to 1980, outputs, imports, and exports were set equal to their actual values, and the actually observed prices were generated as equilibrium prices by ensuring market clearance at these prices through stock accumulation or decumulation. Indeed, that such a procedure did not lead to implausible values for changes in stocks was viewed as a validation of the model. The period after 1980 was the simulation period. The model was greatly simplified by imposing a one-year lag between production and market sale. Thus, in effect, the economy became an exchange economy for the purposes of computing equilibrium prices.

The economy is divided into ten sectors, of which nine produce agricultural commodities and one produces the only nonagricultural good.[3] There are three sets of agents: producers, consumers, and government. Consumers are classified by their residence as rural or urban. Both rural and urban consumers are divided into five classes according to their monthly per capita household consumption expenditure. Means of production (capital), natural resources (land), human resources (labor), and livestock (draft and dairy animals, poultry) generate income, through production activities, that is distributed to consumers. Thus, the behavior of producers—their production activities—determines commodity supplies and incomes. Consumer behavior generates commodity demands—and, implicitly, resource supplies. The government sets policies (investment targets, taxes, tariffs, quotas, rations, price supports and ceilings). Finally, equilibrium is achieved through exchange in which domestic demand, together with export demand by the rest of the world for each sector's output, is equated with the sum of domestic supply (emerging from the previous year's production net of changes in stocks) and (foreign) import supply.

The per capita consumer demand of each of the ten classes of consumers for the output of each sector is modeled as a Stone-Geary linear expenditure system. The growth of total population and the number of households (rural and urban) are exogenously specified. The joint distribution of households according to their per capita income and consumption expenditure was assumed to be lognormal in each period. But the mean of the marginal distribution of the logarithm of per capita income was allowed to change over time with the growth of income. Other parameters, such as the variances, the correlation coefficient, and the intercept of the linear regression of the logarithm of per capita consumption on the per capita income of the household, were assumed to remain constant at their estimated values based on 1976 data. This meant that the mean of the *conditional* distribution of (the logarithm of) per capita household consumption varied linearly with the mean of the logarithm of per capita household income. Thus, the population of households falling within each of the ten expenditure classes, and their mean per capita consumption expenditure, could be determined for each year given aggregate consumer income for that year. The difference between income and consumption expenditure represents household savings.

Admittedly, the above distributional assumptions, including the assumption that only the means of the logarithm of per capita household income (and consumption) vary over time, are strong. They imply that the concentration of the marginal distributions of the logarithms of income and consumption do not change. A more satisfactory procedure would have been to specify an initial distribution of factor endowments and derive the changes in factor endowments from one period to the next, as well as the savings in each period, from an intertemporal optimization procedure, given appropriate assumptions about expectations regarding the path of factor prices, including returns on assets. But implementing such a procedure is beyond the reach of modelers of even industrial countries for which there are more extensive data bases and econometric studies on the savings, investment, and fertility behavior of households. Indeed, modelers most often ignore distributional issues altogether by assuming that the society consists of a single household or avoiding dynamics by concentrating on static distributional effects. Our interest is in dynamics, however, and our strong assumption has an operational justification because it enables us to derive the dynamic distributional effects relatively easily. It is also consistent with econometric studies showing that a lognormal distribution fits the data from the various rounds of India's National Sample Survey on the distribution of households according to per capita private consumption expenditure.

Public consumption is assumed to be a constant proportion of gross domestic product (GDP), and it comprises only nonagricultural goods. The proportion of aggregate investment in GDP is exogenously specified. Income tax rates adjust so as to generate enough public savings (revenues minus consumption), which, together with household savings and exogenously specified foreign capital inflow, will equal aggregate investment. The share of agricultural investment in aggregate investment is a function of the relative price of agricultural goods. Agricultural investment influences the total gross cropped area as well as its irrigated portion. A detailed model of allocation of area among crops, choice of varieties to be cultivated (high-yield and traditional), and fertilizer intensity, based on a version of a Nerlovian adaptive expectations framework, determines the vector of crop outputs. Capital is the only factor used in the production of the nonagricultural good. Capital stock in this sector is updated by net investment. Thus, the value of the outputs of the agricultural and nonagricultural sectors together, net of taxes and transfers, determines the income available to consumers.

The complete algebraic description of the model and its numerical version are available in Narayana, Parikh, and Srinivasan (1991). A more concise description is available in Narayana, Parikh, and Srinivasan (1987). The model has two important weaknesses: the absence of a labor market and the extreme aggregation of all nonagricultural goods into one. By the absence of a labor market we mean, first, that labor is not *formally* treated as a factor of production in any of the ten sectors, so a demand function for labor (let alone for labor distinguished by age, sex, residence, and skill) cannot be derived from producer behavior, given the structure of wage rates, product prices, and so on. Second, leisure does not enter the household utility function, and the value of labor endowment does not explicitly enter the household's budget constraint. Thus, a labor supply function cannot be derived from household behavior. The absence of both demand and supply functions rules out deriving an equilibrium wage rate for each period. There is no capital or land market in the model, so the only real choices for agricultural producers are the allocation of available land (irrigated and nonirrigated) to crops (and varieties of crops) and the amount of fertilizer to use. Nonagricultural producers can choose the rate of capacity utilization. In short, only value added is endogenously derived in the model and not its allocation among factors. This does not preclude an analysis of distributional effects, however, because the joint distribution of household income (which is obtained from value added) and consumption is specified directly. The principal reason for not introducing an explicit labor market is the lack of satisfactory studies of labor supply and demand. Even in industrial countries robust estimates of labor supply elasticities are scarce.

The absence of an explicit labor market could be interpreted as implying that an infinitely elastic labor supply at some real wage level is being assumed. But such an interpretation has no operational significance for most of the analysis, except for the simulations that involve rural works. In these simulations it is assumed that enough labor will find it attractive to be employed in rural works programs offering an exogenously set fixed real wage that is constant over a twenty-year period. It is impossible to say whether this is too strong an assumption without a well-specified labor market that realistically describes rural India. Given the actual rural labor market environment, however, if not enough labor is forthcoming (if there is excess demand for labor at the offered wage), the scale of rural works programs could be reduced without reducing poverty alleviation. It is argued that because of the self-targeting nature of rural works employment, only those with relatively low reservation wages and limited capacity for physical work (women, children, and the elderly) will be attracted to the program, and to the extent that physical effort determines the capacity and durability of roads or irrigation canals constructed with their labor, the quality of such assets may suffer. But the complexity of the relationship between food energy intake and expenditure of energy in work effort precludes any firm conclusion. There are no carefully designed empirical studies on which to base one's judgment on this issue.

The assumption that all goods are internationally traded precludes the analysis of the role of nontraded goods, particularly infrastructural goods, in the development of the Indian economy. The model is better viewed as computing a sequence of temporary equilibria rather than a full-blown intertemporal equilibrium. Strong assumptions on preferences are needed to ensure the intertemporal optimality of the household savings behavior incorporated in the model. The specification that the proportion of aggregate investment in GDP is a function only of time also violates the spirit of models of intertemporal equilibrium. Almost all applied general equilibrium models, including ours, ignore considerations of political economy. The assumption that government policy is set exogenously and agents respond to the policy as if they have no influence in its formulation is extreme. In fact, lobbies form and spend resources to get policies enacted, or to appropriate the benefits of policies in place. These considerations, which form the core of the literature on neoclassical political economy, are absent from our model. Yet, if the model is broadened to generate a political economy general equilibrium, by definition there will be no room for policy change. Only a comparative static analysis is possible with respect to changes in those exogenous variables that determine both equilibrium policies and economic variables.

The reference and policy scenarios

The role of the reference scenario is to serve as a benchmark for comparison with scenarios in which one or more policies are changed from their reference specification. The model is not a forecasting model—all the scenarios, including the reference scenario, are counterfactual simulations. Although in our model—

unlike many models of this type—the values of most of the parameters are econometrically estimated, several are exogenously specified. It is our contention that any alternative specification of the values of these parameters will change both the reference and the policy scenarios in a similar way, so that the effect of policies expressed as changes relative to the reference scenario would be the same regardless of the set of parameter values used. In a way, this is more an article of faith than an analytically or empirically established fact. It is convenient to have a reference scenario in which the relevant policy regimes remain essentially unchanged in the simulation period as compared with the presimulation period.

The following are the most important assumptions and policies in the reference scenario:

- The quantity of food grains distributed in any given year through the public distribution system for urban areas, as a share of the net output of food grains, is a nonlinear function of net output per capita and real nonagricultural income per capita and the change in their levels over the previous year, subject to a ceiling of 135 kilograms per urban resident. (Historically, the largest amount that has been distributed in a year is a little over 150 kilograms per urban resident, in 1966, a year of severe drought.) The price subsidy on publicly distributed grain is 20 percent. (The subsidy is 3 percent according to the 1989-90 budget.) The quantity of food grains purchased at below-market prices was in general related to output and to the ratio of the procurement price to expected open market prices.
- Quantitative restrictions on the net foreign trade of different agricultural commodities range from 5 percent to 15 percent of domestic supply (production plus initial stocks).
- The foreign trade deficit is set at 1.5 percent of GDP.
- Domestic price policy interventions steer the domestic market prices gradually toward exogenously specified world prices—that is, gradual liberalization of markets is postulated.
- Total population grows by 2.26 percent a year, from 674 million in 1980 to 1,048 million in 2000. The proportion of urban population in the total rises from 23 percent in 1950 to 31.5 percent in 2000.
- Aggregate (public plus private) investment as a proportion of GDP was assumed to be a monotonic function of time with an asymptote of 0.45.

We consider several counterfactual policy scenarios:

- Variations in the public distribution system ranging from its abolition to its extension to rural areas, and making food rations free (a 100 percent subsidy).
- A rural works program targeted at the poorest two classes with alternative assumptions regarding the efficiency of its design and execution and its success in targeting.
- Abolition of the fertilizer subsidy and the use of part of the resources saved to augment aggregate investment and the remainder either to institute a rural works program or to expand irrigated area.

Table 17.1 provides data on subsidies relating to fertilizer and food distribution in the central government budget. In 1988-89 these two types of subsidy amounted to 56 billion rupees (Rs). We should add to this figure the budgetary support implicit in water charges and electricity tariffs. Just charging operating costs for water and electricity (excluding capital charges) would have put at least Rs 40 billion more in the hands of central and state governments. The total loss to government budgets was about Rs 96 billion in 1988-89.

Total expenditure by the central government in 1988-89 was Rs 758 billion (revised estimate) and that by the states Rs 542 billion (budget estimate). Subsidies for food, fertilizer, water, and electricity account for roughly 12.5 percent of the central budget and 7.5 percent of the central and state budgets together.

Simulation results

The welfare effect of alternative policies can be seen by comparing the distribution of population according to equivalent expenditure—the consumption expenditure needed at 1970 prices to achieve the welfare achieved under the policy. Because the average equivalent expenditure in each class, as well as its share of population, can vary among policy scenarios, for an overall comparison we adapt the approach of Willig and Bailey (1981). They show that, given a population of individuals ranked from 1 to n, according to their equivalent expenditures, m_i^1 and m_i^2, in two distributions (m_i^j = the expenditure that a person i needs at some base price p^0 to achieve the same welfare that he enjoys at prices p^j and nominal income y^j in distribution j, $j = 1, 2$), the first distribution is preferred to the second according to any social welfare function that satisfies the Pareto principle, anonymity, and aversion to regressive transfer if and only if

$$\sum_{i=1}^{k} m_i^1 > \sum_{i=1}^{k} m_i^2 \quad for \quad k = 1, 2, ..., n.$$

Table 17.1 Food and fertilizer subsidies in central government budget, India, 1979-90
(billions of rupees)

Year	Fertilizer subsidies	Food subsidies
1979-80	6.03	6.00
1980-81	5.05	6.50
1981-82	3.75	7.00
1982-83	6.05	7.10
1983-84	10.42	8.35
1984-85	19.27	11.00
1985-86	19.24	16.50
1986-87	19.33	22.00
1987-88	19.16	22.00
1988-89[a]	32.50	23.60
1989-90[b]	36.51	22.00

a. Revised budget estimate.
b. Budget estimate.
Source: Asha 1986; and central government budget papers for 1989-90.

Person i (the one having the ith lowest equivalent expenditure) in distribution 1 need not be the same as person i in distribution 2. As Willig and Bailey point out, the above inequality for $k = 1$ corresponds to a Rawlsian social welfare function, and the inequality for $k = n$ corresponds to the Hicksian compensation criterion. But for a general social welfare function, the inequality must hold for all k to ensure dominance. Of course, the ranking is not independent of the base price vector p^0, and this serious limitation must be kept in mind in interpreting the results.

Another welfare indicator that we use is average energy intake—kilocalories consumed per capita per day.

Alternative public distribution policies

We compare three public distribution scenarios with the reference scenario. At one extreme, in scenario DPO, the distribution system, including domestic procurement, is abolished. At the other extreme, in scenario FRFD-100W, 100 kilograms of wheat is provided each year to *all* consumers, urban and rural, with the cost financed by increasing income taxes (borne largely by the two richest classes of urban consumers). Policy FRFD-100W-X is the same as FRFD-100W except that the subsidy is financed by reducing investment. The results are shown in tables 17.2 and 17.3. All policy changes relative to the reference scenario are introduced in 1980.

The implications of the simulations presented in tables 17.2 and 17.3 are clear. The differences among the public distribution scenarios in terms of their effects on GDP growth and average energy intake per capita per day are modest. For example, real GDP in 2000 differs by only about 10 percent between the extremes DPO and FRFD-100W.

The policies' distributional consequences differ substantially, however. The massive redistribution scenario FRFD-100W, in which 100 kilograms of wheat is supplied free of cost to all through a distribution financed by increased taxes, results in a substantial reduction in the poorest population in rural areas: by 60 percent from the reference value of 164 million (31.6 percent of the rural population) in 1980, and by 39 percent from the reference value of 148 million (20.5 percent of the rural population) in 2000. For the urban poorest population, which is smaller than the rural poorest population, the reduction in number is smaller, but the reduction as a percentage of the total is considerably larger. The other extreme, DPO, which abolishes the public distribution system that in the reference scenario operates in urban areas only, has a negligible effect on the rural poorest but, as expected, significantly increases the population of urban poorest.

The consequences for growth of financing a free food policy through a reduction in investment under the scenario FRFD-100W-X are marginal—a fall in real GDP of less than 10 percent over a twenty-year period. The poverty reduction achieved under this scenario is virtually the same as that achieved under FRFD-100W, in which the source of financing is additional taxation. In any case, a social welfare measure that is based on equivalent incomes and that incorporates aversion to regressive income transfers shows that a free food policy improves social welfare only modestly (figure 17.1).

In an apparent paradox, abolishing the public distribution system reduces real GDP growth slightly. The paradox is indeed only apparent—it is a consequence of the fact that in the reference scenario the public distribution system generates more revenue through procurement tax than it spends on consumption subsidies in later years. That is because the model does not restrict procurement to equal the amount that is distributed.

In all the food subsidy scenarios the recipient of the food ration is assumed to be able to sell part or all of the ration at open market prices. Thus, the subsidy on the food ration is equivalent to an income subsidy of equivalent value at open market prices. We also examined the consequences of the opposite assumption—one in which open market sale is impossible. Under this assumption the benefits for the poor are smaller because, as long as the ration is not free, the very poor cannot afford to buy and consume their entire ration. They buy only what they can afford, and the ration's effect on their welfare is smaller than when rations can be freely sold.

Table 17.2 Effect of alternative procurement and distribution systems on selected indicators

Indicator	Year	Reference scenario	Percentage change over reference scenario		
			DPO[a]	FRFD-100W[b]	FRFD-100W-X[c]
Total GDP	1980	530.0	0	0	0
(billions of 1970 rupees)	2000	1,429.0	-0.07	0.72	-9.36
Agricultural GDP	1980	220.0	0	0	0
(billions of 1970 rupees)	2000	354.0	0	0.47	-2.50
Nonagricultural GDP	1980	310.0	0	0	0
(billions of 1970 rupees)	2000	1,075.0	-0.09	0.81	-11.62
Total investment	1980	110.0	0	0	-16.71
(billions of 1970 rupees)	2000	492.0	0	1.19	-18.46
Tax rate	1980	2.3	39.0	486.90	160.87
(percent)	2000	9.8	11.2	19.39	0
Ratio of agricultural price index to nonagricultural	1980	0.93	-0.15	12.50	18.44
price index	2000	0.89	0.46	2.89	4.30
GDP per capita	1980	786.0	0	0	0
(1970 rupees)	2000	1,363.0	-0.07	0.72	-9.36
Daily per capita energy	1980	2,162.0	0.42	3.63	5.42
intake (kcal)	2000	2,569.0	0.45	1.59	-1.18
Average per capita	1980	544.0	0	-0.44	3.43
equivalent expenditure[d]	2000	661.0	-0.18	0.46	-2.82

a. No procurement, no distribution.
b. Free food to all, tax rate adjusted.
c. Free food to all, tax rate fixed.
d. Expenditure needed at 1970 prices to provide the same utility as that provided by current consumption at current prices.
Source: Narayana, Parikh, and Srinivasan 1991; and authors' calculations.

Table 17.3 Effect of alternative public distribution policies on the poorest class

Indicator	Reference scenario	Percentage change over reference scenario		
		DPO[a]	FRFD-100W[b]	FRFD-100W-X[c]
		1980		
Rural				
Percentage of total population	31.6	0.00	-60.32	-60.44
Per capita equivalent expenditure (1970-71 rupees)	129.0	1.32	15.49	14.18
Daily per capita energy intake (kcal)[d]	981.0	1.33	14.78	13.15
Urban				
Percentage of total population	1.9	52.63	-89.47	-89.47
Per capita equivalent expenditure (1970-71 rupees)	165.0	-1.03	-7.95	-9.65
Daily per capita energy intake (kcal)[d]	1,085.0	-1.11	-9.77	-11.80
		2000		
Rural				
Percentage of total population	20.5	1.46	-38.54	-34.15
Per capita equivalent expenditure (1970-71 rupees)	133.0	2.64	15.51	15.59
Daily per capita energy intake (kcal)[d]	1,059.0	2.08	15.20	13.22
Urban				
Percentage of total population	0.4	75.00	-50.00	-25.00
Per capita equivalent expenditure (1970-71 rupees)	172.0	-1.51	-0.29	-0.87
Daily per capita energy intake (kcal)[d]	1,252.0	-2.64	-1.92	-4.95

Note: The poorest class comprises those with annual per capita equivalent expenditure of less than Rs 216.
a. No procurement, no distribution.
b. Free food to all, tax rate adjusted.
c. Free food to all, tax rate fixed.
d. As reflected in the data on household expenditure. Excludes consumption provided by employer at place of work.
Source: Narayana, Parikh, and Srinivasan 1991; and authors' calculations.

The above analysis assumes that extending the public distribution system to rural areas does not involve any additional costs—that is, that the unit cost of the distribution system depends neither on its scale, in terms of the volume of grain procured and distributed, nor on its geographical coverage. If there are economies (diseconomies) of scale or scope, the unit cost will fall (rise) as the system is extended. Without any robust empirical evidence, it is difficult to determine how extending the system would affect unit costs. Our results are based on the assumption that they do not change. In addition, our model postulates a fairly high incremental capital-output ratio (ICOR). But because its value is kept the same in both policy and reference scenarios, the growth consequences of alternative policies, expressed as a percentage change from the reference scenario, are not affected by the high ICOR.

Rural works programs

We assume that only the two poorest expenditure classes are targeted under rural works programs.[4] The programs distribute an average quantity of 100 kilograms of food grains a year to each participant as wages. The quantity distributed to those in the poorer of the two classes, however, is fixed at 125 kilograms, so that the quantity r_2 received by the next poorest class is given by $r_2 = (100p - 125p_1)/p_2$, where p is the population of the two classes together, p_1 is the population of class 1, and p_2 is the population of class 2. The value of r_2 var-

Figure 17.1 Social welfare comparison of reference and free food scenarios

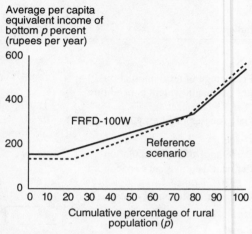

Source: Authors' calculations.

ies between scenarios because of variation in p, p_1, and p_2.

Various inefficiencies and leakages occur in rural works programs. Analytically, these can be viewed as of two types. The first relates to the productivity of the assets created under rural works programs relative to that of other investment in the economy. The second relates to a failure of targeting—the benefits intended for the target groups leaking to nontarget groups.

In our model inefficiencies of the first type are introduced through an efficiency parameter e (which takes three values, 1.0, 0.5, and 0.0), representing the ratio of the productivity of assets created in rural works programs to the economywide average return to investment. Clearly, $e = 1$ represents a well-designed and well-executed rural works program, and $e = 0$ a program that is completely unfruitful as an investment and is simply a transfer program. Targeting efficiency is introduced in the model through a parameter t (taking two values, 1.0 and 0.5), representing the proportion of the wage bill of rural works programs that accrues to the target groups in rural areas. We present the simulation results in table 17.4. A scenario is characterized by its (t, e) combination and the mode of financing of its cost—that is, whether it is through additional taxation or reduction in investment (fixed tax rates). A scenario in which 40 kilograms of wheat is distributed free to all and that is financed by a reduction in investment is also considered. This scenario, denoted as FF40X, costs roughly the same as a rural works program.

The simulation results in show that a well-designed, well-executed, and well-targeted rural works program leads not only to substantial improvement in the welfare of the rural poor, but to slightly faster economic growth (because of the additional investment represented by the rural works), if the resources needed for the program are raised through additional taxation. The additional tax effort needed initially is substantial, however; in 1980 an additional 6 percent of GDP must be raised as income taxes, compared with the reference run value of 2 percent. As the economy grows, however, the additional tax effort required declines substantially and by 2000 falls to about 1 percent of GDP; the reference run value in 2000 is 7 percent. Thus, if foreign aid in the form of grants is available for a limited period, the government can initiate poverty alleviation efforts through a rural works program without straining its fiscal capacity.

If, however, foreign aid is not available and taxes cannot be raised, and a rural works program must be financed through a reduction in investment, real GDP in 2000 is reduced by a marginal 4.6 percent relative to the reference run; the tax-financed rural works program leads to real GDP that is 3.5 percent higher than that in the reference run. Thus, the sacrifice in growth under a program financed by reducing investment is modest and the positive effect on the welfare of the poor is unchanged. Further, social welfare comparisons using the Bailey-Willig criterion show that such a program has greater social welfare benefits than a free food policy that costs just as much (figure 17.2). Finally, if the investment component of a rural works program is completely unfruitful, and 50 percent leakage occurs, the welfare of the poor is roughly halved compared with the results of a well-designed, well-executed, and well-targeted rural works program financed by taxation.

Abolition of the fertilizer subsidy

India's farmers receive a subsidy of roughly 30 percent on the price of the fertilizers they use. In this section we examine the consequences of abolishing

Table 17.4 Effect of alternative rural works programs on growth and rural poor
(percentage change from reference run, 2000)

Scenario	GDP per capita (1970-71 rupees)	GDP growth rate (1980-2000)	Average EQY per capita	ENY per capita	Poorest rural class EQY per capita	Poorest rural class ENY per capita	EQY per capita in two poor-est rural classes
With additional taxation							
RW100-1-1	3.5	0.22	2.2	5.7	67	70	39
With fixed tax rates							
RW100-1-1X	-4.6	-0.25	-0.2	4.7	67	70	39
RW100-1-0.5X	-8.5	-0.47	-2.6	3.8	67	70	39
RW100-1-0X	-13.2	-0.73	-5.4	2.6	67	70	39
RW100-0.5-1X	-3.7	-0.20	0	3.0	33	40	19
RW100-0.5-0.5X	-7.3	-0.40	-2.0	2.1	33	40	19
RW100-0.5-0X	-11.8	-0.66	-4.7	1.0	33	40	19
FF40X	-4.2	-0.23	-0.8	1.3	11	11	10

Note: EQY = equivalent expenditure; ENY = energy intake (kcals per day).
Source: Authors' calculations.

**Figure 17.2 Social welfare comparison
of rural works program and free food
scenario**

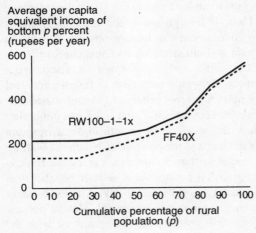

Average per capita
equivalent income of
bottom *p* percent
(rupees per year)

Cumulative percentage of rural
population (*p*)

Source: Authors' calculations.

the subsidy beginning in 1989 and using the resources that had financed the subsidy in three ways. First, in scenario NS the released resources are used to augment aggregate investment. Second, in scenario NS-RW20 some of the released resources are used to finance a rural works program that distributes 20 kilograms of wheat per capita per year as wages to the two poorest rural classes, with *t* and *e* parameters both set at 0.5. The remaining resources are used to augment aggregate investment. Third, in scenario NS-IR+2M some of the released resources are used to create an additional 2 million hectares of irrigated area a year over the reference run, and the remaining resources are used to augment aggregate investment. The simulation results of this section are based on a slightly updated version of the model used for earlier sections; some parameters have been reestimated with data for up to 1984. Therefore, the reference scenario results for these simulations differ from those for the simulations in the sections on public distribution policies and rural works programs, although the policies remain the same. Further policy changes are introduced in 1989. The results are presented in table 17.5.

Increasing aggregate investment (scenario NS), rather than subsidizing the use of fertilizer (reference scenario), increases real GDP by a negligible 1 percent and reduces the output of food grains by about 4 percent in 2000. The proportion of the rural population in the poorest class increases by 4 percent in 1990 and 2000. The proportion of urban poor is unaffected. Using part of the resources saved by abolishing the fertilizer subsidy on rural works and the rest on additional investment (scenario NS-RW20) improves the real income of the poorest in rural areas and leaves GDP, food grain output, and the proportion of urban poor unchanged, compared with investing all of it. And creating an additional 2 million hectares a year of irrigated area with part of the resources and using the rest for increasing investment (scenario NS-IR+2M) increases real GDP by 9 percent, fertilizer use by 5 percent, and food grain output by 12 percent in 2000, compared with the reference scenario. The proportion of the rural population in the poorest class falls by about 1.5 percent. This suggests that augmenting irrigated area, rather than subsidizing the use of fertilizer, not only increases the use of fertilizer, but has a beneficial effect on the rural poor as well.

Compared with the reference scenario, in which the fertilizer subsidy is continued, the three alternative scenarios lead to only small changes in poverty or macroeconomic aggregates. In other words, untargeted and indirect poverty alleviation policies cannot be expected to make much of a dent on poverty.

Table 17.5 Effect of alternative input subsidy schemes on selected indicators

Indicator	Year	Reference scenario	NS	NS-RW20	NS-IR+2M
GDP (billions of 1970 rupees)	1990	746.01	746.23	746.23	748.32
	2000	1,262.93	1,280.43	1,276.09	1,371.80
Agricultural GDP	1990	247.47	247.69	247.69	249.78
(billions of 1970 rupees)	2000	315.55	317.13	314.09	346.65
Fertilizer use					
(millions of metric tons	1990	10.01	8.63	8.63	8.85
of nitrogen)	2000	12.87	11.16	11.15	13.55
Total irrigated area	1990	5.62	5.62	5.62	5.82
(millions of hectares)	2000	7.79	7.92	7.92	10.35
Wheat	1990	57.82	52.78	52.78	53.97
(millions of tons)	2000	82.18	76.67	76.64	92.12
Rice	1990	64.37	63.67	63.67	65.26
(millions of tons)	2000	85.84	85.74	85.69	103.93
Food grains	1990	161.03	154.45	154.45	157.64
(millions of tons)	2000	209.47	201.76	201.70	234.48
Total population					
Daily per capita energy intake	1990	2,129	2,101	2,122	2,104
(kcal)	2000	2,307	2,292	2,305	2,347
Average per capita equivalent	1990	515.7	509.4	512.9	510.2
expenditure (rupees)	2000	580.3	578.0	579.5	601.0
Rural poorest class					
Percentage of rural population	1990	38.9	40.4	40.4	40.3
	2000	30.7	32.0	32.0	30.3
Average per capita equivalent	1990	120.2	118.8	124.4	118.9
expenditure (rupees)	2000	124.7	123.5	128.8	124.7
Urban poorest class					
Percentage of urban population	1990	2.0	2.0	2.0	2.0
	2000	1.0	0.9	0.9	0.9
Average per capita equivalent	1990	172.7	172.7	172.7	172.7
expenditure (rupees)	2000	172.5	172.6	172.5	173.7

Note: In the *reference scenario* the 30 percent fertilizer subsidy is continued. In the other three scenarios the fertilizer subsidy is abolished, beginning in 1989, and the resources released are used as follows: in *scenario NS*, to increase aggregate investment; in *scenario NS-RW20*, to finance a rural works program and increase aggregate investment; and in *scenario NS-IR+2M*, to increase both irrigated area and aggregate investment.
Source: Authors' calculations.

Conclusions

We considered three broad sets of policies for alleviating rural poverty and hunger—an *untargeted* policy of subsidizing part of the food consumption of the entire population, including the poor, a *targeted* policy of providing additional employment opportunities for the rural poor through a rural works program, and an *indirect* policy of subsidizing fertilizer or, alternatively, increasing aggregate investment or the area irrigated *and* aggregate investment. The last leads to increases in food production. It would appear that a well-designed, well-executed, and well-targeted rural works program has the greatest effect on the poor. A free food program that provides 40 kilograms of grain to all would raise the energy intake of the poorest (two poorest) classes in rural areas by 11 percent (10 percent); a rural works program of comparable cost would raise energy intake by 70 percent (40 percent) over its reference run value. Further, the free food program would increase equivalent income by 11 percent (10 percent), and the rural works program would increase it by 67 percent (39 percent). The *indirect* poverty alleviation policies of subsidizing fertilizers or augmenting irrigation have, as expected, only modest effects.

India's policymakers have apparently understood the potential of employment generation for alleviating poverty, as reflected by the introduction in 1989-90 of the Jawahar Rozgar Yojana, an employment program that consolidates and expands preexisting programs.

Notes

The comments of Dipak Mazumdar are gratefully acknowledged without implicating him in any of the errors of omission and commission that may remain.

1. None expressed these concerns better than Prime Minister Nehru, who said in 1960, while introducing the Third Five-Year Plan in Parliament:

...it is said that the national income over the First and Second Plans has gone up by 42 per cent and the per capita income by 20 per cent. A legitimate query is made, where has this gone? It is a very legitimate query; to some extent of course, you can see where it has gone. I sometimes do address large gatherings in the villages and I can see that they are better fed and better clothed, they build brick houses....Nevertheless, this does not apply to everybody in India. Some people probably have hardly benefited. Some people may even be facing various difficulties. The fact remains, however, that this advance in our national income, in our per capita income has taken place, and I think it is desirable that we should enquire more deeply as to where this has gone and appoint some expert committee to enquire into how exactly this additional income that has come to the country or per capita has spread (India, Planning Commission, 1964).

2. This plan is reprinted in Srinivasan and Bardhan (1974).

3. The nine agricultural commodities are rice, wheat, coarse grains, beef and mutton, dairy products, other animal products, protein feeds, other food, and nonfood agriculture.

4. A more complete discussion of the rationale for rural works programs and detailed simulation results are presented in Narayana, Parikh, and Srinivasan (1988).

Part IV
Country Studies

Rural Poverty in India, 1973-87

18 N. Kakwani
K. Subbarao

Much has been written about poverty in India over the last two decades. Initially, attention focused on estimating poverty. Recently, more efforts have gone into explaining its variations, across regions and over time. Controversy still prevails with respect to both the estimation and the explanation of poverty, but several insights have been gained—above all, that faster agricultural growth tends to reduce poverty.

There are two central issues: First, does economic growth reduce poverty—that is, is there a trickle-down mechanism? And second, has economic growth been accompanied by an increase in the inequality of income or consumption? Analysts have examined these issues by looking at the distribution of assets (land) or of income or consumption in the high- and low-growth districts and states, often using single-year, cross-sectional data. To understand the impact of economic growth on poverty, we should measure separately the impact on poverty, over time, of changes in *average* income (consumption) and in its *inequality*. This chapter therefore examines trends in the growth of consumption and its distribution and compares its effects on the poor and the ultrapoor, over time and across states of India.

During 1973-87 India's gross national product (GNP) per capita grew by about 20 percent. Investment and current public expenditure grew as a share of GNP; and the average *private* consumption per person also grew, at an average annual rate of 2 percent. If all households had experienced this rate of growth in consumption, a significant reduction in poverty would have resulted. But if the distribution of per capita consumption had worsened, the effect of growth on poverty would have been much smaller. The important questions, therefore, are these:

- How has the distribution of per capita consumption changed across the states, and to what extent has it nullified the beneficial impact of growth on poverty?
- How have the poor and the ultrapoor fared in the wake of changes in consumption and its distribution?
- What have been the states' patterns in rural poverty, and to what degree can these patterns be explained based on our knowledge of the structural

characteristics of the states and the their performance indicators for antipoverty programs?

The chapter addresses these questions using National Sample Survey (NSS) data for sixteen major states of India. The chapter then analyzes India's poverty alleviation strategies. It analyzes the potential indirect role of agriculture and manufacturing and the contribution of direct poverty alleviation interventions against the backdrop of the results on poverty and inequality. In particular, it examines the extent to which the regional allocation of funds for direct poverty alleviation programs is sensitive to the regional distribution of the poor and the ultrapoor, and whether the recent evidence on the effect of these programs is consistent with the observed patterns in poverty and inequality.

Methodology

To analyze poverty, we need to measure the economic welfare of each individual in the society. Although income is widely used to measure economic welfare, it has many serious drawbacks.[1] One important drawback is that income may have substantial fluctuations that average out in the long run. It has been suggested that consumption may therefore be a better indicator than current income of the actual economic position of a household.[2]

The National Sample Surveys provide reasonably comparable time-series data on the levels and distribution of household consumption expenditures. The data are sorted by population group, based on per capita household expenditure, and give for each group the estimated number of persons and the average consumer expenditures in rupees per person. The monthly per capita expenditure levels are generally grouped into thirteen to fourteen expenditure classes. Estimating poverty from such data requires the use of an extrapolation device. A commonly used procedure is to fit a density function to the entire range of consumption and then compute poverty measures from the parameter of the fitted function. Most studies on poverty in India have employed a two-parameter lognormal distribution (Minhas and others 1987). The lognormal distribution tends to overcorrect for the positive skewness of the income distribution, however, and thus fits poorly to the actual data.

For this chapter we used a general interpolation device proposed by Kakwani (1980a). This method uses, for each range of expenditure, a separate, continuous, differentiable function that exactly fits to the data points. The inequality and poverty measures are then computed by linking this function. We used a polynomial of the third degree to represent the Lorenz curve within each income class, except the first and the last open-ended classes. For these we used a Pareto curve as a further refinement.[3]

We used per capita household expenditure as a measure of household economic welfare.[4] Expenditure comprises all expenditures incurred by the household exclusively on domestic account, including consumption out of homegrown produce or out of transfer receipts, such as gifts and loans. Expenditure on household enterprises is excluded from consumer expenditure, and consumption out of homegrown produce is evaluated at ex-farm rates. Ideally, the depreciated value of consumer durables in stock in the household should be included. But because information on stock values was unavailable, the monetary value of consumer durables acquired during the reference period is included in the total expenditure. This may in some cases distort the results on consumption inequality.

To construct the index of household welfare, the next step is to determine the welfare of the individuals in the households. We derived individual welfare by assigning each individual in a household a welfare value equal to the per capita consumption for that household (Kakwani 1986). If there are severe intrahousehold inequities in the distribution of food and nonfood items, both poverty and inequality will be underestimated. This problem could not be corrected because information on the intrahousehold distribution of resources was unavailable.

Once we have decided on a suitable index of economic welfare for individuals, the next step is to find a threshold welfare level below which an individual is considered poor. In this chapter we have used two poverty lines. India's Planning Commission (1980) has defined the poverty threshold as a per capita monthly expenditure of 49.09 rupees (Rs) in rural India at 1973-74 rural prices. Following the Planning Commission, we adopted Rs 49.1 as our first poverty line. This poverty line corresponds roughly to the per capita expenditure at which a typically structured, typically spending household exactly meets its per capita daily requirement of 2,400 calories in rural areas. Our second poverty line, Rs 39.3, is less than 80 percent of the Planning Commission's poverty threshold of Rs 49.1. We define the households whose per capita consumption is below Rs 39.3 per month as the *ultrapoor*—those whose physical personal maintenance is unstable (Lipton 1988b). The cutoff of Rs 39.3 for the ultrapoor corresponds closely to the poverty line used by Bardhan (1970) and Dandekar and Rath (1971)—Rs 15 at 1960-61 prices, which, at 1973-74 rural prices, is equivalent to per capita expenditure of Rs 42.5.

Price deflators

Comparing poverty across different periods requires adjusting the distributions given in current prices for price changes over time. Minhas (1970) and Dandekar and Rath (1971) used the national income deflator for this purpose. This deflator has been criticized by Bardhan (1974b) because it does not reflect the prices that people actually pay for their consumption goods. We have followed Bardhan in using the Consumer Price Index for Agricultural Laborers (CPIAL) prepared by India's Labor Bureau. This index, based on the monthly retail prices of 62 consumer items collected from selected rural centers, uses the consumption pattern of rural agricultural labor households observed in 1960-61. An important objection to this index is that agricultural labor households constitute only about 30 percent of the rural population; the remaining 70 percent of rural households include a large number of poor small farmers, and thus may have quite a different consumption pattern (Minhas and others 1987). But this objection is not relevant in view of Bardhan's (1974b) observation that the consumption patterns of agricultural labor households differ little from those of other household groups in rural areas.

Minhas and others (1987) have constructed new price indices that depict the movement of consumer prices for the entire rural population (CPITR) and for the rural population in the middle-income range (CPIMR). For poverty analysis Minhas and others (1987) have advocated using the CPIMR, which is based on the consumption pattern of middle-income households in the base period. But middle-income households constitute only 30 percent of the total rural population. Thus, a large proportion of the poor, and almost all ultrapoor households, are not covered by the CPIMR. And the CPITR, although it is based on the average consumption pattern of the entire rural population, and thus includes the poor and the ultrapoor, is nevertheless considered unsuitable for poverty analysis because the *average* consumption pattern of the *entire* rural population may be vastly different from the consumption pattern of the poor and the ultrapoor.

The most attractive feature of the CPITR and the CPIMR is that they are based on more recent consumption patterns (1970-71) than the CPIAL (1960-61). The principal question, therefore, is whether consumption patterns have changed so drastically that the CPIAL has become unusable. To answer this question, we refer to the paper by Minhas and others (1990), which presents the CPITR based on both weighting diagrams—1960-61 and 1970-71. We present their results at the all-India level; patterns at the state level are quite similar.

Year	1960-61 weighting diagram	1970-71 weighting diagram	Percentage difference
1972-73	121.5	121.1	-0.3
1973-74	147.6	146.7	-0.6
1977-78	173.9	172.2	-1.0
1983	274.8	270.1	-1.7

These results indicate that the price indices do not vary significantly when the weighting diagram for the most recent year is used.

The CPIAL series is constructed on the basis of sixty-two consumer items. In the construction of the CPITR and CPIMR, sixty-two consumer items were aggregated into forty-nine items. Because the consumption patterns for the forty-nine items were unavailable for 1970-71, these items were further aggregated into thirteen major groups. The prices for each of these major groups were computed using the consumption patterns observed in 1960-61. The state-specific aggregate consumer price indices were constructed from the thirteen major group indices using the consumption patterns of households in 1970-71.

Thus, the claim that the CPITR and the CPIMR are the best indices because the latest representative consumption patterns are used as the weighting diagram is not entirely valid; in fact, the consumption patterns of households for both years (1960-61 and 1970-71) have been used. Because the income ranges are based on current prices, the households in the middle range for 1960-61 may not have the same level of welfare and the same consumption patterns as those in the middle range for 1970-71. This creates a problem with regard to which households should be selected in 1970-71 to ensure compatibility with those selected in 1960-61.

Because of these difficulties with the most recently proposed indices, we have used the CPIAL as the price deflator. We consider it as the most appropriate index because it depicts the movement of consumer prices for poor and ultrapoor households more accurately than other indices. Gaiha points out that "agricultural labor households (ALH) are the largest occupational group among the rural poor; not only are the bulk of them poor but they also account for a large share of the rural poor" (1989: 6). Although there may be a large number of self-employed small farmers who are poor, their consumption pattern may not differ much from those of agricultural labor households because the two groups of households have almost the same level of economic welfare. Thus, the CPIAL should provide a close approximation to the consumption patterns of the rural poor households. Moreover, because agricultural labor households are typically net buyers of food, the CPIAL can be expected to provide a close approximation to the prices confronting the net buyers of food, who would constitute a much larger share of the rural poor than the agricultural labor households. Finally, the CPIAL is the only index available for the most recent years, 1986-87, the years for which the poverty estimates are presented here.

The CPIAL is published yearly (by calendar or financial year). None of the National Sample Surveys was conducted during either the financial or the calendar year. The months for different surveys are as follows:

NSS round	Survey period
28th	October 1973 to June 1974
32nd	July 1977 to June 1978
38th	January 1983 to December 1983
42nd	July 1986 to June 1987

Because there were substantial fluctuations in the monthly price indices, the yearly average price indices could not be used. We therefore computed a new CPIAL series for the survey periods using the monthly prices corresponding with the survey months. Minhas and others (1987) applied a similar index to compute the incidence of poverty in the rural and urban areas of India for five periods, ranging from 1970-71 to 1983. They performed the poverty computations on the all-India expenditure distributions that are published by the NSS separately for rural and urban areas. These aggregate distributions are derived from the state distributions using population-weighted averages. But this procedure of obtaining the aggregate distributions is unsatisfactory because of widely observed differences in price levels among states. The expenditures in current prices given for each state must be adjusted for the price differences before they can be aggregated. Because this procedure was not adopted in the study by Minhas and others, their all-India estimates of rural poverty are inaccurate despite the advances they made in constructing a new price index.

To obtain comparable poverty levels across different states, we need relative price levels in the rural areas of different states in a given year. Bhattacharya and Chatterjee (1974) worked out these state price relatives for 1963-64 for the entire rural population; these formed the basis for the Bardhan (1974a) study. We have used the price relatives (obtained from Minhas and Jain 1990) based on the weighting diagram of the middle-income group of the rural population. These were considered more appropriate for estimating the incidence of rural poverty (Minhas and Jain 1990). Using these price relatives and the CPIAL available at the state level (table 18.1), we worked out the state-specific poverty lines at the current prices for 1973-74, 1977-78, 1983, and 1986-87 (table 18.2).[5]

The poverty lines vary substantially among the states as well as over time. These differences are due entirely to differences in prices. For instance, West Bengal has the highest poverty line for each of the five years; this means that, for the poor, West Bengal is the most expensive state in which to live. It also had the highest inflation rate, particularly from 1977-78 to 1983.

The incidence of rural poverty for each state was first computed using the state-specific poverty lines given in table 18.2. The poverty for all of India's rural population was then derived from the rural poverty levels computed at the state levels.

Trends in inequality and poverty among all-India's rural population

Having decided on the poverty line, we next compute poverty indices to measure the intensity of poverty. The head count measure, although widely used, is a

Table 18.1 Consumer price index for agricultural laborers and price relatives by state, India, selected years, 1960-61 to 1986-87

State	Price relatives 1960-61	Consumer price index			
		1973-74	1977-78	1983	1986-87
Andhra Pradesh	101	244	297	423	484
Assam	111	270	315	571	606
Bihar	102	350	341	563	594
Gujarat	112	250	285	433	530
Haryana	105	280	332	594	602
Jammu-Kashmir	104	271	342	508	618
Karnataka	99	279	308	491	557
Kerala	107	288	317	534	665
Madhya Pradesh	94	320	345	511	585
Maharashtra	106	277	320	485	581
Orissa	98	340	351	633	616
Punjab	105	280	332	594	602
Rajasthan	103	290	327	456	565
Tamil Nadu	108	251	306	515	575
Uttar Pradesh	95	313	336	518	593
West Bengal	116	288	321	525	607
All-India	100	291	323	511	578

Source: For price relatives, Minhas and Jain 1989; and for consumer price indices, India, Central Statistical Organization, various issues.

Table 18.2 State-specific poverty lines for rural areas, India, selected years, 1973-74 to 1986-87
(rupees per person per month at current prices)

State	Poor				Ultrapoor			
	1973-74	*1977-78*	*1983*	*1986-87*	*1973-74*	*1977-78*	*1983*	*1986-87*
Andhra Pradesh	42	51	72	82	33	41	58	66
Assam	51	59	107	113	40	47	85	91
Bihar	60	59	97	102	48	47	78	82
Gujarat	47	54	82	100	38	43	66	80
Haryana	49	59	105	106	40	47	84	85
Jammu-Kashmir	48	60	89	109	38	48	71	87
Karnataka	46	51	82	93	37	41	65	74
Kerala	52	57	96	120	41	46	77	96
Madhya Pradesh	51	55	81	93	41	44	65	74
Maharashtra	49	57	86	103	39	46	69	83
Orissa	56	58	105	102	45	46	84	81
Punjab	49	59	105	106	40	47	84	85
Rajasthan	51	57	79	98	40	46	64	79
Tamil Nadu	46	56	94	105	37	45	75	84
Uttar Pradesh	50	54	83	95	40	43	66	76
West Bengal	56	63	103	119	45	50	82	95
All-India	49	55	86	98	39	44	69	78

Source: Authors' calculations.

crude poverty index because it does not take into account the income gap among the poor. If the degree of misery suffered by an individual is proportional to that individual's shortfall in income from the poverty line, the sum total of these shortfalls may be considered an adequate measure of poverty. This measure is called the poverty gap ratio and can be written as

$$(18.1) \qquad g = \int_0^z g(x)f(x)dx = H(z-\mu*)/z,$$

where $g(x) = (z - x)/z$, z is the poverty line, $f(x)$ is the density function of income x, H is the head count ratio, and $\mu*$ is the mean consumption of the poor.

The measure g will provide adequate information about the intensity of poverty if all the poor are assumed to have exactly the same income, which is less than the poverty line. In practice, income is unequally distributed among the poor, and therefore g cannot be an adequate measure of poverty. To make g sensitive to the income inequality among the poor, Sen (1976) proposed a poverty measure that led to a large body of theoretical literature on the measurement of poverty.[6] The main difficulty with Sen's measure is that it is not additively decomposable. It is therefore awkward to compute its value for the all-India rural population using the state-level rural expenditure distributions. Moreover, additively decomposable poverty measures are useful because they allow assessment of the effects of changes in the poverty of a subgroup on total poverty.

Watts (1968) proposed an additively decomposable poverty measure that can be obtained by substituting $g(x) = (\log z - \log x)$ in equation 18.1:

(18.2)
$$W = \int_0^z (\log z - \log x) f(x) \, dx$$

Although this is not a well-known measure, it is simple to compute and has all the important attributes: it satisfies both Sen's monotonicity and transfer axioms and Kakwani's (1986) transfer sensitivity axiom. It is also closely related to income inequality. If, rather than z, we use μ (the mean income of the entire population), and evaluate the integral (18.2) over the whole range of x, we obtain

(18.3)
$$T = \int_0^\infty (\log \mu - \log x) f(x) \, dx,$$

which is one of Theil's (1967) two inequality measures. An attractive feature of this measure is that it can be expressed as the sum of the inequalities between and within groups.

In this exercise we have used only additively decomposable poverty and inequality measures. These measures have been used to derive poverty and inequality in each of the sixteen major states of India. The results obtained from individual states have then been aggregated to obtain measures of all-India rural poverty and inequality.[7]

Table 18.3 presents the empirical results on inequality and poverty measures aggregated over the rural areas of the sixteen major states. Average real per capita consumption grew impressively by 3 percent a year from 1973-74 to 1977-78, modestly at 1.3 percent from 1977-78 to 1983, and then again at 2.9 percent from 1983 to 1986-87. The average growth rate for the entire period (1973-74 to 1986-87) was 2.2 percent.

The total inequality in per capita consumption (measured by Theil's index) rose dramatically from 1973-74 to 1977-78, but fell from 1977-78 to 1983. From 1983 to 1986-87, inequality did not change significantly.[8]

Inequality among states contributed 7.7 percent to the total inequality in 1973-74, which means that inequality within states is the main determinant of the inequality at the all-India level. This suggests that policies aimed at redistributing income and assets *within* the poorer states, such as Bihar, deserve greater emphasis. The share of inequality among states grew, however, from 7.7 percent to 9.9 percent between 1973-74 and 1983, but fell dramatically to 7.1 percent between 1983 and 1986-87. Thus, the disparities among states in average living standards showed a tendency to decrease over the most recent period. But this phenomenon was accompanied by an increase in inequality within states. The net increase in total inequality was negligible.

Aggregate poverty in the sixteen major states declined substantially from 1973-74 to 1986-87. The share of rural poor in the population decreased from 59 percent in 1973-74 to 37.5 percent in 1986-87. The poverty gap ratio, which takes into account not only the percentage of poor but their consumption gaps, fell even

Table 18.3 Rural real per capita consumption, inequality, and poverty, India, selected years, 1973-74 to 1986-87

Indicator	1973-74	1977-78	1983	1986-87	Annual growth rate (percent)			
					1973-74 to 1977-78	1977-78 to 1983	1983 to 1986-87	1973-74 to 1986-87
Real per capita monthly consumer expenditure (1973 rupees)	52	58	62	69	3	1	3	2
Theil's inequality measure								
Intrastate inequality[a]	12 (92.3)	16 (91.8)	14 (90.1)	15 (92.9)	6	-2	1	1
Interstate inequality[a]	1 (7.7)	2 (8.2)	2 (9.9)	1 (7.1)	10	0	-9	1
Total inequality[a]	13 (100)	17 (100)	15 (100)	16 (100)	6	-2	1	1
Rural poor								
Head count ratio (percent)	59	53	45	38	-3	-3	-5	-3
Number of poor (millions)	264	253	241	211	-1	-1	-4	-2
Poverty gap ratio (percent)	18	16	12	9	-4	-4	-8	-5
Ultrapoor								
Head count ratio (percent)	40	34	28	20	-4	-4	-8	-5
Number of ultrapoor (millions)	178	166	146	114	-2	-2	-7	-3
Poverty gap ratio (percent)	10	9	6	4	-4	-5	-11	-7

a. Numbers in parentheses are percentage shares of intrastate inequality and interstate inequality in total inequality.
Source: Authors' calculations.

faster. Even the absolute number of rural poor has declined substantially, from 264.3 million in 1973-74 to 210.8 million in 1986-87. These figures demonstrate India's substantial achievements in poverty reduction, particularly in the 1980s.

Furthermore, poverty ratios for the ultrapoor fell more than those for the poor. From 1983 to 1986-87, the head count ratio for the poor fell by 5.3 percent, but that for the ultrapoor by 8.3 percent. The trends in the poverty gap ratio and the Watts measure are similar. These measures showed that, in general, the reduction in poverty was greater for the ultrapoor than for the poor, and the reduction in poverty was greater after 1977-78 than before. This is interesting, because 1973-74 to 1977-78 was a period of higher growth (3 percent) with increasing inequality; 1977-83 was characterized by considerably slower per capita growth in consumption (1.3 percent) but a substantial decrease in intrastate inequality. This decrease in inequality was the main factor behind the substantial reduction in poverty from 1977-78 to 1983. After 1983, inequality did not change significantly, but growth at 2.9 percent led to an even greater reduction in poverty.

No significant changes in the *pattern* of growth could be observed between the periods 1973-74 to 1977-78 and 1977-78 to 1983, but the second period witnessed a spate of direct antipoverty interventions. If this strategy were working with reasonable efficiency, a reduction in consumption inequality would be expected after 1977-78. A reduction is indeed noticeable during the period from 1977-78 to 1983 in table 18.3. Although it is impossible to establish causality, can qualitative inferences nevertheless be drawn about the role of antipoverty programs in the observed reduction in inequality? Why was there no further reduction in inequality observed after 1983? To answer this and other related questions, we need to analyze poverty trends at a disaggregated (state) level. This is done in the following sections.

State trends in average rural per capita consumption and inequality

From 1973-74 to 1977-78 all states except Assam and Maharashtra showed growth in average consumption per capita (table 18.4). That trend continued from 1977-78 to 1986-87 in all states except Bihar, Haryana, Punjab, and Uttar Pradesh, from 1977-78 to 1983, and Karnataka and Rajasthan, from 1983 to 1986-87. Kerala's performance has been consistently good; its per capita consumption increased at an annual rate of 3.3 percent for the entire period (1973-74 to 1986-87). That is not surprising, because Kerala received substantial overseas remittances during this period.[9]

A ranking of states by rural per capita consumption shows that Kerala has substantially improved its relative position from ninth in 1973-74 to thirteenth in 1986-87 (table 18.5). The two largest states, Madhya Pradesh and Uttar Pradesh, also improved their relative positions. The states whose relative positions deteriorated are Assam, Bihar, Gujarat, Karnataka, and Rajasthan. The remaining states maintained more or less the same ranking.

We now turn to trends in inequality in rural per capita consumption. Table 18.6 presents the levels and annual percentage change in inequality as measured by the Gini index, and table 18.7 shows them as measured by the Theil index.[10]

Table 18.4 Rural real per capita consumption by state, India, selected years, 1973-74 to 1986-87
(1973-74 rupees)

State	Per capita consumption (rupees per month)				Annual growth rate (percent)			
	1973-74	*1977-78*	*1983*	*1986-87*	*1973-74 to 1977-78*	*1977-78 to 1983*	*1983 to 1986-87*	*1973-74 to 1986-87*
Andhra Pradesh	60	68	79	84	3	3	2	3
Assam	51	50	52	61	-1	1	5	1
Bihar	46	48	48	56	1	0	5	2
Gujarat	57	64	74	75	3	3	1	2
Haryana	72	77	71	92	2	-2	8	2
Jammu-Kashmir	55	60	71	78	2	3	3	3
Karnataka	55	62	70	69	3	2	-1	2
Kerala	53	64	74	80	5	3	2	3
Madhya Pradesh	49	54	61	65	3	2	2	2
Maharashtra	52	50	63	65	-1	4	1	2
Orissa	37	45	46	55	5	1	5	3
Punjab	75	96	80	98	6	-3	6	2
Rajasthan	62	73	78	78	4	1	0	2
Tamil Nadu	51	56	59	66	2	1	3	2
Uttar Pradesh	50	62	62	72	5	0	4	3
West Bengal	41	46	50	57	3	1	4	3
All-India	52	58	62	69	3	1	3	2

Source: Authors' calculations.

Table 18.5 Ranking of states by rural real per capita consumption, India, selected years, 1973-74 to 1986-87

State	1973-74	1977-78	1983	1986-87
Andhra Pradesh	13	13	15	14
Assam	6	4	4	4
Bihar	3	3	2	2
Gujarat	12	12	12	10
Haryana	15	15	11	15
Jammu-Kashmir	10	8	10	11
Karnataka	11	10	9	8
Kerala	9	11	13	13
Madhya Pradesh	4	6	6	6
Maharashtra	8	5	8	5
Orissa	1	1	1	1
Punjab	16	16	16	16
Rajasthan	14	14	14	12
Tamil Nadu	7	7	5	7
Uttar Pradesh	5	9	7	9
West Bengal	2	2	3	3

Note: A ranking of 1 indicates the lowest level of consumption, 16 the highest.
Source: Authors' calculations.

The results show a wide variation in inequality across states as well as over time. In eleven of sixteen states, inequality measured by the Gini index increased from 1973-74 to 1977-78. Theil's measure, which gives greater weight than the Gini index to income transfers at the bottom end of the distribution, shows that inequality increased in thirteen of sixteen states. Inequality declined significantly in Assam and Bihar. From 1977-78 to 1983, however, thirteen of sixteen states showed a decrease in inequality (all but Assam, Rajasthan, and Tamil Nadu). In the most recent period, between 1983 and 1986-87, inequality increased in eleven states.

Was the widespread decline in inequality from 1977-78 to 1983—especially in the states with better rural administration—due to the major policy change in the late 1970s signaled by the introduction of antipoverty programs? The main objective of these programs was to raise the consumption levels of the poor. Although causality cannot be established, it is possible that this policy contributed to an overall reduction in consumption inequality. Conversely, was the increase in inequality in many states from 1983 to 1986-87 due to a shift toward growth-supporting policies with little emphasis on redistribution? This and other relationships between consumption, inequality, and poverty are investigated in the next section.

Correlates of per capita consumption and inequality

Linear regression and correlation techniques are commonly used to measure relationships between variables. The relationships involving consumption, inequality, and poverty are often nonlinear; thus, the correlation coefficient that

Table 18.6 Inequality of rural per capita consumption as measured by the Gini index, by state, India, selected years, 1973-74 to 1986-87

(percent)

State	Gini index				Annual growth rate			
	1973-74	1977-78	1983	1986-87	1973-74 to 1977-78	1977-78 to 1983	1983 to 1986-87	1973-74 to 1986-87
Andhra Pradesh	29	30	30	31	1	0	1	0
Assam	21	18	20	22	-3	1	2	0
Bihar	28	26	26	25	-2	0	-1	-1
Gujarat	24	29	26	31	5	-2	5	2
Haryana	30	30	28	29	0	-1	2	0
Jammu-Kashmir	23	23	23	28	-1	0	6	2
Karnataka	29	33	30	29	3	-1	-1	0
Kerala	32	36	34	35	3	-1	1	1
Madhya Pradesh	29	34	30	31	4	-2	2	1
Maharashtra	27	29	29	30	2	0	1	1
Orissa	27	31	27	27	3	-2	0	0
Punjab	28	31	29	30	3	-2	2	1
Rajasthan	28	33	35	30	4	1	-4	1
Tamil Nadu	28	32	33	30	4	0	-2	1
Uttar Pradesh	24	30	29	31	6	-1	1	2
West Bengal	30	30	29	24	0	-1	-5	-2

Source: Authors' calculations.

Table 18.7 Inequality of rural per capita consumption as measured by the Theil index, by state, India, selected years, 1973-74 to 1986-87
(percent)

State	Theil index				Annual growth rate			
	1973-74	1977-78	1983	1986-87	1973-74 to 1977-78	1977-78 to 1983	1983 to 1986-87	1973-74 to 1986-87
Andhra Pradesh	15	16	14	18	2	-2	7	2
Assam	7	6	6	8	-5	1	5	0
Bihar	13	11	11	10	-4	-1	-3	-2
Gujarat	9	14	11	19	10	-4	17	6
Haryana	14	15	12	14	1	-3	4	0
Jammu-Kashmir	9	9	8	13	0	-1	14	3
Karnataka	13	18	15	14	7	-3	-3	0
Kerala	17	22	19	21	7	-2	2	2
Madhya Pradesh	14	20	14	17	9	-6	5	2
Maharashtra	12	14	13	15	5	-1	4	2
Orissa	12	16	12	12	8	-5	1	1
Punjab	12	19	13	15	12	-6	4	2
Rajasthan	13	18	20	15	9	1	-8	1
Tamil Nadu	12	19	18	15	12	-2	-4	2
Uttar Pradesh	10	16	14	15	13	-2	2	4
West Bengal	15	14	14	12	-1	-1	-5	-2
All-India	13	17	15	16	6	-2	1	1

Source: Authors' calculations.

426

measures the deviations from linearity may invariably show that the variables either are not related or are weakly related. To take into account the nonlinear features of these variables, some analysts have estimated linear regressions after applying a nonlinear transformation to the original data. Because the exact forms of nonlinear relationships are not known, one may wrongly conclude either that these relationships exist or that they do not exist. In these situations, the rank transformation procedures have been found to be robust and powerful (Iman and Conover 1978). In this section we use Spearman's rank correlation coefficient to test whether there is a relationship between any two variables. The test statistic

$$t = \frac{\rho\sqrt{n-2}}{\sqrt{1-\rho^2}},$$

where ρ is the rank correlation, is distributed approximately as Student's t distribution with $(n-2)$ degrees of freedom. This approximation, suggested by Pitman (1937), has been shown to perform better than the usual normal approximation (Iman and Conover 1978).

We made no attempt to establish a causal relationship between the variables. This would require a more sophisticated model, for which we do not have a sufficient number of observations. Our purpose is limited to testing the hypothesis that there is a significant association between the variables. If the association is found to be statistically insignificant, that would most likely imply that there is no causal relationship. But if the association is statistically significant, it would only mean monotonicity in the relationship between variables. Further investigations to establish causality would then be required.

An important issue in development economics is whether there is a relationship between per capita income and the inequality of its distribution (Kuznets 1955). Much has already been written on this issue, and we do not need to explore it in detail. The correlations between real per capita consumption and the Gini index reported in table 18.8 suggest that the association between the two is positive and significant only in 1986-87. In other years the association is insignificant at the 5 percent level. The states with higher average per capita consumption tended to have greater inequality in 1986-87. Because this relationship holds for only one period, it cannot be said whether higher per capita consumption will necessarily lead to higher inequality.

The next question of interest is whether growth in per capita consumption is associated with the percentage change in inequality. The correlations in table 18.8 suggest that this association is positive and significant only in the first period (1973-74 to 1977-78). The adverse effects of growth on inequality are not evident in the two later periods. The factors that may have contributed to the virtual absence of this relationship in the later periods are difficult to establish empirically. But it is difficult to dismiss entirely the role that the antipoverty interventions introduced in 1977-83 may have played, especially because their scale and delivery surpassed those of the piecemeal efforts of the past.

Next, we examine whether the richer states (in terms of per capita consumption) were growing faster—that is, whether the initial level of per capita con-

Table 18.8 Correlates of real per capita consumption and inequality

Variable	Period	Correlation	t-value
Per capita consumption	1973-74		
Gini index	1973-74	0.13	0.50
	1977-78		
	1977-78	0.30	1.20
	1983		
	1983	0.32	1.30
	1986-87		
	1986-87	0.55	2.50*
Per capita consumption	1973-74		
Theil index	1973-74	0.09	0.40
	1977-78		
	1977-78	0.37	1.5
	1983		
	1983	0.34	1.4
	1986-87		
	1986-87	0.52	2.30*
Per capita consumption	1973-74		
Percentage change in per capita consumption	1973-74 to 1977-78	0.21	0.80
	1977-78		
	1977-78 to 1983	-0.05	-0.20
	1983		
	1983 to 1986-87	-0.30	-1.20
Gini index	1973-74		
Percentage change in Gini index	1973-74 to 1977-78	-0.10	-0.40
	1977-78		
	1977-78 to 1983	-0.34	-1.40
	1983		
	1983 to 1986-87	-0.61	-2.90*
Theil index	1973-74		
Percentage change in Theil index	1973-74 to 1977-78	-0.16	-0.60
	1977-78		
	1977-78 to 1983	-0.48	-2.10*
	1983		
	1983 to 1986-87	-0.54	-2.40*
Per capita consumption	1973-74		
Percentage change in Gini index	1973-74 to 1977-78	0.08	0.30
	1977-78		
	1977-78 to 1983	-0.12	-0.40
	1983		
	1983 to 1986-87	0.27	1.10

Table 18.8 Correlates of real per capita consumption and inequality (cont.)

Variable	Period	Correlation	t-value
Per capita consumption	1973-74		
Percentage change in Theil index	1973-74 to 1977-78	0.20	0.80
	1977-78		
	1977-78 to 1983	-0.28	-1.10
	1983		
	1983 to 1986-87	0.30	1.20
Percentage change in per capita consumption	1973-74 to 1977-78		
Percentage change in Theil index	1973-74 to 1977-78	0.63	3.10*
	1977-78 to 1983		
	1977-78 to 1983	0.19	0.70
	1983 to 1986-87		
	1983 to 1986-87	-0.07	-0.30
Percentage change in per capita consumption	1973-74 to 1977-78		
Percentage change in Gini index	1973-74 to 1977-78	0.57	2.60*
	1977-78 to 1983		
	1977-78 to 1983	0.09	0.30
	1983 to 1986-87		
	1983 to 1986-87	0.11	0.40
Inflation rate	1973-74 to 1977-78		
Percentage change in Theil index	1973-74 to 1977-78	-0.07	-0.20
	1977-78 to 1983		
	1977-78 to 1983	-0.20	-0.80
	1983 to 1986-87		
	1983 to 1986-87	0.11	0.40
Inflation rate	1973-74 to 1977-78		
Percentage change in Gini index	1973-74 to 1977-78	-0.21	-0.80
	1977-78 to 1983		
	1977-78 to 1983	-0.09	-0.30
	1983 to 1986-87		
	1983 to 1986-87	0.0	0.0
Per capita food production	1973-74		
Gini index	1973-74	0.11	0.40
	1977-78		
	1977-78	0.30	1.20
	1983		
	1983	0.15	0.60
	1986-87		
	1986-87	-0.02	-0.10
Per capita food production	1973-74		
Theil index	1973-74	0.06	0.20

Table 18.8 Correlates of real per capita consumption and inequality (cont.)

Variable	Period	Correlation	t-value
	1977-78		
	1977-78	0.30	1.20
	1983		
	1983	0.16	0.60
	1986-87		
	1986-87	-0.17	-0.60
Percentage change in per capita consumption	1973-74 to 1977-78		
Percentage change in per capita			
food production	1973-74 to 1977-78	-0.28	-1.10
	1977-78 to 1983		
	1977-78 to 1983	-0.14	-0.50
	1983 to 1986-87		
	1983 to 1986-87	0.64	3.10*
Percentage change in Gini index	1973-74 to 1971-78		
Percentage change in per capita			
food production	1973-74 to 1977-78	-0.21	-0.80
	1977-78 to 1983		
	1977-78 to 1983	-0.28	-1.10
	1983 to 1986-87		
	1983 to 1986-87	-0.34	-1.40
Percentage change in Theil index	1973-74 to 1977-78		
Percentage change in per capita			
food production	1973-74 to 1977-78	-0.11	-0.40
	1977-78 to 1983		
	1977-78 to 1983	-0.38	-1.50
	1983 to 1986-87		
	1983 to 1986-87	-0.47	-2.00*

* t-values with a significance level of 5 percent or more.
Source: Authors' calculations.

sumption is related to growth. The correlations (table 18.8) suggest that the relationship is insignificant in all three periods, and thus that the rate of growth in per capita consumption is not significantly affected by the initial level of per capita consumption. We also found no significant relationship between the level of per capita consumption and the percentage change in inequality.

Was the percentage change in inequality higher or lower in the states in which inequality was already high? The relationship between the level of inequality and the percentage change in it was found to be insignificant in the first period (1973-74 to 1977-78), but was statistically significant, and negative, in later periods. From 1977-78 to 1986-87, the states with higher levels of inequality tended to have smaller increases (or larger decreases) in inequality.

Recently, there has been considerable discussion on the effect of price changes on poverty (Mellor and Desai 1985). Our results show no significant relationship between the two variables—but this appears counterintuitive. Most of the poor are landless laborers, and net purchasers of subsistence goods. Thus, inflation would almost certainly hurt them and, other things being equal, lead to higher inequality. Clearly, the effect of price changes on inequality is complex, and only well-specified price-endogenous models can help establish causality. We can, however, explore a simpler relationship. To what extent can the changes in inequality in states be explained by the changes in per capita production of food grains? For agricultural production, 1983 was an excellent year; food grain production increased from 129.4 million tons in 1982-83 to 152.4 million tons in 1983-84.

Because we are concerned with inequality in rural areas, we computed per capita food production by dividing total food production by the rural population. The results do not suggest that there is any relationship between per capita food production and inequality. This conclusion seems to hold for all years. We also correlated the percentage change in per capita food production with the percentage change in inequality. Again, the results suggest no significant relationship between them. Thus, the higher rate of growth in per capita food production does not necessarily imply a larger decline in inequality. In other words, the widespread decline in inequality between 1977-78 and 1983 could not be attributed strictly to the larger increases in per capita food production. The antipoverty programs introduced around 1977 probably played an important role in reducing inequality.

State trends in rural poverty

The regional trends in poverty for the poor and the ultrapoor, as measured by the head count and the poverty gap ratios, are presented in tables 18.9-12. The last four columns in each of these tables present the annual percentage change in poverty. Because the results of the Watts measure followed the same pattern as the head count ratio, we did not present them.

From 1973-74 to 1977-78 the head count ratio for both the poor and the ultrapoor decreased in thirteen states; in two states, Assam and Maharashtra, it increased for both groups. The head count ratio for the ultrapoor increased in Tamil Nadu. In Maharashtra the increase in poverty was found to be very large, but during 1977-78 to 1983 the head count ratio for the poor decreased by 6.4 percent and that for the ultrapoor by 10 percent. Andhra Pradesh, Gujarat, Jammu and Kashmir, Karnataka, Kerala, and Madhya Pradesh also had a substantial decline in poverty. Interestingly, poverty increased in the two richest states—Haryana and Punjab. This increase is attributed to the negative growth rate observed in the two states from 1977-78 to 1983.

From 1983 to 1986-87 poverty declined in thirteen of sixteen states; the exceptions were Gujarat, Jammu and Kashmir, and Karnataka, though in Karnataka ultrapoverty declined. The increase in poverty in Gujarat and Jammu

Table 18.9 Head count ratio for rural poor by state, India, selected years, 1973-74 to 1986-87

(percent)

State	Head count ratio				Annual growth rate			
	1973-74	1977-78	1983	1986-87	1973-74 to 1977-78	1977-78 to 1983	1983 to 1986-87	1973-74 to 1986-87
Andhra Pradesh	48	38	26	23	-6	-7	-3	-6
Assam	56	58	54	37	1	-1	-10	-3
Bihar	69	63	64	49	-2	0	-7	-3
Gujarat	47	41	25	29	-4	-9	5	-4
Haryana	36	27	32	20	-7	3	-13	-5
Jammu-Kashmir	53	40	22	24	-7	-11	3	-6
Karnataka	54	47	35	37	-3	-5	1	-3
Kerala	61	49	36	31	-5	-5	-5	-5
Madhya Pradesh	64	61	47	45	-1	-5	-1	-3
Maharashtra	58	63	44	43	2	-6	-1	-2
Orissa	79	72	67	53	-3	-1	-6	-3
Punjab	27	16	23	13	-13	8	-16	-6
Rajasthan	44	35	33	28	-5	-1	-5	-4
Tamil Nadu	60	57	52	41	-1	-2	-7	-3
Uttar Pradesh	59	47	45	35	-5	-1	-7	-4
West Bengal	75	68	62	45	-2	-2	-9	-4
All-India	59	53	45	38	-3	-3	-5	-3

Source: Authors' calculations.

Table 18.10 Head count ratio for rural ultrapoor by state, India, selected years, 1973-74 to 1986-87

(percent)

State	Head count ratio				Annual growth rate			
	1973-74	1977-78	1983	1986-87	1973-74 to 1977-78	1977-78 to 1983	1983 to 1986-87	1973-74 to 1986-87
Andhra Pradesh	27.0	21.1	11.6	9.8	-6.0	-10.3	-4.7	-7.5
Assam	27.8	27.9	25.3	16.6	0.1	-1.8	-11.3	-3.9
Bihar	49.2	42.9	44.2	29.3	-3.4	0.5	-11.1	-3.9
Gujarat	24.7	23.8	9.3	16.9	-0.9	-15.7	18.6	-2.9
Haryana	18.0	11.9	14.9	6.1	-9.8	4.2	-22.5	-8.0
Jammu-Kashmir	28.9	18.0	6.7	9.0	-11.2	-16.4	8.8	-8.6
Karnataka	36.2	30.5	21.6	20.4	-4.2	-6.1	-1.6	-4.3
Kerala	42.8	33.7	19.5	15.4	-5.8	-9.5	-6.5	-7.6
Madhya Pradesh	47.2	43.2	27.5	24.4	-2.2	-7.9	-3.4	-4.9
Maharashtra	37.2	44.5	25.0	24.5	4.6	-10.0	-0.6	-3.2
Orissa	65.4	54.4	44.4	31.1	-4.5	-3.6	-9.7	-5.6
Punjab	14.3	6.6	10.6	4.2	-17.6	9.0	-23.2	-9.0
Rajasthan	25.1	21.0	19.3	14.2	-4.4	-1.5	-8.4	-4.3
Tamil Nadu	38.9	39.4	35.2	24.5	0.3	-2.0	-9.8	-3.5
Uttar Pradesh	38.8	28.2	26.8	18.2	-7.7	-0.9	-10.5	-5.7
West Bengal	59.2	50.4	42.1	24.3	-3.9	-3.2	-14.5	-6.6
All-India	39.7	34.4	27.5	20.3	-3.5	-4.0	-8.3	-5.0

Source: Authors' calculations

Table 18.11 Poverty gap ratio for rural poor by state, India, selected years, 1973-74 to 1986-87
(percent)

State	Poverty gap ratio				Annual growth rate			
	1973-74	1977-78	1983	1986-87	1973-74 to 1977-78	1977-78 to 1983	1983 to 1986-87	1973-74 to 1986-87
Andhra Pradesh	12.6	9.6	5.5	5.1	-6.6	-9.6	-2.1	-6.7
Assam	13.4	12.3	11.2	7.3	-2.1	-1.7	-11.5	-4.6
Bihar	22.8	19.4	19.7	12.4	-4.0	0.3	-12.4	-4.6
Gujarat	11.2	10.7	4.5	7.6	-1.1	-14.6	16.2	-2.9
Haryana	8.2	6.0	6.7	3.3	-7.5	2.0	-18.3	-6.8
Jammu-Kashmir	12.2	8.0	3.5	4.3	-10.0	-14.0	6.1	-7.7
Karnataka	15.5	14.1	9.3	9.4	-2.3	-7.3	0.3	-3.8
Kerala	20.2	15.6	8.7	7.2	-6.3	-10.1	-5.3	-7.6
Madhya Pradesh	21.1	19.6	12.4	10.9	-1.8	-8.0	-3.6	-5.0
Maharashtra	16.7	20.1	10.9	11.0	4.7	-10.5	0.3	-3.2
Orissa	31.7	25.9	21.3	14.6	-4.9	-3.5	-10.2	-5.8
Punjab	5.9	3.4	4.9	2.1	-12.9	6.9	-21.5	-7.6
Rajasthan	11.2	9.8	8.7	6.3	-3.3	-2.1	-8.8	-4.3
Tamil Nadu	17.7	17.6	16.2	11.2	-0.1	-1.5	-10.0	-3.5
Uttar Pradesh	16.2	12.4	11.8	8.2	-6.5	-0.9	-9.9	-5.1
West Bengal	29.0	23.4	19.6	10.9	-5.2	-3.2	-15.4	-7.3
All-India	18.1	15.7	12.4	9.2	-3.5	-4.2	-8.2	-5.1

Source: Authors' calculations.

434

Table 18.12 Poverty gap ratio for rural ultrapoor by state, India, selected years, 1973-74 to 1986-87
(percent)

State	Poverty gap ratio				Annual growth rate			
	1973-74	1977-78	1983	1986-87	1973-74 to 1977-78	1977-78 to 1983	1983 to 1986-87	1973-74 to 1986-87
Andhra Pradesh	6.3	4.7	2.3	2.3	-7.1	-12.2	0	-7.5
Assam	6.0	4.5	4.1	2.5	-6.9	-1.7	-13.2	-6.5
Bihar	13.8	10.9	11.0	5.4	-5.7	0.2	-18.4	-7.0
Gujarat	4.9	5.3	1.5	3.7	2.0	-20.5	29.4	-2.1
Haryana	3.5	2.5	2.7	1.1	-8.1	1.4	-22.6	-8.5
Jammu-Kashmir	5.1	2.7	1.0	1.4	-14.7	-16.5	10.1	-9.5
Karnataka	7.9	7.9	4.6	4.6	0	-9.4	0	-4.1
Kerala	12.1	9.1	3.9	3.3	-6.9	-14.3	-4.7	-9.5
Madhya Pradesh	12.3	11.4	6.1	4.9	-1.9	-10.7	-6.1	-6.8
Maharashtra	8.8	11.7	5.0	5.0	7.4	-14.3	0	-4.3
Orissa	21.4	16.5	12.6	7.3	-6.3	-4.8	-14.4	-7.9
Punjab	2.7	1.6	1.9	0.8	-12.3	3.2	-21.9	-8.9
Rajasthan	5.4	5.2	4.4	2.8	-0.9	-3.0	-12.1	-4.9
Tamil Nadu	9.7	9.9	9.2	5.7	0.5	-1.3	-12.8	-4.0
Uttar Pradesh	7.9	6	5.8	3.5	-6.6	-0.6	-13.4	-6.1
West Bengal	19.2	14.3	11.5	5.2	-7.1	-3.9	-20.3	-9.6
All-India	10.1	8.7	6.4	4.2	-3.7	-5.4	-11.3	-6.5

Source: Authors' calculations.

435

and Kashmir was due to an increase in inequality; in Karnataka, the increase was due to the decline in per capita consumption. In Gujarat and Karnataka, where the proportion of arid regions is high, regional climatic factors also contributed to a rise in poverty.

Tables 18.13 and 18.14 rank states by head count and poverty gap ratios for the poor and the ultrapoor (in ascending order of poverty). They show that there has been substantial change in the ranking. Andhra Pradesh, Jammu and Kashmir, and Kerala have considerably improved their relative position over the entire period. These results are corroborated by trends in the nutritional status of the ultrapoor in these states (Subbarao 1989), which showed an improvement during 1970-80.

An important finding is that, regardless of the way poverty is measured, all states show a considerable reduction in poverty between 1973-74 and 1986-87. Although reductions in poverty were more widespread between 1977-78 and 1983, the reductions were larger in many poorer states (such as Bihar, Tamil Nadu, Uttar Pradesh, and West Bengal) from 1983 to 1986-87. In eight states there was a consistent and sustained reduction in the poverty gap ratio throughout the period. In the remaining states the trends in poverty incidence and inequality are irregular. This is to be expected. Indeed, the purpose of regional disaggregation is to capture these regional and temporal differences.

What explains these differences and changing patterns? Much can be explained by climatic factors and state policies—growth-promoting or inequality-

Table 18.13 Ranking of states by head count ratio for rural poor and ultrapoor, India, selected years, 1973-74 to 1986-87

| | *Head count ratio for poor* | | | | *Head count ratio for ultrapoor* | | | |
State	*1973-74*	*1977-78*	*1983*	*1986-87*	*1973-74*	*1977-78*	*1983*	*1986-87*
Andhra Pradesh	5	4	4	3	5	5	4	4
Assam	8	11	13	10	6	7	10	7
Bihar	14	14	15	15	14	12	15	15
Gujarat	4	6	3	6	3	6	2	8
Haryana	2	2	5	2	2	2	5	2
Jammu-Kashmir	6	5	1	4	7	3	1	3
Karnataka	7	7	7	9	8	9	8	10
Kerala	12	9	8	7	12	10	7	6
Madhya Pradesh	13	12	11	14	13	13	12	12
Maharashtra	9	13	9	12	9	14	9	13
Orissa	16	16	16	16	16	16	16	16
Punjab	1	1	2	1	1	1	3	1
Rajasthan	3	3	6	5	4	4	6	5
Tamil Nadu	11	10	12	11	11	11	13	14
Uttar Pradesh	10	8	10	8	10	8	11	9
West Bengal	15	15	14	13	15	15	14	11

Note: States are ranked in ascending order of poverty, with 1 indicating the lowest level of poverty and 16 the highest.
Source: Authors' calculations.

Table 18.14 Ranking of states by poverty gap ratio for rural poor and ultrapoor, India, selected years, 1973-74 to 1986-87

State	Poverty gap ratio for poor				Poverty gap ratio for ultrapoor			
	1973-74	*1977-78*	*1983*	*1986-87*	*1973-74*	*1977-78*	*1983*	*1986-87*
Andhra Pradesh	6	4	4	4	7	5	4	4
Assam	7	7	10	7	6	4	7	5
Bihar	14	12	15	15	14	12	14	14
Gujarat	4	6	2	8	3	7	2	9
Haryana	2	2	5	2	2	2	5	2
Jammu-Kashmir	5	3	1	3	4	3	1	3
Karnataka	8	9	8	10	9	9	9	10
Kerala	12	10	7	6	12	10	6	7
Madhya Pradesh	13	13	12	12	13	13	12	11
Maharashtra	10	14	9	13	10	14	10	12
Orissa	16	16	16	16	16	16	16	16
Punjab	1	1	3	1	1	1	3	1
Rajasthan	3	5	6	5	5	6	8	6
Tamil Nadu	11	11	13	14	11	11	13	15
Uttar Pradesh	9	8	11	9	8	8	11	8
West Bengal	15	15	14	11	15	15	15	13

Note: States are ranked in ascending order of poverty, with 1 indicating the lowest level of poverty and 16 the highest.
Source: Authors' calculations.

reducing, or both. It is difficult empirically to disentangle them and establish their relative roles in different states. But a few circumstances unique to some states are worth mentioning, to underscore the point that our results for states, despite their irregularity, conform with our knowledge of the states' changing situations.

Maharashtra's impressive reduction in poverty from 1977-78 to 1983 (especially among the ultrapoor) can be attributed to the state's Employment Guarantee Scheme. Kerala combined a fortuitous situation of overseas remittances with a wide-ranging state action equalizing access to food, health care, and minimum wages and providing social security to landless agricultural laborers. And the reduction in poverty in Andhra Pradesh, Gujarat, Karnataka, Orissa, and Rajasthan can be attributed to their impressive growth performance from 1973-74 to 1983.

By contrast, from 1973-74 to 1983 the three large states of Bihar, Tamil Nadu, and Uttar Pradesh had neither an impressive record of economic growth nor substantial interventions providing social security, which explains their slow progress in reducing poverty.

From 1983 to 1986-87 the three major eastern states—Bihar, Uttar Pradesh, and West Bengal—substantially reduced their incidence of poverty. This is attributable largely to the Intensive Rice Production Program, which led to the emergence of high-yield varieties (HYV) of rice as a second crop in many districts in the eastern Gangetic belt. And West Bengal combined production increases with state action to protect tenants and to improve the public distribution system while revitalizing local, decentralized institutions.

Interestingly, Assam's relative position is considerably higher in the ranking based on ultrapoverty than in that based on total poverty. This discrepancy is attributable to the very low degree of inequality in the state, which is predominantly tribal. The low inequality appears to favor the ultrapoor more than the poor.

We ask two questions based on the correlates of poverty in table 18.15. First, did poverty decline faster in the poorer or in the richer states? The correlates indicate that the relationship between the head count ratio and the percentage change in the head count ratio was positive and significant at the 5 percent level in the first period (1973-74 to 1977-78), but not in the second period (1977-78 to 1983). In the first period the rate of reduction in poverty (but not ultrapoverty) tended to be lower in the poorer states. In the second period (1977-78 to 1983) the poorer states did neither better nor worse than the others in reducing either poverty or ultrapoverty. In the most recent period (1983 to 1986-87) the relationship became significantly negative—that is, poverty and, to an even greater extent, ultrapoverty, fell faster in the poorer states. As already noted, the principal impetus for the reduction in poverty in the poorer eastern states may have come from growth stemming from a second rice crop. To gain further insight into this issue, the effects of growth and changing inequality on poverty reduction are separated in the next section.

Second, is there an inverse relationship between rural poverty and agricultural performance, as postulated by Ahluwalia (1978 and 1985)? His own analysis of individual states did not conclusively support this proposition. The correlations in table 18.15 suggest that the inverse relationship between poverty and per capita food production is significant for the head count ratio for the poor in the first (1973-74) and the third (1983) periods. In 1986-87 the relationship becomes insignificant. For the ultrapoor, the relationship is insignificant in all three periods. But if we measure poverty by the poverty gap ratio, the relationship is significant only in the first period, 1973-74. Thus, there appears to be no systematic relationship between either the *extent* or the *intensity* of poverty and food grain production per capita.

But do *changes* in food grain production induce systematic downward *movements* in the extent and intensity of poverty? To examine this, we correlated the percentage change in per capita food production with the percentage change in poverty. Again, there is no relationship between the two. For examining the role of agriculture in explaining poverty, analysis based only on changes in *per capita* food grain production and poverty is clearly inadequate. We need to examine the *growth* and *instability* of the agricultural sector, by region, and then look for patterns in the geographical distribution of the poor and the ultrapoor. This is done later in the chapter.

Effect of economic growth and inequality on poverty

Suppose θ, a poverty index, is a function of three factors: (1) the poverty line, z; (2) mean per capita consumption, μ; and (3) inequality of consumption. Inequality can be measured by a single inequality index (many of which are available in

Table 18.15 Correlates of poverty

Variable	Period	Correlation	t-value
Head count ratio (poor)	1973-74		
Percentage change in head count ratio	1973-74 to 1977-78	0.65	3.20*
	1977-78		
	1977-78 to 1983	0.28	1.20
	1983		
	1983 to 1986-87	-0.72	-2.90*
Head count ratio (ultrapoor)	1973-74		
Percentage change in head count ratio	1973-74 to 1977-78	0.37	1.50
	1977-78		
	1977-78 to 1983	0.25	1.00
	1983		
	1983 to 1986-87	-0.53	-2.30*
Poverty gap ratio (poor)	1973-74		
Percentage change in poverty gap ratio	1973-74 to 1977-78	0.34	1.40
	1977-78		
	1977-78 to 1983	0.27	1.10
	1983		
	1983 to 1986-87	-0.77	-3.20*
Inflation	1973-74 to 1977-78		
Percentage change in head count ratio	1973-74 to 1977-78	0.29	1.10
	1977-78 to 1983		
	1977-78 to 1983	0.57	2.60*
	1983 to 1986-87		
	1983 to 1986-87	0.61	2.90*
Inflation	1973-74 to 1977-78		
Percentage change in head count ratio (ultrapoor)	1973-74 to 1977-78	0.13	0.50
	1977-78 to 1983		
	1977-78 to 1983	0.51	2.20*
	1983 to 1986-87		
	1983 to 1986-87	0.62	2.90*
Inflation rate	1973-74 to 1977-78		
Percentage change in poverty gap ratio	1973-74 to 1977-78	0.17	0.60
	1977-78 to 1983		
	1977-78 to 1983	0.53	2.30*
	1983 to 1986-87		
	1983 to 1986-87	0.66	3.30*
Inflation	1973-74 to 1977-78		
Percentage change in poverty gap (ultrapoor)	1973-74 to 1977-78	0.30	1.20
	1977-78 to 1983		
	1977-78 to 1983	0.52	2.30

Table 18.15 Correlates of poverty (cont.)

Variable	Period	Correlation	t-value
	1983 to 1986-87		
	1983 to 1986-87	0.67	3.40*
Head count ratio (poor)	1973-74		
Per capita food production	1973-74	-0.51	-2.20
	1977-78		
	1977-78	-0.44	-1.80
	1983		
	1983	-0.55	-2.50*
	1986-87		
	1986-87	-0.25	-1.00
Head count ratio (ultrapoor)	1973-74		
Per capita food production	1973-74	-0.43	-1.80
	1977-78		
	1977-78	-0.32	-1.30
	1983		
	1983	-0.44	-1.80
	1986-87		
	1986-87	-0.30	-1.20
Poverty gap ratio (poor)	1973-74		
Per capita food production	1973-74	-0.47	-0.20*
	1977-78		
	1977-78	-0.29	-1.20
	1983		
	1983	-0.42	-1.70
	1986-87		
	1986-87	-0.30	-1.20
Poverty gap ratio (poor)	1973-74		
Per capita food production	1973-74	-0.47	-0.20*
	1977-78		
	1977-78	-0.29	-1.20
	1983		
	1983	-0.42	-1.70
	1986-87		
	1986-87	-0.30	-1.20
Percentage change in head count ratio (poor)	1973-74 to 1977-78		
Percentage change in per capita food production	1973-74 to 1977-78	-0.30	-0.10
	1977-78 to 1983		
	1977-78 to 1983	-0.19	-1.70
	1983 to 1986-87		
	1983 to 1986-87	-0.34	-1.30

Table 18.15 Correlates of poverty (cont.)

Variable	Period	Correlation	t-value
Percentage change in head count ratio (ultrapoor)	1973-74 to 1977-78		
Percentage change in per capita food production	1973-74 to 1977-78	-0.07	-0.30
	1977-78 to 1983		
	1977-78 to 1983	-0.19	-0.70
	1983 to 1986-87		
	1983 to 1986-87	-0.49	-1.90

* t-values with a significance level of 5 percent or more.
Source: Authors' calculations.

the literature), but more generally it is represented by the parameters of the Lorenz curve. If the poverty line z is fixed, we can write

$$(18.4) \qquad d\theta = \frac{\partial\theta}{\partial\mu} d\mu + \sum_{i=1}^{k} \frac{\partial\theta}{\partial m_i} dm_i,$$

where $m_1, m_2, ... m_k$ are the parameters of the Lorenz curve. This decomposes the change in poverty into (1) the effect of growth when the distribution of income does not change, and (2) the effect of income redistribution when the total income of the society remains unchanged.

If consumption per capita is growing, the first component in equation 18.4 will always be negative. If there is any trickle-down mechanism at work, the second component in equation 18.4 is nonpositive.[11] It may be nonpositive even if inequality has increased during the observation period. We now estimate each of the two components of equation 18.4 to assess the extent of the trickle-down effect in each state and in India as a whole.

The decomposition given in equation 18.4 is a linear approximation. Because the poverty measures are nonlinear, the total change in poverty will not be equal to the sum of the growth and inequality effects. We need to compute each of these components separately.

Let us consider two years, the base year and the terminal year. The poverty measure is θ, a function of the mean income and the Lorenz curve. The poverty index in the base year is therefore given by $\theta_{00} = \theta[\mu_0, L_0(p)]$, where μ_0 is the mean income in the base year and $L_0(p)$ the Lorenz curve in the base year, and p varies between 0 and 1.[12] Similarly, the poverty index in the terminal year is given by $\theta_{11} = \theta[\mu_1, L_1(p)]$, where μ_1 and $L_1(p)$ are the mean income and the Lorenz curve in the terminal year. Suppose the base and terminal years are separated by n years; the annual percentage change in total poverty, R_T, is then given by $\theta_{11} = \theta_{00}(1 + R_T)^n$.

The pure growth effect is defined as the annual percentage growth in poverty if the mean income changed but the relative income distribution measured by the Lorenz curve remained unchanged. Denoting the growth effect by R_g, we obtain

$\theta_{10} = \theta_{00}(1 + R_g)^n$, where $\theta_{10} = \theta[\mu_1, L_0(p)]$ is the poverty index that would have obtained with the Lorenz curve in the base year but with the mean income in the terminal year.

Similarly, the inequality effect is defined as the annual percentage change in poverty if the Lorenz curve changed but the mean income remained the same. Thus, the inequality effect denoted by R_I is given by $\theta_{01} = \theta_{00}(1 + R_I)^n$, where $\theta_{01} = \theta[(\mu_0, L_1(p)]$.

The growth effect R_g will be positive (negative) if the growth rate in per capita consumption is negative (positive). The inequality effect can be either negative or positive, however, even for a positive growth rate in per capita consumption. A positive (negative) value for the inequality effect implies that the income redistribution increases (decreases) total poverty.

The change in total poverty R_T will be a function of R_g and R_I. This is an exact mathematical relationship and therefore cannot establish causality between poverty, inequality, and growth. Nonetheless, the methodology enables us to draw interesting inferences. For example, the inequality effect tells us whether economic growth is accompanied by a redistribution of income, although this should not be interpreted as meaning that growth is causing the redistribution. Even if we do not know the cause, it is nonetheless important to know whether redistribution occurs that either favors or does not favor the poor.[13] If the relationship between the growth rate and the inequality effect is found to be significantly positive, we may conclude that growth tends to benefit the rich proportionally more than the poor, even if the causality is not known. In fact, there may not be a one-way causal relationship between growth and inequality; both may affect each other (simultaneous causality). Our concern is limited to assessing the effect on poverty in different states of whatever growth has occurred. Despite the limits of our analysis, stemming from our inability to capture this and other aspects of simultaneity—hence causality—it strongly complements earlier analyses (for example, Ahluwalia 1985) that focused on regressing poverty on agricultural output per capita.

Our numerical estimates of the growth and inequality effects on the head count ratio for the poor and the ultrapoor are presented in tables 18.16 and 18.17. Tables 18.18 and 18.19 show the estimates of these effects on the poverty gap ratio for the two groups.

At the all-India level, total poverty, as measured by the poverty gap ratio, declined at an annual rate of 3.5 percent between 1973-74 and 1977-78. If the inequality, as measured by the Lorenz curve, had not changed during this period, poverty would have declined at an annual rate of 6.4 percent. Thus, the change in the relative distribution between 1973-74 and 1977-78 led to an increase in poverty of 2.4 percent annually. For the ultrapoor, the annual rate of increase in poverty was 4.4 percent. Thus, a less-than-proportional share of the benefits of high growth rates during this period trickled down to the poor, and an even smaller proportional share to the ultrapoor.

At the state level we find that inequality increased in eleven of sixteen states between 1973-74 and 1977-78. This finding holds for all the poverty measures for both the poor and the ultrapoor. Thus, in most of the states, the income redistribution adversely affected the poor during this period.

Table 18.16 Annual percentage change in head count ratio for rural poor due to growth, inequality, and total effects, by state, India, selected years, 1973-74 to 1986-87

State	1973-74 to 1977-78			1977-78 to 1983			1983 to 1986-87		
	Growth	Inequality	Total	Growth	Inequality	Total	Growth	Inequality	Total
Andhra Pradesh	-6.9	0.1	-5.9	-6.6	0.2	-6.7	-6.1	3.3	-3.1
Assam	0.9	-0.4	0.8	-2.2	0.6	-1.3	-12.3	0.1	-10.0
Bihar	-1.6	-0.4	-2.1	0.3	0.1	0.3	-7.5	0.0	-7.2
Gujarat	-7.6	2.1	-3.5	-5.7	-1.6	-8.8	-1.8	5.9	4.8
Haryana	-3.5	-2.5	-7.0	4.0	-1.8	3.0	-22.1	3.8	-12.9
Jammu-Kashmir	-5.1	-0.7	-6.5	-10.2	0.8	-10.8	-11.5	10.5	2.6
Karnataka	-4.4	0.9	-3.3	-3.7	-1.1	-5.2	1.4	0.0	1.3
Kerala	-7.4	0.7	-5.0	-4.1	-0.4	-5.4	-5.3	0.9	-4.8
Madhya Pradesh	-2.9	1.4	-1.3	-3.1	-1.0	-4.7	-3.2	2.0	-1.0
Maharashtra	1.4	0.6	2.0	-6.3	0.0	-6.4	-1.6	0.9	-0.5
Orissa	-3.7	0.7	-2.5	-0.7	-0.4	-1.3	-8.2	0.3	-6.2
Punjab	-15.3	4.3	-13.0	11.0	-3.4	7.5	-17.9	1.8	-15.7
Rajasthan	-9.0	2.3	-5.3	-2.8	1.3	-1.3	0.0	-4.8	-4.8
Tamil Nadu	-3.6	1.6	-1.2	-1.3	-0.3	-1.5	-4.8	-1.7	-6.7
Uttar Pradesh	-8.7	2.2	-5.2	-0.2	-0.8	-0.9	-8.9	1.6	-7.2
West Bengal	-2.6	0.0	-2.4	-1.6	-0.3	-1.9	-6.2	-1.0	-8.5
All-India	-4.3	0.9	-2.9	-2.1	-0.4	-2.6	-6.0	0.6	-5.3

Source: Authors' calculations.

Table 18.17 Annual percentage change in head count ratio for rural ultrapoor due to growth, inequality, and total effects, by state, India, selected years, 1973-74 to 1986-87

State	1973-74 to 1977-78			1977-78 to 1983			1983 to 1986-87		
	Growth	Inequality	Total	Growth	Inequality	Total	Growth	Inequality	Total
Andhra Pradesh	-8.7	2.4	-6.0	-8.7	-0.8	-10.3	-7.0	3.8	-4.7
Assam	1.8	-1.8	0.1	-3.6	2.0	-1.8	-19.0	4.7	-11.3
Bihar	-2.4	-0.8	-3.4	0.4	0.1	0.5	-11.4	0.6	-11.1
Gujarat	-10.0	7.2	-0.9	-7.4	-5.3	-15.7	-2.2	20.2	18.6
Haryana	-6.1	-1.4	-9.8	7.7	-1.9	4.2	-29.0	11.2	-22.5
Jammu-Kashmir	-8.8	-2.3	-11.2	-16.4	-0.8	-16.4	-14.3	23.9	8.8
Karnataka	-8.7	2.2	-4.2	-5.5	-1.2	-6.1	1.7	-3.9	-1.6
Kerala	-11.0	2.7	-5.8	-6.4	-1.9	-9.5	-7.6	0.4	-6.5
Madhya Pradesh	-4.7	2.1	-2.2	-5.1	-2.2	-7.9	-4.5	1.9	-3.4
Maharashtra	2.3	2.4	4.6	-9.6	0.0	-10.0	-2.5	2.7	-0.6
Orissa	-5.7	1.2	-4.5	-1.2	-2.1	-3.6	-9.7	2.9	-9.7
Punjab	-34.1	4.1	-17.6	13.6	-4.6	9.0	-21.7	2.4	-23.2
Rajasthan	-10.6	5.2	-4.4	-3.6	2.1	-1.5	0.0	-8.4	-8.4
Tamil Nadu	-4.3	4.5	0.3	-1.9	-0.1	-2.0	-7.2	-1.9	-9.8
Uttar Pradesh	15.9	4.0	-7.7	-0.3	-0.7	-0.9	-12.2	3.0	-10.5
West Bengal	-4.1	-16.7	-3.9	-2.6	-0.7	-3.2	-8.5	-4.6	-14.5
All-India	-6.4	0.6	-3.5	-3.1	-0.8	-4.0	-8.4	1.0	-8.3

Source: Authors' calculations.

444

From 1977-78 to 1983 total poverty as measured by the poverty gap ratio declined 4.2 percent annually. This faster decline in poverty, which occurred despite a considerably lower rate of growth in per capita consumption (1.3 percent, compared with 3 percent in 1973-74 to 1977-78), can be attributed mainly to income redistribution during the period. The decline in inequality led to a reduction in poverty of 0.9 percent a year. At the state level, inequality increased in only three states. Thus, income redistribution favoring the poor was widespread during 1977-78 to 1983. If there had been no antipoverty interventions in 1973-74 to 1977-78, one could have concluded that the trickle-down effects of growth were stronger in 1977-78 to 1983 than in the earlier period. But, as there were antipoverty interventions in the first period, one could also conclude that inequality declined in the second period in part because the interventions were more successful in that period than in the first.

Although the growth rate in 1983 to 1986-87 was 2.9 percent, little different from that in 1977-78 to 1983, it led to a substantial reduction in poverty, 8.5 percent a year (table 18.18), dwarfing the effect of the increase in inequality, which led to an increase in of 0.5 percent poverty annually. Thus although the poor did not receive the full benefits of growth, poverty, as measured by the poverty gap ratio, declined 8.2 percent annually between 1983 and 1986-87. Distribution and the structure of production seem to have changed between 1977-78 and 1983 so that the poverty incidence became more responsive to the growth rate. For example, the distribution in per capita consumption was more equal in 1983, probably as a result of antipoverty programs. If that is the case, inequality-reducing policies pursued intensively in 1977-78 to 1983 may have enhanced the favorable effect of growth on poverty in the later period. Another explanation is that the pattern and regional distribution of growth from 1983 to 1987 was more labor-absorbing, and thus more poverty-reducing, than in the past. From 1983 to 1987 there was indeed substantial agricultural growth in states with a high concentration of poverty—Bihar, Uttar Pradesh, and West Bengal. The growth led to modest reductions in inequality in two of the states, and substantial reductions in poverty in all three. This suggests that regional relocation of production in favor of the poorer states is greatly desirable for poverty alleviation, even if it does not contribute to a reduction in inequality in India as a whole.

India's experience suggests that increasing inequality retards progress in poverty reduction, as it did in many states from 1973-74 to 1977-78. Poverty declined only because rapid growth more than compensated for the adverse effects on the poor of increasing inequality. The effect of inequality on poverty was especially significant and unfavorable in Gujarat, Madhya Pradesh, Punjab, Rajasthan, Tamil Nadu, Uttar Pradesh, and, to some extent, Karnataka and Orissa. From 1977-78 to 1983, however, growth and a reduction in inequality benefited the poor proportionally more than the nonpoor in all states except Andhra Pradesh, Assam, Jammu and Kashmir, and Rajasthan.

From 1983 to 1986-87 increases in inequality had significant and unfavorable effects on poverty in Andhra Pradesh, Gujarat, Haryana, and Jammu and Kashmir. The effects were less serious in Kerala and Punjab. And in Rajasthan, Tamil Nadu,

Table 18.18 Annual percentage change in poverty gap ratio for rural poor due to growth, inequality, and total effects, by state, India, selected years, 1973-74 to 1986-87

State	1973-74 to 1977-78			1977-78 to 1983			1983 to 1986-87		
	Growth	Inequality	Total	Growth	Inequality	Total	Growth	Inequality	Total
Andhra Pradesh	-8.8	1.7	-6.6	-8.2	-0.8	-9.6	-6.8	4.4	-2.1
Assam	1.6	-4.0	-2.1	-3.3	1.6	-1.7	-17.1	3.7	-11.5
Bihar	-2.6	-1.2	-4.0	0.5	-0.1	0.3	-11.6	-0.4	-12.4
Gujarat	-10.5	7.2	-1.1	-7.4	-5.1	-14.6	-2.0	17.9	16.2
Haryana	-6.4	-1.9	-7.5	5.1	-3.6	2.0	-26.3	8.5	-18.3
Jammu-Kashmir	-7.6	-2.1	-10.0	-13.5	0.0	-14.0	-13.6	18.3	6.1
Karnataka	-7.6	4.2	-2.3	-5.4	-1.7	-7.3	2.1	-1.9	0.3
Kerala	-10.6	3.2	-6.3	-6.0	-2.7	-10.1	-7.2	1.6	-5.3
Madhya Pradesh	-5.4	3.2	-1.8	-5.0	-2.5	-8	-4.6	1.4	-3.6
Maharashtra	2.7	2.3	4.7	-9.8	-0.4	-10.5	-2.4	2.5	0.3
Orissa	-7.1	1.9	-4.9	-1.4	-2.0	-3.5	-10.8	0.7	-10.2
Punjab	-20.1	7.6	-12.9	12.2	-6.9	6.9	-21.5	1.1	-21.5
Rajasthan	-11.4	6.5	-3.3	-3.6	1.6	-2.1	0	-8.8	-8.8
Tamil Nadu	-5.4	4.5	-0.1	-2.2	0.5	-1.5	-7.4	-2.5	-10.0
Uttar Pradesh	-14.9	5.9	-6.5	-0.3	-0.6	-0.9	-12.1	2.4	-9.9
West Bengal	-4.7	-0.4	-5.2	-2.7	-0.4	-3.2	-8.6	-5.1	-15.4
All-India	-6.4	2.4	-3.5	-3.1	-0.9	-4.2	-8.5	0.5	-8.2

Source: Authors' calculations.

446

Table 18.19 Annual percentage change in poverty gap ratio for rural ultrapoor due to growth, inequality, and total effects, by state, India, selected years, 1973-74 to 1986-87

State	1973-74 to 1977-78			1977-78 to 1983			1983 to 1986-87		
	Growth	Inequality	Total	Growth	Inequality	Total	Growth	Inequality	Total
Andhra Pradesh	-9.6	3.0	-7.1	-9.6	-2.0	-12.2	-6.8	6.9	0.0
Assam	2.0	-9.1	-6.9	-4.5	2.7	-1.7	-22.2	8.2	-13.2
Bihar	-3.2	-2.2	-5.7	0.5	-0.3	0.2	-15.1	-1.1	-18.4
Gujarat	-12.3	12.7	2.0	-9.3	-9.8	-20.5	-2.0	31.4	29.4
Haryana	-8.1	-1.5	-8.1	6.3	-5.8	1.4	-32.0	10.3	-22.6
Jammu-Kashmir	-10.3	-4.2	-14.7	-18.1	0.0	-16.5	-13.6	28.4	10.1
Karnataka	-10.4	8.4	0.0	-6.4	-2.4	-9.4	2.4	-2.6	0.0
Kerala	-12.8	11.6	-6.9	-7.6	-5.2	-14.3	-9.0	2.1	-4.7
Madhya Pradesh	-7.3	4.7	-1.9	-6.5	-3.8	-10.7	-5.5	0.5	-6.1
Maharashtra	3.5	4.0	7.4	-12.8	-0.8	-14.3	-3.0	3.3	0.0
Orissa	-9.9	2.7	-6.3	-1.8	-2.9	-4.8	-12.8	0.0	-14.4
Punjab	-38.0	8.2	-12.3	12.1	-14.0	3.2	-28.1	0.0	-21.9
Rajasthan	-14.4	11.0	-0.9	-4.2	1.7	-3.0	0.0	-12.1	-12.1
Tamil Nadu	-6.5	6.8	0.5	-2.9	1.2	-1.3	-9.1	-3.2	-12.8
Uttar Pradesh	-20.9	10.1	-6.6	-0.3	-0.3	-0.6	-15.6	2.9	-13.4
West Bengal	-6.0	-0.7	-7.1	-3.6	-0.4	-3.9	-10.5	-8.9	-20.3
All-India	-7.8	4.4	-3.7	-4.1	-1.5	-5.4	-10.7	-0.4	-11.3

Source: Authors' calculations.

and West Bengal, the reduction in inequality reduced poverty substantially. In many states high growth rates in per capita consumption led to a substantial reduction in poverty. In Rajasthan per capita consumption did not increase, but inequality declined significantly and induced a net reduction in poverty.

The decomposition of the effects of changes in growth and inequality was also done for ultrapoverty. The direction of the results and the differences among states remain broadly the same. But growth seems to benefit the ultrapoor proportionately more than the poor; conversely, a rise in inequality seems to hurt the ultrapoor more than the poor.

Finally, it is important to raise this question: Do the effects on poverty of changes in inequality and growth occur in a *consistent* manner across time periods, and for different measures of poverty? In an earlier section we observed that the association between the growth in per capita consumption and the percentage change in inequality was positive and significant in 1973-74 to 1977-78, but not in the later periods. In that section inequality was measured by the Gini and Theil indices. For analyzing the effect of inequality on poverty, however, changes in Gini and Theil that measure changes in the *entire* distribution are less helpful. We should be concerned more with changes in those segments of the relative consumption distribution (Lorenz curve) that directly affect the poor or the ultrapoor. This inequality effect is measured by the percentage change in poverty if the Lorenz curve were to change, but the mean per capita income were to remain unchanged. Table 18.20 presents correlations between growth in per capita consumption and the inequality effect as defined here, along with other correlations relevant to changes in poverty.

The correlations in table 18.20 suggest that the association between the growth rate and the inequality effect is positive and significant only in the first period (1973-74 to 1977-78), becoming insignificant during the later periods. Thus, the adverse effect of income redistribution on poverty is supported only in the first period but not in the two later periods. These conclusions are similar to the ones we observed in the earlier section in which the inequality was measured by the Gini and Theil indices.

The correlation between the growth rate and the total percentage change in poverty was negative and significant during all three periods (except for the poverty gap ratio for the poor and the ultrapoor during 1973-74 to 1977-78, when the correlation was not significant at the 5 percent level). *It implies that growth generally tended to reduce poverty.* Although these observations tend to support the trickle-down hypothesis, antipoverty interventions may have played a role in suppressing the adverse effects of the increasing income inequality that might have accompanied growth. The effect of growth without the antipoverty interventions could have been smaller than we observed from 1973-74 to 1977-78.

Responsiveness of poverty to growth and changes in inequality

Even if growth is trickling down, the effect on poverty may be small because of initially high levels of inequality. To see how growth in real per capita consump-

Table 18.20 Rank correlations between growth rates in per capita household expenditure and inequality and total poverty effects

	Growth rate and inequality effect		Growth rate and total poverty effect	
Period	*Correlation*	*t-value*	*Correlation*	*t-value*
Head count ratio (poor)				
1973-74 to 1977-78	0.68	3.50*	-0.56	-2.60*
1977-78 to 1983	0.38	1.50	-0.94	-10.70*
1983 to 1986-87	0.09	0.30	-0.83	-5.50*
Head count ratio (ultrapoor)				
1973-74 to 1977-78	0.52	2.30*	-0.56	-2.60*
1977-78 to 1983	0.01	0.00	-0.93	-9.10*
1983 to 1986-87	0.27	1.10	-0.81	-5.20*
Poverty gap ratio (poor)				
1973-74 to 1977-78	0.66	3.50*	-0.44	-1.80
1977-78 to 1983	0.13	0.50	-0.93	-9.50*
1983 to 1986-87	0.08	0.30	-0.83	-5.60*
Poverty gap ratio (ultrapoor)				
1973-74 to 1977-78	0.66	3.50*	-0.18	-0.70
1977-78 to 1983	0.05	0.20	-0.93	-9.20*
1983 to 1986-87	0.08	0.30	-0.82	-5.40*

* Coefficient statistically significant.
Source: Authors' calculations.

tion affects poverty, we computed the poverty elasticities with respect to mean per capita consumption. These *growth elasticities of poverty* have been derived by Kakwani (1990c) for all existing poverty indices. The growth elasticities used in this chapter are

Head count ratio	$z f(z)/H$
Poverty gap ratio	$\mu^*/(z - \mu)^*$
Watts measure	$H/W,$

where W represents the Watts measure, H is the head count ratio, and μ^* is the mean per capita consumption of the poor.

Computing the poverty elasticity with respect to inequality is more difficult because, with per capita consumption held constant, inequality in the distribution can change an infinite number of ways. To compute this elasticity we need to make an assumption about how inequality is changing—for instance, whether inequality is increasing because of a decline in the share of the poor or because of an increase in the share of the rich. Although an increase in the share of the rich has little effect on poverty, a decrease in the share of the poor will substantially increase it. In this section we simply assume that the entire Lorenz curve shifts according to the following formula:

(18.5) $$L^*(p) = L(p) - \lambda[p - L(p)],$$

which implies that when $\lambda > 0$, the Lorenz curve shifts downward, resulting in higher inequality. It can be shown that λ is equal to the proportional change in the Gini index. If $\lambda = 0.01$, the Gini index is increased by 1 percent. Thus, one can derive the elasticity of a poverty measure with respect to the Gini index using this procedure.[14] The elasticities for the three poverty measures used here are

Head count ratio	$[(\mu - z)/H]f(z)$
Poverty gap ratio	$(\mu - \mu^*)/(z - \mu)^*$
Watts measure	$(H/W)[(\mu - h)/h)]$,

where h is the harmonic mean of the income distribution of the poor only.

The inequality elasticities of the poverty gap ratio and the Watts measure will always be positive, meaning that higher income inequality leads to greater poverty. The head count measure does not always produce this result. If and only if $\mu < z$ can the head count measure decrease with an increase in inequality. This result casts doubt on the measure's usefulness for analyzing the impact of inequality on poverty.

Because mean consumption and inequality each affect poverty, an important question arises: What is the tradeoff between them? Put differently, if the Gini index of real private consumption increases by 1 percent, what would the percentage increase in mean real per capita consumption have to be in order for poverty not to increase? This can be answered using the concept of the marginal proportional rate of substitution (MPRS) between mean consumption and inequality (see Kakwani 1990c). It is given by

$$MPRS = \frac{\partial\mu}{\partial G} \frac{G}{\mu} = -\frac{\text{inequality elasticity of poverty}}{\text{growth elasticity of poverty}},$$

which can be computed for each poverty measure.

Growth and inequality elasticities may be related to growth and inequality effects, but they are different concepts. Elasticities measure the responsiveness of poverty to growth and income redistribution; effects measure the *actual change*. Elasticities are computed on the basis of expenditure or income distribution for one year only; growth and inequality effects are computed on the basis of expenditure distributions in two periods. These concepts convey quite different information about the characteristics of poverty.[15] The elasticities are useful for simulating the effects of alternative policies. These elasticities are also of some help in explaining the actual changes in poverty.

The growth and inequality elasticities for the poverty gap ratio for the poor and the ultrapoor are given in tables 18.21 and 18.22. Both growth and inequality elasticities have a general tendency to increase over time, though more slowly in the poorer states. In the two poorest states, Bihar and West Bengal, the elasticities changed little between 1973-74 and 1983, suggesting fairly stable distribution. But in 1986-87 the elasticities increased substantially even in these two states. Thus, poverty has become more sensitive to growth and changes in inequality in recent years.

The inequality elasticity has increased slightly faster than the growth elasticity in most states. This pattern is quite evident from the increasing values of the marginal proportional rate of substitution in table 18.23. This suggests that inequality-reducing policies have an important role in helping the poor maintain their share of consumption during growth. It also suggests that greater, not less, emphasis on growth is required to maintain, if not to improve, the consumption shares of the poor. And because the values of the MPRS are generally higher for the richer states, policies for reducing consumption inequality are imperative even in the high-growth states.

Both growth and inequality elasticities are considerably higher for the ultrapoor than for the poor. This suggests that increasing inequality will hurt the ultrapoor more than the poor, and that growth benefits the ultrapoor proportionately more than the poor. Thus, for the ultrapoor, it is even more imperative to combine high growth with policies aimed at reducing inequality in real per capita consumption. India's basic antipoverty policy response, centered on the provision of public employment and programs to increase the assets (resources) of the ultrapoor and the poor, appears sound. But the effectiveness of the programs needs to be evaluated.

Table 18.21 Growth and inequality elasticities of poverty gap ratio for rural poor, by state, India, selected years, 1973-74 to 1986-87

State	Growth elasticity				Inequality elasticity			
	1973-74	1977-78	1983	1986-87	1973-74	1977-78	1983	1986-87
Andhra Pradesh	-2.8	-2.9	-3.7	-3.5	1.9	2.5	3.8	4.2
Assam	-3.2	-3.7	-3.8	-4.1	1.1	1.1	1.3	2.2
Bihar	-2.0	-2.2	-2.2	-3.0	0.8	1.0	0.9	1.6
Gujarat	-3.2	-2.8	-4.5	-2.8	1.6	2.2	3.7	3.0
Haryana	-3.4	-3.5	-3.7	-4.9	3.0	3.6	3.1	6.1
Jammu-Kashmir	-3.3	-4.0	-5.1	-4.5	1.5	2.1	3.8	4.2
Karnataka	-2.5	-2.4	-2.8	-2.9	1.4	1.9	2.6	2.6
Kerala	-2.0	-2.2	-3.2	-3.3	1.2	1.9	3.1	3.7
Madhya Pradesh	-2.1	-2.1	-2.8	-3.1	0.9	1.3	1.9	2.4
Maharashtra	-2.5	-2.1	-3.0	-2.9	1.2	1.1	2.1	2.2
Orissa	-1.5	-1.8	-2.1	-2.7	0.4	0.7	0.9	1.4
Punjab	-3.6	-3.6	-3.7	-5.0	3.4	5.3	4.0	7.0
Rajasthan	-2.9	-2.6	-2.8	-3.4	2.1	2.7	3.2	3.6
Tamil Nadu	-2.4	-2.2	-2.2	-2.7	1.1	1.5	1.7	2.2
Uttar Pradesh	-2.6	-2.8	-2.8	-3.2	1.1	2.0	2.0	3.0
West Bengal	-1.6	-1.9	-2.1	-3.1	0.6	0.9	1.1	1.7
All-India	-2.3	-2.3	-2.7	-3.1	..	..	..	..

.. Computations not done for all-India level.
Source: Authors' calculations.

Table 18.22 Growth and inequality elasticities of poverty gap ratio for rural ultrapoor, by state, India, selected years, 1973-74 to 1986-87

State	Growth elasticity				Inequality elasticity			
	1973-74	1977-78	1983	1986-87	1973-74	1977-78	1983	1986-87
Andhra Pradesh	-3.3	-3.5	-4.0	-3.3	3.2	4.2	6.1	5.8
Assam	-3.6	-5.2	-5.2	-5.6	2.4	2.6	3.0	4.6
Bihar	-2.6	-2.9	-3.0	-4.4	1.5	1.9	1.9	3.4
Gujarat	-4.0	-3.5	-5.2	-3.6	3.3	3.8	6.4	5.1
Haryana	-4.1	-3.8	-4.5	-4.5	5.3	5.6	5.5	8.5
Jammu-Kashmir	-4.7	-5.7	-5.7	-5.4	3.2	4.4	6.4	7.4
Karnataka	-3.6	-2.9	-3.7	-3.4	2.9	3.2	4.7	4.3
Kerala	-2.5	-2.7	-4.0	-3.7	2.2	3.3	5.5	5.8
Madhya Pradesh	-2.8	-2.8	-3.5	-4.0	2.0	2.4	3.5	4.2
Maharashtra	-3.2	-2.8	-4.0	-3.9	2.4	2.0	4.0	4.2
Orissa	-2.1	-2.3	-2.5	-3.3	0.8	1.4	1.7	2.7
Punjab	-4.3	-3.1	-4.6	-4.3	5.8	7.0	6.7	8.8
Rajasthan	-3.6	-3.0	-3.4	-4.1	3.8	4.5	5.4	6.0
Tamil Nadu	-3.0	-3.0	-2.8	-3.3	2.2	2.6	2.9	3.9
Uttar Pradesh	-3.9	-3.7	-3.6	-4.2	2.4	3.7	3.7	5.3
West Bengal	-2.1	-2.5	-2.7	-3.7	1.1	1.7	2.0	3.1
All-India	-2.9	-3.0	-3.3	-3.8	..	..	..	..

.. Calculations not done for all-India level.
Source: Authors' calculations.

Poverty alleviation policies

The Indian government's strategy for reducing the incidence of poverty is based on a combination of accelerated growth and targeted, direct antipoverty interventions. In the long run, the outlook for poverty reduction depends on the supply of and the demand for labor, and social policies that help improve the basic capabilities of people, especially education and health policies. In this section we assess the policy environment for labor absorption, and programs that have been undertaken to increase the assets of the rural poor and provide employment.

Policies for labor absorption

The number of entrants into India's labor force is unlikely to decrease over the next three decades. This raises two critical issues. To what extent can future growth in agriculture and other sectors absorb the growing labor force? And to what extent can direct interventions help in expanding self-employment and wage employment, especially among the ultrapoor?

Agricultural growth and poverty. In 1983, 65.1 percent of the nation's rural poor and 69.8 percent of its ultrapoor lived in states with agricultural growth at a low or moderate rate and medium or high instability (table 18.24). The states

Table 18.23 Marginal rate of substitution between growth and inequality elasticities obtained from poverty gap ratio

	Growth elasticity				Inequality elasticity			
State	1973-74	1977-78	1983	1986-87	1973-74	1977-78	1983	1986-87
Andhra Pradesh	0.7	0.9	1.0	1.2	1.0	1.2	1.5	1.8
Assam	0.3	0.3	0.3	0.5	0.7	0.5	0.6	0.8
Bihar	0.4	0.5	0.4	0.5	0.6	0.7	0.6	0.8
Gujarat	0.5	0.8	0.8	1.1	0.8	1.1	1.2	1.4
Haryana	0.9	1.0	0.8	1.2	1.3	1.5	1.2	1.9
Jammu-Kashmir	0.5	0.5	0.7	0.9	0.7	0.8	1.1	1.4
Karnataka	0.6	0.8	0.9	0.9	0.8	1.1	1.3	1.3
Kerala	0.6	0.9	1.0	1.1	0.9	1.2	1.4	1.6
Madhya Pradesh	0.4	0.6	0.7	0.8	0.7	0.9	1.0	1.1
Maharashtra	0.5	0.5	0.7	0.8	0.8	0.7	1.0	1.1
Orissa	0.3	0.4	0.4	0.5	0.4	0.6	0.7	0.8
Punjab	0.9	1.5	1.1	1.4	1.3	2.3	1.5	2.0
Rajasthan	0.7	1.0	1.1	1.1	1.1	1.5	1.6	1.5
Tamil Nadu	0.5	0.7	0.8	0.8	0.7	0.9	1.0	1.2
Uttar Pradesh	0.4	0.7	0.7	0.9	0.6	1.0	1.0	1.3
West Bengal	0.4	0.5	0.5	0.5	0.5	0.7	0.7	0.8

Source: Authors' calculations.

experiencing high growth and those with medium growth and low instability account for only 28 percent of the poor and 25 percent of the ultrapoor.

Although no systematic relationship has been established between agricultural growth and poverty reduction, such growth is nevertheless important in reducing poverty. This is because, unlike in manufacturing, the labor-output ratios in Indian agriculture remained favorable, especially in the relatively low-wage, labor-abundant regions of eastern India. Therefore, improved agricultural performance will remain crucial for poverty alleviation for many years in India. What then are the prospects, with stabilizing yields, of growth with stability in the lagging regions? Would accelerated growth in these regions lead to adequate labor absorption?

Recent evidence suggests that the aggregate employment elasticity of agriculture has fallen since the 1970s (Bhalla 1987), but this is a composite estimate over diverse regions and crops. Employment elasticities with respect to output continue to be higher in the low-wage eastern states—for all crops—than in the rest of India. The diffusion of agricultural technology to the low-wage regions is bound to result in greater labor absorption. This is already happening in eastern Uttar Pradesh, where the emergence of HYV rice as a major second crop may have contributed to the substantial reduction in poverty in this state between 1983 and 1986-87.

To accelerate agricultural growth in the eastern region will require strengthening the small-farm sector through a significant reorientation not only of institutional policies but of science and technology policies. Technology and infra-

Table 18.24 Distribution of poor according to growth and instability in food grain production, India, 1983

Category	States	Percentage distribution of newly sown area by level of rainfall			Percentage share of rural population 1983[a]	Percentage share of poor population 1983[a]	Percentage share of ultrapoor population 1983[a]	Agricultural workers per 100 hectares of net sown area, 1980-83
		High (1,150 mm and above)	Medium (750 to 1,150 mm)	Low (up to 750 mm)				
High growth and low instability	Punjab, Jammu and Kashmir	5.3	20.5	74.2	3.3	1.2	0.8	85
High growth and medium instability	Haryana, Uttar Pradesh	8.4	64.1	27.5	19.7	19.1	18.7	148
High growth and high instability	Gujarat	7.3	25.0	67.7	4.6	2.8	1.8	83
Medium growth and low instability	Andhra Pradesh	1.0	66.0	33.0	7.9	4.9	3.7	145
Medium growth and medium instability	Karnataka	9.4	24.3	66.3	5.1	4.1	4.2	95
Medium growth and high instability	Maharashtra, Orissa, Rajasthan	25.0	24.1	50.9	17.7	17.4	17.3	87
Low growth and low instability	Assam, Kerala	100.0	0.0	0.0	7.5	6.7	5.3	173
Low growth and medium instability	Tamil Nadu, West Bengal	54.2	45.8	0.0	14.0	18.0	20.3	188
Low growth and high instability	Bihar, Madhya Pradesh	63.5	33.5	3.0	20.2	25.6	28.0	130
All-India		30.7	35.8	33.5	100.0	100.0	100.0	120

Note: Growth refers to the average rate of growth in food grain production for 1961-85: high—above 3.0 percent; medium—2.0 to 3.0 percent; and low—2.0 percent. *Instability* refers to the standard deviation in the annual output rates of food grains for 1961-85: high—above 20 percent; medium—15 to 20 percent; and low—below 15 percent.
a. Data may not add up to 100 due to rounding.
Source: Rao, Ray, and Subbarao 1988, except population shares, which were computed by the authors.

structure policies should focus on promoting higher cropping intensities, and institutional policies should be geared toward enhancing small farmers' resource base, especially through the consolidation of holdings, and credit and marketing reforms (Rao, Ray, and Subbarao 1988). These policy changes should be combined with the spread of rural nonfarm activities—dairying, poultry, fisheries, forestry and agroprocessing. Progress on all these fronts has been far from satisfactory.

Nonagricultural growth and poverty. In the long run, agriculture's share in employment is bound to fall, so growth in manufacturing and service sector employment will be crucial in the coming decades. Past growth in such employment has been disappointing. Capital intensity in manufacturing was maintained by a policy environment that favored existing workers and thus kept many potential new entrants out of jobs. Industrial labor demand elasticity with respect to the wage rate was about –0.75 from 1973-74 to 1984-85, implying a significant tradeoff between real wages and employment (Hanson and Sengupta 1989). The rising real wage of organized labor in both the public and the private sector in the 1980s also contributed to the slow growth of employment in manufacturing. The prospects for nonfarm employment depend on fiscal and other measures to stimulate labor-intensive light industry, including export industry, and public policy to stimulate the service sector (including the rural informal sector). There has been no policy framework that specifically encourages growth in labor-intensive manufacturing and the service and informal sectors.

Direct antipoverty interventions. Since the mid-1970s the central and state governments have launched numerous direct antipoverty interventions. The scale and variety of these interventions are so large that it is impossible to review them all here.[16] The antipoverty programs initiated from 1977-78 to 1983 merit an assessment, however. During this period, despite slower growth in average consumption per capita, the poverty ratio fell largely due to a decline in inequality in most states. An assessment of the overall impact of the programs must begin with a recognition of the fact that India is experimenting in many directions to reduce poverty-induced human suffering.

The Integrated Rural Development Program (IRDP) has been in operation long enough to be realistically evaluated. It has channeled an unprecedented amount of funding, in the form of loans and subsidies, to the poor to enable them to obtain nonland assets. During the Sixth Plan period assets worth some Rs 50 billion were created and distributed to about 17 million families. During 1987-88, the fourth year of the Seventh Plan, another 4.2 million families were assisted through an investment of Rs 4,471 per family, or Rs 19 billion in total (table 18.25). By 1988, the IRDP had reached about 25 percent of India's rural households.

States' shares of the poor and ultrapoor populations (table 18.26) are compared with their shares of IRDP and National Rural Employment Program expenditures in tables 18.27 and 18.28. This comparison shows that, based on their shares of either the poor or the ultrapoor in 1986-87, the eastern states of Assam, Bihar, Karnataka, Kerala, and West Bengal deserved higher allocations.

Most assessments of the IRDP by the government have been favorable, but microeconomic studies have been more equivocal. The divergence between macroeconomic indicators and microeconomic performance seems to have narrowed in recent years, however.

Moreover, an assessment of success or failure depends on the criterion used. Thus, Subbarao (1985) argued that the usual criterion of "crossing the poverty line" is inappropriate for judging the full benefits of the IRDP, because households far below the poverty line (the ultrapoor) may register incremental income gains, and thus benefit from the program, even if they are unable to cross the poverty line.[17] Pulley (1989) has shown that the program's success rate varied depending on the criterion adopted (table 18.27). By the criterion of "investments remaining intact" (which suggests that households are deriving incremental incomes from the asset), the program is doing reasonably well even in such relatively low-income states as Bihar. But by the usual criterion of "crossing the poverty line," the success rate was very low.

The performance of states suggests an interesting relationship—that between the percentage of eligible beneficiaries and the proportion crossing the poverty line. Except in Himachal Pradesh and Jammu and Kashmir, the higher the proportion of eligible beneficiaries (the lower the percentage of nonpoor) with low initial incomes, the more difficult it is for beneficiaries to cross the poverty line. The program has included very poor people for whom a big increase in income is inadequate to bring them above the poverty line. It is hard for them to overcome poverty and the proportion doing so is small.

Table 18.25 Major poverty alleviation programs, India, 1987-88

Program	Expenditures (millions of rupees)
Credit-based self-employment programs	
Integrated Rural Development Program (IRDP)	
(Investment per beneficiary = Rs 4,471)	19,000
Wage employment programs	
National Rural Employment Program (NREP)	7,850
Rural Landless Employment Guarantee Program (RLEGP)	6,480
Maharashtra's Employment Guarantee Scheme (MEGS)	2,650
Area development programs	
Drought Prone Area Program	900
Desert Development	500
Watershed Development	2,400
All programs	39,780
Percentage of GDP	1
Percentage of plan outlay	9

Program/indicator	Achievements (millions)
Credit-based self-employment programs	
IRDP: Beneficiaries covered	4.2
Wage employment programs	
NREP: Man-days of employment generated	370
RLEGP: Man-days of employment generated	100
MEGS: Man-days of employment generated	150

Source: India, Ministry of Program Evaluation 1988 and 1989.

A major criticism of the IRDP is that the program benefits the households closer to the poverty line but neglects the ultrapoor. It has been suggested that the poorest households may be unable to hold and manage assets, but recent evidence effectively refutes this. In fact, in an administratively weak and relatively poor state such as Uttar Pradesh, panel data for four years show that the poorest households not only managed to hold on to assets, but derived income from them on a sustained basis (Rao and others 1988; and Pulley 1989). Their problem was the continued reluctance of the institutional credit agencies to lend them working capital on a regular basis *even after the households had promptly repaid their IRDP loans*. In other words, the IRDP provided access to institutional credit for the poorest households in a one-shot injection, but failed to open a continuing line of credit for the neediest households despite their proven creditworthiness.

The scale of investments in the IRDP, in combination with the NREP, may give impetus to developing infrastructure and to raising the incomes of the poor at the margin, if the choice of assets matches the level and structure of demand in the region, the assets supplied are labor-intensive, and supporting marketing networks are simultaneously promoted. Decentralizing program administration and involving the beneficiaries in the choice of programs may help realize these preconditions of success. Wherever these conditions were satisfied and the program reached the poorest half of the poor population, its impact on the hard-core poor was substantial (Rao and others 1988). To achieve *sustained* income gen-

Table 18.26 Distribution of poor and ultrapoor by state, rural India, selected years, 1973-74 to 1986-87

(percent)

State	Share of poor				Share of ultrapoor			
	1973-74	*1977-78*	*1983*	*1986-87*	*1973-74*	*1977-78*	*1983*	*1986-87*
Andhra Pradesh	6.6	5.8	4.5	4.8	5.5	4.9	3.4	3.8
Assam	3.0	3.7	4.2	3.6	2.2	2.7	3.2	2.9
Bihar	13.7	14.2	16.8	15.8	14.6	14.8	19.2	17.4
Gujarat	3.6	3.5	2.5	3.5	2.8	3.1	1.5	3.8
Haryana	1.2	1.0	1.4	1.0	0.9	0.7	1.1	0.6
Jammu-Kashmir	0.8	0.7	0.4	0.6	0.6	0.5	0.2	0.4
Karnataka	4.7	4.6	4.0	5.0	4.7	4.5	4.0	5.1
Kerala	4.3	3.9	3.2	3.3	4.5	4.0	2.8	3.0
Madhya Pradesh	8.9	9.5	8.4	9.8	9.7	10.2	8.1	9.7
Maharashtra	7.9	9.5	7.6	9.0	7.5	10.3	7.2	9.5
Orissa	6.3	6.3	6.6	6.3	7.7	7.3	7.3	6.8
Punjab	1.1	0.7	1.2	0.8	0.9	0.5	0.9	0.5
Rajasthan	3.7	3.5	3.9	4.0	3.2	3.1	3.7	3.8
Tamil Nadu	6.7	7.1	7.2	6.7	6.5	7.5	8.0	7.4
Uttar Pradesh	17.4	15.9	17.5	16.3	17.1	14.4	17.3	15.8
West Bengal	10.0	10.2	10.6	9.4	11.6	11.4	12.0	9.4
All-India	100.0	100.0	100.0	100.0	100.0	100.0	100.0	100.0

Note: Data may not add up to 100 due to rounding.
Source: Authors' calculations.

eration, however, it is necessary to ensure that the very poor have continued access to institutional credit.

The overall assessment of the two employment programs, the NREP and the Rural Landless Employment Guarantee Program (RLEGP), is similar to that for the IRDP. Together, the two programs provided, on average, about 450 million man-days of employment a year. But evaluations pointed out that the impact of the programs on the total income of poor households was insignificant because they met only about 9 percent of the demand for work from the poor in rural India; the programs could not create sufficiently useful, wage-intensive works at the times and in the places that they were most needed; the poor could not benefit from the assets created; the assets created were of poor quality; and wages were lower than budgeted because of leakage and corruption. Some of these criticisms are unmerited. For example, the effects of the NREP are not small when judged by the *incremental* employment it generated in the rural areas. One recent estimate (Subbarao 1987) suggests that the NREP

Table 18.27 Distribution of IRDP funds and measures of success by state, India, 1987-88
(percent)

State	Share of IRDP expenditure[a]	Eligible bene-ficiaries[b]	Investments intact[c]	Investments intact with no credit overdue	Eligible bene-ficiaries crossing poverty line[d]
Andhra Pradesh	7.8	68	76	34	9
Assam	2.8	27	70	6	10
Bihar	14.4	76	85	18	3
Gujarat	3.5	78	88	43	4
Haryana	1.4	71	46	15	0
Jammu-Kashmir	1.0	97	80	50	19
Karnataka	3.9	85	64	26	4
Kerala	2.8	89	74	19	5
Madhya Pradesh	11.2	81	73	27	6
Maharashtra	7.1	83	69	30	10
Orissa	5.6	83	68	19	7
Punjab	1.4	30	77	57	18
Rajasthan	4.6	72	48	15	9
Tamil Nadu	6.8	83	63	28	3
Uttar Pradesh	18.6	54	79	41	5
West Bengal	7.1	46	97	23	8
All-India	100.0	70	73	29	7

a. Includes central and state expenditures, but excludes credit mobilized.
b. Beneficiaries with pre-IRDP household income less than or equal to Rs 4,800.
c. IRDP investments that remained fully operational after two years.
d. Beneficiaries with pre-IRDP household income less than or equal to Rs 4,800 and post-IRDP income more than or equal to Rs 6,400 after two years in current price terms.
Source: National Concurrent Evaluation of IRDP, Round 2, 1987, Ministry of Rural Development, as quoted in Pulley 1989; and India, Ministry of Rural Development 1988.

provided nearly 40 percent of the total incremental employment in rural India between 1985 and 1987.

Maharashtra's Employment Guarantee Scheme (MEGS), a state-level program, has a much better record, notably in generating supplementary employment for women and in creating a much better-administered wage structure that reduced gender differences in wage rates. Nonetheless, recent moves to pay statutorily fixed minimum wages may destroy some of the merits of this scheme (Subbarao 1987), such as its self-targeting character.

Only two states—Andhra Pradesh and Tamil Nadu—have been successful in attracting women in large numbers to NREP work sites (table 18.28). Uttar Pradesh, which has one of the largest shares of the ultrapoor population, has a dismal record in employing women in NREP projects.

The rank correlation between the distribution of man-days of employment generated and the distribution of the ultrapoor among states was high at $r = 0.74$, with a t-ratio of 3.96 (significant at the 1 percent level). Bihar and West Bengal, however, had shares of NREP employment that were substantially lower than their shares of the ultrapoor.

Most evaluations of India's public employment programs have expressed concern about states having opted for the construction of rural roads and primary schools, for example, rather than such directly productive activities as soil conservation and watershed development. Yet rural infrastructure (markets and roads)

Table 18.28 Distribution of NREP employment by state, India, 1987-88

State	Employment (millions of man-days)	Women as share of those employed (percent)	Share of employment (percent)	Share of ultra-poor population (percent)
Andhra Pradesh	28.8	41.8	9.0	3.9
Assam	3.4	0.0	0.7	2.1
Bihar	46.8	10.0	12.8	20.0
Gujarat	17.2	28.6	3.5	1.7
Haryana	2.2	0.0	0.7	0.6
Jammu-Kashmir	—	—	—	—
Karnataka	1.9	13.4	5.8	4.6
Kerala	9.9	26.7	4.0	3.0
Madhya Pradesh	50.7	27.1	8.4	8.5
Maharashtra	26.2	26.2	6.9	7.5
Orissa	22.5	25.7	4.9	5.4
Punjab	1.9	0.0	0.8	0.5
Rajasthan	24.0	24.2	6.0	3.2
Tamil Nadu	32.2	44.1	11.8	8.2
Uttar Pradesh	55.3	3.1	21.6	18.3
West Bengal	15.5	3.0	3.1	12.7
All-India	379.6	20.65	100.0	100.0

— Not available.
Source: India, Ministry of Rural Development 1988.

has a significant positive effect on agricultural output (Binswanger, Khandker, and Rosenzweig 1989) and, if appropriate, *is* productive. The most immediate concern ought to be ensuring the quality of works and the maintenance of the infrastructure created.

Employment programs, despite their deficiencies, have desirable features. Because they involve some self-targeting (because of the relative unattractiveness of the employment), they can, in a sense, substitute for a social security system, at least for those able to work. If their deficiencies are tackled (especially in states in which NREP employment lags far behind ultrapoverty), and if women are attracted to work sites, as they are in the MEGS, these programs can reach the poorest fifth of the population more effectively than most alternatives.

Conclusions

The basic conclusion of this study is this: Trickle-down effects can happen but are seldom automatic. The beneficial effects of growth on the incidence of poverty can, but need not, be substantially offset or even nullified by increases in the inequality of consumption. During 1973-77 they were; this is true whether analyzed at the state level or the all-India level. Therefore, India's policy response— a series of antipoverty interventions since the mid-1970s aimed at raising the income and consumption levels of the poor and the ultrapoor—was basically sound.

In 1977-83 average consumption grew slowly, but consumption inequality fell in many states, and the reduction in the incidence of poverty and in the poverty gap was greater than in the earlier period of high growth. The beneficial impact of the reduction in inequality proved more pronounced for the ultrapoor than for the poor; by the same token, a worsening of inequality hurts the ultrapoor proportionately more than the poor. The reduction in inequality and poverty is not just a "dance of the monsoons" because it could not be explained systematically by changes in states' food grain production in this period. Although it is difficult to identify precisely the factors that may have contributed to the decline in inequality in many states during 1977-83, the role of direct interventions cannot be minimized.

From 1983 to 1986-87 growth was high, with almost no change in inequality at the national level. This led to a substantial reduction in poverty, dominated by the growth effect.

During the entire period between 1973-74 and 1986-87, aggregate rural poverty declined substantially; the incidence of poverty declined from 60.6 percent to 41.5 percent, and the severity (the gap between an average poor person's income and the poverty line) from 18.8 percent to 10.5 percent. Even the absolute number of poor declined by about 37 million. These figures demonstrate commendable achievements in poverty reduction, particularly in the 1980s. Both growth and direct poverty alleviation efforts have contributed to this success.

It is noteworthy that the poverty gap ratio has become more responsive (elastic) to growth and to changing inequality in consumption, except in Bihar and West Bengal. Both elasticities are higher for the richer states, and for the ultrapoor.

This suggests that inequality-reducing policies are necessary in the states that are better-off, as well as in the poor states, to compound the beneficial effect of growth on the poor, especially the ultrapoor. Increasingly, and especially for the poorest, growth and antipoverty programs—trickle-down and pull-up—are not substitutes but complements.

These results lend credibility to the consumption-equalizing interventions initiated since the mid-1970s. Yet there is significant variation among states in the effectiveness of the interventions, with effectiveness clearly weaker in poorer states; this needs to be addressed. Our review of microeconomic evidence suggests that there were substantial benefits even in such poor states as Uttar Pradesh, however, consistent with our earlier finding of substantial reduction of consumption inequality.

Employment programs contributed substantially to incremental rural employment and income growth. Their distribution by state largely corresponded with the distribution of the ultrapoor. Two poorer states, Bihar and West Bengal, require greater efforts under the NREP, however.

Notes

The views expressed here are the views of the authors. We are most grateful to Pranab Bardhan, Wil Bussink, Jacques van der Gaag, Michael Lipton, Martin Ravallion, Amartya Sen, and Inderjit Singh for helping us with encouraging comments and very useful suggestions on earlier drafts of this chapter. We are indebted to Maria Felix for cheerfully providing excellent secretarial assistance at all stages of this work.

Preliminary results of this study were reported in a paper entitled "Poverty and its Alleviation in India" in *Economic and Political Weekly* (vol. 26, pp. 1482-86, 1991). This version is extended to cover 1986-87 and has undergone substantial revisions to take into account new evidence.

1. For a detailed discussion of this issue see Kakwani (1986).

2. It would be more appropriate to use permanent income as a proxy for welfare or capability to escape poverty. Because there is no reliable measure of permanent income, we have used household consumption expenditure, which is regarded as a more suitable measure of the household's economic welfare than the current income.

3. It is not clear from the NSS whether the food given to poorer households (often permanent laborers) by richer households (large rural landowners and employers) is included in the consumption of the richer households. If so, the estimates of poverty and inequality will be overestimated. The fitting of the Pareto curve for the first and last expenditure ranges does not remedy this situation. The curve is used only as an interpolation device because information on individual households is not available.

4. A better measure of household welfare would of course be consumption per adult equivalent, which corrects for the differences in the needs of adults and children. But this measure could not be employed because the NSS data were available only in grouped form (the groups formed on the basis of per capita household expenditure). We could have remedied this only by assuming that the ranking of households by per capita consumption is the same as that by consumption per adult equivalent. This assumption, which is unlikely to hold, would result in more serious estimation errors.

5. We performed calculations for both 1972-73 and 1973-74, but this chapter presents the results only for 1973-74 because this was a normal agricultural year.

6. See for instance Kakwani (1980a); Clark, Hemming, and Ulph (1981); Foster, Greer, and Thorbecke (1984); and Takayama (1979).

7. It is worth repeating that this procedure, unlike the procedures adopted earlier by many researchers, appropriately takes into account the regional and seasonal price variations while deriving poverty at the all-India level.

8. It needs to be stressed that these are *rural* growth and inequality trends. These changes trigger changes in urban growth and inequality—an aspect not examined in this chapter.

9. Whether these rural trends reflect *state average* real per capita consumption depends on the trend in rural-urban inequality by state—an aspect not examined in this chapter.

10. In Maharashtra and Rajasthan in 1977-78 there was an implausibly large increase in expenditures on durables for the highest expenditure class; consultations with the NSS office confirmed that these were errors. We therefore adjusted the numbers to conform broadly to the temporal changes in the same states in the years immediately preceding and following 1977-78. The inequality estimates shown in tables 18.6 and 18.7 reflect these adjustments. Because they were required only in the top expenditure range, they would have little effect on the poverty estimates.

11. Generally, economists consider that trickle-down effects have occurred when there is a reduction in poverty, no matter how small, for any positive growth in per capita income or consumption. According to this definition, the inequality component can be positive as long as its adverse effect on poverty is smaller than the pure growth effect. A nonpositive value for the inequality effect implies that the poor are receiving benefits at least equal to the growth rate. Thus, our definition of trickle-down effects is somewhat more demanding.

12. The notations used here are from Datt and Ravallion (1991).

13. An income redistribution can be favorable to the poor but unfavorable to the ultrapoor. From the policy point of view it is important to know such occurrences.

14. Kakwani (1990c) has provided the explicit expressions of this elasticity for all the additively decomposable poverty measures.

15. Note that the inequality elasticity is based on a highly restrictive assumption—nonintersecting movements of the Lorenz curves; no such restriction was necessary in computing the inequality effect.

16. The important direct interventions launched under the initiative of the central government are the Integrated Rural Development Program (IRDP), the National Rural Employment Program (NREP), and the Rural Landless Employment Guarantee Program (RLEGP). There is also an important centrally sponsored program for combating child and maternal malnutrition, the Integrated Child Development Services (ICDS). At the state level, the notable programs are Maharashtra's Employment Guarantee Scheme (MEGS); public distribution systems in Kerala, Tamil Nadu, Gujarat, and Andhra Pradesh; and the Tamil Nadu Integrated Nutrition Project. With regard to each of these programs, there have been many evaluations and much debate (Subbarao 1985, 1987, and 1989; and Pulley 1989).

17. To illustrate, consider a state that assisted households close to the poverty line and helped them all cross the line, and another state that selected households way below the poverty line (the ultrapoor) and helped their incomes grow, but not enough to cross the poverty line. Earlier IRDP evaluations hailed the first state and condemned the second, following the criterion of "crossing the poverty line." Gaiha's (1989) critique misses this important consideration in assessing program effectiveness.

Poverty and Adjustment in Brazil: Past, Present, and Future

19 M. Louise Fox
Samuel A. Morley

The difficulties most Latin American countries have experienced in returning to sustained growth after the world recession and the debt crisis of 1982 have surprised and frustrated many observers. There is growing concern about the social costs of this period of recession and adjustment, especially for the poorest sectors of the population, which had benefited significantly from the more rapid income growth of the 1970s. Nowhere is this concern better placed than Brazil, where roughly 45 million people lived in households below the poverty line in 1987.[1] But in this region, with its record of negative per capita growth, Brazil stands out as having taken a different path. By effectively failing to adjust internal demand to the decline in external funds, Brazil set records in the region in per capita growth and inflation between 1982 and 1988 (table 19.1). Brazil, by choosing an expansionary fiscal path, traded growth in the middle of the decade for inflation and a larger debt later in the decade. Did Brazil make the right policy choices from the point of view of the poor? This chapter attempts to answer that question.

Macroeconomic policy (monetary, aggregate expenditure, and exchange rate policy) affects few people *directly*. Instead, macroeconomic policy operates through factor and product markets to affect the functional distribution of income, and through the functional distribution, to affect individual income. The effect on a household's income depends on its factor endowment. Poor households rarely own much capital; thus, for most, the principal source of income is the labor market. Our approach to analyzing the question of how Brazil's macro-

Table 19.1 Income growth and inflation, Brazil and rest of Latin America, 1982-88

(percent)

Country/region	Average per capita GDP growth	Average yearly inflation
Brazil	0.9	301.9
Latin America (except Brazil)	-1.4	149.8

Source: Cardoso and Dantas 1989.

463

economic policy choices affect the poor therefore focuses on how they affect the labor market. Where possible, we link the labor market outcomes to the flow of income into poor households and to the evolution of poverty.

Using this approach, we address two sets of questions. First, we examine the results of Brazil's macroeconomic policies in some depth, looking at the quantitative record in terms of the evolution of macroeconomic variables, output in the formal and informal sectors, labor market outcomes (employment and earnings), and poverty. Second, we examine the effects of Brazil's macroeconomic choices in the 1980s on its prospects for growth and poverty alleviation in the 1990s. To do so, we use a set of simulation models to elaborate Brazil's macroeconomic policy options for the next decade and derive their income distribution outcomes.

Backdrop to the debt crisis

During the 1970s Brazilians had become accustomed to both high rates of economic growth and significant improvements in living standards. Between 1970 and 1979 real income in Brazil grew an astonishing 6 percent per capita per year, the incidence of poverty fell by roughly 50 percent, and the severity of poverty (the poverty gap) fell by 25 percent (Fox 1990).[2] Brazil's record on poverty alleviation in the 1970s, even in the least affected areas, is the envy of many countries.

The effects of growth on poverty were not uniform across Brazil, however; over the decade poverty fell 67 percent in urban areas, compared with 50 percent in rural areas, and roughly 70 percent in the Southeast, compared with just under 50 percent in the Northeast. Moreover, concentration of income, the perennial black mark on Brazil's growth and development record, does not seem to have improved over the decade,[3] and the country's distribution of income remains one of the most unequal in the world.

Yet recent analyses demonstrate that Brazil's economic growth in the 1970s was accompanied by significant social mobility (Morley 1982; and Pastore 1989). These analyses show that the reduction in poverty was achieved primarily through an expansion in employment in the urban formal sector, where average wages were nearly three times higher than wages in the rest of the economy by the end of the decade. This growth in formal sector employment was heavily concentrated in the Southeast, providing some explanation for the difference between regions in the efficiency of growth in reducing poverty.

External debt played an important role in Brazil's growth performance of the 1970s. Before the second oil shock Brazil's debt was one of the largest in the world, and new lending was increasingly needed just to cover interest obligations. Even if the fall in the price of oil in the early 1980s had not ended the supply of petrodollars for recycling at the same time that rising real interest rates were increasingly eroding Brazil's debt service capacity, Brazil would have faced serious adjustment problems in the 1980s. Thus, the external shocks of 1982—which together have come to be called the world debt crisis—hit Brazil hard. As a result of the crisis, demand had to be cut by roughly 4 percent of GDP (the size of the foreign inflows).

Despite the severity of the crisis Brazil faced by late 1982, most observers believed that Brazil, with its diverse economy and relatively rich resource base, would eventually return to a growth path less dependent on external savings. In 1983 World Bank projections estimated that Brazil could effect the required adjustment if it achieved a savings rate of about 20 to 25 percent of GDP over the next five years (a marginal rate of about 30 percent, as the same projections envisaged a return to growth after a brief period of austerity). By comparison Chile would have had to achieve a marginal savings rate of 50 to 60 percent over the same period to meet its debt service burden. Brazil was viewed as a possible model for the region for adjustment, growth, and external transfer, with minimal tradeoffs among the three objectives.[4] What these projections could not highlight—an element that proved critical in Brazil's failure to adjust—was that all adjustment would have to take place in Brazil's public sector (the owner of the debt, de facto or de jure) to prevent a large public-private transfer problem and significant crowding out. This adjustment in the public sector would have coincided with Brazil's opening up of the political process to groups that had been disenfranchised for twenty years. Politically, the task was to reduce the pie by about 25 percent just as the group standing in line to get a piece was growing dramatically.

Macroeconomic policy in the 1980s

Brazil's macroeconomic policy in the 1980s and the outcomes of the policy can be divided into three periods: (1) recession (1981-83); (2) recovery (1984-85); and (3) boom and bust (1986-89). We briefly review the macroeconomic policies and outcomes in each period; the quantitative record is summarized in table 19.2.[5]

During the recessionary period Brazil used tight money policies, some fiscal restraint, and an active exchange rate policy to lower demand and squeeze out the resources for external transfer.[6] The burden of adjustment fell primarily on the private sector, as rising interest costs led to negative government saving. In an attempt to control inflation and limit the burden of adjustment on the poor, the government also used an incomes policy of cascading wage adjustments, allowing more than 100 percent indexation of wages at lower wage levels, and less than 100 percent indexation at higher wage levels.[7] These policies resulted in Brazil's deepest recession in fifteen years, a 40 percent fall in investment, and, by 1983, an annual transfer abroad of 4 percent of GDP.

During the recovery period (1983-85) Brazil began easing up on interest rates, and at the same time returning to the levels of government expenditure on wages, investment, and goods and services that had been realized in the 1970s, financed by external debt. But this source of financing was unavailable, and interest payments continued to grow. To finance the deficit, the government was forced to sell more government bonds, eventually forcing interest rates back up, and to print money, leading to an acceleration of inflation. Because the recession had left many private sector firms with excess capacity, the decline in investment that had occurred in the previous period was not yet much of a constraint on growth, and the Brazilian economy responded well to the fiscal stimulus. The policy of cascading wage adjustments was abandoned, and a policy of exchange depreciation maintained the trade surplus even as internal demand began to expand, providing Brazil with the foreign exchange to continue debt service payments. The trick was to get the local-currency equivalent of the trade surplus into the hands of the government to meet the fiscal burden of the debt, a feat that was proving increasingly difficult. Nonetheless, Brazil achieved a marginal savings rate well above that required for debt service during this period, investment began to recover, and, except for the troubling inflation, Brazil seemed to be emerging from the debt crisis on a "Baker" path.

By the end of 1985, however, the transfer problem was becoming acute. Inflation was accelerating, velocity was increasing, and financing the government deficit by printing money was becoming more and more difficult. The solution had to be a political consensus on reducing government consumption or increasing revenues. But the newly elected officials, as members of the opposition, had long been denied access to control of the public purse, and for the most part they sought to extend benefits to their constituencies. Brazil's establish-

Table 19.2 Macroeconomic indicators, Brazil, 1980-87

Item	1980	Recession			Recovery		Boom and bust	
		1981	1982	1983	1984	1985	1986	1987
GDP growth, factor cost	1.00	0.95	0.96	0.90	0.95	1.05	1.20	1.16
Agriculture	1.00	1.08	1.08	1.07	1.11	1.22	1.12	1.28
Private formal sector	1.00	0.92	0.92	0.86	0.91	0.97	1.14	1.07
Total formal sector	1.00	0.93	0.94	0.87	0.91	0.99	1.16	1.10
Informal sector	1.00	0.92	0.99	0.95	1.15	1.32	1.62	1.51
GDP growth, market prices	1.00	0.97	0.98	0.95	1.01	1.09	1.18	1.21
Fiscal policy indicators (percentage of GDP)								
Revenue	23.3	23.5	24.9	23.2	20.8	21.1	22.7	22.7
Interest	1.9	2.3	3.4	4.2	6.2	10.8	10.2	9.0
Government savings	1.1	1.9	-0.4	-1.4	-2.8	-8.0	-6.8	-6.1
Debt	—	15.5	19.8	28.4	34.3	36.1	22.7	40.0
Annual rate of inflation (percent)[a]	91	101	97	151	210	235	149	225
Real exchange rate[b]	1.00	0.92	0.92	1.18	1.21	1.25	1.08	1.00
Real interest rates (percent; working capital)	-13.4	25.7	24.6	13.4	36.4	32.1	6.4	30.7
Implicit rate of return Government debt (percent; overnight market)	1.3	18.5	26.5	13.6	17.9	15.9	5.8	7.4

— Not available.
a. GDP deflator, annual rate of change.
b. Exchange rate deflated by cost of living in Brazil times U.S. wholesale price index (WPI); an increase indicates depreciation.
Source: World Bank data; and Brazilian government national accounts data.

ment, represented politically by the President, was likewise unwilling to bear the burden of adjustment. This political stalemate shaped Brazil's macroeconomic policy over the second half of the decade, which was marked by a period of growth (1986), then recession (1987-88), and finally a second growth spurt (1989). Inflation was held in check only through increasingly unsuccessful wage and price control programs inaugurated roughly once every 18 months, and private investment was crowded out.

The first and most famous of Brazil's stabilization programs was the Cruzado Plan, initiated in February 1986. Key elements of this program included (1) real wage increases to pacify organized labor; (2) a monetary reform and price freeze (3) a government-imposed deindexation of the economy, including financial instruments and the exchange rate; and (4) an exchange rate freeze (which implied an appreciation), and a more open import policy to ease shortages. All of these measures increased real purchasing power in the short run, increasing aggregate demand. At the same time, the government failed to take the required action to curb government consumption, despite the breathing space created by the temporarily lower inflation, through interest savings and seigniorage gains, and by the reverse Tanzi effect, through increased tax collections. On the contrary, fiscal pressures were aggravated by the failure to increase public sector prices before the freeze and by the real wage increases granted to government workers as part of the package. The disequilibrium in the balance of supply and demand became evident by July 1986; shortages developed, inflation returned, and the plan collapsed. In addition, because reserves had been used up in the import buying spree stimulated by the appreciated exchange rate (and facilitated by the government import policy), a debt moratorium was finally imposed in 1987.

Brazil has undertaken two more shock stabilization programs since the ill-fated Cruzado Plan. Although both appear to have averted the hyperinflation that threatens Brazil with each recovery in private aggregate demand, neither program succeeded in reversing the negative trend in government saving for more than a month or two. In addition, a new foreign debt agreement reached with commercial banks in 1988 led to renewed savings outflows. With debt service and the government financing needs eating up savings, private investment remained stagnant after a short burst during the Cruzado Plan.

The quantitative results of the tradeoff Brazil made in the second half of the 1980s—less adjustment for more growth, debt, and inflation—are summarized in table 19.3. On the positive side, Brazil managed to increase domestic income by about 16 percent over its level at the beginning of the decade. It met the savings targets required to continue servicing the foreign debt, moving quickly from a trade deficit position in 1980 to a surplus position in 1982, a position it maintained throughout the period except during the Cruzado boom of 1986. Consumption increased over the period, both private and public, helping to protect living standards even though public consumption increased almost 50 percent faster than private. For the period as a whole, however, debt service increased more than domestic savings, leading to a sharp fall in investment. The increasing unwillingness of the private sector to finance government consumption (including debt service payments) led to inflation of more than 50 percent a

Table 19.3 Savings and investment, Brazil, 1980-87

Item	Base 1980 (millions of 1980 Cz$)	Recession 1980-83	Recovery 1983-85	Boom 1985-86	Bust 1986-87	Total 1980-87
Change in GDP (millions of 1980 Cz$)		-615	1,746.9	1,106.7	432.8	2,671
GDP	12,626	*Change as a percentage of change in GDP*				
Consumption	10,014	-34.9	46.3	96.7	92.0	77.2
Government	1,139	-2.4	10.2	18.2	92.9	28.7
Private	8,875	-32.4	36.1	78.5	-0.9	48.5
Exports	1,121	47.2	24.7	-17.0	20.2	23.4
Imports	1,399	-72.7	-1.6	22.0	6.9	9.8
Foreign savings (imports – exports)	278	-120.0	-26.3	39.0	-27.1	-33.1
Domestic savings (GDP – consumption)	2,612	-65.1	53.7	3.3	8.0	22.8
Investment	2,890	-185.1	27.4	42.2	-19.1	-10.3

Source: World Bank data.

month by the end of 1989. The crowding out of investment in the 1980s can be expected to compromise Brazil's growth prospects for the 1990s.

Poverty in the 1980s

The effect of Brazil's macroeconomic policies on the poor and on the incidence of poverty is transmitted primarily through income flows into poor households. Compared with nonpoor households, poor households tend to be larger, to have fewer earners, and, consequently, to have a higher dependency ratio. In 1985 the head of household contributed more than 90 percent of household income in roughly three-quarters of poor households. This ratio holds for both urban and rural regions, indicating that it does not simply represent a correlation of poverty with employment in the agricultural sector, where unpaid family labor is common. Among nonpoor households, only 47 percent relied on the head for more than 90 percent of household income. Heads of poor households tend to be slightly younger than their nonpoor counterparts, and much less educated. In 1980, 59 percent of the heads of poor households lacked any formal education, compared with only 25 percent of the heads of nonpoor households.

Although most of the poor throughout Brazil, urban and rural, live in a household whose head is not employed in the formal sector, in the large cities of the Southeast poor households do depend on formal sector earnings from the head (table 19.4). Two-thirds of the nonpoor population live in a household whose head works in the formal sector, where average earnings are roughly three times earnings in the informal sector, including the agricultural sector (table 19.5). Most heads of poor families are self-employed or sharecroppers, earning income in the agricultural or tertiary sector; in urban areas, however, heads of

Table 19.4 Population in poor households, by occupation of household head, selected areas, Brazil, 1985
(percent)

		Urban		Rural	
Occupation of head	Brazil	Northeast	Southeast	Northeast	Southeast
Technical and administrative	4.4	5.2	6.8	2.7	3.1
Agriculture and mining	39.2	27.6	13.6	85.9	84.9
Manufacturing and construction	10.3	25.8	33.2	5.5	5.1
Commerce and related activities	8.6	12.1	6.7	1.7	0.8
Transport and communications	4.6	4.3	5.7	0.9	0.6
Services	22.4	6.9	12.8	0.7	2.6
Other	13.3	18.2	19.5	2.6	3.0
Formal sector employment	17.7	31.8	50.1	5.5	10.9
Memo item: share of the poor	100.0	20.2	17.2	33.8	10.2

Source: See appendix.

poor households are also found in significant numbers in manufacturing and construction.

An important characteristic of Brazilian labor markets in the 1980s was the increasing integration of rural and urban markets. For example, 25 percent of the heads of poor households in the urban Southeast worked in primary sector activities, and 15 percent of the heads of poor households in the rural Southeast worked in sectors other than agriculture. The agricultural labor force became increasingly proletarianized over the decade; by 1987 more than 50 percent of those earning income in agriculture were employees (even in the Northeast 48 percent are employees). Roughly one-fifth of agricultural employees in Brazil have signed labor cards (indicating formal sector employment), but this ratio varies significantly by region; in the South it is twice that in the Northeast. While most earners in poor households are at the bottom of the earnings distribution, not all low earners belong to poor households. In 1985 roughly 40 percent of those earning minimum wage in the formal sector were secondary earners in households with per capita incomes in the top 40 percent of the distribution (Almeida Reis 1989).

The sluggish growth of the 1980s, unlike the growth in earlier decades, did little to alleviate poverty in Brazil (table 19.5).[8] The recession clearly hurt the poor, but by 1985 mean household incomes had risen to 8 percent above their 1981 level, bringing the incidence and intensity of poverty back to their 1981 levels. The Cruzado Plan appeared to substantially increase the incomes of the poor. It should be noted, however, that our finding of a dramatic decline in poverty must be due at least in part to the price index that we used. This index inadequately measures real purchasing power during this period because the price freeze generated significant shortages of key items in the consumption basket of the poor. Our skepticism about the 1986 numbers is strengthened by the complete reversal in 1987, when inflation accelerated, the economy moved back into recession, and the purchasing power of the poor slipped back to 1985 levels. By 1988 the incidence of poverty had risen above its 1981 levels.

Table 19.5 Poverty and distribution indicators, Brazil, 1981-88

	Poverty indicators						*Share of poor (percent)*	
Indicator	*1981*	*1983*	*1985*	*1986*	*1987*	*1988*	*1981*	*1987*
Incidence of poverty (percent)								
Brazil	24.8	30.9	25.4	16.1	23.3	26.9	100.0	100.0
Urban	14.9	21.6	17.1	9.4	14.8	—	42.5	46.4
Rural	46.8	54.2	47.1	33.7	46.3	—	57.5	53.6
North	18.0	24.8	18.0	10.9	16.8	—	2.0	2.3
Northeast	44.9	52.5	46.3	32.9	44.2	—	54.2	55.7
Urban	31.1	40.2	32.0	21.6	31.4	—	19.8	22.0
Rural	60.5	66.8	63.3	46.2	60.1	—	34.4	33.7
Southeast	13.5	19.4	15.5	8.2	13.0	—	24.3	24.9
Urban	9.3	15.0	11.4	5.4	9.2	—	14.1	15.1
Rural	36.6	43.8	39.1	23.5	34.2	—	10.3	9.8
South	16.6	25.1	17.4	10.8	17.3	—	10.9	11.6
Urban	9.0	16.6	11.7	5.9	10.1	—	3.6	4.5
Rural	28.9	39.4	27.8	20.2	31.6	—	7.2	7.1
Center and west	23.1	28.1	20.9	10.4	18.5	—	6.2	5.5
Income gap ratio	38.1	40.7	37.7	—	39.0	40.5	n.a.	n.a.
Poverty gap index	10.1	13.1	9.9	—	9.5	10.7	n.a.	n.a.
Index of GDP per capita	1.0	0.93	1.01	—	1.08	1.06	n.a.	n.a.
Index of mean household income per capita	1.0	0.93	1.12	—	1.23	1.23	n.a.	n.a.

	Distribution of income per capita							
Population group (ranked by household income per capita)	*Share of income*						*Index of real mean per capita income*	
	1981	*1983*	*1985*	*1986*	*1987*		*1981*	*1988*
Lowest 10 percent	0.88	0.86	0.85	—	0.76		1.0	0.95
Lowest 25 percent	3.86	3.70	3.66	—	3.45		1.0	1.01
Lowest 50 percent	13.21	12.63	12.57	—	12.29		1.0	1.06
Highest 25 percent	68.38	69.46	69.49	—	69.60		1.0	1.32
Highest 10 percent	46.17	47.01	47.36	—	47.52		1.0	1.39

n.a. Not applicable.
— Not available.
Note: A constant poverty line of one-quarter the 1980 minimum salary per capita is used.
Deflator: INPC.
Source: See appendix.

Given such a poor economic growth record, it is somewhat surprising that poverty did not increase even more. Part of the answer to this puzzle lies in the difference between the growth in GDP per capita and the growth in mean household income. For household income to rise three times faster than per capita GDP is unusual; it did not occur during the previous decade (Fox 1990). Most of the divergence occurred between 1983 and 1985. There are several possible explanations for this trend. First, it is possible that the national household survey coverage improved (for example, more income could have been recorded in the later survey than in the earlier surveys). This was not the case. A comparison of the nominal value of survey income with GDP in 1981 and in 1987 shows that survey coverage declined from 46 percent in 1981 to 45 percent in 1987. Second, part of the sharp divergence could represent differences in the speed of change of relative prices during a period of high and accelerating inflation. This does appear to be the case. The GDP numbers are deflated by the implicit GDP deflator, while the household income numbers are deflated by our low-income cost of living index. The accumulated inflation over the period 1981-87 recorded by the INPC (1981 = 100) was 36,931; the implicit GDP deflator for the same period recorded 39,069. How much of this difference is simply "noise" and how much is real gain in the relative price of consumption goods bought by lower-income households compared with prices in the rest of the economy (that is, a real gain in purchasing power for lower-income households) is impossible to tell.

Although the percentage of the population in poverty was roughly constant over the period, the share of household income received by the poor (as measured by the survey data) declined. Between 1983 and 1985 the gain in the average income of the poor offset the negative distributional movement, but during the Cruzado Plan and its aftermath, the income gap ratio widened.[9] The poorest 10 percent of the population benefited the least from the income growth over the period. The mean income of this group actually dropped 3 percent between 1985 and 1987; the mean income of the population as a whole grew 7 percent during the same period.[10]

Among regions, the Northeast—with 27 percent of the population but 50 percent of the poor population at the beginning of the decade—continued to increase its share of the poor. Yet the *incidence* of poverty increased proportionately more between 1981 and 1985 in the South and Southeast, and in urban areas, where the bulk of the population lives. Although the incidence of poverty in urban areas was the same at the beginning of the decade as at the end, the growth in the urban population was strong enough to bring the number of urban poor in 1987 to almost equal the number of rural poor.

Analysis of the 1980s

Brazil's macroeconomic policies of the 1980s produced modest growth in per capita income, external balance, and high inflation. Except for during the recession, they were also somewhat successful in maintaining the incomes of the poorest one-quarter of the population. To seek explanations for this result, we next analyze the effect of the macroeconomic policies on formal, informal,[11] and agricultural sector earnings and employment. Table 19.6 presents details on the labor market outcomes, and table 19.7 summarizes the changes in these indicators, the sectoral output indicators from table 19.2, and the poverty incidence from table 19.5 over the three macroeconomic policy periods.

During the *recessionary* period the formal sector gained slightly at the expense of the informal sector. The big loser appears to have been agriculture, however, where roughly 29 percent of the labor force was employed in 1982.[12]

Table 19.6 Indices of labor market outcomes, Brazil, 1980-87

Item	1980	1981	1982	1983	1984	1985	1986	1987
Employment								
Total	1.00	1.01	1.06	1.04	1.12	1.18	1.22	1.27
Agriculture	1.00	0.96	1.02	0.95	1.08	1.10	1.02	1.01
Formal sector	1.00	1.01	1.03	1.01	1.03	1.11	1.21	1.25
Informal sector	1.00	1.05	1.22	1.27	1.38	1.49	1.54	1.69
Private formal sector[a]	1.00	0.95	0.95	0.89	0.92	0.98	1.02	—
Public sector[a]	1.00	1.06	1.12	1.16	1.25	1.32	1.43	—
Open unemployment (percent)								
São Paulo	7.2	7.2	5.5	6.8	6.8	5.0	3.4	3.8
Average, 6 cities	—	—	6.3	6.7	7.1	5.2	3.6	3.7
Real wages								
Private industry								
(São Paulo)	1.00	1.07	1.14	1.06	0.99	1.05	1.17	1.08
Total formal sector[a]	1.00	1.01	1.07	0.92	0.87	0.98	1.05	—
Government sector[a]	1.00	0.97	1.03	0.86	0.78	0.99	1.16	—
Minimum wage	1.00	0.99	1.01	0.91	0.83	0.86	0.89	0.73
Real average incomes[b]								
Formal sector	1.00[c]	0.86	1.31	0.97	0.89	1.08	1.34	1.09
Informal sector	1.00[c]	0.85	1.30	0.92	1.03	1.20	1.65	1.24
Agriculture	1.00[c]	0.84	0.96	0.77	0.78	0.84	1.16	0.83
Income differentials								
Formal/informal	3.08[c]	3.10	3.11	3.25	2.66	2.76	2.50	2.71
Informal/agriculture	0.63[c]	0.64	0.86	0.75	0.84	0.90	0.90	0.94

— Not available.
Note: Informal sector includes agriculture; it is defined as comprising labor force participants who do not contribute to the social security system.
a. RAIS data.
b. Average earnings, not corrected for hours worked, in main occupation.
c. Data are for 1979.
Source: See appendix. Deflator: INPC

Two government policies appear to have contributed to this result: the policy of guaranteed, twice-yearly overindexation for formal sector workers in lower earnings categories, and the generous government employment policy that kept workers employed in the formal sector, reducing the pressure on wages in the informal sector. Private sector employers shed some workers in response to falling demand, but there clearly was also some labor stockpiling. The government increased employment over the period, so total formal sector employment did not decline. On the wage side, the evidence is somewhat ambiguous. The minimum wage fell by 10 percent, but industrial real wages increased. As a result, there was a large increase in the share of factor income going to labor and an equally large shrinkage in the share of nonfinancial profits. Within the government sector the increase in employment was accompanied by significant real wage compression, causing average wages in the formal sector as a whole to fall. Because employment was stagnant in the formal sector as a whole, and shrinking in agriculture, all the increase in the labor force during the recession was absorbed

Table 19.7 Evolution of key variables, Brazil, 1980-87
(percentage change)

Variable	Recession 1980-83	Recovery 1984-85	Boom 1986	Total period 1980-87
Informal sector				
Output	-5	+38	+22	+7
Employment	+27	+17	+3	+70
Earnings	-8[a]	+29	+38	+25[b]
Formal sector				
Output	-15	+11	+17	+7
Employment	0	+10	+9	+25
Private sector	-11	+10	+4	+2[c]
Wages				
Industry	+6	0	+11	+8
Overall	-8	+6	+7	+9[b]
Labor share	+19	-3	+6	+20
Profit share	-16	+7	+8	-8
Nonfinancial profit share	-25	+10	+25	-17
Agriculture				
Output	+7	+22	-10	+28
Employment	-5	+15	-8	+1
Earnings	-33[a]	+8	+39	-17[b]
Incidence of poverty				
Brazil	+25[d]	-18	-37	-5[e]
Urban	+44[d]	-21	-45	-1[e]
Rural	+16[d]	-13	-29	-1[e]

a. 1979-83.
b. 1979-87.
c. 1980-86.
d. 1981-83.
e. 1981-87.
Source: See appendix.

by the informal sector, where average value added per worker fell by one-fourth. Reflecting this surge in employment (as well as the decline in agricultural incomes), informal sector earnings fell by 8 percent between 1979 and 1983. Somewhat surprisingly, the differential between formal and informal sector incomes remained roughly constant, increasing by only 5 percent for the period.

At the upper end of the income spectrum, profits, especially nonfinancial profits, contracted sharply, as owners of physical capital were hurt by the combination of high interest rates, workers' ability to protect their wages, and sluggish demand. In short, the government's tight money policy, combined with a wage policy that maintained real wages, in effect protected the middle of the earned income distribution against both ends. But the protection of the middle also clearly benefited the urban informal sector by helping to cushion demand for its services, so the policy was not strongly antipoor.[13] Nonetheless, a significant portion of the population was pushed back into poverty, especially in the urban areas in the South and Southeast, where most of the urban population is located. This occurred because of a combination of two effects: the fall in incomes in the agricultural sector, where the majority of the poor earn their incomes, and the crowding of new entrants into the informal sector, where average earnings are one-third those in the formal sector.

During the *recovery* period formal sector holders of capital and informal (including agricultural) workers improved their positions, at the expense of existing private formal sector workers. During this period the earnings differential between the formal and informal sectors fell. Public employment continued to swell, and private sector employment kept pace with output growth. In addition, in 1984, when inflation took a sharp jump upward, formal sector workers appear to have been left behind. These income losses led workers to demand (and, in some sectors, to receive) a halving of the indexation period in 1985. Although private sector workers did not gain over the period, government workers began to recover wages lost during the previous period. The increase in informal sector incomes, combined with the increase in formal sector employment (which automatically raises average wages in the economy because the formal sector is the high-wage sector), led to a significant decrease in urban poverty and in poverty overall. In this period growth did trickle down to the poor, reversing the adverse effects of the previous period.

The Cruzado Plan in 1986 resulted in a short-run gain for all groups that was unsustainable. Interest rates and prices fell and profits and consumption increased, resulting in real income increases across the board. Employment rose, especially in the higher-earnings formal sector. As labor markets tightened, the earnings differential between the formal and informal sectors narrowed further, and the increased demand relative to the supply of labor sharply increased real earnings in the informal sector. Agricultural incomes also took a jump, as employment dropped in response to the urban boom. These real income gains were felt immediately by the poor, as poverty dropped below precrisis levels.

The boom of the Cruzado period was not sustainable, however, and in 1987 inflation returned as the government tried to get the private sector to finance the fiscal stimulus. As prices went up, incomes—in both labor earnings and profits—came back down. The acceleration in inflation clearly hurt labor incomes, especially in the less organized parts of the formal sector, where average earnings fell almost 20 percent. Informal sector earnings also dropped, and the incidence of poverty rose, both returning to 1985 levels.

Although it would appear that the boom and bust cycle of the Cruzado period was neutral with respect to poverty, in fact, the slowdown following the Cruzado Plan lasted through 1988 and led to a further increase in poverty. The absolute income gap of the poorest also widened as their real incomes dropped over the period (table 19.5), indicating that, for the poorest of the poor, the boom and bust cycle was not neutral. In addition, the excesses of the Cruzado Plan exacerbated the future stabilization and adjustment problem by adding to the debt burden. If Brazil had actually stabilized in 1986, allowing a return to sustained economic growth (and the size of the imbalances shown in tables 19.2 and 19.3 are not so great as to render this possibility absurd), the poor might have realized strong income gains by the end of the decade. But as we show in the next section, the longer the stabilization and adjustment is postponed, the worse-off the poor become.

For the seven-year period as a whole, Brazil's macroeconomic policies do not appear to have helped the poor. Given Brazil's lackluster growth performance (which was nonetheless significantly better than most countries in the hemisphere), this is not surprising. What is surprising is how much the lackluster performance in the second half of the decade hurt the poor, compared with the severe recession of 1981-83. The main reason for the difference appears to be the incomes policy during the recession, in which labor was stockpiled, real incomes in the wage earning sectors were maintained, and profits bore the burden of adjustment. During 1986-88 the poor were less fortunate. The large transfers associated with interest payments, combined with the failure of wages to keep pace with accelerating income, meant that negative distributional shifts overwhelmed overall income growth to lower the average incomes of the poorest 25 percent.

In addition to its negative effects in the last years of the 1980s, the policy of continuing government consumption is likely to exact high costs in the future. First, the public sector deficit absorbed a large share of private sector savings, crowding out the private sector investment needed to accelerate growth and improve labor productivity in the 1990s. Second, the high interest rates the government paid on its internal debt represented a significant and regressive income transfer, with the share of national income going to debt service rising to 10 percent of GDP by the middle of the 1980s. Although the household survey data used in this analysis do a poor job of recording capital income, and thus of capturing the effect on the distribution of income of this transfer to holders of government bonds, the transfer can nonetheless be expected to have contributed to the worsening of Brazil's already unequal income distribution over the period.

What if Brazil had successfully adjusted in the early 1980s?

We have described with as much detail as is available what happened to real wages, employment, and poverty during Brazil's adjustment to the debt crisis. Our conclusion from the analysis of the 1980s is that Brazil faced in 1990 essentially the same tradeoffs that it faced in 1981 and 1985, but with a lower stock of capital and a higher stock of debt, it had fewer degrees of freedom. Would a different mix of monetary and fiscal restraint in 1980-87 have helped or hurt the poor? What was the effect of Brazil's relatively generous wage policy? What stabilization choices does the country face, and how will they affect the future prospects of the poor? To answer these questions we built a small simulation model based on a similar analysis by Modigliani and Padoa-Schioppa (1978) for Italy. Here we describe the general structure of the model and report the results of our policy counterfactual simulations for the 1980s and our projections for 1988-95.[14]

In our model we first divide production into the formal (modern) and informal sectors, because macroeconomic policy will affect these sectors differently. In the formal sector, the problem to be analyzed is how to achieve consistency among competing claims of the factors of production and other components of cost, all of which must add up to the total value of the formal sector product.

Workers set target wages, businessmen set their markups, and the government determines the real wage and makes these claims consistent through the inflation rate that it chooses through monetary and fiscal policy. How the government chooses to finance its deficit—through bond sales or money creation—determines both the inflation rate and the interest rate. Financing through bond sales has important negative implications for supply through its effect on working capital and investment. A solution to the model is consistent with the demands of workers, business, and interest, with the informal sector as a residual. Because the informal sector has very little capital, the income distribution issue in the short run is simply how much income is left to be divided within the labor force crowded into this sector.

Our first simulation looks at the tradeoffs between monetary policy and fiscal policy in the first half of the decade with respect to their effects on output and employment. As a result of Brazil's tight money and loose fiscal policies, interest costs rose by 53 percent between 1980 and 1985. This had an unfavorable and perverse effect on employment, output, and the distribution of income. To see how large this interest rate effect was, we ran a counterfactual simulation in which we kept the interest cost at its 1980 level through 1985. Because this increased the level of output, we adjusted the labor productivity parameter to eliminate stockpiling for those years in which output rose above its 1980 level. Our simulation results show that had Brazil curtailed public spending sufficiently to keep interest rates at their 1980 level, by 1985, output would have been 15.5 percent higher, and formal sector labor employment and income would both have been 7.5 percent higher. The big gainer would have been nonfinancial profits, which would have risen by 16 percent because of both lower interest costs and higher labor productivity; these in turn would have reduced the depth of the private sector recession. This counterfactual simulation shows clearly the payoff of a stabilization policy mix that depends more on fiscal and less on monetary policy. Our simulation does not include the possible output cost that such a fiscal contraction might have entailed, however, because our demand side does not include these variables. It is fairly clear from the history of the decade that the fiscal contraction was not politically tenable in 1981-83.

We also ran a simulation to see the effect of rising target wage demands on output and employment. As we pointed out above, a rise in real wages and the labor share were a significant feature of both the period up to 1983 and 1986-87. What would have happened had the government not pursued incomes policies to protect workers in the formal sector? As in the interest rate simulation, we adjusted the labor productivity parameter to eliminate stockpiling in those years in which output exceeded its 1980 level. In our simulation, we get wages equal to the 1980 level. Holding wages down has a significant effect on output, but little effect on employment during the 1981-83 recession. Output in 1983 is only 1.7 percent below its 1980 level rather than 10 percent below, but employment is virtually unchanged because of stockpiling. In the subsequent recovery, through 1986, the simulated output and employment are both about 5 percent higher than the levels observed. Thus, holding down wage demands sharply reduces the recessionary effect of stabilization, and permits an increase in employment during the 1985-86 recovery. But despite the higher levels of real income and employment, formal sector labor is worse-off in the counterfactual world because the decline in the labor share is so pronounced that it more than offsets any increase in employment. Holding down wage demands transfers income to profits, but does not increase employment enough to make up for the gains workers achieved under the incomes policy. In addition, the political viability of this alternative policy regime is suspect; by 1981 labor union federations had formed and the political process was already being opened up to greater participation.

Evaluation of Brazil's policy options for the 1990s

The extreme instability of Brazil's present macroeconomic environment complicates the task of predicting its future growth path. Clearly, Brazil could not have continued along its 1989 path, which would have eventually led to hyperinflation, with ensuing economic disorganization. Brazil can be seen as having two choices. The first choice would be finally to effect the required adjustment, adjusting public consumption to levels consistent with minimal private sector transfers. This would allow a resurgence in private sector investment, stimulating economic growth, reversing the downward trend in labor productivity, and allowing increased employment and real wages. The second choice would be to effect the adjustment only partially—just enough to stabilize the economy and avert hyperinflation. Some scaling back of public consumption, effectively stabilizing the growth of the internal debt, might allow the economy to continue to generate positive growth (zero on a per capita basis) for a few years, until the political consensus for a more ambitious adjustment program is reached.[15] Obviously, either of these future growth paths (or several alternatives in between) can also be reached through the detour of hyperinflation. Our model is not very helpful in analyzing this phenomenon, however.

The purpose of this analysis is to illuminate the implications of a continued failure to adjust, and the two scenarios sketched out above serve this purpose well. The first sets Brazil on a virtuous course of relatively low inflation and high growth, and the second enters Brazil into a vicious circle of inflation and slow growth.

To estimate the effect of alternative macroeconomic scenarios on labor market outcomes and poverty in Brazil, we followed a four-step procedure. First, using a macroeconomic accounting framework to ensure consistency, we estimated growth rates of sectoral outputs, savings, investment, and the external balance, conforming to the normative policy scenarios sketched out above. Second, using estimates plus norms of inflation and interest rates for each scenario, and a behavioral model of portfolio balance (for example, demand for money and bonds), we estimated a financeable government deficit and the government interest bill (including external financing) for each case.[16] Third, using this estimate of the financeable deficit and the interest bill, we estimated the policy measures required to produce a set of government accounts (consumption, investment) consistent with our aggregate macroeconomic projection. In the final step, we plugged the estimates from the first three steps into the model described above, checked again for consistency (making minor modifications where justified), and estimated the effects of the stabilization and growth processes simulated in the first three steps on the functional distribution of income under each scenario. We describe the results of this process and the implications for poverty below.

The first scenario (the high case) is a highly normative one, implying a high degree of consensus among policymakers (legislative, executive, and judiciary) and economic sectors on a stabilization course. It assumes that immediately following the elections, Brazil begins an adjustment program consisting of an incomes policy (wage and price controls) and structural adjustment in fiscal accounts. Subsidies are reduced by 6 percent in the first year, and more rapidly thereafter, as are transfers to the social security and health systems. Government employment is reduced slightly (or wages are cut), as are purchases of goods and services. Public confidence is high, the velocity of money declines dramatically, and tax collections return to their historical levels. Real interest rates fall significantly, because the government is no longer forced to pay high rates to finance the debt. A reduction in debt reduces required interest payments by about 0.5 percent of GDP, aiding in the fiscal adjustment. After the stabilization, the government also initiates major sectoral adjustments, including privatization, trade reform, and deregulation, improving the efficiency of the economy.

The predicted effect of these policy measures on output growth in our normative high scenario is highly positive after a short adjustment period.[17] By 1992 Brazil returns to 5 percent annual growth under a strong resurgence of private investment and could continue along this path through the decade in the absence of any major shocks. Table 19.8 shows what happens to income and employment in both the formal and informal sectors. (Note that informal sector employment is treated as a residual here.) In the formal sector the return to rapid growth by 1992 permits a significant increase in real wage labor income and employment. In our simulations we assumed formal sector productivity growth of 2.3 percent a year, slightly lower than the 2.7 percent rate observed during the 1970s because of the lower overall growth rate. We also assumed that both labor and capital shared the benefit of lower real interest rates through a slight rise in the share of

Table 19.8 Predicted high-case outcomes, Brazil, 1989-95
(1988 = 1.00)

	1989	1990	1991	1992	1993	1994	1995
Formal sector							
Real wages	0.986	0.977	0.987	1.025	1.056	1.090	1.127
Employment	0.961	0.969	0.983	1.010	1.048	1.091	1.125
Labor income	0.943	0.940	0.965	1.032	1.099	1.188	1.262
Profit income	1.071	1.032	1.029	1.064	1.120	1.181	1.252
Nonfinancial profit income	1.094	1.055	1.090	1.150	1.234	1.300	1.378
Informal sector							
Employment	1.181	1.262	1.335	1.395	1.439	1.477	1.535

Source: Authors' calculations.

each factor. Employment, which was sluggish throughout the 1980s, grows at an average rate of 3 percent from 1990 to 1995; real wages grow by 2.9 percent and labor incomes by 6.1 percent a year. This split of the growth dividend permits nonfinancial profits to grow by 30.5 percent over 1990-95, supporting the necessary increase in private investment.

The informal sector, where most of the poor derive incomes, will still be forced to absorb rural workers even in the high-growth scenario because agricultural employment is roughly constant.[18] A good fraction of the increase in informal sector employment occurs during the adjustment period, but even in 1990-95 employment in the sector must grow at 4 percent a year. This does not imply that rapid growth will not have a significant effect on poverty. On the contrary, because average output in the informal sector is growing even faster than the labor force, average informal wages should increase, especially if growth leads to a narrowing in the wage differential between the formal and informal sectors, as it did in the 1980s. In addition, our assumed 3.5 percent productivity growth in agriculture should permit some increase in wages there as well. Nevertheless, the implied growth in the informal sector in the high scenario only underlines the point that 5 percent growth in Brazil must be near the minimum at which significant progress can be made in reducing poverty through growth in formal sector employment alone.

The second scenario (the low case) shows a much less rosy outcome. A stabilization program, again consisting of incomes policy and fiscal reduction, is initiated in 1990. The program averts hyperinflation, but the fiscal reduction is insufficient, and a high real interest rate policy must be maintained in order to finance the deficit. Failure to raise taxes and lower government expenditures makes it impossible to control monetary expansion. As a result, the economy suffers because of two vicious circles. First, deficits financed by bond sales force up the real interest rate; the rate remains at high levels, exacerbating the deficit problem. Second, the continued inflation precludes lengthening the indexing period, and Brazil enters into a fruitless struggle between labor and capital over the distribution of slowly growing formal sector output—a struggle resolved through high inflation.

In the low scenario we have set formal sector growth at 1.85 percent a year. Table 19.9 shows the deleterious effect this has on all participants in the economy. Even though we keep the labor share constant, the real wage grows by only 0.5 percent a year, and labor incomes expand by only 7.4 percent during 1990-95, compared with 35 percent in the high scenario. The growth in profits is equally modest. Slow growth has an important effect in the informal sector because it is the residual employer. One percent growth in the formal sector permits it to absorb only about 250,000 new entrants a year. With agriculture failing to absorb labor, the informal sector must therefore expand by about 1.5 million workers a year (7.7 percent growth). By 1995 there will be about 3 million more workers in the informal sector under the low scenario than in the high scenario, underlining the key role that growth plays in creating good rather than marginal jobs. Because of the expansion in informal sector employment, average value added per worker declines; this implies a falling real wage and an increase in the wage

Table 19.9 Predicted low-case outcomes, Brazil, 1989-95
(1988 = 1.00)

	1989	1990	1991	1992	1993	1994	1995
Formal sector							
Real wages	0.986	0.996	0.990	1.000	1.000	1.010	1.019
Employment	0.961	0.968	0.979	0.987	0.999	1.006	1.018
Labor income	0.943	0.961	0.968	0.982	0.993	1.014	1.032
Profit income	1.071	1.063	1.084	1.010	1.120	1.137	1.157
Nonfinancial profit income	1.094	1.088	1.109	1.123	1.144	1.162	1.181
Informal sector							
Employment	1.181	1.242	1.264	1.342	1.432	1.522	1.710

Source: Authors' calculations.

differential between the formal and informal sectors—exactly what happened between 1986 and 1989.

In the low case the unconvincing stabilization has a high cost. Failing to eliminate the deficit, the government is forced into a high-interest, high-inflation, low-investment, low-growth trajectory. Formal sector growth is insufficient to absorb rural-urban migrants and new entrants. Real wages are roughly constant in the formal sector, and poverty increases in the rapidly expanding informal sector.

Conclusion

From a macroeconomic standpoint, Brazil solved half of the adjustment problem it and other high-debt countries faced in the 1980s—the need for balance of payments surpluses to service the external debt. But Brazil failed to cut from consumption the domestic counterpart of the increased foreign interest burden, preferring to reduce investment instead. Government consumption was financed by extracting resources from the private sector through deficit financing and inflation. As the deficit grew, the government was forced to pay increasingly high rates of interest to extract these resources. Although these policies clearly helped to maintain consumption levels, they had high costs for Brazil's future because they led to declining private sector investment and increasing capital flight. By 1988 the distributional costs of these policies were higher than the income gains, resulting in increasing poverty and a widening of the poverty gap.

Alleviating poverty in Brazil clearly depends on growth in the private formal sector. Virtually all of the net increase in poverty took place during the recession of 1981-83, when formal sector output declined 15 percent. An important factor in that decline in output was Brazil's reliance on tight money policies—which choked off investment and cut nonfinancial profits—rather than fiscal adjustment. Our counterfactual simulations suggest that Brazil could have done far better in alleviating poverty in the 1980s if it had been able to reach a political consensus on reducing consumption in either 1982-83 or 1985 (either by reducing government expenditure, or increasing taxes and thus reducing private consumption). This was very difficult, as the loosening of authoritarian controls gave voice and power to new groups, bringing a rush of pent-up demand for consumption, especially government services. Ironically, the failure to exercise restraint in the early and middle years of the decade compromised growth for the rest of the decade, hurting all groups.

Our review of the macroeconomic record shows that Brazil's wage policies in the 1980s strongly benefited formal sector workers, especially during the recession. This experience differs sharply from that of many other countries during stabilization. Furthermore, during the recession, private sector firms did not reduce employment as fast as output declined, choosing instead to stockpile labor and sacrifice profits. The direct effects of these policies should not be particularly favorable to the poor because most poor households do not receive earnings from this sector. But the indirect effects (the income multiplier effects) appear to have been strong enough to have prevented real incomes in the informal sector (including agriculture) from falling relative to those in the formal sector. Had the government not tried to protect the wages of lower-skilled private sector workers, firms would most likely not have increased employment, increasing profits instead. When private formal sector output increased in 1983-86, employment also increased.

Government sector wage and employment policies seem to have been ill advised from the point of view of poverty reduction. During the recession, the policies helped to maintain formal sector employment, although at lower wages. We could not estimate the cost of the policies in terms of forgone output in the private sector (caused by the deficit financing), nor do our data allow us to estimate how many formal sector jobs went to poor households or near-poor households. Thus, we cannot assess the policies' net effect during the recession, but, owing in part to the wage compression, we suspect that the negative effect they had on poverty through the increased deficit was small. But as government salaries began to recover in the middle of the decade and employment continued to increase, personnel costs at all levels of government became an important expenditure item, rising 30 percent in real terms between 1985 and 1988 to almost 9 percent of GDP. Financing these expenditures must have had a cost in terms of output over the same period. In addition, because government employees with five or more years of service were given permanent tenure under the new constitution, the government's generosity during these years is likely to take its toll in the 1990s as well.

Our scenarios of growth and adjustment in the 1990s suggest that Brazil can still stabilize and return to a sustainable growth path in that decade, and that such a course would bring about a significant reduction in poverty. The trick to embarking on this virtuous course is for all groups (including the poor) to suffer a short-run loss. The loss would be short run *only* if the stabilization is effective within a very short time and if investor confidence brings a resurgence of private investment. Then, repeating the pattern of the 1970s in more sustainable fashion, increases in output in the private formal sector would translate into higher employment and earnings in the higher-wage formal sector and higher earnings in the informal sector, where the poor earn the bulk of their income. Ironically again, pursuing this course would permit government consumption to reach its highest absolute level ever without resorting to inflation. This would permit Brazil to address its long list of social needs, including improving the poor's access to social services.

A repeat of the stabilization failures of 1986-89, on the other hand, would bring with it grim prospects for the poor. The government would be forced to continue a high interest rate policy and an expansionary monetary policy in a fruitless effort to maintain government consumption, which would continue to decline over the decade. Investment would remain flat, and stagnation in the formal sector would crowd workers into the informal sector, reducing earnings in that sector. No expansion of social services would be possible, and the living standards of the poor would deteriorate.

This analysis of the prospects for poverty reduction has focused on an aggregate analysis of the country as a whole. Our prediction of those prospects depends on the mechanism of expansion of the private formal sector. In the 1970s (and again in 1984-85) output growth in this sector brought both growth in formal sector employment (higher-paying jobs) *and* increased incomes in the informal sector through strong linkage effects. This mechanism worked much better in the more developed southern areas of the country, where the degree of formalization is much higher and private sector employment is a much larger share of total formal sector employment. Although we expect that the scenario of stabilization, adjustment, and growth—if it materializes—would benefit the Northeast, we are much less confident about the size of the benefit there than we are about the benefit in the southern areas. The stabilization period will be especially difficult for the major cities in the Northeast, because this period will entail a reduction in either employment or wages, or both, in the public administration sector, and thus the recovery may take longer to bring poverty reduction benefits to these cities. Reducing poverty in this less developed area will clearly require policies that make growth more efficient at doing so—in other words, policies that increase the rate of trickle down.

Data appendix

Tables 19.2 and 19.3. The macroeconomic indicators (fiscal policy, savings, and investment) are from Brazil's national accounts data. The 1987 numbers are preliminary estimates. The estimates of formal and informal sector output were obtained as follows. We defined formal sector earners as those contributing to the social security system (*Previdencia*). Using the distribution of earnings from the main job for formal and informal sector earners reported in the government's household survey (Pesquisa Nacional por Amostra de Domicílios, or PNAD), we calculated mean earnings for each group for each year, and the differential in mean earnings for each year. This differential is reported in table 19.6. The formal share of total output was then $di/cdi + 1 - d$, where d is the share of the labor force in the formal sector and i is the income differential between the formal and informal sectors. We calculated the differential between the informal and the agricultural sector in the same way, except that, here, we used the average income of both contributors and noncontributors because most agricultural workers do not contribute to social security.

Table 19.4. These numbers are compiled from special tabulations of the PNAD survey prepared by Brazil's national statistics agency (Instituto Brasileiro de Geografia e Estatística, or IBGE) for Nelson do Valle Silva. Dr. Silva generously made these tabulations available to us.

Table 19.5. Published tabulations of the distribution of per capita income are available only for selected years and are found in the IBGE series *Mães e Crianças*. Income is reported in minimum salaries (after 1986, the *piso nacional*). Our constant poverty line was obtained by converting minimum salaries for the reference month for each year into constant cruzados, and then converting this value into constant 1980 minimum salaries (correcting for changes in the real minimum wage). The survey reference period often spanned a period of minimum salary change, requiring a reference month. In these cases we chose the reference month identified by IBGE in the published tabulations of the PNAD data. Table A.1 shows this calculation. The income distribution data, mean household income per capita, and poverty gap are the results of our own calculations, based on special tabulations of the PNAD survey data prepared by the National Institute for Economic Planning and Analysis (INPES/IPEA). The methodology is described in Fox (1990).

Table 19.6. The first four employment indices are taken from PNAD and census data as reported in Cacciamali (1989). Formal sector workers are again defined as those contributing to the national social security system, a more inclusive concept than the alternative, workers with a signed labor card. The RAIS (Relação Annual de Informações Sociais) index numbers are from the Ministry of Labor, which used a fixed panel of establishments to calculate the indices. In these data, *public sector* refers to public administration workers only. These numbers are found in Maia and Saldanha (1988). The data on open unemployment are from the monthly employment survey carried out by Brazil's national statistical agency, and the data on real wages in private industry are from the the Fed-

Table A.1 Real minimum wage index for PNAD, census data

Survey reference period	Index reference period	Nominal value (Cz$)	INPC (3/86= 100)	Real value (Cz$)	Index	Poverty line per capita (minimum salaries)
8/01 - 8/31	1980 (average)	4.02	0.48	8.37	1.00	0.250
11/8 - 11/14	11/1981	8.46	1.15	7.35	0.88	0.284
9/19 - 12/11	11/1982	23.57	2.38	9.90	1.18	0.212
9/25 - 1/10	9/1983	34.78	5.58	6.23	0.74	0.337
9/23 - 9/29	9/1984	97.18	16.24	5.98	0.71	0.352
9/22 - 9/28	9/1985	333.10	51.42	6.48	0.77	0.323
9/28 - 10/4	9/1986	804.00	106.15	7.57	0.90	0.276
9/27 - 10/3	9/1987	2,400.00	406.24	5.91	0.71	0.352
—	9/1988	18,960.00	3,093.61	6.13	0.73	0.342

— Not available.
Source: Authors' calculations.

eration of Industries of the state of São Paulo. These numbers are widely available; our source was *Conjuntura Econômica*. The real average income indices and differentials are the same as those used in the calculations for table 19.2.

Table 19.7. Value added per worker is derived from the output and employment data whose indices are displayed in tables 19.2 and 19.6. To derive an estimate of factor shares, we used the definition of the labor share WL/PQ, the observed level of productivity in the formal sector, and the observed average industrial real wage as reported in table 19.6. Financial profit is defined as the share of interest costs (the measurement is described below). We then obtained the nonfinancial profit share as a residual after all other costs (taxes, imports) were subtracted. The indices of factor incomes are the product of the indices of factor shares and an index of total output, which include finance, taxes, and imported inputs in addition to value added. Our estimates, year by year, are shown in table A.2.

Table A.2 Value added per worker, factor shares, and factor incomes, Brazil, 1981-87

(1980 = 1.00)

	1981	1982	1983	1984	1985	1986	1987
Value added per worker							
Total	0.96	0.92	0.91	0.90	0.92	0.96	0.96
Agriculture	1.13	1.05	1.13	1.02	1.11	1.10	1.27
Formal	0.92	0.91	0.87	0.88	0.89	0.95	0.88
Informal	0.88	0.81	0.75	0.83	0.89	1.05	0.90
Index of factor shares							
Labor share	1.16	1.25	1.19	1.09	1.16	1.23	1.20
Profit share	0.85	0.82	0.84	0.93	0.91	0.98	0.92
Nonfinancial profit share	0.77	0.73	0.75	0.85	0.81	1.02	0.83
Index of factor incomes							
Labor (formal only)	1.09	1.17	1.07	1.00	1.12	1.37	1.29
Profit	0.86	0.83	0.82	0.91	0.95	1.06	1.06
Nonfinancial profit	0.80	0.77	0.76	0.86	0.88	1.09	0.99

Source: Authors' calculations.

Notes

A longer version of this paper was prepared as a background paper for *World Development Report 1990*. The findings, interpretations, and conclusions are the authors' own. They should not be attributed to the World Bank, its Board of Directors, its management, or any of its member countries.

1. To put that number into perspective, among Latin American countries, only Mexico has a total population greater than the number of poor people in Brazil.

2. Throughout this chapter, we measure poverty by household income per capita. Our poverty line, constant in real terms, is one-fourth of the 1980 minimum wage. The empirical basis for choosing this poverty line is described in Fox (1990). This income level, roughly $200 per year (in 1985 dollars), represents a lower-bound estimate of the

cost of a basic needs basket of goods. It is roughly equal to the average poverty line used by Fishlow (1972) and Fox (1982) in their analyses of the 1960s. Other estimates using more complex methodology and expenditure data from 1974-75 have found poverty lines 50 to 100 percent higher in metropolitan areas between 1981 and 1986 (Rocha and Tolosa 1989). Fox (1982), using 1970 data, found that if the poverty line is raised by 20 percent, the size of the poor population grows 50 percent, indicating a strong sensitivity of the *absolute size* of the poor population to changes in the poverty line, and implying that there is large scope for measurement error. The trends reported in this chapter are so strong, however, that even if we have understated the absolute size of the poor population, we are confident of our estimates of the trends.

3. According to CEPAL (1989a), the Gini index, which measures the distribution of income across households, ended the 1970s at roughly the same place as, or slightly higher than, it was at the beginning of the decade. Ideally, a measure of the distribution of income per capita across households should be used, as this is a better measure of the distribution of welfare. We have not seen this calculated, however. The distribution of income across earners is the most commonly used measure of income distribution even though it does not measure the distribution of economic welfare as it relates to consumption units. This measure appears to have worsened (Bonelli and Sedlacek 1989).

4. At the time these issues were considered, little or nothing was said from a macroeconomic standpoint about poverty alleviation. The focus was on adjustment; poverty reduction would have to wait. The future was expected to be far worse for the poor without adjustment than with adjustment.

5. This description of Brazil's macroeconomic policy in the 1980s is drawn from various internal World Bank reports.

6. Throughout this period, imports were tightly controlled by a system of import licensing and quantitative restraints. Thus, the exchange rate was used primarily as a tool of export promotion. Throughout the decade, Brazil was able to generate the trade surpluses required with small changes in the real exchange rate. In Brazil, unlike other, more open economies, large real depreciations and devaluations were not required in response to the external shocks of the 1980s, and exchange rate policy played a relatively minor role in stabilization and adjustment programs.

7. In practice, the cascading policy was effective primarily in the public sector, where it succeeded in compressing wages, and at the lowest pay levels in the private sector, where it helped to protect real wages. At the higher pay levels, major private sector and joint public-private companies simply corrected for this policy by paying wage supplements of various kinds to their staff. Other types of wage control policies in Brazil over the decade have generated similar results, leading to a plethora of different types of remuneration other than wages in Brazil's formal sector.

8. Measuring changes in real variables is extremely difficult in Brazil's high-inflation environment. Depending on the deflator chosen, real average wages in the São Paulo manufacturing sector between 1980 and 1988 (1) increased by 50 percent—using the University of São Paulo's cost of living index; (2) decreased by 15 percent—using the Fundação Gétulio Vargas (FGV) broad cost of living index; or (3) increased by 9 percent—using the IBGE narrow cost of living index (INPC). Similar shifts could be recorded for the population in poverty. For purposes of deflating real wages and poverty concepts in this chapter, we used the IBGE narrow cost of living index, as the basket of goods used to calculate this index better approximates the consumption basket of the poor, and it is a national index. It does, however, have a strong urban bias, as do our data, which are from the national labor force survey. This source tends to underestimate rural incomes, but it does so consistently over the period.

9. The *income gap ratio* measures the average distance of the household income of the poor from the poverty line, and thus is a measure of the *severity* of poverty. The *poverty gap index* is the income gap normalized by the population size. This normalization renders the measure distributionally neutral (see Datt and Ravallion 1990 for further discussion).

10. These numbers are not shown in table 19.5 but were computed by the authors from the income distribution data.

11. Note that our definition of the informal sector *includes* agriculture. Where we could separate out output, employment, and earnings for agriculture, we have done so.

12. During this period, the Northeast suffered a major drought. Although agricultural output increased overall, earnings in agriculture must have been affected by the drought conditions, which lasted through the 1982 harvest.

13. The simulation exercise below confirms this result.

14. For a full description of the model and its estimation, see Fox and Morley (1990).

15. Alternatively, Brazil could continue to experience stop-go cycles of stabilization and recession followed by a return to growth as the government loosens its purse strings, with growth each time choked off by a lack of investment, and thus return to inflation again. On average, this scenario would look the same as a low-growth scenario.

16. This model is described in Coutinho (1989).

17. Note that this scenario implies very low costs of adjustment, with only about 18 months of recession. Given Brazil's recent history of failed stabilization policies, such a scenario may be too optimistic.

18. We assume a growth rate for agricultural productivity of 3.5 percent a year, somewhat lower than the rate observed in the 1970s, when the agricultural labor force fell by 3 percent over the decade, or 0.3 percent a year, while output was rising by 4.8 percent a year.

Poverty in Pakistan, 1984-85 to 1987-88

20 *Sohail J. Malik*

Pakistan's growth record over the past two and a half decades has been impressive. Real income per person has almost doubled—no modest record considering Pakistan's 3 percent annual growth in population. The growth in income has been spurred on by a vigorous manufacturing sector and sustained by an innovative agricultural sector. In the 1970s growth was aided by large-scale remittances from Pakistanis in the Middle East.

The gains from this growth have been spread through increasing real wage rates, brought on by the expanding domestic economy, and the strong demand for agricultural labor stemming from the green revolution in the earlier years and the migration of rural workers to the Middle East in the 1970s. Open unemployment has remained low. There is a consensus that the growth has translated into declining poverty, especially since the late 1970s (see, for example, de Kruijk and van Leeuwen 1985; Malik 1988; Ahmad and Ludlow 1989; and Ercelawn 1989). The net effect on overall income inequality is much less clear.

Several studies, starting with Naseem's (1973) pioneering work, have attempted to estimate what percentage of households or persons in Pakistan are poor. But little attention has been given to explaining the variations in poverty over time and across regions. Especially important is the issue of whether times (and places) of more rapid growth in real average income or consumption tend to be associated—causally or otherwise—with simultaneous or later reduction in poverty and changes in the inequality of consumption or income per person. These regional and temporal considerations are especially relevant for Pakistan because of the rapid growth it has experienced since the early 1960s, and the general consensus that most of its direct policy interventions aimed at poverty alleviation have met with mixed success.

Most studies on poverty in Pakistan have simply estimated the head count ratios for single years based on the available Household Income and Expenditure Surveys (HIES); the most recent studies use the 1984-85 data set. The earlier studies were limited by the grouping of the published data from these surveys and by the somewhat arbitrary basis on which poverty lines were set. Only recently, as access to the original household-level data tapes has become easier and the quality of the data sets has improved, has more detailed work been undertaken.

We can now estimate poverty measures that allow not only for incidence, but for the intensity of poverty and for inequitable distribution among the poor. We can thus estimate the additively decomposable class of poverty measures suggested by Foster, Greer, and Thorbecke (1984). Moreover, using Kakwani's method (chapter 2 in this volume), we can estimate standard errors for the different poverty measures so as to provide distribution-free asymptotic confidence intervals; this allows us to state the degree of certainty about changes in poverty measures, about differences among regions or groups, and about whether such differences have narrowed or widened.

This chapter attempts such an analysis for Pakistan, based on the full-sample HIES data sets for 1984-85 and for 1987-88, the most recent year for which HIES data are on tape. Changes in poverty are evaluated in terms of changes in the head count measure (P_0), the poverty gap (P_1), and the Foster-Greer-Thorbecke measure (P_2). Estimates are obtained for region-specific poverty lines based on per capita consumption.[1] Gini coefficients for per capita household income and expenditure are also computed. To examine the relationships between income, income inequality, and poverty, I first evaluate the correlations between poverty, per capita income (and expenditure), and inequality across regions using single-year values. Second, I assess the effect of economic growth on poverty and inequality by evaluating the correlation of changes in poverty and inequality to changes in per capita income (over the period from 1984-85 to 1987-88) to shed some light on whether a trickle-down mechanism is at work in Pakistan. I look also at changes in the nonincome measures of well-being, such as life expectancy and mortality and access to education, health, and sanitation, in order to assess changes in "real" poverty.

The years 1984-85 and 1987-88 have been chosen because of data availability. Can we say anything about general trends based on an analysis of data from the two survey years barely four years apart? Are the two years comparable, with respect to climatic conditions for agriculture and in other relevant respects, in aggregate and for the poor in the different regions? Are the changes over this four-year period fluctuations, random events, or genuine trends? No confident answer can be given, as this would require analysis, within a consistent framework, of several cross-sections over a significant number of years; the data necessary to do this are not yet available. Nevertheless, it may be helpful to review the economic conditions in 1984-85 and 1987-88. The official annual *Economic Survey* (Pakistan, Ministry of Finance 1985) classifies 1984-85 as a good year, with real GDP growth at 8.4 percent and inflation at 5.6 percent, both appreciably better than in 1983-84 (one of the worst agricultural years in Pakistan's history).[2] The year 1987-88 was marred by a persistent drought, a smaller-than-usual wheat crop, and repeated violence and political strife in Karachi (the major port and largest industrial center) that reduced overall industrial production. Growth of real GDP (5.8 percent) was below trend, and inflation was somewhat above trend (about 7 percent, because of the reduction in supplies, due to drought, of perishable agricultural commodities).[3]

Thus, overall, 1987-88 was a below-average year, and 1984-85 an above-average year, in aggregate economic performance. If the data show that poverty, by various measures, had nevertheless declined between two such years, we may be fairly confident that these data are not overstating—are indeed probably understating—the trend of improvement in the well-being of the poor. It is not clear, however, to what extent any reduction in poverty over that period would be due to the culmination in 1987-88 of the then-Prime Minister's Five Point Program, initiated in 1985, which emphasized rural development and the provision of infrastructure, and which was aimed primarily at the alleviation of rural poverty.

Review of previous studies on poverty

The many earlier estimates of the poverty head count used somewhat arbitrary (and different) poverty lines.[4] These estimates are very sensitive to the choice of poverty line, especially because the studies are based on grouped HIES data. So it is difficult to evaluate trends, as can be seen in table 20.1, which presents the results of many of these studies.

Naseem (1973) concluded from his study of real consumption from 1963-64 to 1971-72 that "even though abysmal poverty has to some extent been reduced by the process of growth and by some sharing of the fruits of growth, the proportion of people [above] a sustainable expenditure level has not been appreciably affected" (1973: 358-59). Allaudin (1975), extending Naseem's analysis to real income, confirmed that extreme poverty was declining, and that a slightly less poor group was also beginning to experience a reduction in poverty.

By the mid-1970s and early 1980s the focus of work shifted to estimating the extent of poverty and trends in poverty based on the absorption of a minimum diet for meeting nutritional requirements. Naseem (1977) defined a poverty line in constant 1959-60 prices based on a consumption basket yielding 2,100 calories and constructed lines that would permit the intake of 95 percent, 92 percent, and 90 percent of the minimum required calories. He concluded that poverty, when defined in more extreme terms, appears to have remained roughly unchanged between 1963-64 and 1971-72—about 54 percent of the households were found to be below the poverty line when the norm of 92 percent of recommended intake was used, and about 45 percent when the 90 percent norm was used. Most of this earlier work suffers from two serious limitations: first, it is based on grouped data rather than actual observations, and second, the conversion of the surveyed distribution of income and expenditure by household to one of income and expenditure per capita is built on fairly drastic assumptions.

Irfan and Amjad (1984) avoid these limitations in deriving estimates of the proportion of rural people in poverty in 1979 by using a poverty line that assumes a required intake of 2,550 calories per day per adult equivalent, as suggested by the Nutrition Cell of the Planning and Development Division of Pakistan (Khan and Khan 1980) and actual observations. They analyzed the detailed information available in the Micronutrient Survey of 1976-77 to determine an income-based poverty line of 109 rupees (Rs) per capita per month in 1979 prices. They then used this, and a poverty line for the very poor of Rs 95 per capita per month, to obtain head count measures for 1979 (based on the HIES for the first quarter of

Table 20.1 Prevalence of poverty in Pakistan, 1963-85

Author	Definition of poverty line	Poverty line (rupees)	Percentage below poverty line				
			1963-64	1969-70	1971-72	1978-79	1984-85
Naseem (1973)	Per capita annual expenditure arbitrarily fixed in 1959-60 prices						
					Households		
	Rural	250	43.1	26.0	19.2	—	—
		300	60.5	59.7	58.4	—	—
	Urban	300	54.8	25.0	24.7	—	—
		375	70.0	58.7	62.8	—	—
Allaudin (1975)	Per capita annual income arbitrarily fixed in 1959-60 prices						
	Rural	250	56.5	35.6	41.6	—	—
		300	67.4	61.1	64.8	—	—
	Urban	300	49.6	29.7	41.6	—	—
		375	70.9	60.2	62.4	—	—
Naseem (1977)	Rural; 95 percent of recommended 2,100 calorie intake per capita						
	92 percent		54.0	46.0	55.0	—	—
	90 percent		45.0	36.0	43.0	—	—
Mujahid (1978)	Per capita annual expenditure arbitrarily fixed in 1959-60 prices						
	Rural	250	27.4	35.0	—	—	—
		300	39.5	47.6	—	—	—
	Urban	300	35.5	29.4	—	—	—
		375	51.7	46.2	—	—	—
					Population		
	Rural	250	29.2	39.5	—	—	—
		300	41.6	52.6	—	—	—
	Urban	300	39.0	33.7	—	—	—
		375	55.0	51.9	—	—	—

Table 20.1 Prevalence of poverty in Pakistan, 1963-85 (cont.)

Author	Definition of poverty line	Poverty line (rupees)	Percentage below poverty line				
			1963-64	*1969-70*	*1971-72*	*1978-79*	*1984-85*
Irfan and Amjad (1984)	Monthly per capita income consistent with minimum intake of 2,550 calories in 1979 prices						
					Population		
	Rural poor	109	40.9	54.5	—	41.2	—
	Very poor	95	32.2	43.2	—	29.3	—
de Kruijk and van Leeuwen (1985)	Monthly per household expenditure at 1979 prices						
					Households		
	Overall	700	—	65.0	—	43.0	—
	Rural	700	—	73.0	—	51.0	—
	Urban	700	—	50.0	—	30.0	—
Malik (1988)	Monthly per capita consumption at 1984-85 prices						
	Rural	159	36.79	44.24	—	29.23	24.10
		172	42.69	50.76	—	35.19	29.21
	Urban	185	40.88	34.09	—	23.64	19.40
		207	48.89	42.55	—	30.95	25.61
Akhtar (1988)	Per capita annual expenditure based on 1959-60 estimates converted to 1979 prices						
	Rural	948	—	—	—	12.0	—
	Urban	1,260	—	—	—	20.0	—

Table 20.1 **Prevalence of poverty in Pakistan, 1963-85** (cont.)

Author	Definition of poverty line	Poverty line (rupees)	Percentage below poverty line				
			1963-64	1969-70	1971-72	1978-79	1984-85
Ercelawn (1988)	Per capita annual expenditure for 2,550 calories/ day/a.e. x 0.75; current prices[a]						
					Households		
	Rural	324	—	—	25.0	—	—
		960	—	—	—	19.0	—
		1,716	—	—	—	—	20.0
	Urban	504	—	—	38.0	—	—
		1,404	—	—	—	32.0	—
		2,592	—	—	—	—	36.0
Ercelawn (1989)	Per capita annual expenditure; current prices						
	Urban	1,584	—	—	—	38.0	—
		2,748	—	—	—	—	37.0
	Urban	1,524	—	—	—	36.0	—
		2,436	—	—	—	—	32.0
Ahmad and Allison (1990)	Per capita monthly expenditure in 1979 prices (updated to 1984-85 using GDP deflator from World Bank)						
	Rural	100	—	—	—	25.0	20.0
	Urban	110	—	—	—	20.0	16.0
					Population		
	Rural	100	—	—	—	30.0	24.0
	Urban	110	—	—	—	23.0	20.0

Table 20.1 Prevalence of poverty in Pakistan, 1963-85 (cont.)

Author	Definition of poverty line	Poverty line (rupees)	Percentage below poverty line				
			1963-64	1969-70	1971-72	1978-79	1984-85
Ercelawn (1990)	Monthly per capita expenditure consistent with minimum intake of 2,550 calories/ day/a.e.; in current prices						
					Households		
	Punjab						
	Rural	150	—	—	—	—	21.0
	Urban	150	—	—	—	—	13.0
	Sindh						
	Rural	170	—	—	—	—	21.0
	Urban	170	—	—	—	—	6.0
	Northwest Frontier Province						
	Rural	145	—	—	—	—	10.0
	Urban	145	—	—	—	—	8.0
	Balochistan						
	Rural	160	—	—	—	—	31.0
	Urban	160	—	—	—	—	19.0
	Pakistan (average)						
	Rural	—	—	—	—	—	20.0
	Urban	—	—	—	—	—	10.0

— Not available.
a.e. Adult equivalent.
Note: Some studies show poverty at two different poverty lines since the magnitude of poverty is sensitive to the choice of poverty line.
a. In Ercelawn (1988) the different poverty lines all represent 0.75 of the annual expenditure required to consume 2,550 calories per day per adult equivalent.
Source: Adapted and expanded from Akhtar 1988.

1979). To produce a consistent series, Irfan and Amjad recalculated poverty estimates for 1963-64, 1966-67, and 1969-70 based on the published grouped HIES data. They concluded that the percentage of the very poor increased from about 32 percent in 1963-64 to about 43 percent in 1969-70 and then declined to about 29 percent in 1978-79, close to the 1963-64 level. This pattern is confirmed by Malik's (1988) study of the published grouped data from the HIES from 1963-64 to 1984-85, which show that the percentage of poor and very poor households (and population) increased during the 1960s and then declined. And de Kruijk and van Leeuwen (1985), using the HIES data for 1969-70 and 1979, show that there was a significant decline in poverty between those two years, accompanied by an increase in income inequality.

Akhtar (1988) used the 1979 HIES data to compute a series of poverty and inequality indices. Based on her definition of the poor as the 10 percent of the population with the lowest per capita expenditure, she concluded that poverty in Pakistan is overwhelmingly rural, and is concentrated in Punjab and Sindh. When she used an urban poverty line approximately 25 percent higher than the rural poverty line, however, she found that the incidence of poverty was significantly higher in urban than in rural areas. This is confirmed by Ercelawn (1988 and 1990), but in his studies, too, the finding results from the use of a significantly higher urban poverty line; when Ercelawn (1990) uses the same poverty line for both urban and rural sectors in a province, he finds urban poverty to be significantly lower.

The large number of different estimates show the sensitivity of the poverty measure to the choice of the poverty line. Ahmad and Ludlow (1989) made an effort to clarify this issue; and Ahmad and Allison (1990) took their analysis further. They presented measures of the head count ratio and the Sen index for four poverty lines, based on total per capita expenditure per month, termed *low* (Rs 80), *medium* (Rs 90), *medium-high* (Rs 100), and *high* (Rs 110). The lines were computed for rural Pakistan for 1979 from the full sample data of the Micronutrient Survey of 1976-77 and the HIES for 1979 and 1984-85; the urban poverty lines were assumed to be Rs 10 higher than the corresponding rural ones. Ahmad and Allison regard the cutoff point of 2,550 calories per adult equivalent used by Irfan and Amjad as "absurdly high," but it lies between their medium and medium-high lines.

Their results, which are based on their medium-high poverty line, record a substantial reduction in both rural and urban poverty between 1979 and 1984-85, with the head count measure declining from 25 to 20 percent for the rural sector and from 20 to 16 percent for the urban sector. Although the authors presented estimates within a consistent framework based on household-level data, it is impossible to test statistically for the significance of this decline because they did not present any standard errors of their poverty estimates.

Ercelawn (1990) analyzed the 1984-85 HIES data set, using a concept of undernourishment, to estimate the incidence and intensity of absolute poverty in Pakistan, broken down by province and by rural and urban sectors. He estimated calorie expenditure functions for provinces, rural areas, towns, and cities.[5] Taking the implied poverty line as the monthly expenditure per adult equivalent that a household needs to make to achieve a daily intake of 2,550 calories per adult equivalent, he developed a set of location- and province-specific poverty lines for 1984-85. Not surprisingly, these lie within the range of estimates produced by Ahmad and Allison (1990). Their poverty line of Rs 100 per capita for 1979 inflates to Rs 155 per capita for 1984-85, which lies within Ercelawn's range of province-specific poverty lines.

Ercelawn concluded that the incidence of poverty for Pakistan as a whole may have been quite modest and that Pakistan is "quite fortunate particularly as regards acute poverty with the risk of starvation and malnourishment" (1990: 69). He finds the overall rural head count ratio to be 20 percent of all households: 21 percent for rural Punjab and Sindh, only 10 percent for the Northwest Frontier Province (N.W.F.P.), but 31 percent for Balochistan. Whether rural or urban poverty incidence was higher depends on the choice of poverty line. These estimates, like the others, are difficult to compare across regions or over time because it is not possible to assign any statistical significance to the estimates or to test for differences. The general pattern that emerges is of an increase in poverty during the 1960s, but—according to almost all the studies—a decline since about 1970.

The data sets

The analysis reported in this chapter is based on the data tapes for the HIES for 1984-85 and 1987-88. These surveys cover both rural and urban households in all four provinces of Pakistan, excluding tribal areas, military areas, and certain districts in the N.W.F.P. The surveys were spread over the four quarters of the fiscal year from July to June, and each household was interviewed in a single visit. The sample covers substantially more urban households, and slightly more Sindh and N.W.F.P. households, than their share in the 1981 census. The data tapes correct for this oversampling and thus permit nationally representative estimates. The HIES for 1984-85 covers 16,541 households and that for 1987-88 covers 18,143 households.[6]

Province-specific poverty lines

The poverty lines used in this study are based on those defined by Ercelawn (1990). To compute the poverty lines, Ercelawn estimated calorie expenditure functions of the form $C = a + b \log E$, where C is the calorie intake per adult equivalent and E is the monthly consumption expenditure per adult equivalent. In a series of estimations using location-specific dummies, he found significant differences among rural areas, towns, and cities. He used province dummies to show that province functions are statistically different,[7] but that the effects of location in a province are significant only in rural areas; differences among provinces in urban calorie expenditure are not statistically significant. Using the calorie expenditure functions and a cutoff of 2,550 calories per adult equivalent, Ercelawn obtained the following poverty lines:

Province or sector	Monthly expenditure per adult equivalent (rupees)	Monthly expenditure per capita (rupees)
Punjab	185	150
Sindh	210	170
N.W.F.P.	185	145
Balochistan	200	160
National		
Rural	185	150
Towns	245	200
Cities	355	290

On average across Pakistan, he found the expenditure required per adult equivalent to meet the cutoff of 2,550 calories per adult equivalent to be nearly 33 percent higher for towns than for rural areas, and that for cities another 45 percent higher than for towns. This places his poverty line for cities at nearly 100 percent above the rural one. That seems exceptionally high. Malik (1988), using published grouped data from the 1984-85 HIES, found that poor urban dwellers spend 16 to 26 percent more than poor rural residents to obtain the same number of calories. Havinga and others (1989), using actual data from the 1984-85 HIES to estimate the total expenditure required to obtain between 2,000 and 2,550 calories per adult equivalent, define an urban poverty line about 46 percent higher than the rural one. These differences are substantial, but they can be explained in part through differences across sectors in the nonfood components of total expenditure, especially housing, fuel, and lighting. Most earlier studies avoid the debate by assuming the same poverty line for both sectors; one (Ahmad and Ludlow 1989) has opted for an arbitrary Rs 10 difference. Based on observations in the field, I find Ercelawn's poverty lines for towns and cities to be too high relative to the line for rural areas. I have therefore opted to use his rural poverty lines for both rural and urban sectors in each province; to that extent, I may have tended to underestimate urban poverty.[8] But because more than 70 percent of Pakistan's total population is rural, the bias in total estimates of poverty due to this underestimation is likely to be small.

To update the 1984-85 poverty lines to 1987-88, I obtained regional price indices using the methodology outlined below. This methodology allows, as far as possible, for variations among provinces in the prices facing the poor.

I used the per capita expenditure rural poverty lines for 1984-85 for the provinces and the country as a whole suggested by Ercelawn, and updated them to 1987-88 by computing a price index (Fisher index) as follows:

$$F_{87-84} = \sqrt{\frac{\Sigma_i\, P_i^{87} \cdot Q_i^{84}}{\Sigma_i\, P_i^{84} \cdot Q_i^{84}} \cdot \frac{\Sigma_i\, P_i^{87} \cdot Q_i^{87}}{\Sigma_i\, P_i^{84} \cdot Q_i^{84}}} \times 100,$$

where P_i^t refers to the price, and Q_i^t to the quantity consumed, of good i in year t.

The quantity weights are taken from the HIES for 1984-85 and 1987-88 and reflect the consumption of the lowest expenditure groups. Prices are averages for the province taken from the *Pakistan Statistical Yearbook*, which reports the prices of selected commodities in major cities (Pakistan, Federal Bureau of Statistics 1988b, table 17.3). For Punjab, the average of prices in Lahore, Faisalabad, Rawalpindi, and Multan was taken and then converted into rupees per kilogram, liter, and so on. For Sindh, the average of prices in Karachi, Hyderabad, Sukkur, and Larkana was taken. For Balochistan, prices for Quetta were used, the only city for which they were available. Finally, for the N.W.F.P., prices for Peshawar were used.[9]

The indices computed by this method are reasonable. The index computed for the nation as a whole increased 13 points in the period from 1984-85 to 1987-88. The consumer price index (combined) reported in the *Economic Survey 1988-89* (Pakistan, Ministry of Finance 1989) increased slightly more than 14 points over this period.

Classification of districts of Pakistan by agroclimatic zone

Besides comparing poverty indicators across provinces and between rural and urban sectors, as is traditionally done, this analysis also compares indicators across districts grouped into agroclimatic zones. Such a grouping, besides having the obvious advantage of highlighting differences in poverty in a predominantly agrarian economy, also provides a basis for a comparison of poverty rankings with a ranking of development indicators computed from district-level indices available in the existing literature. In addition, this grouping of districts into agroclimatic zones is necessary because the HIES data sets contain only a small number of observations within the urban or rural sectors of some districts, making it difficult to obtain statistically meaningful estimates at the sectoral level.

The districts of Pakistan are classified into nine agroclimatic or crop zones (chart 20.1), following Pinckney (1989). Rainfed (barani) Punjab, so classified, includes only the districts of Attock, Jhelum, and Rawalpindi/Islamabad. These districts are unusually integrated with the urban centers; a large proportion of the rural population draws its income from service and related sectors. The other, more agricultural barani districts are classified as low-intensity Punjab. The classification of districts is as below:

Zone	District
Rice/wheat Punjab	Sialkot
	Gujarat
	Gujranwala
	Sheikhupura
	Lahore/Kasur
Mixed Punjab	Sargodha/Khushab
	Jhang
	Faisalabad/Toba Tek Singh
	Okara

Cotton/wheat Punjab	Sahiwal
	Bahawalnagar
	Bahawalpur
	Rahim Yar Khan
	Multan/Vehari
Low-intensity Punjab	Dera Ghazi Khan/Rajanpur
	Muzaffargarh/Leiah
	Mianwali/Bhakkar
	Dera Ismail Khan
Barani Punjab	Attock
	Jhelum
	Rawalpindi/Islamabad
Cotton/wheat Sindh	Sukkur
	Khairpur
	Nawabshah
	Hyderabad
	Tharparkaar
Rice/other Sindh	Jacobabad
	Larkana
	Dadu
	Thatta
	Badin
	Shikarpur
	Nasirabad
	Karachi

Other N.W.F.P. except Dera Ismail Khan

Other Balochistan except Nasirabad

Estimates of poverty measures

My estimates of the head count measure for Pakistan as a whole show that, in 1984-85, more than 18 percent of households—21 percent of rural and 11 percent of urban households—were in poverty. These estimates correspond roughly to those of Ahmad and Allison (1990) and Ercelawn (1990).[10] The estimates are presented in table 20.2 along with the test statistic developed by Kakwani (chapter 2 in this volume) for significance of differences in the head count estimates between 1984-85 and 1987-88. (Because the t-statistic for the difference of each of the estimates from zero was significant at 1 percent in each case, the estimated standard errors are not reported.)

Among zones, the highest incidence of poverty for 1984-85 is in rural cotton/wheat Punjab, with about 29 percent of households below the poverty line, followed by rural Balochistan and rural low-intensity Punjab. The lowest incidence is in the urban rice/other zone in Sindh; poverty is low in this zone because it includes the major port and industrial city of Karachi. Barani Punjab, because it contains three of the most developed districts, also has a low incidence of poverty.

The three measures give generally similar results. The poverty gap, P_1, ranges from more than 6 percent for rural low-intensity Punjab to 0.1 percent for urban barani Punjab. The values for P_2 range from 0.019 for rural cotton/wheat Punjab and 0.018 for rural low-intensity Punjab to 0.002 for urban areas of rice/wheat Punjab and rice/other Sindh. Urban rice/wheat Punjab comprises the districts of Sialkot, Gujarat, Gujranwala, Kasur, Lahore, and Sheikhupura, the hub of small-scale industrial activity in Pakistan.

The most striking finding is the substantial reduction in poverty between 1984-85 and 1987-88. For Pakistan as a whole the head count measure declined from about 18 percent to about 13 percent (16 percent for rural Pakistan and 7 percent for urban Pakistan). Most surprising is the big decline in poverty in Balochistan; this decline could be due in part to the price index used, however. Because Balochistan accounts for only 5 percent of the sample households, the

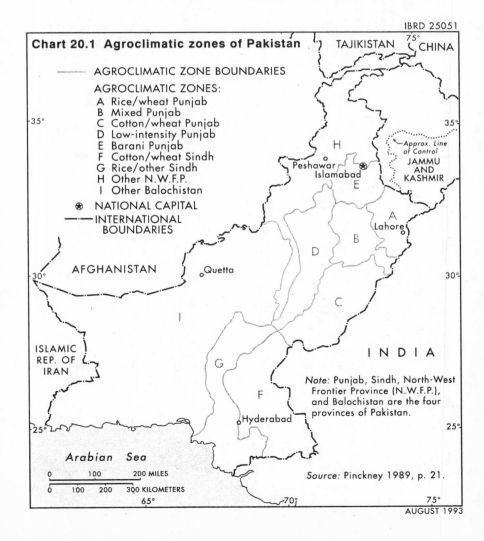

IBRD 25051

Chart 20.1 Agroclimatic zones of Pakistan

AGROCLIMATIC ZONE BOUNDARIES

AGROCLIMATIC ZONES:
A Rice/wheat Punjab
B Mixed Punjab
C Cotton/wheat Punjab
D Low-intensity Punjab
E Barani Punjab
F Cotton/wheat Sindh
G Rice/other Sindh
H Other N.W.F.P.
I Other Balochistan

⊛ NATIONAL CAPITAL

—·— INTERNATIONAL BOUNDARIES

Note: Punjab, Sindh, North-West Frontier Province (N.W.F.P.), and Balochistan are the four provinces of Pakistan.

Source: Pinckney 1989, p. 21.

AUGUST 1993

Table 20.2 Head count, poverty gap, and Foster-Greer-Thorbecke poverty measures by province and agroclimatic zone, Pakistan, 1984-85 and 1987-88

(percentage of households below poverty line)

Area	Head count measure (P_0)		Poverty gap measure (P_1)		Foster-Greer-Thorbecke measure (P_2)		Kakwani's test statistic for P_0
	1984-85	1987-88	1984-85	1987-88	1984-85	1987-88	1984-85 to 1987-88
Pakistan							
Overall	18.3	13.1	3.4	2.1	1.0	0.5	444.12
Rural	21.1	15.5	4.0	2.7	1.2	0.7	428.67
Urban	11.1	6.8	1.9	0.9	0.6	0.3	161.14
Punjab							
Overall	19.0	13.9	3.8	2.4	1.2	0.7	349.79
Rice/Wheat							
Rural	14.3	8.2	2.5	1.2	0.8	0.3	144.28
Urban	7.4	5.0	1.0	0.7	0.2	0.1	47.01
Mixed							
Rural	22.7	15.9	4.7	2.7	1.5	0.7	184.84
Urban	19.0	12.7	3.8	1.9	1.1	0.4	91.31
Cotton/wheat							
Rural	29.3	22.0	5.9	4.0	1.8	1.1	249.41
Urban	22.3	10.6	4.5	1.2	1.4	0.3	130.02
Low-intensity							
Rural	28.0	27.1	6.1	5.0	1.9	1.3	91.22
Urban	19.1	17.6	3.4	4.4	1.0	1.3	12.22
Barani							
Rural	5.7	3.9	0.9	0.5	0.3	0.1	29.13
Urban	1.3	2.3	0.1	0.3	0.0	0.1	-2.64

Table 20.2 Head count, poverty gap, and Foster-Greer-Thorbecke poverty measures by province and agroclimatic zone, Pakistan, 1984-85 and 1987-88 (cont.)

(percentage of households below poverty line)

Area	Head count measure (P_0)		Poverty gap measure (P_1)		Foster-Greer-Thorbecke measure (P_2)		Kakwani's test statistic for P_0
	1984-85	1987-88	1984-85	1987-88	1984-85	1987-88	1984-85 to 1987-88
Sindh							
Overall	15.3	12.8	2.6	1.7	0.7	0.4	137.34
Cotton/wheat							
Rural	20.5	18.9	3.4	2.7	0.9	0.7	86.48
Urban	10.7	8.5	1.9	1.2	0.5	0.3	32.08
Rice/other							
Rural	24.3	20.6	4.3	2.7	1.2	0.5	110.94
Urban	5.9	2.9	0.9	0.4	0.2	0.1	51.72
N.W.F.P.							
Overall	9.6	8.5	1.6	1.2	0.5	0.3	58.88
Other N.W.F.P. (except Dera Ismail Khan)							
Rural	9.1	8.2	1.5	1.2	0.5	0.3	47.85
Urban	7.0	7.0	1.1	0.8	0.3	0.1	11.25
Balochistan							
Overall	27.5	7.3	4.9	1.1	1.4	0.3	262.94
Rural	28.5	8.0	5.1	1.2	1.5	0.3	255.04
Urban	17.0	2.3	3.0	0.1	0.7	0.1	57.76

Note: The poverty line used for each province represents the expenditure required in that province to consume 2,550 calories per capita per day.
Source: Author's calculations based on data from Pakistan, Federal Bureau of Statistics 1988a and 1990.

error on this account in measures for Pakistan as a whole is not likely to be substantial. The only anomalous result is that for urban barani Punjab. This result could be due in part to the large-scale layoff of workers by the Wah Ordinance Factories (the largest single employer in the region) in early 1987. Overall, the test statistic reported in the table shows that the reduction in poverty (on the head count measure) is significant at 1 percent.

The three poverty measures reveal interesting patterns of poverty decline. For Pakistan as a whole, the head count measure (P_0) declined by more than 28 percent from 1984-85 to 1987-88, the poverty gap (P_1) by 38 percent, and the Foster-Greer-Thorbecke measure (P_2) by 50 percent. All three measures confirm the declining trend in poverty.

Wherever P_0 declined, P_1 and P_2 also declined, with one exception: urban low-intensity Punjab. In this region there was a slight improvement in the head count measure, but a marked deterioration in P_1 and P_2. This historically poor region comprises districts that are based on barani agriculture and that have small market (mandi) towns integrated into the local economy of the region. The drought of 1987-88 seems to have adversely affected the urban areas of these districts through reduced market activity; the poorest segments in the urban sector, which have fewer coping strategies, would have suffered disproportionately.

Location of the poor

In 1984-85 more than 83 percent of Pakistan's poor households were located in rural areas (table 20.3). (This is an overestimate, however, because I use the same poverty lines for both urban and rural areas.) Punjab accounted for nearly 62 percent of all poor households, followed by Sindh (18 percent), the N.W.F.P. (7 percent), and Balochistan (9 percent).

A better measure of the location of the poor household, however, is one that incorporates the weight of the number of all households in a category (sector or province) in the total of households in the country. If the percentage share of the poor households in each category is divided by the category's percentage share of all households in the country, it yields a measure that indicates whether that category has more than, equal to, or less than its proportional share of the poor. A value of 100 for this indicator indicates that the share of poor households in a category is equal to its share of all households; a higher value indicates a greater-than-proportional share, and a smaller value a smaller-than-proportional share, of poor households.

The values of this index are presented in table 20.3. Making allowances for differences in living costs, but *not* in urban versus rural "requirements," we see that for Pakistan as a whole the rural sector accounts for more than its share of the poor, and the urban sector for less. This is also the pattern in each province and zone, except the N.W.F.P., rice/wheat Punjab, barani Punjab, and Balochistan (in 1987-88), which, in both the rural and the urban sectors, have a smaller share of the poor than their share of all households. In Balochistan the remarkably low poverty head count may have led to the surprisingly low value of this index in the urban sector.

Table 20.3 Distribution of poor households by province and agroclimatic zone, Pakistan, 1984-85 and 1987-88

| Agroclimatic zone | *1984-85* | | | | *1987-88* | | | |
	P_0 *(percent)*	*Share of poor (percent)*	*Share of population (percent)*	*Index*	P_0 *(percent)*	*Share of poor (percent)*	*Share of population (percent)*	*Index*
Pakistan								
Overall	18.3	100.00	100.00	100	13.1	100.00	100.00	100
Rural	21.1	83.21	72.17	115	15.5	85.82	72.61	118
Urban	11.1	16.79	27.68	61	6.8	14.18	27.53	52
Punjab								
Overall	19.0	61.66	59.39	104	13.9	64.49	60.80	106
Rice/wheat								
Rural	14.3	9.30	11.40	82	8.2	7.92	12.29	64
Urban	7.4	2.82	6.69	42	5.0	2.65	6.71	39
Mixed								
Rural	22.7	13.16	10.15	130	15.9	12.92	10.36	125
Urban	19.0	3.86	3.56	108	12.7	3.20	3.21	100
Cotton/wheat								
Rural	29.3	20.56	12.30	167	21.9	21.43	12.42	173
Urban	22.3	3.81	3.00	127	10.6	2.37	2.85	83
Low-intensity								
Rural	28.0	9.31	5.82	160	27.1	13.65	6.14	222
Urban	19.1	0.99	0.91	109	17.6	1.50	0.86	174
Barani								
Rural	5.7	1.44	4.44	33	3.9	1.51	4.84	31
Urban	1.3	0.12	1.63	7	2.3	0.35	1.96	18
Sindh								
Overall	15.3	18.09	21.64	84	12.8	21.74	22.19	98
Cotton/wheat								
Rural	20.5	7.58	6.48	117	18.9	10.24	6.89	149
Urban	10.7	1.30	2.13	61	8.5	1.40	2.11	67
Rice/other								
Rural	24.3	7.38	5.32	139	20.6	8.92	5.50	162
Urban	5.9	2.60	7.71	34	2.9	1.80	7.89	23
N.W.F.P.								
Overall	9.6	6.83	13.02	52	8.5	8.36	12.93	65
Other N.W.F.P. (except Dera Ismail Khan)								
Rural	9.1	5.53	10.65	52	8.2	6.63	10.28	64
Urban	7.0	0.63	1.58	40	7.0	1.03	1.86	55
Balochistan								
Overall	27.5	9.20	6.12	150	7.3	2.41	4.33	56
Rural	28.5	9.09	5.59	163	7.9	2.38	3.81	61
Urban	17.0	0.50	0.51	97	2.3	0.10	0.56	17

Summaries	*1984-85*	*1987-88*
Households in poverty	2,101,140	1,158,572
Total households	11,989,788	12,041,326
Population in poverty	15,882,517	9,254,673
Total population	74,096,890	75,872,395

Source: Author's calculations.

A comparison of the values of this index between 1984-85 and 1987-88 indicates that the concentration of poor households increased in the rural sectors of five agroclimatic zones in three of the provinces. These agroclimatic zones, as we shall see later, had the lowest growth per capita in income and expenditure.

Income and expenditure inequalities

As we have seen, P_0, P_1, and P_2 were all small and falling between 1984-85 and 1987-88. Yet Gini coefficients increased, both for all households as a group and for households above the poverty line. They generally fell for households below the poverty line (so that P_2 fell faster than P_1), however, not only nationally, but within provinces and agroclimatic zones (table 20.4).

The probable explanation of the finding of both falling poverty and rising overall inequality (Gini coefficients) is that the rise of the vector of all incomes per person outweighed any homothetic rise in the inequality indicators. Two other explanations are also possible. First, lower-end inequality (the proportion of the GNP received by, say, the poorest 20 percent) could have declined, or increased proportionately less than the overall increase in inequality. Second, the prices of commodities consumed by the poor might have gone up less than prices of the GDP taken together. There is evidence that the first effect may have happened (Pakistan, Ministry of Finance 1988) and some evidence that the second effect may also have occurred, since the GDP deflator over this period rose by 17.3 percent as compared with a rise of 15.2 percent in the food price index (Pakistan, Ministry of Finance 1990).

Correlates of consumption per capita, poverty, and inequality

To test for correlation between consumption (and income) per capita and poverty and inequality, I computed Spearman's rank correlation coefficients and the associated t-statistics—as suggested by Kakwani and Subbarao (chapter 18 in this volume)—between rank orderings of poverty (both P_0 and P_2) and different measures of per capita expenditure (*EXP*) and income (*INC*) and their Gini coefficients, for each year and across years. The rankings of the rural and urban sectors of agroclimatic zones for the poverty measures, per capita income, per capita expenditure (*EXP*), and per capita expenditure on health (*HEXP*) and education (*EDEXP*) are presented in table 20.5; the Spearman's rank correlation coefficients are given in table 20.6. For poverty and inequality, the smallest value has rank 1. For all the income and expenditure variables, the highest value has rank 1. Six main findings emerge.

- The two measures of poverty, P_0 and P_2, are strongly and highly significantly correlated in both 1984-85 and 1987-88. The value of the Spearman's rank correlation coefficient is 0.96 for 1984-85 and 0.95 for 1987-88.
- A high rank by poverty and a low rank by income (and by total expenditure) are strongly and significantly correlated in each year. The Spearman's rank correlation coefficients were higher than 0.8 in each case in each year. The corresponding t-statistics were larger than 5.8.

Table 20.4 Income and expenditure inequality overall and for groups above and below poverty line, by province and agroclimatic zone, Pakistan, 1984-85 and 1987-88

| | Gini coefficients 1984-85 | | | | | | Gini coefficients 1987-88 | | | | | |
| | Overall | | Above | | Below | | Overall | | Above | | Below | |
Area	Expend.	Income	Expend.	Income	Expend.	Income	Expend.	Income	Expend.	Income	Expend.	Income
Pakistan												
Overall	0.302	0.338	0.271	0.312	0.099	0.150	0.338	0.341	0.323	0.325	0.087	0.086
Rural	0.305	0.341	0.308	0.312	0.113	0.165	0.325	0.327	0.303	0.305	0.091	0.090
Urban	0.394	0.420	0.367	0.395	0.098	0.124	0.451	0.453	0.438	0.440	0.114	0.117
Punjab												
Overall	0.302	0.329	0.267	0.299	0.095	0.146	0.356	0.358	0.335	0.337	0.087	0.082
Rice/wheat												
Rural	0.289	0.310	0.258	0.283	0.107	0.170	0.355	0.356	0.342	0.342	0.080	0.529
Urban	0.367	0.381	0.351	0.364	0.047	0.106	0.485	0.489	0.478	0.481	0.096	0.108
Mixed												
Rural	0.316	0.329	0.270	0.290	0.092	0.148	0.317	0.317	0.296	0.296	0.107	0.092
Urban	0.294	0.323	0.256	0.290	0.107	0.117	0.382	0.386	0.371	0.376	0.056	0.073
Cotton/wheat												
Rural	0.297	0.348	0.254	0.314	0.107	0.167	0.323	0.325	0.288	0.289	0.083	0.090
Urban	0.305	0.333	0.255	0.288	0.111	0.150	0.343	0.346	0.321	0.325	0.165	0.154
Low-intensity												
Rural	0.288	0.323	0.225	0.269	0.110	0.142	0.302	0.302	0.260	0.262	0.094	0.084
Urban	0.341	0.353	0.304	0.320	0.074	0.117	0.350	0.348	0.305	0.302	0.101	0.084
Barani												
Rural	0.266	0.285	0.255	0.275	0.096	0.120	0.323	0.328	0.316	0.322	0.056	0.066
Urban	0.469	0.515	0.463	0.510	0.057	0.061	0.375	0.374	0.369	0.368	0.032	0.004

Table 20.4 Income and expenditure inequality overall and for groups above and below poverty line, by province and agroclimatic zone, Pakistan, 1984-85 and 1987-88 (cont.)

Area	Gini coefficients 1984-85						Gini coefficients 1987-88					
	Overall		Above		Below		Overall		Above		Below	
	Expend.	Income	Expend.	Income	Expend.	Income	Expend.	Income	Expend.	Income	Expend.	Income
Sindh												
Overall	0.335	0.362	0.307	0.338	0.067	0.115	0.343	0.347	0.329	0.334	0.074	0.077
Cotton/wheat												
Rural	0.272	0.296	0.237	0.268	0.084	0.123	0.237	0.239	0.205	0.207	0.080	0.085
Urban	0.398	0.465	0.362	0.435	0.040	0.043	0.322	0.325	0.305	0.248	0.090	0.100
Rice/other												
Rural	0.308	0.345	0.282	0.327	0.072	0.130	0.217	0.219	0.201	0.203	0.045	0.042
Urban	0.370	0.380	0.344	0.356	0.068	0.096	0.428	0.431	0.415	0.418	0.122	0.097
N.W.F.P.												
Overall	0.259	0.345	0.226	0.319	0.060	0.116	0.285	0.287	0.275	0.277	0.047	0.045
Other N.W.F.P. (except Dera Ismail Khan)												
Rural	0.318	0.387	0.310	0.385	0.167	0.227	0.337	0.338	0.323	0.325	0.079	0.081
Urban	0.350	0.464	0.351	0.468	0.171	0.184	0.323	0.323	0.319	0.320	0.196	0.194
Balochistan												
Overall	0.296	0.338	0.242	0.296	0.249	0.246	0.292	0.297	1.001	0.281	0.134	0.147
Rural	0.340	0.374	0.309	0.351	0.197	0.169	0.343	0.347	0.314	0.318	0.207	0.198
Urban	0.440	0.493	0.425	0.483	0.130	0.216	0.394	0.397	0.390	0.393	0.055	0.032

Note: The poverty line used for each province represents the expenditure required in that province to consume 2,550 calories per capita per day.
Source: Author's calculations based on data from Pakistan, Federal Bureau of Statistics 1988a and 1990.

Table 20.5 Rank ordering of urban and rural sectors by poverty measures, income, expenditures, and inequality by agroclimatic zone, Pakistan, 1984-85 and 1987-88

Zone and sector	P_0 (1984)	P_0 (1987)	INC (1984)	EXP (1984)	EDEXP (1984)	HEXP (1984)	INC (1987)	EXP (1987)	EDEXP (1987)	HEXP (1987)	P_2 (1984)	P_2 (1987)	Gini INC (1984)	Gini INC (1987)	Gini EXP (1984)	Gini EXP (1987)
Rice/wheat Punjab																
Rural	8	8	15	13	11	10	7	7	10	8	9	8	3	13	4	13
Urban	5	5	16	4	3	7	2	2	3	7	2	5	13	18	14	18
Mixed Punjab																
Rural	14	13	16	16	12	17	13	13	12	4	15	14	6	4	9	4
Urban	10	12	9	9	7	15	6	6	4	9	12	12	5	15	5	15
Cotton/wheat Punjab																
Rural	18	16	17	17	14	13	15	15	14	14	17	16	9	7	6	8
Urban	13	11	13	15	8	11	11	11	5	12	14	9	7	10	7	11
Low-intensity Punjab																
Rural	16	18	18	18	15	12	18	18	15	15	18	18	4	3	3	3
Urban	11	17	10	10	6	16	14	14	8	17	11	17	10	12	12	12
Barani Punjab																
Rural	2	4	7	7	10	4	9	9	9	13	4	3	1	8	1	6
Urban	1	1	1	1	1	1	3	3	1	5	1	2	18	14	18	14

Table 20.5 Rank ordering of urban and rural sectors by poverty measures, income, expenditures, and inequality by agroclimatic zone, Pakistan, 1984-85 and 1987-88 (cont.)

Zone and sector	P_0 (1984)	P_0 (1987)	INC (1984)	EXP (1984)	EDEXP (1984)	HEXP (1984)	INC (1987)	EXP (1987)	EDEXP (1987)	HEXP (1987)	P_2 (1984)	P_2 (1987)	Gini INC (1984)	Gini INC (1987)	Gini EXP (1984)	Gini EXP (1987)
Cotton/wheat Sindh																
Rural	12	14	14	12	16	9	17	17	16	11	10	15	2	2	2	2
Urban	7	10	5	5	5	6	10	10	6	6	7	7	16	6	16	5
Rice/other Sindh																
Rural	15	15	12	11	18	8	16	16	17	10	13	13	8	1	8	1
Urban	3	3	2	2	2	2	1	1	2	1	3	6	12	17	15	17
Other N.W.F.P.																
Rural	6	9	8	8	13	5	12	12	13	3	6	11	14	9	10	9
Urban	4	6	3	3	4	3	5	5	7	2	5	4	15	5	13	7
Balochistan																
Rural	17	7	11	14	17	18	8	8	18	18	16	10	11	11	11	10
Urban	9	2	4	6	9	14	4	4	11	16	8	1	17	16	17	16

Note: P_0 is the percentage of the population below the poverty line; P_2 is the Foster-Greer-Thorbecke poverty measure with $\alpha = 2$. *HEXP* and *EDEXP* are per capita monthly expenditure on health and on education, respectively. Ranks are as follows: smallest P_0 has rank 1; smallest Gini coefficient has rank 1; and, for all *INC* and *EXP* variables, highest has rank 1.
Source: Author's calculations.

Table 20.6 Spearman's rank correlation coefficients between measures of poverty and per capita income and expenditure

Measures	Coefficient	t-statistic
P_0 (1984) and P_0 (1987)	0.761	4.686
INC (1984) and *INC* (1987)	0.783	5.040
EXP (1984) and *EXP* (1987)	0.754	4.597
P_0 (1984) and *INC* (1984)	0.825	5.830
P_0 (1987) and *INC* (1987)	0.882	7.500
P_0 (1984) and *EXP* (1984)	0.886	7.662
P_0 (1987) and *EXP* (1987)	0.882	7.500
P_0 (1984) and *HEXP* (1984)	0.789	5.145
P_0 (1984) and *EDEXP* (1984)	0.756	4.626
P_0 (1987) and *HEXP* (1987)	0.352	1.504
P_0 (1987) and *EDEXP* (1987)	0.513	2.390
P_0 (1984) and Gini *INC* (1984)	-0.368	-1.585
P_0 (1984) and Gini *EXP* (1984)	-0.401	-1.753
P_0 (1987) and Gini *INC* (1987)	-0.616	-3.129
P_0 (1987) and Gini *EXP* (1987)	-0.587	-2.902
Gini *INC* (1984) and *INC* (1984)	-0.713	-4.069
Gini *EXP* (1984) and *EXP* (1984)	-0.670	-3.608
Gini *INC* (1987) and *INC* (1987)	-0.810	-5.527
Gini *EXP* (1987) and *EXP* (1987)	-0.810	-5.527
P_0 (1984) and P_2 (1984)	0.963	14.262
P_0 (1987) and P_2 (1987)	0.950	12.231

Note: P_0 is the percentage of the population below the poverty line; P_2 is the Foster-Greer-Thorbecke poverty measure with $\alpha = 2$. *HEXP* and *EDEXP* are per capita monthly expenditure on health and on education, respectively. Ranks are as follows: smallest P_0 has rank 1; smallest Gini coefficient has rank 1; and, for all *INC* and *EXP* variables, highest has rank 1.
Source: Author's calculations.

- Higher per capita health and education expenditures are correlated with lower levels of poverty, except for per capita health expenditure and P_0 in 1987-88.
- Poverty (P_0) and inequality are negatively correlated, though the statistical significance is not always strong.
- Higher average income is significantly correlated with higher inequality.
- Rankings for poverty, income, and expenditure in 1984-85 are significantly correlated with rankings for these indicators in 1987-88.

Correlates of changes in income (expenditure), poverty, and inequality

There is a general interest in determining whether *changes* in income and expenditure are correlated with *changes* in poverty and inequality. To shed some light on this issue, I computed Spearman's rank correlation coefficients between rank orderings of such changes. Agroclimatic zones and their rural and urban sectors were ranked according to the percentage change between 1984-85 and 1987-88 in per capita expenditure and income, poverty, and inequality in both expenditure and income (table 20.7). The changes are ranked in terms of the absolute

Table 20.7 Rank ordering of agroclimatic zones and urban and rural sectors by changes in poverty, income, expenditures, and inequality between 1984-85 and 1987-88, Pakistan

Agroclimatic zone and sector	Change in per capita expenditure	Change in per capita income	Change in poverty (P_0)	Change in Gini coefficient for expenditure	Change in Gini coefficient for income
Rice/wheat Punjab					
Overall	2	2	7	2	2
Rural	3	3	6	4	5
Urban	1	1	9	1	1
Mixed Punjab					
Overall	8	9	10	11	7
Rural	10	10	12	18	11
Urban	4	5	8	3	3
Cotton/wheat Punjab					
Overall	12	11	13	9	12
Rural	13	13	14	10	14
Urban	7	7	4	8	8
Low-intensity Punjab					
Overall	18	18	25	16	16
Rural	16	17	24	14	13
Urban	19	16	26	15	10
Barani Punjab					
Overall	21	20	17	20	17
Rural	15	14	11	5	4
Urban	26	25	27	25	23
Cotton/wheat Sindh					
Overall	25	24	20	27	27
Rural	23	23	22	23	21
Urban	27	26	16	24	24
Rice/other Sindh					
Overall	14	12	15	12	9
Rural	22	22	18	26	26
Urban	11	8	5	6	6
Other N.W.F.P. (except Dera Ismail Khan)					
Overall	20	21	21	7	20
Rural	17	19	19	13	19
Urban	24	27	23	21	25
Balochistan					
Overall	5	6	2	19	18
Rural	6	4	3	17	15
Urban	9	15	1	22	22

Source: Author's calculations.

Table 20.8 Spearman's rank correlation coefficients between changes in poverty, income, expenditure, and inequality

	Income and poverty	Expenditure and poverty	Income and Gini coefficient of income	Poverty and Gini coefficient of income	Expenditure and Gini coefficient of expenditure
Coefficient	0.788	0.812	0.832	0.473	0.708
t-statistic	6.199	6.955	7.502	2.685	5.007

Source: Author's calculations.

values; the highest absolute percentage increase is ranked 1. Because the three measures of poverty move in the same direction, with the relative rankings of each measure more or less maintained over time, I opted to study the changes in poverty in terms of only the head count measure (P_0).

The Spearman's rank correlation coefficients are all statistically significant (table 20.8). Increase in average income—and, even more strongly, increase in average expenditure—is correlated with decline in poverty. Increase in income (expenditure) and growing inequality of income (expenditure) are strongly correlated. Declining poverty and increasing overall inequality are also correlated, though not as strongly. The t-statistic for this correlation is 2.685, which is significant at the 5 percent level. The other correlations are statistically significant at the 1 percent level.

The correlates suggest that at the *regional* level, higher income growth is accompanied by greater reduction in poverty and increased inequality. Thus, both trickle-down and trickle-up effects seem to be at work for Pakistan. This finding strongly supports the finding across countries (Lecaillon and others 1986) that inequality does indeed increase in early development (and decrease in late development)—the Kuznets hypothesis—but only between the wealthiest 5 percent of persons and others; the cross-national data show no systematic variation in inequality among the other 95 percent as average real income varies. This appears to parallel the findings for England between 1803 and 1867 reported by Pulak and Williamson (chapter 10 in this volume).

Real indicators of welfare outcomes

The foregoing analysis tends to confirm a number of trends. There has been a significant increase in private income and consumption per capita in Pakistan, accompanied by a decrease in the incidence and intensity of poverty, and a reduction in inequality *among the poor*. Thus, the relative position of the poorest has improved despite a rising Gini coefficient for Pakistan as a whole.

A large part of the reduction in poverty is due to the overall increase in cereal production following gains associated with the green revolution. Food grain production increased about 55 percent between 1970 and 1986 (Pakistan, Ministry of Food, Agriculture and Cooperatives 1991). Despite the rapid population growth, the average number of calories available per capita increased from about 2,200 calories per day in 1970 to 2,384 calories per day in 1988 (Burney and others 1990). The foregoing analysis and the earlier studies suggest that the poor were not completely excluded from these gains. The aggregate evidence may mask differences across regions and groups, however. The *incidence* of malnutrition remains rather high, especially among women and children (and, above all, among rural children), and the *intensity* of malnutrition is higher in urban areas than in rural areas. Malnutrution is also a significant problem among pregnant and lactating mothers, with iron, iodine, and vitamin A deficiencies prevalent in this group (Pakistan, National Institute of Health, Nutrition Division 1988).

Although access to decent health facilities remains inadequate, the real indicators of the welfare outcomes of growth and development in Pakistan reveal significant improvements. Life expectancy has increased significantly, from about 39 years in 1961 to 61 years in 1988 (table 20.9). Differences persist, however, between rural and urban areas and between the sexes, with life expectancy significantly higher in urban areas and among males (table 20.10). The crude death rate has declined significantly in the last three decades, and there has been an appreciable decline in the infant mortality rates. But here again the data from the different demographic surveys indicate differences among regions; as in India (Mitra 1978), infant mortality rates are significantly lower, and the decline in rates more pronounced, in urban areas than in rural areas (table 20.11).

Table 20.9 Real indicators of welfare outcomes, Pakistan, selected years, 1961-88

Year	Life expectancy (years)	Infant mortality rate (per 1,000)	Crude death rate (per 1,000)
1961	38.7	131	19.0[a]
1971	48.0[b]	106	10.6
1981	52.0	—	11.8
1985	58.6	112	10.0
1988	61.0	113	10.5

— Not available.
a. Rate is for 1962.
b. Figure is for 1972.
Source: Burney and others 1990.

Table 20.10 Life expectancy at birth by region and sex, Pakistan, 1976-79
(years)

Region	Survey[a]	Male	Female
Rural	PGS-II	55.1	54.8
Urban	PGS-II	60.5	58.4

a. PGS denotes Population Growth Survey.
Source: Burney and others 1990.

Table 20.11 Infant mortality rate, Pakistan, selected years, 1981-87
(per 1,000)

Survey[a]	All areas	Urban	Rural
PDS-1981	126.7	105.2	135.2
PDS-1985	115.9	90.2	126.3
PDS-1986	105.6	79.4	116.3
PDS-1987	104.9	79.0	113.5

a. PDS denotes Pakistan Demographic Survey.
Source: Burney and others 1990.

Table 20.12 Literacy rate, Pakistan, selected years, 1951-88

Year	Percent
1951	13.2
1961	18.4
1972	21.7
1981	26.2
1985	29.4
1988	32.1
Annual growth rate	2.4

Source: Burney and others 1990.

The literacy rate has continued to improve at an annual rate of about 2.4 percent despite population growth of about 3 percent (table 20.12). There are, however, considerable differences across regions, and literacy rates are significantly higher in urban areas and for males (table 20.13).

Access to basic services

Differences among regions and groups also show up in access to education, health care, and sanitation.[11] The differences observed in literacy rates are paralleled by the differences in school enrollment rates (table 20.14). Rural enrollment rates are significantly lower than urban rates. And enrollment rates for females are much lower than those for males, although they have increased much more rapidly despite the cultural and religious environment and the virtual absence of a tradition of sending girls for formal education (table 20.15).

Government expenditures on education as a proportion of GNP continue to be small. Increases in private incomes (and expenditures) seem to have shrunk the "food adequacy gap" much more effectively than increases in public sector activity have shrunk the corresponding gaps in access to education (and health care). Although primary enrollment rates (adjusted for underage, but not overage, children) increased from 37 percent to 48 percent between 1979-80 and 1984-85, the imbalance between rural and urban areas disadvantages the poor, since they are relatively concentrated in rural areas (Benson 1989). Primary enrollment rates are more than 80 percent higher in urban areas than in rural areas in Punjab; in Sindh urban rates are 65 percent higher than rural rates. Urban areas also account for a highly disproportionate share of girls attending primary school, so that poor *girls* are especially discriminated against. The differences in enrollment rates show up across microregions, not just between urban and rural areas. For example, in Sindh, the poor and less urbanized districts of Larkana, Jacobabad, and Nawabshah were characterized by lower primary enrollment rates, for both boys and girls, in part because fewer settlements in these districts had primary

Table 20.13 Literacy rates by province, Pakistan, 1972 and 1981
(percent; age 10 and older)

	1972			1981		
Province	Overall	Rural	Urban	Overall	Rural	Urban
Pakistan	21.7	14.3	41.5	26.2	17.3	47.1
Punjab	20.7	14.7	38.9	27.4	20.0	46.7
Sindh	30.2	17.6	47.4	31.5	15.6	50.8
N.W.F.P.	14.5	11.0	33.7	16.7	13.2	35.8
Balochistan	10.1	5.6	32.3	10.3	6.2	32.2

Source: Burney and others 1990.

**Table 20.14 Urban and rural enroll-
ment rates for population age 10 to
24, by province, Pakistan, 1981**
(percent)

Region	Rural	Urban
Pakistan	11.40	31.30
Punjab	12.83	28.37
Sindh	8.18	37.52
N.W.F.P.	11.09	24.55
Balochistan	5.14	22.25

Source: Burney and others 1990.

schools. Among those enrolled, the incidence of dropouts was also higher; fewer than half of the boys enrolled in the first grade in Larkana and Jacobabad made it to the fifth grade, compared with 80 percent or more in the more urbanized and affluent districts of Sukkur and Hyderabad (Benson 1989).

The enrollment rate for boys is at least double that for girls in every province; it is even higher in Punjab, the least poor province. In Punjab a finer mesh reveals that the rural male-female student ratio in five of the six poorest districts was higher (3 or 4 to 1) than in the more affluent districts (less than 2 to 1). In addition, there is a shortage of female teachers; the shortage is even more acute in poor areas. Benson (1989) points out that in Jacobabad (Sindh), for example, the ratio of male teachers to female teachers was 7 to 1; in Hyderabad the ratio was 2 to 1. Imbalances in enrollment and teachers are closely related; the small number of girls attending primary school means that the potential pool from which female teachers are drawn is likewise small. The resulting shortage of female teachers, in turn, inhibits expansion of female enrollment. Girls in poor districts fared even worse in terms of enrollment and transition rates.

Health expenditures as a proportion of GNP also continue to be small (table 20.16). There has been, on aggregate, a significant improvement in the provision of health facilities, with a substantial decrease in the population per hospital bed and per doctor. Rural health coverage improved significantly during the Sixth Plan (1983-88; table 20.17). The average distance from rural households to a health facility has decreased to just over 6 km, about a one-and-a-half-hour walk.

As with education, the overall improvement is soured by several factors unfavorable to the poor. First, because most of the poor live in rural areas, the concentration of medical facilities and personnel in the towns, especially the

**Table 20.15 Enrollment and educational expenditure, Pakistan, selected
years, 1961-88**
(thousands, except expenditure)

Year	Primary enrollment		Secondary enrollment		Expenditure as
	Male	*Female*	*Male*	*Female*	*percentage of GNP*
1961	1,710	455	134	25	1.28
1965	2,380	725	186	48	1.98
1972	3,140	1,190	302	76	2.59
1975	3,655	1,490	375	103	1.71
1981	3,769	1,839	394	133	1.58
1985	4,653	2,309	488	169	2.07
1988	5,425	2,708	552	201	3.04

Source: Burney and others 1990.

Table 20.16 Population per hospital and doctor, and health expenditure, Pakistan, selected years, 1961-88

Year	Population per hospital bed	Population per doctor	Total expenditure on health care as a share of GNP (percent)
1961	2,063	6,368	0.46
1971	1,804	4,137	0.39
1975	1,852	3,912	0.74
1981	1,731	3,144	0.68
1985	1,695	2,229	0.82
1988	1,610	1,880	1.02

Source: Burney and others 1990.

provincial capitals, clearly limits their availability to the poor. Rural health centers and basic health units—the only public sector facilities that the poor use more than proportionately as a first source of health care—are located primarily in rural areas, but they account for less than 15 percent of the government hospital beds in each province (Pakistan, Institute of Health Economics and Technology Assessment 1988). Therefore, rural households usually need to travel considerably farther to reach health facilities than do urban households. The average distance for rural households to a rural health center is more than 11 km, and to a basic health unit, more than 8 km, compared with an average distance for urban households of 2 to 3 km to the closest maternity and child health center.

Second, the distribution of facilities is quite uneven across provinces. In Sindh the physical coverage ratios (population to doctor and population to nurse, for example) are good—boosted no doubt by the presence of Karachi. But the average distance for rural households to a rural health facility in Sindh is twice that in Punjab and the N.W.F.P. Excluding Karachi, Sindh's rural population was more than four times its urban population. Yet rural facilities had only 20 percent as many doctors and 6 percent as many nurses as urban facilities.

Just as in education, these disparities are particularly disadvantageous to the poor. In Sindh, the only province for which district-level indicators for health are available, the poorest districts had considerably larger ratios of population to basic health units and to rural health centers than other districts. The use of these facilities was also lower in poor districts. Outpatient attendance rates were a third of those in more affluent districts, and hospital bed occupancy

Table 20.17 Doctors per 100,000 residents, and health facilities, Pakistan, 1982-83 and 1987-88

	1982-83	1987-88
Doctors per 100,000 residents		
Urban	72	44
Rural	4	12
Rural health centers	374	576
Basic health units	4,262	3,635

Note: The substantial decline in the number of doctors per 100,000 residents in the urban areas and the threefold increase in their numbers in the rural areas is, to some extent, the result of the changed government policy requiring doctors to register in the rural areas, rather than of genuine movements of doctors.
Source: Burney and others 1990.

rates only a fifth (see Jeffrey 1989; and Pakistan, Institute of Health Economics and Technology Assessment 1988).

Disparities between provinces and between urban and rural areas are both quantitative and qualitative. In rural and remote areas, not only is access more difficult but health facilities are more poorly staffed. Although no data are available, vacancy rates for medical personnel in rural areas are certainly higher than the national averages of 40 to 50 percent (more than 80 percent for female doctors, and about 40 percent for male doctors). Staff imbalances are also particularly acute between doctors and nurses, with some 3.5 doctors to 1 nurse the national average (Pakistan, Institute of Health Economics and Technology Assessment 1988). The unavailability of female personnel severely constrains women's access to health services, especially in rural areas.

There are also significant differences in access to safe drinking water and sanitation. Although the proportion of the population with access to these has increased considerably, the rural population still has far less access than the urban population (table 20.18).

Direct policy intervention for poverty alleviation

The alleviation of poverty has been an express goal of all development plans in Pakistan. Among the direct government measures to alleviate poverty have been minimum wage legislation, special rural development programs, subsidies on selected consumer goods and agricultural inputs, and such fiscal instruments as progressive income taxation, regional tax holidays, and higher public expenditure allocations for the development of backward regions.

These policies have not always achieved their objectives. Subsidies intended for the poor did not always reach the target population, as shown by the experience of the subsidized rural credit program. This program of markup-free production loans, introduced by the government in 1979, was intended for small farmers. The scheme grew rapidly, so that by 1986-87 more than 61 percent of all commercial bank loans to the rural sector were at zero nominal and explicit interest.[12] But Malik (1989), in a comparison of two large data sets based on national surveys conducted in 1973 and 1985, showed that access to institu-

Table 20.18 Population with access to safe drinking water and sanitation facilities, Pakistan, selected years, 1976-89
(percent)

	Drinking water			Sanitation		
Year	Total	Rural	Urban	Total	Rural	Urban
1976	22	11	54	—	—	22
1980	31	17	68	—	—	37
1980	44	25	79	20	—	53
1988	66	40	80	27	15	59
1989	69	44	80	32	19	66

— Not available.
Source: Burney and others 1990.

tional credit for small-farm households (those operating holdings of less than five acres) was generally limited to start with, and in nearly all cases worsened over time.

Public sector direct interventions presently include a few social insurance programs, restricted primarily to the formal and government sectors, and the quasi-official *zakat* and *ushr* system, which was introduced in 1979 to assist "the needy, the indigent, and the poor." *Zakat* is a wealth tax, assessed at 2.5 percent on financial assets owned by individuals, and *ushr* is a tax on agricultural produce, charged at 5 percent of crop output, from every landowner, lessee, leaseholder, and landholder. The lessons of the zakat and ushr system for poverty-oriented social security are discussed by Ahmed (chapter 15 in this volume).

The zakat and ushr collected are disbursed by zakat councils at three levels: national, provincial, and individual. Zakat deducted at source is paid into a central zakat fund, and a portion of the funds is disbursed to institutions operating at the national level or in more than one province. Zakat and ushr collections accounted in 1987-88 for only 0.3 percent of GNP, however, and disbursements to individuals and institutions have lagged behind even these modest collections.

Available evidence suggests that the program has had only a minimal effect on poverty. It is beset with a number of problems in its implementation, especially in the targeting of what are very small income subsidies to households.

Conclusions

This analysis of poverty in Pakistan indicates that the poverty gap (P_1) was small and falling over the period from 1984-85 to 1987-88, as were the head counts of poor households (P_0). The Foster-Greer-Thorbecke index (P_2), which assigns a higher weight to the welfare of the poorest, also improved over the period, in part because inequality among the poor fell. Yet inequality in income and expenditure per person among *all* households increased (as did inequality among households above the poverty line). These trends were all also found within provinces and agroclimatic zones. The most likely explanation for the clear and widespread fall in the poverty measures is that the rise in the vector of all incomes per person reduced poverty more than the worsening overall inequality increased it—though there are other possible explanations.

The marked decline in the incidence and intensity of poverty in Pakistan over the four years covered appears to continue a longer-term trend. This process has resulted from the growth in private incomes, and has occurred despite the increased inequality in income associated with that growth. "Public incomes" in the form of social services and infrastructure have also increased in aggregate. Although no detailed data are available with which to assess the trends in the nonincome indicators of welfare as they affect the poorest, the available information suggests that there has been a marked improvement, in aggregate, in the provision of social services. This improvement is indicated by the declining infant mortality rates and crude death rates and by improving trends in education and health statistics and in access to clean water and sanitation. Although there is evidence that these nonincome welfare improvements have favored more advantaged groups and regions—for example, males over females, and urban areas over rural areas—there are indications that the disadvantaged have nevertheless benefited from the improvements.

Although there has been a conscious effort at the policy level in Pakistan to redress poverty through the increased and better provision of social services, infrastructure, and public goods, such policies need to do much more to redress the inherent bias toward adult males and urban areas, and against remote places and disadvantaged groups. Allocations of public funds for education and health historically have been quite low. There is a need to increase these. Any increase in the public incomes of the poor will inevitably lead to even greater declines in poverty.

Notes

1. The poverty line is based on estimated calorie expenditure functions for 1984-85 in which calorie intake per 'adult equivalent is regressed upon the logarithm of total expenditure per adult equivalent. The cutoff is 2,550 calories per adult equivalent. Households are counted as poor if the expenditure per adult equivalent is below the poverty line.

2. The year 1984-85 had seen the installation of a government elected on a mandate of Islamizing the economy, deregulating private industrial activity, providing energy and physical infrastructure, and giving special attention to agriculture and rural development and the provision of health, education, and other social services.

3. The *Economic Survey 1984-85* states that estimates suggest that "virtually the entire population enjoys a consumption level which while low by comparison to richer countries is nevertheless adequate to meet minimal levels of nutrition and to provide for the basic necessities of life" (Pakistan, Ministry of Finance 1985: 7). By 1987-88, despite the relatively poor economic conditions in the country in that year, according to the *Economic Survey 1987-88*, the situation had improved so that "the average caloric intake by the lowest income groups has virtually reached the required nutritional standards," though "social services in the society have not reached the poor effectively" (Pakistan, Ministry of Finance 1988: 18).

4. See Akhtar (1988), on which some of the following is based, for a detailed review.

5. The calorie expenditure function was estimated separately for provinces, rural areas, towns, and cities. To confirm underlying differences in the function, dummy variables for towns and cities were used in a regression based on the pooled (rural and urban) sample. An additional regression with a dummy variable for cities was run on the pooled urban sample. The results suggested that a distinction in the functional relationships, both between rural and urban and between towns and cities, could be maintained with a high degree of confidence (Ercelawn 1990: 26).

6. Earlier studies using these data tapes have tended to clean the data for outliers. For example, Ercelawn uses only 15,399 out of the total of 16,541 households, throwing out more than 1,100 observations, approximately 7 percent of the sample. This study does not undertake such a cleaning exercise.

7. Ercelawn's calorie expenditure function for provinces (reported in Ercelawn 1990: 30), in which he uses both slope and intercept dummies for provinces, has an R^2 of 0.33, and all the estimated coefficients are significantly different from zero.

8. The overall provincial poverty lines estimated by Ercelawn from the pooled rural and urban populations are only marginally different from his rural poverty lines. His comparative table (Ercelawn 1990: 76, table A.4) shows the overall poverty lines only less than 3 percent different from the corresponding rural poverty lines in Punjab and the N.W.F.P. The difference in Sindh is about 10 percent. There is no difference in Balochistan. It is interesting to note that his overall line is actually about 3 percent lower than the rural line for the N.W.F.P.

9. Details of the commodity classification and weights are available from the author.

10. The differences from Ercelawn's estimate may be due to his data cleaning, which excluded more than 1,100 households from the analysis.

11. The author would like to thank Kee-Cheok Cheong for providing material on which part of this section is based.

12. There were several implicit charges, however, such as travel expenditures and bribes.

References

Adams, Dale, and Douglas Graham. 1981. "A Critique of Traditional Agricultural Credit Projects." *Journal of Development Economics* 8 (2):347-66.

Adelman, Irma. 1984. "Beyond Export-Led Growth." *World Development* 12 (9):937-49.

Adelman, Irma, and Cynthia Taft Morris. 1978. "Growth and Impoverishment in the Middle of the Nineteenth Century." *World Development* 6 (3):245-73.

African Business. 1989. "Zimbabwe Heads for Renewed Clash over Land Rights." (August):12-13.

Ahluwalia, M.S. 1978. "Rural Poverty and Agricultural Performance in India." *Journal of Development Studies* 14 (3):298-323.

———. 1985. "Rural Poverty, Agricultural Production and Prices: A Re-examination." In Mellor and Desai (1985).

Ahmad, Ehtisham. 1991. "Social Security and the Poor: Choices for Developing Countries." *World Bank Research Observer* 6 (1):105-27.

Ahmad, Ehtisham, and Christine Allison. 1990. "Poverty, Growth and Public Policy in Pakistan." Paper presented at World Bank/International Food Policy Research Institute Poverty Research Conference, October 25-28, 1989, Airlie, Virginia.

Ahmad, Ehtisham, Jean Drèze, J. Hills, and Amartya K. Sen, eds. 1991. *Social Security in Developing Countries.* Oxford: Clarendon Press.

Ahmad, Ehtisham, and Athar Hussain. 1991. "Public Action for Social Security in China." In Ahmad and others (1991).

Ahmad, Ehtisham, and Stephen Ludlow. 1989. "Poverty, Inequality and Growth in Pakistan." Background paper for *World Development Report 1990.* World Bank, Washington, D.C.

Ahmad, Ehtisham, and Nicholas Stern. 1987. "Alternative Sources of Government Revenue, Illustrations from India." In David Newbery and Nicholas Stern, eds., *The Theory of Taxation for Developing Countries.* New York: Oxford University Press.

———. 1991. *The Theory and Practice of Tax Reform in Developing Countries.* New York: Cambridge University Press.

Ahmad, Ehtisham, and Yan Wang. 1991. "Inequality and Poverty in China: Institutional Change and Public Policy, 1978-1987." *World Bank Economic Review* 5 (2):231-57.

Ahmed, Bashir. 1987. "Determinants of Contraceptive Use in Rural Bangladesh: The Demand for Children, Supply of Children, and Costs of Fertility Regulation." *Demography* 24 (3):361-73.

Ahmed, Raisuddin, and Mahabub Hossain. 1990. *Developmental Impact of Rural Infrastructure in Bangladesh.* International Food Policy Research Institute Research Report 83. Washington, D.C.

Aimei, Jia. 1988. "New Experiments with Elderly Care in Rural China." *Journal of Cross-Cultural Gerontology* 3 (3):139-48.

Akerlof, George. 1978. "The Economics of 'Tagging' as Applied to the Optimal Income Tax, Welfare Programs and Manpower Planning." *American Economic Review* 68 (1):8-19.

Akhtar, Shamshad. 1988. "Poverty in Pakistan." World Bank, Islamabad.

Akin, John S., Nancy Birdsall, and David M. de Ferranti. 1987. *Financing Health Services in Developing Countries: An Agenda for Reform.* Washington, D.C.: World Bank.

Alberts, Thomas. 1983. *Agrarian Reform and Rural Poverty: A Case Study of Peru.* Boulder, Colo.: Westview Press.

Alderman, Harold. 1986. *The Effect of Food Price and Income Changes on the Acquisition of Food by Low-Income Households.* Washington, D.C.: International Food Policy Research Institute.

————. 1987a. "Allocation of Goods Through Non-Price Mechanisms: Evidence on Distribution by Willingness to Wait." *Journal of Development Economics* 25 (1):105-24.

————. 1987b. *Cooperative Dairy Development in Karnataka, India: An Assessment.* International Food Policy Research Institute Research Report 64. Washington, D.C.

————. 1989. "The Impact of Changes in Income and Schooling on the Demand for Food Quantity and Quality in Rural Pakistan." International Food Policy Research Institute, Washington, D.C.

————. 1990. *Nutritional Status in Ghana and Its Determinants.* Social Dimensions of Adjustment in Sub-Saharan Africa Working Paper 3. Washington, D.C.: World Bank.

Alderman, Harold, and Marito Garcia. 1991. "Poverty, Household Food Security and Nutrition in Rural Pakistan: A Longitudinal Study." International Food Policy Research Institute, Washington, D.C.

————. Forthcoming. "Food Security and Health Security: Explaining the Levels of Nutritional Status in Pakistan." Economic Development and Cultural Change.

Alderman, Harold, and Paul Gertler. 1989. *The Substitutability of Public and Private Health Care for the Treatment of Children in Pakistan.* Living Standards Measurement Study Working Paper 57. Washington, D.C.: World Bank.

Alderman, Harold, George Mergos, and Roger Slade. 1987. "Cooperatives and the Commercialization of Milk Production in India: A Literature Review." Working Paper on Commercialization of Agriculture and Nutrition 2. International Food Policy Research Institute, Washington, D.C.

Alderman, Harold, and Joachim von Braun. 1984. *The Effects of the Egyptian Food Ration and Subsidy System on Income Distribution and Consumption.* International Food Policy Research Institute Research Report 45. Washington, D.C.

Allaudin, Talat. 1975. "Mass Poverty in Pakistan — A Further Study." *Pakistan Development Review* 14 (4): 431-50.

Almeida Reis, Jose Guilherme. 1989. "Salario Minimo e Distribuição de Renda." In *Perspectivas da Economia Brasileira 1989.* Rio de Janeiro: Instituto de Planejamento Economico e Social/Instituto de Pesquisas.

Altieri, Miguel, and Andrés Yurjevic. 1989. "The Latin American Consortium on Agroecology and Development: A New Institutional Arrangement to Foster Sustainable Agriculture Among Resource-Poor Farmers." *Bulletin of the Institute of Development Anthropology* 7 (1):17-19.

Anand, Sudhir, and Ravi Kanbur. 1990. "Public Policy and Basic Needs Provision: Intervention and Achievement in Sri Lanka." In Jean Drèze and Amartya K. Sen, eds., *The Political Economy of Hunger.* Vol. 3, *Endemic Hunger.* Oxford: Clarendon Press.

Anderson, Michael. 1972. "Household Structure and the Industrial Revolution: Mid 19th Century Preston in Comparative Perspective." In Peter Laslett, ed., *Household and Family in Past Times.* Cambridge: Cambridge University Press.

Armitage, Jane, and Richard H. Sabot. 1990. "Educational Policy and Intergenerational Mobility." In Knight and Sabot (1990).

Arun, T.K. 1989. "Poverty Ratio as a Devolution Criterion: A Note." *Economic and Political Weekly* 24:319-21.

Asha, P. 1986. "Trends in Growth and Pattern of Subsidies in Budgetary Operations of Central Government." *Reserve Bank of India Occasional Papers* 7 (2):209-50.

Ashenfelter, Orly, Angus Deaton, and George Solon. 1985. "Does It Make Sense to Collect Panel Data for Developing Countries?" Woodrow Wilson School Discussion Paper 119. Princeton University, Princeton, N.J.

Atkinson, A.B. 1986. "Social Insurance and Income Maintenance." LSE/STICERD Welfare State Program Paper 11. London School of Economics, London.

———. 1987a. "Income Maintenance and Social Insurance." In Alan J. Auerbach and Martin S. Feldstein, eds., *Handbook of Public Economics.* Vol. 2. Amsterdam: North-Holland.

———. 1987b. "On the Measurement of Poverty." *Econometrica* 55 (4):749-64.

———. 1989. *Poverty and Social Security.* London: Harvester Wheatsheaf.

———. 1990. "Poverty, Economic Performance and Income Transfer Policy in OECD Countries." Background paper for *World Development Report 1990.* World Bank, Washington, D.C.

Atkinson, A.B., and John Hills. 1991. "Social Security in Developed Countries: Are There Lessons for Developing Countries?" In Ahmad and others (1991).

Auzemary, Claire, and Michel Eresue. 1986. "El Proceso de Parcelación de las Cooperativas Agrarias del Valle de Cañeta." *Bulletin del Institut Français d'Etudes Andines* 15 (1-2):179-205.

Azariadis, Costas, and Allan Drazen. 1990. "Threshold Externalities in Economic Development." *Quarterly Journal of Economics* 105 (May):501-26.

Babu, S.C., R. Ayoade, and D. Bisika. 1990. "Agricultural Economy of Malawi: A Food Security and Nutrition Perspective." Working Paper 1, Food Security and Nutrition Monitoring Project. Malawi Ministry of Agriculture, Lilongwe.

Bardhan, Pranab K. 1970. "On the Minimum Level of Living and the Rural Poor." *Indian Economic Review* 5:129-36.

———. 1974a. "On the Incidence of Poverty in Rural India in the Sixties." In P.K. Bardhan and T.N. Srinivasan, eds., *Poverty and Income Distribution in India.* Calcutta: Statistical Publishing Society.

———. 1974b. "Poverty and Income Distribution in India: A Review." In P.K. Bardhan and T.N. Srinivasan, eds., *Poverty and Income Distribution in India.* Calcutta: Statistical Publishing Society.

———. 1983. "Regional Variations in the Rural Economy." *Economic and Political Weekly* 18 (July 23):1319-34.

———. 1984. *Land, Labor and Rural Poverty: Essays in Development Economics.* New York: Columbia University Press.

Bardhan, Pranab K., and Ashok Rudra. 1981. "Terms and Conditions of Labor Contracts in Agriculture: Results of a Survey in West Bengal in 1979." *Oxford Bulletin of Economics and Statistics* 43 (1):89-111.

Barraclough, Solon, ed. 1973. *Agrarian Structure in Latin America: A Resume of the CIDA Land Tenure Studies of Argentina, Brazil, Chile, Colombia, Ecuador, Guatemala, Peru.* Lexington, Mass.: Lexington Books.

———. 1982. *A Preliminary Analysis of the Nicaraguan Food System.* Geneva: United Nations Research Institute for Social Development.

Barraclough, Solon, and Arthur Domike. 1966. "Agrarian Structure in Seven Latin American Countries." *Land Economics* 42 (4):391-424.

Barrera, Albino. 1990. "The Role of Maternal Schooling and Its Interaction with Public Health Programs in Child Health Production." *Journal of Development Economics* 32 (1):69-91.

Barro, R.J. 1974. "Are Government Bonds Net Wealth?" *Journal of Political Economy* 82:1095-1117.

Barsky, Osvaldo. 1984. *La Reforma Agraria Ecuatoriana.* Quito: Corporacion Editora Nacional.

Barzel, Yoram. 1974. "A Theory of Rationing by Waiting." *Journal of Law and Economics* 17 (1):73-95.

Bastiansen, J. 1988. "The Peasantry and Post-Revolutionary Agrarian Policy in Nicaragua: 1979-1986." *EADI Bulletin* (Antwerp) 1:29-41.

Basu, D.D. 1983. *Introduction to the Constitution of India.* 10th ed. New Delhi: Prentice-Hall.

Bates, Robert H. 1981. *Markets and States in Tropical Africa: The Political Basis of Agricultural Policies.* Berkeley and Los Angeles: University of California Press.

Baumeister, Eduardo. 1985. "Estructuras Productivas y Reforma Agraria en Nicaragua." In R. Harris and C. Vilas, eds., *Revolución en Nicaragua.* Mexico, D.F: Ediciones Era.

Baumol, William J. 1959. *Theory of Economic Dynamics: An Introduction.* 2nd ed. New York: Macmillan.

Beaton, George. 1989. "Small but Healthy? Are We Asking the Right Question?" *Human Organization* 48 (Spring):30-39.

Beaton, G.H., and H. Ghassemi. 1982. "Supplementary Feeding Programs for Young Children in Developing Countries." *American Journal of Clinical Nutrition* 35 (supplement):864-916.

Becker, Charles M., Jeffrey G. Williamson, and Edwin S. Mills. 1992. *Indian Urbanization and Economic Growth since 1960.* Baltimore: Johns Hopkins University Press.

Becker, G.S. 1983. "A Theory of Competition among Pressure Groups for Political Influence." *Quarterly Journal of Economics* 98 (1):371-400.

Becker, Gary S., and H. Gregg Lewis. 1974. "Interaction Between the Quantity and Quality of Children." In T.W. Schultz, ed., *Economics of the Family.* Chicago: University of Chicago Press.

Behrman, Jere R. 1988. *Nutrition and Incomes: Tightly Wedded or Loosely Meshed?* Pew/Cornell Lecture Series on Food and Nutrition Policy. Ithaca, N.Y.: Cornell Food and Nutrition Policy Program.

Behrman, Jere R., and Nancy Birdsall. 1983. "The Quality of Schooling: Quantity Alone is Misleading." *American Economic Review* 73 (5):928-46.

———. 1987. "Communication on 'Returns to Education: A Further International Update and Implications.'" *Journal of Human Resources* 22 (4):603-10.

———. 1988a. "The Equity-Productivity Tradeoff: Public School Resources in Brazil." *European Economic Review* 32 (October):1585-1601.

———. 1988b. "The Reward for Good Timing: Cohort Effects and Earnings Functions for Brazilian Males." *Review of Economics and Statistics* 70 (1):129-35.

Behrman, Jere R., and Anil B. Deolalikar. 1987. "Will Developing Country Nutrition Improve with Income? A Case Study for Rural South India." *Journal of Political Economy* 95 (3):108-38.

———. 1990. "The Intrahousehold Demand for Nutrients in Rural South India: Individual Estimates, Fixed Effects and Permanent Income." *Journal of Human Resources* 25 (4):665-96.

Behrman, Jere R., Anil Deolalikar, and Barbara Wolfe. 1988. "Nutrients: Impacts and Determinants." *World Bank Economic Review* 2 (3):299-320.

Behrman, Jere R., and Barbara L. Wolfe. 1984. "More Evidence on Nutrition Demand: Income Seems Overrated and Women's Schooling Underemphasized." *Journal of Development Economics* 14 (January-February):105-28.

————. 1987. "How Does Mother's Schooling Affect the Family's Health, Nutrition, Medical Care Usage, and Household Sanitation?" *Journal of Econometrics* 36 (2):185-204.

Bell, Clive. 1977. "Alternative Theories of Sharecropping: Some Tests Using Evidence from Northeast India." *Journal of Development Studies* 13 (4): 317-46.

Bell, Clive, Peter Hazell, and Roger Slade. 1982. *Project Evaluation in Regional Perspective: A Study of an Irrigation Project in Northwest Malaysia.* Baltimore: Johns Hopkins University Press.

Benson, Christopher. 1989. "Primary Education for the Poor in Pakistan."

Berg, Alan. 1987. *Malnutrition: What Can Be Done? Lessons from World Bank Experience.* Baltimore: Johns Hopkins University Press.

Berrian, David, and Erik Thorbecke. 1992. "Budgetary Rules to Minimize Societal Poverty in a General Equilibrium Context." *Journal of Development Economics* (Netherlands) 39(October):189-205.

Berry, Albert, and Richard H. Sabot. 1981. "Labor Market Performance in Developing Countries: A Survey." In Paul Streeten and Richard Jolly, eds., *Recent Issues in World Development.* Oxford: Pergamon Press.

Berry, R. Albert, and William R. Cline. 1979. *Agrarian Structure and Productivity in Developing Countries.* Baltimore: Johns Hopkins University Press.

Besley, Timothy J. 1990. "Means Testing Versus Universal Provision in Poverty Alleviation Programs." *Economica* 57 (225):119-29.

Besley, Timothy J., and Stephen Coate. 1991. "Public Provision of Private Goods and the Redistribution of Income." *American Economic Review* 81 (4):979-84.

————. 1992. "Workfare vs. Welfare: Incentive Arguments for Work Requirements in Poverty-Alleviation Programs." *American Economic Review* 82 (1):249-61.

Besley, Timothy J., and Ravi Kanbur. 1988. "Food Subsidies and Poverty Alleviation." *Economic Journal* 98 (392):701-19.

————. 1990. "The Principles of Targeting." Policy Research Working Paper 385. World Bank, Washington, D.C.

Beveridge, Lord. 1942. *Social Insurance and Allied Services.* Cmnd. 6404. London: HMSO.

Bhaduri, Amit. 1973. "A Study in Agricultural Economic Backwardness under Semi-Feudalism." *Economic Journal* 83 (1):120-37.

Bhalla, Sheila. 1987. "Trends in Employment in Indian Agriculture, Land and Asset Distribution." *Indian Journal of Agricultural Economics* 42 (4):537-60.

Bhatt, P.N. Mari. 1989. "Mortality and Fertility in India, 1881-1961: A Reassessment." In Tim Dyson, ed., *India's Historical Demography.* London: Curzon.

Bhattacharya, Nikhilesh, and G.S. Chatterjee. 1974. "On Disparities in Per Capita Household Consumption in India." In P.K. Bardhan and T.N. Srinivasan, eds., *Poverty and Income Distribution in India.* Calcutta: Statistical Publishing Society.

Bhattacharya, Nikhilesh, G.S. Chatterjee, and Padmaja Pal. 1988. "Variations in Level of Living Across Regions and Social Groups in Rural India, 1963/64 and 1973/74." In T.N. Srinivasan and P.K. Bardhan, eds., *Rural Poverty in South Asia.* New York: Columbia University Press.

Bhattacharya, Nikhilesh, P.D. Joshi, and A.B. Roychoudhury. 1980. "Regional Price Indices Based on Nss 28th Round Consumer Expenditure Survey Data." *Sarvekshana* 3:107-21.

Bienen, Henry S., and Mark Gersovitz. 1985. "Economic Stabilization, Conditionality and Political Stability." *International Organization* 39 (4):728-54.

Binswanger, Hans P. 1987. "Fiscal and Legal Incentives with Environmental Effects on the Brazilian Amazon." World Bank, Agricultural and Rural Development Department, Research Unit, Washington, D.C.

Binswanger, Hans P., and M. Elgin. 1988. "What Are the Prospects for Land Reform?" In A. Maunder and A. Valdez, eds., *Agriculture and Governments in an Interdependent World, Proceedings of the Twentieth Conference of Agricultural Economists, 1988.* Brookfield, Vt.: Gower.

Binswanger, Hans P., Y. Mundlak, M.-C. Yang, and A. Bowers. 1985. "Estimation of Aggregate Supply Response." Discussion Paper. World Bank, Agricultural Research Unit, Washington, D.C.

Binswanger, Hans P., Shahidur R. Khandker, and Mark R. Rosenzweig. 1989. "How Infrastructure and Financial Institutions Affect Agricultural Output and Investment in India." Policy Research Working Paper 163. World Bank, Washington, D.C.

Binswanger, Hans P., and Mark Rosenzweig. 1984. *Contractual Agreements, Employment and Wages in Rural Labor Markets: A Critical Review.* New York: Agricultural Development Council.

————. 1986. "Behavioral and Material Determinants of Production Relations in Agriculture." *Journal of Development Studies* 22 (3):503-39.

Binswanger, Hans P., and S.V.R. Shetty. 1977. "Economic Aspects of Weed Control in the Semi-arid Tropical Areas of India." Occasional Paper 13. International Crops Research Institute for the Semi-Arid Tropics (ICRISAT), Economic Department, Hyderabad, India.

Binswanger, Hans P., Maw-Cheng Yang, Alan Bowers, and Yair Mundlak. 1987. "On the Determinants of Cross-Country Aggregate Supply." *Journal of Econometrics* 36:111-31.

Birdsall, Nancy. 1988. "Economic Approaches to Population Growth." In Chenery and Srinivasan (1988).

————. 1989. "Thoughts on Good Health and Good Government." *Daedalus* 118 (1):89-124.

————. 1990. "Public Spending on Higher Education in Developing Countries: Too Much or Too Little?" World Bank, Country Economics Department, Washington, D.C. Draft.

————. 1992. "Pragmatism, Robin Hood and Other Themes: Good Government and Social Well-Being in Developing Countries." In L.C. Chen, A.M. Kleinman, and N.C. Wade, eds., *Social Dimensions of Health Transitions: An International Perspective.* New York: Oxford University Press.

Birdsall, Nancy, and Lauren A. Chester. 1987. "Contraception and the Status of Women: What is the Link?" *Family Planning Perspectives* 19 (1):14-18.

Birdsall, Nancy, and Charles C. Griffin. 1988. "Fertility and Poverty in Developing Countries." *Journal of Policy Modeling* 10 (1):29-56.

Blankstein, Charles S., and Clarence Zuvekas, Jr. 1973. "Agrarian Reform in Ecuador: An Analysis of Past Efforts and the Development of a New Approach." *Economic Development and Cultural Change* 22 (1):73-94.

Blinder, Alan S. 1987. *Hard Heads, Soft Hearts.* Reading, Mass.: Addison Wesley.

Bliss, C.J., and Nicholas H. Stern. 1982. *Palanpur: The Economy of an Indian Village.* Oxford: Clarendon Press.

Bond, M. (1983). "Agricultural Response to Price in Sub-Saharan African Countries." *IMF Staff Papers* 30 (4).

Bonelli, Regis, and Guilherme Luis Sedlacek. 1989. "Distribuição de Renda: Evolução no Ultimo Quarto de Seculo." In Guilherme Luis Sedlacek and Ricardo Paes de Barros, eds., *Mercado de Trabalho e Distribuição de Renda: Uma Coletânea.* IPEA, Série Monográfica. Rio de Janeiro: Instituto de Planejamento Economico e Social/Instituto de Pesquisas.

Borcherding, Thomas. 1985. "The Causes of Government Expenditure Growth: A Survey of the U.S. Evidence." *Journal of Public Economics* 28 (December):359-82.

Borcherding, Thomas E., Werner W. Pommerehne, and Friedrich Schneider. 1982. "Comparing the Efficiency of Private and Public Production: The Evidence from Five Countries." *Zeitschrift für National–Ökonomie* 42 (supplement 2):127-56.

Bouis, Howarth E., and Lawrence J. Haddad. 1990. *Effects of Agricultural Commercialization on Land Tenure, Household Resource Allocation, and Nutrition in the Philippines.* International Food Policy Research Institute Research Report 79. Washington, D.C.

———. 1992. "Are Estimates of Calorie-Income Elasticities Too High? A Recalibration of the Plausible Range." *Journal of Development Economics* 39(2): 333-64.

Boulier, Bryan L. 1985. "Evaluating Unmet Need for Contraception." In R.A. Bulatao and R.D. Lee, eds., *Determinants of Fertility in Developing Countries.* New York: Academic Press.

Bourguignon, Francois. 1991. "Optimal Poverty Reduction, Adjustment and Growth: An Applied Framework." *World Bank Economic Review* 5 (2):315-38.

Bowley, Arthur L., and A.R. Burnett-Hurst. 1915. *Livelihood and Poverty.* London: Ratan Tata Foundation, Bell and Sons.

Bowley, Arthur L., and Margaret H. Hogg. 1925. *Has Poverty Diminished?* London: King and Son.

Boyer, George B. 1990. *An Economic History of the English Poor Law, 1750-1850.* Cambridge: Cambridge University Press.

Boyer, George B., and Jeffrey G. Williamson. 1989. "A Quantitative Assessment of the Fertility Transition in England, 1851-1911." *Research in Economic History* 12:93-117.

Braverman, Avishay, and Ravi Kanbur. 1987. "Urban Bias and the Political Economy of Agricultural Reform." *World Development* 15 (9):1179-87.

Braverman, Avishay, and Joseph E. Stiglitz. 1982. "Sharecropping and the Interlinkage of Agrarian Markets." *American Economic Review* 72 (4):695-715.

Buchanan, James M. 1967. *Fiscal Institutions and Individual Choice.* Chapel Hill: University of North Carolina Press.

Buchanan, James M., Robert D. Tollison, and Gordon Tullock. 1980. *Toward a Theory of the Rent-Seeking Society.* College Station: Texas A&M University Press.

Burger, Susan, and Steven Esrey. 1989. "Water and Sanitation: Health Benefits to Children." Paper prepared for Cornell/Rockefeller Workshop on Beyond Child Survival, July. Cornell University, Department of Nutrition, Ithaca, N.Y.

Burney, Nadeem A., and others. 1990. "Human Development Report on Pakistan." Pakistan Institute of Development Economics, Islamabad.

Burtless, Gary. 1986. "Public Spending for the Poor: Trends, Prospects and Economic Limits." In S.H. Danziger and D.H. Weinberg, eds., *Fighting Poverty.* Cambridge, Mass.: Harvard University Press.

Byerlee, Derek. 1973. "Indirect Employment and Income Distribution Effects of Agricultural Development Strategies: A Simulation Approach Applied to Nigeria." African Rural Employment Paper 9. Michigan State University, Department of Agricultural Economics, East Lansing.

Cacciamali, Maria Cristina. 1989. "Emprego no Brasil Durante a Primeira Metade da Decada de 80." In Guilherme Luis Sedlacek and Ricardo Paes de Barros, eds., *Mercado de Trabalho e Distribuição de Renda: Uma Coletânea.* IPEA, Série Monográfica. Rio de Janeiro: Instituto de Planejamento Economico e Social/Instituto de Pesquisas.

CAHI (Central American Historical Institute). 1985. "Los Campesinos Nicaragüensas Dan un Nuevo Gira a la Reforma Agraria." *Envio* 51:1c-19c.

Calloway, Doris, Suzanne Murphy, and George Beaton. 1988. *Food Intake and Human Function: A Cross-Project Perspective.* Berkeley: University of California Press.

Cardoso, Eliana, and Daniel Dantas. 1989. "Brazil After 1982: Adjusting or Accommodating?" Tufts University, Boston.

Carlson, Beverly, and Teresa Wardlaw. 1990. "A Global, Regional and Country Assessment of Child Malnutrition." UNICEF Staff Working Paper 7. New York.

Carlyle, T. 1852. *Past and Present.* Reprint. London: Dent, 1967.

Carr, S.J. 1988. "Modification and Extension of the National Rural Development Program." Paper presented at the Symposium on Agricultural Policies for Growth and Development, Magnochi, Malawi, October 31-November 4. World Bank, Washington, D.C.

Carter, Michael R. 1984a. "Identification of the Inverse Relationship between Farm Size and Productivity: An Empirical Analysis of Peasant Agricultural Production." *Oxford Economic Papers* 36 (1):131-45.

————. 1984b. "Resource Allocation and Use under Collective Rights and Labor Management in Peruvian Coastal Agriculture." *Economic Journal* 94 (4):826-46.

————. 1985. "Parcelación y Productividad del Sector Reformado: Cuestiones Teóricas y una Eficiente Alternativa Institucional Mixta." In A. Gonzales and H. Torre, eds., *Las Parcelaciones de las Cooperativas Agrarias del Perú*. Chiclayo, Peru: Centro de Estudios Sociales - Solidaridad.

————. 1987. "Risk Sharing and Incentives in the Decollectivization of Agriculture." *Oxford Economic Papers* 39 (2):577-95.

————. 1988. "Equilibrium Credit Rationing of Small Farm Agriculture." *Journal of Development Economics* 28 (1):83-103.

————. 1990. "The Microeconomics of Class Differentiation and Agrarian Structural Evolution in Imperfect Market Environments: Theory and Analysis of Agricultural Decollectivization in Peru." Paper presented at conference on the Theory of Rural Organization and Agricultural Development Policy, Annapolis, Md. University of Wisconsin, Madison.

Carter, Michael R., and Elena Alvarez. 1989. "Changing Paths: The Decollectivization of Agrarian Reform Agriculture in Coastal Peru." In W.C. Thiesenhusen, ed., *Searching for Agrarian Reform in Latin America*. Boston: Unwin Hyman.

Carter, Michael R., and John Kalfayan. 1989. "A General Equilibrium Exploration of Agrarian Class Structure and Production Relations." University of Wisconsin-Madison Agricultural Economics Staff Paper 279 (revised).

Carter, Michael R., and Karen Luz. 1990. "What Is To Be Done About Land Reform Cooperatives in Nicaragua?" University of Wisconsin-Madison Department of Agricultural Economics Staff Paper 318.

Carter, Michael R., and W.C. Walker. 1989. "The Evolution of Agrarian Structure in Latin America: An Econometric Investigation of Brazil." University of Wisconsin-Madison Agricultural Economics Staff Paper 298 (revised August 1989).

Carter, Michael R., Keith Wiebe, and Benoit Blarel. 1989. "Tenure Security for Whom: An Econometric Analysis of the Differential Impacts of Land Titling in Kenya." Land Tenure Center Research Report, University of Wisconsin-Madison.

CASAR (Comité de Acción para la Seguridad Alimentaria Regional). 1986. *National Food Programs in Latin America and the Caribbean: A Response to the Economic Crisis*. Buenos Aires.

Case, Anne. 1987. "On the Use of Spatial Autoregressive Models in Demand Analysis." Woodrow Wilson School Discussion Paper 135. Princeton University, Princeton, N.J.

Castañeda, Tarusio. 1985. "Determinantes del Descenso de la Mortalidad Infantil en Chile, 1975-1983." *Cuadernos de Economía* 2 (66):195-214.

Castillo, Leonardo, and David Lehmann. 1983. "Agrarian Reform and Structural Change in Chile 1965-1979." In A.K. Ghose, ed., *Agrarian Reform in Contemporary Developing Countries*. New York: St. Martin's Press.

Cavallo, Domingo, and Yair Mundlak. 1982. *Agriculture and Economic Growth in an Open Economy: The Case of Argentina.* International Food Policy Research Institute Research Report 36. Washington, D.C.

Centre for Social Research. 1988. *The Characteristics of Nutritionally Vulnerable Sub-Groups within the Smallholder Sector of Malawi: A Report from the 1980/81 NSSA.* Zomba: Center for Social Research, University of Malawi.

CEPAL (Comisión Económica para América Latina). 1989a. *Antecedentes Estadísticos de la Distribución del Ingreso: Brasil 1960-1983.* Santiago: United Nations.

————. 1989b. "Ronda de Uruguay. Hacia una Posición Latino Americana sobre los Productos Agrícolas." *Comercio Exterior* 39 (6): 458-84.

Cerqueira, Maria Teresa, and Christine M. Olson. Forthcoming. "Nutrition Education in Developing Countries: An Examination of Recent Successful Projects." In Per Pinstrup-Andersen, David Pelletier, and Harold Alderman, eds., *Beyond Child Survival: Enhancing Child Growth and Nutrition in Developing Countries.* Ithaca, N.Y.: Cornell University Press.

Chaloult, Y. 1988. "Governo de Transição com Velhas Praticas: O que Sobra par o Trabalhador do Campo?" Paper presented to the VII International Congress of Rural Sociology, Bologna, Italy, June 26-July 1.

Chavez, Arturo. 1988. "A Propósito de las Parcelaciones." *Debate Agrario* 3:123-34.

Chayanov, A.V. 1967. *The Theory of Peasant Economy.* Edited by D. Thorner, B. Kerblay, and R.E.F. Smith. Homewood, Ill.: Irwin and Co.

Chen, L.C., A.K.M. Chowdhury, and S.L. Huffman. 1980. "Anthropometric Assessment of Energy-Protein Malnutrition and Subsequent Risk of Mortality Among Preschool-Aged Children." *American Journal of Clinical Nutrition* 33 (8):1836-45.

Chenery, Hollis B., and T.N. Srinivasan, eds. 1988. *Handbook of Development Economics.* Amsterdam: North-Holland.

Chipande, Graham. 1983. "Socio-Economic Aspects of Female Headed Households and Rural Development Efforts: With Special Reference to the Phalomba Area of Southern Malawi." Chancellor College, University of Malawi.

Chomitz, Kenneth M., and Nancy Birdsall. 1991. "Incentives for Small Families: Concepts and Issues." *Proceedings of the World Bank Annual Conference on Development Economics 1990.* Supplement to *World Bank Economic Review and World Bank Research Observer.*

Christiansen, Robert E., and J.G. Kydd. 1987. "The Political Economy of Agricultural Policy Formulation in Malawi, 1964-1985." World Bank, Southern Africa Department, Washington, D.C.

Chuta, Enyinna, and Carl Liedholm. 1979. "Rural Nonfarm Employment: A Review of the State of the Art." MSU Rural Development Paper 4. Michigan State University, Department of Agricultural Economics, East Lansing.

CIERA (Centro de Investigaciones y Estudios de la Reforma Agraria). 1984. *Historia Agraria de las Segovias Occidentales.* Managua.

————. 1985a. "Estudio de las Cooperativas de Producción de Santa Lucía, Petacatepe, Los Ébanos, Masaya y Santa Teresa." Managua: Centro de Investigaciones y Estudios de la Reforma Agraria.

————. 1985b. "Problemas y Perspectivas de la Migración Campo-Ciudad." *Revolución y Desarollo* 3.

————. 1989. *Reforma Agraria en Nicaragua.* Vol. 10. Managua: Centro de Investigaciones y Estudios de la Reforma Agraria.

Clark, Stephen, Richard Hemming, and David Ulph. 1981. "On Indices for the Measurement of Poverty." *Economic Journal* 91 (June):514-26.

Cline, William R. 1975. "Policy Instruments for Rural Income Redistribution." Paper prepared for the Princeton University-Brookings Institution project on Income Distribution in Less Developed Countries. Princeton University, Department of Economics, Princeton, N.J.

Coale, A.J., and E.M. Hoover. 1958. *Population Growth and Economic Development in Low-Income Countries.* Princeton, N.J.: Princeton University Press.

Coate, Stephen. 1989. "Cash versus Direct Food Relief." *Journal of Development Economics* 30 (2):199-224.

Coder, John, Lee Rainwater, and Timothy Smeeding. 1989. "Inequality among Children and the Elderly in Ten Modern Nations: The United States in an International Context." *American Economic Review* 79 (May):320-24.

Cohen, John M. 1975. "Effects of Green Revolution Strategies on Tenants and Small Landowners in the Chilalo Region of Ethiopia." *Journal of Developing Areas* 9 (3):335-58.

Collier, Paul, and Deepak Lal. 1980. *Poverty and Growth in Kenya.* World Bank Staff Working Paper 389. Washington, D.C.

Commander, Simon, ed. 1989. *Structural Adjustment and Agriculture: Theory and Practice in Africa and Latin America.* London: Overseas Development Institute.

Connell, John. 1976. *Migration from Rural Areas: The Evidence from Village Studies.* Delhi: Oxford University Press.

Corbo, Vittorio, Stanley Fischer, and Steven Webb. 1992. *Adjustment Lending Revisited: Policies to Restore Growth.* Washington, D.C.: World Bank.

Cornia, Giovanni A., Richard Jolly, and Frances Stewart, eds. 1987. *Adjustment with a Human Face.* 2 volumes. Oxford: Clarendon Press.

Coutinho, Rui. 1989. "A Portfolio Allocation Model for Brazil." World Bank, Washington, D.C.

Cox, Donald, and Emmanuel Jimenez. 1989. "Private Transfers and Public Policy in Developing Countries: A Case Study for Peru." Policy Research Working Paper 365. World Bank, Washington, D.C.

————. 1990. "Achieving Social Objectives Through Private Transfers: A Review." *World Bank Research Observer* 5 (2):205-18.

Cramer, Herold. 1946. *Mathematical Methods of Statistics.* Princeton, N.J.: Princeton University Press.

Dandekar, V.M., and Nilakanth Rath. 1971. "Poverty in India." Pune: Indian School of Political Economy.

Dasgupta, Biplab, with Roy L. Laishley, Henry Lucas, and Brian Mitchell. 1977. *Village Society and Labor Use.* Delhi: Oxford University Press.

Datt, Gaurav, and Martin Ravallion. 1990. "Growth and Distribution Components of Changes in Poverty Indices." World Bank, Population and Human Resources Department, Washington, D.C.

————. 1991. "Growth and Redistribution Components of Changes in Poverty Measures: A Decomposition with Applications to Brazil and India in the 1980s." World Bank, Population and Human Resources Department, Washington, D.C. (Also published in *Journal of Development Economics* 38:275-95, 1992.)

Datta, Gautam, and Jacob Meerman. 1980. *Household Income or Household Income Per Capita in Welfare Comparisons?* World Bank Staff Working Paper 378. Washington, D.C.

Davison, Jean. 1988. "Who Owns What? Land Registration and Tensions in Gender Relations of Production in Kenya." In Jean Davison, ed., *Agriculture, Women and Land: The African Experience.* Boulder, Colo., and London: Westview Press.

Deaton, Angus. 1987. "Estimation of Own- and Cross-Price Elasticities from Household Survey Data." *Journal of Econometrics* 36 (1):7-30.

Deaton, Angus, and Nicholas H. Stern. 1985. "Optimally Uniform Commodity Taxes, Taste Differences and Lump-Sum Grants." Discussion Paper 123. Princeton University, Woodrow Wilson School, Research Program in Development Studies, Princeton, N.J.

Deere, Carmen D., and Peter Marchetti. 1981. "The Worker-Peasant Alliance in the First Year of the Nicaraguan Agrarian Reform." *Latin American Perspectives* 8 (2):40-73.

de Janvry, Alain. 1981. *The Agrarian Question and Reformism in Latin America.* Baltimore: Johns Hopkins University Press.

de Janvry, Alain, and Raúl Garcia. 1988. "Rural Poverty and Environmental Degradation in Latin America: Causes, Effects, and Alternative Solutions." International Fund for Agricultural Development, Rome.

de Janvry, Alain, Robin Marsh, Dave Runsten, Elisabeth Sadoulet, and Carol Zabin. 1989. *Rural Development in Latin America: An Evaluation and a Proposal.* San José, Costa Rica: Inter-American Institute for Cooperation on Agriculture.

de Janvry, Alain, Dave Runsten, and Elisabeth Sadoulet. 1987. *Technological Innovations in Latin American Agriculture.* San José, Costa Rica: Inter-American Institute for Cooperation on Agriculture.

de Janvry, Alain, and Elisabeth Sadoulet. 1988. "Alternative Approaches to the Political Economy of Agricultural Policies: Convergence of Analytics, Divergence of Implications." Paper for 20th International Conference of Agricultural Economists, Buenos Aires, Argentina, August. University of California at Berkeley.

————. 1989. "Efficiency, Welfare Effects, and Political Feasibility of Alternative Antipoverty and Adjustment Programs." Working Paper 6. OECD Development Center, Paris.

de Janvry, Alain, Elisabeth Sadoulet, and Linda Wilcox. 1989. "Land and Labor in Latin American Agriculture from the 1950s to the 1980s." *Journal of Peasant Studies* 16 (3):396-424.

de Janvry, Alain, and K. Subbarao. 1986. *Agricultural Price Policy and Income Distribution in India.* Delhi: Oxford University Press.

de Kruijk, Hans, and Myrna van Leeuwen. 1985. "Changes in Poverty and Income Inequality in Pakistan during the 1970's." *Pakistan Development Review* 24 (3 and 4):407-19.

Delgado, Christopher. 1989. "Why is Rice and Wheat Consumption Increasing in West Africa?" Paper for 19th European seminar of the European Association of Agricultural Economists, Montpellier, France, June. International Food Policy Research Institute, Washington, D.C.

Demsetz, Harold. 1982. "The Growth of Government." In de Vries Lectures, no. 4, *Economic, Legal and Political Dimensions of Competition.* Amsterdam: North-Holland.

Denslow, David, Jr., and William Tyler. 1983. *Perspectives on Poverty and Income Inequality in Brazil: An Analysis of the Changes during the 1970s.* World Bank Staff Working Paper 601. Washington, D.C.: World Bank.

Deolalikar, Anil B. 1988. "Do Health and Nutrition Influence Labor Productivity in Agriculture? Econometric Estimates for Rural South India." *Review of Economics and Statistics* 70 (2).

de Soto, Hernando. 1989. *The Other Path: The Invisible Revolution in the Third World.* New York: Harper and Row.

Dev, S. Mahendra. 1985. "Direction of Change in Performance of All Crops in Indian Agriculture in Late 1970s." *Economic and Political Weekly* 20 (December 21-28):A130-38.

————. 1988. "Regional Disparities in Agricultural Labor Productivity and Rural Poverty in India." *Indian Economic Review* 23:167-205.

Dickerman, Carol W., and Peter C. Bloch. 1989. "Land Tenure and Agricultural Productivity in Malawi." Land Tenure Center, University of Wisconsin, Madison. Draft.

Dorner, Peter, and Don Kanel. 1971. "The Economic Case for Land Reform." In Peter Dorner, ed., *Land Reform.* Madison: Land Economics for the Land Tenure Center, University of Wisconsin-Madison.

Downs, Anthony. 1982. "Comment on Tullock." In Garfinkel (1982).

Drèze, Jean. 1990a. "Famine Prevention in India." In Jean Drèze and Amartya K. Sen, eds., *The Political Economy of Hunger.* Vol. 2, *Famine Prevention.* Oxford: Clarendon Press.

————. 1990b. "Poverty in India and the IRDP Delusion." *Economic and Political Weekly* 25 (September 29):A95-104.

————. 1990c. "Widows in Rural India." Development Economics Research Program Discussion Paper. London School of Economics, London.

Drèze, Jean, and Amartya K. Sen. 1989. *Hunger and Public Action.* Oxford: Clarendon Press.

Duncan, A. 1990. "The Impact of Pricing Policy on Tobacco Tenancy in Malawi." Oxford University, Food Studies Group. Draft.

ECLAC (Economic Commission for Latin America and the Caribbean). 1988. *Statistical Yearbook for Latin America and the Caribbean.* Santiago.

Edirisinghe, Neville. 1987. *The Food Stamp Scheme in Sri Lanka: Costs, Benefits, and Options for Modification.* International Food Policy Research Institute Research Report 58. Washington, D.C.

————. 1988. "Food Subsidy Changes in Sri Lanka: The Short-Run Effect on the Poor." In Pinstrup-Andersen (1988).

Elhassan, A. Mohammed. 1988. "The Encroachment of Large-scale Mechanized Agriculture: Elements of Differentiation Among the Peasantry in Sudan." In Tony Barnett and Abos Abdelkarim, eds., *State, Capital, and Transformation.* New York: Croom Helm.

Engels, Friedrich. 1845. *The Conditions of the Working Class in England in 1844.* Leipzig. Reprinted in *Karl Marx and Friedrich Engels on Britain.* Moscow: Foreign Languages Publishing House, 1953.

————. 1971. *The Conditions of the Working Class in England.* Edited and translated by W.O. Henderson and W.H. Chaloner. 2nd ed. Oxford: Basil Blackwell.

Epstein, Trude S. 1973. *South India: Yesterday, Today, Tomorrow.* London: Macmillan.

————. 1982. *Urban Food Marketing and Third World Rural Development.* London: Croom Helm.

Ercelawn, Aly A. 1986. "Poverty in Pakistan: A Study of Villages." In I. Nabi, ed., *The Quality of Life in Pakistan.* Lahore: Vanguard.

————. 1988. Tables presented at seminar sponsored by World Bank, Population and Human Resources Department, Washington, D.C., May. Available from author, University of Karachi, Applied Economics Research Centre.

————. 1989. "Poverty in Pakistan: Choice of Poverty Criteria." University of Karachi, Applied Economics Research Centre.

————. 1990. "Absolute Poverty in Pakistan: Poverty Lines, Incidence, Intensity." University of Karachi, Applied Economics Research Centre.

Eswaran, Mukesh, and Ashok Kotwal. 1986. "Access to Capital as a Determinant of the Organization of Production and Resource Allocation in an Agrarian Economy." *Economic Journal* 96 (2):482-96.

FAO (Food and Agriculture Organization). 1988. *Potentials for Agricultural and Rural Development in Latin America and the Caribbean.* Rome.

————. Various years. *Production Yearbook.* Rome.

————. Various years. *Trade Yearbook.* Rome.

Fagundes, Maria Helena. 1988. "Comentarios sobre o Crédito Rural no Brasil e sua Evolução Recente." *Coleçao de Estudos Especiais* (Companhia de Financiamento da Produção, Ministério de Agricultura, Brazil) 21 (September).

Feder, Gershon. 1985. "The Relation Between Farm Size and Farm Productivity: The Role of Family Labor, Supervision and Credit Constraints." *Journal of Development Economics* 18 (2-3):297-313.

Feder, Gershon, and Raymond Noronha. 1987. "Land Rights Systems and Agricultural Development in Sub-Saharan Africa." World Bank, Department of Agriculture and Rural Development, Research Unit, Washington, D.C.

Fields, Gary S. 1989a. "Changes in Poverty and Inequality in Developing Countries." *World Bank Research Observer* 4 (July):167-85.

———. 1989b. "Poverty, Inequality, and Economic Growth." Cornell University, Economics Department, Ithaca, New York. D.C.

Figallo, Flavio. 1990. "Parceleros: Tierras, Trabajo e Ingresos." In A. Fernandez and Alberto Gonzales, eds., *La Reforma Agraria Peruana, 20 Años Después*. Chiclayo, Peru: Centro de Estudios Sociales Solidaridad.

Figueroa, Adolfo. 1975. "La Redistribución del Ingreso y de la Propriedad en el Perú: 1968-73." In R. Webb and A. Figueroa, eds., *Distribución del Ingreso en el Perú* Lima: Instituto de Estudios Peruanos.

Fiorina, Morris, and Roger G. Noll. 1978. "Voters, Bureaucrats and Legislators: A Rational Choice Perspective on the Growth of Bureaucracy." *Journal of Public Economics* 9 (2):239-54.

Fishlow, Albert. 1972. "Brazilian Size Distribution of Income." *American Economic Review* (May):391-402.

Fitzgerald, Edmund V.K. 1985. "Agrarian Reform as a Model of Accumulation: The Case of Nicaragua since 1979." *Journal of Development Studies* 22 (8):208-26.

Fluitmen, Fred. 1983. "The Socio-Economic Impact of Rural Electrification in Developing Countries: A Review of Evidence." World Employment Programme Working Paper WEP 2-22/WP 126. International Labour Organisation, Geneva.

Fogel, Robert W. 1989. "Second Thoughts on the European Escape from Hunger: Famine, Price Elasticities, Entitlements, Chronic Malnutrition, and Mortality Rates." NBER/DAE Working Paper 1. Cambridge, Mass.: National Bureau of Economic Research.

Forster, Nancy R. 1989. "When the State Sidesteps Land Reform: Alternative Peasant Strategies in Tungurahua, Ecuador." Land Tenure Center Paper 133. University of Wisconsin-Madison.

Foster, James, Joel Greer, and Erik Thorbecke. 1984. "A Class of Decomposable Poverty Measures." *Econometrica* 52 (3):761-66.

Fox, M. Louise. 1982. "Income Distribution in Brazil: Better Numbers and New Findings." Ph.D. dissertation. Vanderbilt University, Department of Economics, Nashville, Tenn.

———. 1990. "Poverty Alleviation in Brazil, 1970-1987." Latin America and Caribbean Region Internal Discussion Paper, Report IDP 072. World Bank, Washington, D.C.

Fox, M. Louise, and Samuel A. Morley. 1990. "Who Paid the Bill? Adjustment and Poverty in Brazil, 1980-1995." Policy Research Working Paper 648. World Bank, Washington, D.C.

Fraker, Thomas, Barbara Devaney, and Edward Cavin. 1986. "An Evaluation of the Effect of Cashing Out Food Stamps on Food Expenditures." *American Economic Review* 76 (May):230-34.

Gaiha, Raghav. 1989. "Poverty Alleviation Programmes in Rural India: An Assessment." Delhi University, Faculty of Management Studies, Delhi.

Garcia, Marito, and Per Pinstrup-Andersen. 1987. *The Pilot Food Price Subsidy Scheme in the Philippines: Its Impact on Income, Food Consumption, and Nutritional Status.* International Food Policy Research Institute Research Report 61. Washington, D.C.

Garfinkel, Irwin, ed. 1982. *Income-Tested Transfer Programs: The Case For and Against.* New York: Academic Press.

Garramón, Carlos J. 1988. "Introducción." In Carlos J. Garramón and others, eds., *Ajuste Macroeconómico y Sector Agropecuario en América Latina.* Buenos Aires: Inter-American Institute for Cooperation on Agriculture.

George, P.S. 1988. "Costs and Benefits of Food Subsidies in India." In Pinstrup-Andersen (1988).

Gershoff, Stan, Robert McGundy, Amorn Nundasutin, and Puangton Tantiwongse. 1988. "Nutritional Studies in Thailand: Effects of Calories, Nutrient Supplements, and Health Interventions on Growth of Preschool Thai Village Children." *American Journal of Clinical Nutrition* 48 (5):1214-18.

Gertler, Paul, Luis Locay, and Warren Sanderson. 1987. "Are User Fees Regressive? The Welfare Implications of Health Care Financing Proposals in Peru." *Journal of Econometrics* 36 (1):67-88.

Gertler, Paul, and Jacques van der Gaag. 1990. *The Willingness to Pay for Medical Care: Evidence from Two Developing Countries.* Baltimore: Johns Hopkins University Press.

Gibb, Arthur. 1974. "Agricultural Modernization, Nonfarm Employment and Low Level Urbanization: A Case Study of Central Luzon Sub-Region." Ph.D. dissertation. University of Michigan, Department of Economics, Ann Arbor.

Glewwe, Paul. 1988. *The Distribution of Welfare in Côte d'Ivoire in 1985.* Living Standards Measurement Study Working Paper 29. Washington, D.C.: World Bank.

———. 1990a. *Efficient Allocation of Transfers to the Poor: The Problems of Unobserved Household Incomes.* Living Standards Measurement Study Working Paper 70. Washington, D.C.: World Bank.

———. 1990b. *Investigating the Determinants of Household Welfare in Côte d'Ivoire.* Living Standards Measurement Study Working Paper 71. Washington, D.C.: World Bank.

Glewwe, Paul, and Dennis de Tray. 1988. *The Poor during Adjustment: A Case Study of Côte d'Ivoire.* Living Standards Measurement Study Working Paper 47. Washington, D.C.: World Bank.

———. 1989. *The Poor in Latin America during Adjustment: A Case Study of Peru.* Living Standards Measurement Study Working Paper 56. Washington, D.C.: World Bank.

Glewwe, Paul, and Oussama Kanaan. 1989. "Targeting Assistance to the Poor Using Household Survey Data." Policy Research Working Paper 225. World Bank, Washington, D.C.

Glewwe, Paul, and K.A. Twum-Baah. 1991. *The Distribution of Welfare in Ghana, 1987-88.* Living Standards Measurement Study Working Paper 75. Washington, D.C.: World Bank.

Gols, José. 1985. "La Parcelación de las Empresas Asociativas de la Costa Peruana: El Caso del Valle de Canete." Bachelor's thesis. Universidad Nacional Agraria-La Molina, Peru.

Gómez, Sergio, and Jorge Echenique. 1988. *La Agricultura Chilena: Las Dos Caras de la Modernización.* Santiago: Faculdad Latino Americana de Ciencias Sociales (FLACSO)/Agraria.

Graham, G.G., H.M. Creed, W.C. MacLean, Jr., C.H. Kallman, and J. Rabold. 1981. "Determinants of Growth among Poor Children: Nutrient Intake-Achieved Growth Relationships." *American Journal of Clinical Nutrition* 34 (3):539-54.

Griffin, Charles. 1989. *Strengthening Health Services in Developing Countries through the Private Sector.* IFC Discussion Paper 4. Washington, D.C.: World Bank.

Grosh, Margaret, Frederic Louat, and Jacques van der Gaag. Forthcoming. *The Welfare Implications of Female Headship in Jamaica.* Living Standards Measurement Study Working Paper. Washington, D.C.: World Bank.

Guhan, S. 1988. "Social Security in India: Looking One Step Ahead." *Bulletin of the Madras Development Seminar Series* 18:438-58.

Guilkey, David, Barry Popkin, John Akin, and Emelita Wong. 1989. "Prenatal Care and Pregnancy Outcomes in Cebu, Philippines." *Journal of Development Economics* 30 (2):241-72.

Gulati, Leela. 1977. "Rationing in a Peri-urban Community." *Economic and Political Weekly* (March 19):501-06.

Haddad, Lawrence J., and Howarth E. Bouis. 1991. "The Impact of Nutritional Status on Agricultural Productivity: Wage Evidence from the Philippines." *Oxford Bulletin of Economics and Statistics* 53 (1):45-68.

Haggblade, Steven. 1982. *Rural Industrial Officer's Handbook.* Gaborone, Botswana: Ministry of Commerce and Industry.

Haggblade, Steven, Jeffrey Hammer, and Peter Hazell. 1991. "Modelling Agricultural Growth Multipliers." *American Journal of Agricultural Economics* 73 (2):361-74.

Haggblade, Steven, and Peter Hazell. 1989. "Agricultural Technology and Farm-Nonfarm Growth Linkages." *Agricultural Economics* 3 (4):345-64.

Haggblade, Steven, Peter Hazell, and James Brown. 1989. "Farm-Nonfarm Linkages in Rural Sub-Saharan Africa." *World Development* 17 (8):1173-1201.

Hajnal, John. 1982. "Two Kinds of Pre-Industrial Family Formation." *Population and Development Review* 8 (3):449-94.

Haney, Emil, and Wava Haney. 1989. "The Agrarian Transition in Highland Ecuador: From Precapitalism to Agrarian Capitalism in Chimborazo." In W.C. Thiesenhusen, ed., *Searching for Agrarian Reform in Latin America.* Boston: Unwin Hyman.

Hannon, Joan U. 1984a. "The Generosity of Antebellum Poor Relief." *Journal of Economic History* 44 (3):810-21.

————. 1984b. "Poverty in the Antebellum Northeast: The View from New York State's Poor Relief Rolls." *Journal of Economic History* 44 (4):1007-32.

————. 1986. "Dollars, Morals and Markets: The Shaping of Nineteenth Century Poor Relief Policy." Paper for the University of California Intercampus Group in Economic History Conference on Searching for Security: Poverty, Old Age, and Dependency in the Nineteenth Century, Berkeley, California, March.

Hansen, W. Lee, and Burton A. Weisbrod. 1969. *Benefits, Cost and Finance of Public Higher Education.* Chicago: Markham Publishing Co.

Hanson, James, and Sunanda Sengupta. 1989. "India's Manufacturing Sector and Employment Creation: A Comparison of the 1970s and 1980s." World Bank, Asia Country Department, Washington, D.C.

Hanushek, Eric. 1986. "The Economics of Schooling: Production and Efficiency in Public Schools." *Journal of Economic Literature* 24 (September):1141-77.

Hart, Gillian P. 1986. *Power, Labor and Livelihood: Processes of Change in Rural Java.* Berkeley: University of California Press.

Haveman, Robert. 1989. "Economics and Public Policy: On the Relevance of Conventional Economic Advice." *Quarterly Review of Economics and Business* 29 (Autumn):6-20.

Havinga, Ivo C., and others. 1989. "Poverty and Inequality in Pakistan, 1984-85." Project on Improvement of National Account Statistics. Federal Bureau of Statistics, Islamabad, and Institute of Social Studies, The Hague.

Hazell, Peter, and Steven Haggblade. 1991. "Rural-Urban Growth Linkages in India." *Indian Journal of Agricultural Economics* 46 (4):515-29.

Hazell, Peter, and C. Ramasamy, eds. 1991. *The Green Revolution Reconsidered: The Impact of High-Yielding Rice Varieties in South India.* Baltimore: Johns Hopkins University Press.

Hazell, Peter, and Ailsa Roell. 1983. *Rural Growth Linkages: Household Expenditure Patterns in Malaysia and Nigeria.* International Food Policy Research Institute Research Report 41. Washington, D.C.

Heaver, Richard. 1989. *Improving Family Planning, Health, and Nutrition in India: Experience from Some World Bank-Assisted Programs.* World Bank Discussion Paper 59. Washington, D.C.

Hill, Kenneth, and Ann R. Pebley. 1989. "Levels, Trends, and Patterns of Child Mortality in the Developing World." Prepared for the Workshop on Child Survival Programs: Issues for the 1990s, School of Hygiene and Public Health, Johns Hopkins University, Baltimore, Md., November 20-21.

Ho, Samuel P.S. 1986. "Off-farm Employment and Farm Households in Taiwan." In R.T. Shand, ed., *Off-farm Employment in the Development of Rural Asia.* Canberra, Australia: National Center for Development Studies, the Australian National University.

Hochman, Harold M., and J.D. Rodgers. 1969. "Pareto Optimal Redistribution." *American Economic Review* 59 (4, part 1):542-57.

Hopkins, Raymond F. 1988. "Political Calculations in Subsidizing Food." In Pinstrup-Andersen (1988).

Hornik, R.C. 1985. *Nutrition Education: A State-of-the-Art Review.* Nutrition Policy Discussion Paper 1. Geneva: United Nations, Administrative Committee on Coordination, Subcommittee on Nutrition.

Hossain, Mahabub. 1988a. *Credit for Alleviation of Poverty: The Grameen Bank in Bangladesh.* International Food Policy Research Institute Research Report 65. Washington DC.

————. 1988b. *Nature and Impact of the Green Revolution in Bangladesh.* International Food Policy Research Institute Research Report 67. Washington, D.C.

Howes, Michael. 1982. "The Creation and Appropriation of Value in Irrigated Agriculture." In Michael Howes and Martin Greeley, eds., *Rural Technology, Rural Institutions and the Rural Poorest.* Dhaka: CIRDAP/IDS.

Howes, Stephen. 1990. "Statewise Variations in Poverty Alleviation in India: An Early Progress Report." ST/ICERD, London School of Economics, London.

Husain, S. Shahid. 1989. "Reviving Growth in Latin America." *Finance and Development* 26 (2):2-6.

Hymer, Stephen, and Stephen Resnick. 1969. "A Model of An Agrarian Economy with Nonagricultural Activities." *American Economic Review* 59 (September):493-506.

IDB (Inter-American Development Bank). 1988. *Economic and Social Progress in Latin America, 1987 Report.* Washington, D.C.

Iliffe, John. 1987. *The African Poor.* Cambridge: Cambridge University Press.

ILO (International Labour Office). 1984. *Into the Twenty-first Century: The Development of Social Security.* Geneva.

Iman, R.L., and W.J. Conover. 1978. "Approximation of the Critical Region for Spearman's Rho with and without Ties Present." *Communications in Statistics,* series B, 7:269-82.

IMF (International Monetary Fund). Various years. *International Financial Statistics.* Washington, D.C.

————. Various years. *Yearbook of Government Finance Statistics.* Washington, D.C.

India, Central Statistical Organization. Various issues. *Monthly Abstract of Statistics.* New Delhi.

India, Economic Administration Reforms Commission. 1984. *Report of the Working Group on Social Security.* New Delhi.

India, Finance Commission. 1880. *Report of the Indian Famine Commission 1880.* London: HMSO.

India, Finance Commission. 1988. *First Report of the Ninth Finance Commission.* Delhi.

India, Ministry of Program Evaluation. 1988. "Progress Report of the 20-Point Program." New Delhi.

————. 1989. "Progress Report of the 20-Point Program." New Delhi.

India, Ministry of Rural Development. 1988. *Rural Development Statistics.* New Delhi.

India, Planning Commission. 1964. *Report of the Committee on Distribution of Income and Levels of Living.* New Delhi: Controller of Publications.

————. 1980. *Sixth Five Yecr Plan.* New Delhi: Controller of Publications.

IPEA/IPLAN (Instituto de Planejamento Economico e Social/Instituto de Planejamento). 1988. *Educação e Cultura—1987: Sítuação e Políticos Governamentais.* Brasilia: IPEA/IPLAN, Coordenadoria de Educação e Cultura.

Irfan, Mohammed, and R. Amjad. 1984. "Poverty in Rural Pakistan." In Azizur R. Khan and Eddy Lee, eds., *Poverty in Rural Asia.* Bangkok: International Labour Office/Asian Employment Program.

Islam, Rizwanul. 1984. "Nonfarm Employment in Rural Asia: Dynamic Growth or Proletarianisation?" *Journal of Contemporary Asia* (U.K.) 14 (3):306-24.

Jain, L.R., K. Sundaram, and Suresh D. Tendulkar. 1988. "Dimensions of Rural Poverty: An Inter-Regional Profile." *Economic and Political Weekly* 23:2395-408.

Jain, L.R., and Suresh D. Tendulkar. 1990. "Role of Growth and Distribution in the Observed Change of Head-count Ratio—Measure of Poverty: A Decomposition Exercise for India." *Indian Economic Review* 25 (July-December):165-205.

James, Estelle. 1986. "The Private Nonprofit Provision of Education: A Theoretical Model and Application to Japan." *Journal of Comparative Economics* 10 (September):255-76.

————. 1988. "Difference Between the Public and Private Sectors in Higher Education." Working paper. Yale University, Program on Nonprofit Organizations, New Haven.

————. 1989a. "Higher Education in Asia: A Proposal for Further Study." World Bank, Country Economics Department, Washington, D.C.

————. 1989b. "The Private Provision of Public Services: A Comparison of Sweden and Holland." In Estelle James, ed., *The Nonprofit Sector in International Perspective: Studies in Comparative Culture and Policy.* New York: Oxford University Press.

————. 1991. "Public Policies Toward Private Education." *International Journal of Educational Research* 15 (5):359-76.

James, Estelle, Nabeel Alsalam, Joseph Conaty, and Duc-Le To. 1989. "College Quality and Future Earnings: Where Should You Send Your Child to College?" *American Economic Review* 79 (2):247-52.

James, Estelle, and Gail Benjamin. 1987a. "Educational Distribution and Redistribution Through Education in Japan." *Journal of Human Resources* 22 (Fall):469-89.

————. 1987b. *Public Policy and Private Education in Japan.* New York: St. Martin's Press.

Jarvis, Lovell S. 1989. "The Unraveling of Chile's Agrarian Reform." In W.C. Thiesenhusen, ed., *Searching for Agrarian Reform in Latin America.* Boston: Unwin Hyman.

Jayasuriya, Sisira, and Richard T. Shand. 1986. "Technical Change and Labour Absorption in Asian Agriculture: Some Emerging Trends." *World Development* 14 (3):415-28.

Jeffrey, Roger. 1989. "Health and Nutrition Services in Pakistan: Their Contribution to Improving the Living Standards of the Poor."

Jimenez, Emmanuel. 1987. *Pricing Policy in the Social Sectors: Cost Recovery for Education and Health in Developing Countries.* Baltimore: Johns Hopkins University Press.

Jodha, N.S. 1985. "Population Growth and the Decline of Common Property Resources in India." *Population and Development Review* 2 (2):247-64.

————. 1991. "Rural Common Property Resources: A Growing Crisis." Gatekeeper Series no. S24. International Institute for Environment and Development, London.

Johnston, Bruce, and Peter Kilby. 1975. *Agriculture and Structural Transformation: Economic Strategies in Late-Developing Countries.* London: Oxford University Press.

Kaimowitz, David. 1986. "Agrarian Structure in Nicaragua and Its Implications for Policies towards the Rural Poor." Ph.D. dissertation. University of Wisconsin-Madison, Department of Agricultural Economics.

————. 1988. "Nicaragua's Experience with Agricultural Planning: From State-Centered Accumulation to the Strategic Alliance with the Peasantry." In E.V.K. Fitzgerald and M. Wuyts, eds., *Markets Within Planning: Socialist Economic Management in the Third World.* London: Frank Cass.

Kakwani, N. 1977. "On the Estimation of Engel Elasticities from Grouped Observations with Application to Indonesian Data." *Journal of Econometrics* 6 (July):1-19.

————. 1980a. *Income Inequality and Poverty: Methods of Estimation and Policy Applications.* New York: Oxford University Press.

————. 1980b. "On a Class of Poverty Measures." *Econometrica* 48(March):437-46.

————. 1984. "Issues in Measuring Poverty." In *Advances in Econometrics* 3. Greenwich, Conn.: Jai Press.

————. 1986. *Analyzing Redistribution Policies: A Study Using Australian Data.* New York: Cambridge University Press.

————. 1990a. "Growth Rates and Aggregate Welfare: An International Comparison." University of New South Wales, Department of Econometrics, Australia.

————. 1990b. "On Measuring Changes in Living Standards." University of New South Wales, Department of Econometrics, Australia.

————. 1990c. *Poverty and Economic Growth: With Application to Côte d'Ivoire.* Living Standards Measurement Study Working Paper 63. Washington, D.C.: World Bank.

————. 1990d. *Testing for Significance of Poverty Differences: With Application to Côte d'Ivoire.* Living Standards Measurement Study Working Paper 62. Washington, D.C.: World Bank.

————. Forthcoming. "Statistical Inference in the Measurement of Poverty." *Review of Economics and Statistics.*

Kakwani, N., and Kalinidhi Subbarao. 1991. "Rural Poverty and Its Alleviation in India." *Economic and Political Weekly* 26:1482-86.

Kanbur, Ravi. 1986. "Budgetary Rules for Poverty Alleviation." Seminar Paper 363. University of Stockholm, Institute for International Economic Studies, Stockholm.

————. 1987a. "Measurement and Alleviation of Poverty: With an Application to the Effects of Macroeconomic Adjustment." *IMF Staff Papers* 34 (1):60-85.

————. 1987b. "Structural Adjustment, Macroeconomic Adjustment and Poverty: A Methodology for Analysis." *World Development* 15 (12):1515-26.

————. 1987c. "Transfers, Targeting and Poverty." *Economic Policy: A European Forum* 2 (4):111-47.

————. 1988. "Poverty Alleviation under Structural Adjustment: A Conceptual Framework and Its Application to Côte d'Ivoire." World Bank, Africa Technical Department, Poverty and Social Policy Division, Washington, D.C.

————. 1990a. "Malnutrition and Poverty in Latin America." In Jean Drèze and Amartya K. Sen, eds., *The Political Economy of Hunger.* Vol. 3, *Endemic Hunger.* Oxford: Clarendon Press.

————. 1990b. *Poverty and the Social Dimensions of Structural Adjustment in Côte d'Ivoire.* Social Dimensions of Adjustment in Sub-Saharan Africa Working Paper 2. Washington, D.C.: World Bank.

Kanbur, Ravi, and M.J. Keen. 1987. "Optimum Income Taxation for Poverty Alleviation." University of Warwick, Department of Economics.

Katz, Elizabeth. 1989. "The Socio-Economic Impact of Non-Traditional Agricultural Export Promotion in Guatemala: Final Report for the Tinker Field Research Grant." University of Wisconsin-Madison, Department of Agricultural Economics.

Kay, John A., and Mervyn A. King. 1980. *The British Tax System.* New York: Oxford University Press.

Kelley, Allen C. 1988. "Economic Consequences of Population Change in the Third World." *Journal of Economic Literature* 26 (4):1685-1728.

Kennedy, Eileen. 1987. "The Nutritional Effects of Subsidized Milk Distribution Schemes: Evidence and Justification." Paper presented at Dairy Development Workshop, Copenhagen, January. International Food Policy Research Institute, Washington, D.C.

————. 1989. "Health and Nutrition Effects of the Commercialization of Agriculture: A Comparative Analysis." International Food Policy Research Institute, Washington, D.C.

Kennedy, Eileen, and Bruce Cogill. 1987. *Income and Nutritional Effects of the Commercialization of Agriculture in Southwestern Kenya.* International Food Policy Research Institute Research Report 63. Washington, D.C.

————. 1988. "Alternatives to Consumer-Oriented Food Subsidies for Achieving Nutritional Objectives." In Pinstrup-Andersen (1988).

Kennedy, Eileen, and Odin Knudsen. 1985. "A Review of Supplementary Feeding Programmes and Recommendations on Their Design." In Margaret Biswas and Per Pinstrup-Andersen, eds., *Nutrition and Development.* London: Oxford University Press.

Kesselman, J.R. 1982. "Taxpayer Behavior and the Design of a Credit Income Tax." In Garfinkel (1982).

Khan, Azizur R. 1977. "Poverty and Inequality in Rural Bangladesh." In K. Griffin and Azizur R. Khan, eds., *Poverty and Landlessness in Rural Asia.* Geneva: International Labour Office.

Khan, Azizur R., and Eddy Lee, eds. 1984. *Poverty in Rural Asia.* Bangkok: International Labour Office/Asian Employment Program.

Khan, Mushtaq A., and M.A. Khan. 1980. *Nutritional Standards of Growth for Infants and Young Children and Recommended Dietary Allowances of Pakistani Population.* Islamabad: Government of Pakistan, Planning and Development Division.

Khandker, Shahidur. 1989. "Improving Rural Wages in India." Policy Research Working Paper 276. World Bank, Washington, D.C.

Kielmann, Arnfried, C.E. Taylor, and R.L. Parker. 1978. "The Narangwal Nutrition Study: A Summary Review." *American Journal of Clinical Nutrition* 31:2040-52.

Kikuchi, M.A., A. Huysman, and L. Res. 1983. "Agriculture, Labor Absorption and Migration: Comparative Histories of Two Philippine Rice Villages." IRRI Research Paper Series 90. International Rice Research Institute, Los Banos, Philippines.

Kilby, Peter. 1979. "Evaluating Technical Assistance." *World Development* 7 (3):309-23.

Kilby, Peter, and David D'Zmura. 1985. "Searching for Benefits." U.S. Agency for International Development Evaluation Special Study 28. Washington, D.C.

King, Robert P., and Derek Byerlee. 1978. "Factor Intensities and Locational Linkages of Rural Consumption Patterns in Rural Sierra Leone." *American Journal of Agricultural Economics* 60 (2):197-206.

Klitgaard, Robert. 1989. "Incentive Myopia." *World Development* 17 (4):447-59.

Knight, John B., and Richard H. Sabot. 1990. *Education, Productivity and Inequality: The East African Natural Experiment.* New York: Oxford University Press.

Knudsen, Odin, and John Nash. 1989. "Agricultural Sector Adjustment Lending and Agricultural Policy." Paper presented at seminar on Policy-Based Lending in Agriculture, Agricultural Policies Division, World Bank, Washington, D.C., May.

Konjing, Chaiwat. 1989. "Trends and Prospects for Cassava in Thailand." Working Paper 6 on Cassava. International Food Policy Research Institute, Washington, D.C.

Korea, Republic of, National Bureau of Statistics. 1987. *Korea Statistical Yearbook.* Seoul.

Kouwenaar, Arend. 1988. *A Basic Needs Policy Model: A General Equilibrium Analysis with Special Reference to Ecuador.* Amsterdam: North-Holland.

Krishna, Raj. 1975. "Measurement of the Direct and Indirect Employment Linkages of Agricultural Growth with Technical Change." In Earl O. Heady and Larry R. Whiting, eds., *Externalities in the Transformation of Agriculture.* Ames, Iowa: Iowa State University Press.

Krueger, Anne O. 1974. "The Political Economy of the Rent-Seeking Society." *American Economic Review* 64 (3):291-303.

Kumar, Shubh K. 1979. *Impact of Subsidized Rice on Food Consumption and Nutrition in Kerala.* International Food Policy Research Institute Research Report 5. Washington, D.C.

Kusterer, K.C., M.R. Estrada de Batres, and J. Xuya Cuxil. 1981. "The Social Impact of Agribusiness: A Case Study of ALCOSA in Guatemala." U.S. Agency for International Development Evaluation Special Study 4. Washington, D.C.

Kuznets, Simon. 1955. "Economic Growth and Income Inequality." *American Economic Review* 45 (1):1-28.

————. 1974. "Demographic Aspects of the Distribution of Incomes among Families: Recent Trends in the United States." In Willy Sellekaerts, ed., *Econometrics and Economic Theory: Essays in Honour of Jan Trinbergen.* London: Macmillan.

————. 1976. "Demographic Aspects of the Size Distribution of Income: An Exploratory Essay." *Economic Development and Cultural Change* 25 (1):1-94.

Kydd, Jonathan. 1990. "Maize Research in Malawi: Lessons from Failure." *Journal of International Development* 1 (1):112-44.

Lamptey, Peter, and Fred Sai. 1985. "Integrated Health/Nutrition/Population Programmes." In Margaret Biswas and Per Pinstrup-Andersen, eds., *Nutrition and Development.* London: Oxford University Press.

Laraki, Karim. 1989. *Food Subsidies: A Case Study of Price Reform in Morocco.* Living Standards Measurement Study Working Paper 50. Washington, D.C.: World Bank.

Laslett, Peter. 1985. "Gregory King, Robert Malthus, and the Origins of English Social Realism." *Popular Studies* 39 (3):351-63.

Laslett, Peter, and Richard Wall, eds. 1972. *Household and Family in Past Time.* Cambridge: Cambridge University Press.

Lecaillon, Jacques, F. Paukert, C. Morrison, and D. Germidis. 1986. *Income Distribution and Economic Development: An Analytical Survey.* 2nd ed. Geneva: International Labour Office.

Lee, Ronald, and Timothy Miller. 1991. "Population Growth, Externalities to Childbearing, and Fertility Policy in Developing Countries." In *Proceedings of the World Bank Annual Conference on Development Economics 1990.* Supplement to *World Bank Economic Review* and *World Bank Research Observer.*

LeGrand, Julian, and David Winter. 1987. "The Middle Classes and the Defence of the British Welfare State." In R.E. Goodin and J. LeGrand, eds., *Not Only the Poor: The Middle Classes and the Welfare State*. London: Allen and Unwin.

Lehmann, David. 1978. "The Death of Land Reform: A Polemic." *World Development* 6 (3):339-45.

———. 1982. "After Lenin and Chayanov: New Paths of Agrarian Capitalism." *Journal of Development Economics* 11 (1):133-61.

———. 1986a. "Sharecropping and the Capitalist Transition in Agriculture: Some Evidence from the Highlands of Ecuador." *Journal of Development Economics* 23 (2):333-54.

———. 1986b. "Two Paths of Agrarian Capitalism: A Critique of Chayanovian Marxism." *Comparative Studies in Society and History* 28 (3):601-27.

Lele, Uma, and Manmohan Agarwal. 1990. *Smallholder and Large-Scale Agriculture: Are There Tradeoffs in Growth and Equity?* MADIA Discussion Paper 6. Washington, D.C.: World Bank.

Lele, Uma, and John Mellor. 1988. "Agricultural Growth, Its Determinants, and Their Relationship to World Development: An Overview." Paper presented at the 20th International Conference of Agricultural Economists, Buenos Aires, Argentina, August 24-31. World Bank, Washington, D.C.; and International Food Policy Research Institute, Washington, D.C.

Lele, Uma, Nicolas van de Walle, and Mathurin Gbetibouo. 1990. *Cotton in Africa: An Analysis of Differences in Performance*. MADIA Discussion Paper 7. Washington, D.C.: World Bank.

Lemer, Andrew. 1990. "Building Firm Foundations: Africa's Infrastructure." In World Bank, *Long-Term Perspective Study of Sub-Saharan Africa*. Vol. 2, *Economic and Sectoral Policy Issues*. Washington, D.C.

Lenin, Vladimir Ilyich. 1974. *The Development of Capitalism in Russia*. Moscow: Progress Publishers.

Leonard, David. 1984. "Disintegrating Agricultural Development." *Food Research Institute Studies* 19 (2):177-86.

Leslie, Joan, and Michael Paolisso. 1989. *Women's Work and Child Welfare*. Boulder, Colo.: Westview Press.

Levy, Daniel. 1986. *Higher Education and the State in Latin America: Private Challenges to Public Dominance*. Chicago: University of Chicago Press.

Lewis, W. Arthur. 1978. *The Evolution of the International Economic Order*. Princeton, N.J.: Princeton University Press.

Lindert, Peter H. 1989. "Modern Fiscal Redistribution: A Preliminary Essay." University of California, Davis, Department of Economics.

Lindert, Peter H., and Jeffrey G. Williamson. 1983. "English Workers' Living Standards During the Industrial Revolution: A New Look." *Economic History Review*, second series, 36 (1):1-25.

———. 1985. "Growth, Equality and History." *Explorations in Economic History* 22 (4):341-77.

Lipton, Michael. 1977. *Why Poor People Stay Poor: A Study of Urban Bias in World Development*. Canberra: Australian National University Press.

————. 1982a. "Migration from Rural Areas of Poor Countries: The Impact on Rural Productivity and Income Distribution." In R.H. Sabot, ed., *Migration and Labor Markets in Developing Countries*. Boulder, Colo.: Westview Press.

————. 1982b. "Rural Development and the Retention of the Rural Population in the Countryside of Developing Countries." *Canadian Journal of Development Studies* 3 (1):11-37.

————. 1983a. *Demography and Poverty*. World Bank Staff Working Paper 623. Washington, D.C.

————. 1983b. *Labor and Poverty*. World Bank Staff Working Paper 616. Washington, D.C.

————. 1983c. *Poverty, Undernutrition, and Hunger*. World Bank Staff Working Paper 597. Washington, D.C.

————. 1984a. "Family, Fungibility, and Formality." In S. Amin, ed., *Human Resources, Employment, and Development*. Vol. 5, *Developing Countries*. London: Macmillan.

————. 1984b. "Urban Bias Revisited." *Journal of Development Studies* 20 (3):139-66.

————. 1985. *Land Assets and Rural Poverty*. World Bank Staff Working Paper 744. Washington, D.C.

————. 1987. "Limits to Agricultural Price Policy: Which Way at the World Bank?" *Development Policy Review* 5 (June):197-215.

————. 1988a. *Attacking Undernutrition and Poverty: Some Issues of Adaptation and Sustainability*. Pew/Cornell Lecture Series on Food and Nutrition Policy. Ithaca, N.Y.: Cornell Food and Nutrition Policy Program.

————. 1988b. "Poverty: Concepts, Thresholds and Equity Concepts." International Food Policy Research Institute, Washington, D.C.

————. 1989. "State Compression: Friend or Foe of Agricultural Liberalization?" In M. Dantwala and V. Dandekar, eds., *Indian Society of Agricultural Economics, Golden Jubilee Volume*. Delhi.

Lipton, Michael, with Richard Longhurst. 1989. *New Seeds and Poor People*. London: Unwin Hyman.

Lipton, Michael, and John Toye. 1990. *Does Aid Work in India?* Routledge: London.

Liviatan, Nissan. 1961. "Errors in Variables and Engel Curve Analysis." *Econometrica* 29 (3):336.

Lustig, Nora. 1986. "Economic Crisis and Living Standards in Mexico: 1982-1985." El Colegio de Mexico, Department of Economics, Mexico City.

Luz, Karen. 1989. "Cooperation and the Competitive Edge: The Relationship Between Organization and Productivity in Nicaraguan Collective Agriculture." Master's thesis. University of Wisconsin-Madison, Department of Agricultural Economics.

Luzuriaga, C.C., and C. Zuvekas, Jr. 1983. "Income Distribution and Poverty in Rural Ecuador, 1950-1979: A Survey of the Literature." Arizona State University, Center for Latin American Studies, Tempe, Ariz.

Macedo, R. 1987. "The Mistargeting of Social Programs in Brazil: The Federal Health and Nutrition Programs." University of São Paulo.

MacKinnon, Mary. 1985. "Poverty and Policy: The English Poor Law 1860-1910." D.Phil. thesis. Oxford University, Faculty of Economics.

―――. 1986. "Poor Law Policy, Unemployment and Pauperism." *Explorations in Economic History* 23 (3):299-336.

―――. 1987. "English Poor Law Policy and the Crusade Against Outrelief." *Journal of Economic History.* 47 (3):603-25.

Madison, Bernice. 1990. "The Soviet Pension System and Social Security for the Aged." In G. Lapidus and G. Swanson, eds., *State and Welfare: USA/USSR.* Berkeley: Institute of International Studies, University of California.

Maia, Rosane, and Rosangela Saldanha. 1988. "Abrindo a Caixa Preta: Estudo Sobre a Evolução do Emprego na Administração Publica Estatal e Municipal." Brazil Ministry of Labor, Brasilia.

Malawi, Economic Planning Division. 1971. *Statement of Development Policies 1971-1980.* Zomba.

Malawi, Ministry of Agriculture. 1988. "Crop Industry Economic Studies." Vol. 2. Prepared by Lanell Mills Associates, Bath, U.K.

―――. Various years. "Annual Agricultural Survey (ASA)." Summary Tables. Computer print-outs. Lilongwe.

Malawi, National Statistical Office. 1978. *Malawi Statistical Yearbook 1978.* Zomba.

―――. 1987. *Malawi Population and Housing Census 1987: Preliminary Report.* Zomba.

―――. 1988. *Malawi Statistical Yearbook 1986.* Zomba.

―――. Various issues. *Monthly Statistical Bulletin.* Zomba.

―――. Various years. *Reported Employment and Earnings Annual Report.* Zomba.

Malawi, Office of the President and Cabinet, Department of Economic Planning and Development. 1989. *Economic Report 1989.* Lilongwe.

Malik, Mohammed H. 1988. "Some New Evidence on the Incidence of Poverty in Pakistan." *Pakistan Development Review* 27 (4):509-15.

Malik, Sohail J. 1989. "The Source Structure and Utilization Patterns of Rural Credit in Pakistan: Implications for Policy." International Food Policy Research Institute, Washington, D.C.

Manoff, R.K. 1985. *Social Marketing.* New York: Praeger.

Martorell, Raynaldo, and Teresa Gonzalez-Cossio. 1987. "Maternal Nutrition and Birth Weight." *Yearbook of Physical Anthropology* 30:195-220.

Matlon, Peter, Thomas Eponou, Steven Franzel, Derek Byerlee, and Doyle Baker. 1979. "Poor Rural Households, Technical Change and Income Distribution in Developing Countries: Two Case Studies from West Africa." Michigan State University International Development Working Paper 29. Michigan State University, Department of Agricultural Economics, East Lansing.

Matos Mar, José, and J.M. Mejia. 1980. *La Reforma Agraria en el Perú.* Lima: Instituto de Estudios Peruanos.

McClintock, Cynthia. 1981. *Peasant Cooperatives and Political Change in Peru.* Princeton, N.J.: Princeton University Press.

McInerney, John P., and Graham F. Donaldson. 1975. *Consequences of Farm Tractors in Pakistan.* World Bank Staff Working Paper 210. Washington, D.C.

Meade, J.E. 1964. *Efficiency, Equality and Ownership of Property.* London: Allen and Unwin.

Meeker, Edward. 1974. "The Social Rate of Return on Investment in Public Health, 1880-1910." *Journal of Economic History* 34 (2):392-73.

Meerman, Jacob. 1979. *Public Expenditure in Malaysia: Who Benefits and Why.* New York: Oxford University Press.

Mellor, John W. 1976. *The New Economics of Growth: A Strategy for India and the Developing World.* Ithaca, N.Y.: Cornell University Press.

———. 1986. "Agriculture on the Road to Industrialization." In John P. Lewis and Valeriana Kallab, eds., *Development Strategies Reconsidered.* New Brunswick, N.J.: Transaction Books.

Mellor, John W., and Gunvant M. Desai, eds. 1985. *Agricultural Change and Rural Poverty: Variations on a Theme by Dharm Narain.* Baltimore: Johns Hopkins University Press.

Mellor, John W., and Bruce F. Johnston. 1984. "The World Food Equation: Interrelations Among Development, Employment and Food Consumption." *Journal of Economic Literature* 22 (June):524-31.

Mellor, John, and Uma Lele. 1973. "Growth Linkages of the New Food Grain Technologies." *Indian Journal of Agricultural Economics* 18 (1):35-55.

Melmed, Jolyne. 1987. "Perspectives on the Parcellation of Agrarian Reform Cooperatives: The Peruvian Case." Ph.D. dissertation. University of Wisconsin-Madison, Department of Agricultural Economics.

Melmed-Sanjak, Jolyne, and Michael R. Carter. 1992. "The Economic Viability and Stability of Capitalized Family Farming: An Analysis of Agricultural Decollectivization in Peru." *Journal of Development Studies* 27 (2):190-210.

Meltzer, A.H., and S.F. Richard. 1978. "Why Government Grows (and Grows) in a Democracy." *Public Interest* 52 (Summer):111-18.

———. 1981. "Tests of a Rational Theory of the Size of Government." *Journal of Political Economy* 89 (5):914-27.

Mesa-Lago, Carmelo. 1991. "Formal Social Security in Latin America and the Caribbean." In Ahmad and others (1991).

Meyer, Carrie A. 1989. *Land Reform in Latin America: The Dominican Case.* New York: Praeger.

Mingat, Alain, and Jee-Peng Tan. 1985. "Subsidization of Higher Education Versus Expansion of Primary Enrollments: What Can a Shift of Resources Achieve in Sub-Saharan Africa?" *International Journal of Educational Development* 5 (4):259-68.

Minhas, B.S. 1970. "Rural Poverty, Land Distribution and Development." *Indian Economic Review* 5 (1):97-128.

————. 1991. "On Estimating the Inadequacy of Energy Intake: Revealed Food Consumption Behaviour versus Nutritional Norms." *Journal of Development Studies* 28 (1):1-38.

Minhas, B.S., and L.R. Jain. 1990. "Incidence of Rural Poverty in Different States and All India: 1970-71 to 1983." In Indian Society of Agricultural Economics, ed., *Agricultural Development Policy*. New Delhi: Oxford and IBH Publishing.

Minhas, B.S., L.R. Jain, S.M. Kansal, and M.R. Saluja. 1987. "On the Choice of Appropriate Consumer Price Indices and Data Sets for Estimating the Incidence of Poverty in India." *Indian Economic Review* 22 (1):19-50.

————. 1988. "Measurement of General Cost of Living for Urban India: All-India and Different States." *Sarvekshana* 12:1-23.

————. 1990. "Cost of Living in Rural India: 1970-71 to 1983; Statewise and All-India." *Indian Economic Review* 25 (1):75-104.

Mirrlees, James A. 1971. "An Exploration in the Theory of Optimum Income Taxation." *Review of Economic Studies* 38 (114):175-208.

Mishra, G., ed. 1985. Regional Structure of Development and Growth in India. Delhi: Ashish Publishing House.

Mitra, Asok. 1978. *India's Population: Aspects of Quality and Control*. New Delhi: Abhinav Publications.

Mkandawire, Richard, Steven Jaffee, and Sandra Bertoli. 1990. "Beyond 'Dualism': The Changing Face of the Leasehold Estate Sub-sector of Malawi." Bunda College and the Institute for Development Anthropology, Lilongwe, Malawi.

Mkandawire, Richard, and Chimimba D. Phiri. 1987. "Land Policy Study: Assessment of Land Transfers from Smallholder to Estates." Bunda College of Agriculture, Lilongwe, Malawi.

Modigliani, Franco, and Tommaso Padoa-Schioppa. 1978. "The Management of an Open Economy with '100 percent Plus' Wage Indexation." Princeton Essays in International Finance 130. Princeton University, Princeton, N.J.

Moffitt, Robert. 1983. "An Economic Model of Welfare Stigma." *American Economic Review* 73 (5):1023-35.

Morley, Samuel A. 1981. "The Effect of Changes in the Population on Several Measures of Income Distribution." *American Economic Review* 71 (3):285-94.

————. 1982. *Labor Markets and Inequitable Growth: The Case of Authoritarian Capitalism in Brazil*. Cambridge: Cambridge University Press.

Morris, Cynthia Taft, and Irma Adelman. 1988. *Comparative Patterns of Economic Development 1850-1914*. Baltimore: Johns Hopkins University Press.

Mosley, Paul, and Lawrence Smith. 1989. "Structural Adjustment and Agricultural Performance in Sub-Saharan Africa, 1980-87." *Journal of International Development* 1 (July):321-55.

Moulton, Kirby, and Dave Runsten. 1986. "Frozen Vegetable Industry in Mexico." University of California, Berkeley, Department of Agricultural and Resource Economics.

Mtawali, K.M. 1989. "An Analysis of Characteristics of Households Facing Food Insecurity in Malawi." Research paper submitted to the Kellogg International Program in Food Systems, Michigan State University, East Lansing.

Mueller, D.C. 1979. *Public Choice.* New York: Cambridge University Press.

Mujahid, G.B.S. 1978. "A Note on Measurement of Poverty and Income Inequalities in Pakistan: Some Observations on Methodology." *Pakistan Development Review* 17 (3):365-77.

Murray, Charles A. 1984. *Losing Ground: American Social Policy, 1950-1980.* New York: Basic Books.

Musgrave, R.A. 1959. *The Theory of Public Finance: A Study in Political Economy.* New York: McGraw Hill.

Nabi, Ijaz, Naved Hamid, and Shahid Zahid. 1986. *The Agrarian Economy of Pakistan: Issues and Policy.* Oxford: Oxford University Press.

Nankumba, J.S. 1985. "Tenancy Arrangements and Rural Development in Malawi: A Study of Mitundu (Burley Tobacco) Estate." Paper presented at the National Workshop on Rural Development Projects and Agrarian Change in Malawi, December 1985-January 1986.

———. 1990. *A Case Study of Tenancy Arrangements on Private Burley Tobacco Estates in Malawi.* African Rural Social Science Series, Research Report 4. Morrilton, Ark.: Winrock International Institute for Agricultural Development.

Narayana, N.S.S., K.S. Parikh, and T.N. Srinivasan. 1987. "Indian Agricultural Policy: An Applied General Equilibrium Model." *Journal of Policy Modeling* 9 (4):527-58.

———. 1988. "Rural Works Programs in India: Costs and Benefits." *Journal of Development Economics* 29 (2):131-56.

———. 1991. *Agriculture, Growth and Redistribution of Income—Policy Analysis with an Applied General Equilibrium Model.* Amsterdam: North-Holland.

Naseem, S.M. 1973. "Mass Poverty in Pakistan: Some Preliminary Findings." *Pakistan Development Review* 13 (4):317-60.

———. 1977. "Rural Poverty and Landlessness in Pakistan." In *ILO Report on Poverty and Landlessness in Asia.* Geneva: International Labour Office.

National Council of Applied Economic Research. 1975. *Changes in Rural Income in India 1968-69, 1969-70, 1970-71.* New Delhi.

National Research Council. 1986. *Population Growth and Economic Development: Policy Questions.* Washington, D.C.: National Academy Press.

Nelson, Joan. 1989. "The Politics of Pro-Poor Adjustment." In Joan M. Nelson and contributors, *Fragile Coalitions: The Politics of Economic Adjustment.* Overseas Development Council, U.S.-Third World Policy Perspectives, 12. New Brunswick, N.J.: Transaction Books.

Nerlove, Marc. 1988. "Modernizing Traditional Agriculture." Occasional Papers 16. International Center for Economic Growth, Panama City.

Nerlove, Marc, Assaf Razin, and Efraim Sadka. 1987. *Household and Economy: Welfare Economics of Endogenous Fertility.* New York: Academic Press.

Ng, Yew-Kwang. 1986. "On the Welfare Economics of Population Control." *Population and Development Review* 12 (2):247-66.

Nichols, Albert L., and Richard Zeckhauser. 1982. "Targeting Transfers through Restrictions on Recipients." *American Economic Review* 72 (2):372-77.

Niskanen, William A. 1971. *Bureaucracy and Representative Government.* Chicago: Aldine-Atherton.

Noronha, Raymond. 1985. "A Review of the Literature on Land Tenure Systems in Sub-Saharan Africa." Discussion Paper ARU 43. World Bank, Washington, D.C.

Nozick, Robert. 1974. *Anarchy, State and Utopia.* New York: Basic Books.

NSSO (National Sample Survey Organization). 1986. "A Report on the Third Quinquennial Survey on Consumer Expenditure, NSS 38th Round." *Sarvekshana* 9:S1-S102.

Nugent, Jeffrey, and Rudolf Walther. 1981. "Old-Age Security, Household Structure, Marriage and Fertility." University of Southern California, Department of Economics, Los Angeles.

Nyanda, Macleod E. 1989. "The Labour Market in Malawi's Estate Sub-Sector." Centre for Social Research, Zomba.

Nyanda, Macleod E., and Gerald Shively. 1989. "Sources of and Factors Influencing the Incomes of Tenants on Agricultural Estates: The Case for Malawi." Cornell University Food and Nutrition Policy Program, Washington, D.C.

Okelo, Jasper A. 1973. "Rural Enterprise Survey in Kakamega District, Kenya: A Report of the Consultant to DANIDA." Nairobi, Kenya.

Okun, Arthur. 1975. *Equality and Efficiency: The Big Trade-Off.* Washington, D.C.: The Brookings Institution.

Okyere, William A. 1990. "The Response of Farmers to Ghana's Adjustment Policies." In World Bank, *The Long-Term Perspective Study of Sub-Saharan Africa.* Vol. 2, *Economic and Sectoral Policy Issues.* Washington, D.C.

O'Rourke, Kevin, and Jeffrey G. Williamson. 1992. "Were Hecksher and Ohlin Right? Putting the Factor-Price-Equalization Theorem Back into History." NBER/DAE Working Paper 37. National Bureau of Economic Research, Cambridge, Mass.

Ostrom, Elinor. 1990. *Governing the Commons: The Evolution of Institutions for Collective Action.* New York: Cambridge University Press.

PAHO (Pan-American Health Organization). 1989. "Health and Development: Repercussions of the Economic Crisis." Washington, D.C.

Paige, Jeffrey. 1975. *Agrarian Revolution.* New York: Free Press.

Pakistan, Federal Bureau of Statistics. 1983. *Household Income and Expenditure Survey 1979.* Karachi.

———. 1988a. *Household Income and Expenditure Survey 1984-85.* Karachi.

———. 1988b. *Pakistan Statistical Yearbook 1988.* Karachi.

———. 1988c. *Survey of the Social and Economic Impact of Zakat and Ushr on Individuals and Households.* Karachi.

———. 1990. *Household Income and Expenditure Survey 1987-88.* Karachi.

Pakistan, Institute of Health Economics and Technology Assessment. 1988. *Health Sector in Pakistan: A Financing and Expenditure Study*. Islamabad.

Pakistan, Ministry of Finance. 1985. *Economic Survey, 1984-85*. Islamabad.

————. 1988. *Economic Survey, 1987-88*. Islamabad.

————. 1989. *Economic Survey, 1988-89*. Islamabad.

————. 1990. *Economic Survey, 1989-90*. Islamabad.

Pakistan, Ministry of Food, Agriculture and Cooperatives. 1991. *Agricultural Statistics of Pakistan 1989-90*. Islamabad.

Pakistan, National Institute of Health, Nutrition Division. 1988. *National Nutrition Survey, 1985-87, Final Report*. Islamabad.

Pakistan, Planning and Development Division, Nutrition Cell. 1978. *Micro-Nutrient Survey of Pakistan*. Islamabad.

Pakistan, Planning Commission. 1988a. "The Sixth Five-Year Plan 1983-1988." Islamabad.

————. 1988b. "The Seventh Five-Year Plan 1988-1993 and Perspective Plan 1988-2003." Islamabad.

Pastore, Jose. 1989. "Inequality and Social Mobility: Ten Years Later." In Edmar L. Bacha and Herbert S. Klein, eds., *Social Change in Brazil 1945-1985: The Incomplete Transition*. Albuquerque: University of New Mexico Press.

Pathak, R.P., K.R. Ganpathy, and Y.U.K. Sarma. 1977. "Shifts in Pattern of Asset-Holdings of Rural Households, 1961-62 to 1971-72." *Economic and Political Weekly* 12 (March 19):507-17.

Paulino, Leonardo. 1986. *Food in the Third World: Past Trends and Projections to 2000*. International Food Policy Research Institute Research Report 52. Washington, D.C.

Payne, Philip, and Michael Lipton. 1991. "How Third World Rural Households Adapt to Dietary Energy Stress." International Food Policy Research Institute, Washington, D.C.

Peek, Peter. 1983. "Agrarian Reform and Rural Development in Nicaragua, 1979-1981." In A.K. Ghose, ed., *Agrarian Reform in Contemporary Developing Countries*. New York: St. Martin's Press.

Peltzman, Sam. 1976. "Toward a More General Theory of Regulation." *Journal of Law and Economics* 19 (2):211-40.

————. 1980. "The Growth of Government." *Journal of Law and Economics* 23 (2):209-87.

Pervis, D.W. 1984. "An Economic Analysis of a Land Registration Program in the Lilongwe Agricultural Development Division, Malawi, 1979-1983."

Peters, Pauline E., and M. Guillermo Herrera. 1989. "Cash Cropping, Food Security and Nutrition: The Effects of Agricultural Commercialization Among Smallholders in Malawi." USAID/HIID Study. Harvard Institute for International Development, Cambridge, Mass.

Petrei, A. Humberto. 1987. "El Gasto Público Social y Sus Efectos Distribuidos: Un Examen Comparativo de Cinco Paises de América Latina." Programa de Estudios Conjuntos sobre Integración Económica Latinoamericana, Rio de Janeiro.

Pfeffermann, Guy. 1986. "Poverty in Latin America: The Impact of Depression." World Bank, Latin America and the Caribbean Regional Office, Washington, D.C.

Phongpaichit, P. 1982. *Employment, Income and Mobilization of Resources in Three Thai Villages*. New Delhi: International Labour Organisation.

Pinckney, Thomas C. 1989. *The Demand for Public Storage of Wheat in Pakistan*. International Food Policy Research Institute Research Report 85. Washington, D.C.

Pinstrup-Andersen, Per. 1984. "The Nutritional Impact of the Colombian Food and Nutrition Program in the State of Cauca, Colombia." International Food Policy Research Institute, Washington, D.C.

————. 1985. "Food Prices and the Poor in Developing Countries." *European Review of Agricultural Economics* 12 (1/2):69-81.

————. 1989. "The Impact of Macroeconomic Adjustment: Food Security and Nutrition." In Commander (1989).

Pinstrup-Andersen, Per, ed. 1988. *Food Subsidies in Developing Countries: Costs, Benefits, and Policy Options*. Baltimore: Johns Hopkins University Press.

————. Forthcoming. *The Political Economy of Food and Nutrition Policies*. Baltimore: Johns Hopkins University Press.

Pinstrup-Andersen, Per, Alan Berg, and Martin Foreman, eds. 1984. *International Agricultural Research and Human Nutrition*. Washington, D.C.: International Food Policy Research Institute, and Rome: U.N. Subcommittee on Nutrition.

Pinstrup-Andersen, Per, and Elizabeth Caicedo. 1978. "The Potential Impact of Changes in Income Distribution on Food Demand and Human Nutrition." *American Journal of Agricultural Economics* 60 (3):402-15.

Pinstrup-Andersen, Per, Norha Ruiz de Londono, and Edward Hoover. 1976. "The Impact of Increasing Food Supply on Human Nutrition: Implications for Commodity Priorities in Agricultural Research and Policy." *American Journal of Agricultural Economics* 58 (1):131-42.

Pinstrup-Andersen, Per, and Peter Hazell. 1985. "The Impact of the Green Revolution and Prospects for the Future." *Food Reviews International* 1 (1):1-25.

Pinstrup-Andersen, Per, Mauricio Jaramillo, and Frances Stewart. 1987. "The Impact on Government Expenditures." In Cornia, Jolly, and Stewart (1987).

Pinstrup-Andersen, Per, Karen Peterson, Susan Burger, and J.P. Habicht. Forthcoming. "Protein-Energy Malnutrition." In D.T. Jamison and W.H. Mosley, eds., *The Health Sector in Developing Countries: Evolving Priorities for the 1990s*. Baltimore: Johns Hopkins University Press.

Pitman, E.J.G. 1937. "Significance Tests which May Be Applied to Samples from any Population: II. The Correlation Coefficient Test." *Journal of Royal Statistical Society* (supplement 4):225-32.

Pitt, Mark. 1983. "Food Preferences and Nutrition in Rural Bangladesh." *Review of Economics and Statistics* 65 (1):105-14.

Pitt, Mark, and Mark Rosenzweig. 1985. "Health and Nutrient Consumption Across and Within Farm Households." *Review of Economics and Statistics* 67 (May):212-23.

Pitt, Mark, Mark Rosenzweig, and Mohammad Nasmul Hassan. 1990. "Productivity, Health and Inequality in the Intrahousehold Distribution of Food in Low-Income Countries." *American Economic Review* 80 (5):1139-56.

Platteau, Jean-Philippe. 1991. "Traditional Systems of Social Security and Hunger Insurance: Past Achievements and Modern Challenges." In Ahmad and others (1991).

Polanyi, Karl. 1944. *The Great Transformation: The Political Origins of Our Time.* Reprint. Boston: Beacon Press, 1985.

Pommerehne, Werner W., and Friedrich Schneider. 1978. "Fiscal Illusions, Political Institutions, and Local Public Spending." *Kyklos* 31 (3):381-408.

Prahladachar, M. 1983. "Income Distribution Effects of the Green Revolution in India: A Review of Empirical Evidence." *World Development* 11 (November):927-44.

Prais, S., and Hendrik Houthakker. 1955. *The Analysis of Family Budgets.* Cambridge: Cambridge University Press.

Prasad, Pradhan H. 1988. "Roots of Uneven Regional Growth in India." *Economic and Political Weekly* 23:1689-92.

Preston, Samuel. 1986. "Review of Richard Jolly and Giovanni Andrea Cornia, eds., The Impact of World Recession on Children." *Journal of Development Economics* 21 (2):374-76.

Prosterman, Roy, and Jeffrey Riedinger. 1987. *Land Reform and Democratic Development.* Baltimore: Johns Hopkins University Press.

Pryor, Frederic L. 1977. *The Origins of the Economy: A Comparative Study of Distribution in Primitive and Peasant Societies.* New York: Academic Press.

————. 1988. *Income Distribution and Economic Development in Malawi: Some Historical Statistics.* World Bank Discussion Paper 36. Washington D.C.: World Bank.

Psacharopoulos, George, Jee-Peng Tan, and Emmanuel Jimenez. 1986. *Financing Education in Developing Countries: An Exploration of Policy Options.* Washington, D.C.: World Bank.

Pulley, Robert V. 1989. *Making the Poor Creditworthy: A Case Study of the Integrated Rural Development Program in India.* World Bank Discussion Paper 58. Washington, D.C.

Quinn, Victoria, Mabel Chiligo, and J. Price Gittinger. 1988. "Household Food and Nutritional Security in Malawi." Paper presented at Symposium on Agricultural Policies for Growth and Development, Mangochi, Malawi, November.

Quizon, Jaime, and Hans Binswanger. 1986a. "The Impact of Agricultural Growth and Selected Government Policies on the Distribution of Income in India: Regional Analyses." World Bank, Washington, D.C.

————. 1986b. "Modeling the Impact of Agricultural Growth and Government Policy on Income Distribution in India." *World Bank Economic Review* 1 (1):103-48.

Rangarajan, C. 1982. *Agricultural Growth and Industrial Performance in India.* International Food Policy Research Institute Research Report 33. Washington, D.C.

Ranis, Gustav, and T. Paul Schultz, eds. 1988. *The State of Development Economics: Progress and Perspectives.* New York: Basil Blackwell.

Rao, C.H.H., S.K. Ray, and K. Subbarao. 1988. *Unstable Agriculture and Droughts: Implications for Policy.* New Delhi: Vikas.

Ravallion, Martin. 1984. "How Much is a Transfer Payment Worth to a Rural Worker?" *Oxford Economic Papers* 36:478-89.

———. 1988. "Expected Poverty under Risk Induced Welfare Variability." *Economic Journal* 98:1171-82.

———. 1989. "Land-Contingent Poverty Alleviation Schemes." *World Development* 17 (8):1223-33.

———. 1990. "Income Effects on Undernutrition." *Economic Development and Cultural Change* (April):489-516.

———. 1991. "Reaching the Rural Poor through Public Employment: Arguments, Evidence, and Lessons from South Asia." *World Bank Research Observer* 6 (2):153-75.

———. 1993. "Poverty Alleviation Through Regional Targeting: A Case Study for Indonesia." In K. Hoff, A. Braverman, and J.E. Stiglitz, eds., *The Economics of Rural Organization.* Oxford: Oxford University Press.

Ravallion, Martin, and Kalvin Chao. 1989. "Targeted Policies for Poverty Alleviation under Imperfect Information: Algorithms and Applications." *Journal of Policy Modeling* 11 (2):213-24.

Ravallion, Martin, Gaurav Datt, and Shubham Chaudhuri. 1991. "Higher Wages for Relief Work Can Make Many of the Poor Worse Off: Recent Evidence from Maharashtra's 'Employment Guarantee Scheme.'" Policy Research Working Paper 568. World Bank, Washington, D.C.

Ravallion, Martin, Gaurav Datt, Dominique van de Walle, and Elaine Chan. 1991. "Quantifying the Magnitude and Severity of Absolute Poverty in the Developing World in the Mid-1980s." Policy Research Working Paper 587. World Bank, Washington, D.C.

Ravallion, Martin, and Monika Huppi. 1989. "Poverty and Undernutrition in Indonesia during the 1980s." Policy Research Working Paper 286. World Bank, Washington, D.C.

Rawls, John. 1971. *A Theory of Justice.* Cambridge, Mass.: Belknap Press of Harvard.

Redclift, Michael. 1978. *Agrarian Reform and Peasant Organization on the Ecuadorian Coast.* London: University of London Press.

Reserve Bank of Malawi. 1987. *Financial and Economic Review* 19 (2). Lilongwe.

———. 1988. *Financial and Economic Review* 20 (4). Lilongwe.

Reutlinger, Schlomo, and Marcelo Selowsky. 1976. *Malnutrition and Poverty: Magnitude and Policy Options.* Baltimore: Johns Hopkins University Press.

RGCCI (Registrar General and Census Commissioner of India). 1982. *Final Population Totals.* Census of India, ser. 1, no. 1. Delhi: Controller of Publication.

Richardson, Harry W. 1985. "Input-Output and Economic Base Multipliers: Looking Backward and Looking Forward." *Journal of Regional Science* 25 (4):607-61.

Ridell, James C. 1985. "Customary Tenure in Malawi." University of Wisconsin, Land Tenure Center, Madison.

Roberts, Kevin. 1984. "The Theoretical Limits of Redistribution." *Review of Economic Studies* 51 (2):177-95.

Rocha, Sonia, and Hamilton Tolosa. 1989. "Pobreza Metropolitana e Politicas Sociais." In *Perspectivas da Economia Brasileira 1989*. Rio de Janeiro: Instituto de Planejamento Economico e Social/Instituto de Pesquisas.

Romer, P.M. 1986. "Increasing Returns and Long-Run Growth." *Journal of Political Economy* 94 (5):1002-37.

————. 1989. "Increasing Returns and New Developments in the Theory of Growth." NBER Working Paper 3098 (September):1-37.

Romer, Thomas, and Howard Rosenthal. 1978. "Political Resource Allocation, Controlled Agendas and the Status Quo." *Public Choice* 33 (4):27-43.

Rondinelli, Dennis A. 1983. *Secondary Cities in Developing Countries: Policies for Diffusing Urbanization.* Beverly Hills, Calif.: Sage Publications.

Rondinelli, Dennis A., and K. Ruddle. 1978. *Urbanization and Rural Development: A Spatial Policy for Equitable Growth.* New York: Praeger.

Rosenzweig, Mark R., and T. Paul Schultz. 1983. "Estimating a Household Production Function: Heterogeneity, the Demand for Health Inputs and Their Effects on Birth Weight." *Journal of Political Economy* 91 (5):723-46.

————. 1987. "Fertility and Investments in Human Capital: Estimates of the Consequences of Imperfect Fertility Control in Malaysia." *Journal of Econometrics* 36 (September-October):163-84.

Rosenzweig, Mark R., and Kenneth Wolpin. 1980. "Testing the Quantity-Quality Fertility Model: The Use of Twins as a Natural Experiment." *Econometrica* 48 (1):227-40.

Rouse, C. 1990. "A Study of the Poor in Sri Lanka." World Bank, South Asia Regional Office, Washington, D.C.

Rowntree, B. Seebohm. 1901 (new edition 1908). *Poverty: A Study of Town Life.* London: Macmillan.

Ruel, M. Forthcoming. "Growth Monitoring as an Education Tool, an Integrating Strategy and a Source of Information: A Review of Experience." In Per Pinstrup-Andersen, David Pelletier, and Harold Alderman, eds., *Beyond Child Survival: Enhancing Child Growth and Nutrition in Developing Countries.* Ithaca, N.Y.: Cornell University Press.

Ruttan, Vernon W., and Hans P. Binswanger. 1978. "Induced Innovation and the Green Revolution." In Hans P. Binswanger and Vernon W. Ruttan, eds., *Induced Innovation: Technology, Institutions, and Development.* Baltimore: Johns Hopkins University Press.

Ryan, J.G., and M.S. Rathore. 1980. "Factor Proportions, Factor Market Access and the Development and Transfer of Technology." In *Indian Agricultural Research Institute, Proceedings of the Seminar on Economic Problems in Transfer of Agricultural Technology.* New Delhi: IARI.

Sabel, C.F. 1987. "Changing Models of Economic Efficiency and Their Implications for Industrialization in the Third World." Massachusetts Institute of Technology, Department of City and Regional Planning, Cambridge.

Sadka, E., I. Garfinkel, and K. Moreland. 1982. "Income Testing and Social Welfare: An Optimal Tax-Transfer Model." In Garfinkel (1982).

Sahn, David E. 1988. "The Effect of Price and Income Changes on Food-Energy Intake in Sri Lanka." *Economic Development and Cultural Change* 36:325-40.

————. 1990. *The Causes of Malnutrition in West Africa: Evidence on the Role of Income.* Social Dimensions of Adjustment in Sub-Saharan Africa Working Paper 4. Washington, D.C.: World Bank.

Sahn, David E., and Harold Alderman. 1988. "The Effect of Human Capital on Wages and the Determinants of Labor Supply in a Developing Country." *Journal of Development Economics* 29 (September):157-83.

Sahn, David E., and Jehan Arulpragasam. 1991. "Development Through Dualism? Land Tenure, Policy, and Poverty in Malawi." Working Paper 9. Cornell University Food and Nutrition Policy Program, Washington, D.C.

Sahn, David E., Jehan Arulpragasam, and Lemma Merid. 1990. *Policy Reform and Poverty in Malawi: A Survey of a Decade of Experience.* Monograph 7. Washington, D.C.: Cornell University Food and Nutrition Policy Program.

Sanderson, Steven E. 1986. *The Transformation of Mexican Agriculture: International Structure and the Politics of Rural Change.* Princeton, N.J.: Princeton University Press.

Schiff, Maurice, and Alberto Valdés. 1990. "Nutrition: Alternative Definitions and Policy Implications." *Economic Development and Cultural Change* 38 (2):281-92.

Scobie, Grant. 1988. "Macroeconomic and Trade Implications of Consumer-Oriented Food Subsidies." In P. Pinstrup-Andersen, ed., *Consumer-oriented Food Subsidies: Costs, Benefits, and Policy Options for Developing Countries.* Baltimore: Johns Hopkins University Press.

Scott, A.J. 1988. *Metropolis: From the Division of Labor to Urban Form.* Berkeley: University of California Press.

Scott, Christopher. 1985. "El Ascenso de la Mediana Producción en la Agricultura Latinoamericana." Paper presented at conference on the Ascent of Medium-size Farms in Latin American Agriculture, Food and Agriculture Organization, Rome.

Scott, James C. 1976. *The Moral Economy of the Peasant.* New Haven: Yale.

Seckler, David. 1982. "Small But Healthy: A Basic Hypothesis in the Theory, Measurement and Policy of Malnutrition." In P.V. Sukhatme, ed., *Newer Concepts in Nutrition and Their Implications for Policy.* Maharashtra Association for the Cultivation of Science Research Institute, India.

Selowsky, Marcelo. 1979. *Who Benefits From Government Expenditure? A Case Study of Colombia.* New York: Oxford University Press.

Sen, Amartya K. 1966. "Peasants and Dualism With or Without Surplus Labor." *Journal of Political Economy* 74 (5):425-50.

————. 1967. "Isolation, Assurance and the Social Rate of Discount." *Quarterly Journal of Economics* 81 (1):112-24.

————. 1976. "Poverty: An Ordinal Approach to Measurement." *Econometrica* 44 (March):219-31.

————. 1977. "Starvation and Exchange Entitlements." *Cambridge Journal of Economics* 1 (1):33-59.

————. 1979. "Issues in the Measurement of Poverty." *Scandinavian Journal of Economics* 81:285-307.

————. 1981a. *Poverty and Famines: An Essay on Entitlement and Deprivation.* Oxford: Clarendon Press.

————. 1981b. "Public Action and the Quality of Life in Developing Countries." *Oxford Bulletin of Economics and Statistics* 43 (4):287-319.

Senauer, Benjamin, David Sahn, and Harold Alderman. 1986. "The Effect of the Value of Time on Food Consumption Patterns in Developing Countries: Evidence from Sri Lanka." *American Journal of Agricultural Economics* 68 (4):920-27.

Senauer, Benjamin, and Nathan Young. 1986. "The Impact of Food Stamps on Food Expenditures: Rejection of the Traditional Model." *American Journal of Agricultural Economics* 68:37-43

Shah, A.M. 1979. *Household Dimensions of the Family in India.* Berkeley: University of California Press.

Shah, Chandrahas H. 1979. "Food Preferences and Nutrition: A Perspective on Poverty." Presidential Address. Indian Society of Agricultural Economics. Bangalore.

Shekar, Meera. Forthcoming. *The Tamil Nadu Integrated Nutrition Project: A Review of the Project with Special Emphasis on the Monitoring and Information System.* Cornell Food and Nutrition Policy Program Working Paper. Ithaca, N.Y.

Shipton, Parker. 1987. *The Kenyan Land Tenure Reform: Misunderstandings in the Public Creation of Private Property.* Development Discussion Paper 239. Cambridge, Mass.: Harvard Institute for International Development.

Sidhu, Surjit S. 1972. "Economics of Technical Change in Wheat Production in Punjab, India." Ph.D. dissertation. University of Minnesota, Department of Agricultural and Applied Economics, St. Paul, Minn.

Singh, Inderjit. 1990. *The Great Ascent: The Rural Poor in South Asia.* Baltimore: Johns Hopkins University Press.

Singh, Inderjit, Lyn Squire, and John Strauss. 1986. *Agricultural Household Models.* Baltimore: Johns Hopkins University Press.

Smedmen, Lars, Geran Stuky, Lotta Mellander, and Stig Wall. 1987. "Anthropometry and Subsequent Mortality in Groups of Children Aged 6-59 Months in Guinea-Bissau." *American Journal of Clinical Nutrition* 46 (3):369-73.

Smith, J.E. 1984. "Widowhood and Aging in Traditional English Society." *Aging and Society* 4 (4):429-49.

Smith, Richard M. 1981. "Fertility, Economy, and Household Formation in England over Three Centuries." *Population and Development Review* 7 (4):595-622.

Snell, K.D.M. 1985. *Annals of the Labouring Poor.* Cambridge: Cambridge University Press.

Srinivasan, T.N., and P.K. Bardhan, eds. 1974. *Poverty and Income Distribution in India.* Calcutta: Statistical Publishing Society.

Stark, Oded. 1991. *The Migration of Labor.* Oxford: Basil Blackwell.

Stern, Nicholas H. 1989. "The Economics of Development: A Survey." *Economic Journal* 99 (September):597-85.

Stigler, George. 1970. "Director's Law of Public Income Distribution." *Journal of Law and Economics* 13 (1):1-10.

———. 1971. "The Theory of Economic Regulation." *Bell Journal of Economics and Management Science* 2 (1):3-21.

Stiglitz, Joseph E. 1988. "Economic Organization, Information and Development." In Chenery and Srinivasan (1988).

Stiglitz, Joseph E., and Andrew Weiss. 1981. "Credit Rationing in Markets with Imperfect Information." *American Economic Review* 71 (3):393-410.

Strauss, John. 1989. "The Impact of Improved Nutrition on Labor Productivity and Human Resource Development: An Economic Perspective." Rand Corporation, Santa Monica, Calif.

———. 1990. "Households, Communities and Preschool Children's Nutrition Outcomes: Evidence from Rural Côte d'Ivoire." *Economic Development and Cultural Change* 38 (2):231-62.

Strauss, John, and Duncan Thomas. 1990. "The Shape of the Expenditure-Calorie Curve." Economic Growth Center Discussion Paper 595. Yale University, New Haven, Conn.

Subbarao, K. 1985. "Regional Variations in Impact of Anti-Poverty Programmes." *Economic and Political Weekly* 20 (October 26):1829-34.

———. 1987. "Interventions to Fill Nutrition Gaps at the Household Level: A Review of India's Experience." Paper presented at a workshop on Poverty in India: Research and Policy, Queen Elizabeth House, Oxford University. Institute of Economic Growth, Delhi.

———. 1989. *Improving Nutrition in India: Programs and Policies and Their Impact.* World Bank Discussion Paper 49. Washington, D.C.

Sudan, Republic of, Ministry of Health and Social Welfare. 1988. *Sudan emergency and recovery information and surveillance system (SERISS).* Khartoum.

Summers, Robert, and Alan Heston. 1988. "A New Set of International Comparisons of Real Product and Price Levels Estimates for 130 Countries, 1950-1985." *Review of Income and Wealth* Series 34, no. 1 (March):1-24.

Sundaram, K., and Suresh D. Tendulkar. 1988. "Toward an Explanation of Interregional Variations in Poverty and Unemployment in Rural India." In T.N. Srinivasan and P. Bardhan, eds., *Rural Poverty in South Asia.* New York: Columbia University Press.

Sundrum, R.M. 1987. *Growth and Income Distribution in India: Policy and Performance since Independence.* New Delhi: Sage Publications.

Swynnerton, R.J.M. 1954. *A Plan to Intensify the Development of African Agriculture in Kenya.* Nairobi: Government Printer.

Takayama, Noriyuki. 1979. "Poverty, Income Inequality and Their Measures: Professor Sen's Axiomatic Approach Reconsidered." *Econometrica* 47 (May):747-60.

Tan, Jee-Peng. 1992. *Education in Asia: A Comparative Study of Cost and Financing.* Washington, D.C.: World Bank.

Tanzi, Vito. 1987. "Quantitative Characteristics of the Tax Systems of Developing Countries." In David Newbery and Nicholas Stern, eds., *The Theory of Taxation for Developing Countries.* New York: Oxford University Press.

Taylor, Carl E., A.A. Kielmann, C. De Sweener, I.S. Uberoi, H.S. Takulia, C.G. Neumann, W. Blot, H. Shankar, S. Vohra, G. Subbulakshmi, R.S. Sarma, R.L. Parker, C. McCord, N. Masih, D. Laliberte, N.S. Kielmann, D.N. Kakar, and A. Forman. 1978. "The Narangwal Experiment on Interactions of Nutrition and Infections: 1. Project Design and Effects upon Growth." *Indian Journal of Medical Research* 68 (supplement):1-20.

Tendler, Judith. 1988. "Northeast Brazil Rural Development Evaluation: First Impressions." Department of Urban Studies and Planning, Massachusetts Institute of Technology, Cambridge.

Theil, Henri. 1967. *Economics and Information Theory: Studies in Mathematical and Managerial Economics.* Vol. 7. Amsterdam: North-Holland.

Thiesenhusen, William. 1977. "Reaching the Rural Poor and the Poorest: A Goal Unmet." In H. Newby, ed., *International Perspectives in Rural Sociology.* New York: John Wiley.

Thiesenhusen, William, and Jolyne Melmed-Sanjak. 1990. "Brazil's Agrarian Structure: Changes from 1970 to 1980." *World Development* 18 (3):393-415.

Thomas, Duncan. 1990. "Intrahousehold Resource Allocation: An Inferential Approach." *Journal of Human Resources* 25 (4):635-64.

Thomas, Duncan, John Strauss, and Maria Helena Henriques. 1990. "Child Survival, Height for Age and Household Characteristics in Brazil." *Journal of Development Economics* 33 (2):197-234.

———. 1991. "How Does Mother's Education Affect Child Height?" *Journal of Human Resources* 26 (2):183-211.

Thompson, Edward P. 1971. "The Moral Economy of the English Crowd in the Eighteenth Century." *Past and Present* 50 (1):76-136.

Thomson, David. 1984. "The Decline of Social Welfare: Falling State Support for the Elderly since Early Victorian Times." *Aging and Society* 4 (4):451-82.

Thon, Dominique. 1983. "A Note on a Troublesome Axiom for Poverty Indices." *Economic Journal* 93:199-200.

Thorbecke, Erik, and David Berrian. 1989. "Budgetary Rules to Minimize Societal Poverty in a General Equilibrium Context." Cornell University, Ithaca, N.Y. (Also published in *Journal of Development Economics* 39:189-206, 1992.)

Tobin, James. 1970. "On Limiting the Domain of Inequality." *Journal of Law and Economics* 13 (October):263-77.

Torre, Herman. 1985. "La Parcelación y Alternativas Organizativas en las Cooperativas Agrarias de la Costa." In A. Gonzales and H. Torre, eds., *Las Parcelaciones de las Cooperativas Agrarias del Perú.* Chiclayo, Peru: Centro de Estudios Sociales-Solidaridad.

Tullock, Gordon. 1982. "Income Testing and Politics: A Theoretical Model." In Garfinkel (1982).

Twomey, Michael J. 1988. "The Debt Crisis and Latin American Agriculture." Paper presented at the LADA Conference, New Orleans, Louisiana, March. University of Michigan, Department of Economics, Dearborn.

UNDP (United Nations Development Programme). 1990. *Human Development Report 1990.* New York: Oxford University Press.

UNDP and World Bank. 1989. *African Economic and Financial Data.* Washington, D.C.

UNICEF. 1989. *1989 State of the World's Children.* New York.

United Kingdom, Parliament. 1900. *Report of the Committee on the Aged Deserving Poor.* Vol X, Appendix II. Cd. 67.

————. 1910. *Report of the Royal Commission on the Poor Laws and Relief of Distress.* Vol. LIII, Statistical appendix, part 2. Cd. 5077.

United Nations, ACC/SCN (Administrative Committee on Coordination, Subcommittee on Nutrition). 1987. *First Report on the World Nutrition Situation.* Geneva.

————. 1989. *Update on the Nutrition Situation: Recent Trends in Nutrition in 33 Countries.* Geneva.

United Nations Statistical Office. 1988. *Demographic Yearbook.* New York.

USAID (U.S. Agency for International Development). 1988. *Growth Monitoring and Nutrition Education: Impact Evaluation of an Effective Applied Nutrition Program in the Dominican Republic.* Washington, D.C.: USAID, Bureau of Science and Technology, Office of Nutrition.

van der Gaag, Jacques, and Paul Glewwe. 1988. *Confronting Poverty in Developing Countries: Definitions, Information, and Policies.* Living Standards Measurement Study Working Paper 48. Washington, D.C.: World Bank.

van der Gaag, Jacques, Morton Stelcner, and Wim Vijverberg. 1989. "Wage Differentials and Moonlighting by Civil Servants: Evidence from Côte d'Ivoire and Peru." *World Bank Economic Review* 3 (1):67-95.

Vaughan, M., and G.H.R. Chipande. 1986. *Women in the Estate Sector of Malawi: The Tea and Tobacco Industries.* World Employment Programme Research Working Paper. Geneva: International Labour Office.

Villa, M. R. 1977. *El Mercado de Trabajo y la Adopción de Tecnología Nueva de Producción Agrícola: El Caso del Plan Puebla.* Chapingo, Mexico: Colegio de Postgraduados, Centro de Economía Agrícola.

Visaria, Pravin M., with Shyamalendu Pal. 1980. *Poverty and Living Standards in Asia: An Overview of the Main Results and Lessons of Selected Household Surveys.* Living Standards Measurement Study Working Paper 2. Washington, D.C.: World Bank.

von Braun, Joachim. 1989. "Production, Income, and Employment Effects of Commercialization: Implications for Household Food Security and Lessons for Agricultural Policy." Paper presented at IFPRI/INCAP Policy Workshop, Antigua, Guatemala, March 9-11.

————. 1991. "Social Security in Sub-Saharan Africa." In Ahmed and others (1991).

von Braun, Joachim, Hartwig de Haen, and Juergen Blanken. 1991. *Commercialization of Agriculture under Population Pressure: Production, Consumption and Nutritional Effects in Rwanda.* International Food Policy Research Institute Research Report 85. Washington, D.C.

von Braun, Joachim, David Hotchkiss, and Maarten Immink. 1989. *Nontraditional Export Crops in Guatemala: Effects on Production, Income, and Nutrition.* International Food Policy Research Institute Research Report 73. Washington, D.C.

von Braun, Joachim, and Eileen Kennedy. 1986. "Commercialization of Subsistence Agriculture: Income and Nutritional Effects in Developing Countries." Working Paper on Commercialization of Agriculture and Nutrition 1. International Food Policy Research Institute, Washington, D.C.

von Braun, Joachim, Eileen Kennedy, and Howarth Bouis. 1989. "Comparative Analyses of the Effects of Increased Commercialization of Subsistence Agriculture on Production, Consumption, and Nutrition." Report to USAID. International Food Policy Research Institute, Washington, D.C.

von Braun, Joachim, Detlev Puetz, and Patrick Webb. 1989. *Irrigation Technology and Commercialization of Rice in The Gambia: Effects on Income and Nutrition.* International Food Policy Research Institute Research Report 75. Washington, D.C.

von Oppen, Mathias. 1989. "Regional Production and Interregional Trade of Agricultural Commodities in Benin." Paper for 19th European seminar of the European Association of Agricultural Economists, Montpellier, France, June.

Wachter, Kenneth W., E. Hammell, and Peter Laslett. 1978. *Statistical Studies of Historical Social Structure.* New York: Academic Press.

Wade, Robert. 1982. "The System of Administrative and Political Corruption: Canal Irrigation in South India." *Journal of Development Studies* 18 (3):287-328.

Ward, Benjamin. 1958. "The Firm in Illyria." *American Economic Review* 48 (4):556-89.

Watts, H.W. 1968. "An Economic Definition of Poverty." In D.P. Moynihan, ed., *On Understanding Poverty.* New York: Basic Books.

Webb, Patrick. 1989. "When Projects Collapse: The Impact of Agricultural Project Failure in The Gambia from a Household Perspective." International Food Policy Research Institute, Washington, D.C.

Wheeler, David. 1985. "Female Education, Family Planning, Income and Population: A Long-Run Econometric Simulation Model." In Nancy Birdsall, ed., *The Effects of Family Planning Programs on Fertility in the Developing World.* World Bank Staff Working Paper 677. Washington, D.C.: World Bank.

Wilcox, Linda. 1987. "Internationalization of the Labor Process in Agriculture: A Case Study of Agro-Industrial Development in Mexico, El Bajio." Ph.D. dissertation. University of California, Berkeley, Department of Agricultural and Resource Economics.

Williams, Karel. 1981. *From Pauperism to Poverty.* London: Routledge and Kegan Paul.

Williams, Robert. 1986. *Export Agriculture and the Crisis in Central America.* Chapel Hill: University of North Carolina Press.

Williamson, Jeffrey G. 1976. "American Prices and Urban Inequality since 1820." *Journal of Economic History* 36 (2):303-33.

————. 1984. "Why Was British Growth So Slow during the Industrial Revolution?" *Journal of Economic History* 44 (3):687-712.

————. 1985. *Did British Capitalism Breed Inequality?* Boston: Allen and Unwin.

————. 1986. "Did Rising Emigration Cause Fertility to Decline in 19th Century Rural England? Child Costs, Old-Age Pensions, and Child Default." Paper presented to the Tenth Conference of the University of California Intercampus Group in Economic History, Laguna Beach, California, May 2-4.

————. 1987. "Did English Factor Markets Fail during the Industrial Revolution?" *Oxford Economic Papers* 39 (4):641-78.

————. 1988. "Migration and Urbanization in the Third World." In Chenery and Srinivasan (1988).

————. 1990a. *Coping With City Growth during the British Industrial Revolution.* Cambridge: Cambridge University Press.

————. 1990b. "The Impact of the Corn Laws Just Prior to Repeal." *Explorations in Economic History* 27 (2):123-56.

————. 1991. *Inequality, Poverty, and History.* Cambridge, Mass.: Basil Blackwell.

Williamson, Jeffrey G., and Peter H. Lindert. 1980. *American Inequality: A Macroeconomic History.* New York: Academic Press.

Willig, R.D., and E.E. Bailey. 1981. "Income Distribution Concerns in Regulatory Policy Making." In G. Fromm, ed., *Studies in Public Regulation.* Chicago: University of Chicago Press.

Willis, Robert J. 1987. "Externalities and Population." In D. Gale Johnson and Ronald D. Lee, eds., *Population Growth and Economic Development: Issues and Evidence.* Madison: University of Wisconsin Press.

Winkler, Donald. 1990. "Higher Education in Latin America: Issues of Efficiency and Equity." Discussion Paper 77. World Bank, Latin America Technical Department, Public Sector Management Division, Washington, D.C.

Wohl, Anthony S. 1983. *Endangered Lives: Public Health in Victorian Britain.* Cambridge: Cambridge University Press.

Wolfe, Barbara L., and Jere R. Behrman. 1987. "Women's Schooling and Children's Health: Are the Effects Robust with Adult Sibling Control for the Women's Childhood Background?" *Journal of Health Economics* 6 (3):239-54.

Wood, Geoffrey D. 1984. "Provision of Irrigation Assets by the Landless: An Approach to Agrarian Reform in Bangladesh." *Agricultural Administration* 17 (2):55-80.

World Bank. 1978a. *Employment and Development of Small Enterprises.* Sector Policy Paper. Washington, D.C.

————. 1978b. *Rural Enterprise and Nonfarm Employment.* Washington, D.C.

————. 1980. *World Development Report 1980.* New York: Oxford University Press.

————. 1981. *World Development Report 1981.* New York: Oxford University Press.

————. 1984. *World Development Report 1984.* New York: Oxford University Press.

————. 1986a. *Poverty and Hunger: Issues and Options for Food Security in Developing Countries.* Washington, D.C.

————. 1986b. *World Development Report 1986.* New York: Oxford University Press.

————. 1987. *Agricultural Mechanization: Issues and Options.* A World Bank Policy Study. Washington, D.C.

————. 1988. *Adjustment Lending: An Evaluation of Ten Years of Experience.* Policy and Research Series 1. Washington, D.C.

————. 1989a. *World Bank Atlas 1989.* Washington, D.C.

————. 1989b. *World Development Report 1989.* New York: Oxford University Press.

————. 1990a. *India: Poverty, Employment, and Social Services.* A World Bank Country Study. World Bank, Washington, D.C.

————. 1990b. *World Development Report 1990.* New York: Oxford University Press.

————. 1992. *Poverty Reduction Handbook.* Washington, D.C.

————. Various years. *World Tables.* Baltimore: Johns Hopkins University Press.

World Health Organization. 1989. "World Immunization Reaches 2/3 Mark." Press Release WHO/35, August 17, Geneva.

Yambi, Olivia, Urban Jonsson, and Bjorn Ljungqvist. 1989. *The Role of Government in Promoting Community Based Nutrition Programs: Experience from Tanzania and Lessons for Africa.* Pew/Cornell Lecture Series on Food and Nutrition Policy. Ithaca, N.Y.: Cornell Food and Nutrition Policy Program.

Zeitlin, Marian F., Mohamed Mansour, and J. Bajrai. 1987. "Positive Deviance in Nutrition." In D. Jelliffe, ed., *Advances in International Maternal and Child Health.* Vol. 7. Oxford: Clarendon Press.

Zevallos, Jose V. 1989. "Agrarian Reform and Structural Change: Ecuador since 1964." In W.C. Thiesenhusen, ed., *Searching for Agrarian Reform in Latin America.* Boston: Unwin Hyman.

Name Index

Subject Index

Absentee landlords, in estate sector in Malawi, and underutilization of leased land, 324, 331n, 333n

Absolute deprivation, 45

Additively absorbed transfers, impact on national head count index of poverty, 94-96

Additively decomposable poverty measures, 45, 46-47; and poverty measurement in Pakistan in 1984-85 to 1987-88, 488; in rural poverty study in India, 419-420; sample estimate of class of, 48-49

Adjustment with a Human Face (UNICEF), 136

Adjustment policies: and agricultural growth rates, 23; and complementary state activities, 23; and creation of employment in commercial agriculture, 266; and cuts in social welfare expenditures, 144-145; favoring labor-intensive employment and production of food, 23; impact on poor people, 135-137, 163-164; International Monetary Fund– and World Bank–supported, 24, 135, 164n; and living conditions in developing countries, and causality problem, 136; objections to, and wage rates, 39n; and options for Brazil in 1990s, 477-480; and pricing, 23; reasons for failures of, 24-25; and reforms in economic policy and political regimes, 249-250; simulation model for Brazil in 1980s, 475-477; temporary protective and compen-satory measures and, 369-370; time lags in effects on basic social indicators, 136; and World Bank loans, 135, 164n. *See also* Government policy; Macroeconomic policy and poverty in Brazil; Structural adjustment

Administration: and declines in consumption inequality in rural India, 424; of food-linked income transfers, 387-388, 390; of pilot projects, success rates and, 384-385; reforms of, economic growth and, 272; and success of integrated nutrition and health programs, 385. *See also* Administrative costs

Administrative cost function, 71f

Administrative costs of antipoverty programs, 8; and choice of poverty indicators for targeting, 75, 76-77; of food-linked income transfers, 382; and general subsidy schemes, 373; in Great Britain, 89n; and land-contingent transfers, 77; quantification of, 71-72; and targeting costs, 82; and targeting methods, 69-72

Africa: antipoverty policies in, 23; colonial period in, and exclusion of native smallholders, 182; demographic changes after control of malaria, 11; economic conditions in 1980s, 142-143; effects of International Monetary Fund– and World Bank–supported stabilization and adjustment measures in, 24; expenditures on colleges and universities in public education budget in, 342-343; incidence of poverty in, 1; lack of poverty measurement in, 3; life expectancy at birth in, 13; proportion of children under five in, and cost of social security, 361; public works programs in, 375; share of rural labor force employed primarily in nonfarm activities in, 191t; technological change and commercialization in agriculture and tenant eviction in, 181. *See also* Living conditions in developing countries *and under specific countries*